Exploring
Teaching

Exploring Teaching

FIRST EDITION

Richard I. Arends
Central Connecticut State University

Nancy E. Winitzky
The University of Utah

Margaret D. Tannenbaum
Rowan University

Boston, Massachusetts   Burr Ridge, Illinois   Dubuque, Iowa
Madison, Wisconsin   New York, New York   San Francisco, California   St. Louis, Missouri

McGraw-Hill

A Division of The McGraw-Hill Companies

EXPLORING TEACHING

Copyright © 1998 by The McGraw-Hill Companies, Inc. All rights reserved. Printed in the United States of America. Except as permitted under the United States Copyright Act of 1976, no part of this publication may be reproduced or distributed in any form or by any means, or stored in a data base or retrieval system, without the prior written permission of the publisher.

This book is printed on acid-free paper.

1 2 3 4 5 7 8 9 0 VNH/VNH 9 0 9 8 7

ISBN 0-07-003045-6

Editorial director: *Jane Vaicunas*
Sponsoring editor: *Beth Kaufman*
Editorial coordinator: *Adrienne D'Ambrosio*
Marketing manager: *Daniel M. Loch*
Project manager: *Pat Frederickson*
Production supervisor: *Lori Koetters*
Senior designer: *Laurie J. Entringer*
Photo research coordinator: *Sharon Miller/Keri Johnson*
Compositor: *Carlisle Communications, Ltd.*
Typeface: *9.5/12 Cheltenham Book*
Printer: *Von Hoffmann Press, Inc.*

Library of Congress Cataloging-in-Publication Data

Arends, Richard.
    Exploring teaching / Richard I. Arends, Nancy Winitzky, Margaret Tannenbaum.
        p.   cm.
    Includes bibliographical references and index.
    ISBN 0-07-003045-6
    1. Teaching—United States. 2. Classroom management—United States. 3. Education—United States—Curricula. 4. School management and organization—United States. I. Winitzky, Nancy.
II. Tannenbaum, Margaret D. III. Title.
LB1025.3.A753   1998
371.102—dc21   97-29508
                                                                    CIP

http://www.mhhe.com/socscience/education/intro/atw/

*To Nancy Winitzky's parents Norm
and Camille Stolba*

*To Margaret Tannenbaum's parents Otto
and Ida Denner*

To Richard Arends' mother Mildred Williams

This text is intended for people contemplating careers in teaching. It takes them on a journey of exploration into the world and work of teaching, both past and present, and into themselves as future inhabitants of that world. Whereas most introductory texts provide descriptive accounts of the contemporary world of education—teaching, schooling, and the foundational disciplines underlying it all—none make a sustained effort to help students explore themselves in terms of that world. To do so, we think, means projecting oneself into the ever-widening contexts within which teaching unfolds, that is, classrooms, schools, the school-society relationship, and the profession of teaching. We also think that in order to understand these contexts, one must have a knowledge of their origins and how they developed into their current condition. Finally, we believe that a healthy dose of firsthand experiences and personal reflections must be stirred into one's book-driven knowledge of self and job.

We structured this text in accordance with these beliefs. Part I begins with an overview of the world and work of teaching and the teachers (past and present) who inhabit that world. Next we look at what is known about effective teachers and speculate about their future. Part I concludes with a discussion of the need for a personal philosophy of teaching and provides guidance in building one. Parts II through V profile the various contexts of teaching—classroom, school, sociopolitical, and professional—and examine the role demands of each. Each part ends with a series of self-assessment activities that help students evaluate themselves in terms of these roles and settings. Thus, the book's overall structure involves an ongoing attempt to match self with the job of teaching.

Content Coverage and Organization

Since the first step in any career exploration process is to acquire a broad and coherent view of the field in question, the topical coverage of this text is quite comprehensive. In addition to all the usual chapters, we have included a chapter on classroom *Instruction and Management* and another on the *Ethical Dimensions of Teaching*. And unlike many introductory texts, this one has a coherent, organizing framework—the various contexts that surround and shape the work-life of teachers. Organizing topics in this manner gives them a more personal and interactive quality than merely providing discrete but unrelated discussions of one topic after another.

Historical Perspectives

Rather than including the traditional, fact-laden chapter on the history of American education, each of the book's five major parts opens with a chapter-length introduction that provides historical perspectives on the material that follows. Thus, the introduction to Part I provides a broad overview of how teaching has evolved in this country from colonial times to the present. Likewise, Part II begins with a historical account of how American classrooms, students, and instruction have changed—or not—over the years. The introductions to Parts III, IV, and V provide similar perspectives on how schools, the school-society relationship, and the profession of teaching have evolved. These focused historical accounts of the major contexts of teaching provide a meaningful backdrop for organizing and retaining the information that follows.

Part-Ending Assessment Activities

Just as each part opens with a historical perspective on the chapters that follow, each ends with a set of assessment activities (reflection, observation, interview) designed to help students match themselves with the teaching context and roles described in the part. Taken together, these part-ending activities comprise a useful portfolio that extends the book's content into field settings and helps students evaluate their general fitness for teaching or for a specific type of teaching career.

Focus Boxes

To emphasize the fact that teaching has (1) a multitude of unresolved issues, (2) a rich and growing research base on which to draw, and (3) an increasingly multicultural and global perspective, we include the following types of special interest boxes in each chapter.

1. *Issues.* These boxes present the pros and cons surrounding educational issues of current concern.

2. *Research.* These boxes summarize a relevant study or group of studies related to the topic at hand.

3. *Global/Multicultural.* These boxes provide a cross-cultural focus to one or more of the chapter topics.

Diversity-Repertoire Theme

A central theme of this book is our belief that teaching is a situation-driven profession in which good practice demands that knowledgeable teachers adapt themselves to a never-ending string of unique situations. Thus, in Chapter 3, we present a variety of educational philosophies that students can draw on as they build their own set of beliefs about the nature of teaching. Likewise, in Chapter 6, we present a number of different instructional strategies that all teachers should master in order to adapt their instruction to fit diverse teaching situations and contexts. This theme, which resurfaces again and again throughout the book, reminds aspiring professionals that the explorations begun in this book are but a first step in a lifelong journey of study, reflection, and creative adaptation.

Acknowledgments

Directly or indirectly, many people have contributed to the preparation of this book. We will begin by acknowledging the reviewers, whose support and insightful comments have helped shape the final version of this text. These include John Engelhardt, Northern Arizona University; Robert Farrell, Florida International University; Joel Levin, Youngstown State University; Elaine McNeese, University of Central Arkansas; Susan Mintz, University of Virginia; and Ralph Shart, University of Central Arkansas.

We are grateful to Shelly Clemson for her early work on the text and to our many other colleagues who offered their ideas and support. Any book of this nature rests on the support of many individuals who contribute in important ways: these include: Lisa Manousos, of Connecticut State University, who coordinated many aspects of the book during its early stages; Sharon Lambuth, of Seattle University, who provided research and secretarial support to the project during the final stages of revisions and production; Arlene Burek, of Connecticut State University, and Mark Hallerman, of Seattle University, who provided research assistance and worked on the instructor's manual; Steve Winitzky who worked on the index; and Christy Faison, of Rowan University, who carefully read and commented on numerous chapters. They all did magnificent work and their contributions have been invaluable. Thanks are also due Seattle University for the time and support afforded Richard Arends.

We thank and are grateful for the continued support of our families—Steve, Jessie, and Alex Winitzky, Ted, Jessica, and Steven Tannenbaum, and William Arends. Their patience and understanding always make this type of project easier.

Finally, a very special thanks goes to Lane Akers for his initial conception of and tireless commitment to this book.

ABOUT THE AUTHORS

Richard I. Arends, formerly William Allen Chair at Seattle University, is dean of the School of Education and Professional Studies at Central Connecticut State University. Prior to his coming to Connecticut, Professor Arends was on the faculty at the University of Oregon and chair of the department of Curriculum and Instruction at the University of Maryland, College Park. A former elementary, junior high, and high school teacher, his special interests are the social psychology of education, teacher education, and organizational development and school improvement. Professor Arends has authored or contributed to over a dozen books on education and has worked widely with schools and universities throughout North America and the Pacific Rim.

Dr. Nancy Winitzky is currently Associate Professor of Educational Studies at the University of Utah. Experienced in elementary through adult education, she has been involved in teacher education for 11 years. Her areas of specialization include teacher thinking, preservice teacher education reform, and cooperative learning. Dr. Winitzky has focused most recently on applying constructivist theory to understanding beginning teacher learning.

Margaret D. Tannenbaum received her Ed.D. in Foundations of Education from Temple University in 1972. She is currently a Professor of Education, having served as department chair for 4 years in the Secondary Education/Foundations of Education Department of Rowan University (formerly Glassboro State College) where she has taught for 26 years. Formerly a preschool, elementary, junior high, and high school teacher, her special interests include school choice, vouchers, charter schools, and the restructuring of early childhood education.

PART I

Teachers and Their Work   3

CHAPTER 1
The World and Work of Teaching   **11**

CHAPTER 2
The Effective Teacher   **36**

CHAPTER 3
Defining a Philosophy of Education   **55**

PART II

Teachers and Their Classrooms   91

CHAPTER 4
Classrooms   **100**

CHAPTER 5
Students   **123**

CHAPTER 6
Instruction and Management   **150**

PART III

**American Schools and
Their Curricula   197**

CHAPTER 7
Schools: Organization, Culture, and
Effectiveness   **206**

CHAPTER 8
Curriculum   **234**

PART IV

**Relationships between School
and Society   275**

CHAPTER 9
Schools and Society   **283**

CHAPTER 10
School Governance and Finance   **305**

CHAPTER 11
Legal Foundations of Education
and Teaching   **335**

PART V

**The Professionalization
of Teaching   381**

CHAPTER 12
Becoming a Professional Teacher   **388**

CHAPTER 13
Ethical Dimensions of Teaching   **412**

PART I

Teachers and Their Work   3

Teaching in the Colonial Era   4

Teaching in the Nineteenth Century   5

Teaching in the Twentieth Century   7

Teaching in the Information Age   10

CHAPTER 1

The World and Work of Teaching   11

Why Be a Teacher?   12
  Motives for Teaching   12
  Who Teaches Today?   14

The Context and Nature of Teaching   18
  Teaching Is a Professional Career   18
  Teachers' Work   20
  Teachers' Workplace   28

A Quick Tour through Exploring Teaching   30
  Self-Regulated Learning in Democratic Classrooms   31
  Social Context of Teaching   31
  Repertoire of Best Practice Based on Research   32
  Multicultural Crossroads   33
  Schools Reflect Society   33

Assessing Your Motives and Skills for Teaching in the Twenty-First Century   33

Summary   33

Readings for the Professional   35

CHAPTER 2

The Effective Teacher   36

Images of Effective Teachers   37
  Remembering Effective Teachers   37
  Media Images of Teachers   38
  Young Children's Images of Teachers   38

What Research Says about Effective Teachers   39
  Do Teachers Make a Difference?   39
  Personal Qualities of Effective Teachers   40
  Behaviors of Effective Teachers   44
  Teachers' Knowledge and Thought Processes   46

The Effective Teacher for the Twenty-First Century   50

Summary   53

Readings for the Professional   54

CHAPTER 3

Defining a Philosophy of Education   55

The Meaning and Relevance of Philosophy   57
  The Meaning of Philosophy   57
  The Relevance of Philosophy   57

Philosophical Questions and Contemporary Educational Issues   58
  Questions   58
  Issues   61

Philosophies   66
  Branches of Philosophy   66
  Systems of Philosophy   66
  Comparing Philosophical Systems   69

Philosophies of Education   70
  Perennialism   71
  Progressivism   72
  Essentialism   72
  Social Reconstructionism   73
  Examples of the Four Philosophies of Education   75

Defining a Personal Philosophy of Education   77
  Two Approaches   77
  Positioning Yourself   78

Summary   79

Readings for the Professional   80

PART I

Application and Portfolio Activities   81

Self-Assessments   82
  Assessing Your Motivations for Teaching   82
  Teachers I Remember   83
  Thinking through Your Educational Philosophy   84

Observations   86
  Observing School Board Politics   86
  Becoming an Effective Teacher   86
  Indicators of Educational Philosophy   87

Interviews **88**

  Principals' Views on Teacher Supply and
  Demand **88**

  Students Talk about "The Good Teacher" **88**

  One Teacher's Philosophy of Education **89**

PART II

Teachers and Their Classrooms **91**

Colonial Classrooms **92**

Nineteenth Century One-Classroom Schools **92**

Classrooms from the Late Nineteenth Century to
the Present **94**

  Teacher-Centered Instruction at the Turn of the
  Century **94**

  Student-Centered Instruction and the Progressive
  Era **95**

  Inquiry-Oriented Teaching and Open Education **96**

Where We Are Today **97**

  Schools as a Factor of Social Control **98**

  Organizational Structures Support Teacher-
  Centered Instruction **98**

  The Culture of Teaching **98**

  Teacher Characteristics **98**

CHAPTER 4

Classrooms **100**

Expectations **101**

  Expectations and Student Learning **101**

  Expectations Shape Perceptions **101**

  Your Expectations **101**

  Research on Beginning Teachers'
  Expectations **102**

Classroom Similarities **103**

  Life in Classrooms **103**

  A Place Called School **104**

  Social Psychology of Classrooms **105**

  Classroom Properties **108**

  Performance-for-Grade Exchange **110**

  Ambiguity and Risk in Teacher Preparation **111**

Classroom Differences **112**

  Social Class Differences **112**

  Grade-Level and Subject Matter Differences **113**

  Alternative Classrooms **117**

  Classrooms versus Other Workplaces **118**

  Classrooms in Other Cultures **120**

Putting It All Together **121**

Summary **121**

Readings for the Professional **122**

CHAPTER 5

Students **123**

Student Diversity **124**

  Ethnicity and Culture **124**

  Language **130**

  Social Class **132**

  Gender **132**

  Special Needs **134**

  Demographic Trends **138**

  At-Risk versus Resilient Students **138**

Student Development **139**

  Cognitive Domain **139**

  Affective Domain **144**

Schools' Responses to Diversity **145**

  Pull-Out Programs **145**

  Mainstreaming and Inclusion **146**

  Multicultural Education **146**

The Problem and Opportunity of Diversity **147**

Summary **148**

Readings for the Professional **149**

CHAPTER 6

Instruction and Management **150**

Organizing the Classroom **151**

  Long-Range Planning **152**

  Physical Arrangement of Classroom **152**

  Rules and Procedures **156**

  Organization and Classroom Management **157**

  Beyond the Classroom **157**

Planning **157**

  Teachers' Thought Processes **158**

  Cycles of Planning **158**

  Use of Time **159**

Instructing **160**

  Repertoire **161**

  Classroom Discourse **165**

Managing and Disciplining Students **169**

  Student Cooperation and Classroom
  Management **169**

  Communication and Management **172**

Discipline   172

Classroom Meeting   173

Assessing   174

Purposes   174

Alternatives   178

Summary   179

Readings for the Professional   180

PART II

Application and Portfolio Activities   181

Self-Assessments   182

Managing the Classroom Context   182

Teacher Candidates' Expectations   183

What Are Your Teaching Goals?   184

Observations   186

Classroom Climate and SES   186

Classroom Interaction   188

Asking Questions   190

Interviews   193

What Is Hard and What Is Easy in Preservice
Teacher Education   193

Learning about Students from Different
Cultures   194

How Students Make Sense of School   195

PART III

American Schools and Their
Curricula   197

Colonial Roots   197

Dame Schools and Reading and Writing
Schools   197

Latin Grammar Schools   198

Academies   198

Creation of the Common School:
1825–1865   199

Expansion of the Elementary School
Curriculum   200

Creation of Secondary Schools   201

Creation of Modern Schools: 1865–1940   202

The Comprehensive High School   202

Standardization and Reform   203

The Contemporary Debate   204

CHAPTER 7

Schools: Organization, Culture, and
Effectiveness   206

How Schools Work   206

The Culture of Schools   207

Schools as Social Organizations   211

Schools as Communities   213

How Good Are Today's Schools?   215

Cycles of Criticism and Reform   215

A More Positive View of Schools   216

Good Schools for the Future   222

Making Traditional Schools Work Better   223

Experimenting with Innovative Schools   224

Prototype of the Twenty-First Century School   227

Will We Get the Schools We Want?   232

Summary   232

Readings for the Professional   233

CHAPTER 8

Curriculum   234

Curriculum Defined   235

Who Controls the Curriculum?   235

National Influences   236

State Influences   239

Local Influences   239

Cultural Hegemony   243

Curriculum in Other Countries   244

The American Curriculum   246

Literacy, Language Arts, and English   246

Mathematics   248

Science   248

Social Studies   250

Foreign Language   254

The Arts   255

Physical and Health Education   255

Vocational Education   256

Curriculum Trends   257

Curriculum Choices   259

Choosing What to Teach   259

Selecting Curriculum Materials   260

Supplementing the Curriculum   260

Summary   261

Readings for the Professional   264

PART III

Application and Portfolio Activities 265

Self-Assessments 266
You and the Standards 266
Assessing Your Workplace Skills 267
Observations 268
Making Textbook Selections 268
Observing for School Effectiveness 269
Interviews 271
Teachers' Curriculum Decisions 271
Perceptions about the Effectiveness of Schools 272

PART IV

Relationships between School and Society 275

Features of American Education 275
Major Periods in American Education 276
Colonial Roots: 1620–1780 277
The Early Republic: 1780–1820 277
The Common School Era: 1820–1870 277
The Progressive Era: 1870–1920 278
The Post-World War II Era: 1945–1980 279
The Contemporary Era: 1980–the Present 282

CHAPTER 9

Schools and Society 283

Why We Have Schools 285
Purposes of Schooling 286
Transmitting the Culture 286
Developing Human Potential 289
Reconstructing Society 290
Social Problems Come to School 291
Social Class and Poverty 291
Family Configurations and Distress 296
Child Abuse 296
Drug and Alcohol Abuse 297
Teen Pregnancy 297
Crime, Violence, and Social Tensions 298
Kids and Television 300
Other Social Problems 300
Perspective on School Problems 300

Schools, Social Reform, and the Next Millennium 301
Schools and Social Reform 301
Schools, Society, and the Third Millennium 302
Summary 303
Readings for the Professional 304

CHAPTER 10

School Governance and Finance 305

Background 306
Role of State Government 306
Legislatures 306
Governors 307
State Courts 307
Role of Local Government 308
School Boards 308
Superintendents and Central Administration 309
Principals 310
Policy Development and Implementation 310
School District Organization 311
Role of Federal Government 318
Legislative Influence 318
Executive Influence 320
Judicial Influence 321
Other Federal Education Agencies 321
Nongovernmental Influences on School Governance 322
Teachers' Organizations 322
School Boards' Associations 322
Professional Educational Organizations 323
Parent Organizations 323
Business Organizations 323
Funding of Public Education 324
Collection of Revenues 324
Distribution of Funds 326
Funding Reform 327
Other Financial Concerns 329
New Funding Practices 331
New Approaches for the Twenty-First Century 332
Summary 332
Readings for the Professional 334

CHAPTER 11

Legal Foundations of Education and Teaching 335

Historical Perspective **336**
    Early Legislation **336**
    Constitutional Basis for Education **336**
How Will the Law Affect Your Life as a Teacher? **337**
    Certification Requirements **338**
    The Interview Process **338**
    Acquiring Tenure **338**
    Grounds for Dismissal **339**
    Collective Bargaining **341**
Teachers' and Students' Legal Rights **342**
    Freedom of Expression **342**
    Religious Freedom **345**
    Freedom of Association **347**
    Personal Freedom **350**
    Freedom from Discrimination **351**
    Due Process Rights **359**
Legal Bases for Curriculum and Teaching Issues **362**
    Curriculum **362**
    Student Testing **363**
    Copyright Laws **363**
    Access to Student Records **365**
    Liability **366**
Summary **368**
Readings for the Professional **368**

PART IV

Application and Portfolio Activities 369

Self-Assessments **370**
    The Purposes of Schooling **370**
    You and the System **371**
    Knowing the Law **372**
Observations **373**
    The Resource Room **373**
    Site-Based Decision Making **374**
    Shadowing the Principal **375**
Interviews **376**
    Programs for At-Risk Kids **376**
    Getting to Know a School Board Member **377**
    The Principal on Job Interviewing **378**

PART V

The Professionalization of Teaching 381

What Does Professionalization of Teaching Mean? **381**
The Colonial and Early Republic Eras: 1620–1820 **382**
The Common School Era: 1820–1870 **382**
The Progressive Era: 1870–1920 **383**
    Teacher Preparation and Licensure **383**
    Professional Associations **384**
The Post-World War II Era: 1945–1980 **385**
    Postwar Criticism **385**
    Postwar Teacher Activism **385**
The Contemporary Era: 1980–the Present **386**
    Specialized Knowledge **386**
    Preparation and Accreditation **386**
    Teacher Licensing and Certification **386**
    Autonomy and Accountability **386**

CHAPTER 12

Becoming a Professional Teacher 388

What Is a Professional Teacher? **388**
    Features of a Profession **389**
    Is Teaching a Profession? **390**
Becoming a Teacher Today **395**
    Phases of Professional Preparation **395**
    Preservice Preparation and Accreditation **396**
    Certification **399**
    Continuing Education and Advanced and National Certification **400**
Teachers' Organizations and Collective Bargaining **405**
    Teachers' Organizations **405**
    National Education Association **406**
    American Federation of Teachers **407**
    Collective Bargaining **407**
A Look Ahead **408**
    Research and Performance-Based Teacher Education **408**
    Testing to Assure Teacher Quality **409**
    Restructured Schools for Teacher and Student Success **409**
Summary **410**
Readings for the Professional **411**

CHAPTER 13

Ethical Dimensions of Teaching **412**

History of Moral Education **413**

Research on Moral Development **414**

Piagetian Perspective **414**

Kohlberg's Stage Theory **415**

Kohlberg's Critics **419**

Ethics in the Classroom **420**

Should Morals Be Taught in the Classroom? **421**

Teaching Values **422**

Professional Ethics **425**

Codes of Ethics **425**

Moral Problem Solving **428**

Becoming an Ethical Teacher **429**

Summary **432**

Readings for the Professional **433**

PART V

Application and Portfolio Activities **435**

Self-Assessments **436**

Measuring Up to the Standards **436**

Assessing Your Level of Moral Development **437**

Observations **438**

Professional Boards in Action **438**

The Moral Tone of the Classroom **439**

Interviews **441**

The Unions and Professionalism **441**

Students' Views about Ethics **442**

APPENDIX A

Observing in Communities, Schools, and Classrooms **443**

APPENDIX B

Getting Certified and Employed **452**

APPENDIX C

State Licensing Agencies **458**

APPENDIX D

Professional Associations **461**

References **462**

Glossary **478**

Exploring
Teaching

Teachers and Their Work

Humans are a learning species, so long before there were formal classrooms and professional teachers, people were teaching one another. Parents were teaching their children; ministers were teaching their congregations; and crafts people were teaching their apprentices. In early colonial America, the church and the family were the principal educators of young people. Formal, classroom-based instruction did not become the norm until well into the nineteenth century, at which time teaching began its long and still unfinished evolution into a professional occupation.

This evolution has been characterized by both constancy and change. An example of constancy within teaching can be seen in the fact that for over a century most classrooms have been teacher dominated; that is, teachers talk while students listen. Also, compared to other occupations, such as law or medicine, teaching has been perceived as a temporary occupation in which inadequately prepared practitioners plied their trade until marriage or a better paying position came along. This perception of teaching as a temporary occupation has been one of the major deterrents to investing public money in professional training programs for teachers, which, in turn, has deterred teaching from becoming a true profession.

Despite such constancy, teachers and their work have undergone substantial changes over the centuries. For example, during the colonial period in America, teaching was primarily an occupation for middle class educated males. However, the explosion of more lucrative commercial positions that came with the industrial revolution lured many of these men away and helped transform teaching into a primarily female occupation by the middle of the nineteenth century. This conversion to a mostly female teaching force was fueled by two additional facts: state and local boards of education found they could hire women for lower wages than men demanded and woman were more compliant about the social restrictions that accompanied the job. However, the strong moral restrictions once placed on teachers have gradually disappeared, and most teachers today enter and stay in education-related jobs for their lifetimes. And with this long-term commitment has come an increased willingness within communities and governing bodies to invest in professional training programs for teachers and to hold them accountable for the practices they use. Let's look at how all of this has come about.

The evolution of teaching in the United States can be divided into four major eras: the early colonial times; the agrarian society of the eighteenth and early nineteenth centuries; the industrial age that emerged in the middle of the nineteenth century and has extended to the present; and the information age, which is currently in its infancy but is predicted to extend well into the next century and to have significant impact on teachers and their work.

TEACHING IN THE COLONIAL ERA

Early North American settlers brought with them distinctly European ideas about how their children should be educated. Consequently, the patterns of education that developed in the various colonies had many features in common. Most teaching and learning was organized through the home and church. In both the South and the North, for instance, parents and grandparents were responsible for teaching their children manners, social graces, and many of the vocational skills associated with farming and the trades. However, regional differences also emerged. In the northern colonies, the Puritan church played a significant role in promoting education, since Puritans believed that salvation depended on being able to read the Bible. Children learned religious doctrine at a very young age in Sunday school and in special religious classes held during the week. The preparation of ministers was also important to the Puritans and led to the opening of Harvard College in 1636 for that exclusive purpose.

In the southern colonies, religion played a lesser role in education. The Anglican church did not emphasize individual accountability for personal salvation and thus did not encourage everyone to learn to read for religious reasons. Furthermore, the plantation system created a situation in which people lived far apart instead of clustered in small towns as they did in the North. Thus, the South established schools and colleges more slowly than the North. Wealthy southern plantation owners continued to use in-home tutors for their younger children and to send their older children to European schools much longer than their northern neighbors did.

Professional teachers, as we understand that role today, did not exist in the colonial period. Initially, literate individuals were hired by wealthy families or by a local church to help children learn to read and write. Later, towns began employing teachers on a part-time basis. As we already mentioned, teachers in the northern colonies were mainly men from the middle class. Remember, this was a time when legal and social restrictions placed on women and African slaves prevented them from participating in many aspects of community life, including teaching the community's children. Formal education was a private and expensive affair and, consequently, remained the privilege of the middle and upper classes. Rury (1989) explained this situation:

> In an age when the egalitarian ethic of modern public education had not yet been articulated, it is little wonder that representatives of the most privileged social group—white middle- and upper-class males—appear to have constituted the vast majority of the period's teachers. (p. 12)

In the southern colonies, educational patterns were slightly different than in New England. Southerners who could afford education lived mainly on plantations in rural areas. The prevailing practice of plantation owners was to hire masters (teachers) who would tutor their children. These masters often spent a few weeks at one plantation and then moved on the next, similar to the practice of circuit-riding preachers of that day. As in the northern colonies, teachers were almost always young white men, since education was denied African slaves in the South and traveling from one plantation to another was deemed unsuitable for young women.

In both the northern and southern colonies, young men were attracted to teaching mainly for the economic support it provided while they were preparing for some other career, such as law or the ministry. The result, of course, was a high turnover rate among teachers that, in turn, contributed to an inexperienced teaching force. For example, Preston (1982) studied teachers in Dedham, Massachusetts, between 1653 and 1703 and found that half of them taught for no longer than 1 year and none for over 5 years (Rury, 1989).

Elementary schools for young girls, called Dame Schools, were started in the northern colonies in the late seventeenth century. These schools, often conducted in a home by a housewife, provided the first teaching opportunities for women. The overall numbers of girls who attended these schools and the women who taught in them, however, remained very small.

Few teachers in colonial America really trained themselves to be teachers, so most were ill prepared for the job. The typical practice in filling a teaching position was to employ a literate young man who was studying for the ministry. There are some reported instances of individuals being apprenticed to experienced teachers, as was the case with a young man from New York described by Sedlak (1989).

> This Indenture witnesseth that John Campbel Son of Robert Campbel of the City of New York with the Consent of his father and mother hath put himself and by these presents doth Voluntarily put and bind himself Apprentice to George Brownell of the Same City Schoolmaster to learn the Art Trade or Mastery—for and during the term of ten years . . . And the said George Brownell Doth hereby Covenant and Promise to teach and instruct or Cause the said Apprentice to be taught and instructed in the Art Trade or Calling of Schoolmaster by the best way or means he or his wife may or can. (p. 263)

Most often, however, teachers did not receive any formal training, and the qualifications deemed important by the community were minimal, as illustrated by an advertisement that appeared in the *Virginia Gazette* in 1772.

> Wanted Immediately: A sober diligent Schoolmaster capable of teaching READING, WRITING, ARITH-METICK, and the Latin TONGUE. The school is quite new, has a convenient Lodging Room over it, is situated in a cheap Neighborhood, and its Income estimated at between sixty and eighty Pounds a Year. Any person qualified as above, and well recommended, will be put into immediate Possession of the School, on applying to the Minister of Charles Parish, York County. (Sedlak, 1989, p. 259)

As might be expected, communities in both the North and the South had high moral expectations for their teachers. This was particularly true in the Puritan towns of New England. Teachers were expected to provide a moral example for their students and to live prudent, righteous lives. Because the Puritans placed so many personal and social restrictions on all members of their community, it is unlikely that their teachers resented the restrictions placed on them. It is important to point out that teachers during colonial times, as in later times, were afforded a special status within the community, mainly because they were among the few who possessed even a minimal education.

In sum, teaching situations and the makeup of the teaching force changed little throughout the colonial period. Teaching was not considered a long-term career and, consequently, it was not an occupation for which one prepared. Instead, teaching drew middle- and upper-class men for short periods of time as they prepared for some other more lucrative line of work.

TEACHING IN THE NINETEENTH CENTURY

American society in the early to mid-nineteenth century remained basically agrarian as it had been in the eighteenth century. For instance, over two-thirds of the people in the United States were independent farmers or small town artisans and traders when the colonies won independence from England (Tozer et al., 1995). Teaching remained mainly the province of men who were poorly trained and waiting for a better job to come along. However, several important societal changes emerged at the beginning of the nineteenth century that radically changed the composition of the teaching force and the expectations society held for teachers.

Leaders of the new nation, such as Thomas Jefferson, believed strongly that a free, democratic society was possible only through education. As early as 1779, Jefferson introduced "A Bill for the More General Diffusion of Knowledge" into the Virginia legislature specifying that a system of free public education be established. Although it was not enacted, Jefferson's bill anticipated a system of public education that received wider support in later years and influenced the educational reforms that came after the election of Andrew Jackson in 1828. Generally referred to as the Common School Movement and attributed to the leadership of Horace Mann, legislation was passed first in Massachusetts and then in many other states calling for community support of schools. States created boards of education to ensure community compliance with educational laws. Mann, who became the first secretary of the Massachusetts State Board of Education in 1837, used his position to argue for an enlarged system of public education and to remind communities of their legal and moral obligations to support schools.

The work of Jackson and Jefferson and common school reformers such as Mann had considerable influence on American education. Their advocacy of free public education resulted in compulsory school attendance laws being passed in Massachusetts in 1852 and soon enacted in almost every state. Their reform efforts also resulted in an increased public awareness of how poorly prepared most teachers were and the need for special schools to remedy that situation.

The early part of the nineteenth century saw some radical changes in the geography and demography of the United States. It was during this time that settlers expanded into the middle and western parts of the country and that the industrial age had its beginnings. A simultaneous western migration and emerging factory system prompted a shortage of labor, which generated an increasing flow of immigrants to the United States, many of whom could not read or write English. It also generated poor working conditions and an increasing interest in trade unions. Common school reformers proclaimed the importance of educating immigrant children, and, at the same time, union leaders made free public education one of their early political planks.

The Common School Movement thus created a system of public schools, and the children of immigrant factory workers helped fill them. Together these conditions created a demand for teachers that could not be met by young men in search of other careers. Consequently, large numbers of women were recruited into the teaching ranks for the first time, women who had only recently been able to acquire the formal education demanded of teachers.

Women's access to formal schooling can be traced back to the beginnings of the nineteenth century, which saw the emergence of the first women's movement in the United States. At the turn of the century, Mary Wollstonecraft (1797) published a treatise entitled *Vindication of the Rights of Women* in which she argued for women's equal status with men and the importance of education in helping women to attain this status. As the women's movement gradually expanded, several schools for women were established. These included the Troy Female Seminary, established by Emma Willard in Troy, New York; the Mount Holyoke Seminary, started by Mary Lyon in Holyoke, Massachusetts; and the Hartford Female Seminary, begun by Catherine Beecher in Hartford, Connecticut. The establishment of these institutions, along with the first normal schools, or public colleges for teachers, in 1839, made it possible for women to acquire enough formal education to satisfy the teaching requirements of most communities.

It was not just teacher shortages and increasing educational opportunities that turned women to teaching. Equally important was the emerging view that women were more suited to teaching than men were. For centuries, Christian theology had proclaimed that women were rationally inferior but more loving and nurturing than men. Building on these beliefs and the view that teaching was essentially a nurturing process, reformers such as Mann began advocating women's natural fitness for teaching. An additional argument asserted that women were better in the role of teachers, because they had no need to support a family and, consequently, would work for less money. The following statement made by a member of the Boston Board of Education in 1841 illustrates this point of view:

> As a class they [women] never look forward, as young men almost invariably do, to a period of legal emancipation of parental control, when they are to break away from the domestic circle and go abroad into the world, to build up a fortune for themselves; and hence, the sphere of hope and of effort is narrower, and the whole forces of mind are more readily concentrated upon present duties. (Elsbree, as cited in Spring, 1996, p. 43)

By 1850, according to Rury (1989), 60 percent of the teachers in the United States were women and 80 percent of those in New England were women. By 1900, the percentage of women teachers nationwide had grown to 74 percent, a figure that has remained essentially unchanged to the present day. (See the related discussion in Chapter 1.)

What some historians have referred to as the "feminization of teaching" has had both positive and negative effects on the teaching profession. On one hand, the emergence of seminaries and normal schools provided women with access to education and greatly expanded the available pool of capable teachers. On the other hand, the fact that teaching became a "women's profession" caused educators in the late nineteenth and early twentieth centuries to develop systems in which teachers' work was tightly supervised, poorly paid, and characterized by a lack of respect. Susan B. Anthony, after hearing male teachers complain about their own low status as teachers, had this to say:

> None of you comprehend the cause of the disrespect of which you complain. Do you not see that so long as society says a woman is incompetent to be a lawyer, a minister, a doctor, but has ample ability to be a teacher, that every man of you who chooses that profession tacitly acknowledges that he has no more brains than a woman . . . Would you exalt your profession, exalt those who labor with you. (Sedlak, 1989, p. 122)

The training of teachers started to improve in the middle of the nineteenth century. In 1839, the first state normal school was opened in Lexington, Massachusetts. The idea for normal schools came from the common school reformers who visited Europe in the 1820s and 1830s and observed the teacher-training seminaries in Prussia. These reformers became convinced that good schools required good teachers. Although only three students appeared at the opening of the first normal school, within time it became a thriving institution and spawned others throughout New England. The idea spread quickly into the Midwest and West, and by 1890, the U.S. Commissioner of Education reported that 135 state-operated normal schools existed in the United States with over 25,000 teacher candidates in attendance. During this time, however, graduation from a normal school, or from any other school, was not required in order to teach, and most communities continued the practice of hiring poorly prepared teachers.

In addition to being mainly women, teachers during the nineteenth century were usually drawn from the local community. As in earlier times with male teachers, many were keeping school only until something better came along. Standards governing teaching practices were usually minimal or nonexistent. However, some communities took steps to make sure that teachers had minimal knowledge of the subjects they were to teach. The curriculum of the early normal schools emphasized subjects such as spelling, arithmetic, and grammar. Initial teaching certificates, such as the one illustrated in Figure P1.1, certified that teachers had passed tests in the subjects they were expected to teach. Generally, however, local school authorities made up their own exams and were more often concerned with order and discipline than they were with knowledge of subject matter or pedagogy. This point is illustrated in the following rendition of an exam given to a teacher candidate in a small New England town at the time of the Civil War:

> Chairman: How old are you?
> Candidate: I was eighteen years old the 27th of last May
> Chairman: Where did you last attend school?
> Candidate: At the Academy of S.
> Chairman: Do you think you can make the big youngsters mind?
> Candidate: Yes, I think I can.
> Chairman: Well, I am satisfied. I guess you will do for our school. I will send over the certificate by the children tomorrow. (Sedlak, 1989, p. 261)

Another illustration of a test given to teacher candidates in Maine in the 1840s follows:

> How would you deal with a child who was: (1) obstinately disobedient? (2) physically and mentally indolent? (3) addicted to falsehood? (4) impulsive? (Sedlak, 1989, p. 261)

As with their counterparts in the colonial era, teachers in the nineteenth century were expected to perform various community duties in addition to teaching school. Lortie (1975) reported that teachers "rang the church bells . . . swept up . . . taught Bible lessons, and occasionally substituted for the ailing pastor" (p. 18). In addition, teachers were expected to subject their personal lives to strict community regulation, as evidenced in the set of promises required of women teachers in a North Carolina community shown in Figure P1.2. Although this particular list may have been more stringent than in most communities, it nonetheless gives a clear indication of the concern nineteenth century communities had for their teachers' moral character and conduct.

TEACHING IN THE TWENTIETH CENTURY

During the second half of the nineteenth century and the first part of the twentieth century, great changes occurred in the United States. The Industrial Revolution exploded and grew to maturity. Urban centers were created and fed by millions of new immigrants who came from Europe and Asia to work in the factories as well as by newly emancipated workers—African Americans from the south and women from rural farms. Between 1850 and 1920, the population of the United States more than tripled, and the number of cities with over a half-million people grew from 2 to 12 (Edwards & Riche, 1963). The combined forces of industrialization, immigration, and urbanization lay the groundwork for today's educational system as well as for many of the social and educational problems Americans still face.

The schools that were created between 1870 and 1920 reflected the changes that were occurring in the larger society in three important ways. First, the industrial age sought large, bureaucratic forms of organization. This trend caused educators of the day to create large schools characterized by standardization, specialization, and differentiation between teachers and administrators. Second, the factory system's need for large numbers of workers brought to the United States waves of immigrants whose children needed to be educated. Educators had to seek ways to teach large numbers of children efficiently. Third, the industrial age embraced science. The emerging field of psychology, the science of how people learn and behave, was embraced by educators and used to defend the educational system they were building. These situations, as you will see, had lasting effects on teachers and their work.

Figure P1.1   **Nineteenth Century Teaching Certificate**

Teacher's ....2nd.... Grade Certificate.

I, County Superintendent of Public Instruction of......*Guilford*.... County, North Carolina, certify that I have thoroughly and fully examined ....*Julia E. Ross*........... an applicant for a Teacher's Certificate, on the several branches of study named below, and that ....*her*..... true grade of Scholarship in each is indicated by the number annexed to it, 100 indicating the highest. (See section 38, School Law of 1881.)

Spelling, (including sounds of letters,)	90
Defining,	85
Reading,	90
Writing,	85
Arithmetic, (Mental and Written,)	80
English Grammer,	90
Geography,	85
History of North Carolina,	75
History of the United States,	75

The said applicant has also furnished satisfactory evidence of good moral character. This certificate will therefore authorize the said ....*Julia E. Ross*.... to teach in the Public Schools in ..*Guilford*.. County during one year only from date hereof.

This ....*3rd*............ day of ....*Aug*.......... 188 *3*.......

....*J. R. Wharten*....
County Superintendent of Public Instruction

Source: After Porkay & Sanford, 1992, p. 176.

The effects of all this bureaucratic standardization and supervision on the teaching profession and its future were immense, and the elaborate systems that were created to supervise the work of teachers were particularly far reaching. One superintendent wrote:

> In industrial establishments, as well as in enterprises requiring unskilled manual labor, employers insist upon abundant supervision. A great railroad company places one man to boss three or four. Every factory, large or small, has its foremen and its bosses. Experience has taught that such an arrangement pays financially. The conclusions are quite as reasonable in the conduct of schools. (Tyack, 1974, p. 129)

Superintendents and principals, thus, became bosses, and teachers became workers, a condition

Figure P1.2   **Typical Restrictions Placed on Nineteenth Century Teachers**

> I promise to take a vital interest in all phases of Sunday-school work, donating of my time, service and money without stint for the benefit and uplift of the community.
>
> I promise to abstain from dancing, immodest dressing, and any other conduct unbecoming a teacher and a lady.
>
> I promise not to go out with any young man except as it may be necessary to stimulate Sunday-school work.
>
> I promise not to fall in love, to become engaged or secretly married.
>
> I promise to remain in the dormitory or on the school grounds when not actively engaged in school or church work elsewhere.
>
> I promise not to encourage or tolerate the least familiarity on the part of any of my boy pupils.
>
> I promise to sleep eight hours a night, eat carefully. . .

Source: Brenton, 1970, p. 74.

that is still evident today. David Tyack (1974) wrote about how the role of the principal evolved and how school administration became separated from teaching and learning:

> Principals were the inspectors and disciplinarians . . . Nothing was left to chance in the duties of teachers. They were told when to open the windows at recess; how to suspend the thermometer from the ceilings and to keep their rooms between 67 and 71 degrees; when to assemble, for at least two hours, at the monthly institute (they were fined two dollars for failing to attend and one dollar for being tardy); to subscribe for, take and read at least one periodical devoted to educational work; and how to cheerfully cooperate with the City Superintendent in executing the prescribed work of the grades. (p. 143)

As local schools strove to standardize the curriculum and to supervise the work of teachers, states began setting standards for teachers that later became requirements for certification. Teacher testing also became commonplace in most states, although the tests remained primarily tests of general knowledge rather than of pedagogy. The salary schedules used today, based on training and years of experience, were adopted at the turn of the century.

Many teachers still lacked formal training and skills, but this situation was starting to improve. Teacher preparation began expanding beyond the 2-year normal schools to universities, and by the middle of the twentieth century, virtually all teachers held bachelors' degrees. Even so, the profession did not improve substantially during the early twentieth century. Education's bureaucratic form of organization prevented the development of a culture in which teachers were encouraged toward professional growth and self-regulation. The supervisory and regulatory practices of the age restricted these through an elaborate system of externally imposed rules. A class system in education emerged in which men assumed the dominant supervisory roles and women the submissive teaching positions.

It was also during this time that educators began to embrace the emerging discipline of psychology and to use it as a means for understanding and defending the educational system being developed. Ideas from psychology provided the foundation for new standardized testing systems that were being used to measure student achievement and intelligence and, thereby, to segregate students into different academic tracts. A theory of learning was also developing that envisioned a child's mind as an empty vessel waiting to be filled. A child, the theory asserted, is motivated to activity (learning) primarily through a system of externally imposed rewards and punishments. This view of the child and the learning process, which will be described in the introduction to Part 2, led to a system of teacher-centered instruction that has dominated the practice of teaching until the present time.

As the twentieth century progressed, communities began replacing the social restrictions imposed on teachers with new expectations. Increasingly, communities sought to hire teachers who liked children and who taught them effectively. The criteria used to judge effective teaching, however, were based on individual personal attributes of teachers, such as "displays warmth," "acts in professional manner," "has good rapport with students," and "dresses appropriately" rather than on specific teaching behaviors. Personal attributes and their relevance to effective teaching are discussed in more detail in Chapter 2.

TEACHING IN THE INFORMATION AGE

Many features of schools and teaching were so permanently institutionalized in American culture in the early part of the twentieth century that they still dominate the educational landscape today. However, our educational system is currently in transition and is beginning to take on the organizational features of the emerging information age. These features are discussed in later part openers and in Chapters 7 and 9 so will not be detailed here. It is important to point out, however, that public expectations for teachers are changing rapidly. Rather than emphasizing social restrictions on teachers' personal lives, today's public wants teachers who are highly trained and who can be held accountable for demonstrating best teaching practices. Whereas they were previously evaluated by a set of personal attributes, teachers are currently required to demonstrate their knowledge of subject matter and pedagogy. Teacher testing has become and will continue to become more prevalent. For instance, in 1996, 43 states required teachers to pass some type of test before issuing them a teaching certificate. Plans are under way to institute the same requirements in all remaining states. Most states use Praxis, a set of paper-and-pencil tests developed and administered by the Education Testing Service (ETS), which measures teachers' knowledge of both subject matter and pedagogy. Alternative and more difficult performance-based tests are currently being developed and pilot tested.

Furthermore, competency in academic subjects alone will no longer be a sufficient measure of an effective teacher, particularly for teaching in classrooms that are culturally diverse and include students with various handicapping conditions. Neither will the criteria of liking children, in and of itself, be enough for tomorrow's teachers. Twenty-first century teachers will be required to have a command of various knowledge bases—academic, pedagogical, social, and cultural—and to be reflective, problem-solving professionals. The following description of teachers appeared in *A Nation Prepared: Teachers for the Twenty-First Century,* a document sponsored by The Carnegie Forum on Education and the Economy (1986):

> Teachers should have a good grasp of the ways in which all kinds of physical and social systems work; a feeling for what data are and the uses to which they can be put; an ability to help students see patterns of meaning where others see only confusion; an ability to foster genuine creativity in students; and the ability to work with other people in work groups that decide for themselves how to get the job done. They must be able to learn all the time, as the knowledge required to do their work twists and turns with new challenges and the progress of science and technology. Teachers will not come to the school knowing all they have to know, but knowing how to figure out what they need to know, where to get it, and how to help others make meaning out of it.
>
> Teachers must think for themselves if they are to help others think for themselves, be able to act independently and collaborate with others, and render critical judgment. They must be people whose knowledge is wide ranging and whose understanding runs deep. (p. 25)

If current trends, which include expanded expectations for teachers and more and better teacher testing, continue into the next century, it is likely that training programs for teachers will have to be extended. Many of you may be in extended programs now that require a bachelor's degree with a strong subject matter major before you can be admitted to a masters level teacher-training program centered around pedagogy and field experiences.

Current trends are also leading to a system of national certification of teachers. The Carnegie Forum on Education and the Economy has helped organize the National Board for Professional Teaching Standards. This board, formally created in May 1987, has the support of many important education groups, including the two major teachers' unions, the American Federation of Teachers (AFT) and the National Educational Association (NEA). The board's aim has been to set standards for the teaching profession and to issue a national teaching certificate. The board began its formal assessments in 1993, and the first teachers were nationally certified in 1994. Requirements for the national professional certificate include: an undergraduate degree in one of the arts or sciences, successful teaching or internship experiences, and a passing score on a series of very difficult and thorough oral, written, and performance exams.

We return to the attributes of effective teachers in Chapter 2 and to the professionalization of teaching in Chapter 12, where we review more recent history such as the unionization of teachers after World War II and the evolution of teaching over the past quarter of a century into a true profession.

The World and Work of Teaching

Every day nearly 3 million people get up in the morning, eat their low-fat, high-fiber cereals, and then go out to teach school. If we include those who teach in early childhood centers and in business and industrial settings, this figure might well be doubled. In short, education occupies a prominent place in our society, and many people devote their lives to teaching. Because you are reading this text, it is likely that you too are contemplating a teaching career. Perhaps you are an 18-year-old high school graduate who has been thinking of teaching since the eighth grade. Perhaps you are 29, and after working at several routine jobs, you have re-entered college and are considering a teacher education program at the advice of your college's academic counselor. Or, it may be that you are a bit older, in your early forties, and are seeking a new, more meaningful and people-oriented career after working for years as a successful corporate accountant. You believe that teaching offers the personal satisfaction that you missed in your previous job.

But is teaching really for you? Although you know quite a bit about schools and teaching from having spent approximately 15,000 hours in elementary and high school classrooms, your view of classroom life has been from in front of rather than behind the teacher's desk. What, for instance, do you know about the noninstructional work that teachers do? What do you know about schools as organizational settings that constrain or support teachers' efforts? What do you know about the teaching profession? As you consider these questions, you will find that some of your images of teaching are not only incomplete but, in some instances, altogether wrong.

We have written this book to help you explore teaching as a career and understand more fully the complexity of classrooms and schools. To make a wise career choice requires an in-depth understanding of two things. First, you need to understand the world and work of teachers—what it is like now and what it might become in the years ahead. Second, you need to understand yourself—your needs, your goals, and your motivations. Finally, you need to match those two bodies of knowledge; that is, to match knowledge of yourself against that of teaching. That is the purpose of this book, to help you

Why Be a Teacher?
Motives for Teaching
Who Teaches Today?
Teacher Supply
Teacher Gender
Teacher Race and Ethnicity
Teacher Quality

The Context and Nature of Teaching
Teaching Is a Professional Career
Teachers' Work
Goals
Tasks
Tools and Technologies
Time and Work Schedules
Preparation Requirements
Rewards of Teaching and Advancement Opportunities

Teachers' Workplace
Physical Characteristics of Schools
Organizational Features of Schools

A Quick Tour through Exploring Teaching
Self-Regulated Learning in Democratic Classrooms
Social Context of Teaching
Repertoire of Best Practice Based on Research
Multicultural Crossroads
Schools Reflect Society

Assessing Your Motives and Skills for Teaching in the Twenty First Century

Summary

Readings for the Professional

explore the world of teaching and your ability to work in that world. If you understand and value the many things that teachers do on a day-to-day basis, it is likely that you will find satisfaction in a teaching career. On the other hand, if you perceive our description of teachers' work as uninteresting or unchallenging, then you should probably begin looking for another career.

Chapter 1 begins with a brief overview of the world and work of teaching that includes a glimpse into why people choose to become teachers and what kinds of individuals make this choice. This is followed by a more in-depth look at the work teachers do and at the place where they do it. The work of teachers, unlike that of lawyers, doctors, or marriage counselors, is *not* conducted in an office with private clients. Instead, most teaching is public and takes place in unique organizational settings we call *classrooms* and *schools*. The fact that schools are highly visible public organizations accounts for many of the often-conflicting expectations that society has for teachers. It also influences the nature of teachers' work and the rewards and status that accompany that work. The chapter concludes with a brief discussion of changes—social, organizational, technological, and pedagogical—that seem destined to have impact on the world and work of teaching over the next 20 years and with a short section that provides you with a preview of the rest of the book.

WHY BE A TEACHER?

You have been having a stimulating discussion with a group of good friends. The topics this evening have ranged widely, from politics to religion to the meaning of life. Finally, the subject moves to one that is very meaningful to everyone: your careers and the lifestyles you envision for yourselves.

Ben says that he wants to live a life characterized by simplicity, with few obligations and only essential material goods. He wants his work to pay enough to support a modest lifestyle, but most important, he wants to be free from the demands that characterize many professional careers. He wants time to pursue his personal artistic interests and to raise a family. He believes that working in a book store in some similar capacity will provide him with what he wants from a job.

Marie has different plans. She believes that financial success is the key to her life goals and that she will not be happy until she is recognized for her professional accomplishments. Marie plans to enter law school next fall and looks forward to the competition and stress associated with most legal careers. She thrives on hard work and doubts that she will have children, at least not until she is financially secure and professionally recognized.

Suddenly, the conversation turns to you, and you begin talking about your desire to be a teacher. Some of your friends groan at your choice, but others listen as you explain what teaching means to you and how you have wanted to be a teacher since you were 10 years old. You explain your desire to help young people and to enjoy the benefits and lifestyle that a career in teaching affords. As you talk, you wonder if your motives are similar to others who have chosen to be teachers.

Motives for Teaching

People choose teaching for many reasons. For some, the desire to teach has always been there, having been planted early in life by a parent or an admired teacher. For others, it comes later in life, as the desire to help others supplanted more materialistic goals. For still others, the combination of intellectual stimulation and free time for travel and additional pursuits is the lure. Think for a moment about the motives behind your desire to teach. Think also about goals you may have that work against choosing a teaching career.

From the research information presented in the accompanying Research Box, you can see that individuals choose teaching for a variety of intrinsic and extrinsic reasons, the overwhelming reason being a desire to work with young people.

Teachers, it seems, have a special liking for children and young people, and teaching provides a rewarding, day-to-day interaction with them. The experience of helping a classroom of young people form into a cohesive learning community and the subsequent teacher-student bonding that occurs is intrinsically rewarding. Teachers like knowing that they are needed and that their efforts can make a difference in the lives of young people. Knowing this sustains them during the difficult and stressful aspects of their work.

Liking children is not all that attracts people to teaching, however. Many teachers have an intense interest in the subjects they teach, and teaching affords them the opportunity to pursue these interests. As part of their job, they read books and attend seminars about their subjects. Often they receive extra pay for these activities. Teaching about something can intensify one's knowledge and bring about new understandings. The old adage that you never really understand or appreciate something until you have taught it to another person is true and, for those who love their subjects, makes teaching a worthwhile career.

Also, it seems that teachers and parents have an enormous influence on an individual's choice to become a teacher as well as on the type of teacher a person becomes. In many ways, this is a positive situation. It means that many beginning teachers have been inspired by good models over the years. This situation, however, can also have a negative impact, particularly when former teachers looked on as role models have used teaching methods that do not represent best practice. Continued experiences with poor teachers may also cause some otherwise qualified individuals to reject teaching as a career.

Additionally, many individuals choose a teaching career because of its unique mixture of benefits, another topic we treat in more detail later in the chapter. Here it suffices to say that teacher salaries, although not immense, have risen to respectable levels over the past three decades. And while the hours are often long, teaching offers more flexibility than most other jobs or professions. Holiday and vacation times for teachers are likewise quite generous in comparision to those offered by other jobs.

Some of the more altruistic motives for teaching may be overstated because they are socially acceptable, but other motives, such as wanting lengthy summer vacations, may be just as influential. Below we provide three vignettes about real people who chose to make teaching their career. As you read about these people, consider whether any of their characteristics or motives match your own.

John, who is 20 years old, was admitted into the elementary teacher education program at a major state university last fall. John's mother is a teacher in a nearby community, and although he always considered teaching a possible career choice, he went to college as a chemistry major. After his sophomore year, during which he tutored several young children in science, John decided that teaching was for him. His tutoring experience caused him to spend considerable time and effort considering how to make science interesting to young children. He now believes that teaching will provide not only the intellectual stimulation he wants from a job but will also satisfy his desire to help people. John's university requires him to have a double major, one in a subject area and the other in education. It will take John 5 years to graduate and to obtain his teaching certificate.

Rosalie is a 37-year-old mother who was admitted to the same teacher education program as John but

followed a different route to get there. Rosalie was married right after high school, and although she wanted to go to college, she wasn't interested in teaching at that time. In fact, Rosalie never really enjoyed school or her teachers very much. She never had a favorite teacher with whom she identified.

Rosalie soon became the mother of two children and abandoned her thoughts of college. When her children started school, she volunteered to be a parent helper and began assisting her children's teachers with reading groups and other classroom activities. Three years ago, she was invited by one of the teachers to attend a workshop on the whole-language approach to reading, and she became fascinated with the subject. Gradually Rosalie started to think about teaching as a possible career. She believes not only that she can become a good teacher but that the school calendar will give her more free time to devote to her family than other jobs will.

With the support of her husband and children, Rosalie started taking courses at the local community college. At first she took only one or two courses at a time but later switched to a full-time schedule. She graduated with an associate degree in English, then applied and was accepted to the university's elementary teacher preparation program. Rosalie's fascination with language and how children acquire language skills has remained constant. At the university, she will pursue a subject matter major in English and a degree in elementary education. By the time Rosalie's children are in college, she will have her degree and her teaching certificate. She expects her teaching career to carry her through to her retirement years.

David is 44 years old and has worked for NASA since graduating 20 years ago from MIT with a master's degree in physics. Although David's work on the cutting edge of space exploration has been exciting, he has been increasingly bothered by feelings that he would like to spend more time working with people and applying his skills to social rather than technical problems. He also has hobbies there isn't time to pursue. David's wife is an attorney, and she has encouraged him to leave NASA and prepare for another career if that's what he wants. After attending several workshops for career changers, David decided that teaching would be a good second career for him. His background in science and his years of experience in the space industry make him uniquely qualified to work with youth in middle schools and to encourage them to pursue studies and careers in science. The work schedule of teaching and the lengthy summer vacations will allow him more time to spend with his family and with his gardening hobby.

As these brief sketches show, people choose teaching for a variety of reasons. Most believe it will offer them meaningful challenges and both intrinsic and extrinsic rewards. The challenges will come from daily engagement with young people, helping them to develop and grow intellectually, emotionally, and socially. Challenges will also come from serving as advocates for youth and their schools. After reading this section, what do you now think of these various motives and how they may work for or against choosing a teaching career? Do you have a desire to work with young children or youth? Will helping them develop bring you satisfaction? Are you interested in your subject field, and will you find it satisfying to teach it to others? What about the extrinsic aspects of teaching? Are you the type of person who wants a long summer vacation and job security?

Who Teaches Today?

In addition to examining your motives for teaching, you need to consider who today's teachers are, because if you decide to pursue a teaching career, they will be your colleagues.

As you read in the introduction to Part 1, the demographic profile of teachers has changed dramatically over the course of this nation's history. In colonial times, teaching attracted mostly young men who worked as tutors and kept school for only a few weeks each year. Teaching did not represent a ca-

RESEARCH

Reasons People Give for Choosing a Career in Teaching

Several major studies conducted over the past 30 years have produced pretty consistent results about the reasons individuals give for choosing teaching as a career. One of the most famous studies was done in the late 1960s and early 1970s by Daniel Lortie, a sociologist at the University of Chicago. In his study, Lortie was interested in a variety of issues about teaching as a career, particularly how teachers' work was organized and the sentiments teachers held toward their work. To find answers to questions about teaching, Lortie used information from a national survey of teachers as well as from 94 teachers he interviewed. Lortie found that many teachers in his study had been influenced by other adults and attributed their career choice to an inspirational teacher or to a parent who was a teacher. They reported that their choice occurred very early in life. Here is what one teacher told Lortie (1975) about the influence a parent had on her decision to teach:

My mother was a teacher, her sisters were teachers—it's a family occupation. I always wanted to go into teaching. I can't remember when I didn't want to . . . I remember as a little girl sometimes seeing teachers having a hard time. I thought , well, I will be careful because some day I'll be on the other side of the desk. (p. 61)

Other teachers told Lortie how their decision to teach and their teaching styles had been greatly influenced by their own teachers, for instance:

The teacher I had in sixth grade was good, interesting. There are few things I used this year that I don't remember having done in her room. (p. 63)

I had (a teacher) in United States history and she whetted my appetite for history and for teaching . . . I (as a teacher) may be one of her protégés. I think I am. (p. 64)

Between 1986 and 1994, a group of researchers working under the auspices of the American Association of Colleges for Teacher Education

reer; rather, it provided a convenient way station while preparing or waiting for some other more attractive opportunity to come along. Then, educational opportunities expanded, and market forces began the feminization of teaching. By 1930, this trend resulted in a teaching force that was 80 percent women, most of whom were quite young. Although teaching during the nineteenth and early twentieth centuries took on some characteristics of a career, low pay and easy entry made it an interim occupation for many women also, until more important work or marriage and family materialized.

Today, there are still far more women than men in teaching, and some individuals still view teaching as a place holder until something better comes along. However, most people today enter teaching with the view that it or some education-related career will be a lifetime endeavor. It is also common today for people to enter teaching at various stages of their lives, not just as young college graduates. The next section describes some important characteristics of today's teaching force. Two aspects that you might find of interest to your own career choice include: the overall supply (quantity) of those willing to teach and the overall demographic profile of the teaching profession.

Teacher Supply

Over time, the number of teachers in the United States has increased dramatically. However, without specific policies to guide the supply of teachers, the United States has experienced extreme shifts in teacher supply and demand. This is particularly true for the 50 years since World War II. First, the postwar

RESEARCH

Continued

(AACTE) conducted yearly studies about teacher education. Over a 9-year period they surveyed thousands of teacher education students from a random sample of colleges and universities in the United States. Among many other questions, students were asked about why they chose to go into teaching. The National Education Association also asks its members on a regular basis why they chose to be teachers. The list here represents a composite of results from these studies. (See AACTE, 1989; AACTE, 1991; NEA, 1993).

Reasons Given for Choosing Teaching as a Career

Reason	Approximate Range for This Reason (in percentages)
• Desire to work with young people	65–75
• Value of teaching to society	35–40
• Interest in my subject matter	35–45
• Influence of family	20–25
• Long summer vacation	15–25
• Job security	15–20
• Self-growth and actualization	10–20

How do these reasons compare with yours for considering a career in teaching? Is your primary motive a desire to work with young people? What about your friends who are considering teaching? What reasons have they discussed with you?

Figure 1.1   **Elementary and Secondary School Enrollments 1970–2006**

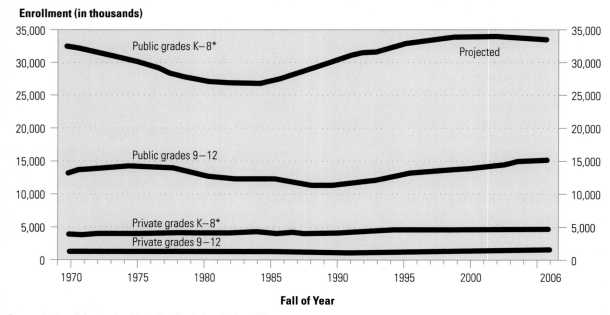

Enrollment (in thousands)

Source: *National Center for Education Statistics,* 1996, p. 127.

baby boom of the 1950s and 1960s brought critical shortages of teachers. This was followed by decreases in school enrollments in the 1970s and a corresponding teacher surplus. By the mid-1980s, however, the children of the postwar baby boomers began entering schools, so enrollments and the demand for teachers once again increased. The changes in public and private school enrollments between 1970 and 1995 and projected through 2006 are displayed in Figure 1.1. As you can see, total public school enrollment rose almost 15 percent between 1985 and 1995, and it is expected to increase by 6 percent by the year 2006. Of course, such demographic factors as birth rate and immigration could change these predictions.

Figure 1.2 shows that the overall number of teachers has increased steadily since 1960. It also shows the flat growth rate in the 1970s and the early 1980s, which corresponds to the decline in student enrollments during that time. In the 10-year period between 1985 and 1995, the number of classroom teachers increased from slightly over 2.2 million to over 2.5 million. Currently, teacher shortages exist in some subject areas (e.g., math and science) and in some geographical areas (e.g., inner city and rural) but not in others. Special education and bilingual teachers are in great demand. Overall, however, there is a slight surplus of teachers in most parts of the United States, and this condition is expected to continue until the beginning of the twenty-first century.

A traditionally serious problem with the supply and demand of teachers is that, unlike in other fields where services are curtailed if there is a shortage of trained providers, shortages of qualified teachers have been solved by hiring unqualified teachers. For instance, many senior faculty in schools today were hired during the shortages that occurred in the 1950s and 1960s when virtually anyone with a college degree could secure a teaching position. Alternative certification procedures practiced today in some states perpetuate this potentially harmful means of coping with teacher shortages, particularly in the inner cities and poor rural areas. This practice of hiring unqualified teachers has caused long-range problems for education and for the teaching profession in the United States. For example, unqualified teachers are frequently hired to teach in the most unattractive and difficult situations, such as inner city schools, where experienced and highly trained teachers are most needed. Furthermore, scarce resources that could be spent for crucial supplies and improved facilities are often spent on in-service training for recently hired, unqualified teachers.

Teacher Gender

We described earlier how, except for in its very early stages, teaching in the United States has been traditionally considered the domain of women and how at one time as many as 85 percent of U.S. teachers were women. Today, that trend has changed some-

Figure 1.2   **Number of Elementary and Secondary Teachers 1960–1996**

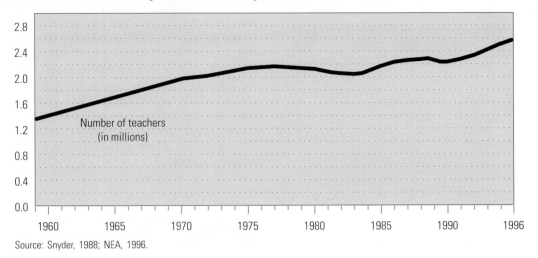

Source: Snyder, 1988; NEA, 1996.

what, but still the vast majority of teachers are women. Table 1.1 shows the percentages of male and female elementary and secondary teachers in the United States for three time periods.

As you can see, overall, there are slightly fewer males in teaching today than in 1965. Male teachers are more likely to work in secondary schools, but also, there has been an increase in men teachers in elementary education during the past decades.

The profile and demographics of people entering teaching today are very similar to those of the current teaching force. For instance, from 1987 to 1990, a team of researchers surveyed candidates entering teaching from various kinds of colleges and universities in the United States. When candidates

Table 1.1   **Male and Female Teachers by Type of School: 1965–1995** (in percentages)

Gender	Year		
	1965	**1984**	**1995**
Male			
Elementary	11	15	15
Middle	n/a	42	35
Secondary	54	62	53
Total	31	34	30
Female			
Elementary	89	85	85
Middle	n/a	58	65
Secondary	46	38	47
Total	69	66	70

Source: After Metropolitan Life, 1995, p. 70.

preparing for secondary teaching were surveyed, it was found that slightly over three-fourths (76 percent) were women (AACTE, 1987). When elementary teacher candidates were surveyed a year later, 90 percent were found to be women (AACTE, 1988).

Teacher Race and Ethnicity

During the past three decades, the demographics of the student population in America's schools has changed dramatically. A third of all public school students in the United States today are of African American, Asian, or Hispanic descent. The proportion of students from non-European backgrounds approaches 90 percent in many large urban areas. This trend toward an increasingly non-European student population is expected to continue well into the next century. However, as students in public schools have become more diverse, the ethnic and racial backgrounds of their teachers have changed very little. In fact, African American and Hispanic teachers have remained a very small proportion of the teaching profession over the past decade, as Table 1.2 illustrates.

The majority of U.S. teachers (89 percent) is white. Six percent of teachers are African American and 5 percent are Hispanic. This discrepancy between the backgrounds of teachers and students is troublesome for a number of reasons. In the first place, it is important that children from non-European backgrounds have positive role models, people from their own race or ethnic background who can help them learn and develop positive self-esteem. It is equally important that children with European or majority culture backgrounds are taught by competent minority teachers, individuals

Table 1.2 **Distribution of Teachers by Race**

(in percentages)

Race	1988	1995
White	90	89
African American	7	6
Asian	.5	1
Native American	n/a	1
Other	1	3
Hispanic*	4	5

*Hispanic could also be included in other races
Source: After Metropolitan Life, 1995, p. 73.

who can help them overcome their mistrust or stereotypic views of other cultural groups. Simply, it is important for the country's social health that all our professions reflect the racial and cultural diversity of the overall population.

The shortage of minority teachers is not something that will be solved quickly. Rather, it is a problem that will require considerable attention and resources in the future. One deterrent to its solution has been the steadily improving access of minority groups to other professions with higher salaries and more status. This access has diverted members of minority cultures, who previously might have chosen a teaching career, to other professions. Also, the lack of good minority teachers has contributed to the bad school experiences of minority students. This, in turn, makes it less likely that minority students will choose a teaching career. Overcoming the shortage of minority teachers will depend on the continued improvement of teachers' salaries and working conditions. It will also require increased financial aid and incentives for those who are willing to enter teaching. Providing student loans that are forgiven after three to five years of teaching is an example of a financial aid policy currently being considered in some states. Starting future teacher clubs in high schools with large minority populations is another strategy for attracting minority youngsters into teaching.

Teacher Quality

Quality is an additional demographic characteristic of the teaching profession that may influence your career choice. Some school critics have maintained that the best and brightest do not become teachers.

This assertion, however, has been challenged in recent years, and data have illustrated that teachers are every bit as talented as people in other professional fields. In 1992, the U.S. Department of Education studied adult literacy in the United States and compared prose literacy scores among various occupation groups. As you can see in Figure 1.3, teachers' literacy skills tested lower than those of many private sector executives and managers, but they scored higher than writers, social workers, and registered nurses. They also scored higher than school administrators.

THE CONTEXT AND NATURE OF TEACHING

When most people think of teaching, they imagine the *act of teaching,* that is, of a teacher interacting with one or more students. Although such teacher-student interactions may appear to be spontaneous, highly personal activities, in reality they are greatly influenced by a variety of invisible forces that penetrate the school and classroom walls. These invisible forces are the cultural norms, values, beliefs, and organizational arrangements that exist in the various contexts (classroom, school, community, society, and professional) that surround and shape the act of teaching. Although invisible, they are nevertheless powerful and greatly influence the interpersonal side of teaching. The section that follows describes some of the contextual aspects of teaching, and we will return to this topic at end of the chapter to illustrate how they have influenced the organization and content of the book.

Teaching Is a Professional Career

In everyday conversation, we use the words *job, occupation,* and *career* interchangeably—"my job," "my occupation," "my career." There are differences, however, among these terms. A *job* normally refers to activity at a place of employment: "I have a job at McDonalds." Often a job is simply considered something we do for money. An *occupation,* on the other hand, is a more general term and refers to the *type of work* performed by an individual or to a group of similar jobs: "My occupation is a fry cook," or "My occupation is a business manager."

The term **career,** on the other hand, describes various jobs or occupations that have been hierarchically arranged within some broad field of work. For example, law careers encompass such occupations as paralegals, law clerks, attorneys, legal sec-

Figure 1.3   **Prose Literacy Scores of Employed Bachelor's Degree Recipients by Selected Occupations: 1992**

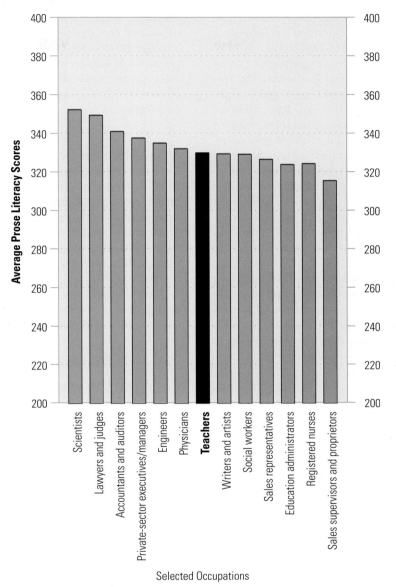

Selected Occupations

Source: National Center for Education Statistics, 1996, p. 58.

retaries, and judges. One needs to have a law degree and to practice law before becoming a judge. Likewise, careers in education encompass not only classroom teachers but also teacher's aides, resource room teachers, special educators, deans of students, principals, coaches, superintendents, teacher educators, and so on. Careers, particularly those in the professions, necessitate special preparation for entrance, and they demand continuing education. In most instances, professional careers require advanced degrees if one wants to change occupations within the overall career field. For instance, a high school biology teacher would normally be required to have a Ph.D. before becoming a college biology teacher. Similarly, an elementary school teacher needs to obtain a special certificate and a master's degree in school administration before he or she becomes a principal. Finally, most careers exist within a larger profession, such as the legal profession, the medical profession, the counseling profession. Teaching exists within the larger education profession, a topic covered in some detail in Chapter 12.

The process of choosing an occupation or career is complex and should be approached with care. Too often, individuals look back and regret their career decisions. Building on the work of John Holland (1992), a famous occupational counselor, and of Richard Bolles (1995), the author of the highly popular *What Color Is Your Parachute,* we suggest that anyone can make a more rationale career choice by considering the following three aspects of a career: the nature of the work, the setting in which the work is performed, and how well your own talents, knowledge, characteristics, and attitudes match this work and its settings. Figure 1.4 illustrates this basic model.

In the following section we examine the first two aspects of this model, and in Chapter 2 on effective teaching, we discuss the third, the attitudes, knowledge, and orientations of effective teachers. In each instance, we pose questions that ask you to assess yourself in terms of the criteria discussed.

Teachers' Work

Think for a moment about the work experiences you have had. What was the purpose of your work? What were you required to do? Did the work require any special preparation, or could just about anyone start doing the work immediately? Did you enjoy the work, or did you find it boring? Were opportunities for advancement in the workplace available, or was it a dead-end job? These are questions anyone can

ask about any work experience and ones that obviously need to be answered before one makes a long-term career decision. To help you match what teachers do to your own career choice, we have organized our discussion of the nature of teaching into the six categories illustrated in Figure 1.5: goals, tasks, tools and technologies, time and work schedules, preparation requirements, and rewards and advancement opportunities. A brief discussion of each follows.

Goals

All work is driven by goals or outcomes that people want to accomplish. Normally, people find their work satisfying when they value what they accomplish and unsatisfying when the outcomes of their work conflict with their basic values. For instance, it is hard to conceive of a pacifist finding much satisfaction working in a weapons factory or a person who dislikes animals finding happiness working in a pet store.

Many individuals choose teaching because its altruistic goal of helping others is considered a noble and significant public service. Even people

Figure 1.5 **Features of Teachers' Work**

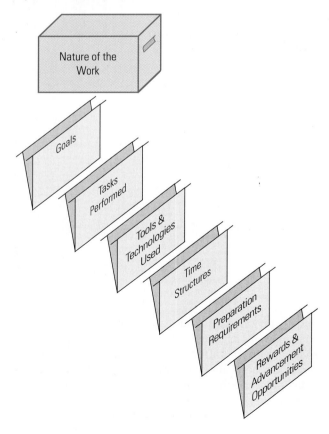

Figure 1.4 **Making a Career Choice**

Career Considerations

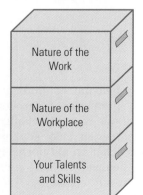

who criticize the schools generally believe that educating the young is important. Although they may grumble about the taxes that pay teachers' salaries, they generally respect the work that teachers do and see teaching as a socially important profession whose goals they embrace. The data presented in Figure 1.6 illustrates the positive status afforded teachers because of the important and demanding work they do. Notice that of all the jobs listed, teachers are perceived to be in the middle in terms of prestige and second only to doctors in terms of how demanding the work is.

On the other hand, because education has to do with matters of the mind, many individuals in our materialistic society view its devotion to learning as an end in itself with some skepticism. Some college graduates, for example, report that they really did not go to college for the sake of learning but for economic advancement. This deep and abiding anti-intellectualism that permeates American culture has been evident for many years. It seems unreasonable to expect a person whose materialistic goals far outweigh their intellectual and altruistic goals to find much satisfaction in teaching. *How do the goals teachers are expected to accomplish match your own values, goals, and motivations?*

Tasks

All jobs are partially defined by the specific tasks an individual is expected to perform. Some jobs, such as sorting parts on an assembly line, have very little variety and are quite routine. On the other hand, highly specialized work, such as that of a surgeon or an air controller, presents the job holder with many specific and highly technical tasks. Teachers are among those required to perform an array of diverse tasks in complex and unpredictable settings. These tasks can be broadly organized into the following three categories: interactive tasks, leadership tasks, and organizational tasks. A word about each of these task categories follows.

Part of a teacher's work consists of working directly with students: instructing them, promoting collaboration among them, counseling them, and otherwise helping them accomplish assigned learning tasks. We have labeled these the **interactive tasks** of teaching. Another aspect of a teacher's work has to do with providing leadership. **Leadership tasks** performed by teachers are not much different from those performed by leaders or executives in other work settings. They include such things as planning, managing, evaluating, motivating, and empowering individuals and groups in order to accomplish valued work.

Additionally, teachers work in unique organizations called *schools* and, as organizational members, are required to perform numerous tasks to help sustain and improve the organization. Working with parents, principals, curriculum specialists, and fellow teachers are examples of important **organizational**

Figure 1.6   **How the Public Views Teachers and Their Work**

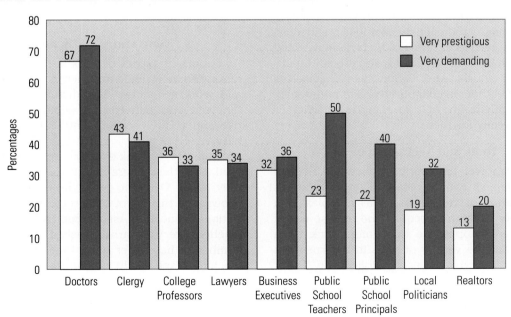

Source: NEA/Gallup Public Opinion Poll, 1985.

tasks performed by teachers. These noninstructional tasks are often ignored when exploring a teaching career. Although the interactive and leadership tasks of teaching are what attract most people into the profession, a review of Table 1.4 presented later in this section shows just how prevalent and important the organizational tasks of teaching are.

Indeed, contrary to popular belief, today's teachers do not spend the vast majority of their time working face-to-face with students in self-contained classrooms. Increasingly, both teachers and students spend time working with others. In the case of teachers, this means working with other adults—parents, fellow teachers, staff specialists, and administrators—in pursuit of both schoolwide and individual student goals. *Can you see yourself becoming a member of a resource team that includes a parent, a school counselor, a nurse, a social worker, and a special educator?*

Working with other adults is not the only form of **collaboration** that confronts today's teachers. Recent advances in pedagogy have demonstrated the effectiveness of student collaboration in producing both academic and social achievement. Thus, just as teachers are expected to work effectively with other adults in organizational settings, they are also expected to use collaborative learning strategies, such as cooperative learning and project-based learning, both of which are discussed in Chapter 6.

Research on effective schools has repeatedly shown that the most effective schools—those that consistently produce above-average student achievement—are those which achieve a high degree of faculty, parent, and student collaboration. For this reason, applicants for teaching positions are increasingly being screened in terms of their demonstrated ability to work well in group situations. Consequently, individuals who cannot see themselves working with others in collaborative and interdependent ways might do well to reconsider whether teaching is really for them.

Tools and Technologies

Tools are whatever humans have invented to help them accomplish valued goals. They can be as simple as a set of chopsticks or as complex as a laser scanner. Some jobs require the precise use of many tools. To appreciate this point, think for a moment about the variety of tools in a carpenter's toolbox or those on a surgeon's surgical tray. Other jobs require the use of only a few tools. A cleaning person relies mainly on a vacuum cleaner, a broom, and a mop. Some tools, such as those used by air traffic controllers, are quite complex, whereas others, such as the thermometers used by nurses, are technologically simple. Tools help determine the nature of particular jobs, and learning how to use the "tools of the trade" is a major goal in most professional preparation programs.

Some who have studied education have observed that teaching, for whatever reasons, has not required the use of very many technological tools. In fact, many recent technological advances, such as computers, that have significantly influenced other professions, have been slow to impact the work of teachers. The tools most closely associated with teaching are books, pencils and papers, chalk and chalkboards. These have been around for a long time, and just about everyone in our society knows how to use them. Perhaps this is one reason that many people think they can teach without special preparation. They know how to use the simple tools and technologies most closely associated with teaching.

Many experts believe that teachers of the future will be required to use a much more complex and powerful array of technological tools. They anticipate twenty-first century teachers making multimedia presentations and students using interactive technologies to explore the world in ways that chalkboards and books cannot. Some believe that computers will replace paper-and-pencil lessons and perhaps even books as we now know them. The use of complex technological tools will make teaching seem more attractive for some, whereas it will have a negative effect on others. *Does involvement with new technology appeal to you, or are you worried about its use?*

Time and Work Schedules

An important aspect of work is the way that goals, tasks, and tools come together to create unique time and work schedules. The distinctly characteristic time and work patterns of teaching have both negative and positive components, which we describe here.

Some people think that teachers do not work very hard, that their hours match those of the children they teach. Over the years, however, studies have shown that this is not at all the case. Since 1961, the National Education Association (NEA) has surveyed teachers every 5 years and asked them to report the number of hours per week they spend on various teaching responsibilities. For 30 years, the findings of these reports have remained pretty consistent. Elementary teachers report that they work between 45 and 49 hours per week, while secondary teachers say that they work from 46 to 50 hours per week

(NEA, 1992). A recent survey confirmed that the majority of teachers today spend at least 46 hours in an average week on school-related responsibilities and over one-third spend more than 55 hours per week (Metropolitan Life, 1995). Table 1.3 shows the number of hours per week teachers spend on school-related activities.

In order to validate these findings, that is, to guard against inflated self-reporting, researchers have shadowed teachers to find out precisely what kind of work they do and for how long. One particular study done by Cypher and Willower (1984) found that teachers averaged a 48.5-hour working week, spending approximately 38 hours in school and 10.5 hours in after-school work. Table 1.4 summarizes data from Cypher and Willower's and the Metropolitan Life survey. Among other things, it shows that most teachers spend less than 40 percent of their work week on instructional activity and that a sizable portion of their work consists of meetings and exchanges with other adults, such as parents, the principal, and professional colleagues. We described this hidden side of teaching in the previous section.

The following two vignettes illustrate how a teacher's day might look based on the data collected by the NEA and by researchers such as Cypher and Willower. *As you read these vignettes, consider whether or not this is the way you would like to spend your working hours.*

Gina Leonardi has been teaching at Webster Elementary School for the past 5 years. She began her career at Webster teaching first grade in a self-contained classroom. Today she is the team leader of a four-member teaching team responsible for all 6- and 7-year-old children in the school. This is the way a typical day looks in Gina's world.

Gina scoots through the office at exactly 7:40 A.M., picking up her mail before a 7:45 meeting with her team. Today, the team meeting has been scheduled to put the finishing touches on the logistics for Friday's field trip to the local science museum and to

Table 1.3 Amount of Time Teachers Spend on School-related Responsibilities in Elementary, Middle and Secondary Schools (in percentages)

Hours per Week Categories	Elementary	Middle	Secondary	Total
Fewer than 40 hours	12	8	9	9
41–45 hours	11	15	9	12
46–50 hours	31	28	29	30
51–55 hours	16	9	14	14
More than 55 hours	35	40	39	35
Median hours	51	51	55	51

Source: After Metropolitan Life, 1996, p. 67.

Table 1.4 How Teachers Spend Their Time

Activity	Total Time in Minutes	Percentage of Time
Instruction		
Direct instruction	95.4	20.6
Organizing	15.9	3.4
Reviewing	21.0	4.5
Testing	22.9	5.0
Monitoring	23.6	5.1
Other work with students		
Study hall supervision	17.4	3.8
Assemblies and clubs	5.9	1.3
Control and supervision	12.7	2.7
Interaction with colleagues and others		
Planned meetings	2.7	1.0
Unscheduled meetings	46.5	10.0
Exchanges	67.5	14.6
Desk and routine work	89.8	20.0
Travel time	24.6	5.3
Private time	16.2	3.5

Source: After Metropolitan Life, 1995; Cypher & Willower, 1984.

discuss the unit on Africa that will begin in 2 weeks. Team members will also use this meeting to make sure the details for today's lessons are clear and that both teachers and their assistants understand their respective assignments.

Children begin arriving at 8:30. They are greeted by Gina and Marie, one of the teaching assistants. At 8:45, Gina reviews the daily schedule with the children in her group, and she reminds them of today's helper roles. Reading and language arts (using a whole-language approach mainly) and instruction in mathematics take up most of the morning. Throughout this time, children work in various cooperative learning groups—sometimes facilitated by Gina, sometimes by other teachers on the team, and sometimes by Marie. Independent learning centers are also available for students at particular times during the morning, and because this is Tuesday, Gina's group goes to the library. Marie supervises the library period, leaving Gina free to prepare for the afternoon science lesson. Marie also supervises the children during their recess at 10:15.

Gina eats her lunch in the teacher's lounge and spends the 25 minutes talking about personal things with her friends. Before returning to her classroom, she sticks her head into the principal's office to remind her of their meeting with Joey's parents later in the day.

Gina's afternoon, like most afternoons, is spent on science and social studies. She takes the lead role for science lessons because she likes science and had a biology minor in college. One of her teammates provides the leadership for the social studies lessons.

After school, while the teaching assistant helps students board the buses, Gina greets the parents of Joey Fisher. Joey, who is a very bright little boy, has had a difficult time working with other children and has been in fights twice during the past week. Gina has asked the principal to join her in the conference, because some of Joey's misbehavior has been with students in other teachers' classes. Gina is not looking forward to this conference. From earlier exchanges with Joey's mother, she knows that Mrs. Fisher can become defensive and place the blame for Joey's behavior on other children and their teachers.

The conference actually goes quite well. After a frank discussion, everyone leaves with an agreed upon plan for how to work with Joey and help him learn alternative strategies for dealing with conflict.

Because this is Tuesday, Gina has to leave immediately following the conference to attend a class at the local university. She is working on her master's degree in reading and hopes to become a reading specialist sometime in the future. The class has been helpful to her, and has given her ideas for how to work with both the other teachers and with the assistants on her team. When the class is over, Gina leaves for home, getting there at 7:30 P.M., almost 12 hours after her departure that morning.

A similarly busy day is experienced by Charles Carter, a mathematics teacher at Eisenhower High School just down the road from Webster Elementary School.

Today Charles leaves his home at 7:15 A.M. However, he doesn't go directly to school. A substitute has been hired to teach his morning classes, so he can attend a meeting at the state department of education in a nearby city. Charles, a 10-year teaching veteran and chairman of the mathematics department at Eisenhower, has been invited by the state's commissioner of education to serve on a blue-ribbon task force that is helping to develop a new K–12 mathematics curriculum. Charles considers it an honor to serve on this task force, because he thinks their work will influence mathematics instruction in the state for years to come.

The meeting of the task force adjourns at 11:30 so teachers can get back to their schools for afternoon classes. For Charles, this means grabbing a sandwich at a nearby deli and rushing back to school. There, he quickly prepares a test for his advanced placement math class, which meets during sixth period, and also prepares to meet his fifth-period algebra class at 12:50. He has repeatedly taught both these classes, so he isn't worried about this tight schedule and lack of prior preparation.

Charles is released from teaching during seventh period, which begins at 2:30, so he can carry out his department chair responsibilities. Today, he has made plans to visit Elizabeth Fraser's classroom. Elizabeth is a first-year mathematics teacher working under Charles's supervision. After Charles observes her classroom for the full period, he and Elizabeth meet to discuss the lesson. Both agree that the sequencing of the various learning tasks was much smoother than in previous lessons and that Elizabeth made very effective use of cooperative learning groups. However, Charles points out that, in his judgment, Elizabeth is still trying to cover too much material in a single period. They discuss the importance of teaching a few things well rather than rushing through a huge amount of material.

After his meeting with Elizabeth, Charles returns to his office, where he corrects the test he gave to his sixth-period class. He likes to return all papers the next day, so students can get immediate feedback on their performances. Finally, Charles prepares the agenda for Wednesday's department meeting before he goes home in time to watch the 6:00 P.M. evening news.

We hope these brief glimpses into the lives of Ms. Leonardi and Mr. Carter give you a better sense of the way teachers use time and will dispel any thoughts that teaching is an easy job with a short workday. Most teachers, as these cases illustrate, begin work early in the morning and do not return home until late afternoon or early evening. These cases should also help eliminate the common misconception that teaching consists mainly of providing direct instruction to students. Both examples illustrate teachers who are involved in a broad range of noninstructional activities, from meetings with parents and colleagues to involvement in long-term planning at the district and state level. With Gina's and Charles's daily routines in mind, read the accompanying Global Box to learn similarities and differences between their and a Japanese teacher's teaching experiences. If you are the type of person who thrives on a busy schedule, and if you get enjoyment and satisfaction from helping children learn and providing professional leadership to parents and colleagues, you are likely to find the work and world of teaching both challenging and rewarding. *How do you see yourself relating to the time schedules and the type of work U.S. teachers are asked to perform?*

Preparation Requirements

Historically, many people chose teaching because the preparation requirements were minimal. For those wishing to teach in high schools, preparation consisted of getting a bachelor's degree in a particular subject, taking two or three education courses, and doing a semester of student teaching. These requirements were met quite easily during a 4-year baccalaureate program. Also, as previously described, licensing boards have frequently offered emergency certificates to unprepared persons during times of teacher shortages.

Except in a few states and a few large cities, most school systems today require teachers to be certified before they are employed. Increasingly, this means that elementary and secondary teacher candidates must obtain a bachelor's degree in a particular subject field, such as history, biology, or English, and then obtain a teaching certificate through study of **pedagogy,** or teaching methods. Also, before issuing a teaching certificate, many states today require teachers to pass **competency exams.** These gener-

ally consist of a written test of their subject area and a **performance test,** in which they demonstrate competence in the principles of teaching and learning. Preparation for teaching, thus, is far more demanding and time-consuming than it once was. Nonetheless, preparation time for teaching still remains less than that for many other professions, such as law and medicine, and many other skilled occupations, such as lab technologist, computer technician, and physical therapist. A more detailed discussion of teacher preparation and certification is presented in Chapter 12.

Rewards of Teaching and Advancement Opportunities

The rewards of teaching take many forms, but they generally fall into two broad categories—extrinsic rewards and intrinsic rewards. **Extrinsic rewards** include those that are part of one's external environment, such as salary, job security, and career advancement opportunities. **Intrinsic rewards** encompass the internal satisfactions of teaching, such as sense of accomplishment, intellectual stimulation, social relationships, or just the enjoyment of working.

Although few people enter teaching solely for the money, salaries are too important an extrinsic reward to ignore. Teaching salaries are not generally as high as those in other professions, but today, in many parts of the country, they are quite substantial and they are far better than they were in previous eras. Figure 1.7 shows salaries for experienced elementary and secondary teachers and beginning teachers in the United States between 1960 and 1995. Salaries in this figure have been adjusted to account for inflation and are reported in 1995 dollars.

As you can see, teachers' salaries over the past 30 years have improved significantly. Note, however, their decline in the 1980s, which reflects the previously described period of the decrease in school enrollments and surplus of teachers. Not shown are salary variations among regions of the country. For example, in states such as California, New York, and Connecticut the average beginning teacher's salary in 1995 was over $35,000, whereas in states such as Idaho and Mississippi, the average salary was under $20,000. Furthermore, most public school salary schedules are tied to one's years of teaching experience and amount of education. In most instances, teachers who obtain an advanced degree and 10 to 15 years of experience will earn double the salary of beginning teachers. In 1995, experienced teachers in Hartford, Connecticut, thus made as much as $70,000 a year. It is likely that salaries for teachers will continue to improve in the

Life as a Teacher in Japan

As you will read in more detail in Chapter 12, a *professional* is someone who possesses a specialized body of knowledge, is respected for that knowledge by the larger community, is given a degree of autonomy for performing work, and is accountable to peer review. Many believe that Japanese teachers have obtained higher professional status than American teachers have.

The road to becoming a teacher is very competitive in Japan. Elementary school teachers are prepared at national teachers' colleges, and high school teachers at universities. After graduation, all teachers must take what are called *recruitment exams.* Recruitment exams are extremely difficult, but there are always many applicants. Teaching is considered a high-status occupation, and there are as many as five or six applicants for every available teaching position. Over 55 percent of the teachers in Japan are male, a proportion significantly higher than in the United States.

The typical Japanese teacher arrives at school at 7:30 A.M. and remains there until 6:00 P.M. This amounts to about 20 hours more time in school than for American teachers, who normally go home between 3:30 P.M. and 4:30 P.M.. Teaching in Japan is definitely a 12-month job. Teachers work a 240-day school year, and they are often found at school when students are on vacation. By law, teachers are forbidden to have part-time jobs.

Class size in Japan is typically around 40 students, and Japanese teachers spend only about 15 hours per week with direct classroom instruction. This compares to the 25 to 30 hours a week spent by American teachers. Japanese teachers, on the other hand, use these extra hours to perform many leadership roles in the school, such as planning, scheduling, and curriculum development. Indeed, Japanese teachers are much more involved in school governance, and they run every aspect of their school. They attend short planning meetings with their colleagues every morning and longer meetings after school once a week. They hold regular group meetings to discuss teaching techniques and to engage in cooperative planning. Teachers, not principals, chair these meetings.

Japanese teachers report that they assign the highest priority to their work. They take full responsibility for all aspects of their students' education, including what students do outside school and during vacation time. In return, they are given a great deal of autonomy in how they go about performing their work.

About two-thirds of Japanese teachers belong to unions, but they do not have the right to bargain collectively or to strike. Salaries are determined by national authorities and are set to make sure there is a continuous supply of highly qualified teachers. In the late 1980s and early 1990s, Japanese teachers' salaries were almost twice that of manufacturing workers in Japan. However, their salaries typically have been slightly less (95 percent) than American teachers.

How do you react to the nature of work of Japanese teachers? Would you exchange the longer hours for higher status and more autonomy? Would you prefer to spend less time working directly with students and more time with colleagues? What about responsibility toward students? Should teachers take responsibility for students' out-of-school learning and deportment?

Source: After Sato & McLaughlin, 1992; Phi Delta Kappan, 1996.

Figure 1.7   **Average Annual Salaries for Teachers, 1960-1995**

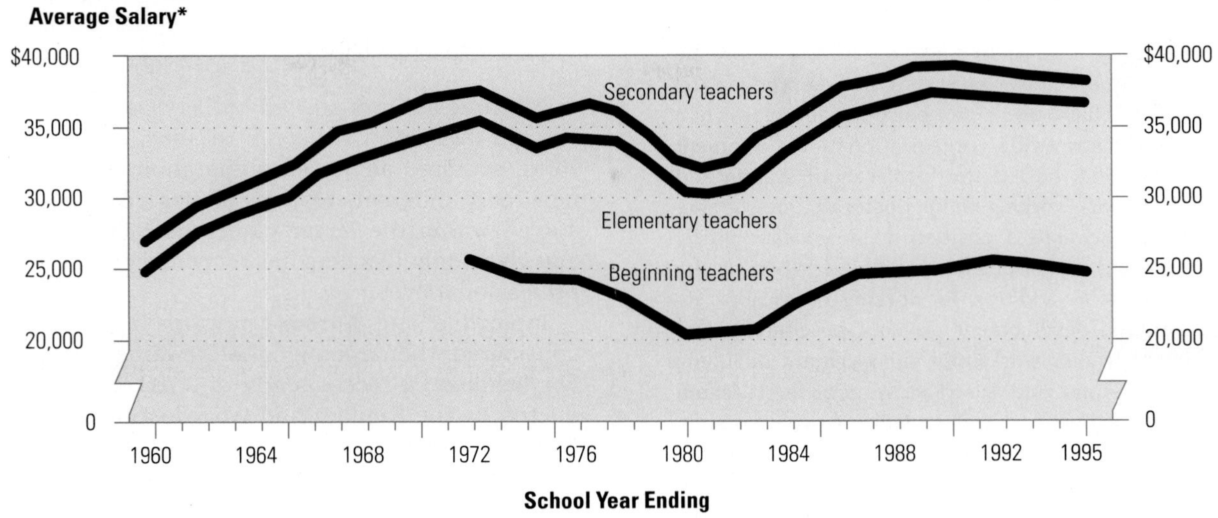

Average Salary*

*Plotted points for average annual salaries for public school teachers are even years 1960—1968 and all years 1970—1995.
Plotted points for average beginning salaries for public school teachers are even years 1972—1988 and all years 1990—1995.

Source: National Center for Education Statistics, 1996, p. 169.

future, although some reform proposals call for drastic changes in the nature of salary schedules. *Do you think that the teaching salaries in the part of the country in which you wish to teach will sustain the lifestyle you require?*

Job security is another important external reward to consider when choosing a career. Most people believe that teaching and related educational jobs, such as school administration, counseling, and nursing, are highly secure. In most situations this is true. New teachers today go through a 2- to 3-year trial period during which their teaching effectiveness is judged by school leaders and peers. Once they are judged to be sufficiently effective, beginning teachers are then granted **tenure.** By law and tradition, tenured teachers in the United States cannot be removed from their teaching positions without "just cause" or unless a school system is facing an extreme financial emergency. Thus, a teacher's job, once tenured, is normally secure for life. The issue of teacher tenure and some of the proposed changes to the tenure system are explored more fully in Chapter 12.

Career advancement is another extrinsic reward that prospective teachers should consider. Advancement opportunities vary according to one's desire to stay in or to move beyond the classroom. Historically, teachers who have remained in the classroom throughout their careers have retired performing essentially the same tasks and having the same

responsibilities as when they first began teaching. To combat this lack of a **career ladder,** numerous experiments during the past 50 years have attempted to introduce new and differentiated roles for classroom teachers. In some cases, experienced teachers were asked to work face-to-face with students for part of the day and to take on additional responsibilities, such as team leader or teacher mentor, for the remainder of the day. Many experts believe that differentiated staffing will increase in the future, but most career ladder experiments to date have been abandoned.

On the other hand, if a potential teacher views classroom teaching as only one role within the larger field of education, then prospects for career advancement are substantial. It is very common for individuals, after a few years of classroom teaching, to qualify themselves for another more specialized role in education, such as a reading specialist or a curriculum coordinator. This new role can, in turn, serve as a stepping stone to school administration, a position some teachers aspire to. Similarly, many experienced teachers leave kindergarten through twelfth-grade classrooms altogether for related careers as college teachers, industrial trainers, or publishers of educational materials. The career biographies of the three authors of this text provide you with examples of these types of career changes and advancements.

Dick Arends began his education career in Walla Walla, Washington, teaching mornings in an elementary classroom and afternoons in a junior high. After 4 years, he moved to Eugene, Oregon, where he taught twelfth-grade social studies, served as department chairperson, and became coordinator of a special districtwide organizational development project. Next, he left the local school system and spent 3 years working on his doctorate. After graduation, he secured a position at an educational research and development laboratory. While at the laboratory, in addition to working on various research and development projects, he continued to teach by leading workshops and seminars, including some in Samoa and Australia. Work at the research and development laboratory led to a professorship, first at the University of Oregon and later at the University of Maryland. It also led to an interest in higher education administration and his current position as dean of the school of education at Connecticut State University.

Nancy Winitzky attended the University of California at San Diego and graduated with a bachelor of science in general science from the University of Oregon in 1973. She taught junior high math, health, life science, and physical science in Veneta, Oregon, for 3 years. During her tenure there, she served as department chair and was active in developing innovative programs and team-teaching arrangements. After taking time to start a family, Nancy completed her master's degree in curriculum and instruction at the University of Oregon in 1985 and her doctorate at the University of Maryland at College Park in 1987. She has worked in teacher education ever since, in secondary education at Utah State University and in elementary education at the University of Utah. Her interests include teacher thinking, teacher education, school improvement, and cooperative learning.

Margaret Tannenbaum's first teaching position was in Knoxville, Tennessee. She taught seventh grade reading and geography and eighth grade American history. Following that, she served as a long-term substitute teacher in secondary English in the Delaware County Christian Day School and taught 4- and 5-year olds in Head Start in Chester, Pennsylvania. In 1966, she acquired a full-time job teaching fifth grade in Pottstown, Pennsylvania. The following year, she taught seventh, eighth, and ninth grade developmental reading in that same district and the year after that eighth grade reading for the Centennial Pennsylvania School District. She then became a teaching assistant at Temple University in Philadelphia, where she completed residence requirements for her doctorate. Following that, she

continued her teaching career as an instructor and department chair at Glassboro State College (now Rowan College of New Jersey), where she has been preparing future teachers.

All three authors started out as classroom teachers and then, for a variety of reasons, assumed new roles, acquired advanced preparation, and took on new and different responsibilities. All, however, stayed within the larger career field of education, and classroom teaching has remained central to our professional lives.

Intangible and intrinsic rewards must also be considered when examining the rewards of teaching. For instance, a recent study of 3,700 workers conducted by the Families and Work Institute (1993), a New York-based research organization, found that many workers do not find satisfaction in the pursuit of money and career advancement alone. Instead, they are happiest working where they are afforded respect from their supervisors and peers and where they are given a great deal of autonomy. This study also found that most workers want open communication in the workplace and conditions which allow them time for themselves and for their families (*Hartford Courant*, 1993). Teaching allows individuals to realize these types of intrinsic rewards more fully than many other higher paying occupations.

Teachers also report that working with their colleagues and being involved in work that is interesting and not routine provides important intrinsic rewards. Every day, indeed every hour, presents a teacher with new challenges and situations. As you saw in the cases of Ms. Leonardi and Mr. Carter, although teachers spend a large portion of their time with children, in today's schools, they also do many other things that can be equally interesting and rewarding. Of course, as you read at the beginning of this chapter, most teachers say that their most important intrinsic rewards come from helping young people and from the sense that they are making significant social contributions.

Teachers' Workplace

Equally important as the nature of teachers' work is the nature of the workplace itself. With few exceptions, teachers perform their work inside, rather than outside an organizational setting. Western societies have labeled this organizational setting the *school* and those who have a role in teaching *school teachers*. If you choose to be a teacher, a school is the place you will go to every morning, and it is, as you have read, the place where you will spend at least 45 hours of your waking hours each week. Two important aspects of schools are their physical characteristics and their organizational features. The nature of each will influence the amount of satisfaction you will derive from teaching.

Physical Characteristics of Schools

An important component of a teacher's workplace is the physical space itself, and schools in the United States vary immensely in their physical characteristics. In some wealthy districts, they are aesthetically pleasing, have beautiful furnishings and superb art, music, and athletic facilities. In such schools, teachers have attractive offices and are assured the amenities afforded other professionals in our society. On the other hand, in many poorer districts, schools are physically atrocious, having been poorly constructed in the first place and then neglected for years. Many observers have described school buildings in which plaster falls from classroom ceilings, chairs and tables are broken, and noxious smells emanate from plugged toilets and urinals. Teachers in such schools seldom have offices and sometimes are required to teach in any available space, including in janitors' closets and in hallways. Generally, however, the physical settings for schools are moderately pleasant and environmentally safe and healthy.

Organizational Features of Schools

There are numerous organizational features of schools that impact on the work of teachers. Later chapters deal with school organization and culture in more depth, but a brief glimpse in this direction is appropriate at this point.

Except in very rural areas, schools are usually large organizations designed around policies, rules, and procedures that characterize most other large **bureaucracies** in our society. As with most formal, bureaucratic organizations, schools are directed toward accomplishing specific goals. Whereas the goal of an auto manufacturing plant is to make cars, the goal of schools is to provide purposeful learning experiences for students. To accomplish valued goals requires schools, like other formal organizations, to have a division of labor and rules, norms, and procedures to coordinate effort and reward members. These mechanisms work in schools in much the same way as they do in other organizations.

Schools also have special features not found in other organizations. Figure 1.8 illustrates the special features of schools that have a direct impact on teachers' work and include ambiguous and conflicting goals, political visibility and vulnerability, a loosely coupled organizational structure, and under-

Figure 1.8   Special Feature of Schools

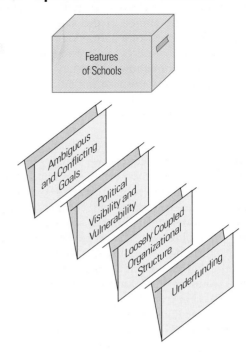

funding. Some aspects of these special features are described here briefly. They are more thoroughly discussed in Chapter 7.

Ambiguous and Conflicting Goals   In some instances, the goals of an organization are very clear, and the success of job holders can be measured quite precisely. For example, the success of realtors can be easily quantified by adding up their annual sales of property. An attorney's success can be determined by the number of cases she wins. Although the overriding goal of schools appears to be straightforward—to facilitate important learning for students—people often differ in their thinking about what learning is most important and how to know when it has been achieved. Thus, teachers who work in schools are often faced with ambiguous and conflicting goals. As an example of the ambiguity and potential conflict embedded in school goals, let's examine the almost universally accepted goal of citizenship education.

Most people agree that schools should prepare students to be good, productive citizens in a rather complex, democratic political system. This broad goal becomes ambiguous, however, when it comes to defining the specifics of good citizenship and deciding how teaching it is to be accomplished. Does good citizenship mean embracing the values of one's parents or of the dominant culture at a particular point in time? Does it mean espousing values that are considered "politically correct"? Or, does it mean adopting the stance of the skeptic and being constructively critical of existing values or contemporary political structures and processes? How do parents and teachers know when they have successfully helped students prepare for citizenship? Does voting regularly constitute success? Does serving on community agencies or boards display the hallmark of a good citizen?

Goal statements made about health education and multicultural education are other examples of ambiguous goals that generate conflict. Likewise, conflict between the subject matter teachers are supposed to teach and certain community groups' reaction to that subject matter have existed since the beginning of formal schooling. The most famous and long-standing examples are the conflicts between science teachers and certain religious groups over the teaching of evolution. Condom distribution is a contemporary issue that creates conflict among various well-meaning groups in all kinds of communities. Many teachers find goal ambiguity and conflict very disconcerting, but others seem to thrive on it. *If you are the type of person who is unable to function effectively in situations in which criticism and conflict exist, then teaching may not be for you. What do you think?*

Political Visibility and Vulnerability   Schools are also unique in that they are organizations that have a high degree of political visibility. In most communities, people take a very active interest in their schools. This is particularly true in small rural communities, where school activities often form the hub of the community's social and intellectual life. It is also the case in very large urban areas, such as New York City, where many political and social issues are played out in the educational arena. Large portions of many newspapers are devoted to school news, and many individuals consider exercising their citizenship mostly a matter of attending school meetings and voicing opinions about the schools. Some teachers seem to thrive on the fact that schools are so politically visible and permeable. These teachers like being in the spotlight and often serve on school boards and other politically oriented councils and committees. Other teachers find the political aspect of schools distasteful and view politics as an intrusion on their work with students. They argue that teaching should be left in the hands of the professionals and that every effort should be made to buffer schools and teachers from the whim

of local politics. *It is unlikely that schools in a democratic society will ever be free from politics. How will you relate to this aspect of teaching?*

Loosely Coupled Organizational Structure   Schools differ from many business organizations in that they have an organizational arrangement sociologists have labeled **loosely coupled.** This means that what goes on in one part of the organization is not very tightly connected, or coupled, to what goes on in another part. In teaching, teachers can do pretty much what they want to in their own classrooms. On a daily basis, they work independently of administrators, peers, and others. The school board may adopt a policy, but some in the school system may choose to ignore it. On the positive side, loose coupling gives teachers a great deal of freedom and autonomy. On the other hand, it prevents teachers from having much influence on their peers, and it stymies efforts to work on common goals and to coordinate important schoolwide activities. *What do you think? Would you find satisfaction in a loosely coupled situation? Or, would you prefer an arrangement in which the work in one part is connected to the work in other parts?*

Underfunding   As with most other public agencies and institutions, schools tend to be underfunded, always striving to satisfy increasing demands without increasing resources. Limited resources are particularly acute in those communities in which few citizens have schoolage children, such as retirement communities, or in communities in which a large proportion of citizens are very poor. Limited resources pose one of the major frustrations for teachers, leading not only to poor salaries but also to poor working conditions and lack of instructional technologies and materials. *Could you find satisfaction working in an underfunded school?*

A QUICK TOUR THROUGH EXPLORING TEACHING

Now that we have explored teachers and the nature of teachers' work, let's conclude this chapter with a brief tour of what you will find in the pages that follow and a rationale for how the book is organized. Five major themes guided the planning and writing of *Exploring Teaching.* You will find them incorporated throughout the book.

Theme 1:   The purpose of teaching is to help students become *self-regulated learners* within a *democratic classroom* community.

Theme 2:   Teaching and learning take place within the *social context* of the classroom, the school, the profession, and the larger society.

Theme 3:   Effective teaching is characterized by teachers who command a *repertoire of best practice* and who recognize the situational nature of teaching.

Theme 4:   Classrooms and schools in today's world have become *multicultural crossroads* and contact points from which teachers serve as mediators of *cultural diversity.*

Theme 5:   Schools *reflect changes* in the larger society and act as *change agents,* or mediators, of the society.

Self-Regulated Learning in Democratic Classrooms

This first theme stems from a contemporary view about knowledge and learning and from an old idea about classrooms. Today, most learning theorists work from a **constructivist perspective,** using a view of knowledge different from those held in earlier times. Rather than thinking of knowledge as eternally fixed and transmittable through language from teacher to learner, constructivists see knowledge as subjective, that is, as something that individuals actively construct through personal experience. This theory focuses on learning as a social process, in which learners construct knowledge through interaction with their teachers, peers, and others. Teaching from a constructivist perspective is not limited to telling or transmitting fixed bodies of knowledge but instead provides students with a variety of meaningful learning experiences and the intellectual support to understand those experiences.

Students can construct their own knowledge and teachers can orchestrate tasks and conversations better in classrooms that are free from traditional constraints and characterized by open, democratic processes. This current approach stems from an old idea, dating back to John Dewey and the early part of the twentieth century, but the goal of creating democratic learning communities, as you will see, has been a difficult one to achieve. The theme of helping students become self-regulated learners in a democratic learning community opens up many new and exciting avenues for twenty-first century teachers.

Social Context of Teaching

The second theme guiding the information you find in this book is that teaching takes place within a social context. Embedded in the act of teaching are four particular contexts, as illustrated in Figure 1.9, that surround and influence the act of teaching. The most immediate context is the classroom, a place that is characterized by considerable complexity. Whereas classroom influences are strong and immediate, they exist within a set of larger, surrounding contexts: the organizational context of the school and the sociopolitical contexts of the community and the larger society. Schools and communities have histories, norms, values, and organizational arrangements that impact teaching and determine the ease or difficulty of the work teachers do. Furthermore, because teaching is a profession, it is governed by norms and a code of ethics embraced by the professional community as well.

The organizing framework for *Exploring Teaching* stems from this social context perspective. Part 1 (Chapters 1 through 3) begins with the personal aspects of teaching. We explore the nature of teaching and examine the characteristics of effective teachers, including their motives, understandings, beliefs, skills, and philosophies. Part 1 also provides you with an opportunity to begin exploring how well your motives, beliefs, and personal characteristics match up with the expectations and demands of a teacher's career and work.

Part 2 (Chapters 4 through 6) focuses on the classroom, the students that inhabit classrooms, and the methods of instruction used by teachers. You will learn that classrooms today are becoming more and more diverse and that teachers are expected to work with all kinds of students. Although this task is difficult, today's teachers have available to them a much broader repertoire of effective teaching practices than was available to teachers in earlier times.

Part 3 (Chapters 7 and 8) focuses on the school context and the curriculum arrangements found in schools. We will examine the evolution of the school from its humble beginnings to its present state, which is characterized by complexity and bureaucratization. We also explore the effectiveness of today's schools and provide a glimpse of what schools may look like in the future. We believe that schools and the curricula of the future will be

Figure 1.9   **The Contexts of Teaching**

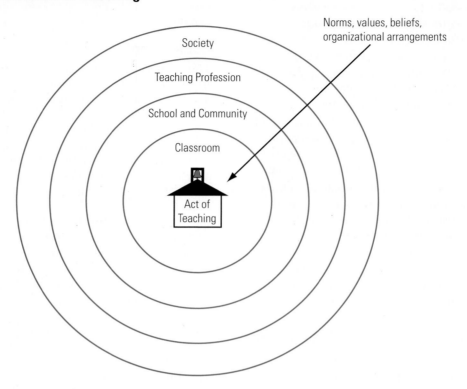

conceived and structured differently. Trends currently underway suggest that twenty-first century schools will be smaller than schools today. Also, the traditional academic curriculum, with its division into a number of largely unrelated subjects, will be replaced by a more focused curriculum in which students solve real-world problems by integrating relevant knowledge from all academic subjects. In these smaller, more focused schools, teaching will become much more personalized, and teachers will be given broader responsibility for their students' education. Many teachers believe this situation will make their jobs much more stimulating and satisfying.

Part 4 (Chapters 9 through 11) explores the sociopolitical aspects of teaching. The focus is on the ever-changing nature of the school-society relationship and how teaching is affected by governance, finance, and school law. Many educators and theorists believe that schools of the twenty-first century will have closer links to society and the surrounding community. Instead of working in isolation and in competition with their fellow students, twenty-first century students will increasingly work in cooperative teams in which they will learn to pool their

individual knowledge and skills in the pursuit of meaningful problems. In fact, schools, classrooms, and neighborhoods may become **learning communities** in which students, teachers, administrators, parents, and others will work together to achieve important adult and student learning goals.

Finally, Part 5 (Chapters 12 and 13) examines the professional context of teaching. You will learn how the teaching profession has expanded and changed over time. Trends are currently underway that will radically change the professional nature of teaching as we know it. Currently, reforms have been initiated to upgrade teacher preparation programs and to require that teachers demonstrate their knowledge of subject matter, human development, and pedagogy prior to being issued a teaching certificate. In the future, teachers will be held accountable throughout their careers for keeping abreast of trends in their subject field, for using best teaching practices, and for adhering to high ethical standards. Many educators believe that accepting higher standards and more accountability will strengthen the teaching profession in the long term and raise it to the level of other major professions.

Repertoire of Best Practice based on Research

The third theme you will find running through *Exploring Teaching* is that effective teaching requires teachers with a broad repertoire of effective teaching practices, not just a few pet methods. This idea is highlighted in each chapter with special boxes that summarize and highlight research particularly appropriate to beginning teachers. Tightly tied to this idea of best practice is the idea that all acts of teaching are situational and methods that work with one group of students may be inappropriate for another group. Effective teachers, therefore, must have the ability to accurately diagnose a teaching-learning situation, select a teaching strategy to use, and then monitor and assess its success. You will find that new cognitive approaches to acquiring knowledge and human learning have led to new methods of teaching. Twenty-first century teachers will not be limited to teacher-centered methods, such as lecture and direct instruction, but also will have available to them such new strategies as cooperative learning and project-based instruction. Cognitive research has also shown teachers that students acquire new knowledge by linking it to what they already know. More and more, teachers will readily diagnose students' existing knowledge, activate that knowledge when needed, and tie new knowledge into students' existing knowledge base.

Multicultural Crossroads

The fourth theme incorporated in *Exploring Teaching* as well as the focus of special multicultural and global boxes is that today's classrooms are multicultural crossroads where teachers serve as mediators of cultural diversity. For the past several decades, schools have experienced important demographic shifts, gaining an increasing number of students of ethnic and racial backgrounds that are non-European. Today, these young people represent over 30 percent of the school population nationwide and in many urban areas are now an overwhelming majority. In the future, society will demand that these students do well in school. This situation will necessitate that all teachers have a familiarity with other cultures and languages and a repertoire of teaching strategies to accommodate diverse groups of students. Accomplishing learning in diverse classrooms will be one of the most interesting and challenging aspects of teaching in the twenty-first century.

Schools Reflect Society

A final theme you will find in *Exploring Teaching* is that schools reflect the larger society in two ways. First, changes in the larger society, such as an increasing concern with civil rights, usually bring a corresponding change in schools. Second, schools occasionally become agents of change for the larger society, as when they work to help the overall society become more literate and socially responsible. Take a moment to consider the accompanying Issues Box, for instance, which exemplifies this school-social change connection. Part openings provide brief historical accounts about how teaching, classrooms, and schools have changed over the years and how these changes have reflected the larger demographic, social, political, and economic changes occurring in American society. Some part openers also suggest future directions in education to accommodate our transition from an industry-based to an information-based society. Since many of these changes are controversial, each chapter contains an issues box that examines the pros and cons of a current controversial educational topic.

ASSESSING YOUR MOTIVES AND SKILLS FOR TEACHING IN THE TWENTY-FIRST CENTURY

This chapter described the world and work of teaching and has highlighted many of the issues and questions related to a career in that world. We now encourage you to begin the career-assessment process, that is, to assess your own needs, skills, and attitudes and match them with the realities of teaching. At the end of Part 1, you can find several self-assessment tools. These will help you explore your motives for teaching and how well suited your attitudes and personal characteristics are for the work of teaching. We urge you to spend some time with these self-assessment activities and to reflect on your potential for being an effective teacher.

SUMMARY

- Teaching is a demanding and complex profession, and individuals should carefully consider their decision to become teachers. Although everyone knows something about teaching as a result of their school days, individuals preparing to teach should make a special effort to acquire an accurate view of the world and work of teachers. After all, a wise career choice requires the ability to match your own needs, goals, and abilities with this world.

- Most teachers and teacher candidates say they enter teaching because they like working with children and because teachers can make a difference in the lives of young people and in society. Other less altruistic but nevertheless valid motivations include reasonable and improving salary levels, better than average job security, intellectual

stimulation, above average vacation periods, and considerable job autonomy.

- The supply and demand for teachers has changed over time. Today and in the future, the demand for teachers will remain moderately high overall with considerable variations among both geographic locations and subject areas. In general, the demand will be highest for teachers in poor rural and urban areas and for teachers who are bilingual or teach in the math or science fields.

- Since the mid-nineteenth century, teaching has been considered work for women, and although more men teach today than in

ISSUES

EXTRA

Should We Expect Teachers to Be Moral Role Models?

Recently, in a moderately large New England community, the high school's student council passed a resolution encouraging the local board of education to ban smoking for everybody on the high school campus. Currently, students cannot smoke, but faculty are permitted to smoke outside the school building. The local newspaper editorialized that the students had made a fair request and urged the board of education to honor it. The editor argued that the ban would promote good health, but more important, he pointed out that teachers should set a good moral example for students. The editor wrote:

> *Students need and seek role models. Teachers and administrators who puff on cigarettes while standing outside doorways are hardly an inspiring sight for students resisting the temptation to engage in the harmful habit.*
> (Hartford Courant, 1994)

This interesting situation has produced considerable controversy. One side holds the view that teachers should set a moral and ethical example for their students. Their perspective represents a long tradition in which a teacher's character is considered one of the most important attributes of effective teaching. As you recall from the Part Opener, many early teaching contracts required their teachers to attend church and to abstain from dancing, smoking, and drinking. Some teachers even promised not to fall in love or to marry.

On the other hand, the smoking ban for teachers seems to run counter to recent efforts by teachers to escape the social restrictions placed on them in earlier times. During the 1970s and 1980s, the teaching profession became more professional and teachers more empowered. Most teachers and their professional associations believe that society should not ask teachers to follow a higher moral standard than they do for people in other occupations. They reject the idea that they should be setting moral examples for students who themselves come from diverse family backgrounds representing a variety of moral and ethical beliefs.

How do you stand on this issue? Should teachers, most of whom come from white, middle-class backgrounds, serve as moral examples for their students, many of whom come from different backgrounds? Should a board of education restrict teacher smoking? If you had a magic wand and could dictate policy to govern the situation, what would you decree? Why?

earlier times, the profession is still predominately female. It is also dominated by individuals with middle class, European American backgrounds, most of whom are monolingual and monocultural. Therefore, there is a great need to attract people from non-European backgrounds—African-Americans, Native Americans, Asians, and Hispanics—into the teaching profession.

- Teachers perform their work in the highly visible and political environment of schools, which, in turn, are embedded in the larger social and cultural traditions of society. Teaching, thus, is influenced by five contexts: the personal, the classroom, the school, the sociopolitical, and the professional.

- Before choosing a teaching career, one should consider the nature of the work teachers do, the place where that work is performed (the school), and how one's own talents, needs, and attitudes will fit that work and workplace.

- Six features of work distinguish one career from another. Applied to teaching, this involves considering the goals of teaching, its primary tasks, its tools and technologies, its time and work schedules, its preparation requirements, and its rewards and opportunities.

- The goals of teaching involve helping others to learn and to develop and, as such, are considered noble and socially significant. Therefore, teachers accrue rather high status because of the social importance of these goals.

- Teachers perform a wide variety of tasks in complex, unpredictable settings. The tasks of teaching can be divided into three main categories: working directly with students (interactive tasks); performing routine planning, management, and evaluation (leadership tasks); and working with others to develop and implement schoolwide improvements (organizational tasks).

- Historically, teaching has required the use of relatively simple tools, such as books, chalk, and chalkboards. This is changing, as teachers start to use computers and other new technologies in their classrooms.

- Some people think that teachers do not work very hard and that they work mainly with children. In reality, teachers work long hours and much of their time is spent on planning and evaluation activities and collaborating with other adults in the school, community, or profession.

- Teaching offers incredible challenges and opportunities. The rewards of teaching are both extrinsic and intrinsic. Extrinsic rewards consist of reasonable and improving salaries, better than average job security, liberal vacations, and time off in the summers. Intrinsic rewards include the satisfaction of helping children learn and develop and the stimulation of intellectual activity.

- The workplace of teachers, the school, includes not only the physical setting but also such unique organizational features as goal ambiguity, loosely coupled parts, high political visibility, and insufficient resources.

- The twenty-first century will present teachers with many new challenges and promises. Important new challenges include the changing nature of the student population and new demands for teacher accountability. New promises include discoveries about human cognition and learning, new student-centered teaching methods, such as cooperative learning and project-based teaching, and new conceptions of schooling that consider classrooms and schools learning communities in which students work cooperatively on authentic problems.

READINGS FOR THE PROFESSIONAL

Glasser, W. *The Quality School Teacher.* New York: HarperCollins, 1993.
This book describes in plain terms the ingredients that go into making a quality teacher and why having quality teachers is important.

Grossman, P. L. *The Making of a Teacher.* New York: Teachers College Press, 1990.
This research study shows how individuals become teachers, with particular attention to changes that occur in their belief systems about children and their subject matter.

Little, J. W. & M. W. McLaughlin (eds.). *Teachers' Work: Individuals, Colleagues, and Contexts.* New York: Teachers College Press, 1993.
This excellent selection of readings describes the nature of teacher's work and the context in which teaching occurs.

Sarason, S. B. *You Are Thinking of Teaching: Opportunities, Problems, Realities.* San Francisco: Jossey Bass, 1993.
This is a clearly written and informative book about the challenges and problems of a career in teaching.

CHAPTER 2

The Effective Teacher

What is a good teacher? What is good teaching? What makes some teachers better than others? What can be done to make sure all teachers are effective? These are important questions asked by parents and taxpayers, by teachers and teacher educators, and by individuals like you who intend to become teachers. They are questions that have been examined by scholars and philosophers for a very long time and for which hundreds of answers have been proposed.

Although we know a great deal about the effective teacher, there is still much to learn. We know, for instance, that effective teachers have positive relationships with their students, but that these relationships consist of more than just liking children. We know that teaching effectively requires command of what is being taught, but that knowledge alone does not produce student learning. We know that teaching takes place in a complex environment that necessitates an endless stream of decisions every day. We also know that good teaching is not confined to classrooms, that it can be found in homes, museums, and corporate offices. Good teaching requires individuals with appropriate dispositions who have acquired important knowledge about their subject fields, learning, and human development and can translate their knowledge into effective examples, illustrations, and activities.

This chapter explores various images and conceptions of an effective teacher. These images are important because they form the expectations many people have for teachers, and they may form the perceptions you have about good teaching. Next we examine what research has to say about what effective teachers *believe*, what they *know*, and what they *can do*. We will consider how certain attributes distinguish effective from ineffective teachers and from other well-educated people in our society. We conclude the chapter with our own attempt to define the effective teacher based on a synthesis of contemporary knowledge about learning and teaching. Our definition will highlight the view that effective teaching cannot be thought of apart from the contexts in which it occurs. That is, the highest level of professional practice, whether it occurs in courtrooms, boardrooms, or classrooms, involves adapting one's repertoire of professional skills and strategies to fit the demands of specific situations and contexts.

Images of Effective Teachers
   Remembering Effective Teachers
   Media Images of Teachers
   Young Children's Images of Teachers

What Research Says about Effective Teachers
   Do Teachers Make a Difference?
   Personal Qualities of Effective Teachers
     Dispositions toward Children and Youth
      Teacher Caring
      Teacher Expectations
     Dispositions toward Knowledge
      Intellectual Orientation
      Enthusiasm
     Dispositions toward Colleagues and Other Adults

Behaviors of Effective Teachers
Teachers' Knowledge and Thought Processes
   Teachers' Knowledge
   Teachers' Thought Process
     Expert & Novice Teachers
     Reflective Teachers
     Constructivist Teaching

The Effective Teacher for the Twenty-First Century

Summary

Readings for the Professional

IMAGES OF EFFECTIVE TEACHERS

Since nearly everyone can remember teachers who made an impact in their lives, let's begin our discussion with these memories. This section looks at images of teachers using our own memories, those of prominent historical figures and the mass media, and the most neglected of all voices, children and youth. See Figure 2.1.

Remembering Effective Teachers

Most of us have known hundreds of teachers in our lifetimes. They have loved us and scolded us. They have made us learn our multiplication tables and memorize important dates in history. They have introduced us to Plato, Shakespeare, and Martin Luther King. When the media interview famous people and ask about their success, people often attribute it to one or more teachers they encountered somewhere along the way. It may have been a teacher who made them work hard by coaxing and scolding them to do better. It may even have been a teacher who, at the time, seemed mean and treated them cruelly. Read, for instance, the following example:

> As a child I had the good fortune to attend a small country school. The best year of my school career

Figure 2.1   Contributing Perspectives on Effective Teachers

Memories

Media

Research

Children

was spent in the sixth grade with Mr. Deutscher. "Mr. D." was from Holland and spoke with a curious (to us) accent. He was a rather imposing man (large, bald, small spectacles); all the kids were afraid of him. This fear was not unfounded, for he administered discipline with a firm hand.

In spite of his menacing image, I liked Mr. D. His class was always a place of learning and adventure. We studied French, read about pirates, collected stamps, sculpted models of African wildlife in clay, drew maps, and much more. I read many books that year in sixth grade. Among my favorites were *The Adventure of Tom Sawyer, Robinson Crusoe,* and the entire collection of *Tarzan* books by Edgar Rice Burroughs!

Today I am very thankful that Mr. D. was my teacher. He inspired in me a love of learning and a thirst for knowledge that has never left me. (Parkay, 1992, p. 28)

Take a moment to conjure up your own image of a teacher who made a difference in your life. What kind of individual was this teacher? What did he or she know and do that made a difference? Did this teacher make a difference for all students or just for you? If just for you, why you and not others?

In addition to our own memories of effective teachers, there are the memories of others to consider. Think for a moment of the voices of some prominent historical figures whose admiration of great teaching can be traced back to their own teachers.

Albert Einstein: It is the supreme art of the teacher to awaken joy in creative expression and knowledge.

Plato: Those who have torches will pass them along to others.

Aristotle: The one exclusive sign of a thorough knowledge is the power of teaching.

Ralph Waldo Emerson: The person who can make hard things easy is the true teacher.

Horace Mann: A teacher who is attempting to teach without inspiring the pupil with a desire to learn is hammering on cold iron.

Thomas Wolfe: I put the relation of a fine teacher to a student just below the relationship of a mother to a son, and I don't think I could say more than this.

This list of quotes could go on and on. The important point is that many people have been highly motivated by some special teacher whose influence contributed much to their later success. As Henry Adams said, "A teacher affects eternity; he never knows where his influence stops."

Media Images of Teachers

More recent images of effective teaching come from the mass media: television, movies, film, and literature. In American culture, according to Joseph and Burnaford (1994), these media-created images have been positive, unrealistic, and negative. On the negative side, teachers have been portrayed as bumblers and buffoons (Mr. Chips), as rigid authoritarians who bully students while simultaneously fighting for them (Joe Clark of *Lean on Me* fame), even as witches and mishap-prone teenagers (the adolescent-like Our Miss Brooks). On the unrealistic side are movies that portray an eager, idealistic teacher moving into blackboard-jungle teaching situation, having hair-raising confrontations with classroom thugs, winning over the toughest kid, and resulting in the thugs' rallying behind the teacher and suddenly becoming the best students in the school. On the positive side are television and film portrayals of teachers—such as Gabe in "Welcome Back Kotter," and Mr. Moore in "Head of the Class"—with a sense of calling, who advance the cause of their students against great odds. Recent film examples of positive teacher images include Jaime Escalante of *Stand and Deliver* fame, a teacher in an East Los Angeles high school who successfully taught advanced calculus to previously low-achieving students, and David Holland of *Mr. Holland's Opus,* who helped all kinds of students achieve their goals through music. Following is what the president of a national teacher's union said about Mr. Holland:

"Mr. Holland's Opus" is good on a lot of things about teaching. It suggests how physically grueling and emotionally demanding the work is; how great a commitment of time and self is required; where the motivation to teach comes from (love, not money); and how odd and unexpected gifts, and more than a little courage, can make an ordinary person into an extraordinary teacher. (Shanker, 1996)

Young Children's Images of Teachers

Often ignored in discussions of good and bad teachers are the voices of the consumers themselves—the children. It appears that children develop their perceptions of "good" teachers at a very young age. W. Nikola-Lisa and Gail Burnaford (1994) studied children's perceptions of their teachers in 32 public and private classrooms in urban and suburban Chicago. The researchers worked with children from diverse socioeconomic and racial backgrounds in kindergarten through Grade 6

In small groups or individual interviews students responded to a number of open-ended questions, such as:

- "If I were a teacher, I would . . ."
- "What do you think makes a good teacher?"

Nikola-Lisa and Burnaford divided student perceptions of teachers into 9 categories: teacher as novice, teacher as pushover, teacher as tyrant, teacher as incompetent, teacher as mother, teacher as witch, teacher as friend, teacher as problem-solver, and teacher as victim. What they found in regard to young children's perception of good (effective) teachers is particularly relevant for our discussion here. Several of the children's responses follow.

> Thomas (Grade 2): If I was a teacher I would be a good teacher. I would take care of my class and be useful and do my best . . . Even if I could not make it to school, I would try to. I do like my teacher she helps me with some of my work and when I grow up I will thank her for that. She is just like my mom. (p. 131)
>
> Mary Jane (Grade 2): All teachers are very nice people. Everybody should like teachers. Teachers are people to help you learn so when your a grown person you have lot of things to tell your children. (p. 140)
>
> Cindy (Grade 4): I will always remember my third grade teacher, Mrs. Schram. When my aunt died she was comforting, understanding and helpful. (p. 133)
>
> Mike (Grade 6): A good teacher is a teacher that does stuff that catches your interest. Sometimes you start learning and you don't even realize it. A good teacher is a teacher that does stuff that makes you think. (p. 139)
>
> Lee (Grade 6): A good teacher would be a smart, well educated one. Someone who would be nice but would still teach (just in a fun way). Someone who would reward student for good work. Someone who would bring in many interesting things to show. Someone who would be fair and not put people down at anytime. (p. 141)

What young children say about teachers is not too much different from what research about effective teachers found later in this chapter says. Children want teachers who are well educated, who understand the subjects they teach, who attend to them as human beings, and who can create classrooms and relationships that are caring and just. Many of these attributes are supported by the research on effective teaching.

WHAT RESEARCH SAYS ABOUT EFFECTIVE TEACHERS

While personal memories and the voices of historical figures, the mass media, and young children all contribute to our understanding of good and bad teachers, we must turn to research on teaching if we are to form a truly honest and objective portrait of effective teachers. Only then is it possible to escape oversimplified views of teaching based on only one or two factors, such as loving children or being a subject-matter expert. We also need to turn to research to counter those who argue that teachers really do not make much difference. Let's begin with that assertion.

Do Teachers Make a Difference?

In the late 1960s, several large, comprehensive research projects questioned the concept of teacher effectiveness. The most famous of these studies was directed by a sociologist at the University of Chicago, James Coleman (Coleman, Campbell, Wood, Weinfeld, & York, 1966). The Coleman project, as well as one conducted by Jencks (1972), studied what effect various factors, such as students' verbal abilities, social class backgrounds, and teacher characteristics, had on student achievement scores. Among other things, the Coleman and Jencks studies claimed that teachers seemed to have little impact on school achievement. Instead, students' intellectual abilities and the social class of their parents seemed to account for most of the differences found in student learning. This finding was widely disseminated at the time, and it was used by those who were critics of the public schools and of teachers.

Later, other researchers criticized the research methods used by Coleman and Jencks (Good, 1983, for example). Educational researchers pointed out that Coleman and Jencks looked only at schoolwide achievement and did not look at achievement of students in individual classrooms. They did not study the relationship between the behaviors of particular teachers and the achievement of their students. However, more important than the methodological debate concerning these studies was their aftereffect. The Coleman and Jencks studies ignited 2 decades of intense research aimed at discovering what, if any, teacher characteristics and behaviors seem to make a difference in student learning. We look more closely at this research in the remainder of this section.

Personal Qualities of Effective Teachers

You read in the Introduction to Part 1 how early American communities had few standards governing teaching practices but a great many regulations governing teachers' personal lives and moral conduct. Although concern for teachers' moral character had diminished by the early part of the twentieth century, citizens and many educators continued to believe that a teacher's personal qualities were among the most important attributes for effective teaching. They believed that teachers who were warm and loving and truly empathetic toward children and their problems were those who could best help children learn. Teachers without these personal qualities, those perceived as cold or aloof, were judged ineffective.

This view of the effective teacher was also shared by the educational research community of that time. Indeed, studies that attempted to identify the personal characteristics of effective teachers dominated the research conducted between 1930 and 1960. Researchers developed a variety of personality inventories, such as the Minnesota Teacher Attitude Inventory, the Authoritarianism F Scale, and the Guilford-Zimmerman Temperament Survey. In each instance, the researcher tried to measure some feature of a teacher's personality to see if this feature correlated with good teaching. One of the most comprehensive studies in this research tradition was the Teacher Characteristic Study done by David Ryan (1960). Over a period of 6 years, Ryan collected personal information from over 6,000 teachers in 1,700 schools and found that several characteristics, which are summarized in Figure 2.2, seemed to be related to effective teaching.

Ryan concluded that effective teachers exhibited the characteristics of warmth, fairness, and responsiveness, that they were understanding, democratic, kind, alert, attractive, steady, poised, and confident. He contrasted these positive characteristics with less desirable ones, such as aloofness, egocentrism, dullness, and authoritarianism.

Like most beliefs held over a long period of time, those concerning the importance of teacher characteristics and personality had, and still has, a measure of truth to it. Think about your own teachers again. Many you liked were probably warm and caring, whereas those you did not like seemed cold and aloof. However, this single-minded focus on the personal qualities of teachers eventually fell into disrepute for reasons summarized by Getzels and Jackson in 1963.

Figure 2.2   Selected Characteristics of Effective Teachers

- Superior intellectual abilities
- Good emotional adjustment
- Favorable attitudes toward pupils
- Enjoyment of pupil relationships
- Generosity in the appraisal of others
- Strong interests in reading and literary matters
- Interest in music and painting
- Participation in social and community affairs
- Early experiences in caring for and liking children
- History of teaching in the family
- Family support of teaching as a vocation
- Strong social service interest

Source: After Ryan, 1960, p. 366-370.

The regrettable fact is that many of the studies so far have *not* produced significant results. Many others have produced only pedestrian findings. For example, it is said that after the usual inventory tabulation that good teachers are friendly, cheerful, sympathetic and morally virtuous rather than cruel, depressed, unsympathetic, and morally depraved. But when this has been said, not very much that is especially useful has been revealed. For what conceivable human interaction—and teaching implies first and foremost a human interaction—is not the better if the people involved are friendly, cheerful, sympathetic, and virtuous rather than the opposite. (p. 574)

Furthermore, even though most of the characteristics identified by Ryan may have been desirable, it is unlikely that individuals who did not possess these characteristics could readily obtain them, even with extensive training. The human personality is simply too complex to be manipulated and changed, at least over short periods of time.

Today's educational researchers take a slightly different perspective when studying the characteristics of effective teachers. Rather than focusing on specific characteristics, such as those identified by Ryan, most tend to focus on more broadly defined *dispositions* possessed by teachers. A **disposition** is a person's inclination or tendency to act in certain ways under particular circumstances. Unlike basic personality traits, researchers believe dispositions are learned and are thus changeable through training or experience. For our discussion here, we consider three types of teacher dispositions that impact on what students learn and are deemed important for effective teaching. These include positive dispositions toward children and youth, knowledge, and working with other adults.

Dispositions toward Children and Youth

In general, we believe that teachers should demonstrate caring dispositions toward children and youth and believe in the ability of all children to learn. Let's look more closely at these two dispositions.

Teacher Caring   Even though teacher-characteristic research has never been conclusive, it nonetheless supports the common-sense view that some measure of caring, friendliness, sensitivity, and understanding are important to effective teaching. Teachers who are friendly and warm have students who like them. Teachers who show that they "really" care and have concern for their students create conditions where students work harder for longer periods of time and thus learn more. At the same time, we have to be careful about over generalizing in this regard. For instance, there are many ways in which a teacher can show friendliness and caring. Some may do it with hugs and smiles and others with exacting demands and high work standards. Also, we need to realize that what constitutes caring can be ambiguous and even appear contradictory and often can fluctuate as situations change. What passes for understanding and caring within one culture, class, or situation may be regarded as insensitive and thoughtless in another. For example, in Western cultures, making eye contact with another person during a conversation shows that you care about the person and that you are interested in their ideas. In some Asian cultures, on the other hand, respect, a form of caring, is shown by listening with eyes downcast. Similarly, the way individuals accept and display warmth may vary significantly within and between social and cultural groups. In some instances, warmth is characterized by lots of touching. In other situations, touching can be construed as intrusive or sexually motivated. Nonetheless, it is probably safe to conclude that people believe caring, credibility and trust, and encouragement and support are important dispositions for teachers to have. It is the way they are communicated that varies.

Teacher Expectations   Perhaps the most important, and certainly the most studied, teacher disposition is their **expectations.** These are the attitudes and beliefs teachers have about how well their students can do and how much they can learn. Over the past 3 decades, researchers have discovered that teachers who communicate clear academic and social goals for students, who hold high expectations for all children, and who convey a "can do" attitude motivate students to engage in learning and to aspire to excellence. Unfortunately, not all teachers hold high expectations for their students or treat all students the same. Instead, it is a well-documented fact that some teachers hold differential expectations for students and interact with them accordingly. For example, the white, European culture of most American teachers causes them to *unconsciously* expect more from students who share their background and less from students whose cultural backgrounds and language differ from their own.

A classic study that explored the effects on students of teacher expectations was done by Ray Rist (1970). Rist observed a single class of African American children twice weekly for 90 minutes. Observations were conducted throughout the year when the children were in kindergarten and again when they were in first and second grades. Observers kept an account of interactions that occurred, and they interviewed the teachers. What Rist found was insightful but also disturbing. The kindergarten teachers in the study practiced ability grouping. They placed children into low-, middle- and high-ability groups on the eighth day of school. They made these placements on the basis of perceptions and such nonacademic data as whose mother was on welfare, the child's behavior as described by the mother, and the child's dress. Children in each group were seated together and received similar instruction for the remainder of the year. Rist reported that teachers gave more positive attention to children in the high group and spent more time with them. Children in the low group were not only reprimanded more often by the teacher but were often ridiculed (without reprimand from the teacher) by children in the high group.

When this group of children moved to the first grade, they remained essentially in the same subgroups, which were labeled Group A, Group B, and Group C. The children in Groups B and C did not work on the first-grade curriculum early in the year; instead they completed kindergarten lessons.

The second-grade teacher continued the grouping practice started in kindergarten. Group A children became "tigers"; Group B, "cardinals"; and Group C, which now included some students who were repeating the second grade, were called "clowns." The different groups were assigned different books for reading. The students in the high group were given time for independent reading; students in the low group were not. Rist concluded that children in the low group were locked out of ever advancing into the higher group and wrote, "The child's journey through the early grades of school at one reading level and in one social grouping appeared to be pre-ordained from the eighth day of kindergarten" (p. 435).

It is likely, given all the attention the teacher-expectation research received, that teachers in most schools today no longer ability group students the way teachers did in the Rist Study. Nonetheless, Rist's findings remain important, because they demonstrated that teachers' dispositions and expectations toward children profoundly influence their learning opportunities and, ultimately, their academic and social achievement. Unfortunately, expectations are usually influenced by group characteristics, such as social class, race, ethnicity, and gender. Children who do not fit the white, middle-class mold suffer from the lower expectations most teachers hold for them. Furthermore, teacher expectations create a cyclical pattern of behaviors for both teachers and students as Figure 2.3 illustrates.

It is important that you consider teacher expectations as you think about becoming a teacher. Do you have perceptions that some children are more capable than others? On what are these perceptions based? Do you think you could learn to have high

expectations for all children? Will your own cultural background influence the way you behave toward culturally different children?

Dispositions toward Knowledge

It should be self-evident that knowledge and "things of the mind" are central to teaching and learning. Without a love of knowledge that encompasses both the subject matter they teach and the methods they use to teach it, teachers have little hope of ever being effective in their work. An enormous part of a teacher's job has to do with knowledge. Teachers' dispositions about knowledge are crucial to both their success and their job satisfaction.

Intellectual Orientation   Teachers who do not value knowledge, either subject matter or pedagogical, are like swimmers uncomfortable in the water. They are simply ill suited to their environment. Unfortunately, American culture has been characterized as anti-intellectual, as devaluing knowledge, the intellect, and reason. Indeed, several observers dating back as early as the 1960s (Hofstader, 1962, for example) have described the anti-intellectualism in American life. They note the anti-intellectual views of some teachers and the public's anti-intellectual attitude toward teachers and scholars whom they sometimes disparage as "egg heads," "nerds" or individuals with their "heads in the clouds." We also see anti-intellectualism at work when we find parents more concerned about their childrens' popularity or acquiring a diploma than they are about their academic learning. It is commonplace to find parents who believe that the "school of hard knocks" is the best teacher, and they convey this attitude to their children.

Whether or not mainstream America is anti-intellectual and therefore suspicious of intellectually oriented teachers is a matter that is open to debate. What seems important, however, is the fact that schools exist for the purpose of acquiring knowledge and that any teacher who is uncomfortable in a knowledge-oriented environment is ill suited to a teaching career. To test your own intellectual dispositions, consider the following questions. Do you rely mainly on evidence and knowledge or on your own personal experience to clarify difficult problems? Are you inclined to believe or doubt the results of scientific research in such areas as medicine, nutrition, and children's learning? Do you approach complex situations rationally or intuitively? How would you react if your best friend swears by a new vitamin, but you read about several studies that

Figure 2.3   **Cyclical Process of Teacher Expectations**

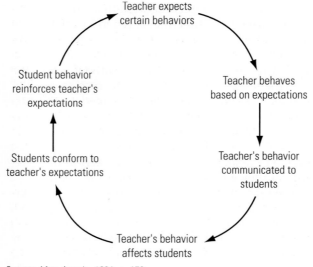

Teacher expects certain behaviors

Teacher behaves based on expectations

Teacher's behavior communicated to students

Teacher's behavior affects students

Students conform to teacher's expectations

Student behavior reinforces teacher's expectations

Source: After Arends, 1994, p. 150

question its efficacy? Similarly, how would you react to a teaching colleague who commits to a new classroom management system that has been criticized by the research community? How likely are you to implement that management system in your own classroom? How likely are you to tell your friend what you know about the system?

Enthusiasm   Obviously, it is important for teachers to have a command of important facts and concepts associated with the subjects they teach as well as an intellectual orientation toward knowledge and learning. Equally as important is their attitude toward this knowledge and how enthusiastically they can communicate this attitude to their students. Teacher enthusiasm is a disposition that some teachers display more than others and one that has been studied rather thoroughly.

In 1970, Barak Rosenshine reviewed the research on teacher enthusiasm. He and Furst reported that **teacher enthusiasm** was consistently shown to have a positive relationship to student learning (Rosenshine & Furst, 1973). Seeing the connections between enthusiasm and student achievement led some researchers, such as Collins (1978), to develop particular training programs aimed at helping teachers become more enthusiastic and testing whether or not enthusiasm displayed under experimental conditions would produce higher student learning. Collins taught teachers to display the behaviors shown in Figure 2.4 when they were talking about or dealing with their subject areas.

Collins found that students of enthusiasm-trained teachers did better on targeted achievement tests than students of untrained teachers did. However, other studies that replicated Collins's study, such as Bettencourt (1979), could find no significant differences between enthusiasm-trained and untrained teachers. Currently, some evidence, as well as common sense, point to the importance of enthusiasm in effective teachers' dispositions. However, an exact recipe for imparting enthusiasm does not exist. Questions about enthusiasm that you may want to consider include: How enthusiastic are you toward the subject matter you plan to teach? Do you read in these subjects beyond required assignments? Do you voluntarily read or pursue research in these subjects? How do you display your enthusiasm or lack of enthusiasm? If you simply are not very enthusiastic about particular subjects, do you think you can encourage your students' enthusiasm? Can you communicate enthusiasm to students without the behaviors recommended by Collins?

Figure 2.4   Elements of Enthusiasm

Vocal Delivery
  Varied, lilting, uplifting intonations, many changes in tone, pitch
Eyes
  Shining, frequently opened wide, eyebrows raised, eye contact with total group
Gestures
  Frequent movements of body, head, arms, hands and face, sweeping motions; clapping hands; head nodding rapidly
Movements
  Makes large body movements, swings around, changes pace, bends body
Facial Expression
  Changes denoting surprise, sadness, joy, thoughtfulness, awe, excitement
Word Selection
  Highly descriptive, many adjectives, great variety
Acceptance of Ideas and Feelings
  Accepts ideas and feelings quickly with vigor and animation; ready to accept, praise, encourage, or clarify in a nonthreatening manner; many variations in responding to pupils
Overall Energy
  High degree of spirit throughout lesson

Source: After Collins 1978 p. 53-57.

Dispositions toward Colleagues and Other Adults

At one time, most people believed that teachers' work consisted mainly of their classroom interactions with children. However, as you read in Chapter 1, this simplistic view has been replaced with an expanded view of teaching and schooling. Today, educators believe that schoolwide efforts impact on student learning and that schools where teachers work effectively with each other and with parents are crucial. Where this cooperation exists a synergy is achieved, which results in far greater student learning than in schools where teachers work alone.

Achieving **synergy** and **interdependence,** however, has not been easy to accomplish. Part of the difficulty is that many veteran teachers have been socialized into working alone, and they prefer it that way. Some of your own friends are probably more enthusiastic about working in interdependent ways than others are. However, it is likely that tomorrow's schools will seek teachers who are comfortable working in cooperative team arrangements with colleagues and with parents. Some schools are starting to query teachers during job interviews about their disposition toward working in teams, helping colleagues draft schoolwide goals, and finding ways to involve parents in their children's education. These schools want teachers who value working together, not those who resist interdependent action. Questions you will want to consider about your own dispositions include: On important tasks, do you enjoy working with others or do you prefer working alone? As a student, have you ever helped establish or belonged to a study group? Do you believe that teaching includes working with parents as well as children? What "people skills" do you have?

Behaviors of Effective Teachers

Possessing favorable personal qualities and positive dispositions toward people and knowledge are important for effective teaching. Equally important is that at some point these must be transformed into action. Doctors who know how the heart works are asked to perform bypass surgery. Architects who understand the physics of stress must design buildings that will withstand earthquakes. The same reality is true for teachers. Knowledge about human development and children's learning are of little value unless they guide the actions of some teacher with a class of 25 children. Fortunately, we have a knowledge base that tells us what effective teachers "do" and how their behavior differs from ineffective teachers', particularly when providing basic-skills instruction to students. The nature of this research and the way it was produced is the subject of the accompanying Research Box.

The process-product research described in the Research Box identified several domains of teacher behavior that were strongly associated with student learning. We describe these here.

- *Effective use of time.* Researchers found that there was a strong relationship between student academic engagement rates, also called "time on task," and student achievement. Teachers who ran businesslike, task-focused classrooms and who allocated a great amount of time to academic learning were more effective than teachers whose classrooms were more informal and who consumed more time with nonacademic and housekeeping activities.

- *High performance expectations.* Effective teachers, researchers discovered, communicated higher performance expectations to students, assigned more work, and moved through the curriculum at a brisker pace than less effective teachers did.

They exhibited a "can do" attitude toward all their students.

- *Clear rules and procedures.* Effective teachers' classrooms were characterized by clear *rules and procedures* that governed student talk, participation, movement, turning in work, and what to do during downtimes. *Instructions* in their classrooms were *clearly stated* and student *misbehavior was handled quickly.*

- *Work requirements and feedback.* Effective teachers had clear work requirements, monitored student work carefully, and provided students with feedback on how they were doing. They particularly provided students with feedback that was immediate and nonevaluative, thereby helping students accomplish the task at hand.

- *Appropriate use of praise.* Researchers consistently found that effective teachers provide less praise and a different kind of praise than ineffective teachers. When the finding about less praise was first discovered, it contradicted the common wisdom of the time that encouraged teachers to use praise liberally. Studies about praise were summarized by Jere Brophy in 1981. Figure 2.5 illustrates guidelines for effective and ineffective praise.

- *Clarity of presentations.* Process-product researchers observed that some teachers' lessons were characterized by vagueness, indicating that the teacher either did not know the information or else could not present it clearly. In 1986, Rosenshine and Stevens reviewed a number of studies that had found significant relationships between teacher clarity or verbal fluency and student achievement. From these studies they developed the list of suggested behaviors for clear presentations found in Figure 2.6.

- *Active teaching.* Last, process-product researchers found that teachers who were focused on academic tasks, who were businesslike and conducted briskly paced, teacher-directed lessons produced higher student achievement than teachers who used more informal and less teacher-directed approaches. The instructional method associated with this type of teaching came to be called *direct instruction,* described in Chapter 6. We provide an example of this approach to teaching in Table 2.1.

Process-product research has had profound effects on our views of effective teaching. For example, many tests used today to certify teachers have test items based on this research, and most state departments of education have developed evaluation systems for beginning teachers that use it. Figure 2.7 illustrates the list of teacher behaviors used by the state of Florida.

Active teaching (direct instruction) came under criticism almost as soon as its effectiveness was

RESEARCH

Process-Product Research and the Effective Teacher

Prior to the 1970s, educational researchers focused mainly on teachers' personal characteristics and how they related to student learning. They also examined the relationships between a principal's judgment of a teacher's effectiveness and student achievement scores. Researchers eventually became disillusioned with this line of inquiry, and in the early 1970s, a new paradigm for research on teaching and learning emerged. Called *process-product* research, this line of inquiry had profound effects on our views of effective teaching.

Process-product research was characterized by both the type of questions asked and the methods of inquiry used by the researcher. The overriding question guiding process-product research was, What do individual teachers do that make a difference in the academic achievement of their students? There are two important words in this question. One, the word *do,* suggests teacher action or behaviors as contrasted with earlier concerns about their personal attributes or characteristics. The researchers labeled these teacher behaviors *process*. The second important word is *achievement.* For the process-product researchers, achievement was the *product* of instruction. In most instances, they defined achievement as the acquisition of those skills and knowledge that can be measured on standardized tests. Effective teachers were individuals who acted in ways that produced average to above-average student achievement. Process-product research, thus, can be summarized as the search for those teacher behaviors (process) that lead to above average student achievement scores (product).

Particular methods of inquiry also characterized process-product research. Typically, process-product researchers went directly into classrooms and observed teachers in natural (regular) classroom settings. This was something that few researchers had done before the 1970s. Teacher behaviors were recorded using a variety of low-inference observation devices, and student achievement was measured over several time periods, often at the beginning and the end of a school year. Particular teacher behaviors were then correlated with student achievement scores, and successful and unsuccessful teacher behaviors were identified.

Researchers completed hundreds of process-product studies in the 1970s and 1980s. In general, process-product researchers found that teachers who had well-organized classrooms in which structured learning experiences prevailed produced certain kinds of student achievement better than did teachers who did not use these practices. It is important to note that process-product researchers did not try to invent and test new ways of teaching. Mainly, they were content to study teaching as it occurred in regular classroom settings.

Figure 2.5   **Guidelines for Effective Praise**

Effective Praise	Ineffective Praise
1. Is delivered contingently	1. Is delivered randomly or unsystematically
2. Specifies the particulars of the accomplishment	2. Is restricted to global positive reactions
3. Shows spontaneity, variety, and other signs of credibility; suggests clear attention to the student's accomplishment	3. Shows a bland uniformity that suggests a conditioned response made with minimal attention
4. Rewards attainment of specified performance criteria (which can include effort criteria, however)	4. Rewards mere participation without consideration of performance processes or outcomes
5. Provides information to students about their competence or the value of their accomplishments	5. Provides no information at all or gives students information about their status
6. Orients students toward better appreciation of their own task-related behavior and thinking about problem solving	6. Orients students toward comparing themselves with others and thinking about competing
7. Uses students' own prior accomplishments as the context for describing present accomplishments	7. Uses the accomplishments of peers as the context for describing students' present accomplishments
8. Is given in recognition of noteworthy effort or success at difficult (for *this* student) tasks	8. Is given without regard to the effort expended or the meaning of the accomplishment
9. Attributes success to effort and ability, implying that similar successes can be expected in the future	9. Attributes success to ability alone or to external factors such as luck or low task difficulty
10. Fosters endogenous attributions (students believe that they expend effort on the task because they enjoy the task and/or want to develop task-relevant skills)	10. Fosters exogenous attributions (students believe that they expend effort on the task for external reasons—to please the teacher, win a competition or reward, etc.)
11. Focuses students' attention on their own task-relevant behavior	11. Focuses students' attention on the teacher as an external authority figure who is manipulating them
12. Fosters appreciation of, and desirable attributions about, task-relevant behavior after the process is completed	12. Intrudes into the ongoing process, distracting attention from task-relevant behavior

Source: Brophy, 1981, pp. 5–32.

being established. Critics argued that the approach was limited because it showed results only for teaching basic skills and not for accomplishing higher-level thinking objectives, such as analyzing, synthesizing, or evaluating. Some researchers criticized this concept of effective teaching because of the underlying behavioral theory that viewed students primarily as empty vessels waiting to be filled with information. This relegated teaching to transmitting segmented knowledge into the empty vessels. Still others criticized the teacher effectiveness research because of the overzealous way it was implemented in classrooms. For example, in one large public school system on the East Coast, every teacher was expected to provide the same kind of active teaching lesson every day. If other approaches were used while the teacher was being observed by a supervisor, the teacher received a negative evaluation. The pros and cons for using direct instruction are further highlighted in the accompanying Issues Box.

You will read in the next section that most educators today hold a more balanced view of what constitutes an effective teacher, considering teacher behavior only one aspect of a complex role. Also, as Chapter 6 shows in more detail, the overall key to

effective teaching is the teachers' ability to match their instructional approaches to the context of their classrooms and to the type of learning goals they are trying to achieve with their students.

Teachers' Knowledge and Thought Processes

Process-product research dominated conceptions of effective teaching between 1970 and 1990. This research paradigm and the approach to teaching it embodied were consistent with philosophical views that see knowledge as fixed and eternal and teaching as the clear transmission of that knowledge. **Constructivism,** an alternative view about knowledge and teaching, started to gain ground in the 1980s and continues to in the present time. Rather than viewing knowledge as fixed, knowable, and transmittable, the constructivist perspective holds that some aspects of knowledge are necessarily personal in nature, that is, that learners actively construct knowledge which is meaningful to them by interacting with their social and physical environment. Constructivist teaching provides students with relevant experiences for interaction and dia-

Figure 2.6   **Aspects of Clear Presentation**

1. Clarity of Goals and Main Points
   a. State the goals or objectives of the presentation
   b. Focus on one thought (point, direction) at a time
   c. Avoid digressions
   d. Avoid ambiguous phrases and pronouns
2. Step-by-Step Presentations
   a. Present the material in small steps
   b. Organize and present the material so that one point is mastered before the next point is given
   c. Give explicit, step-by-step directions (when possible)
   d. Present an outline when the material is complex
3. Specific and Concrete Procedures
   a. Model the skill or process (when appropriate)
   b. Give detailed and redundant explanations for difficult points
   c. Provide students with concrete and varied examples
4. Checking for Students' Understanding
   a. Be sure that students understand one point before proceeding to the next point
   b. Ask the students questions to monitor their comprehension of what has been presented
   c. Have students summarize the main points in their own words
   d. Reteach the parts of the presentation that the students have difficulty comprehending, either by further teacher explanation or by students tutoring other students

Source: After Rosenshine & Stevens, 1986, p. 378.

Figure 2.7   **Florida's Teaching Competencies**

1. Begins instruction promptly
2. Handles materials in an orderly manner
3. Orients students to classwork/maintains academic focus
4. Conducts beginning/ending review
5. Asks single factual question
6. Recognizes response/amplifies/gives corrective feedback
7. Gives specific academic praise
8. Provides for practice
9. Gives direction/assigns/checks comprehension of homework, seatwork assignment/gives feedback
10. Circulates and assists students
11. Treats concept-definition/attributes/examples/nonexamples
12. Discusses cause-effect/uses linking words—applies law or principle
13. States and applies academic rule
14. Develops criteria and evidence for value judgment
15. Emphasizes important points
16. Expresses enthusiasm verbally/challenges students
17. Uses body behavior that shows interest—smiles, gestures
18. Stops misconduct
19. Maintains instructional momentum

Source: After Florida Department of Education, 1991.

Teachers' Knowledge

It appears that effective teachers draw on many sources of knowledge when they are making decisions about what to teach and how to teach it. Lee Shulman (1987), one of America's foremost educational researchers, and some of his colleagues organized important knowledge for teachers into the seven categories illustrated in Figure 2.8. Teachers must have knowledge of the subject fields they teach and of other related fields, such as mathematics, science, English, and history. They must also know how to transform their knowledge into teaching activities for students. Teachers who know the facts, concepts, and the big organizing ideas of the subjects they teach can make clearer presentations, engage students in the inquiry process, and better assist their students in understanding important relationships among ideas.

Pedagogical content knowledge is knowledge about how to represent ideas, that is, how to provide effective examples, analogies, explanations, and demonstrations of the ideas in a subject field. Read, for example, how one teacher decided to use the

logue. This perspective shifts the definition of effective teaching from what teachers *do* to what they *know* and how they *think*. It also shifts the ways that educational researchers approach the study of effective teachers. Instead of focusing on observable teacher and student behaviors, as you read in Chapter 2's Research Box, researchers who hold a constructivist perspective are more interested in what teachers and students know and what they are thinking.

In the sections that follow we explore the nature of teacher knowledge and teacher thinking and the effects these are believed to have on teachers' work. We conclude with a description of a lesson designed from a constructivist perspective and compare it with one designed from a direct-instruction perspective.

Figure 2.8   **Categories of Professional Knowledge Base for Teachers**

Knowledge of Subject Matter	Knowledge of Curriculum
Pedagogical Content Knowledge	Knowledge of Learners
Knowledge of Other Content	Knowledge of Educational Aims
	General Pedagogical Knowledge

Source: After Wilson, Schulman, & Richert, 1989.

concept of moral conflict to introduce Julius Caesar to his students.

Julius Caesar is basically a play about internal conflicts, a moral decision for which there is really no wrong or right answer. If we kill this man, we might save our republic but we endanger ourselves. If we don't kill him, we could be endangered. One man's struggle with a moral decision, the consequences of his actions and how people turn against him. And so what I had them do was . . . I gave them an artificial scenario. I said, "You are the first officer on the Starship Enterprise. Captain Kirk has been getting

ISSUES

EXTRA

What Is the Best Approach for Teaching At-risk or Learning Disabled Students?

There have been many recommendations over the past 2 decades on how best to teach students who are **at risk,** that is, students who have trouble learning the school's curriculum. On one side of this issue are those who support the use of direct-instruction approaches, because highly structured, teacher-directed lessons have been shown to produce higher learning of basic skills. Some educators believe that at-risk students and students who are learning disabled (for whatever reason) require instruction that focuses on basic skills and information that is prerequisite to both self-care and higher-level learning. Advocates of direct introduction offer the following advice to teachers.

- Break information or skills to be taught into small chunks or steps, and avoid complex materials that may be confusing to students.

- Provide teacher-centered activities that are clear, carefully sequenced, and relatively brief, and avoid activities in which a teacher is not in charge and students are not following the teacher's directions.

- Teach students in whole-class settings, and avoid small-group and independent activities.

- Emphasize paper-and-pencil exercises, and provide lots of practice with feedback. Avoid open-ended assignments, discovery activities, and interest centers.

- Ask questions that require recall or convergent thinking, and avoid open-ended and divergent questions that do not have correct answers.

Over 2 decades of process-product research has shown the effectiveness of direct instruction in producing high student achievement on standardized tests as compared to more informal and student-centered instructional methods. Much of this research has been done in classrooms in which many of the students are from low-socioeconomic backgrounds and who have been identified as being at risk.

On the other side of this issue are educators who say that using direct-instruction strategies with at-risk students does not work, and that it is the worst thing teachers can do. Martin Haberman (1991), for example,

out of hand. He's a good captain, he's been made Commander of the Fleet. But you, his closest friend, and your fellow officers have been noticing that he's been getting too risky, a little big-headed. You're afraid that he's going to endanger the Federation Fleet and might just seek glory in some farcical campaign." And they really took off on that . . . they said they found out there really wasn't a right answer. They argued back and forth. You couldn't just kill him because the whole fleet likes him. If you kill him, it's your head on the chopping block, too. But you also have a moral obligation to your country and you can't let him go on. What they finally came

up with was that it's a pretty tough decision to make. (Wilson, Shulman, Richert, 1989)

Effective teachers also draw on knowledge from the field of education. Knowledge of educational aims and curriculum contribute to making wise decisions about what should be taught and justifying these decisions to students and to their parents. Teachers use knowledge of learners, their characteristics and cognitive processes for the purpose of designing particular learning activities and making sure they are developmentally appropriate. Additionally, general pedagogical knowledge, such as

ISSUES

Continued

labeled direct instruction, particularly as it is practiced in urban classrooms, the "pedagogy of poverty." He argued:

> *[A] classroom atmosphere created by constant teacher direction and student compliance seethes with passive resentment that sometimes bubbles up into overt resistance . . . In reality the pedagogy of poverty is not a professional methodology at all. It is not supported by research, by theory, or by the best practice of superior urban teachers. It is actually certain ritualistic acts that, much like the ceremonies performed by religious functionaries, have come to be conducted for their intrinsic value rather than to foster learning. (308)*

Haberman and educators who hold a more cognitive and student-centered view of learning would recommend the following for teaching at-risk students.

- Involve students in problems and concerns vital to their lives, and focus on complex but meaningful problems.
- Help students see major concepts, the big ideas, and general principles. Embed basic-skills instruction within these larger ideas and problems.
- Involve students in planning what they will be doing.
- Get students actively involved in their own learning and in constructing their own knowledge. Provide help connecting new material to students' prior knowledge.
- Make dialogue rather than completion of paper-and-pencil exercises central to the tasks of teaching and learning.
- Get students involved in real-life experiences, such as field trips and community work. Help them connect back to their families and culture and the cultures of others.

What do you think about this issue? If you were given a magic wand and could get teachers and others in schools to do whatever you command, what would you prescribe as the best approach for working with at-risk students?

how to question effectively, how to create a positive learning environment, and how to structure a lesson is also needed.

Recent research has found that many teachers have limited content and pedagogical knowledge (Amarel & Feiman-Nemser, 1988; Ball, 1988; Carter, 1990; Feiman-Nemser & Remillard 1996; Gomez 1988). How much this lack of knowledge impacts student learning has not yet been fully documented. However, teachers who have deep and flexible knowledge are known to provide more appropriate instruction that in turn stimulates more meaningful student discourse. Conversely, teachers with limited knowledge, generally present their subjects as a collection of facts and tend to rely on seatwork assignments. For example, read the following.

> Several secondary biology majors are discussing their plans for teaching one-week units. Most of the unit plans share a common problem: They include far too much content for the time available. One student, for example, plans to cover the following topics in five-day units on fishes: evolution of fishes, classes of fishes (named in Latin) and their characteristics, adaptation of fishes to their environment, structure, and function of fish body systems (down to the level of parts of the brain). The methods course instructors immediately begin suggesting ways to reduce and simplify the content that she plans to teach. She demurs, "But it's all interconnected!" (Anderson, 1989, p. 96)

Teachers' Thought Processes

In addition to studying what effective teachers know, there is also an emerging interest in how teachers think and in the relationships between their reflective capacities and their effectiveness. That is, researchers are interested in how teachers use their knowledge. Two particularly interesting areas of teacher thinking are relevant to our discussion of effective teachers: expert teachers' thinking processes and teachers' ability to think reflectively about their work.

Expert and Novice Teachers   Researchers have investigated the different thought processes used by expert and novice teachers [Borko & Livingston, (1989); Housner & Griffey (1985); Leinhardt & Greeno (1986)]. They found that expert teachers have more highly developed knowledge systems that lead them to think differently about problems and to use different problem-solving strategies. An expert teacher, for instance, creates lessons that connect new subject matter to what students already know. An expert teacher also can explain things in ways that students understand. Novice teachers, on the other hand, seem unable to think about or to tailor subject matter to a particular group of students. In short, thorough knowledge and considerable experience allow expert teachers to diagnose a complex teaching situation before making a decision, whereas novice teachers, lacking this flexibility, may adopt the first method that comes to mind.

Reflective Teachers   A final feature of teacher thought processes has to do with the way teachers reflect on their work and stems mainly from the work of Donald Schon (1983; 1986). According to Schon, good practice requires more than a firm grasp of professional knowledge, because the teachers' problems, as with those of doctors, lawyers, and other professionals, are characterized by their uniqueness. To support this argument, Schon cited an eminent physician who claimed that "85 percent of the problems a doctor sees in his office are not in the book." (Schon, 1983) Schon also pointed out that many of the problems facing teachers center around values and priorities. For example, teachers are often asked to increase their effectiveness while their budgets are being cut, or they are asked to teach for higher-level thinking while being held accountable for student scores on standardized tests of basic skills.

Additionally, Schon explains how much of what we know is intuitive and tacit. That is, in addition to being grounded in important knowledge and skills, the most effective teachers are usually individuals who can approach unique and value-laden situations with a reflective, problem-solving orientation. They know how to examine their own values, and they trust their intuition to provide an appropriate guide for action. They think about and reflect on their practice and use this reflection to build both the art and science of effective teaching.

Table 2.1 concludes this section by showing the contrasting techniques of the two major conceptions of effective teaching—constructivism and direct instruction—in teaching a math lesson.

THE EFFECTIVE TEACHER FOR THE TWENTY-FIRST CENTURY

What several decades of painstaking research tell us is that teaching is a very complex job, and although we know a great deal about being an effective

Table 2.1   **Comparing a Direct Instruction and a Constructivist Math Lesson**

Direct Instruction Lesson	Constructivist Lesson
• *Daily review:* Review yesterday's work and check homework	• Promote students' autonomy by insisting that they try to solve problems
	• Promote commitment to answers through questioning
• *Presentation:* Focus on lesson objective and provide materials in small steps and at rapid pace	• Develop students' reflective processes by asking them to restate problem and explain answers
• *Guided practice:* Have students practice under teacher's supervision; check for understanding	• Construct a case history of each student: Note how student approaches problem and note misconceptions
• *Feedback:* Provide students with quick, firm feedback	
• *Independent practice:* Assign seatwork and practice to accomplish overlearning	• If students unable to solve problem, intervene to negotiate a possible solution Guide to think about possible solution and, if frustrated, ask direct, problem-oriented questions
• *Weekly and monthly reviews:* Systematically review all previously learned materials and homework	
	• When the problem is solved, review the solution, encourage reflection, and note what they did well

Source: After Good & Grouws, 1979; Rosenshine & Stevens, 1986; Confrey, (1990).

teacher, there is still much to learn. The eternal search for the perfect teacher, the one that we can all model ourselves after, will always entice us but forever elude us. Teaching is simply too complex to know perfectly, and it grows more complex everyday. Research also tells us that teaching is situation driven, meaning that what may be effective in one school or classroom situation may be ineffective in another. For instance, we know that certain types of teachers and teaching methods work well with some kinds of students but not with others. What may be very effective with an at-risk student from a working-class background may be very ineffective with a student from a middle-class background whose parents have different expectations for their children's education. Similarly, a teacher who is highly effective in lecturing to college students may find herself ineffective teaching a group of middle-school students with limited attention spans.

Decades of research have also left us with the conception that some aspects of effectiveness stem from teachers' personal qualities, others from what they know and can do, and others from the way they think and reflect on their work. Society wants teachers who are caring and nurturing toward children and who can create classrooms in which children are motivated to work hard and to learn. Although

communities no longer apply tight social restrictions to teachers' personal lives, nevertheless, they want teachers who can bring a moral perspective to their work. Likewise, what teachers know and can do is critical if children are to learn. Effective teachers for the twenty-first century must have thorough and flexible understanding of subject matter, pedagogy, and student development in order to make lessons meaningful. However, we come back to the point that teaching is always situational. This means that all knowledge, whether derived from research or from practice, must be adapted to fit the nature of a particular classroom situation. Knowing how to diagnose situations and to adapt the use of one's professional knowledge accordingly are critical and exciting aspects of teaching. A summary of the four attributes that describe effective teachers of the twenty-first century follows.

1. Effective teachers should have personal qualities that allow them to develop authentic human relationships with students, parents, and colleagues and to create democratic classrooms for children and adolescents.

2. Effective teachers should have positive dispositions toward knowledge. They should command at least three broad knowledge

bases: subject matter, human development and learning, and teaching practices.

3. Effective teachers should command a repertoire of teaching practices known to stimulate student motivation, to enhance student achievement of basic skills, to develop higher-level thinking, and to produced self-regulated learners.

4. Effective teachers should be personally disposed toward reflection and problem solving. They should consider learning to teach a lifelong process in which they learn to diagnose situations and then adapt their professional knowledge to fit those situations.

Figure 2.9 illustrates this view of effectiveness and the four attributes deemed essential in order to be an effective teacher. Teachers who possess these attributes should be able to teach like the German teachers described in the accompanying Global Box.

What about you? Do you possess the personal qualities needed to be a teacher? Do you like children and want to work with them? What about your colleagues and parents? Do you have or are you willing to acquire the knowledge required of contemporary teachers? Are you willing to acquire a repertoire of teaching practices so you can create democratic classrooms and develop self-regulated learners? Are you the type of person who will be reflective about your work and see learning to teach as a life-long endeavor?

GLOBAL

Teaching for Thinking in German Schools

Most industrialized countries face the same problems of school reform as does the United States. These countries have schools that were created in earlier eras to accomplish purposes of an industrial age and not those of contemporary societies. Recently, American educators have looked to other countries for models of teaching and schooling that may inform our own reform efforts.

Germany has been of particular interest. According to Zahorik and Dichanz (1994), German schools have been guided by a constructivist perspective for quite some time and have implemented several practices that are currently being proposed in the United States. These include multi-year grouping, community-based curriculum, and responsive teaching. **Multi-Year Grouping.**   In German elementary schools students are formed into heterogeneous groups in the first grade and then remain together with the same teachers for 4 years. This arrangement helps teachers to build a long-range relationship with their students and to know their students' learning styles, interests, and cognitive and emotional development. Students also get to know each other, which allows the formation of a supportive learning community.

Community- and Project-Based Curriculum.   Curriculum in German elementary schools draws its themes from a variety of subject fields, and students are involved in projects that incorporate a variety of subjects and activities. Here is a report by two American educators who observed a third-grade classroom.

> Students prior to our day at the school had visited the community bakery, and one of the student's grandmother had visited the class to tell how bread was baked when she was young.
>
> On the day of our visit, the teacher continued bakery-related activities for three hours ... During that time we watched students construct sentences at the board using bakery terms, create stories about their bakery visit, discuss the history of breadmaking using historical

Figure 2.9 **Attributes of Effective Teachers**

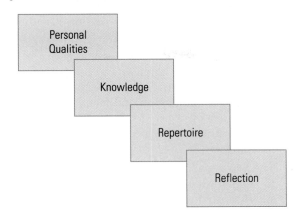

SUMMARY

- Definitions and images of effective teachers abound. Some are based on our own memories of effective teachers, some have been provided by writers and philosophers throughout the ages, and some come from the media.

- People's memories of effective teachers are important, because they form the perceptions most people have about teachers and their work. They also shape the beliefs individuals preparing to teach have about effective teaching.

GLOBAL

Continued

photographs and drawings, and read aloud and discuss selections about bakeries ... Then, after some mathematics warm-up exercises, the teacher involved students in multiplication problems related to the bakery. (p. 76)

Responsive Teaching.   Teachers in German elementary schools use what they call *responsive teaching*. Instead of presenting information and demonstrating and practicing skills, the dominant method in American schools, German teachers work with students to help them identify problems and projects and to facilitate student inquiry and problem solving. Project teaching and group activity and dialogue characterize classroom activities. Here is another example from Zahorik and Dichanz:

In a fourth-grade lesson on community health, the teacher began by displaying a model of the human brain and then asked students to examine the model and describe their impressions. Following their comments—which focused on texture, shape, color, parts, weight, and size—the teacher introduced the topic of the brain's function and how to research them. A wide-ranging discussion followed. Students voiced research suggestions that were clarified through group interaction. This verbalizing enabled teachers to see the state of students' internal knowledge structures and thinking processes and to adapt their responses to individual students. (p. 76)

Some of these features may be found in a few American elementary classrooms. They do not occur regularly, however, nor do they pervade classroom life as they seem to in Germany.

What are your ideas about the German style of schooling and teaching? Are German students learning important things that U. S. students are not? Do you suppose German students are missing out on important knowledge and skills? How would you feel about teaching in a German elementary school?

- Media representations of teachers have been both negative and positive. On the negative side, teachers are portrayed as bumblers with their "heads in the clouds." On the positive side, recent television shows and films have portrayed teachers as strong individuals who are willing to challenge and stand up for their students regardless of the odds.

- At a very early age, children begin to develop strong and persistent perceptions about effective teachers. Our own experiences as students have strongly influenced the views we have about teaching and about being an effective teacher. There are many parallels between children's perceptions and what research says about effective teachers.

- For most of this century, educational researchers focused their attention on the personal characteristics of teachers. This research did not produce significant results, but it lead to new paradigms for studying teaching and confirmed some common-sense ideas about the type of person we want teachers to be.

- Teachers who are warm and caring are better at motivating students to work harder and to persevere on academic tasks for longer periods of time.

- Effective teachers hold expectations that all children have potential and can learn. They do not interact differentially with particular groups of students. They treat students from non-European cultures and from lower social-economic backgrounds with the same regard as students from the middle class and the dominant culture.

- Effective teachers are enthusiastic toward the subjects they teach and can demonstrate this enthusiasm to their students.

- Effective teachers know that their work extends beyond the classroom door. They have positive dispositions toward working with their colleagues in the school and with the parents of their students.

- Effective teachers value knowledge and intellectual things. They do not represent the anti-intellectual attitudes found in some segments of American culture.

- Most contemporary knowledge about effective teaching stems from the process-product research of the past 25 years. This research aimed at discovering relationships between what teachers do in their classrooms (process) and student achievement levels as measured on standardized tests (products).

- Process-product research has codified effective teaching behaviors in the following domains: use of time, teacher expectations, classroom organization and management, teacher use of praise, teacher clarity, and teaching behaviors associated with active teaching.

- The ways teachers use time and their ability to keep students engaged and on-task significantly influences student learning.

- Classrooms that are well organized and have clearly defined rules and procedures in which lessons move along smoothly without disruptions result in higher student engagement and learning.

- The reinforcer most readily available to teachers is praise. Guidelines for the effective use of praise include giving it immediately and sincerely and specifying the particulars of the accomplishment.

- Teachers who are verbally fluent and who can present their ideas clearly to students are more effective than teachers who are vague. Guidelines for clear presentations include clearly stating your instructional goals, making step-by-step presentations, modeling skills and providing examples, and checking for understanding.

- A particular set of instructional behaviors labeled active or direct teaching are characterized by teacher-centered lessons conducted in an orderly, businesslike way.

- Instructional approaches such as direct instruction have been criticized by cognitive theorists and educators. Although acknowledged to be effective in teaching basic skills, these approaches are deemed inappropriate for teaching more complex processes, such as higher-order thinking and self-regulated learning.

- The constructivist perspective of teaching and learning provides an alternative to behavioral views. Cognitivists see knowledge as having a subjective or personal element in which unique individuals interact with others in ever-shifting contexts to construct knowledge that is personally meaningful. This perspective shifts the definition of effective teaching from what teachers can do to what they know and how they think.

- Effective teachers have control over the professional knowledge bases they need to perform their work. This is what separates teachers from educated laypersons who lack this command.

- Seven areas of research-based knowledge that are important for teachers to have command of are subject-matter knowledge; pedagogical content knowledge; knowledge of learners; general pedagogical knowledge; knowledge of the context of education; curriculum knowledge; and knowledge about educational ends and purposes.

- Effective teachers can translate their knowledge into specific teaching actions. The deeper a teacher's knowledge, the more able he or she is to plan lessons tied to students' prior knowledge and to explain subject matter in ways students can understand.

- Effective teachers possess: personal qualities and beliefs appropriate for the job, strong understandings of the subjects they teach, and knowledge of human development and teaching and learning. They also command a repertoire of effective teaching practices and can approach their work in a reflective, problem-solving fashion. They are adept at diagnosing complex teaching situations and at adapting the use of their professional knowledge accordingly.

READINGS FOR THE PROFESSIONAL

Harel, I. & S. Papert. *Constructionism.* Norwood NJ: Ablex Publishing, 1993. This is an excellent collection of research reports and essays on the constructivist perspective.

Schon, D. A. *The Reflective Practitioner.* San Francisco: Jossey-Bass, 1983. This book, now 15 years old, is still the best discussion of the complexities of professional practice and the importance of reflection.

Wittrock, M. C. (ed). *Handbook of Research on Teaching* (3rd ed.). New York: Macmillan, 1986. This book is the most authoritative review of the mountain of research on effective teaching. A fourth edition is currently under preparation and is due out soon.

CHAPTER 3

Defining a Philosophy of Education

As discussed in Chapter 1, making a wise career choice involves an in-depth understanding of two things: the world and work of teachers and the interests, needs, goals, and beliefs that you bring to this world. This chapter pursues these issues by asking you to explore your beliefs about the world in general and education and teaching in particular. It is important that you be aware of your own beliefs, because they will give direction to your thinking and actions as a teacher. Inasmuch as education and teaching involve passing on to youth the knowledge, ideas, and values that a society embraces, it is also important that we understand what counts as knowledge and how we decide what our values are. This is what philosophy attempts to do—to provide systems of analysis to help us examine and understand what we believe we know and value. The tools of philosophy directed toward education further help us ask and answer the broad questions about what we know and value that will help us become better teachers as we attempt to pass this knowledge and these values on to those we teach.

Before we begin to examine the tools of philosophy, consider for a moment how you would react to the following situations.

You are a middle-school teacher, and one of your students—a boy from a poor home with slightly below average academic talents—asks whether he should pursue a college preparation program or one

The Meaning and Relevance of Philosophy
The Meaning of Philosophy
The Relevance of Philosophy

Philosophical Questions and Contemporary Educational Issues
Questions
What Is the Purpose of Education?
What Should Be Taught and How Should It Be Taught?
What Should Be the Role of Teachers and What Types of Relationship Should They Develop with Their Students?
Issues
Inclusion: Exploring the Purposes of Education
National Standards: Exploring What Should be Taught and Who Should Control the Curriculum
The Education and Testing of Teachers: Exploring the Role of the Teacher

Philosophies
Branches of Philosophy
Metaphysics
Epistemology

Axiology
Logic
Systems of Philosophy
Idealism and Realism
Pragmatism
Existentialism
Comparing Philosophical Systems

Philosophies of Education
Perennialism
Progressivism
Essentialism
Social Reconstructionism
Examples of the Four Philosophies of Education

Defining a Personal Philosophy of Education
Two Approaches
Choose and Follow
Mix and Match
Positioning Yourself

Summary

Readings for the Professional

that is mostly vocational when he gets to high school. How would you advise him? Why?

You are a member of the high school's disciplinary committee and have to consider the case of Connie, a girl who frequently misses school, has been kicked out of school seven times in the past month, and has been caught threatening another girl with a knife. How would you deal with Connie? Would you recommend that she be expelled or assigned to another counselor more accustomed to this type of student? Why?

You are a member of a site-based school council and are informed that budget difficulties necessitate cutting at least one major school program. Would you be inclined to cut the athletic program or the music program? Why?

Before reading on, take a few minutes to jot down your answers to these questions. But, more important, explain your reasons for answering the way you do. Put your answers aside and we will look at them later. Your answers to these questions and the reasons you give for them provide a convenient starting point for examining your personal beliefs about teaching. These beliefs, continually examined, clarified, and logically organized throughout your teaching career, will become the basis for developing a personal philosophy of education that will guide you in your classroom decisions and practices as well as in analyzing educational issues. If you want to become a teacher with a sense of vision, one who can probe beneath the surface of educational issues, one who can teach with integrity and conviction, then it is crucial that you also become an educational philosopher.

We begin this exploration by discussing the meaning of philosophy and its relevance to teaching. Next we examine three fundamental questions that lie at the heart of all philosophical debate in education, and we illustrate how these questions can be used to analyze the educational issues of inclusion, national standards, and testing teachers. Following this, we briefly examine the branches of philosophy and the four major philosophical systems out of which systems of philosophy of education are derived. The next section presents these four specific philosophies of education. Finally, we discuss how to weave your own core beliefs about education and teaching into a personal philosophy that will help guide your classroom practice. It is our hope that this inductive approach to educational philosophy will prove more interesting and useful than a mere description of a variety of contemporary philosophies.

THE MEANING AND RELEVANCE OF PHILOSOPHY

The Meaning of Philosophy

Consider the following four definitions of philosophy, all of which appear in respected dictionaries.

1. Love and pursuit of knowledge by intellectual means and moral self-discipline
2. Inquiry into the nature of things based on logical reasoning
3. The critique and analysis of fundamental beliefs
4. The rational investigation of the truths and principles of being, knowledge, or conduct

Although these definitions vary somewhat, what they have in common is a focus on the mental activities of pursuit, inquiry, critique, and investigation. In short, philosophy seems to be centered more on thought processes than on any intellectual product, or organized body of thought, that might emerge from that process. Building on this process-oriented view of philosophy, we adopt the following working definition for purposes of this book: ***philosophy*** *is the process of systematically reflecting on the world around us in an attempt to build a coherent set of beliefs and values with which to guide our actions.* Philosophy in this sense might be likened to the dispositions discussed in Chapter 2. Good teachers are those who are reflective about their classroom planning and activities.

The Relevance of Philosophy

Is a reflective disposition really essential to being an effective teacher, you may be wondering? Can I be a good teacher simply by studying what is already known about teaching and applying that knowledge in my everyday practice? The answers to these questions depend on just how good you want to be. Conscientiously assimilating and applying the growing knowledge base on teaching will certainly assure you of being a capable teacher, probably of being a better than average one. However, it will not allow you to "be the best you can be," to use the slogan from the U.S. Army recruitment program. To perform at your highest level, that is, to be a master teacher, you must have more than a firm grasp of the professional knowledge base. You must be prepared to face unique situations on a daily basis that will demand on-your-feet problem solving that goes far beyond simply applying a body of knowledge. Teachers are faced with hundreds of immediate daily decisions that must be made in the context of constantly doing several things simultaneously, including maintaining control over as many as 20 or 30 energetic young people. To be a master teacher, you must be a reflective problem solver who can adapt existing knowledge to unique classroom situations with consistency and integrity. Philosophy will help you to come to grips with the large questions about existence, knowledge, and meaning in life that will help give purpose and direction to your teaching.

Chapter 2 briefly discussed the work of Donald Schon, who more than anyone else has studied the nature of professional practice in such fields as medicine, law, and education. He found that *effective* and *reflective* usually go together. That is, the most effective practitioners are generally individuals who are able to analyze the never-ending flow of unique situations that confront them and to adapt their knowledge to particular situations. In terms of teaching, this means being able to reflect on and adapt to such situations as a class with an unusual number of disruptive, handicapped, or non-English-speaking students. It means being able to adapt your teaching to new, sometimes unrealistic, curriculum guidelines or to budget cuts that increase your class size while simultaneously reducing your access to needed supplies and outside help.

Philosophical reflection on your classroom practices can also enhance your teaching effectiveness by helping you to be consistent. In order to establish a stable and trusting classroom environment, where students "know the ropes" and behave accordingly, teachers need to maintain a high degree of consistency in their teaching. This does not mean being dull and predictable from one day to the next. However, it does mean establishing and maintaining fair and equitable classroom rules and routines and establishing a classroom persona that students can adapt to. Without such consistency, it becomes virtually impossible to form a diverse and self-conscious group of young people into a classroom learning community in which students can develop into cooperative, self-regulated learners.

Reflective teachers are also better able to analyze and understand divergent viewpoints in the never-ending debate about educational policies and practices. They are able to search out the underlying and "unprovable" assumptions people make about knowledge and values and to determine what impact these assumptions have on education and teaching. Once these hidden assumptions are understood, it is possible to evaluate them in terms of one's own beliefs and values and to support, resist, or replace them with new proposals. Such critical thinking is the beginning of intellectual empowerment. If, for example, you are opposed to students' being suspended from school as a result of disciplinary infractions, you will be able to explain why and offer alternative means of addressing discipline problems. Take a moment to read the accompanying Research Box about multiage grouping, and reflect on its pros and cons as you continue to learn how to develop your own educational philosophy.

PHILOSOPHICAL QUESTIONS AND CONTEMPORARY EDUCATIONAL ISSUES

Questions

Most human beings appear to want to know the answers to such basic questions as, Who am I? What is my place in the universe? What is the purpose of life? What happens to me when I die? What constitutes a good or a bad person? What are truth, justice, love, and beauty? Notice that none of these questions is of the sort that we can answer by looking at the world around us. Answers to questions such as these are based on personal beliefs formed from various mixtures of personal experience, indoctrination, study, and reason. The amount of each ingredient and how they are mixed, however, varies widely. For this reason, each person has a somewhat unique set of core beliefs about the answers to life's fundamental questions.

Education, as with life in general, has been a central concern of philosophers dating back to the ancient Greek and Asian cultures. Philosophers such as Socrates, Plato, and Aristotle spent a great deal of time thinking and writing about such fundamental education questions as the following.

1. What Are the Purposes of Education?

Should education primarily address the needs and interests of individual students or the needs of a society as a whole? If the answer is "both," whose needs prevail when a conflict of interest arises—the individual's or the larger group's? Likewise, is society better served by distributing its limited educational resources equally among all its members or by focusing on the education of an identifiable segment, such as the very bright or the handicapped? Is equal educational opportunity a good or bad social policy?

2. What Should Be Taught, and How Should It Be Taught?

Should all students be required to take a common curriculum, or should students be placed in different programs based on their interests and abilities? If students are placed in different programs, who should determine placement, and what evidence should be used to support them? Should the curriculum be

Multiage Grouping

Defined most basically, multiage grouping describes a classroom purposefully composed of children who are more than one year apart in age. Such grouping is random rather than selective. For example, classrooms do not consist of the most advanced first graders in combination with the least advanced second graders. The rationale for multiage grouping is based on meeting students' individual needs. Students are grouped together across ages in combinations most beneficial to their educational stimulation and success.

Our families, neighborhoods, and communities are all multiage learning environments, yet the composition of most schools today does not reflect the natural groupings found in the world. Multiage classrooms, as representations of these environments, provide opportunities for the exchange of ideas, modeling of behaviors, practice of responsibility and nurturance, and development of leadership and social skills.

There are a number of basic principles and practices that underlie multiage classrooms:

1. Developmentally appropriate curricula and practices
2. Active, child-centered, and continuous learning
3. Attention to the education of the whole child
4. The teacher as facilitator
5. Integrated curriculum across subjects
6. The absence of rigid instructional strategies and assessments

A developmental, child-centered philosophy of learning guides multiage classroom practices.

The National Association for the Education of Young Children (NAEYC) has proposed that educators follow practices that are both developmentally and individually appropriate for young children. Such practices involve (a) hands-on learning through play and exploration; (b) activities that meet the needs of wide ranges of ability and interest levels; (c) responsive teacher-pupil relationships that are sensitive to the needs, interests, and readiness of the whole child; and (d) child-centered environments that demand problem solving, student interactions, and the enhancement of creative and critical thinking. Multiage grouping reflects the NAEYC guidelines for educational practices that are developmentally appropriate.

Social Effects

Studies of children's social perceptions in multiage groups reveal that children associate specific expectations with specific age groups. Younger

primarily academic, or should it include social and moral dimensions as well? Should attempts be made to relate what is taught to students' background experiences?

3. What Should the Role of Teachers Be, and What Types of Relationships Should They Develop with Their Students?

Should society view teachers as experts whose responsibility is to transmit the collective wisdom of the ages? Or, should we view teachers as facilitators and coaches whose primary task is to help students understand themselves and their relationship to the world? Should we expect teachers to know all the answers to students' questions? Should students feel free to challenge teachers' answers? Should society expect teachers to be better moral exemplars than other adults? How close and personal should teacher-student relationships be?

RESEARCH

Continued

children assign roles of leadership and skills of instruction to older children, and older children perceive younger students in need of help and instruction (French, 1984). Such perceptions tend to create a climate of cooperation that is beneficial to both younger and older children. There often exists increased competition and aggression among same-age peers (Hartup, 1979), and increased harmony and nurturance within multiage groups (Wakefield, 1979). Studies have found older children exhibiting leadership roles in mixed-age groups (Stright & French, 1988).

Buckholdt and Wodarski (1978) found that multiage preschool groupings, in which children are allowed to occasionally serve as teacher, promoted interpersonal and cooperative skills, social perspectives, role taking, and empathy. Social interaction in the form of leadership skills was studied by Mobley (1976), who found improvement in the self-concepts of students in grades 1 to 3 in multiage settings but no noticeable improvement in homogeneous settings. Sociability was found to be enhanced in mixed-age groupings with children interacting more frequently with peers than adults (Reuter & Yunik, 1973).

Prosocial behavior has also been found to be enhanced within mixed-age groups. Graziano, French, Brownell, and Hartup (1976) found first and third graders to be more sensitive to complex interactions inherent in multiage settings. Positive, spontaneous attention to peers, plus affection and reciprocation, are traits demonstrated in multiage settings (Lougee, Grueneich, & Hartup, 1977). Older children's self-regulation has been found to improve when they remind younger children of rules. The multiage classroom atmosphere fosters more cooperation and less competition. Roopnarine and Mounts (1987) found that younger children in multiage groups were able to participate in more complex play situations when more competent children initiated the situation.

Attitudes Toward School and Self-Concept

In a study of therapeutic effects of multiage grouping, Furman, Rahe, and Hartup (1979) found that withdrawn preschoolers' interaction with younger children enhanced the former's social skills of leadership and sociability. Younger children who are experiencing social difficulties have also been found to benefit from cross-age interaction (Kim, 1990). Carbone (1961/62) reported that children in nongraded schools had more positive attitudes about their teachers. They were described as quiet, interesting, soft, bright, smooth, sweet, relaxed, and good, as compared to graded schools where

Notice that all these questions, like the more lofty ones posed earlier, have no "correct" answers. Their answers depend on the beliefs that individuals and societies have acquired that often stem from philosophical reasoning about the nature of reality, knowledge, and goodness. Let's now apply some philosophical reasoning to three contemporary educational issues, each of which corresponds to one of the questions posed in this section.

Issues

Inclusion: Exploring the Purposes of Education

Before passage of the Education for All Handicapped Children Act in 1975 (PL 94–142), the type of education received by physically and intellectually handicapped youngsters was left up to individual school districts, and the quality of these experiences varied widely from one community to the next. The

RESEARCH

Continued

teachers were described as little, loud, boring, hard, dull, rough, sour, stiff, and bad.

Utilizing the Piers-Harris Children's Self-Concept Scale in a study of elementary multiage and traditional classrooms, Way (1981) found significant differences on the factors of Happiness and Satisfaction, with students in multiage classrooms demonstrating a more positive score than those from traditional classrooms.

Cognitive Development

Brown and Palincsar (1986) found that children's mixed-age interactions can result in cognitive conflict, or intellectual discord, which leads to cognitive growth. Slavin's (1980; 1989) research on cooperative learning has revealed that individuals can grow cognitively through cooperative efforts. Multiage students spend a great deal of time working in cooperative groups and have considerable opportunity to learn from each other.

Problem-solving ability has been found to be enhanced within multiage settings when older children offer information, guidance, and new viewpoints, and demonstrate social skills such as negotiation, argumentation, and cooperative work skills (Azmitia, 1988). Younger children in mixed-age groups have been shown to develop such language skills as sentence length and complexity by the children adjusting their communication for each other (Gelman & Baillargeon, 1983; Lougee et al., 1977; Shatz & Gelman, 1973).

Reflection on the evidence suggests that there is nothing natural about age segregation. A natural learning group, like a natural social group, is one in which a commonality of interest and a shared readiness for a task is complemented by a diversity of age and other characteristics. If schools could approach this ideal, they might become more natural and more educative places. (p. 31)

Although current research provides convincing evidence as to the necessity of and justification for this educational model, most attention is directed to the social aspects of multiage grouping. What perhaps should become more of a focus is the interrelationship between a child's psychological/emotional self and his or her ability to develop cognitively. Meanwhile, there is a great need for continued study of the multiage concept.

How do you react to this information on multiage grouping? What values and beliefs do you bring to bear in evaluating multiage grouping?

Handicapped Children's Act has several important features. The most far-reaching was the requirement that handicapped students be educated in the *least restrictive* environment. This meant that children with handicaps should be **mainstreamed** into regular classrooms for as much of the school day as possible. In the 1990s, the discussion of mainstreaming became encompassed in the movement for **inclusion.** This practice involves keeping special education students in regular education classrooms and bringing support services to the child, rather than taking the child to the support services. In an inclusionary setting, special education teachers work with regular education teachers in regular classrooms. There is much debate about the educational value of inclusion to both the regular and special students. Consider the following discussion, which might take place in a middle-school teachers' lounge.

> "I think that all students, regardless of their abilities, backgrounds, or handicaps, should be included in regular classrooms and in all schoolwide activities," argues Mrs. Hackley, the school's special education teacher. "Isolating these students from the others is immoral."
>
> "I couldn't agree more," pipes in Mr. Sanchez. "Placing students in special classes hasn't improved their learning, and being separated from their peers causes lots of anxiety and loss of self-esteem."
>
> "Well, I disagree with that perspective," says Mrs. Boyd, who has taught sixth grade at the school for 13 years. "Students who are learning disabled or disruptive take a disproportionate amount of my scarce time and energy. This detracts from the attention I'm able to devote to the rest of my class and that just isn't fair. Besides, some of my inclusion kids don't learn a single thing, nor do they interact very much with the other students. What's the point?"
>
> Miss Davidson agrees. "You are absolutely right. If I have to spend all my time working with the disruptive and handicapped kids, I don't have time to help the bright ones who will go on to college and become our next generation of leaders. And, if we *are* going to have special ed kids in our classrooms, we should be given the resources we need, and this community is simply unwilling to provide that type of help."
>
> "Well that's all well and good," declares Mrs. Hackley, "but the primary issue for me isn't how much subject matter children learn in my class but how well they learn to accept and get along with one another. We can't expect children with different backgrounds and abilities to live together in the same communities as adults unless we help them to

live together as children. This is such an important learning goal in today's world."

Think about the wide range of opinions represented in this discussion about the purposes of schooling and who should be educated. On one side are those who argue that the main purposes of education are academic. Although they may be sympathetic to social and emotional goals, they worry that nonhandicapped students will be cheated if teachers spend too much time with students who are handicapped or with students who present discipline problems. They also argue that handicapped students, themselves, may learn less if placed in regular classrooms. The following excerpt summarizes this point of view about the purposes of education:

> [T]he primary purpose of education is just that, to educate. While social agendas do exist in schools, these matters must take a back seat to educational goals. All teachers would prefer that their charges make friends, learn tolerance, understand differences, and be reasonably happy in school as long as they are learning at the same time. Given two schools, one in which all the children are happy but learn nothing and one in which all the children are unhappy but learn everything, which one best serves education? Thankfully, we are seldom presented with two such absurd alternatives, but to place a higher priority on social relationships than on academic need is not, we suspect, what the general society expects us to do with its tax dollars. If this is not the case, then we ought to start calling ourselves "social engineers" rather than "educators." (Smelter, Rasch, & Yudewitz, 1994, p. 36)

These educators are clear about their philosophical stance in relation to education. They believe that students should acquire important knowledge and that the curriculum should be structured around traditional academic subjects. Class time should be spent teaching these subjects, not dealing with the social problems of disruptive or special needs students.

On the other side of the spectrum are those who argue that education should be focused on social goals as much as, if not more than, on academic goals. Education should prepare children to live together in a complicated and problem-ridden society and to provide them with the social and academic skills to cooperatively solve some of the problems that face them. Those who hold this view generally want schools to address *all* the needs of *all* the children, not just the academic needs of the best prepared students. They maintain that the curriculum should be flexible enough to accommodate the needs and interests of individual children, not just the learning of academic subjects. They also want to see a flexible curriculum that is constantly changing to reflect ongoing changes in the real world. In their view, a major part of a teacher's role is to facilitate students' progress in understanding and adapting to these changes.

Those who believe in a broader, more socially oriented curriculum generally believe that handicapped and disruptive students should not be separated from their peers. They maintain that what is accomplished through integration of these students with their less troubled classmates—role modeling, understanding of handicapped people, social adaptability—may ultimately be more important to both them and society as a whole than how much subject matter knowledge students acquire.

Cast in a larger context, questions about the inclusion of handicapped and disruptive students is an extension of the basic questions about the purposes of education. Does your view of education support the inclusion of handicapped and disruptive children? Should schools' first priority be toward academic or social goals? Should all schools share a common curriculum, or should some students pursue college preparatory courses while others attend basic-skills and vocational classes? Should handicapped students be placed in special or regular classrooms? What about disruptive students? When it comes to education, is society best served by focusing on students' individual needs rather than on the welfare of the group as a whole?

National Standards: Exploring What Should Be Taught and Who Should Control the Curriculum

Disagreements over the purposes of education often pale when compared to questions about what to teach and who should control the curriculum. Should teachers decide what is in the best interest of their students to teach? Or should this decision be left to the local school board? Or is that the responsibility of each state? Or should we have a set of national curriculum standards developed by a board of political, business, and educational leaders? The following vignette, looks at some beliefs people have about these questions by listening in on a legislative hearing in the state of Massachusetts.

It is a cold January day in New England. The Massachusetts Committee on Education has invited Phil Holcroft, a nationally recognized mathematics educator, to testify on national curriculum standards, a topic that has drawn a large cross section of people

to today's hearing. Holcroft previously chaired the committee created by the National Council for Teaching Mathematics (NCTM) for the purpose of developing mathematics standards for all levels of education. The NCTM standards have been widely praised for bringing a much needed set of curriculum goals and strategies into what was previously one of the most misunderstood, poorly taught, and feared subject areas.

Holcroft begins his testimony by describing how American students have fallen behind students in other countries and explains that one reason for this situation is the lack of consistent and high curriculum standards in the United States. He tells committee members "it is possible to define what children should know and be able to do at various ages," and he argues his belief that "all children everywhere in the country should be held to the same standards, so they will receive the same high quality education." He further insists that "once we have agreed upon national standards, we can then develop valid and reliable tests to measure student performance and hold states, local districts, and teachers accountable for achieving these targeted learning outcomes."

An array of unsolicited presentations by teachers and community members follows Holcroft's testimony. Mrs. Perez, a local middle-school teacher, tells the committee, "I believe in high standards, and I hold my students accountable to them. If you don't believe me, just ask them. However, I am closer to my students and their academic needs than anyone, and as a professional teacher, I should be allowed to deliver what I believe to be a valid curriculum based on my own assessment of their needs. I shouldn't be forced to follow a curriculum designed thousands of miles away by a group of well-meaning but out-of-touch college professors and politically oriented bureaucrats."

She is followed by Dr. Pyle, a teacher-education professor at a nearby university. Professor Pyle testifies that, "We don't know and never will know what every student should be able to do either now or in the future. So why bother?" "Furthermore," he argues, "curriculum should respond to the diversity of students and their individual learning styles. Finally, the most important learning outcomes really can't be assessed by the type of tests described by Dr. Holcroft." He ends his speech by encouraging committee members to oppose national standards and to establish a state committee to develop standards uniquely appropriate to Massachusetts.

The last presenter is a woman who represents a fundamental Christian group in the state. She argues that the government, federal or state, should stay out of the business of education. It definitely should not be prescribing what the local schools should teach. That decision should be left to the citizens and parents in local communities. She says she has organized a curriculum committee composed of local citizens, and she stands ready to share the work of her committee with members of the local school board.

In this vignette, an expert in mathematics education explains why it is important to have national standards in the subject area of mathematics. A public school teacher, an education professor, and a spokesperson for an interest group respond to his point of view, each from a particular perspective. Let's step back a minute and examine how the debate for and against national standards illustrates the perennial problem of who should determine what the curriculum should be.

One of the more interesting features of this issue is the fact that proponents of a national curriculum come from both those who believe the primary focus of the curriculum should be to achieve social goals and those who believe the focus should be primarily academic, such as Holcroft.

Many of those who are committed to using the schools to improve society have raised questions of equity. Because children in certain areas, such as inner cities and rural communities, perform less well on standardized tests than those in more affluent areas, particularly the suburbs, some proponents argue that a national curriculum will provide these less-advantaged students with an education comparable to that in other areas of the country. Motivated by concerns of educational equity, these reformers need a measuring rod, such as a national curriculum with standardized tests, with which to measure equity gains.

On the other hand, many who support national standards do so not because of equity considerations but because they believe in the primacy of academic goals. These proponents feel that a concentrated focus on an academically oriented curriculum must not be diluted by well-meaning efforts to achieve social goals. This movement reached its zenith during the presidency of George Bush, with a program of national educational goals labeled *America 2000.* Later named *Goals 2000* by President Clinton, both programs support an objective means of measuring the students' academic performance beyond local report cards and grade point averages. Thus, calls for a testing-focused national curriculum that could be used to compare schools and school systems across the country arose from both academically and socially oriented camps.

It is easy to see how quickly a discussion of national standards or goals leads to a consideration of a national curriculum. But there is a difference: **National standards** refer to levels of knowledge and performance that are to be acquired by designated points in the schooling experience. This is what has been proposed by the NCTM for that discipline area. By contrast, a **national curriculum** lays down exactly what specific subject matter is to be covered in each year of schooling.

Those opposed to national standards and curriculum maintain that such standards show an underlying mistrust of teachers. Under such a scheme, they say, teachers would cease being self-directed professionals and become mere technicians dispensing someone else's knowledge. National standards would inevitably limit teachers' authority to tailor curriculum to the specific needs and interests of students.

An intense argument against national standards and a national curriculum also comes from those who question the idea of testing and accountability.

> The vision of education that could suggest a national curriculum, a national testing program, and national standards for teachers could be advanced only by individuals convinced of their claim to Truth. Certainty of this sort comes either from religious belief or from scientific conviction . . . The (testing) tradition has consistently argued through the decades that science is the answer to all our curriculum and instructional questions. This certainty is generated by that premier scientific instrument, the test.
>
> For this reason, it should not be particularly surprising that contemporary leaders of (testing) forces have . . . equated accountability with tests. They would have us believe that all of society's ills can be cured if only we make schools accountable. The wisdom of this strategy is embedded in such logic as this: "If we make schools more accountable, they'll improve our position in the engineering race with the Germans and Japanese." Throughout the 1980's and into the 1990's, the push for accountability has been indistinguishable from the push for more standardized testing, which has been indistinguishable from the push for a better global economic position. (Theobold & Mills, 1995, p. 465)

Theobold and Mills go on to argue that "what constitutes an educated person is a question properly answered by local communities, not by a national or quasi national testing service" (p. 466). They emphasize the importance of each community seeking answers to the question, What is our vision of the good life? Everyone, not just an appointed few, should deliberate about what constitutes prosperity, goodness, love, and happiness.

Still others opposed to national standards argue that such a notion makes it more difficult to respond to students with different cultural and cognitive learning styles. They point out that national standards focus on *what* to learn but not *how* to learn. Furthermore, they point out, national standards are usually keyed to culturally mainstream, college-bound students who comprise less than half the student population. In place of national standards, they argue that we should develop curriculum based on the needs and interests of students at the local level. Such flexible, localized curriculums, they maintain, are more adaptable in the ever-changing modern world.

Which of the above views seem more compelling to you? Would national standards written by experts at the national level have an equalizing effect on student achievement across the United States and make us more academically competitive with students in other industrialized countries? Or would they mostly benefit mainstream, college-bound students from better schools and penalize minority students and those from poorer schools? Is it even possible to develop culturally fair standardized tests? Would national standards, curriculums, and tests reverse a century-old movement to professionalize teaching and make teachers into mindless technocrats? Or would they provide the means to assure that we expect all students to reach the same high level of academic performance?

The Education and Testing of Teachers: Exploring the Role of the Teacher

The movement to raise students' academic standards has been paralleled by a similar movement to raise teachers' professional standards. And once again at the center of the teacher-performance debate is the question of whether standardized testing is the most appropriate means of ensuring teacher competency. The following debate that took place at the monthly meeting of the Auburn School Board illustrates this issue.

Richard Allen sparks the debate by saying, "I am sick and tired of hearing parents complain about the teachers in the Auburn schools who are barely literate and don't know their subjects. Our schools' job is to teach essential knowledge to our children, and that can't be done unless teachers, themselves, have this knowledge. I think we should require all teachers to have a major in at least one of the subjects they are going to teach, no matter what level they are going to teach, and to pass a general competency test before we let them teach."

"Well, I agree that it's important for teachers to be well educated," says Janice Munroe, "but there is

so much more to teaching than simply passing on one's subject-matter knowledge. If teachers don't know how to motivate their students and how to make subject matter meaningful to them, then all the subject-matter knowledge in the world won't bring about learning. Besides, it's just as important that children learn how to solve problems and get along with one another as it is to absorb facts. All this requires teachers who are tuned in to students, who are just as knowledgeable at turning them on to learning as they are at passing on the wisdom of the past."

"That's just so much educational gobbledygook," yells Richard. "All this student-centered stuff has only led to schools that are out of control and students who don't know anything. Look at all the students who graduate from high school and can't even read and write. Look at the SAT scores over the past 20 years. I say we need teachers who know their subject and who can present it clearly to students."

"Richard," replies Janice, "the world simply isn't that black and white. Teaching is a complex role, and it requires a complex set of understandings that goes well beyond merely knowing one's subject. Many teachers who might have difficulty passing a standardized test are excellent in the classroom with their students."

As the preceding debate illustrates, those who favor testing teachers often begin by saying something like, "You can't teach what you don't know." In their minds, this justifies requiring all secondary teachers to pass in-depth tests on the subjects they plan to teach and requiring all elementary teachers to pass tests of general knowledge covering all subjects. In addition, many argue, teachers ought to know pedagogy, that is, how to teach. This, of course, includes knowledge of how students learn. If they can't at least pass paper-and-pencil tests in these areas, the argument goes, they are unlikely to be effective teachers.

Some who oppose teacher testing argue that content knowledge is not the most important part of being a good teacher. In their minds, liking and understanding students, being able to relate well to them, and providing guidance and support in a perilous and fast-changing world are more important than being on the cutting edge of academic knowledge. Some even go so far as to say one doesn't need to know "the what" of teaching, just "the how," that is, how to guide students in their learning. Still others argue that it is a waste of time and money to require teachers to pass paper-and-pencil tests, that teachers' knowledge of subject matter and pedagogy can only truly be demonstrated in the context of real classrooms.

Each of these views of teacher testing derives from different philosophical beliefs. On one side of the philosophical spectrum are those who believe that the fundamental purpose of schools is to transmit knowledge through a curriculum based on traditional academic disciplines. These people believe that teachers should demonstrate knowledge of their subjects before being given a license to teach. On the other side are those who believe that the essence of education is helping individual children learn according to their own interests and needs. They maintain that teaching *how to learn* is more important than teaching *specific content* and recommend that teachers be evaluated by being observed at work in real classrooms rather than by using written tests to attempt to determine their competence.

What are your views on this issue? Should teachers be required to demonstrate their knowledge of subject matter before certification? Is subject-matter knowledge the most important knowledge for teachers? In your experience, have your most knowledgeable teachers also been your best teachers? Your favorite teachers? Why or why not?

PHILOSOPHIES

As the preceding section illustrates, a wide variety of sensible answers can be given to any of the fundamental questions in education or, for that matter, in any area of life. Over the years, however, the most effective thinkers have been those who sought broad connective ideas that would allow them to tie specific questions and issues together so that their answers fit into an intellectually coherent scheme. These broad intellectual schemes eventually came to be known as **schools of philosophy** and the various parts of these schemes as the **branches of philosophy.** This section briefly examines four of the major schools of thought that have survived the test of time. In each case, core tenets have spawned specific philosophies of education that we can observe in today's schools. This discussion begins with a look at the various branches of philosophy, which then will be used as a means of comparing the major schools of philosophy.

Branches of Philosophy

Metaphysics is the branch of philosophy that attempts to answer the question, What is the nature of reality? **Epistemology** is the branch that poses answers to the question, What is the nature of knowl-

edge and knowing? The branch that addresses the question, What is the nature of values and valuing? is **axiology.** Finally, **logic** is the study of the principles of reasoning. **Deductive logic** begins with general statements and moves to particular or specific instances of application. **Inductive logic** examines the particulars or specifics in an attempt to develop generalizations. We apply logic when we ask, What is the relationship between metaphysics, epistemology, and axiology? For example, one's views concerning the nature of reality have logical implications for one's answers about how we come to know reality and what is of most value.

Although these terms are not found in most people's everyday language, they are important conceptual tools in the analysis and understanding of philosophy and philosophy of education. Just as it is impossible, for instance, to practice psychology effectively without understanding the concepts of psychometrics, psychoanalysis, and cognition, it is equally difficult to engage in meaningful philosophical discussion, that is, to be systematically reflective, without understanding the concepts of metaphysics, epistemology, axiology, and logic.

It is important to understand, however, that the philosophical systems we discuss here are what we refer to as **logical constructs.** What goes on in real life, including education, is unstructured, unsystematic, and often inconsistent. Logical constructs are not assumed to be reality; rather they are a set of concepts we use to analyze real events. Freudian psychology could not be understood without the concepts of *id, ego,* and *superego,* but no one would ask a Freudian psychologist where the id, ego, and superego are. They are simply logical constructs used to analyze the real events that comprise human development and behavior. Not only are *metaphysics, epistemology,* and *axiology* logical constructs to help us organize our thinking about the world around us, so too are systems of philosophy even more elaborate logical constructs. They are not meant to represent entities that can actually be found in the real world, but are meant to be used to help us analyze and systematize our own thinking.

Systems of Philosophy

Throughout history, there have been systematic attempts to understand the nature of reality, how we come to know reality, and what is worth knowing. That there is a logical relationship among these three broad intellectual issues is obvious. From the time of Socrates and Plato through the twentieth century, four major philosophical systems have addressed these metaphysical, epistemological, and axiological questions. They are Idealism, Realism,

Pragmatism (or Experimentalism), and Existentialism. We examine these philosophical systems in terms of their metaphysical, epistemological, and axiological assumptions and then examine four philosophies of education that have been derived from them. Armed with these contending philosophies, you will be in a better position to understand your own and others underlying assumptions regarding the three basic educational questions listed earlier.

Idealism and Realism

The first two systems we address are Idealism and Realism.

Metaphysics and epistemology The term *metaphysics* comes from the Greek roots: *meta,* a prefix meaning *beyond* and *ta physika* meaning *the physics. Ta meta ta physika,* the things after the physics, was Aristotle's treatise on transcendental philosophy, so called because it followed his work on physics. As the term has survived the centuries, it has come to include the idea of *beyond*—metaphysics is the study of that which is beyond the merely physical. Again, the basic question of metaphysics is, What is the nature of reality? or more simply, What is real?

You may think the answer to this question is obvious; whatever we can see, hear, and touch is real. But it is not quite that simple. For example, do you think people have souls that exist after death? Can you see, hear, or touch them? Do you believe human beings have memories? Can you see, hear, or touch them? If not, how do you know they are real? Already, it is evident that as soon as we begin to consider what the nature of reality is, we are into a discussion of epistemology as well. How do we know that something is real? Thus, we discuss the metaphysics and epistemology of the various philosophical systems together.

Western civilization has produced two basic answers to the question of what is real. Plato's ideas form the basis for the philosophical system of Idealism, which maintains that reality is nonmaterial, that it inheres primarily in ideas and only secondarily in their physical manifestation. Idealists believe that individuals come to know reality through mental-spiritual processes, such as meditation, inspiration, intuition, and reflection. In contrast, Plato's student, Aristotle, argued that reality is exclusively physical, that only the things we can see, hear, and touch are real. His philosophy of Realism maintains that the way we come to know reality is through the interaction of our senses with the world around us. Reality is objective, knowing is a rational process, and claims about knowledge can be tested empirically.

How do these views differ in their impact on our understanding of life? Let's start with the nature of human beings and a very well known twentieth century phenomenon, psychological problems. Freudian psychologists propose to solve psychological problems through psychoanalysis, a process whereby a psychologist helps a therapy patient examine his or her own psyche and its development through infancy and childhood to its current state of distress. But, what is the *psyche?* Can we determine its existence through the senses? Most would say not, that it is the "inner being" of the individual, the personality, maybe even the soul, of the person and that it is shaped through life's experiences. Freudian psychologists hold that in order to remedy our present problems, one must, through the process of psychoanalysis, "go back" to when those problems first developed and attempt to understand the origin of the problem. To hold such views, we need to assume there is a reality beyond the senses that is not part of the material world and can be stored in something called *memory.* The philosophical system that best supports this view is Idealism.

In contrast, behavioral psychology holds that understanding human beings comes from observing behavior, and the way to change undesirable behavior is to change the environment that stimulates and shapes that behavior. Behaviorists do not look for logical constructs by which to explain some abstract inner component of the individual. We might say that the motto of the behavioral psychologist is "what you see is what you get." Such a view is grounded in the metaphysical and epistemological assumptions of Realism. Reality, what is and what can be known, is accessible only through the senses. Human beings are the sum total of observable behaviors—no soul, no spirit, no abstract inner being. Therefore, behavioral psychologists argue, to change an individual, you change his or her behavior. Like nutritionists who maintain that "you are what you eat," behavioral psychologists believe you are what you do—behave differently, and you will be a different person. Furthermore, they claim, behavior, not thoughts or intentions, are what educators should be concerned with as well. These views are consistent with Realism.

Let's continue the comparison in the field of education. The early New England settlers, the Puritans, believed that all children are born evil and the role of education is to bring them to an understanding of God and his will. Parents and teachers are to provide the appropriate role models, the discipline, and the Bible-reading skills to accomplish this. In contrast, the English philosopher John Locke, known as "the empiricist educator," proposed the notion of **tabula rasa**—that human beings are born "blank slates" and that we acquire information about the world through our senses. The French philosopher Jean-Jacques Rousseau, known as the "naturalist educator," further emphasized the importance of a child's interacting with nature and exploring the environment in order to learn. The underlying assumption of the Puritans is that there is some inner being—a soul—to be depraved. This belief is rooted in Idealism. Locke and Rousseau, by contrast, argue that humans are shaped as a result of their interaction with the environment, that is, by manipulating objects and receiving information through their senses. These ideas find their basis in Realism.

Axiology   We can see that Idealism and Realism differ substantially in their metaphysical and epistemological assumptions. This difference continues into the area of axiology. Axiology is comprised of two areas of study: *aesthetics* and **ethics.** We focus here on ethics, the study of right and wrong, since it is the most germane to education. Schools are, to some extent, responsible for moral education (not religious), which, in turn, is based on underlying assumptions about what is or is not ethical.

Those who believe that moral values are handed down from God or from a holy book or from some authoritative individual accept the assumptions of Idealism. In contrast, Realists argue that moral values are determined by looking to the world of nature and the natural order of the universe.

How does this play out in everyday life? Let's examine a controversial moral issue to compare these views, the issue of bigamy. One can argue that having multiple mates is wrong because the Bible says, "Thou shalt not commit adultery." Or one can say there is nothing wrong with it because many of the patriarchs of the Old Testament had more than one wife. In either case, a source beyond human observation and reasoning is the authority, so one's justification comes out of the assumptions of Idealism. If, however, an individual maintains that the way to answer this question is to observe the natural world around us, pointing out that animals are rarely monogamous, he or she is rejecting authority and calling for observation of and reflection on the natural world as the basis for determining right and wrong. This approach is firmly rooted in Realism.

An important point to be made here is that it is not so much what you believe that determines your philosophical orientation as it is the reasons you give for those beliefs. Thus you could believe that bigamy is right or wrong and still be either an Idealist or a Realist. This point will be reillustrated throughout the ensuing discussion of both philosophy and philosophy of education.

As different as they are, Idealism and Realism are alike in one major way. Both hold that reality, knowledge, and values are absolute, universal, and unchanging. According to these philosophies, what counts as real, what can be known, and what is right and wrong are the same for all people in all times. Idealists turn to sources of authority whereas Realists to the natural world. As discussed earlier, however, Idealists and Realists differ in what they believe is the source, or basis, of reality, knowledge, and values.

Pragmatism

The third system we consider is pragmatism.

Metaphysics and epistemology   The philosophical views of Idealism and Realism have prevailed throughout ancient, medieval, and early modern times. During the nineteenth century, there was a major new development in philosophical thinking. As Charles Darwin's *Origin of the Species* began to raise questions about how life began and about the nature of the universe, the philosophy of Pragmatism emerged, first in Europe and Great Britain, then in the United States. One of its major proponents in this country was John Dewey, also considered to be the father of Progressivism, the educational philosophy derived from Pragmatism.

Pragmatism and Realism have much in common. Both maintain that reality is exclusively physical, that knowledge is acquired through the senses, and that for a claim to be valid it has to be verified through the scientific method. They differ, however, in one major way. Whereas Realists insist that reality is universal, absolute, and unchanging, Pragmatists argue that reality is relative and ever-changing. Evolution best typifies Pragmatists' beliefs about reality. Just as the physical universe is in a constant state of change, so too are society and individuals.

Dewey proposed that claims of truth be replaced with claims of *warranted assertability,* that is, base knowledge on the best evidence available at any particular time. As instruments of observation, such as telescopes and microscopes improve our scientific evidence, the degree of warranted assertability should also improve. Such improvements in warranted assertability are what Dewey and other Pragmatists based their conception of progress on.

For example, consider the change in the way physicists described the relationship between space and time before and after Einstein. Realists would argue that the pre-Einsteinian physicists were mistaken, while Pragmatists would maintain that physicists' theories preceding Einstein's discoveries counted as knowledge at that time. They would argue that because the universe changes, as does our ability to observe and understand it, there is no such thing as absolute knowledge. In fact, Pragmatists say, what counts as scientific knowledge is that which garners a high degree of consensus—warranted assertability—among scientists who conduct repeated experiments to test hypotheses.

What is the point of all this, you ask? It is to make clear the way in which Pragmatism differs from Realism. Both agree that reality inheres in objects, not ideas, and that the way one comes to know what is real is through the interaction of one's senses with the natural world. Realism, however, maintains that this objective and natural world is unchanging and absolute. Pragmatism contends that it and our perceptions of it are continually changing. For Pragmatists, relativity, not constancy, defines reality and knowing. What can be said to count for knowledge at one time, whether in the physical world, society, or an individual life, may not count as knowledge at another time. Reality and knowing are relative to place, time, and circumstances.

Axiology   As you might expect the difference between Pragmatism and Realism becomes especially significant when we consider ethics. What sort of moral justifications fit Pragmatism? Let's return to the issue of bigamy. If one argues that in a society in which there is a shortage of either men or women (an observation), bigamy is an acceptable life style, that would fit Pragmatism. A Pragmatist might also argue that under normal circumstances extramarital sex is wrong, but if one's mate is permanently incapacitated, it is all right. Such a Pragmatic view is sometimes labeled **situation ethics,** because right and wrong are not seen as absolutes but as being determined by the particular time, place, and circumstances.

Existentialism

We turn now to our fourth and last philosophical system, Existentialism.

Metaphysics and epistemology   Existentialism is the most contemporary and liberal system of philosophy. The Existentialist maintains that not only is reality not absolute, it is not even relative. Rather, there are as many different realities as there are people to construct them. The French playwright, Jean Paul Sartre, proposed that *existence precedes essence,* meaning that there is no universal human nature and no common point of reference for observing the world, so each person must construct his or her own unique reality. It follows that if there is no common reality to be shared, then there can be no systematic body of knowledge to be passed on. This is not to say that Existentialists have no metaphysics or epistemology, just that there is no common reality or knowledge to share. Every individual must construct his or her own.

Axiology   What implications does this philosophy have for identifying values? Existentialism's views on values are based on an understanding of the German term *angst*—dread in the face of death. Although no human being has the choice of whether or not to be born, we come to recognize that at any point in our lives we could choose to die. Not to do so is to make a choice to live, and we are responsible for the consequences of that choice. Existentialism holds that there is no system of values, no rights and wrongs, only individuals making choices and accepting the consequence of those choices. Thus, one might maintain, as Norman Mailer seems to in *The Executioner's Song,* the fictionalized story of the mass murderer Gary Gilmore, that even cold-blooded murder is not in and of itself evil.

Having examined these four philosophical systems, you may have begun to realize that there is a continuum along which they fall in terms of their metaphysics, epistemology, and axiology. Referring to Table 3.1, you can see that this continuum moves from left to right, from the traditional and conservative view that there is a fixed, unchanging reality that we can know and pass on to others to the more contemporary and liberal views that see reality in terms of change and individual perception. At this point, stop a few minutes to think about where your own philosophical inclinations place you on this continuum. Do you believe there is a god? An afterlife? Do you think there is an objective reality that exists apart from any mind that might know it? Or do you feel that reality is totally subjective and varies according to the experiences of each individual? Do you think there is an absolute moral code that all individuals should abide by? If so, what is the basis of that code? Do any of your answers to these questions seem to contradict other answers?

Comparing Philosophical Systems

Let's now consider differences in these philosophical systems for examining every day events. Imagine a fight on the school playground that has several participants and observers. A teacher comes along after the fight is over and attempts to determine

Table 3.1 **Philosophical Systems**

	Idealism	Realism	Pragmatism	Existentialism
Metaphysics	Universal Ideas	Physical Objects	Physical Objects	Individual Ideas
Epistemology	Inspiration Revelation Intuition Meditation	Senses/experience absolute	Senses/experience consensus	Introspection
Axiology	Absolute/external authority	Absolute/nature	Relative/social group	Individual

what took place. The normal procedure would be to interview as many observers as possible. One might assume in this process, possibly unconsciously, one of the following:

- The facts are there to be gathered. It is just a matter of talking to enough people, then figuring it out.

- Interviewing enough people will bring about a high degree of consensus about what took place, and we can then assume that the consensus represents reality and act accordingly.

- Everyone sees things differently, even who threw the first punch. Therefore, it is impossible to come to a conclusion about what happened because no "one thing" took place.

It takes very little analysis to realize that the first of these viewpoints assumes that there is an absolute reality that can be known (Idealism or Realism). The second assumes that reality is jointly constructed by a group of people and is relative (Pragmatism). The third assumes that reality is a totally individual experience (Existentialism). How a teacher might proceed after such a fight might vary depending on her view of reality. For instance, if the teacher insists on finding out who was right and who was wrong and then punishing that individual on the basis of some fixed vision of right and wrong, she is acting on the premises of Idealism. However, the teacher might try to reconcile the students' differences because of her belief that nature looks for harmony (Realism) or because the class will not be able to accomplish its goals if everyone does not work together (Pragmatism). Finally, the teacher's focus might be to help the students examine their own inner drives, consider choices, and accept the consequences of their behavior (Existentialism).

PHILOSOPHIES OF EDUCATION

This section examines four philosophies of education—Perennialism, Essentialism, Progressivism, and Reconstructionism—that derive from the larger philosophical systems we have been discussing. We chose these particular educational philosophies because each one has stood the test of time and has had a significant impact on the development of educational policies and practices in the United States. We describe and compare each in terms of how it deals with the three fundamental questions presented at the start of this chapter: What are the purposes of education? What should be taught and how should it be taught? What should the role of teachers be and what types of relationships should they develop with their students? Table 3.2 displays the characteristics of each educational philosophy.

We can think of these four educational philosophies as existing along a continuum in the same way the larger philosophical systems do. On one end is Perennialism, a school of thought that emphasizes the constancy of human nature and knowledge and the enduring aspects of society. On the other end is Reconstructionism, which emphasizes the changes in human nature and knowledge and the need to constantly reconstruct society to meet these changes. In some ways, this philosophical continuum is similar to the conservative/liberal continuum that is used to label political positions and other schools of thought. Generally, people with conservative political beliefs tend to support schooling practices that conserve existing knowledge, values, and practices. People with liberal beliefs, on the other hand, tend to support school programs designed to accommodate changing knowledge and social conditions.

Table 3.2 **Educational Philosophies**

	Perennialism	**Essentialism**	**Progressivism**	**Reconstructionism**
Purpose of education?	Conserve society/train intellect	Transmit essentials to all	Prepare for change	Reconstruct society
What is to be taught?	Classics	Basic academic subjects	Based on needs and interests of students	What is needed to reconstruct society to meet new challenges
Role of teacher?	Authority	Leader	Facilitator	Leader/facilitator

Perennialism

The educational philosophy of **Perennialism** is derived from both Idealism and Realism. From Idealism comes the combination of ideas that truth is universal and unchanging. It is independent of time, place, and the immediate physical reality that surrounds us. From Realism comes an emphasis on rationality and the importance of education in training our intellect in the search for truth.

Perennialism maintains that the purpose of schools is to prepare children to accept their places in a society built on long and tested tradition. Society has a natural order, and schools should operate as testing grounds to determine where children will fit in this order. To do this, schools should offer all children an academic curriculum based on the classics, compendiums of human knowledge that have been tested over time. The purpose of such a curriculum is to train the intellect in a broad, general way. As a result, it will become evident who are the brightest and best, who will be fit to be the leaders in society. Perennialism contends that schools should not address either the fleeting, narrow interests of students or the immediate needs of society. These concerns are left to other social institutions. The role of the teacher, who has been trained in the same type of academic curriculum, is that of moral and intellectual authority figure. Perennialists hold that courses in academic subjects are a far more important part of teacher education than courses in how to teach. Teachers should be role models of educated people.

Perennialism has its roots in the Greek classics, which dominated early education in this country. Its clearest articulation in the United States, however, occurred primarily in the twentieth century. One of its foremost advocates was Robert Hutchins, president of the University of Chicago during the 1960s. His famous "Great Books" curriculum centered on the classics of Western thought—books such as *Darwin's Origin of the Species* and Homer's *Iliad* and *Odyssey*. It is in these great works, he argued, that

students can find the best representations of eternal truth, and it is through these works that their intellects are best developed.

In 1982, Mortimer J. Adler published *The Paideia Proposal: An Educational Manifesto*. In it he emphasized the importance of a broad and intellectually demanding curriculum built around the great works and traditions of the liberal arts and sciences. According to Adler and his colleagues, immersion in great works helps students reach a state called *paideia*, that is, a state of moral goodness and intellectual enlightenment. Adler, Hutchins, and other Perennialists argue that requiring students to take an intellectually demanding curriculum is the only way to ensure equal opportunity for all. Other, more diverse, curricula that separate students into various tracks are elitist in that they deny many students access to the richest and most demanding intellectual traditions.

However, critics of the Perennialist perspective argue that as long as we expect all children to learn in a single way, through an abstract and mainly book-oriented curriculum, only those students whose cultures have conditioned them to learn in this way are likely to be successful. Other children, whose cultural or cognitive learning styles condition them to learn through hands-on or group-oriented activities, will find school boring and meaningless. Furthermore, critics argue, the books and ideas proposed by Hutchins and Adler promote a Eurocentric view of the world. They tend to ignore the contributions of women and minorities and the great works produced by other cultures. The curriculum, they argue, should represent the wisdom of the world, not just a small portion of it.

In sum, those educators who identify themselves as Perennialists are likely to stress the importance of students' acquiring broad and thorough subject-matter knowledge through the study of the classics; schools' maintaining demanding academic standards with rewards for those who perform at the highest levels; and schools and classrooms in which teachers and students demonstrate the decorum in their relationships and behavior that is necessary to achieve these goals. Perennialism continues to be the prevailing view on which most schooling in Western society is based.

Progressivism

At the end of the nineteenth century, John Dewey, one of America's leading philosophers and a prominent proponent of Pragmatism, began to channel his interests toward education, challenging the long-standing grip of Perennialism on American education. Although such individuals as Rousseau and the Swiss educational reformer Johann Pestalozzi were forerunners of Progressive views of education, it was Dewey who systematically developed and tested the tenets of American Progressivism.

As the chairman of the departments of psychology, philosophy, and pedagogy at the University of Chicago, Dewey established his famous laboratory school in 1895. The two announced purposes of the school were to exhibit, test, and criticize ideas about how children learn and to watch children to discover how they learn. Such an approach was in stark contrast to the static, tradition-oriented views of Perennialism.

Progressivism purports that the purpose of education is to prepare children to live in society, but that since society is in a constant state of change, schools should prepare students to confront the changing world. Dewey rejected the notion that reality and ways of knowing and behaving are absolute and of divine origin. Rather, he argued, reality is continually reconstructed, based on an ever-changing universe and the changing needs and interests of human beings. This, Progressivism maintains, is the world for which children should be prepared.

Whereas the curriculum emphasized by Perennialists is academic and teacher centered, that proposed by Progressives is highly social and student centered. Rejecting the notion that the function of schools is simply to train the intellect, Dewey argued that children should acquire knowledge through meaningful activities and apply it to real social situations. Thus, Progressivism rejects classroom practices that involve children passively learning information "poured" into them by authoritarian teachers or from books. Further, Progressivism stresses the importance of addressing the needs and experiences of the whole child, not just a child's intellect. As much as possible, what a child studies should be determined by his or her own experiences and interests. Moreover, the best method of intellectual training is through helping children learn to work cooperatively to solve problems, not through

studying a fixed body of knowledge. In short, Progressive educators see cooperation and problem solving as the key to human adaptation in an ever-changing world.

Progressivism maintains that the role of the teacher is as a facilitator who helps children to examine their experiences as they interact with the physical and social worlds and to sort out a satisfactory role in this world. Teachers are not considered authority figures handing down knowledge and precepts by which children should live. Rather, it is important that they prepare a wide repertoire of classroom activities to stimulate and satisfy the interests of all their students. They need to give students as much contact with real-life situations as they possibly can, so students can learn and test their ideas.

How do differences in the tenets of Perennialism and Progressivism manifest themselves in the classroom? In his study of constancy and change in American classrooms from 1880 to 1990, Larry Cuban (1993) proposed that the following six classroom indicators be used to analyze the dominant form of instruction taking place in a classroom.

1. Arrangement of classroom furniture

2. Ratio of teacher talk to student talk

3. Whether most instruction occurs individually, in small groups, or with the entire class

4. Presence or absence of learning or interest centers used by students as part of the regular school day

5. Degree of physical movement students are allowed without asking the teacher

6. Degree of reliance on tests and use of varied instructional materials

Using these indicators, we can see in Table 3.3 the differences in Perennialism and Progressivism as they are likely to play out in the classroom.

Essentialism

Beginning in the 1930s and reemerging with increased strength in the 1950s and 1980s, Essentialism has decried Progressivism's focus on *how* children learn rather than on *what* children learn. A kind of neoPerennialism with roots in both Idealism and Realism, **Essentialism** maintains that the purpose of schools is both to preserve the knowledge and values of the past and to provide children with the skills essential to live successful and meaningful lives in present society. Academic subject matter has priority in the curriculum, but its primary purpose is to transmit useful skills. In response to the

Table 3.3 **Comparison of Perennialism and Progressivism**

Indicator	Perennialism	Progressivism
Arrangement of desks	Straight rows/facing teacher	Squares/horseshoe/scattered
Teacher-student talk	Predominantly teacher	Predominantly students
Instructional grouping	Entire class	Individuals/small groups
Learning centers	Absent or used only with teacher permission	Use determined freely by students
Student physical movement	Only with teacher permission	At will
Instructional materials	Structured/standardized/routine	Flexible/created with and by students/varied

growing Progressive movement, Essentialism argued that teachers must be returned to their traditional authoritarian place in the classroom as dispensers of knowledge and skills and as role models of useful and competent citizens. Essentialism shares with Perennialism the view that schools should conserve important social traditions and the curriculum should be teacher and subject centered. But there is more emphasis in Essentialism on education's relevance in preparing individuals to live in the current society and less on absolutism and enduring issues. Perennialism focuses more on the value of studying the classics for their own sake, because they help individuals to become liberally educated. Essentialism focuses more on the utilitarian value of these great works that helps individuals develop high-order thinking skills and acquire knowledge which will better society.

In the last few decades, there have been several well-publicized manifestations of Essentialism. The **back-to-basics movement** of the 1970s and 1980s criticized Progressive educators for becoming so preoccupied with children's social needs that they failed to teach the basics of reading, writing, and arithmetic. During the 1970s alternative school movement—primarily a Progressive response to the needs of students who did not fit in highly structured public schools—back-to-basic schools emerged in many urban areas. Then, as now, these schools often have long waiting lists.

The back-to-basics movement reached its height with the publication in 1983 of *A Nation at Risk,* the report of the National Commission on Excellence in Education, which recommended "five new basics"—English, social studies, science, mathematics, and computer science. In reality, computer science was the only new entry. This report has been the touchstone for educational policy making at the federal level since its publication and has generated volumes of response among both educators and state governments.

Another publication that helped publicize the Essentialist view was E. D. Hirsch's book, *Cultural Literacy: What Every American Needs to Know* (1987). Hirsch states that there is an essential core of background knowledge that all Americans need to know in order to participate in public discourse and to transmit our cultural heritage. He maintained that it is the responsibility of the schools to provide this cultural literacy. To some extent, this viewpoint is a reaction against the growing emphasis on nonwestern, nonmainstream literature that many Progressive educators advocate.

In summary, Essentialism, which in the post-World War II era has come to replace Perennialism as the dominant educational philosophy in American public schools, holds that the purpose of the schools is to prepare students for their roles in society, through a curriculum focused on basic skills and traditional academic content, taught by teachers who expect respect for authority and discipline.

Social Reconstructionism

The Progressive Education Association was organized in 1919. Members were unanimous in rejecting traditionally structured, authoritarian, teacher-centered classrooms, but their different views regarding the primary purpose of education eventually led to the formulation of a related but somewhat distinct educational philosophy, Social Reconstructionism. First articulated in the 1930s in George S. Count's book *Dare the World Build a New Social Order?,* this offshoot of Progressivism paralleled the growth of Essentialism.

Progressives who identified themselves as Social Reconstructionists believe that the purpose of schools is to address the needs of society as a whole, not just the social needs of individual students.

Education should encompass broad multicultural and global concerns and prepare students to deal with social problems on a large scale. **Reconstructionism** asserts that curriculum should focus on such issues as technology, the interdependence of human beings for survival, social inequities, and population and environmental problems. Like other Progressives, Reconstructionists believe that schools must make students social problem solvers and agents of change if the society is going to survive. Read the accompanying Global Box, which shows that this way of thinking is not unique to the United States.

Reconstructionists also argue that schools should model the solutions to social problems and the role of the teacher is to help students examine major social problems and controversial issues. This is consistent with Dewey's views that, as much as possible, schools should, themselves, be working societies, in many ways microcosms of the larger society. This perspective was manifest, for instance, in the decision on the part of the federal government, first in the 1954 *Brown v. Board of Education* decision and subsequently in the 1964 *Civil Rights Act*, that the way to achieve an integrated society is to integrate schools. Many argued, in fact, that it is

MULTICULTURAL

The "Perfect European": An Impossible Dream?

As the European Union (EU) expands, and new frameworks are established for developing the European dimension in all levels of education, the expectation is that national barriers will continue to be eroded away. The focus on education is especially important when one considers the high proportion of young people now living in the different member states.

An important step toward achieving the educational aim of eroding barriers is to link schools, colleges, and universities through networks. These networks are being supported by EU funding and will enable participants to share expertise and experience with regard to a range of topics related to the European dimension. Matters of pupil and teacher exchanges receive high priority, as does the development of links between schools and universities. Behind such activity is the important matter of breaking down stereotypes, national prejudices, and intolerance—all related to a lack of direct knowledge, contact, and communication. It will be obvious, therefore, why recent and current EU legislation has increasingly supported a number of educational initiatives designed to promote the opportunities available for young people to work together.

Despite all these efforts, a range of evidence supports the conclusion that it may well take some time for national stereotyping to disappear (if, indeed, it ever will). One of the more substantial studies, which focused on civic morals across Europe, was conducted by the European Value Systems Study Group, a network of academics who surveyed nearly 19,000 individuals about their attitudes toward 10 "antisocial" activities. Respondents in each of the EU countries were asked to what extent they felt the activities listed could be justified. The list included such matters as claiming state benefits to which one was unentitled, avoiding fares on public transport, cheating on taxes, joy riding, accepting a bribe, littering the environment, and driving while drunk.

The results, published in 1992, suggested that the Portuguese were Europe's biggest fare dodgers, that the Swedes were the greatest litterers, and that the Belgians were considered to be the most prominent tax cheats! By contrast, the Danes were seen to be the most righteous of all Europe's citizens.

impossible to achieve social integration without school integration. The growing level of concern about the decrease in minority teachers in our schools, even as the minority population increases, reflects the Social Reconstructionist's view that schools should be a model of the way we believe the world should be.

Examples of the Four Philosophies of Education

Let's return to the three situations posed at the outset of this chapter and examine some possible responses.

You are a middle-school teacher, and one of your students—a boy from a poor home with slightly below average academic talents—asks whether he should pursue a college preparation program or one that is mostly vocational when he gets to high school. How would you advise him? Why?

A Perennialist response: You advise this student to take the college preparation program when he gets to high school whether or not he ever goes to college, because you believe that everyone should be exposed to great works of literature and study the other academic disciplines and high school is likely

MULTICULTURAL

Continued

What is significant, of course, is the continued inclination to assume the existence of some kind of national character or characteristic and to regard the behavior of another group or "nation" as homogeneous. This feature also emerged quite clearly from the studies of a research team from the University of Utrecht that investigated attitudes on stereotypes and national characteristics. Nearly 300 students in secondary schools located in Denmark, Belgium, Germany, Italy, the United Kingdom, France, and the Netherlands participated. They were invited to indicate on a scale of zero to 100 percent, how well people from different countries fit 22 characteristics.

The students collectively characterized Danes as being particularly efficient, confident, life loving, proud, and honest. The English were viewed as aggressive, egoistic, and industrious—and the Germans were seen to be self-confident, dominant, and aggressive. The Italians were universally characterized as helpful and life loving.

A related survey, and the first study in nearly 20 years of English children's attitudes toward Europeans, was conducted by a researcher in London and published in 1993 in the *British Journal of Developmental Psychology*. Martin Barrett questioned more than 200 children in primary schools west of London. Perhaps the most encouraging finding was that the children became less prejudiced as they became older and better informed. Those between 5 and 7 years of age, however, see Spaniards as "sunburned, happy, clean, poor, and lazy" and the French as "sunburned, rich, clean, clever, and hard-working." Germans were considered to be the villains of Europe and "white, rich, clean, hard-working, and aggressive."

The "truth" may not always be what is reported by others but may lie instead in the eye of the beholder. What does seem clear is that elementary school is a key time to affect children's ideas about foreigners and that there is nothing better than to encourage direct contact, connections, and exchanges of all kinds. This is what the European Commission is intent on doing. It remains to be seen how quickly attitudes will change and how soon the stereotypes will become diluted.

Source: Peck, 1996, p. 389.

the only opportunity he will ever have to do so. Your advice is consistent with the Perennialist view that schools are responsible for developing everyone's intellect to the fullest extent possible and that the best means of accomplishing this goal is through teaching the classics and the academic disciplines.

Another Perennialist response: You advise him that, based on his past performance, he is not likely to be successful in a college preparation program and that the appropriate place for him is in a vocational program, which will prepare him for the world he is likely to be part of when he graduates from high school. This advice is consistent with the Perennialist view that society has a natural order and that a major role of the schools is to determine where students fit in this order.

That you can give such different advice from the same philosophical orientation illustrates that it is not only the view you have or the position you hold that identifies your underlying philosophy but the reasons you give for those views and positions as well. The same assumptions about the purposes of schools, who should control the curriculum, and the role of teachers can lead to very different actions and advice in educational practice.

A Progressive response: If, on the other hand, you advise this student to take the vocational course, because it seems best suited to his interest in mechanical things and to his hands-on learning style, your advice is based in the Progressive view that students learn best when engaged in tasks that draw on their natural interests and inclinations. You hope that the vocational teachers use hands-on learning tasks to teach students how to read, compute, and work cooperatively in groups, not just teach mechanical skills.

Once again, it is the underlying reasons for some recommended course of action that signals one's philosophy of education, not the course of action itself. Two teachers can give the very same advice to a student for completely opposite reasons. It is important always to ask yourself and others why a person puts forth a particular position. You may be surprised at the areas of agreement and disagreement you uncover. Analyzing reasons for your views is the first step toward becoming a reflective educator whose practices are integrated and consistent.

You are a member of the high school's disciplinary committee and have to consider the case of Connie, a girl who frequently misses school, has been kicked out of school seven times in the past month, and has been caught threatening another girl with a knife. How would you deal with Connie? Would you recommend that she be expelled or assigned to another counselor more accustomed to this type of student? Why?

A Perennialist response: You recommend that Connie be expelled, arguing that she has had plenty of opportunity to find her place in the academic environment, and it is clear that she is not going to, that she does not belong in school interfering with the education of the students who really want to learn. This reasoning is consistent with the Perennialist view that schools exist primarily to develop students' intellect through study of the academic disciplines and that other goals, such as developing social skills, cannot be permitted to interfere with these academic goals.

A Progressive response: You recommend that Connie be assigned to another counselor or that the school find or develop a learning environment more suited to Connie's temperament and needs. This position is consistent with the Progressive view that schools should address the needs and experiences of the whole child, not just his or her intellectual growth. This view further holds that students' social and emotional growth are just as crucial to a healthy society as are the goals of the traditional academic curriculum.

You are a member of a site-based school council and are informed that budget difficulties necessitate cutting at least one major school program. Would you be inclined to cut the athletic program or the music program? Why?

A Perennialist response: You support the music program, citing research that indicates students who study music do better in their academic subjects than students who do not. Your arguments come from a Perennialist perspective, which holds that academic achievement is the most important criterion on which to base decisions about school curriculum.

A Progressive response: You favor funding the athletic program, because it serves more students and addresses a broader array of student needs than the music program. Your views are based in the Progressive perspective that schools should be democratic institutions which promote the full development of as many students as possible.

An Essentialist response: You support keeping the athletic program, because a substantial number of marginal students keep up with their studies only so they can participate in sports. Thus, having an athletic program not only helps to lower the dropout rate, but provides many students with the essential skills they will need to function in contemporary society. This argument is consistent with an Essentialist philosophy of education.

A Reconstructionist Response: You argue for cutting both the athletic and the music program. Your aim is to use the funds to support the expansion of technology in all the schools, including hardware, software, and teacher training for complete integration of technology into the curriculum. The basis of your argument is that schools must live up to their clear responsibility for preparing students to lead society into the twenty-first century and to meet the demands of a global culture. This is the argument of a Reconstructionist.

Although many policy statements and classroom practices are clearly rooted in one or another educational philosophy, in most cases, discovering the underlying assumptions of your own views or those of other educators or educational policy makers is rarely that clear-cut and straightforward. It is often necessary to examine justifications for these views, since it is often the case that a variety of people endorse what appear to be the same practices but for very different reasons and with very different outcomes in mind, as the first case illustrated. The educational philosophies and the larger philosophical systems examined in this chapter are analytical tools, or logical constructs for "peeling the intellectual onions"—positions, arguments, and actions—to see what assumptions lie within.

DEFINING A PERSONAL PHILOSOPHY OF EDUCATION

At the beginning of this chapter, we discussed the relevance of philosophy to your becoming a professional teacher. As Chapter 12 discusses more fully, being a professional involves more than having highly developed pedagogical skills. It involves understanding how and why classrooms and schools have come to operate as they do and what possibilities there are for them to be otherwise. This means that you will need to examine your own classroom practices and analyze your underlying assumptions when you choose to do one thing rather than another. Additionally, you need to be able to define where a particular practice fits in with your overall vision of what teaching and learning are all about and whether or not it is consistent with other things you say and do. Philosophy is a critical tool in the quest to become this kind of teacher, because it

provides you with logically consistent schemes of analysis and the skills for informed reflection.

Furthermore, as you develop your own educational philosophy—an on-going activity throughout your career—you will be better able to respond to those frequent, unique situations that teachers face almost every day. Thinking on your feet and doing the appropriate thing in the middle of a classroom situation is probably one of the most daunting tasks new teachers face. Building a philosophy of education through your reflections will not only enable you to become a truly professional classroom practitioner, it will help you to better understand practices and policy statements of others. As you participate in the profession beyond the classroom, whether it is on a site-based management committee, in the teachers' association, working with a districtwide committee, or collaborating with the state department of education in an activity such as standardized test development, you will want to have at least the beginnings of your own educational philosophy from which you can analyze information.

Two Approaches

At this point, you are probably asking how you, as a beginning teacher, can go about the task of critically reflecting on your beliefs, assumptions, and values. Many students studying these systems of analysis say they agree with *some* components of each philosophical system and philosophy of education. Many professors of education endorse doing this, calling it an *eclectic* approach, selecting the best from various views. On the surface, this solution may appear harmless, perhaps even a good idea. However, as you pursue a deeper understanding of both your own and others beliefs and practices, such eclecticism can lead to confusing inconsistencies in your professional practice.

Other professors argue that it is important that you adopt one philosophy of education—often their own—and insist that you plan your classroom practices around the precepts of that educational philosophy. This approach to working with teacher-education students is most likely to be evident during your student teaching, when your college supervisor or your cooperating teacher might insist that you do things a particular way. If you, as a future teacher, are going to have the opportunity to experiment with various ways of doing things during your student teaching, you will want to be able to articulate which educational philosophy most represents your views and why you, too, want to do things in certain ways. Let's examine more fully the two approaches you might take to developing your own coherent philosophy of education.

Choose and Follow

Reflective people who have a strong need for consistency are inclined to adopt a particular educational philosophy, such as Perennialism or Progressivism, and to follow it as closely as possible. In fact, many of the educational reform movements that proliferated during the 1970s and 1980s were centered on two concepts that are an integral part of Perennialism: a curriculum that focuses on the academic disciplines and using objective test scores to sort students according to their academic performance.

The danger in using this choose-and-follow approach when forming your own philosophy of education is the possibility of becoming too narrow in your outlook on the world and on education, especially as a beginning teacher. As we repeatedly point out, being a professional involves adapting your professional knowledge and practice to a never-ending variety of situations and contexts. Just as no single-teaching methodology can be stretched to fit all teaching situations, it is unlikely that any single philosophy of education can be stretched to fit all conceivable educational situations. While adherence to some coordinated set of beliefs does bring much needed consistency to one's teaching, slavish adherence to any set of beliefs can cause one to become an overly rigid, nonadaptive teacher. Try to own ideas rather than letting ideas own you.

Mix and Match

As already suggested, in reading about educational philosophies, you probably responded positively to some but not all tenets within each. And it is tempting to select what you feel are the best ideas from each and weave them into your own eclectic philosophy of education. This is an appealing prospect to those who like to think of themselves as open-minded, adaptive thinkers. The danger here is that too much adaptability can lead to inconsistency because core beliefs do not exist.

Such inconsistencies in school systems abound. Let's consider a couple of examples. Currently many high schools have advanced placement (AP) courses that students can take for college credit if they are able to pass the standardized tests given at their completion. This is clearly a form of tracking, providing intensive courses for the most academically able students. It is also clearly in keeping with the Perennialist view of education. In one high school in which these courses had been taken for decades almost exclusively by only the highest achieving students, parental accusations of elitism eventually resulted in school officials' opening the courses, which previously had performance requirements for

admittance, to anyone who wanted to take them. As you might expect, the teachers were no longer able to teach these courses at a college level inasmuch as some students' reading ability was at the third- or fourth-grade level. As a result, no one was satisfied. The academically prepared students were not receiving the level of instruction needed to pass the college-level tests, and poorly prepared students were not able to keep up with instruction, even though it had been slowed to accommodate the mixed classes. It seems clear that this high school should resume the advanced courses and maintain admittance standards or abandon them completely and have all students grouped heterogeneously.

If you think about your own school experience, you can probably identify examples of such inconsistencies. For example, imagine a teacher who goes through the lengthy "democratic" activity of having students make up their own classroom rules at the beginning of the year, a popular idea among those who consider themselves Progressive educators. She encourages them to agree on the class rules and write them on the board. If this teacher makes a practice of disciplining students for violating rules that never appeared on the board that first day of school, though, she will lose credibility with her students. Before long they will learn that she believes she is the authority figure in the classroom despite her proclamations about building a democratic learning community.

Positioning Yourself

How much consistency versus how much adaptability? This is a question you will grapple with throughout your teaching career. No one can give you the answer. As you prepare for a career in teaching, you need to closely study other educators and ask probing questions about their practices to help you develop your own coherent educational philosophy. Before you are actually teaching in a classroom, you may not know what you will do in particular instances, but a sound philosophical basis can help you be prepared to deal with a variety of situations. It is important to emphasize that no one educational philosophy in and of itself is better. As you begin the pursuit of identifying and defining your own philosophy of education, you will probably find yourself embracing tenets from different philosophies, in spite of the drawbacks we mentioned.

The first step in your reflection process is to identify your beliefs. How do you do this? As your field experience begins to involve such activities as tutoring and small-group instruction, step back frequently and examine what you tell students about your expectations for them in both their classroom behavior and their academic performance. Where do your expectations fall on the philosophical continuum? Look closely at whether your own motivations to teach have more to do with helping young people develop socially or with getting them to develop academic competence. How do you envision your role as a teacher? Is it more as a leader and standard setter, or is it more as a guide and facilitator? Every time a question about curriculum arises, ask yourself what you would recommend. But more important, *examine your reasons* and, once again, attempt to identify where they fall on the philosophical continuum from Perennialism to Reconstructionism.

Once you are a student teacher with full responsibility for planning and teaching classes, you may feel overwhelmed with the demands this places on you. Nevertheless, you need to spend time regularly to reflect on what you say and do in your classroom and why. Student teaching is a time of experimentation and learning, a time when you can begin to discover whether you are more inclined to adopt a single educational philosophy and work out its tenets in your classroom or to try a variety of things that you will eventually meld into your own coherent philosophy of education.

As you continue your professional career, we urge you to engage in a relentless analysis of your views and practices, thereby reducing the likelihood of confusing your students through inconsistency and contradiction. How do you go about doing this? Engage in frequent discussion with your colleagues and supervisors about what you do and why you do it. Solicit their critique of your views and methods. Take every opportunity that arises to observe your colleagues and analyze their practices. As you become more experienced and confident in your classroom, invite your students to critique your practices and use the opportunity to respond to them to further explore your philosophical justifications. Finally, continue your own professional development by reading a wide variety of educational journals that deal with classroom and policy issues and by participating in in-service and graduate classes that can further help you explore and expand your views.

It is important that teachers and prospective teachers engage in reflection as a routine part of their educational activities. This chapter has attempted to provide you with the tools to begin to discover and to define your own philosophy of education. It is not something that appears ready made on the first day you walk into the classroom as a teacher. Rather, you need to actively develop it while you are preparing to be a teacher. It will continue to develop throughout your professional career.

SUMMARY

- It is important to examine and analyze your own beliefs about education and teaching, since they will give direction to your thinking and actions as a teacher.

- Philosophy is the process of systematically reflecting on the world around us in an attempt to build a coherent set of beliefs and values with which to guide our actions.

- Reflective teachers will be better able to develop problem-solving skills, adapt their knowledge to new situations, establish stable and trusting classrooms, and understand divergent points of view.

- The four branches of philosophy are metaphysics, the study of the nature of reality; epistemology, the study of knowledge and knowing; axiology, the study of values and valuing; and logic, the study of the principles of reasoning.

- There are four major philosophical systems. Idealism maintains that reality is mental or spiritual; knowledge is acquired through such processes as meditation, inspiration, intuition, and reflection; and values are determined by those in authority. Realism maintains that reality is physical; knowledge is acquired through the senses; and values are found by observing nature. Both Idealism and Realism purport that reality, knowledge, and values are absolute. Pragmatism, like Realism, maintains that knowledge is determined by the senses but that reality and values are ever-changing, not absolute. Existentialism maintains that reality, knowledge, and values are totally individual.

- Philosophies of education address three basic questions: What is the purpose of education? What should be taught and how? What should be the role of teachers and what types of relationships should they develop with their students?

- There are four basic philosophies of education. Perennialism, derived from both Idealism and Realism, maintains that schools should offer an academic curriculum by teachers as authority figures to provide a testing ground to identify students' place in society. Progressivism, developed directly out of Pragmatism, asserts that the schools should offer a varied and student-centered curriculum with teachers as facilitators to prepare children to live in a constantly changing society. Essentialism, a kind of neoPerennialism and also derived from both Idealism and Realism, believes that the curriculum should be primarily academic but should be made relevant to present society by teachers as role models of the useful and competent person. Social Reconstructionism, an extreme form of Progressivism, maintains the primary purpose of schools and teachers is to prepare students to be agents of social change and the curriculum should focus on that goal.

- There are two approaches to developing one's own philosophy of education. The choose-and-follow approach entails identifying one educational philosophy that most represents your views and attempting to carry out its tenets in your classroom. The mix-and-match approach involves experimenting with the beliefs and practices of various philosophies in order to develop your own coherent educational philosophy. Whatever method you follow, it is important that professional educators achieve both consistency and adaptability in their classroom practices.

- Using philosophy to reflect on your educational views and practices should become a life-long enterprise if you are to become a professional educator. This endeavor should begin during your teacher-preparation program and continue throughout your career.

READINGS FOR THE PROFESSIONAL

Griese, A. A. *Your Philosophy of Education: What is it?* Santa Monica, CA: Goodyear Publishing, 1981.
The purpose of this book is to link the formal structure of philosophy to future teachers' life experiences and to relate philosophy to their future experiences as teachers or educators.
Hargreaves, A. *Changing Teachers, Changing Times: Teachers Work and Culture in the Postmodern Age.* New York: Teachers College Press, 1994.
This book describes the political, economic, and social context in which schools are embedded in order to connect educational change to the changes taking place in society.
Knight, G. R. *Issues and Alternatives in Educational Philosophy.* Berrien Springs, MI: Andrews University Press, 1982.
This book is a survey of philosophies and philosophic issues that are relevant to the educational profession. It highlights the relationship between philosophic starting points and educational outcomes—between theory and practice.

PART I

Teachers and Their Work

Application and Portfolio Activities

Self-Assessments

Assessing Your Motivations for Teaching 82

Teachers I Remember 83

Thinking through Your Educational Philosophy 84

Observations

Observing School Board Politics 86

Becoming an Effective Teacher 86

Indicators of Educational Philosophy 87

Interviews

Principals' Views on Teacher Supply and Demand .88

Students Talk about The "Good Teacher" 88

One Teacher's Philosophy of Education 89

Assessing Your Motivations for Teaching

Purpose   Teachers bring a variety of needs and desires to their career decision. Clarifying your own motivations can help you think through whether a teaching career is for you.

Directions   Rate each of the statements below on a scale of 1 to 5, depending on how strongly that factor influences your thinking about the desirability of teaching (1 = Doesn't appeal to me at all; 2 = Not very appealing; 3 = Neither here nor there; 4 = Somewhat appealing; 5 = Appeals to me a great deal). Total your score. Higher scores indicate stronger and multiple sources of motivation for teaching.

What Draws Me to Teaching	Rating
Dealing with complex problems every day	_____
Unpredictability and spontaneity of classroom life	_____
Intellectual stimulation	_____
Working with children and adolescents	_____
Inspiring students as my teachers inspired me	_____
Love of my subject	_____
Opportunity for creativity and self-expression	_____
The chance to master a tough job	_____
Salary and benefits	_____
Job security	_____
Convenient daily, weekly, and annual schedule	_____
Order and structure of daily schedule	_____
Opportunity for career advancement	_____
Collegial friendships	_____
Encouragement of my family	_____
Status of teachers	_____
Religious/spiritual fulfillment	_____
Working for social justice, peace, and equality	_____

Reflection   Look for patterns in your responses. What types of needs, interests, and goals attract you to teaching? How can you use this information in making your career decision?

Teachers I Remember

Purpose
Many teacher-education students point to a particular teacher who inspired them and whom they wish to emulate. Often the image of these influential teachers unconsciously shapes one's perceptions about what constitutes effective teaching. This exercise will help you uncover your unconscious images of effective teaching so that you may explicitly examine them.

Directions
Write a letter to a teacher you remember fondly and tell what made him or her an effective teacher. You can even mail it if you want to! Next, write a paragraph or two describing what you consider the ideal teacher.

Reflection
Compare and contrast your descriptions of effective teaching with the attributes of effectiveness identified by research described in Chapter 2. What has led you to hold your views? Explain the similarities and differences between the research literature and your current perspectives. What questions does this raise for you?

For example, you may have greatly admired a high school history teacher who was an excellent lecturer. But current research puts lecture rather low on the list of important teaching strategies, not eliminated certainly, but not in first place either. You may have liked this teacher and developed the view of teaching as telling, because it was a teaching strategy that worked well for you. You may be wondering why, if lecture worked so well for you, it isn't more highly valued by the research community. What in the world will you do in your own classroom if you can't lecture all the time?

Would you include this exercise in a portfolio for application to a teacher-education program? For a teaching job? Why or why not?

Thinking Through Your Educational Philosophy

Purpose   As Chapter 3 stressed, a thorough understanding of one's own philosophy of teaching is important for several reasons. Illuminating your philosophy will smooth the path to new learning, allow for a critical reappraisal of your views, and ultimately afford you the ability to teach more effectively. This survey will get you started in clarifying and developing your own educational philosophy.

Directions   Circle the one response for each item below that best describes your views. Use the chart at the end of the survey to analyze your responses to see if you are progressivist, perennialist, essentialist, or existentialist.

1. What is the essence of education?
   A. Reason and intuition
   B. Growth
   C. Knowledge and skills
   D. Choice

2. What is the nature of the learner?
   A. Experiencing organism
   B. Unique, free choosing, and responsible, made up of intellect and emotion
   C. Rational and intuitive
   D. Storehouse of knowledge and skills which, once learned, can be applied and used

3. How should education provide for human needs?
   A. By providing a passionate encounter with the perennial problems of life: the agony and joy of love, reality of choice, anguish of freedom, consequences of actions, and inevitability of death
   B. By inculcating children with the essential skills and knowledge that all should possess
   C. By concentrating on developing the intellectual potential of students
   D. By developing the unique capacities of each individual student

4. What should be the concern of the school?
   A. Students' minds, and developing their rationality
   B. The whole child, and developing the needs and interests of each student
   C. Basic knowledge, and helping students attain what is necessary to understand the real world outside the school
   D. Helping each student on the journey to self-realization

5. What should the atmosphere of the school be?
   A. Democracy in which cooperation is fostered
   B. Authentic freedom in which all are allowed to find their own truth and fulfillment through non-conforming choice making
   C. Intellectualism, creative thinking, and individuality
   D. Mental discipline, innovation, and self-examination

6. What should the curriculum include?
   A. That which has survived the test of time, including the symbols and ideas of literature, history, science, and mathematics
   B. How to manage change through problem-solving activities in the social and physical sciences and vocational technology
   C. Intellectual subject matter, including English, languages, history, mathematics, natural sciences, fine arts, and philosophy
   D. The humanities—history, literature, philosophy, art—where greater depth into the nature of humanity's conflict with the world is revealed

7. What should the preferred teaching method be?
   A. Projects in which students can be guided through problem-solving experiences
   B. Lectures, readings, and discussions
   C. Demonstrations
   D. Socratic dialogue
   SOURCE: After Glickman, 1985.

Reflection   Circle the answers you selected in the chart below. Total the number of circles below each column. Did most of your responses fall in one category? Are you comfortable with that category? Or are your answers spread around? If so, what do you think the significance of that is? Are you undecided or unclear about your beliefs? Do you have values or perspectives that were not tapped by this survey? What is the degree of fit between your preferred philosophy and the recommendations for professional teachers advanced in this text?

Item	Progressivism	Perennialism	Essentialism	Existentialism
1	B	A	C	D
2	A	C	D	B
3	D	C	B	A
4	B	A	C	D
5	A	C	D	B
6	B	C	A	D
7	A	B	C	D

Observing School Board Politics

Purpose   Although teachers can and often do shut their classroom door and teach in isolation from others, politics still impinge on teachers' lives. This observation is designed to help you see politics in action and to think through its impact on you as a teacher.

Directions   Attend a school board meeting in your community. (Call the school district office to find out about meeting time and place.) Take notes of the discussion. What are the issues under discussion? What arguments are advanced in support of various positions on these issues? Who is in attendance? Who comprises the various factions? What do they want, and why? How do school board members interact with each other and with other participants in the meeting? What is the superintendent's role? To what extent are professional views sought out and considered in decision making?

Reflection   What decisions did the school board make? How will those decisions be communicated to teachers and the community? What impact will the decisions have on teachers' work lives? How will the decisions affect students and parents? If you were a teacher in this district, how would you react to the board's decisions? How do you feel about the impact local and national politics have on life in classrooms?

Becoming an Effective Teacher

Purpose   Chapter 2 discussed the characteristics of effective teachers. The purpose of this exercise is give you a feel for effective teaching.

Directions   Contact a teacher and make arrangements to present a lesson in his or her class. Many teachers host guest speakers on special topics; consider planning a lesson in your area of special expertise. Review the ideas in Chapter 2, and put together a lesson that you believe captures all we know about effective teaching. Present the lesson, and ask the teacher to observe you and give you feedback.

Reflection   What are your reactions to this experience? How long did it take you to plan your lesson? What were the strengths and weaknesses of your lesson? What feedback did the teacher give you? Did the students learn what you intended them to learn? What was expected and what was unexpected about the experience? How would you feel about doing this every day?

Indicators of Educational Philosophy

Purpose　　There are many ways to uncover one's educational philosophy. One of these is to observe teachers' practices and infer their philosophy from their actions. The purpose of this observation is to give you experience in seeing the links between philosophy and practice.

Directions　　Observe a class at the grade level and subject area you are interested in teaching. Describe the following:

Indicator	Description
Arrangement of desks	
Teacher v. student talk	
Grouping arrangements	
Learning centers	
Student movement	
Instructional materials	
Assessment materials	
Curriculum	

Reflection　　Review Chapter 3's description of the various philosophical schools. How would you classify the teacher you observed? What aspects of his or her practice lead you to this conclusion? Would you feel comfortable teaching this way? Why or why not?

Principals' Views on Teacher Supply and Demand

Purpose   An important factor in considering whether to pursue teaching as a career is the availability of jobs. The purpose of this exercise is to acquaint you with the job market.

Directions   Interview a principal in your area, either secondary or elementary, whichever you are more interested in. Use the following questions to guide your interview:

1. What's your impression of the number of teachers looking for jobs in this area versus the number of job openings? How does this break down for subject area and grade level? How long do you think this pattern will continue?

2. What's the mix of male versus female teachers? What can you tell me about the ethnic distribution of teachers?

3. How do the gender and ethnic breakdown for teachers compare to these proportions in the student population?

4. Do you think it's important for students to be taught by teachers who are like them? Why or why not?

Reflection   Pool and compare your results with those of other students in your class. What patterns and trends do you notice? In what ways does this inform your career decision?

Students Talk about the "Good Teacher"

Purpose   Beginning teachers often overlook the perspectives of their students. One of our goals is to assist you in becoming more sensitive to your prospective students. The purpose of this exercise is to alert you to the views of students.

Directions   Interview a child and an adolescent about the qualities they see as important to good teaching. Use the following questions as a guideline:

1. Is there one teacher from your past who was especially good? Why?

2. Is there one in particular who was especially bad? What made that teacher bad?

3. What do you think good teachers need to know and be able to do?

4. If you could create a perfect teacher, what would he or she be like?

Reflection   What are the differences and similarities between the responses of children and adolescents? Did other students in your class get comparable answers? How do your results compare with this textbook's research? In what ways has this exercise informed your own views about good teaching? How will you use this information?

One Teacher's Philosophy of Education

Purpose   How does your own philosophy stack up against the views of practicing teachers? How might other teachers' philosophies affect your own work life? The purpose of this interview is to probe the philosophy of a working teacher and to explore the impact of others' philosophical views on you.

Directions   Using the following questions as a guide, interview a teacher at the grade level or in the subject area you're interested in.

1. Describe how you organize your class. What types of instruction do you use? What do you think your students should learn in your class?

2. Why do you structure your class in this way?

3. What do you believe is the purpose of public schooling? Why do you believe this is important?

4. What do you believe teachers' responsibilities in their classes should be? Students' responsibilities? What do you believe the nature of the relationship between students and teachers should be?

Reflection   Compare and contrast your own emerging philosophy with this teacher's. Given your own orientation, would you find the teacher you interviewed enjoyable and easy to work with? Why or why not? If this teacher were in the classroom next door to yours, how might you foster a good working relationship with him or her? Do you anticipate strong agreement in philosophy with most teachers, strong disagreement, or something in between? How might you deal with colleagues who you disagreed with over basic philosophy?

Teachers and Their Classrooms

The images of habitation that people envision are expressions of their visions of themselves. Churches are expressions not only of man's vision of God but of man's vision of man. They represent not only conceptions of places for worshipping but also conceptions of the worshipper. The classrooms we envision for our children represent not only conceptions of spaces for learning but also our conceptions of the learner. And the dwellings, churches, and classrooms we create also create us. The classrooms we build for our children are not only places where lessons intended by the teacher are taught. These classrooms teach lessons of

their own; they tell the child[ren] who [they are] supposed to be (or at least who we think [they are]) and how [they are] supposed to learn. One classroom tells the child[ren they are] empty organisms learning through the operation of rewards and punishments at the command of the teacher; a second classroom tells [them they] are active organisms learning through the solution of problems that satisfy [their] needs; a third classroom tells the child[ren they] are social organisms learning through interaction with others; the fourth classroom tells the child[ren they] are a stimulus-seeking organism learning because [they] intrinsically have to. (Getzels, 1977, p. 16)

The acts of teaching and learning do not occur in isolation. Instead they occur in a social context. The classroom is the primary context that mediates what goes on between teachers and learners. And as Getzels described, we build our classrooms based on our beliefs and conceptions about children and how they learn. However, once classrooms have been created, they influence greatly the ways teachers teach and what children learn. What is particularly interesting about American classrooms, when viewed from a historical perspective, is the duality of constancy and change that has characterized them. Classrooms certainly have changed over time. In their physical appearance, today's classrooms bear little resemblance to the one-room school of 200 years ago. At the same time, many aspects of contemporary classroom life have remained remarkably the same. The introduction to Part II provides a brief history of American classrooms and how they and the instructional practices used in them have changed over time. Also, it describes certain constancies in classroom life over the past century.

COLONIAL CLASSROOMS

There is little information about the design and nature of classrooms in the colonial era. Laws were passed shortly after the first settlers arrived in America requiring towns to hire teachers so children could learn how to read the Bible and to write. The curriculum in these early reading and writing schools was a simple matter; students were taught the ABCs, the rudiments of reading and spelling, and some arithmetic. Students, particularly in the northern colonies, were also provided a large dose of religion.

Instruction in the colonies was rarely carried out in a setting constructed specifically for that purpose but instead occurred in a church or a home. This was particularly true of eighteenth century dame schools taught by housewives. It is reported that in the South, classes were sometimes held in a small building built near the plantation house. In both the North and South it was common for teachers to move from location to location and to "keep school" in whatever facility was available. Sometimes, however, actual schoolhouses were constructed. Samuel Griswold Goodrich provided the following description of his classroom and the methods used by teachers in eighteenth century rural Connecticut:

> The schoolhouse chimney was of stone, and the fireplace was six feet wide and four deep. The flue was so ample and so perpendicular that the rain, sleet, and snow fell directly to the hearth. In winter the battle for life with green sizzling fuel, which was brought in lengths and cut up by the scholars, was a stern one.... My teacher was "Aunt Delight," a maiden lady of fifty, short and bent, of sallow complexion and solemn aspect. We were seated upon benches made of slabs.... They had each four supports, consisting of straddling wooden legs set into auger holes.
>
> The children were called up one by one to Aunt Delight, who sat on a low chair, and required each, as a preliminary, "to make his manners," which consisted of a small, sudden nod. She then placed the spelling-book before the pupil, and with a pen-

knife pointed, one by one, to the letters of the alphabet, saying, "What's that?"

> Two years later I went to the winter school at the same place kept by Lewis Olmstead—a man who made a business of ploughing, mowing, carting manure, etc., in the summer, and of teaching school in the winter. He was a celebrity in ciphering, and Squire Seymour declared that he was the greatest "arithmeticker" in Fairfield County. There was not a grammar, a geography, or a history of any kind in the school. Reading, writing, and arithmetic were the only things taught, and these very indifferently—not wholly from the stupidity of the teacher, but because he had forty scholars, and the custom of the age required no more than he performed. (Edward & Ritchey, 1963)

Methods of instruction used by colonial teachers were not intended to develop children's initiative or creativity but instead to encourage conformity and self-restraint. Or, as one historian wrote, teaching methods of this era were "heavily inclined to the inculcation of obedience, in point of good manners, and dutiful behavior toward all" (cited in Katz, 1973, p. 30). The *New England Primer,* for instance, was built around the catechism. It was used by colonial teachers to teach children not only religious doctrine but also how to read and write (see Figure P2.1). Teachers drilled children in the *Primer* long before they knew the meaning of what they were saying. (Zukerman, 1970). Most often children were called one by one to be drilled in front of the teacher's desk similar to the scene described by Griswold.

NINETEENTH CENTURY ONE-CLASSROOM SCHOOLS

By the early part of the nineteenth century, public education was becoming established in both urban and rural areas. The classrooms and the instructional practices that emerged during this time were forerunners of those we know today. Most communities before the Civil War had a one-classroom school, similar to the ones from 1837 described here.

> They consisted, with few exceptions, of a single room, with a chimney at one end, on one side of which was the door and entrance.... There were generally no outhouses of any kind whatever. Even

Figure P2.1   **Examples of Text from New England Primer**

Let him learn these
and such like sentences by
Heart,
whereby he will be both
instructed in his
Duty
and encouraged in his
learning

In Adam's Fall
We finned all.

Thy Life to mend,
This Book attend.

The Cat doth play,
And after flay.

A Dog will bite
A Thief at Night.

An Eagle' flight
Is out of fight.

The idle Fool
Is whipt at School.

Source: *New England Primer* (Public Domain)

the wood lay exposed to the snow and rain. The furniture consisted of a chair, a table, a few benches, and writing desks; and the latter were usually attached to the walls, on three sides of the room. The benches consisted of slabs, with pegs for support; and they were without backs. The schoolroom was in general so small that the pupils were obliged to economize as much as possible in regard to space, at the risk of crowding and jostling each other, and a thousand other evils. Thus we say, was the general state of things. (Edwards & Ritchey, 1963, p. 225)

Books to assist teachers became more widely available during this era. Noah Webster's *Speller* first appeared in 1783. Murray's *Grammar* text was published in 1795. A text, *Elements of Geography,* was also published in 1795, followed by *A History of the United States,* which appeared in 1822. These texts served to standardize the curriculum for the first

time, and they helped poorly prepared teachers in one-room schools extend their instruction beyond the basics of reading, writing, and arithmetic.

As the nineteenth century progressed, educators began to pay more attention to teaching methods. Communities demanded good educations for their children but were reluctant to pay for it. Thus, a quest began to find teaching practices that could be used to educate large numbers of students as cheaply as possible. The Lancaster Plan, developed in England and India to teach orphan children, was introduced in the United States in the early nineteenth century. Its essential feature was to use older children, called monitors, to teach younger ones. The Lancaster Plan called for gathering many children in one room—a few hundred was considered manageable—sorting them into groups of similar abilities, and having the monitors work with the various groups. Detailed lesson plans were given to the older children to guide pupil recitation, and an elaborate system was developed to check attendance and to keep order. Discipline was strict.

Although Lancaster, himself, did not believe in using "the rod," he developed an elaborate system of punishment for students who misbehaved, including "suspending them from the roof in baskets or leaving them tied up in a blanket in the schoolroom overnight so they could reflect on their misdeeds" (Edwards & Ritchey, 1963, pp. 242–243). Although the Lancaster Plan was never widely adopted, many particular features of it were and can be observed today in classrooms with such labels as *peer tutoring, ability grouping,* and *teacher-proof materials.*

In the early nineteenth century, educators such as Horace Mann and Henry Barnard visited Europe to study teaching practices in England and Germany. Educational ideas they brought back included considering education a science, systematic teaching, and more rigorous teacher preparation. These ideas formed the intellectual basis for the evolution of classrooms and teaching practices that dominate instruction to the present day.

CLASSROOMS FROM THE LATE NINETEENTH CENTURY TO THE PRESENT

In the 1970s, J. W. Getzel, a prominent educator at the University of Chicago, described classrooms in four different schools, all of which he observed from his university office.

> In one building dating from the turn of the century, the spaces called classrooms are rectangular in shape, the pupils' chairs are firmly bolted to the floor in straight rows, and the teacher's desk is front and center. In the second building, dating from the 1930s, the classrooms are square, the pupils' chairs are movable into various patterns around the room, and the teacher's desk is out of the way in a corner. In the third building, dating from the 1950s, the classrooms are also square, but the pupils' movable desks are now trapezoidal in shape, so that when they are placed next to each other they make a circle, and the teacher's desk has vanished! In the fourth building, there is a classroom, constructed a year or so ago, that is four times the size of the ordinary classroom. It has no teacher's or pupils' desks at all but is filled instead with odds and ends, from fish bowls and birds' nests to drawing boards and Cuisinare rods. If one were not told it was a

classroom, this space might be mistaken for an overgrown playroom or a warehouse full of children's paraphernalia. (Getzel, 1977, p. 7)

Getzel goes on to describe how the succession of rectangular, square, circular, and open classrooms was not accidental but, instead, reflected transformations in architecture and changing conceptions of the child as a learner and of the learning process. We use these changing views to describe classrooms and instructional practices used by teachers between 1890 and the present.

Teacher-Centered Instruction at the Turn of the Century

Using historical photographs of teachers and students in their classrooms, reports from educators and journalists who visited classrooms, and descriptions of over 1,200 classrooms between 1890 and 1980, Larry Cuban (1984) summarized classrooms and teaching practices during the twentieth century.[1] His chronicle shows clearly how many of the reforms of the past century, although embraced by educational leaders of the time, have failed to become an enduring part of classroom life. This section looks at efforts to reform classrooms since 1890 and describes why it has been so difficult to get teachers to change the ways they teach.

By 1890, the reforms of the common school movement, which had begun a half-century earlier, had spread throughout most parts of the United States. Most communities supported a system of public education, and nearly every state had laws requiring children to attend school until the age of 14 or 16. Many of the educational practices familiar to us today had been firmly established by that time. The age-grade organizational structure, dividing the day into periods, and giving credits for time spent on particular subjects (called Carnegie units) had been widely implemented. Schools in most parts of the country ran for 9 months, from September until June. Except in instances in which shortages existed, society expected teachers—by this time mainly women—to have formal training, and the practice of giving each teacher her own classroom had become the norm. Curriculum had been standardized; homework and report cards as we know them today had become commonplace.

In 1890, the classroom itself was rectangular in shape with fixed straight rows of chairs facing the

---

[1]Much of the information we provide in this section draws from the excellent study done by L. Cuban, *How Teachers Taught: Constancy and Change in American Classrooms, 1890–1980* (New York: Longman, 1984).

teacher's desk and a chalkboard. Many communities had completely institutionalized and standardized this arrangement. In New York City, for instance, the district's policy manual in the late nineteenth century specified 48 fixed desks for Grades 1 through 4, 45 fixed desks for Grades 5 and 6, and 40 permanent desks for Grades 7 and 8. (Cuban, 1984)

This physical arrangement reflected nineteenth century traditions of constructing rectangular buildings and met the physical requirements of housing large numbers of students (30 to 50) in a space conducive to inexpensive lighting and heating. More important, the rectangular fixed-seat classroom reflected the prevailing views of children and the learning process at the turn of the century. These views conceived of children as "empty organisms" responding to environmental stimuli in order to maximize rewards and to minimize pain and punishment. People believed that the stimulus (what was to be learned) and the response (what students did) should be determined solely by the teacher. Putting the teacher at the front of a rectangular classroom, sometimes on a platform, maximized her ability to gain pupil attention and emphasized her authority. The straight rows told the students "to look ahead and ignore everything except the teacher" (Getzel, 1977, p. 8).

Instructional practices did not differ significantly in urban and rural classrooms, nor were many differences found between elementary and secondary classrooms. Barbara Finkelstein (1970) studied over 1,000 classrooms of that era. She concluded that elementary students spent most of their time reciting passages from textbooks, working on assignments at their desks, or listening to their teachers talk. Finkelstein noted that teachers told students:

> when they should sit, when they should stand, when they should hang their coats, [and] when they should turn their heads.... Students often entered and exited the room, rose and sat, wrote and spoke as one.... Teachers assigned lessons, asked questions and created standards of achievement designed to compel students to assimilate knowledge and practice skills in a particular fashion. It was a fashion dictated by the textbooks usually ... and often with dogmatic determination. (Cuban, 1984, p. 19)

Similar practices were observed in William Chatfield's U.S. history classroom in 1900:

> The general method has been to first furnish the pupils with an outline of the work to be covered and to assign lessons from the text in conformity with this, and then to lead them by conversation to discover the reasons and think out the results.

A part of the time each week is given to oral instruction and at the end of the week a written exercise is required of each pupil. In this he attempts to show what he has gathered from the oral work, his reading and the text book.

> Maps and pictures are freely used to illustrate the work, the former being drawn upon the blackboard and copied by the pupil. Upon these maps are indicated the movements of the opposing forces; and brief statements are made of events which have made certain places and localities noted. (Cuban, 1984, p. 17)

Student-Centered Instruction and the Progressive Era

During the early part of the twentieth century, conceptions of learners and the learning process began to change. Psychologists challenged the prevailing empty organism view and replaced it with one that viewed children as inherently active and seeking solutions to real problems. A teacher's role, accordingly, was to nurture and guide the inquiry process, which led to a pedagogy known as *project method,* or inquiry-based teaching (Kirkpatrick, 1918). This new perception of students and pedagogy came under the influence of *progressive education.* In general terms, the progressive movement was a reaction against teacher-centered, textbook-oriented methods, and it reflected changing conceptions about the role of a child in the learning process. Progressive educators believed that children's first-hand experiences should be the focus of the curriculum, and that self-expression rather than restraint should be encouraged. A teacher's role was as a facilitator and guide rather than a lecturer or drill master. Chapters 4 and 6 describe this perspective in more detail.

John Dewey was progressive education's most famous philosopher and spokesperson. In *Democracy and Education,* Dewey (1916) presented a view of education in which the school mirrored the larger society and classrooms served as laboratories for real-life problem solving. Dewey's pedagogy encouraged teachers to engage students in problem-oriented projects and to help them inquire into the important social and intellectual problems of the day. In addition to being child centered, education should be purposeful rather than abstract. Such education, according to Dewey, is best accomplished through "learning by doing," which translates into children's working in small groups on projects of their own interest and choosing.

Fixed desks with the teacher at the front of the room were not appropriate for the inquiry-oriented instruction and project methods progressive educators favored. The arrangement did not permit students to work together on projects or allow teachers to move easily around the room. Progressives preferred a square classroom with movable pupil desks, which allowed learners to be the focus of attention and the center of the learning process. The pupil-centered classroom moved the teacher's desk to the side and eliminated the fixed straight rows of student chairs.

In the late 1930s and 1940s, the emerging fields of social psychology and group dynamics added other dimensions to educators' perceptions of children and how they learn. In addition to supporting a child-centered curriculum, social psychologists believed children learn through social interactions with others. In classrooms this meant learning from teachers and peers. Such learning required classrooms with positive interpersonal and group processes, conditions best accomplished with a circular arrangement of desks and chairs, so that everyone could face one another.

Thus, during the period between 1900 and World War II, child-centered classrooms and small-group methods of instruction became accepted practice among educational leaders, if not by most teachers. These classrooms and methods can be summarized as a set of conditions and practices in which:

- Classrooms are arranged in a manner that permitted students to work together or separately, in small groups or in individual work space; no dominant pattern exists, and much movement of desks, tables, and chairs occurs as a result of shifting activities.

- Student talk is encouraged and often exceeds the amount of teacher talk.

- Most instruction occurs either individually, in small (2 to 6 students) or medium-sized (7 to 12 students) groups rather than as whole-class activities.

- Students help choose and organize the content to be learned.

- Teachers permit students to determine, partially or wholly, classroom rules, rewards, and penalties and how they are enforced.

- Varied instructional materials are available so that students can use them independently or in small groups, e.g., interest centers, teaching stations, and activity centers.

- Use of these materials is either scheduled by the teacher or determined by students for at least half the academic time available.

Although the tenets of child-centered pedagogy were widely embraced by the educational establishment of the day, including most teacher educators in colleges and universities, they were enacted in very few classrooms. For reasons that will be explored later, most teachers did not adopt child-centered practices and continued in the didactic, teacher-centered mode prevalent at the turn of the century.

In the early 1940s and following World War II, progressive, child-centered education came under severe attack and was blamed for many of the ills confronting the larger society at that time. Critics argued that student-centered pedagogy made students "soft" and that classroom teachers serving as "facilitators" were unable to discipline students. They saw the emphasis on real-life problems stemming from the interests of children as anti-intellectual and nonacademic. Thus, in the 1940s and early 1950s, progressive education declined and traditional subject-centered curricula and teacher-centered pedagogy reemerged. By 1955, the Progressive Education Association, which was founded in 1919, had vanished.

Inquiry-Oriented Teaching and Open Education

The Soviet Union launched Sputnik, the first space satellite, in 1957. Almost immediately, citizens blamed the educational system for the United States' not being first in space. Some critics argued that the schools had not prepared enough scientists, engineers, or technicians. Other critics said Americans were behind the Russians because schools had neglected traditional academic subjects or taught them poorly. This criticism precipitated passage of the National Defense Education Act (NDEA) in 1958, the first effort to provide general rather than single-purpose federal aid to education. The NDEA provided resources for research and curriculum-development projects in most disciplines. From these research and development projects came new curricula in mathematics, the sciences, history, the social sciences, and foreign languages.

Chapters 7 and 8 and Part III describe the curriculum reforms of the 1950s and 1960s in more detail. Here the focus remains on classrooms and teaching methods. What is interesting about this reform, however, is that although it was a response to criticism leveled at progressive education, it nevertheless relied on the student-centered, inquiry-based teaching methods developed during the progressive era. The new math, science, and social studies curricula shifted primary focus from teacher-centered activities for the transmission of existing knowledge to student-centered activities designed to teach the *processes* of scientific inquiry. The new curricula expected students to assume responsibility for their own learning by participation in problem-solving activities. Laboratory manuals and primary source materials replaced textbooks. Teachers were encouraged to facilitate and to ask questions rather than to lecture and to drill.

Discovery learning, developed by Harvard psychologist Jerome Bruner, was one of the primary teaching models associated with post-Sputnik reform efforts. **Discovery learning** emphasized the importance of the inquiry processes through which students *discover* key ideas rather than memorize long lists of factual information. Bruner believed teaching students to think was the ultimate goal of education and that actively involving students in the learning process accomplished that. True learning, according to Bruner, was the result of personal discovery, and it was the teacher's job to assist the discovery process.

The concept of informal or **open education** was also introduced in the United States during the 1960s and early 1970s. Open educators' goal was to create a more informal classroom in which children were free to exercise their imagination and creativity. In the United States, open education became popular following the publication of *Summerhill* by A. S. Neill (1962). *Summerhill* described an open school in England that gave students complete freedom to study what they wanted and to run the school as they saw fit. Adult direction was kept to a minimum. Open-classroom reformers attacked teacher-centered, textbook-oriented teaching methods in much the same way that progressives had criticized autocratic teaching methods a half-century earlier.

Open education was not just a restatement of progressive education, however. It reflected changing conceptions of learners and the learning process as well. The open-classroom advocates of the 1970s, like today's advocates of constructivist-oriented classrooms, embraced cognitive theories of learning. Advocates believed that children have an intrinsic motivation to learn that can best be satisfied through exploration and problem solving. Given this starting point, teachers facilitate learning best when they encourage students to take responsibility for their own learning and to construct meaning from their own experiences with ideas and the environment.

Roland Barth described the classroom space required to support open classrooms and informal teaching methods in 1975:

The teacher in the open classroom organizes his classroom not to produce optimal conditions for transmission of knowledge but to extend the range of possibilities children can explore. Children's desks are often removed from the room, and only chairs and tables are left. . . . Space within the classroom is divided, often by movable screens or furniture, into an "interest area" . . . While in the traditional classroom the child learns at his desk, in the open classroom the locus of learning is where something of particular interest to the child happens to be. (Getzel, 1977, p. 15)

The intellectual links between progressive reform in the early part of the twentieth century and discovery learning and open education at mid-century are clear. All three encouraged learners' active involvement, which, in turn, necessitated teacher-facilitators of student discovery rather than transmitters of a predetermined curriculum. Informal and flexible classroom space enhanced such facilitation.

WHERE ARE WE TODAY?

The inquiry-oriented curriculum and the open-education reforms of the post-Sputnik era were short lived as the progressive reforms had been earlier in the century. Classroom teachers ignored most parts of the new curricula, and more important, by the 1970s, parents and other citizens were calling for schools to get "back to the basics." The idea of moving back to traditional education is particularly interesting in view of the enlightened conceptions that grew between 1890 and 1980 of the learner and learning, including the changes in classroom architecture. Despite intellectual and architectural innovations, most teaching practices and use of classroom space seem to favor more traditional modes, as reported by Getzel (1977):

The movable chairs [had been] placed in straight rows and the trapezoidal desks [were] lined up behind one another rather than joined in the circle for which they were designed. In one renovated classroom I visited, the movable chairs were placed exactly on the bolt marks left by the fixed chairs they had supplanted. (p. 8)

Larry Cuban (1984) argued that the core of progressive practices that started to appear at the turn of the century and were later recycled through the post-Sputnik reforms never reached a majority of elementary or high school classrooms. Where these practices appeared, they appeared as hybrid versions. For example, a teacher might use small-group teaching methods once in a while, but would not give students autonomy in deciding what their groups should study. How can it be that classrooms and teaching practices have remained virtually the same for most of a century, when so many other aspects of our society have changed significantly? Why has changing instructional methods been so hard to accomplish? Cuban (1984) and others (Arends, 1991; Sharan & Sharan, 1991) have provided several hypotheses worth exploring.

Schooling as Social Control

Schools reflect the larger social and economic order of their parent society. In Western cultures, schools are assigned the function of sorting students for various economic and social roles (Spring, 1996). This sorting function is facilitated by certain instructional practices and is restrained by others. For example, teacher-centered practices, such as teaching the whole class, accepting a standardized curriculum, grouping according to ability levels, using norm-referenced tests, and grading on a curve all aid the school's sorting function and prepare students to live in a certain kind of world—one that is standardized, competitive, and socially stratified. A standard curriculum teaches acceptance of uniformity. Teaching to the whole class and grading on a curve encourage students to be competitive. And grouping by ability levels influences students' achievement expectations. These practices allow teachers to compare and judge students. Student-centered practices, on the other hand, which allow the curriculum to grow out of the interests of children and encourage each child to pursue his or her own learning goals, provide few means for teachers to compare or sort students according to particular social and economic roles.

Organizational Structures Support Teacher-Centered Instruction

Compulsory attendance, age-graded classrooms, standardized curricula, and the Carnegie unit are all organizational structures that were thoroughly institutionalized by the late nineteenth century. Their purpose was to make schools more orderly and to provide inexpensive education for large numbers of students. Over a period of time, teaching practices most compatible with these structures were adopted. Teacher-centered methods allowed large amounts of required curriculum material to be "cov-ered" in the least amount of time. They helped teachers monitor student behavior and manage large groups of students with a minimum amount of disruptions. Student-centered practices, on the other hand, required more flexibility and energy from teachers. Managing and facilitating varied tasks presented more ambiguity and risk. Student-centered instruction and open classrooms are more complex, are messier, and simply take more work. Furthermore, their benefits can never be clearly demonstrated as long as school goals and evaluation remain focused on objective, norm-referenced test scores keyed to a standardized curriculum.

The Culture of Teaching

A third hypothesis about why it is so hard to change classroom instructional practices involves teacher culture, which in most schools is characterized by two very strong norms: the autonomy norm and the hands-off norm. The **autonomy norm** permits teachers to do almost anything they want once they are inside their classrooms; the **hands-off norm** makes it unacceptable for teachers to ask for or provide professional advice to their colleagues. Both characteristics are particularly evident in the two most important aspects of teachers' work—classroom management and pedagogy. Together these norms tend to discourage collegial interaction and teachers' active participation in schoolwide decisions. They make it difficult for teachers to learn from one another as practitioners do in other professions and, in turn, restrain efforts at reform, particularly reform that requires learning how to teach in different ways. Chapters 7 and 12 explore aspects of the culture of teaching in more detail.

Teacher Characteristics

Another hypothesis argues that teachers as a group possess certain characteristics that make them resistant to change. Recently, a team of researchers (AACTE, 1990) asked students in over 90 colleges and universities who were preparing to teach why they chose the schools they were attending, where they wanted to teach after graduation, and what kind of students they wanted to work with. An overwhelming percentage reported that they chose their college or university because of its proximity to their home, and that they planned to teach close to their homes. A large majority also said that they wanted to teach normal, middle-income students and had little interest in teaching students with disabilities or in working with culturally diverse students. Could it be that this type of "culturally insulated" individual is satisfied with the way schools are and is unprepared to challenge the existing culture of schools and teachers?

We face a particularly puzzling situation. On the one hand, it appears that for almost one hundred years the leaders of the educational establishment have felt that classrooms and teaching methods should be child-centered. On the other hand, the average teacher has not embraced these practices. Didactic, teacher-centered pedagogy still persists, while reform efforts produce only piecemeal change.

What hypotheses do you have about this situation? Do you think your generation of teachers will embrace student-centered teaching or will tomorrow's teachers teach in the same ways they were taught? Can it be that the educational establishment is wrong to embrace student-centered methods? Perhaps teacher-centered methods work best in classrooms with lots of students. Will the spirit of progressive classrooms, discovery learning, and student-centered pedagogy soon be realized, or will it continue to be a part of *future* reform agendas?

CHAPTER 4

Classrooms

Mr. Sperry paused and surveyed the class. Seventh period was never easy. Most of his eighth graders were not paying attention; they were staring out the window, passing notes back and forth, and quietly chatting when his back was turned. Sperry had just asked a question about the Reconstruction period, and he saw the same hands go up. The ones who wanted the good grade. He'd like to separate the noisy ones, but where would he put them? Was it time to call Yolanda's parents again? She was getting more withdrawn. With 35 students, all different from each other, how do you get them all engaged? Not much time left in the period; was it today that he had bus duty, or tomorrow?

Yolanda stared out the window. What had Sperry just asked? Oh yes, what does Reconstruction mean. She knew the answer, but why bother to raise her hand? He never called on her anyway. It was so distracting the way so many other students were passing notes and talking. She wished she could sit closer to the teacher. Patti passed her a note about what Rob had said during lunch, so she scribbled a hurried reply the next time Sperry turned to write on the board.

If you are like others contemplating a teaching career, you bring with you strong, often unconscious, expectations about what teaching is like and what it is like to work in a classroom. However, seeing classrooms through the eyes of a teacher is very different from seeing them through the eyes of a student. The experience of the classroom for Yolanda, in the opening vignette, is almost the opposite of what it is for Sperry. Understanding what the classroom looks like and feels like from a teacher's perspective is critical to making an informed decision about teaching as a career. This chapter gives you the opportunity to compare your own expectations about teaching, framed from your own personal experiences as a student and from the popular media, to the realities of classrooms.

Expectations
Expectations and Student Learning
Expectations Shape Perceptions
Your Expectations
Research on Beginning Teachers' Expectations

Classroom Similarities
Life in Classrooms
A Place Called School
Social Psychology of Classrooms
Stage 1: Facilitating Psychological Membership
Stage 2: Establishing Rules and Routines
Stage 3: Establishing Shared Influence
Stage 4: Pursuing Academic Goals
Stage 5: Transition and Closure
Classroom Properties
Multidimensionality
Simultaneity
Immediacy
Unpredictability

History
Publicness
Performance-for-Grade Exchange
Ambiguity and Risk in Teacher Preparation

Classroom Differences
Social Class Differences
Grade Level and Subject Matter Differences
Teachers' Conceptions of Subject Matter
Alternative Classrooms
Classrooms versus Other Workplaces
Solitary versus Group Work
Mental Work versus Technology
Organization
Classrooms in Other Cultures

Putting It All Together

Summary

Readings for the Professional

EXPECTATIONS

Expectations exert powerful emotional effects. This is vividly illustrated by *culture shock,* the emotional reaction that first-time travelers to foreign countries experience as they encounter strange behavior patterns that violate their own cultural norms. For example, many Americans are very time-conscious, and when they travel to places like the Mediterranean or Latin America, they often become very uncomfortable with the local people's slower pace and lack of concern about punctuality. Likewise, if your first teaching job turns out to be very different from what you expected, you will experience a kind of work-related culture shock, not unlike that of travelers to foreign countries. Bringing your expectations into closer alignment with how teaching really is will minimize these negative emotional experiences.

Expectations and Student Learning

Nearly all teachers hold expectations about their students, and these expectations can have a powerful effect on their students' learning, as we discussed in Chapter 2. For example, many beginning teachers naively assume that their love of the subjects they teach will infect their students. However, their students often disappoint them in this regard, and if instruction has been predicated on students' love of subject, then learning will undoubtably suffer.

Expectations can affect learning in other ways, too. In one case, Goldenberg (1989) described a first-grade girl, Sylvia, and how her teacher's expectations strongly influenced her learning:

> Sylvia began first grade with every indication of becoming a strong reader, including high reading readiness scores, and the teacher predicted that Sylvia would learn to read rapidly. However, Sylvia began to have serious difficulties early on; she fell farther behind, and made little progress. The teacher failed to revise her early high estimation of Sylvia's aptitude, expecting her difficulties would be temporary and would clear themselves up, and thus did not intervene. By the end of the year, Sylvia was one of the poorest readers in the class. If her teacher had adjusted her expectations and instruction to fit Sylvia's real performance, rather than her predicted performance, Sylvia could have developed into a good reader. (p. 19)

Expectations Shape Perception

Expectations also influence our perceptions and interpretations of events. For example, we interpret the actions of politicians we like very differently from those we do not like. Think back to the various scandals that have afflicted U.S. presidents in recent decades. What are your feelings about Bill Clinton, and how have those feelings influenced your interpretation of the Whitewater affair? If you expected honesty and integrity from the president, you likely dismissed the news of scandal as scurrilous partisanship. If you expected ignoble behavior, you likely welcomed the charges as confirming your already low opinion.

We interpret any new information in ways consistent with our previous beliefs, whether about politics or teaching. If you hold certain beliefs about classrooms, these will color how and what you learn in your teacher-education program. Just as in evaluating news of presidential scandal, you attend to, value, and believe information that is consistent with your beliefs about teaching. Conversely, you tend to repudiate or ignore information that is inconsistent with your beliefs, whether those beliefs are accurate or not. Figure 4.1 shows the relationship between beginning teacher expectations and learning.

For example, many secondary teacher candidates strongly identify with their discipline, thinking of themselves as biologists, say, more than as biology teachers. This leads them to value their own discipline over others, whether these have a bearing on teaching or not. They may disregard, for instance, information about how people learn, clearly important knowledge for teachers, because they do not think educational psychology is as important as biology. Unfortunately, lack of understanding about learning processes will negatively affect their effectiveness in teaching biology.

Obviously, accurate expectations are very important. Faulty expectations can lead, at best, to emotional discomfort and, at worst, to lost opportunities to learn, both for you and your future students. Let's examine, then, your own expectations and those of other beginning teachers who have been the subject of careful research. Once revealed, these two sets of expectations can be evaluated and, if need be, adjusted to the realities of teaching.

Your Expectations

There are at least a couple of ways to uncover expectations. One is to review one's own memories of classrooms, and another is to examine how classrooms are portrayed in books, movies, and television. Comparing these images can help create a full picture of one's assumptions and beliefs, rendering them accessible to reflection and analysis.

Take a moment now to visualize a specific classroom from your own childhood or adolescence, and jot down your images.

- What do you see?
- What is the teacher doing?
- What are you doing?
- What are other students doing?
- How is the physical space arranged?
- What is your overall impression of the classroom?

Here is what one of the authors of this text came up with for this exercise:

> I am 9 years old. The classroom is a large, square room, high-ceilinged, with big windows along one wall. I can see the asphalt playground outside. No one is out playing, because it isn't recess. The teacher sits at the front of the room, and the students are working individually at their desks. I am writing and illustrating a report on tuna following a field trip to the harbor. I have to draw the different varieties of tuna exactly right or I won't get a good grade. Students who have problems go up to the front of the room to get help from our teacher, Mrs. Haggarty, an older lady whom we all think is very mean. The desks are placed in rows, and we're all supposed to be working quietly by ourselves. Some students are side-talking; the ones who won't stop are banished to the cloak room.

Let's now look at an example from popular culture. In one popular film from the 1980s, *Ferris Bueller's Day Off*, the high school social studies teacher stands at the front of the class by the chalkboard. He drones on and on without expression, reciting events and dates in a monotone. He asks a question, "When did the Civil War end?" He pauses and he waits. No one responds. He asks nasally, "Anyone...? Anyone...?" Finally he answers himself, "1865," and moves on to the next question, which will also be ignored. Students sit passively in various slouch postures, at desks arranged in rows, putting more thought into how to avoid academics than in mastering the content.

In these examples, the classroom is a quiet place. The only person who talks is the teacher. If students are talking, it is usually off-task remarks. Students perceive the work as boring, and consequently, they feel justified in tuning the lesson out. When they do comply, it is only because the teacher controls important rewards and punishments. Students sit at desks arranged in orderly rows listening to the teacher or working by themselves. The teachers pass along information that students are somehow expected to absorb. Time is tightly scheduled, with specific times set aside for specific activities. How

Figure 4.1 **Expectations about Teaching Influence Professional Learning**

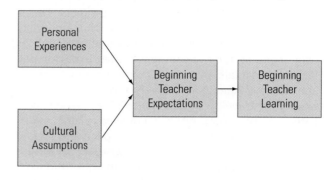

do these impressions compare with your own memories?

Research on Beginning Teachers' Expectations

Another way to explore the expectations of beginning teachers is to delve into research on the topic. Weinstein (1989) studied the expectations that students bring with them to their teacher education programs. Building on previous research in teacher socialization, Weinstein surveyed students in educational foundations classes about their beliefs concerning good teaching. She also asked them to rate how successful they thought they would be as student teachers and first-year teachers. She found that they shared a very rosy outlook, which she dubbed an *optimistic bias*. A whopping 75 percent of elementary and 80 percent of secondary teacher education students rated themselves slightly to much above average in teaching ability. These findings suggest that prospective teachers may be so optimistic about their natural teaching abilities that they underestimate the importance of professional training.

This has been confirmed by other scholars who have observed similar optimism in teacher candidates. Crow (1987) found that beginning secondary teachers felt very confident about teaching, that they did not think they had much to learn from their teacher education programs, and that they assumed they would learn what they needed on the job. These students had difficulty seeing the connection between their liberal arts and professional coursework and the knowledge they would need in order to be effective teachers.

Overconfidence is not unique to beginning teachers. In fact, it appears to be a general human characteristic. Baumeister, Heatherton, and Tice (1993), in a study on the negative consequences of high self-esteem, noted:

People tend to overestimate their abilities and good qualities, their capacity to control their outcomes, and the likelihood that good things will happen to them. . . . Recent studies suggest that self-prediction processes suffer from pervasive overconfidence. . . . These inflated self-views may help people feel better about themselves and maintain the positive affective states associated with healthy adjustment . . . . but they increase the risk of making overly ambitious decisions that lead into situations where the person is likely to fail. (p. 142)

There appear to be other similarities in beginning teachers' expectations and assumptions about classroom life. For example, most beginners think teaching primarily involves telling students what they know and then testing them on that information (Ball, 1988). They see the learner's job as simply memorizing and practicing. When students have difficulty with schoolwork, especially minority or low-income students, novices tend to blame the trouble on students' low ability, lack of motivation, or inadequate support from home. They rarely look for factors under the teacher's control that might improve student achievement (Brousseau & Freeman, 1989; Freeman & Kalaian, 1989). Most beginners headed for elementary teaching value the affective over the intellectual; that is, they believe that building students' self-esteem and other "warm fuzzies" take precedence over building students' academic achievements (Book, Byers, & Freeman, 1983). In contrast, many secondary teacher candidates tend to place much more emphasis on academics, overlooking affective factors important to learning (Crow, 1987).

Personal memories of classroom life, images from popular culture, and research on beginning teachers' expectations all converge on a similar set of assumptions about classrooms that are shared by most Americans, even by teachers. At the outset of their careers, most teachers assume that classrooms are rather tame and boring, and that teaching is a fairly simple, straightforward job. Many also assume that they will somehow be different and better than previous generations of teachers, that they will be more interesting, more caring, more effective, and more appreciated by their students. Moreover, many beginning teachers also think that they already possess the knowledge and skills needed to accomplish all this.

Are these your expectations? Are they realistic? These are critical questions, because realistic expectations will not only aid your decision about whether to pursue teaching as a career but will influence how you prepare for such a career. As you read the rest of

this chapter, ask yourself: What really are my beliefs about the nature of teaching and of classroom life? Are they consistent with the information in this chapter? Should I revise my beliefs or not? If so, in what way? What are the consequences of these decisions for my own learning and for the learning of my future students?

CLASSROOM SIMILARITIES

A number of investigators have systematically explored life in classrooms. Their research provides a broader and more accurate portrayal of classrooms than could possibly be created by any one individual, no matter how broad their personal experience might be. Examined here are studies conducted by Philip Jackson, John Goodlad, Walter Doyle, and others who have contributed to our knowledge about life in classrooms.

Life in Classrooms

One of the classic studies in this area was conducted by Phillip Jackson (Jackson, 1968). Jackson analyzed life in classrooms from the perspective of both the teacher and the student. A key insight concerned the crowded nature of classrooms and how this crowding was experienced differently by teachers and students. From a student's point of view school means waiting—waiting in line for a drink of water, waiting for the teacher to call on you, waiting for your assignment to be checked and handed back. Classroom life for students means delay and deferred gratification, weathering long periods of quiescence during which they put their own needs on hold.

The picture from the teacher's perspective is quite the reverse. The teacher sees 25 thirsty students, one drinking fountain, and a crowd control situation to be managed. The teacher sees 25 hands raised and must instantly decide whom to call on (who has talked the most? who is likely to give a good answer? how long to wait for students to respond before the momentum of the class slows?). The teacher sees 25 assignments that need checking and thoughtful feedback and must be recorded in her gradebook, at least an hour's work she must somehow manage in the 25 minutes remaining in her prep period.

Classroom life for teachers, then, is a whirlwind of activity, with every moment filled with important decisions to make and immediate actions to take. Jackson (1968) estimated that a typical elementary teacher averages at least 300 interactions with students daily and that secondary teachers log an even greater number. In summing up what ⸑lementary classrooms are like, he said:

> The job of managing the activities of 25 or 30 children for 5 or 6 hours a day, 5 days a week, 40 weeks a year, is quite a bit different from what an abstract consideration of the learning process might lead us to believe. In the small but crowded world of the classroom, events come and go with an astonishing rapidity. . . . The personal qualities enabling teachers to withstand the demands of classroom life have never been adequately described. But among those qualities is surely the ability to tolerate the enormous amount of ambiguity, unpredictability, and occasional chaos created each hour by 25 or 30 not-so-willing learners. (p. 149)

The picture for secondary classrooms is much the same, if not exacerbated, because of the sheer number of students teachers see every day.

A Place Called School

Several years after *Life in Classrooms* was published, John Goodlad (1984) released the findings of his extensive research on schools in a book entitled *A Place Called School.* Goodlad's research team visited elementary, junior high, and senior high schools in every region of the United States, 38 schools in all. The selected schools varied in their size, the income and ethnicity of families whose children attended, the type of neighborhood (urban, suburban, rural), and other demographic factors. In short, Goodlad's team closely examined a representative cross-section of American schools. The team observed classrooms, collected survey data from many sources, including students, and interviewed teachers and parents. Because of the meticulous way the schools were selected and the thoroughness with which the data were collected, we can be very confident that Goodlad's findings apply to most American schools.

Here's how Goodlad described one day during the research project:

> I stood in the open doorway of a classroom in one of the junior high schools we studied. It was one of a series of classes located side by side down a long hallway. The day was a warm one and the doors of three of the classrooms were open. Inside each, the teacher sat at a desk, watching the class or reading. The students sat at table-type desks arranged in rows. Most were writing, a few were stretching, and the remainder were looking contemplatively or blankly into space. In one of the two other rooms with closed doors, the students were watching a film. . . . In the other, the teacher was putting an algebraic equation on the chalkboard and explaining its components to the class. In visits to several other academic classes that day, I witnessed no marked variations on these pedagogical procedures and student activities. (p. 93)

Does this description sound familiar? According to Goodlad's research, the range of pedagogical practices across the country is very narrow, especially at the secondary level. From the 1,000-plus classrooms his group studied in depth, it appears that teachers primarily speak to their students as a whole group and that most instruction is very teacher centered. Teachers are highly autonomous, making instructional and curricular decisions, selecting materials, and so on, without much input from colleagues, students, parents, or others. Teachers spend most of their time front and center, presenting information to students, monitoring student seat work, and giving tests. Students work alone and achieve alone; small-group work is rare. Students experience few field trips, audio-visual materials, guest speakers, or hands-on activities of any kind, except in physical education, the arts, and vocational education. Students frequently report that they neither understand their assignments nor have enough time to complete them. The emotional atmosphere of classrooms is mostly neutral, neither joy nor anger are evident. Surprisingly, despite this picture of classroom *anomie,* students and parents appear to be fairly content with schools. Schmuck and Schmuck (1990) later confirmed most of these findings in a broad study of rural schools.

Goodlad also noted how teachers and students interacted in the classroom. These communication patterns are termed **discourse patterns.** Despite 100 years of reform reports calling for more student involvement and discussion, Goodlad found that teachers still dominate classroom talk. That certainly confirms one of the public's assumptions about schools. Teachers not only talk the most, they determine which students will have the floor, and the rules students must follow to gain the floor. Classroom discourse is important, because communication, either oral or written, is the medium through which student learning occurs. As you will see in Chapter 5, although classrooms look much the same, the students who occupy these classrooms do not. Students' linguistic, cultural, and socioeconomic diversity strongly influences the quality of communication in classrooms and, thus, exert powerful effects on learning. Before going on, read the accompanying Issue Box, which examines a very different kind of classroom.

Social Psychology of Classrooms

All classrooms are social places. Wherever groups of people congregate, social psychological forces operate. Social psychologists have examined the process of group development in classrooms. Teachers who attend to this research will be more likely to capitalize on students' readiness to learn. Sometimes, though, this can necessitate actions that at first glance may seem counterproductive. Read and evaluate the following vignette about how one elementary teacher launched the first day of school:

> On the first day of school, the teacher, Mrs. Forero, stayed near the door. As the students entered the room, she greeted each one individually. She called them by name or asked their names, and she looked each one directly in the eyes as she greeted him/her. She asked each student about a family member, a pet, or some personal matter. She introduced students to each other, saying, "Tim, do you know Javier? Javier, this is Tim. Please go over to the desks and see if you can find the one with your name taped to it. If you see someone having a hard time finding the right desk, you can help. Then sit in your seat. We have a lot to do today." She kept an eye on the students as they looked for the desks with their names on them. If a student was having difficulty, she said, for example, "Tim, William is having a hard time finding his desk. Can you find his name?" . . .
>
> When everyone was in his/her seat, Forero started a whole-class session by asking the students to fold their hands and look directly in her eyes. Then she said, "We've got to get to know each other. You can call me Janet. I think that Forero is a hard name to say". . . . Then she walked around the group and mentioned each student's name and something the student had said to her upon entering the room. "Michael said he was sorry summer was over. Michael, what was the reason?" Michael responded, "I want to go to the lake to swim some more." Then she put her hand on one student's shoulder and asked the group who knew that student's name. She listened to callouts; after several people had said the name, she asked a student who had not volunteered. When possible, she made connections between what was of interest to one student and what was of interest to another student, mentioning both students' names. (Putnam & Burke, 1992, p. 122)

Does the heavy emphasis placed on helping the children get to know each other surprise you? Did you expect that immediate attention should have been given to academics? Most novices, especially those headed for secondary teaching, believe that in order to maintain high academic standards they should immediately start the school year with academic assignments. Actually, expert teachers realize that attending to the social and emotional, as well as academic, needs of a new group of students will help develop a positive classroom environment that will lead to heightened achievement benefits later.

What behavior patterns can you expect in classrooms over the course of the year? Several social psychologists studied classrooms closely, and found similar patterns (Schmuck & Schmuck, 1979; Stanford, 1977). The following stages of classroom group development represent a synthesis of their ideas:

Stage 1: Facilitating Psychological Membership

Everyone wants to feel that they belong, that they are accepted by significant others. This is especially important in a classroom setting, because being a learner is a risky business. In order to have the courage to make the mistakes that are a natural part of learning, students need to feel that they are in an emotionally safe environment. This sense of safety comes only when you feel accepted and liked by those around you. That is why Ms. Forero spent so much time the first day of school forging her own personal connections with each student and assisting them in building relationships with each other. She realized that this is a key first step in creating a productive learning environment for her students.

Stage 2: Establishing Rules and Routines

It is important that everyone in the classroom understand how the class will operate. What are the rules, procedures, policies, and expectations for behavior in the classroom? Sometimes this stage follows Facilitating Psychological Membership, but it can and often does happen concurrently. Following is an example of how one junior high math teacher navigated Stage 1 and Stage 2 simultaneously.

Day One On the first day of school, Henderson follows her plans for the individual classes. For example, in the third-hour math class, she meets the students at the door and asks them to hand her their bar-coded identification cards so that she can scan them with the computer wand, then to select a seat and fill out the information sheet that is on each desk. . . . By the time all the students are in the room, seated, and filling out the information sheets, Henderson has already entered the attendance data from the computer wand into her computer, and pressed the printer code for her attendance record. . . .

Next, Henderson carries out activities designed to help students answer their questions about who is in the group, how they will be treated, and norms

Home Schooling

Not all classrooms are located in schools. Within the last 15 years, home schooling has become quite popular. Although home schooling's roots lie in the alternative school movement of the 1960s, the majority of home schoolers today turn to educating their own children for religious reasons. About 70 percent of home-schooling parents believe the environment of public schools is too secular and that their children will not be thoroughly grounded in moral and religious principles (Knowles, 1989; Ray, 1989). Estimates of the number of home-schooling families range as high as 260,000 (Lines, 1987).

Home schooling became acceptable after a series of rough battles in the mid-1980s in which some home-schooling parents were actually jailed (Lines, 1987). Currently, every state allows home schooling in some form. Acceptance of it, though, is uneasy. Home schooling remains controversial, and home-schooling families are looked on askance. The controversy centers around what the role of public education ought to be in a democracy. We turn now to examining the arguments pro and con.

The Case For

Most parents choose to home school because they find public schools intolerable. Van Galen (1988) divides home-schooling parents into two camps, the ideologues and the pedagogues. Each finds fault with the ways of public schooling and elect home schooling to overcome these faults. The ideologues are the majority, and they have chosen to withdraw their kids from the public schools because they object to its curriculum. Their religious life is central to them, and public schools fall far short of the education they envision for their children. They argue that with home schooling, they can give their children a proper education as Christians and can develop closer relationships with them. One of the ideologue parents whom Van Galen interviewed elaborated:

> I think it comes down to the principle of what they [the public educators] consider education and what we consider education are two different things. My idea of success is that my child has strong Christian values and is a strong Christian, no matter what area of life they choose to go into. Someone else's idea of success is maybe for their child to be a doctor or lawyer. They're looking at it from a worldly point of view . . . whereas we're looking at it biblically. (p. 56)

For the ideologues, then, the secular nature of public school is untenable.

In contrast, the pedagogues do not mind the curriculum, they criticize instead the methods of teaching used in public schools. *Overly regimented, insensitive to individual students' needs, mindless,* and *undemocratic* are some of the unflattering terms pedagogues use to describe schools. They see home schooling as a personal solution to the ineptitude of public education.

Home-schooling supporters contend that the public schools cannot meet the needs of all children: its curriculum, its values, its separating of parent from child, and/or its methods of instruction are unacceptable. They argue further that in a democracy, citizens ought to be able to choose the kind of education they want for their children.

The Case Against

The arguments for home schooling are very persuasive. After all, why should the government be able to intervene in parents' private decisions

about how to educate their own child? Unfortunately, the situation is not that simple. There are also powerful arguments against home schooling.

First, many opponents reason that a democracy as diverse as our own needs some institution that serves a uniting function. No one as yet has created a better means to do that than through the public schools. Where else does everyone come together? Where else will the shared experiences necessary for creating a citizenry committed to democracy occur? Where else can we practice working out our differences in a peaceful, mutually respectful way? For many policy makers, this philosophical objection is compelling, by itself sufficient enough to warrant a ban on home schooling.

There are other, more pragmatic arguments against home schooling as well. Many educators maintain that they are the professionals who are specially trained to provide top-quality education for young people. Parents are not so trained, and students may get an inferior education as a result. These opponents also point out that public schools are funded through attendance; that is, schools receive money based on the number of students who attend each day. A drop in attendance means a drop in the available resources, and schools, they aver, are already stretched too thin as it is.

Educators also contend that home schooling, because it isolates students from their peers, risks hampering their social and emotional development. They counter the argument that public schools do not meet individual students' needs by saying that schools are improving on this point all the time. Further, without activist parents' support, the external impetus that schools need to continue to improve services would be missing. Schools need involved parents and patrons in order to change and grow.

What Does Research Have to Say?

Unhappily, most of the writing on home schools is hortatory. Writers carry on eloquently but provide little hard data to support or disconfirm the arguments of detractors. Some evidence, albeit spotty and methodologically weak, indicates that students' academic and socioemotional development are not adversely affected by home schooling (Lines, 1987). This provides some tentative reassurance on pragmatic grounds, but the philosophical problems remain. It is very difficult to balance the valid claims on both sides of the issue. The American Civil Liberties Union juggled the competing values in this way:

> In the interest of parental right to choose an alternative to public education, [home instruction with safeguards, such as approval of curriculum or testing of the child] ... should be extended to all jurisdictions because the state's interest in assuring minimum levels of education does not extend to control of the means by which that interest is realized. (cited in Lines, 1987, p. 514)

In the years to come, the issue of home schooling promises to remain controversial. Those who pursue careers in education are sure to confront the problem at some time. They will be forced to make some resolution of the profoundly competing values inherent in the debate.

and role expectations. She begins with an orientation activity that has two purposes: first, for the students to introduce themselves, and second, for each student to practice listening and paraphrasing what another student has said. She tells the students to introduce themselves to the group by telling their names . . . and telling about a mathematical problem they encountered and solved during the summer months. Several students call out, "I don't use math!" She says, "That could be so; listen to the examples, and if you still need some help, I'll work with you." . . . To illustrate the assignment, she gives two examples. Then she calls on two students to restate her directions. . . .

She then gives the students time to think about a problem . . . and to talk quietly to themselves to rehearse what they will say when she calls on them. She then provides directions: "Listen very carefully to each speaker. After a speaker has finished, we will ask clarifying questions. Negative comments are not permissible. Once a person has finished their introduction and answered . . . questions, she/he will draw the name of a person out of an envelope, and that person will be the next speaker." (Putnam & Burke, 1992, 149–150)

Notice how Henderson weaves academic expectations (an emphasis on math problem solving) with interpersonal expectations (learning names) with behavioral expectations (the prohibition on negative comments). She has very efficiently and skillfully established an environment in which students can expect to work hard on math within a safe, supportive climate. One day will not be sufficient to cement these norms, but within another week or so, students will learn to operate appropriately.

Stage 3: Establishing Shared Influence

It does not take very long, even with very young children, to facilitate psychological membership and establish rules and routines. However, inevitably there will be problems. Some students probably will resent the teacher's authority, whereas others will jockey with each other for position and status within the group. These are signals that the classroom has entered Stage 3, in which individuals begin struggling to establish their influence within the group. As a teacher, your job will be to help students through this phase in a productive way and help all students feel they have a voice in classroom decision making. During the course of your teacher education program, you will learn a variety of techniques for dealing with such situations: classroom meetings, conflict resolution, role playing, active listening, dis-

ciplining, and many others. At this point, it is enough to know that such unpleasant experiences as challenges to your authority, fights between students, and off-task behavior are all normal occurrences on the road to establishing classroom social order.

Stage 4: Pursuing Academic Goals

At this stage, the classroom group is functioning smoothly and productively. Students feel comfortable in the class and are confident that difficulties can be worked out. The frequency of conflicts and off-task behavior decreases, and when they do happen, they are dealt with quickly and effectively. Learning goes into high gear. This stage is probably close to what you imagine your classroom will be like. Students "know the ropes," and little time is lost in miscommunication, conflict, or confusion.

Stage 5: Transition and Closure

As the semester or year comes to an end, so too does the classroom group. Having worked side by side for several months, students develop close ties with each other, and teachers must address the heartache involved in breaking those ties. Similar moments of emotional strain can happen during the year as students move to new schools or as long vacations cause separations. The teacher's job in Stage 5 is to monitor for these emotional changes, be ready to assist the group in revisiting and reworking previous stages as needed, and aid students in synthesizing and bringing to closure the bonds they have formed. Additionally, teachers must help prepare students for what is to come next—the next grade, teacher, or school. Teachers need to develop a great deal of emotional sensitivity and an extensive repertoire of techniques and activities to assist their students through Stage 5.

If you are considering becoming a secondary teacher, you may have difficulty accepting the need to attend to the social and emotional needs of students in your classroom. Elementary teachers are generally more attuned to these student needs, but sometimes they fail to see the link between students' socioemotional and intellectual growth (Weinstein, 1989). As you think through your career decision, you need to consider your willingness to learn about and to skillfully balance students' emotional, social, physical, and intellectual needs.

Classroom Properties

Walter Doyle is a noted educational researcher and scholar who, like Jackson in the 1960s, analyzed the common properties of classrooms (Doyle, 1986). His perceptive analysis reveals a great deal about how the classroom environment affects teachers and students. Among other things, Doyle's analysis focused heavily on the physical and temporal organization patterns of most classrooms. He found that most schools are physically organized in an "egg-crate" pattern: rows of rectangular classrooms within which a single adult is responsible for coordinating the activities of 25 to 30 students. Most schools must also impose standardized time patterns on their constituents, because they have to simultaneously orchestrate the activities of many classes totaling anywhere from hundreds to thousands of students. According to Doyle, this egg-crate architectural arrangement coupled with standardized time patterns and large student-to-teacher ratios conspire to create six universal characteristics of classroom life. Doyle argued that neither the teacher's philosophy or training nor the students' abilities or culture can modify these six characteristics, which are discussed here.

Multidimensionality

Multidimensionality refers to the very large number of events and tasks that go on in classrooms. It is related to Jackson's insights about the crowded nature of schools. Because so many people, all with different needs and goals, are crowded into a small space with limited resources, a lot of structure is needed to keep things moving in a productive direction. Teachers need to keep written and mental records of student learning, behavior, social competence, and emotional status. They need to plan lessons and evaluate student work. They need to teach lessons within tight schedules, monitor 25 or 30 students' engagement and learning during that lesson, and when necessary, make "in-flight" adjustments to the lesson. Bulletin boards must be created; furniture arranged; supplies ordered, stored, and distributed; student work collected, assessed, and reported; communication with colleagues and parents maintained; lunch counts and head lice checks conducted. Sometimes teachers must also supervise volunteers, aides, and student teachers; sometimes they must deal with students who have serious emotional or health problems. The list of tasks is long and varied.

Simultaneity

Closely related to multidimensionality is **simultaneity,** which highlights the fact that not only are many things happening in classrooms, many are happening all at once. This means that, in order to be effective, teachers must pay attention to many things at the same time. Picture yourself leading a discussion with 30 junior high students. You need to constantly keep your learning goals in mind, to keep formulating clear and worthwhile questions, to scan for off-task behavior and, when necessary, to smoothly intervene without disturbing the flow of the discussion. You need to maintain an appropriate pace for the lesson, to ensure broad participation, and to respond to students appropriately—elaborating on their comments, connecting them to other comments and to your learning goals, making corrections, and giving encouragement. Moreover, all this must be done while you keep one eye on the clock. From this partial description of just one classroom event, it is obvious that teaching is a juggling act, and beginning teachers find they often drop a plate or two.

Immediacy

Many things are happening in classrooms (multidimensionality), they are happening all at once (simultaneity), and they must be dealt with "right now" (immediacy). Like simultaneity, **immediacy** has to do with the rapid pace of classroom life, at least from the standpoint of the teacher. Mentioned earlier was Jackson's estimate that elementary teachers have at least 300 interactions per day with students, each one needing immediate attention. Another researcher looked specifically at the number of purely evaluative comments teachers made, and found that teachers praised or reprimanded students 15.89 times per hour on average, about once every 4 minutes (Sieber, 1979). As Doyle (1986) pointed out, "teachers have little leisure time to reflect before acting" (p. 394).

Unpredictability

Because classrooms house so many different people and tasks, events often take unexpected turns. Thus **unpredictability** is another universal property of classrooms. Although teachers and students work together to make things happen, even the most structured lesson can go in unanticipated directions, sometimes negative, sometimes positive. For example, a tightly planned meteorological demonstration on atmospheric inversion layers goes awry when equipment malfunctions, or a student's grandparent drops by for an unannounced visit and quickly becomes the focal point for a spontaneous oral history lesson on the Korean War. Sometimes students bring the aftermath of a lunchtime fight into the classroom; sometimes they change the course of discussions by leaping to unexpected insights; and sometimes everything gets derailed by a surprise fire drill. Such events are but the tip of the iceberg when it comes to the unpredictability of classroom life.

History

Classroom groups are not temporary; students live together for 9 months and gradually form themselves into a classroom community with a **history** of shared events and experiences. In so doing, they develop their own set of norms and expectations for how everyone should behave, and they share a set of experiences with each other that build a sense of community. Events, actions, and words can carry special meanings understood only by members of that classroom. You undoubtably have experienced being a part of a group and understanding an "in" joke, where knowing the people and their collective history was essential to "getting it." The same applies to classrooms.

Doyle's history property also refers to the developmental nature of classroom groups, and to the cyclical nature of the school year. For example, there is always a "honeymoon" period at the beginning of the year. Next, students often test the teacher's authority. Later, the group's ability to accomplish academic work soars. Holidays also affect the emotional tone of a classroom in predictable ways. Halloween or a looming Christmas vacation usually increase students' activity level. If new students move into the classroom, the group dynamic will change, revolving back to earlier phases of the cycle. You can see that the history property is closely related to the work social psychologists have done on group development in the classroom.

Publicness

Finally, **publicness** refers to the fact that events in classrooms are public events: Everyone can see what happens to everyone else. When the teacher reprimands one student and praises another, everyone knows. The presence of others also means that there is an audience for classroom events, and this factor can influence how individuals behave. For example, some kids revel in negative attention and in publicly flaunting their ability to rile the teacher. Thus, because classroom events are public occurrences, individual teacher-student or student-student interactions can influence group norms and expectations. Likewise, group norms influence the behavior of individual students and teachers. Figure 4.2 summarizes the similarities that exist among classrooms.

Performance-for-Grade Exchange

Doyle argued that the highly public and evaluative nature of classroom life produces a unique bartering or exchange system between teachers and students (Doyle, 1979). Students do academic work, and in

Figure 4.2 Classroom Similarities

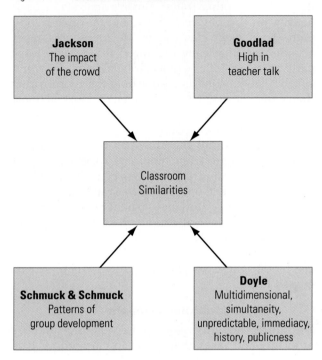

exchange, teachers give them grades commensurate with that work. Doyle termed this the **performance-for-grade exchange.** There is a contractual feel to this interaction, and teachers have a sense of obligation to make their assignments and evaluation criteria clear. Likewise, students have a sense of injustice if they feel teachers have not rewarded them adequately for work done.

In executing this exchange, students have to worry about two things: ambiguity and risk. The tasks the teacher assigns may be very clear and straightforward, as when students are asked to recall facts, or they may be vague and ambiguous, as when they must complete an open-ended assignment, such as "write an essay on a topic of your choice." Furthermore, the amount of risk associated with a task may vary. For example, completing a worksheet at your seat has much less risk than giving an oral book report in front of the class. Some tasks are high in both ambiguity and risk, some low in both, and some are high in one and low in the other.

Doyle and Carter (1984) conducted a study of a junior high English class, looking at how ambiguity and risk affected teacher-student interactions and the performance-grade exchange. When the teacher assigned a relatively open-ended writing project (a high-ambiguity assignment), the students pressured her to reduce ambiguity by continually asking for more specific guidelines on how to complete the project. Over the three periods devoted to the assignment, the teacher became increasingly explicit in her directions. The dynamics of the performance-grade exchange system require that the assigned work be clearly defined in order that students may know precisely how much and what kind of work they have to do for a given grade. Consequently, it is in the interest of students to reduce ambiguity, and they do so by pressuring their teachers to make assignments simpler and more oriented to factual recall than to critical or creative thinking. Consider your own experience as a student. When teachers assign papers, how often have you heard students ask, "How many pages should it be? How many references should we include? Should we use footnotes?" These questions are all attempts to reduce the ambiguity of the assignment and have the unfortunate side effect of also reducing critical thinking.

Interestingly, the teacher in the Doyle and Carter study was unaware of this pressure toward making the assignment more explicit until it was brought to her attention. Typically when students press for more detail, teachers capitulate and provide what appears at the moment merely to be greater clarification. When teachers are aware that students are attempting to make the work simpler, they often feel frustrated by the difficulty in promoting creative thought in their students. Beginning teachers need to be alert to their students' need for risk and ambiguity reduction. Virtually everyone believes in the importance of critical thinking, creativity, and problem solving in schools, but students resist these sorts of activities because of the performance-for-grade exchange dynamic. Teachers need to think ahead and plan strategies that support their students through these risky ventures. Start paying attention to this dynamic in your current classes; observing how your teachers deal with this problem may provide you with strategies of your own.

Ambiguity and Risk in Teacher Preparation

Ambiguity, risk, and the performance-grade exchange will also affect your education for the teaching profession. Let's apply Doyle's analysis to what happens in teacher education programs. The goals and practices common to most teacher education programs stretch the limits (even violate) the terms of the performance-for-grade exchange contract. Consider how professional education differs from your previous educational experiences. In most of your preprofessional college classes, you could decide what grade you wanted and thus how hard you

wanted to work. In teacher education, however, because it is a professional program based as much on live performance as on paper-and-pencil tests, there is no easy, predictable performance-grade exchange rate. Often teacher candidates are required to work until they achieve a professional standard of performance, no matter how long or how much work it takes. Sometimes this upsets students who feel that the implicit performance-grade contractual arrangement they are accustomed to and their autonomous status as students are being violated.

Let's turn now to the concept of risk and see how it plays out in teacher education. Candidates lose much of their academic privacy when they enter into the very public world of teacher education. Everyone is watching them: their university supervisor, the students in their charge, their cooperating teachers, their peers, perhaps the principal, sometimes even parents. No longer are they slaving alone over a computer composing a paper that only one instructor will read. Now they are doing their assignments, their learning, in front of other people, and this increased risk causes many candidates to experience a great deal of anxiety. Furthermore, despite their best efforts (and unlike the junior high students in the Doyle and Carter study), prospective teachers are unable to influence their professors to reduce the risk. It is not because the professors are unsympathetic. It is simply in the nature of the enterprise to be public, thus, risky. For the first time in their academic careers, teacher candidates—people who have been very successful students—are experiencing much more anxiety and much less control of their academic lives than they are accustomed to.

Just as with risk, most students, including teacher education students, strive to reduce any ambiguity in their assignments, thus ensuring a fair, predictable deal in the performance-grade exchange. Once again, however, the very nature of classrooms (multidimensional, simultaneous, immediate, unpredictable, historical, public) makes them ambiguous environments in which it is often difficult to know exactly the right thing to do at any given time. Although teacher candidates want clear, detailed guidelines on how to do their student-teaching assignments, these assignments are done in the unpredictable world of the classroom, rendering specific guidelines impossible. Candidates naturally pressure professors to reduce ambiguity, but the nature of classrooms again makes this impossible. The result, again, is to increase candidates' anxiety.

The element of expectations also plays a significant role in the lives of many teacher education students. Recall that beginning teachers often underestimate what they need to learn about teaching. Because of their unrealistic optimism, some feel that their teacher education courses are not essential to their teaching effectiveness. Consequently, candidates sometimes wonder why they are working so hard and feeling so stressed for information they neither need nor want. This line of thought only serves to exacerbate their anxiety.

CLASSROOM DIFFERENCES

We have reviewed the many ways classrooms resemble each other: the typical teaching patterns, the nature of the group, classroom characteristics, typical communication patterns, and the performance-for-grade exchange. However, there is more to the story of classrooms than their similarities; there are also variations in classroom life. Figure 4.3 shows the influences on classrooms that contribute to their differences. This section presents research on how classrooms differ from each other and from other work settings. Again, keep in mind your expectations and beliefs, reviewing them in light of any differences between them and research-based descriptions.

Social Class Differences

Jean Anyon (1980) examined differences in classrooms based on the type of neighborhood in which schools were located. Anyon studied how fifth grade work assignments differed in schools in contrasting social class communities. She observed classrooms, interviewed students, teachers, principals, and district staff, and reviewed curriculum materials. Two schools in the sample were *working-class* schools in which parents held blue-collar jobs with relatively low incomes. In another school, termed *middle class,* parents worked in a variety of highly skilled blue-collar jobs, in white-collar office jobs, in city services (including teaching), and in middle management. The fourth school was labeled *affluent professional,* and those parents worked as professionals in medicine, design, law, and engineering. In the final school, which Anyon called *executive elite,* most fathers were top Wall Street executives and many mothers volunteered for service organizations, such as Junior League. At each progressively higher social level, average family income increased. The percentage of minorities was low in all five schools.

Anyon found that students' academic work differed greatly depending on the school's social class milieu. In the working-class schools, children believed that learning meant "following the steps of a procedure" (p. 73). The work to be done was very mechanical, rote learning with little student choice. Teachers seldom explained the rationale for the work, nor did they show how it connected to other assignments. Children were evaluated more for *following directions* than on the quality of their academic performance. You will learn more in Chapter 5 about this type of learning environment, which has been called the *pedagogy of poverty* by Martin Haberman.

In contrast, *getting the right answer* signified learning in the middle-class school. Right answers earn you a good grade. (Remember the performance-for-grade exchange?) Children were still expected to follow directions, but the purpose was to obtain the right answer, not just to follow directions for the sake of following directions. Some problem solving was expected of the students. For example, they often had to "figure out by themselves what the directions ask(ed) them to do, and how to get the answer" (p. 77).

Independent, creative activity characterized academic work in the affluent professional school. Anyon described the classroom this way:

> The students are continually asked to express and apply ideas and concepts. Work involved individual thought and expressiveness, expansion and illustration of ideas, and choice of appropriate method and material. . . . The products of work in this class are often written stories, editorials and essays, or representations of ideas in mural, graph, or craft form. . . .

Figure 4.3   **Classroom Differences**

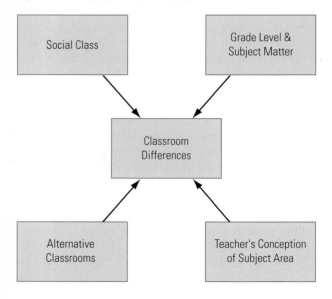

It is important that the children decide on an answer as a result of thinking about the idea involved in what they're being asked to do. (Anyon, 1980, pp. 78–79)

Finally, in the executive elite school, learning meant *developing one's analytical and intellectual powers*. The purpose of school was made explicit—to help you excel and to prepare for life. Children were expected to reason through problems, to derive rules for solving classes of problems, to fit these rules together in logical systems, and to apply these rules in solving novel problems. For example, in one math lesson, the teacher used class discussion to help students arrive at a formula for solving problems involving area. Next she asked, "Can anyone make up a formula for perimeter? Can you figure that out yourselves? (pause) Knowing what we know, can we think of a formula?" (p. 83).

What is the relationship between social class and academic work according to Anyon's data? It appears that as social class increases, so too do expectations for children to work more independently, more democratically, more creatively, and more meaningfully. Children at the lower end of the socioeconomic scale appear to receive instruction that is more autocratic and oriented to control than to personal development. Does this mean that our society, despite public utterances about providing equal education for all students, is subconsciously grooming lower social class students for roles as followers rather than leaders? Or does it mean that children and their parents in the various socioeconomic strata transmit to teachers their own expectations for learning which teachers, in turn, comply with? How much do community members and parents tug schools to operate in particular ways?

What do these differences in schooling mean for you in a teaching career? If you do go into teaching, will you focus your job search in affluent communities? In working class or poor communities? Which would be the more comfortable or interesting position? Which would be more frustrating or stressful? What are the obligations of professional teachers in working to ameliorate economic injustice? To what extent is the teaching in working-class schools poor teaching? If you find yourself employed in a working-class school, how will you ensure that your teaching meets professional standards? As highlighted in previous chapters, an important consideration for you is the extent to which you mold yourself to fit into schools as they are, versus the extent to which you are prepared to act as a change agent. The research Anyon conducted provides some important points of reference as you think through your teaching commitments.

Anyon's research is also thought provoking. Why do these class differences produce different classroom learning environments? Where do they come from? How do they perpetuate themselves? You will have the opportunity to explore these questions and others concerning the relationship between school and society later in this text and in your teacher preparation program.

Grade Level and Subject Matter Differences

While Goodlad's (1984) book *A Place Called School* showed that there is a very narrow range of teaching methods used across the country, he did find some variation based on subject area and grade level. Table 4.1 displays grade level differences in the use of classroom time for the following: instruction, routines, behavior control, and social activities. You can see that more time is devoted to instruction at the junior and senior high levels than at the elementary level. Also, whereas the time needed for routines (collecting lunch money, lining up for assemblies, listening to announcements, etc.) is roughly the same at each level, the time needed for behavior control decreases with each increase in grade level. The implications for teachers are clear; the younger the students, the more time teachers must spend in socializing them to the norms of school. Read the accompanying Research Box to learn more about one important classroom variable, class size.

Goodlad's team also found that subject matter influenced the use of time at the secondary level. Foreign language consistently came out at the top, with a mean of 84 percent of class time devoted to instruction. The lowest percentage of time spent on instruction was in vocational education at the junior high level and, surprisingly, English at the senior high level, both clocking in at 73 percent.

Table 4.1   **Mean Percentage Use of Classroom Time at Different Grade Levels**

Level	Instruction	Routines	Behavior	Social
Lower elementary	73.22	18.99	5.52	2.27
Upper elementary	72.89	20.71	4.39	2.01
Junior high	77.42	18.02	2.88	1.68
Senior high	76.12	20.39	1.29	2.20

In addition to differences in time use between grade levels and subject matters, Goodlad's team also found considerable variation within each category. For example, time spent on instruction at the elementary level ranged from a low of 18.5 hours to a high of 27.5 hours per week. Younger students spend more class time doing written work, whereas older students spend more time listening to lectures. Children in Grades 1 through 3 engage in more interactive and hands-on learning activities than older students do. Classes in foreign language, arts, vocational education, and physical education involve secondary students in more interactive, hands-on activities than classes in the four core academic subjects, English, math, science, and social studies. In particular, foreign language classes provide more student-teacher and student-student interaction, more corrective feedback, and a more businesslike atmosphere than other subject areas.

RESEARCH

Class Size

The Problem

One of the most important classroom variables is class size. From the point of view of the teacher as well as the students, class size makes a big difference in the quality of classroom life. Fewer students means the teacher can devote more time to each one. But how much difference does class size actually make on student achievement?

First, a caveat. Because of problems with measurement and absenteeism, most estimates of class size greatly underestimate the actual number of students a teacher is responsible for. With that in mind, pupil-teacher ratios range from a low of 14 to 1 in Connecticut to a high of 27 to 1 in Utah. Ratios also vary by grade level and subject areas, with lower ratios found in lower grades. The highest class sizes are found at the secondary level in physical education classes.

The Evidence

The issue of class size has generated much controversy. For years, many policy makers and scholars argued that class size does not have an impact on student achievement. They contended that within the typical range of class size, usually considered to be between 20 and 40 students, there is no evidence that lowered class size increases achievement. The only reason to lower class size, they maintain, is to make life easier for teachers and students. Others have countered that smaller classes do promote achievement, as well as other more intangible benefits, such as reduced stress and absenteeism.

Intensifying the heat of the dispute is the importance of class size at every level of the educational enterprise. For teachers and students, life in a crowded classroom is much more frenetic, unsatisfying, and much harder work. For districts, class size has a significant impact on salary and facilities budgets, and small decreases in class size can mean big increases in expenditures. For government policy makers, class size is the largest factor in the educational price tag (Geary, 1988).

Researchers have been examining class size for 100 years, and have published numerous studies on the topic (Mitchell & Beach, 1990). The results of this large literature conflicted. Recently a new technique of statistical analysis termed **meta-analysis** was invented, and this provided a very powerful way to synthesize results from many different studies, enabling statisticians to more easily identify patterns. The new technique was immediately brought to bear on the large and messy class size

The reasons for these differences are unclear. Perhaps students who gravitate to different classes have different needs and abilities; perhaps the nature of certain subjects necessitates more time on routine tasks; perhaps the norms and expectations for work vary in the different disciplines. Whatever the reasons, the subject area and grade level you select will definitely have an impact on your work life as a teacher.

Teachers' Conceptions of Subject Matter

In addition to differences between different disciplines, how teachers think about their subject matter also has a great bearing on what their classrooms are like. Grossman (1990), for example, studied several English teachers, some of whom had certified through alternative programs and others who had taken traditional teacher education programs. Two beginning English teachers she studied took very

RESEARCH

Continued

literature (Glass, Cahen, Smith, & Filby, 1982; Glass & Smith, 1979; Smith & Glass, 1980). Glass, Smith, and their colleagues used meta-analysis to show that when students were added to small classes, achievement dropped off, but that the magnitude of that impact decreased as the classes grew larger. That is, making small classes bigger lowered achievement markedly, but making big classes bigger had relatively little effect. Specifically, achievement increased when class size was lowered to 20 students, with a pronounced increase when lowered to 15 students. Glass and Smith (1979) also showed that teacher morale and quality of instruction were higher in smaller classes.

Smith and Glass were criticized, however, on methodological grounds. Slavin (1989) charged that many of the studies included in the Glass and Smith meta-analyses were flawed. Some of the studies had been conducted in nonschool settings (eg., tennis classes) and, in some, the instruction only lasted 30 minutes. When Slavin reanalyzed the data without these studies, he found that the purported relationship between class size and achievement evaporated. No benefit was found to reducing class size until the "class" consisted of only three students.

Are we back to square one? Fortunately, no. New evidence has emerged that helps clarify the relationship between class size and achievement. The new evidence satisfies Slavin's legitimate concerns over methodological rigor; it is based on long-term, methodologically strong experimental studies conducted in schools. Project STAR (Student/Teacher Achievement Ratio) was initiated in the mid-1980s by the Tennessee legislature to examine the effects of reducing class size in the lower grades. The investigators in charge of the research, Finn and Achilles (1990), randomly assigned 6,500 kindergarten students to either a small class (13 to 17 students), a regular class (22 to 25 students), or a regular class with an aide. These classes were located in 76 schools representing inner-city, urban, suburban, and rural settings. Each school had three kindergarten classes, one of each type. Teachers were also randomly assigned to the classes, and those assigned to the small classes received no special training. The initial study lasted 5 years, and follow-up work continues.

Finn and Achilles found substantial sustained effects for reduced class size. Examine the data in Table 4.2. Note the dramatic increases in achievement in math and reading between the small classes and regular classes. These differences are statistically significant ($p < .001$). Also note

different approaches to teaching Shakespeare. Jake had a degree in English literature, but no teacher education, whereas Steven had an undergraduate English degree, plus a masters degree and a teaching certificate in secondary education.

In Jake's planning, he decided that his goals in teaching *Hamlet* to his seniors were to introduce the process of contextual analysis and to demonstrate the connections between *Hamlet's* themes and its language. He taught the play by examining it line by line, emphasizing its linguistic aspects. Jake said he learned how to teach literature this way from his undergraduate college courses in English. After the *Hamlet* unit, Jake was discouraged. The students appeared unwilling to work hard and had not really grasped the key ideas about themes and language. He questioned how much they had really understood.

Jake met even more frustration in trying to teach *The Merchant of Venice* to freshmen. He decided to

RESEARCH

Continued

that the achievement for regular classes with aide more closely resembles regular class performance than small-class performance; in fact, there were no statistically significant differences between regular classes and regular classes with aides. Interestingly, although there were major differences in achievement, virtually no differences were found for motivation or academic self-concept.

Table 4.2 **Effects of Reducing Class Size in Kindergarten**

		Measure		
Group	**SAT Reading**	**SAT Math**	**Motivation**	**Self-Concept**
White				
Small	530.3	545.8	50.1	48.0
Aide	525.3	538.2	50.2	47.7
Regular	518.1	535.4	50.2	47.4
Minority				
Small	507.1	521.3	49.9	48.6
Aide	491.7	510.3	49.9	48.3
Regular	489.0	509.2	49.9	48.5

Finn and Achilles continued to track the achievement of 2,291 children who remained in the same class-size configurations they began in kindergarten into the first grade. They found that small classes increased their superiority over regular classes by the end of the first grade. In contrast to the first year of the study, aides made an important impact. Teacher-aide classes gained as much as small classes during first grade, almost closing the gap.

The work in Tennessee has continued, and the achievement gains have been documented through seventh grade. Gains in other subject areas have been demonstrated, and referrals to special education and retention rates have slowed (Bracey, 1995). The Tennessee work has not received the attention it deserves, but that may be changing as more scholars recognize and publicize the findings.

It appears, then, that the issue may be settled. A large, longitudinal, well-designed, and well-executed study has demonstrated that decreases in class size bring about substantial gains in achievement. But these gains cost a lot of money. Are the benefits worth the cost? That issue is one for policy makers and taxpayers!

spoon-feed them just to get through the play. He really did not have many ideas about how to make Shakespeare accessible to ninth-grade students, and he came to blame the students for being unmotivated and unwilling to work hard. Disappointed in his attempts to teach literature as he had been taught, Jake decided that perhaps he should obtain a graduate degree, so that he could teach at the college level.

In contrast, in his teaching of *Hamlet,* Steven focused less on the language and more on helping his seniors see the connections between the play and their lives. For example, he allowed them to watch a videotape of the play, and he gave them summaries of each act. He oriented discussions so they centered on such issues as separation and divorce and student experiences with these topics. As Steven reflected on his teaching, he was glad that students took a more active interest in the play and that they seemed to understand more about it. He was less sanguine, though, about class discussions, in which most of the time students focused on their personal experience and not on the play. The previous year Steven had used an approach similar to Jake's and had gotten a similar lackluster response from students. He thought about the levels of engagement and understanding that both approaches had elicited, and he decided the next time to merge the two strategies, hoping to capitalize on the best of both of them.

These contrasting stories of Jake and Steven illustrate the power of one's conception of teaching, learning, and subject matter on planning, instruction, and even career choices. Because Jake had a rather unyielding, narrow, scholarly view of English literature, he was inflexible in his ability to rethink his teaching. Steven, on the other hand, maintained a scholarly vision but kept his feet pragmatically grounded in student knowledge, motivation, and understanding. Since he could think and plan more flexibly, and since he had more tools to draw on to make the content accessible for students, he could teach more flexibly and, ultimately, more effectively. The moral of these stories is that beginners need to examine very closely their conceptions of the disciplines they will teach. Is the way you think about subject matter compatible with student learning?

Alternative Classrooms

As you learned in Chapter 3, different philosophies of education can result in very different classrooms. For example, one large group of educational reformers have long advocated an **open-classroom approach** to schooling. These reformers (e.g., Dewey) begin with the twin assumptions that the purpose of schools in a democracy is to prepare students to be active, socially responsible citizens, and that in order to achieve this goal, schools should help each student develop to his or her full potential. With this philosophy as a foundation, open-classroom teachers prefer "a style of teaching involving flexibility of space, student choice of activity, richness of learning materials, integration of curriculum areas, and more individual or small-group than large-group instruction" (Horwitz, 1979, p. 92). Take a moment to read about three Australian teachers' open-classroom experiences in the accompanying Global Box.

Open classrooms look very different from conventional classrooms. Students are often up and moving about and talking to each other. The teacher is not stationed front and center but tends to move about, interacting with individual students or small groups. In one open classroom that we are familiar with, children begin the day by making a plan for what they will do that day. They are then responsible for executing that plan. The day may involve a variety of small-group activities with different sets of classmates (of varying age, gender, and ethnicity) to work on math or science problems, to critique each other's written work, to program a computer or work with a variety of construction toys, or to participate in field trips. Alternatively, students may spend substantial portions of the day in solitude, reading books of their choice. The teacher's job is to help students create an appropriate plan, to conduct small-group lessons, and to assist children throughout the day. At the end of each day, the teacher facilitates a discussion in which students evaluate their own learning, motivation, and goals and begin to think about what they need to work on the next day.

What does research have to say about the effectiveness of open classrooms? As you might expect, evaluating their success depends on what outcomes you are looking for. Based on a review of many studies that compared open classrooms to conventional ones, Peterson (1979) found that there was a very small difference favoring conventional classrooms in terms of academic achievement on standardized tests but that open classrooms appeared to produce greater creativity and problem-solving ability. Open classrooms were also superior in developing curiosity, independence, and positive attitudes toward school. The results were mixed for outcomes like positive self-concept, sense of self-determination, and anxiety. It is interesting to consider Peterson's findings in light of Anyon's work on social class differences in pedagogy. Given what you know about the relationship between social class and schooling, in what kinds of neighborhoods would you predict to find a greater proportion of open classrooms?

Classrooms versus Other Workplaces

It is also instructive to compare life in classrooms with life in other types of workplaces. Does the classroom behavior we require of students differ from what is expected in the real world of work? The answer is yes; there are several significant differences.

Solitary versus Group Work

First, most school work is conducted solo; students generally work by themselves to learn academic material. In contrast, out-of-school work, whether at home, on the job, in recreation, in volunteer activities, or other situations, is normally shared. One person's ability to function depends on the behavior of everyone else. Think, for example, about the

GLOBAL

An Open Classroom in Australia

Three teachers in Australia have written about their experiences in developing open classrooms in their country. Their approach could also be termed *constructivist,* an orientation toward teaching and learning that we introduced in Chapter 2. It is a concept likely to receive major attention in your teacher education program. Constructivist classrooms the world around will exhibit many similarities, so examining an Australian classroom can teach American teachers much about student-centered learning.

First, Baker, Semple, and Stead contrast traditional classrooms with their problem-centered approach.

> *Traditionally ... (teachers) have moved from the meaningless part to the meaningful whole, and children who couldn't make sense of the abstract nature of the parts fell by the wayside. There was nothing in the ... learning that they could link into their existing understanding. In the part-to-whole approach, children who have difficulty with skills or concepts are "stuck" with meaningless experiences. For instance, in maths, traditionally, we have taught children the basic number facts and operations, exposed them to a variety of number concepts and then presented them with problems to solve. In many cases the problems we gave them to solve were of the meaningless variety—"If apples cost 23 cents each and you bought six, how much would it cost you altogether?" If we looked carefully at how we divided our time between these issues, we would probably find that we devoted 60 to 70 percent to the basic operations, 10 to 20 percent to applied number and 10 percent to problem solving.*
>
> *We have found that we can help children learn ... best if we reverse this approach. We begin by allowing children to explore real-life problems or issues that are meaningful to them and within the context of this exploration we help them to come to terms with the relevant facts, skills, concepts and processes. (pp. 7–8)*

How do these Australian teachers accomplish this? First, they focus on their students' learning needs in light of the learning goals that they hold for the children. For example, the teachers created a unit on time because they noticed that many of their elementary students were having difficulty in that area. They introduced the unit by posing questions to the class having to do with time differences between different parts of the world. The children worked in small groups to solve these problems, and turned

interdependence required to successfully run a fast-food restaurant, and compare that with the independence required of young people in schools. The contrast is striking.

Mental Work versus Technology

A second major difference is the focus on purely mental work in schools versus the dependence on technology and tools to aid mental effort in other settings. One of the authors once observed an elementary teacher laboriously averaging all of her pupils' test scores by hand, eschewing a calculator because "it's a crutch." She did not allow her students to use such crutches either. This teacher is not alone; traditionally there has been a dearth of tools in most classrooms. This is slowly changing,

GLOBAL

Continued

to a variety of materials in the room to help them: calculators, atlases, phone books, and encyclopedias. Then they gathered back together and shared their results.

This activity launched a 5-week unit in which children explored their own questions about time, sometimes with other children, sometimes on their own. The teacher's role during the unit is to help students clarify what it is they know, do not know, and would like to explore in order to make this a successful learning experience. The teacher also provides assistance in how students will go about researching their questions.

During this period, the teachers offer "clinics" on special topics. When the students discover that they need a particular skill in order to advance their own explorations, the teacher will provide direct instruction on that skill to those students. For example, in the unit on time, clinics were provided on telling time from a clock face.

After children have completed their explorations and answered their own questions, they report on what they have discovered to the rest of the class. These reports often lead to further discussions about new questions, and these discussions launch a new cycle of exploration. The format in the Semple, Baker, and Stead classes, then, alternates between teacher-directed and student-directed activities.

Visitors to this classroom observe a place rich in reference materials, with a variety of spaces supporting many different kinds of activities: a library and reference section; an individual study section; a small-group work area; a whole-class meeting area; a multimedia work space; chalkboards; computers; storage spaces; bulletin boards displaying student projects; and animals and plants. They also observe a variety of activities taking place. Sometimes the teacher will be addressing the whole class, sometimes students will. At other times, teachers will be working with one small group while the rest of the class works independently. Sometimes students will be working quietly by themselves, at other times, in vocal small groups. Students can be observed reading, writing, computing, calculating, discussing, measuring, and thinking. This is a very different picture from that of the conventional classroom with the teacher front and center lecturing and students sitting in rows of desks passively listening.

SOURCE: After Baker, Semple, & Stead, 1990.

with computers and other technological tools becoming more prevalent. Currently, about 50 percent of students report using computers with some regularity in school (Bracy, 1995). However, for the most part, these technological advances are not used in the same way they are used in the workplace, to help solve actual problems or to do the work more efficiently. If computers are present in the classroom, they are most frequently used for drill and practice, as a kind of automated worksheet, not as tools for solving problems or getting academic work done. Calculators have made great inroads at the secondary level but are less common in elementary schools. Think about places you have worked, and try to imagine operating them, or any other modern business, without calculators, computers, or the other forms of technology used to help solve business problems.

Organization

A third way classrooms differ from real-life settings lies in how they are organized. Picture a typical day for an average high school student. He is crammed into a small space with 30 other people who resemble him quite closely in terms of age, skills, and other background factors, and whom he is supposed to ignore. He is given some work to do that he often does not completely understand. He works on it for a limited period of time, usually under an hour. Then this job is interrupted, he gets up, moves to another room, gathers with another set of 30 similar people with whom he is not to interact, and launches into another vaguely understood task totally unrelated to the first one. And so it goes. Again the contrast with the workplace is striking. In most offices, factories, and other work settings, people must interact in order to complete tasks; they vary in terms of their age, skills, and other characteristics; they are generally provided with reasonable space and time in which to do their work; they understand how to do their job; they work until the job gets done; and tasks are usually related to each other.

You can probably think of additional ways classrooms differ from other settings. Take a moment to list a few of these right now, and consider whether and in what ways these differences influence your beliefs about teaching, your interest in pursuing a teaching career, and how you will operate as a teacher. In case you are wondering how schools differ from other workplaces from the standpoint of the teacher, that issue is addressed in Chapter 7.

Classrooms in Other Cultures

Classrooms also differ by culture. It is instructive to observe how other nations organize their classrooms, because it highlights some of our taken-for-granted, "common sense" ideas about what is natural or right. It also helps us understand how children whose native culture is not mainstream may have difficulty navigating the typical American classroom.

Take, for example, the performance-for-grade exchange discussed earlier. It is hard to imagine thinking it is okay for a teacher not to be explicit about her expectations. After all, if the teacher has the power to grade students, then she should be very clear about what students need to do in order to earn that grade. How would you feel if you took a class and the professor did not tell you what you were expected to read? How would you know what to study? My guess is that you would think that unfair in the extreme. But consider this story told by a colleague who studied at the Sorbonne in Paris:

> I was excited to be attending my first day of class at the Sorbonne. The professor began lecturing immediately, and fascinated me with his comments on French philosophy. But I was a little confused because he didn't hand out a syllabus, he didn't provide an overview of the course, he didn't talk about the required work and readings. So after the lecture I went up to him and asked what books I should buy for the class. He said to me, "You're American, aren't you?" A bit startled, I said yes. He said, "I thought so. Here is how it works here. Each day that we meet, I will mention certain books in my lectures. Maybe you have read those books; if so, it doesn't make any sense for you to buy and read them again. If you haven't, then you can buy and read them. At the end of class, when you write your paper, I will see what you have learned.

You can see that this is a very different view of teaching and learning from the contractual approach Americans favor. What do you think this signifies about French assumptions as to the status of teachers, the desired relationship between student and teacher, the nature of knowledge, the process of learning, the responsibilities of the learner? What is the same and what is different between French and American assumptions? For one thing, it appears that teachers may be trusted more in France than they are here. To give this much power and discretion to the teacher must mean that teachers are held in higher regard, and that students are willing to relinquish more of their power to them than American students are willing to do. As Americans, we want to strike bargains with our teachers; the French, on the other hand, seem quite content to defer to the teacher's judgment. The French also seem to have different expectations about learners and motivation. American teachers assume that students will not do anything unless they are required to do so, whereas French teachers expect students to show more initiative and self-direction.

Another illustrative example comes from Mexico. Here is how an educational anthropologist described a typical elementary classroom in one Mexican town:

> Characteristic of instruction in the *Primaria* was its oral, group interactive quality.... Students talk throughout the class ... teachers are always available to repeat, explain, and motivate; silent seat work is rare; and often a crescendo of sound ... is indicative of instructional activity.... (This) first grade classroom illustrates this pattern of verbal and physical activity:

> As she instructs children to glue sheets of paper in their books and write several consonant-vowel pairs, the teacher sometimes shouts her directions to compete with the clamor of kids asking for glue, repeating instructions to each other, sharing small toys, sharpening pencils, asking to go to the bathroom, etc. This activity and "noise" is compounded by the large number in the classroom, 35, but things somehow seem to get done.... Then the teacher has the children recite the word pairs taped to the chalkboard. They shout these out loudly as a group as she points to each combination with an old broken broom handle. Sometimes she calls out the pairs in order; other times, out of order to check their attention. Then she calls individual children to the board, gives them the stick, they choose a pair of sounds, but then have to pronounce them loudly and quickly as she presses them for correct responses. (Macias, 1990, p. 304)

Most Americans think that classrooms ought to be quiet places, that noise interferes with learning. And, in fact, as we have seen from the work of Goodlad and others, most American classrooms *are* quiet. Most of us could also probably give personal anecdotes about how noise is bothersome when we are trying to concentrate. But the Mexican classroom shows us that it is not some immutable law of pedagogy or human nature that pushes us toward quietness. Our common-sense notions about the need for quiet are simply cultural norms that we have deeply internalized. This does not make them any less real; it just means that others can carry totally different assumptions that make just as much sense to them.

PUTTING IT ALL TOGETHER

As you think about what kind of teacher you want to be, you will need to consider the information presented in this chapter.

- What are your beliefs, expectations, and values about classrooms? Are classrooms always boring? Should teachers strive to entertain students?

- How much should you focus on students' emotional needs versus their academic needs?

- Can you deal with the unpredictability, simultaneity, and other facets of classroom life?

- What grade level or subject area are you best suited to teach?

- What balance should you strike between fitting in with schools as they are and trying to improve or reform them?

- What new knowledge and skills do you need to acquire in order to become an effective teacher?

- With what attitude will you approach your teacher education program?

At the end of Part 2, we have provided self-exploratory questionnaires, interview guides, observation frameworks, reflection exercises, and other materials to help you sort out your beliefs and values in order to begin resolving these important questions.

SUMMARY

- Teachers' expectations of students greatly influence student learning. Teachers need to regularly monitor their expectations and to adjust them appropriately in order to maximize student learning.

- One's own expectations shape one's perceptions and judgments about the world. Unrealistic expectations can lead to emotional discomfort and can negatively affect one's own learning. For these reasons, it is important to recognize and consciously reflect on one's expectations.

- Like most people, prospective teachers generally have unrealistically positive expectations about their own teaching ability and about the job of teaching itself.

- Life in classrooms is crowded, and much of a teacher's job involves managing large numbers of young people in productive ways. For students, this makes the classroom a "hurry-up-and-wait" kind of place, whereas for teachers it is a whirl of activity, interactions, and decisions.

- In most classrooms, teacher talk dominates. Most instruction is very teacher centered.

- Classroom groups progress through a predictable series of stages of group development in ways akin to other kinds of groups. These stages are facilitating group membership, establishing rules and routines, establishing shared influence, pursuing academic goals, and transition and closure.

- Schools' large student-to-teacher ratios and separation into an egg-crate organizational structure create properties that all classrooms share. These are multidimensionality, simultaneity, immediacy, unpredictability, history, and publicness.

- In exchange for the work students perform, teachers give them grades. From the students' point of view, reducing the ambiguity and risk of assignments as much as possible makes it easier to come out ahead on the exchange. Because of this, there is a constant press from students to "dumb down" their assignments.

- Because of the nature of teacher education, many of the customary rules of the performance-for-grade exchange may be violated. The added ambiguity and risk is often very stressful for teacher candidates.

- Schools in different neighborhoods often differ in their curricular and instructional practices. Schools located in low-income areas tend to be more hierarchical and autocratic, whereas schools in high-income areas tend to focus more on developing students' intellect and autonomy.

- Teachers of younger children generally must devote more time to management. Foreign language classes generally spend the most time on instruction and also devote more time to interaction than other subjects do.

- Some teachers create very different classrooms with more student-centered learning, more student movement, and more interaction. Research suggests that these open classrooms perform about as well academically as conventional classrooms. Open classrooms differ in that they produce more curiosity, independence, creativity, and problem-solving ability.

- Conventional classrooms differ from conventional workplaces in that students typically work alone, they do not use technology and tools as often, and their work is more fragmented and less meaningful.

- Classrooms in other cultures often operate very differently in terms of student-teacher relationship, performance-for-grade exchange, student motivation, and acceptable noise levels among other characteristics. It is important to examine other cultures' practices as a way of gaining insight into our own.

READING FOR THE PROFESSIONAL

Goodlad, J. I. *A Place Called School.* New York: McGraw-Hill, 1984.
This classic work paints a picture of the regularities of schooling and classroom life.
Sizer, T. R. *Horace's Compromise: The Dilemma of the American High School.* Boston: Houghton Mifflin, 1985.
Goodlad's book is replete with facts and figures, but Sizer fleshes out this skeleton with an inside look at how life is lived inside the typical American high school. Also, it provides a vision of what high schools could be like.

CHAPTER 5

Students

Teachers spend their professional lives with young people. What are kids like? Who are these people you are thinking about spending so much time with? As a prospective teacher, you should be aware that although students share many attributes, no two of them are identical. On virtually every dimension you can imagine, students vary. As a teacher, you must be sensitive to, indeed capitalize on, student differences. This chapter introduces you to students from the teacher's perspective, to the ways students are the same and different from each other and from their teachers, and to the school's evolving role in managing this diversity. The following vignettes illustrate how student diversity presents itself to teachers.

Ms. Farmer, engrossed in planning for her ninth-grade algebra class, became more and more excited about the potential her diverse students brought to her classroom. "The middle-class kids are going to get a dose of reality when they interact with the poorer ones around problems involving money," she mused, "And the Hispanic, Asian, and white kids will all see things differently. I'm lucky to have a classroom this varied. Our cooperative learning and class discussions are going to be very rich!"

Mr. Allred sighed as he reviewed the latest enrollment figures for his fifth-grade class in rural Colorado. How was he going to manage with his new multiple-disabilities student? He'd figured out how to cope with the Spanish-speaking kids; he'd figured out how to cope with the mistrust between the white and Native American kids; he'd figured out how to cope with an achievement span spreading from first grade to high school. But how was he going to deal with a child who needed someone to accompany her to the bathroom? How was he going to make his erosion box learning center accessible to her wheelchair? Was there a way to meet her educational needs *and* the needs of the rest of the class?

Student Diversity
   Ethnicity and Culture
      School Patterns
      Cultural Deficit Theory
      Cultural Difference Theory
      Voluntary and Involuntary Minorities
   Language
      Dialect
      English as a Second Language
   Social Class
   Gender
      School Patterns
      Biological Explanations
      Sociological Explanations
      Testing Differences
   Special Needs
      Intellectual
      Physical
      Emotional
      Teachers' Responsibilities

   Demographic Trends
   At-Risk versus Resilient Students
Student Development
   Cognitive Domain
      Intellectual Development
      Multiple Intelligences
   Affective Domain
      Social-Emotional Development
      Development and Culture

Schools' Responses to Diversity
   Pull-Out Programs
   Mainstreaming and Inclusion
   Multicultural Education

The Problem and Opportunity of Diversity

Summary

Readings for the Professional

STUDENT DIVERSITY

Like Mr. Allred and Ms. Farmer, teachers everywhere are confronted with many forms of student diversity. Sometimes they need extra resources to support them, sometimes not. Sometimes these resources are provided, sometimes not. Sometimes teachers welcome diversity with grace, sometimes not. The vignettes illustrate some of the ways students can express differences. Students come from a variety of ethnic, racial, and cultural backgrounds; they may be rich or poor or somewhere in between; they speak a variety of languages; and they possess a range of physical, emotional, interpersonal, and intellectual abilities. As you read this section, be especially aware of the ways students might differ from you, and the ways their background experiences might lead them to see the world a little differently. Consider as well how these differences might affect your teaching effectiveness.

Ethnicity and Culture

We are becoming an increasingly diverse nation. Over the last 20 years, white student enrollment in schools decreased 13 percent, Hispanic enrollment increased 45 percent, and Asian-Pacific Islander increased 116 percent (Garcia, 1993). The proportion of African Americans and other minority groups enrolled in schools also went up. These shifts are felt most acutely in urban areas, but rural and suburban regions are experiencing similar trends. Every teacher can expect to teach students from a wide variety of ethnic and cultural backgrounds.

School Patterns

What typically happens to minority students in schools? Unfortunately, it appears that the quality of their education is generally lower than that for European Americans. Their enrollment patterns are different, the curriculum they receive is different, they bear the brunt of ability grouping and tracking, and their interactions with teachers are not as positive.

Minorities are disproportionately placed in vocational and special education programs but are underenrolled in college preparation and gifted programs. Minority enrollment in advanced coursework is up, but whites still maintain a lead, as Figure 5.1 shows. Even when the courses are nominally the same, there are inequalities. The College Entrance Examination Board (1985) found that African Americans who had taken 3 or more years of mathematics were less likely than whites to have covered algebra, geometry, and calculus. The curriculum covered in vocational classes differs, too, with blacks receiving training for low-paying jobs, such as cosmetology

Figure 5.1   High School Enrollment in Core Subjects

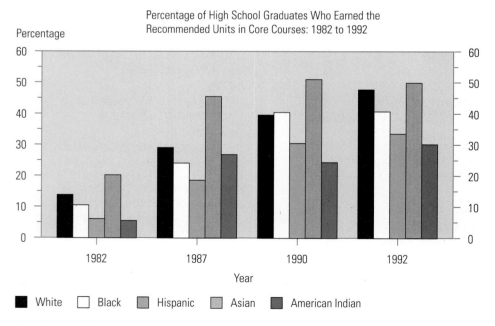

Percentage of High School Graduates Who Earned the Recommended Units in Core Courses: 1982 to 1992

Note: The graph shows the recommended 4 units of English, 3 units of science, 3 units of social studies, 3 units of mathematics, but does not include the recommended one-half year of computer science.

Source: U.S. Department of Education, 1987; NAEP High School Transcripts Studies, 1992.

and mill work, and whites gaining experience with business, finance, and management (Oakes, 1985).

Tracking is a more formalized version of these curricular practices. In elementary school, tracking usually consists of creating reading groups within a class based on ability level. By the time students get to high school, within-class ability grouping has given way to grouping whole classes by ability. Most high schools offer honors English, regular English, and remedial English; they provide a similar range of offerings in math and other subjects. Many investigators have documented the deleterious effects of

tracking on classroom life and learning for minority students (Goodlad, 1984; Oakes, 1985). For instance, the lessons given lower-track classes and lower-ability groups emphasize memorization of basic facts and skills, whereas higher classes and ability groups receive instruction in critical thinking, problem solving, and conceptual understanding. Interestingly, heterogeneous and middle-track classes more closely resemble higher tracks in learning goals and activities; in other words, minority students are more likely to receive a high-quality education in mixed-ability classes and groups.

Figure 5.2   **Trends in Standardized Test Scores**

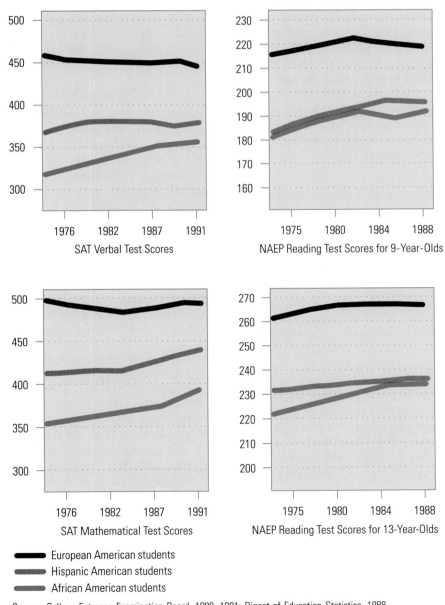

SAT Verbal Test Scores

NAEP Reading Test Scores for 9-Year-Olds

SAT Mathematical Test Scores

NAEP Reading Test Scores for 13-Year-Olds

— European American students
— Hispanic American students
— African American students

Source: College Entrance Examination Board, 1988, 1991; Digest of Education Statistics, 1988.

Teachers also interact differently with minority children. Minority students are asked fewer questions, are given less time to respond to questions, and are less often praised or encouraged (Gay, 1974). These patterns hold no matter the teacher's race.

Minority students have different achievement patterns as well. Look at the graphs in Figure 5.2, which display trends in standardized achievement test scores for African, Hispanic, and European Americans. Performance for other minorities, except certain Asian groups, is similar. It is clear that achievement for minority children lags behind. Although they appear to be closing the gap in recent years, it is still quite wide.

Cultural Deficit Theory

Many people have used the **cultural deficit theory** to account for minority students' poor performance in schools. If these kids have problems with achievement, so this theory goes, it must be because their culture, class, or race is deficient in some way. Books like *The Bell Curve* (1995) promote this view. Sometimes teachers subscribe to this view because of experiences they have had with minority kids. Puerto Rican scholar Sonia Nieto (1992) described teachers' reactions to the low achievement of cultural minorities:

> I have made scores of presentations on multicultural and bilingual education in many different school systems. After each session, a number of teachers invariably approach me with the same concern: Why do some of their students (usually African American, Latino, or Indian . . .) fail, no matter what they, their teachers, do, while other (usually middle-class European-American students . . .) succeed? Although a small number of these teachers are convinced that students of color or . . . (low-income) students are genetically or culturally inferior and simply want verification of their racist and classist beliefs, this is certainly not true in the vast majority of cases. Another group, who may have begun as committed and idealistic teachers, have simply tired of confronting hostile and nonachieving students in their classrooms every day. These teachers genuinely do not want to believe that some children are inferior. (p. xxiii)

Given these patterns of school failure, what is a typical white, middle-class teacher to think? After all, she has tried everything she knows how to do to reach those students in difficulty; she has made tasks simpler, she has given them more practice exercises, she has provided easier reading materials, but they still cannot seem to make the grade. There are also many special federal programs designed to aid disadvantaged students, such as Title I, resource classes, and self-esteem building. However, nothing seems to help. What else can be the cause of school failure, then, if not cultural, class, or racial inferiority?

Despite its apparent appeal (to whites), there are reasons to doubt the cultural deficit theory. Research demonstrating the lower-quality education that minorities often receive challenges this explanation, as does the fact that achievement differences between majority and minority students get worse as they progress through school. That is, the difference between whites and blacks is smaller at first grade than it is at eighth grade. If the minority culture or race were inferior, one would expect that schooling would help, that contact with the dominant culture would in some way "cure" the deficits, and, consequently, the gap would be widest when children first started school and then progressively narrow over time. The fact that the opposite happens makes one question the cultural deficit theory.

Cultural Difference Theory

Villegas (1991) has offered another more compelling explanation. She asserted that school failure is grounded in the cultural *differences* of minority students, not cultural deficiencies. Consider the typical classroom we discussed in Chapter 4. The teacher is usually at the front of the room, talking and asking questions. Students are to sit quietly, to learn by listening, and to answer questions in front of the whole class when the teacher calls on them. If they do not do these things, they are considered behavior problems or learning disabled. It all seems straightforward enough. However, the following vignette about a second-grade reading lesson in New Mexico illustrates how some Native American students respond to this "normal" situation:

> The teacher said, "Look at the illustration at the beginning of the chapter and tell me what you think is going to happen." A few students raised their hands. The teacher called on a boy in the back row. He said, "I think the boy is going to meet his grandfather." Then the teacher asked, "Based on what you know, how does the boy feel about meeting his grandfather?" Trying to involve the whole class, the teacher called on another student—one of four Native Americans in the group—even though she had not raised her hand. When she didn't answer, the teacher tried rephrasing the question, but again the student sat in silence. Feeling exasperated, the teacher wondered if there was something in the way the lesson was being conducted that made it difficult for the student to respond. She sensed that the student . . . understood the story and was enjoying it. Why, then, wouldn't she answer . . . a simple

question? The teacher recalled that this was not the first time this had happened, and that, in fact, the other Native American students in the class rarely answered questions. . . . She wanted to involve them, wanted them to participate in class, but could not think of ways to get them to talk. (p. 3)

How can we explain the difficulty the Native American students had with the lesson? Researchers have demonstrated over the last several years that cultures differ in their use of language and in the ways they teach their children and that these differences can adversely affect children's school performance. For example, Phillips (1972) found that learning practices in Native American homes in Oregon differed greatly from school practices. She, too, had observed that Native American children were silent during lessons, sometimes even when asked a direct question by the teacher. Most European Americans would assume that these children were shy, that they had a learning disability, or that they were being subtly defiant. However, Phillips found that within their own homes, these Native American children were expected to learn by watching adults, not by interacting with them; that they were expected to turn to older siblings, not adults, when they needed assistance; and that they were accustomed to a great deal more self-determination at home than was permissible in the school environment. Given this divergence between the home and the school, it is much easier to understand Native American children's quietness in the classroom.

In another landmark study, Brice-Heath (1983) examined home-school cultural differences in the Piedmont region of the Carolinas. Specifically, she investigated differences in communicative style between working-class African Americans and middle-class European Americans. One of the many differences she documented in her fascinating book involved the use of questions. Brice-Heath found that at home, African American adults did not ask children very many questions, and when they did, they were real questions, really seeking information that the adult did not have. In school, however, teachers expected children to answer questions all the time, and the questions themselves were artificial in that the teacher already knew the answer. From the African American students' perspective, these questions did not make any sense at all, and they had difficulty bridging the cultural gap.

These and related studies have led researchers to postulate that minority children have difficulty in school because of cultural differences, not cultural deficits. For many educators, this **cultural difference theory** provides a better explanation for minority students' achievement difficulties than does the cul-

tural deficit theory. Armed with this improved understanding, teachers have a better chance to effect solutions. One approach that future teachers will certainly be expected to master is **culturally responsive teaching.** Obviously it is unreasonable to thoroughly ground every teacher in each culture they could conceivably come in contact with, but it is very reasonable to expect teachers to be sensitive to the impact of cultural differences on learning, to carry an attitude of respect for these differences, to be familiar with procedures for getting to know more about their students' cultural backgrounds, and to be able to use this knowledge to inform their instructional and curricular practices (Villegas, 1991). These skills and dispositions are the essence of culturally responsive teaching. The accompanying Multicultural Box discussion of the Kamehameha/Rough Rock Project provides an example of culturally responsive teaching.

Voluntary and Involuntary Minorities

Cultural difference theory helps us understand why minority children have difficulty in school and gives some helpful guidelines about how teachers can help them. But another question lingers. Why do some minority children have difficulty but not others? For example, some Asian children, particularly Japanese and Vietnamese, do quite well in school. The Japanese culture is certainly different from North American, so why do they not struggle the way African Americans, Hispanic Americans, and Native Americans do? According to John Ogbu (1992) of the University of California, one reason may be their status differences relative to the majority group. Ogbu divided subcultures into two categories: voluntary and involuntary minorities. Africans were brought to North America as slaves, and, as such, constitute an **involuntary minority.** Similarly, Native Americans and Puerto Ricans were conquered by invading Europeans and their cultures subordinated to that of the invaders. The Japanese, in contrast, immigrated freely, and represent a **voluntary minority.** Ogbu argued that it is the group's status as a voluntary or involuntary minority that better explains achievement differences between minority groups, whether the groups live in the United States or elsewhere. Ogbu elaborated on his argument:

The Koreans in Japan are an . . . example. In Japan, where they went originally as colonial forced labor, they do very poorly in school. But in Hawaii and the continental United States, Korean students do as well as other Asians; yet Korean culture is more similar to Japanese culture than to American mainstream culture. . . . West Indians are a similar example. They are academically successful in the continental

KEEP/Rough Rock Project

Researchers have been intrigued with the issue of how culture might influence learning. Do all people basically learn the same way, or does culture influence the way people learn? If culture does influence the learning process, how can instruction be adapted to meet the needs of different cultural groups? A multidisciplinary team of educational researchers in Hawaii has examined these questions carefully over the last 15 years and has developed and field tested classroom teaching methods that embody their findings. They formed the Kamehameha Early Education Project (KEEP) to study these issues.

The initial task the team set for itself was to improve the academic achievement of native Hawaiian children. They studied language interaction patterns in Hawaiian communities and found them to be quite different from those common in typical American classrooms. They began to modify classroom processes to make them more culturally compatible. Jordan (1994) described **cultural compatibility** as using knowledge of students' cultures to design classroom learning activities that would elicit behavior which was more congruent with school achievement. Cultural compatibility does *not* mean that school practices are identical with those of the home culture. It does mean that they are similar enough to make sense and to feel comfortable to students, but at the same time, to lead them to greater success with the school curriculum. Cultural compatibility in practice means the same thing as the Villegas term *culturally responsive teaching*.

What did culturally compatible, or responsive, teaching look like at the Kamehameha school? After analyzing children's home life and cultural practices, the research team found that Hawaiian children are accustomed to living and playing in large groups and in looking out for each other without much adult supervision. Children were aware of each other's needs, and did not hesitate to ask each other for help if they needed it. When they talked to each other, they used a pattern of interaction termed the **talk story.** Talk story involves a group of children, one of whom initiates describing something that happened, with other children chiming in as they think of related events, or contributing their perspective on the story. Interruptions are frequent and signify to participants that all are participating and listening to each other.

The KEEP elementary school language arts program organized learning centers in alignment with these findings about Hawaiian culture. Students worked in mixed-ability and mixed-gender groups of four to six, analogous to their play groups, on a variety of reading and writing projects. Lessons further capitalized on Hawaiian culture by allowing the talk story interaction pattern for discussions of reading material. A management system grounded in the teacher being "tough and nice," adult attributes that Hawaiian children value, was initiated. Children were permitted to help each other on their assignments, and were given a lot of latitude in moving about the room and talking during learning center time. These culturally compatible (responsive) changes in classroom organization and interaction

Continued

patterns brought about significant increases in the children's reading and writing achievement.

The KEEP team then wanted to test whether the program they had developed was simply good educational practice, applicable anywhere, or whether it was something uniquely appropriate to Hawaiian children. In order to investigate this problem, they sought another culturally homogeneous setting in which achievement outcomes were poor and the culture differed markedly from Hawaii. Just the right site was found in a third-grade classroom at the Rough Rock Demonstration School on the Navajo reservation in northeast Arizona. The KEEP team worked with the Native American teachers there to implement KEEP practices, and they studied the outcomes for Navajo children.

They discovered that what worked well for Hawaiian students did not work so well for Navajo students. One problem was the learning centers. Navajo students responded to them differently. Although compliant with their teachers, they seemed to find the learning centers uncomfortable: They moved their chairs away from each other, they did not scan for others having difficulty, and when they had trouble understanding, they tended to tough it out on their own. Most important, achievement did not improve.

The KEEP team turned to the Navajo teachers for help in understanding students' discomfort and for ways to adapt instruction to make it more compatible for Navajo students. They found that Navajos, unlike Hawaiians, live great distances from each other, and that children do not spend a great deal of time in groups together. Like Hawaiian children, Navajos are expected to take on significant family responsibilities at a young age, but unlike Hawaiian kids, Navajos' responsibilities take them far away from their peers. For example, many of the Rough Rock third graders were in charge of shepherding the family flock in distant fields, by themselves, for long periods. In contrast, Hawaiian children work and play in large companion groups. Thus, Navajo kids had to develop a great deal of independence at a young age and to learn how to manage problems on their own. They had not had the opportunity to develop skill in monitoring for peers needing assistance or in asking peers for assistance.

Another significant difference had to do with gender. Hawaiian children operate in mixed-sex groups, but Navajo boys are told to stay away from their sisters, and the sexes tend to segregate themselves from each other.

Based on this analysis of Navajo culture, the KEEP/Rough Rock team redesigned their pedagogy. They retained the learning centers and group work but modified the way they were organized. The size of the groups was reduced to 2 or 3 and were homogeneous by gender. These changes have been recent and it is too early to tell whether achievement will increase, but the children have responded positively and have become much more productive in the centers. All indications are that achievement will follow suit.

United States and in the U.S. Virgin Islands, where they regard themselves as "immigrants" . . . ; less successful in Canada, where they regard themselves as members of "the Commonwealth" . . . ; and least successful in Britain, which they regard as their "motherland" . . . (pp. 7–8)

Why do involuntary minorities fare so poorly? Ogbu suggests that members of these groups tend to avoid behaviors and attitudes they associate with the dominant group and to adopt opposing behaviors and attitudes. This **oppositional identity** appears to interfere with achievement. If doing well in school means you have to "act white," which feels like a betrayal of yourself and your people, then you are not going to try to excel academically. To compound the problem, other minority students are likely to reject the one struggling for academic success. At the same time, it is uncertain whether white students will pick up the slack. For the individual minority student, trying for academic success is a dicey business.

Ogbu made several suggestions to teachers to ameliorate this situation. Many are similar to those offered by Villegas: recognize and respect cultural and linguistic differences, learn about the cultures and languages of the students in your charge, and get to know your students well. He also suggested multicultural education, which we discuss in more detail later. He further advised that teachers guide involuntary minority students toward being bicultural to help them accommodate but not assimilate into the majority culture:

> The essence of this strategy is that students should recognize and accept the fact that they can participate in two cultural or language frames of reference for different purposes without losing their own cultural and language identity or undermining their loyalty to the minority community. They should learn to practice "when in Rome, do as the Romans do," without becoming Romans. (p. 12)

Language

Closely related to culture and race, language is another major form of diversity teachers frequently confront in their classrooms. Language diversity comes in two forms. Children's first language may be something other than English, in which case they are considered **limited English proficiency (LEP)** or **English as a second language (ESL)** students. Or they may speak English as their native tongue but use a nonstandard dialect like Black English, Hawaiian Creole, or Brooklynese. In either case they may experience difficulties at school. We examine the effects of dialect differences first and then turn to a discussion of native languages.

Dialect

Dialect or accent differences are quite common. You, yourself, may speak a variation of standard English if you hail from the South, New Jersey, New England, Australia, or other regions of the English-speaking world. Recent estimates of African American children who speak Black English are in the 60 percent to 70 percent range (Lucas, 1987). In the past, most people considered dialects like Black English substandard and inferior. However, linguistic research dating back 20 years reveals that language variation is quite natural, and that dialects such as Black English operate from a distinct and strict set of rules and syntax (Labov, 1972). Furthermore, attitudes about the value of any particular dialect stem from society's class structure rather than any inherent goodness of the prevailing standard (Garcia, 1993). In other words, those in power define their speech as right and the speech of those out of power as wrong. Although it is vital for members of a society to share a common language, it is important to keep in mind that what counts as "correct" speech is really quite arbitrary. Anyone who has studied English literature will be familiar with the works of Chaucer and other old texts. Only a cursory inspection is sufficient to realize that what constitutes standard English has changed dramatically over the centuries.

What happens to children who speak a nonstandard dialect of English in the classroom? Many assume that the dialect will adversely affect their academic performance. However, it appears that any learning losses are the result of teachers' response to minority dialects, not to any inherent deficiency in the dialect itself. Researchers have found, for example, that teachers rate students of equal ability who speak a different dialect less competent and that they are more apt to be supportive toward those speaking standard English (Cherry, 1981). As Chapter 4 discussed, when teachers hold low expectations for students or when they interact with them less often, students may not achieve to their potential. Researchers have shown also that, at least in the case of African American students, these children do acquire the standard English dialect in school and can use both the standard and dialect forms of the language in the appropriate contexts. That is, they use Black English on the playground with their friends, and in the classroom, they use the standard dialect at least half the time in first grade and most of the time by sixth grade (Destefano, 1972; Lucas, 1987; Melmed, 1971). Although it is clear that the achievement of African American children of the inner city is too low, these findings suggest that it is not the black dialect that is the cause but rather factors such as cultural differences between home and school and involuntary immigrant status.

A teacher's job is to understand and honor children who speak dialects and, at the same time, support their learning of standard English. It is important, as you think through the impact of dialect diversity on your life as a teacher, that you resolve to maintain high and reasonable expectations of all students, no matter what form of English they speak. To get you started on the process of understanding other dialects, here are some of the rules for the most-studied dialect, Black English:

- Double and triple negatives are acceptable and are used for dramatic emphasis. For example, Alice Walker (1982) opens her novel *The Color Purple* with this sentence: "You better not never tell nobody but God."

- Use a minimal number of words for every idea. For example, "She going out with him," rather than "She is going out with him," and "What you think?" rather than "What do you think?"

- Don't use the *-ed* suffix to indicate the past tense. Instead of "She closed the door," say "She close the door." The context will convey when the action occurred. (Jordan, 1988)

English as a Second Language

In addition to dialect variations, the United States is home to a number of people for whom English is a second language. In the last 20 years, the proportion of language minorities has dramatically increased, with California leading the way as we become a minority-majority nation. Garcia (1993) estimated that half the students in California speak a language other than English. Figure 5.3 displays the languages spoken by America's students. Spanish is the most common non-English language, but there are many others including Russian, Vietnamese, Farsi, Tagalog, and Navajo. School means double duty for these students, as they try and master English as well as the subjects under study.

How do they go about this difficult task? Investigators who have studied second-language acquisition say that it is a creative process, not just a matter of memorizing huge amounts of new vocabulary. Second-language learners must listen attentively, rely on social and situational cues to help them generate guesses about how to speak, test out their guesses, and revise accordingly. This does not mean that memorization and imitation are unimportant; they are, especially in the early stages. At every level of proficiency, ESL students need a high degree of English input and opportunities to try out the language in meaningful ways.

Several factors influence how successful children will be at learning English as a second language. Social skills, for example, play a big role. Children who are outgoing and gregarious, who are willing to join a group of native speakers and behave as if they understand, who can convey understanding with a few well-chosen words, and who seek out assistance from their friends learn English faster than children who do not. Another important factor is the attitude the learner has toward English speakers; if they have a positive regard for English-speaking people, they learn faster. The implications for involuntary minorities are clear.

Although the advantages of learning English for anyone living in the United States are obvious, the advantages of helping LEP students maintain their mother tongue is less so. From a political standpoint, this is a tangled issue. However, a consensus is beginning to emerge among scholars investigating the effects of bilingualism. It was once thought that it prevented deep language development in either language and thereby lowered intelligence, but it is now clear that this is not so. In fact, the ability to speak more than one language may enhance intellectual development (Goncz & Kodzepeljic, 1991). Bilingual children consistently outperform monolinguals on a variety of cognitive tasks (Garcia, 1993). They display greater cognitive flexibility as a result of their linguistic problem-solving efforts. These findings seem to hold even when the bilingual children are from a lower socioeconomic group than the monolinguals they are compared to.

Surprisingly, research in language learning shows that it is better for children's academic success if their family continues to speak the native language at home. This finding makes sense when you consider that for children to develop sophisticated language skills, they need to be immersed in a sophisticated language environment. LEP families cannot provide that kind of environment when they speak halting English. Therefore it is important for teachers to encourage language-minority families to continue using their native language in the home.

How can teachers help ESL students master English, maintain their home language, and learn the curriculum all at the same time? These imposing goals are not only desirable but mandated by laws that require schools to provide comprehensible instruction to all students, whatever language they speak. Although this is a tall order, researchers are beginning to identify specific programs and practices that teachers can use to help their LEP students (Allen, 1991), including cooperative learning (Kagan, 1994) and bilingual curriculum materials (Cohen, 1986; DeAvila & Duncan, 1980).

Figure 5.3   **Languages Spoken in U.S. Homes**

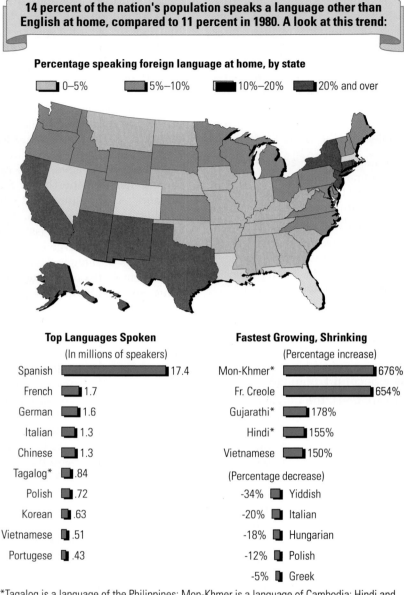

14 percent of the nation's population speaks a language other than English at home, compared to 11 percent in 1980. A look at this trend:

Percentage speaking foreign language at home, by state

☐ 0–5%   ▨ 5%–10%   ▰ 10%–20%   ▨ 20% and over

Top Languages Spoken
(In millions of speakers)

Language	Speakers
Spanish	17.4
French	1.7
German	1.6
Italian	1.3
Chinese	1.3
Tagalog*	.84
Polish	.72
Korean	.63
Vietnamese	.51
Portugese	.43

Fastest Growing, Shrinking
(Percentage increase)

Language	Percentage
Mon-Khmer*	676%
Fr. Creole	654%
Gujarathi*	178%
Hindi*	155%
Vietnamese	150%

(Percentage decrease)

Percentage	Language
-34%	Yiddish
-20%	Italian
-18%	Hungarian
-12%	Polish
-5%	Greek

*Tagalog is a language of the Philippines; Mon-Khmer is a language of Cambodia; Hindi and Gujarathi are languages of India.

Source: *Spokesman Review,* 1993, p. 2A.

Social Class

One of the most important ways students differ is by class, or socioeconomic status (SES). Class differences manifest themselves in different values and priorities, different ways of using language, and different expectations about schooling. Sociologists define class membership in terms of factors like income, education, and job type. As we saw in Chapter 4, schools differ based on the class characteristics of the neighborhoods they are located in, and these differences can have serious consequences for children's education. We explore the relationship between SES and education in detail in Chapter 9. For now, be aware that students' class is an important consideration for teachers.

Gender

Just as societal inequities of class and race are reflected in schools, so too are inequities of gender.

This section discusses the differences between boys' and girls' achievement and analyzes the causes for these differences.

School Patterns

There is much evidence of unequal achievement between boys and girls in schools. Girls outscore boys on tests in the elementary grades, but boys gradually catch up and surpass them by high school. For example, the National Assessment of Educational Progress found that 9-year-old girls outperformed boys of the same age on reading tests (Sadker & Sadker, 1994). However, on the verbal portion of the 1994 Scholastic Achievement Test (SAT), the college entrance exam, boys slightly outscored girls (Education Week, 1994). This pattern is more pronounced in math achievement, whereby high school boys outscored girls by 41 points on the SAT (1994). Girls comprise the only group that starts out ahead and then falls behind as they progress through school.

Biological Explanations

What accounts for this unequal achievement? Several possible explanations have been advanced. Some have argued that achievement differences are biologically based. Males are said to be superior in perceptual and cognitive skills like spatial reasoning, and this accounts for their higher math performance. Girls are thought to be better readers and writers in elementary school because these are quiet activities that suit their earlier maturation and longer attention spans, and that ill suit the more energetic and rambunctious boys.

There are problems, however, with these biologically based explanations. For example, the difference in spatial reasoning between boys and girls is actually small, and so is the purported relationship between spatial skills and math achievement (Linn & Hyde, 1989). Spatial skills are also quite malleable, and when girls are trained in spatial reasoning, their scores match those of boys. Further, in some other countries, like England and Nigeria, boys learn to read earlier than girls (Johnson, 1976). Yet another weakness of the biological explanation is that in this country, girls start out ahead and then fall behind in both verbal and quantitative achievement. Finally, the gap in achievement and other cognitive measures has been steadily declining over the last two decades (Jacklin, 1989; Linn & Hyde, 1989). These findings challenge the view that gender differences in achievement are grounded in physiology.

Sociological Explanations

Classroom interaction research provides another set of explanations. Researchers have found that both male and female teachers treat boys and girls differently. Boys get more attention from teachers, both positive and negative. They get asked more questions and more cognitively demanding questions. They get praise for their creativity, but girls get praise for conforming to rules (Grant, 1984; Sadker, Sadker, & Klein, 1991). When boys call out responses to teacher questions, teachers more often accept their callouts and continue, whereas with girls' callouts, teachers are more likely to reprimand and correct their behavior. Not surprisingly, boys are much more prone to callouts than girls.

Cultural conditioning makes it very difficult for teachers to spot this unequal treatment without systematic observation. For example, in one study, teachers viewed videotapes of classroom interactions in which boys' verbal participation was three times that of girls, but in follow-up interviews the teachers thought the girls had received more attention. This finding is not unique to teachers. Overestimation of female participation has been documented in a variety of settings, including corporate offices, law school classrooms, and informal social gatherings (Tannen, 1990). As a result of this differential treatment over the years, female-initiated questions and comments drop from 41 percent to only 30 percent between the seventh and eighth grades. By high school, male and female students display different enrollment patterns, with girls taking fewer high level math and science classes, although in recent years this enrollment gap has been closing. These findings suggest that boys and girls in the same school experience different educational environments, with boys receiving much more reinforcement for their assertiveness, both academic and nonacademic.

Nonschool socialization experiences may also help explain gender differences. Parents and other adults socialize girls to be more compliant with authority, but aggression in boys is encouraged. These socialization patterns can affect school performance. For example, boys and girls respond differently to the anxiety that studying math engenders in both of them. Boys say to themselves, "Well, this is just anxiety, I have to be brave and carry on," but girls tend to withdraw from whatever is provoking the anxiety. These sex-stereotyped responses clearly affect student learning and persistence on academic tasks.

Testing Differences

Test-taking behavior, and thus test scores, are also affected by gender. The SAT is a timed, multiple-choice test, and sometimes intelligent estimating is the most effective way to proceed. Girls are more rule-bound than boys, and their test-taking strategies are often ineffective in dealing with the timed nature of the test. Specifically, in the mathematics portion they tend to carry out the entire computation the way they were taught, even though they might be able to quickly figure out the correct answer by simple inspection of the available choices. Boys, on the other hand, being less rule-bound, make the necessary intuitive leaps, thus completing more problems faster and obtaining higher scores.

Finally, research has also shown that on standardized math tests, boys do better on problems concerning measurement, sports, and science, whereas girls do better on items involving aesthetics, human relationships, typing, and sewing (Linn & Hyde, 1989). To the extent that boys and girls continue to develop stereotyped interests, there will be the potential for bias in test items, which will in turn affect performance.

As a society, we have responded to the gender problem in schools through legislation called **Title IX.** Title IX was one of the Education Amendments passed in 1972, and it prohibits discrimination on the basis of sex in schools that receive federal funding. Title IX applies to public schools and higher education in a broad array of circumstances: admissions, guidance and counseling, athletics, facilities, and availability of programs. It also applies to employment practices such as hiring, promotion, and compensation. Most educators agree that one of the ways females have gained under Title IX has been in athletics; more high school girls participate in sports now than did 20 years ago.

It is critical to emphasize that gender stereotyping hurts boys as well as girls. For example, boys not only get more positive attention, they get more negative attention. Boys are more likely to be reprimanded by teachers, even when their behavior is the same as girls'. More boys are diagnosed with learning disabilities, and more boys drop out of school. Boys are also more often identified as having emotional problems and commit suicide at a higher rate. Socialization into the male sex role starts earlier and is reinforced more harshly by both adults and peers than it is for girls, which in turn leads to higher anxiety levels for boys.

Even though gender inequity is an immense social problem, teachers have some influence in positively affecting it. When teachers systematically monitor and study their interaction patterns with students, they can learn how to communicate high expectations for all students and to provide more leadership opportunities for girls and more nurturing opportunities for boys. They can gradually even out their responses to males and females and make their disciplinary actions more fair. Also, through careful lesson preparation, they can correct sex stereotyping in curriculum materials.

Special Needs

During the 1992–1993 school year, over 5.1 million young people between birth and 21 years of age, or about 7.4 percent, received special educational services because of some intellectual, emotional, or physical condition that makes them exceptional in terms of the normal distribution of human traits (U.S. Department of Education, 1994). This represents a 39 percent increase since data were first collected 20 years ago. Figure 5.4 depicts the changes in the number of children identified as having various disabilities over the last 15 years. The next section describes the special intellectual, emotional, and physical conditions that characterize this population. First, read the accompanying Issue Box to learn about some of the consequences of the labeling process that is involved with special needs students.

Intellectual

Students at both ends of the intellectual spectrum have special learning needs. Currently about 6 percent of the school age population is considered intellectually disabled in some way. The prevalence of giftedness is estimated variously at 3 percent to 15 percent, depending on how it is assessed.

Mental disabilities are classified into three major groups. At the most severe level are those who suffer from profound mental retardation with IQs below 35. They comprise only 0.1 percent of the general population and are educated in separate facilities and group homes rather than in regular schools. At the next level are the moderately, or trainable, mentally retarded, whose IQs range from 35–50. These students, who represent 0.3 percent of the general population, are usually educated in special resource rooms and classes often held in regular schools. Next are the mildly, or educable, mentally retarded. With IQs ranging from 50–70, they are capable of participating to a limited extent in regular classrooms but also spend much of their school time in resource classrooms. These children are usually expected to learn basic academic and survival skills.

What are these students like in the classroom? Consider the case of Kim, a second-grader with mild mental retardation. Kim's IQ is 60, and her reading and math scores are predictably low for her age. Her social skill development also lags behind the other children in her class, with her behavior matching that of a child 3 or 4 years younger. She is capable of

Figure 5.4   **Percentage of Children in Federal Programs for Students with Disabilities**

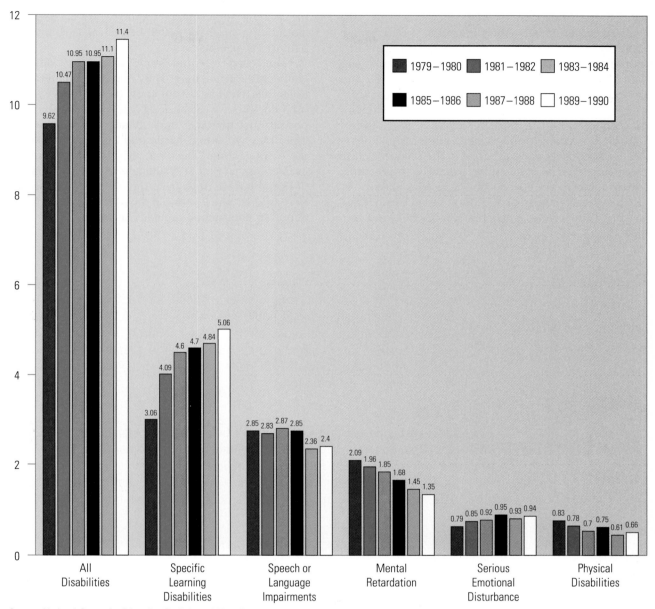

Source: National Center for Education Statistics, 1992, p. 64.

interacting with the other children during play time, but she withdraws if the game is complicated or involves more than a few children. She has learned how to dress and feed herself and to take care of her own hygiene needs. She also has a stuttering problem. While the other students are reading stories, Kim is still struggling with **decoding,** that is, with identifying and pronouncing letters correctly. Her math skills are slightly closer to age-level expectations for computation, but she cannot solve story problems that have been read and explained to her

(Hardman, Drew, Egan, & Wolf, 1996). A reasonable academic goal for Kim is to equip her with a survival reading vocabulary, such as the ability to recognize her own name and words like *danger* and *stop.*

Students of normal intelligence can still experience academic difficulties and may suffer from **specific learning disabilities.** Specific learning disabilities hamper learning in a particular domain. Experts assume that these difficulties are due to some disorder within the central nervous system and that this interferes with the development and use of a specific language, mathematical, or reasoning skills. One well-known learning disability is **attention deficit disorder,** or **ADD.** Students with ADD have trouble focusing their attention on a learning task. Symptoms include problems with listening, completing work, concentrating, awaiting turns, and the tendency to be easily distracted, impulsive, and to frequently call out.

The "average" learning disabled (LD) student, according to Kavale and Reese (1992), is a 13-year-old male, halfway through sixth grade, whose IQ is 96. He spends 78 minutes a day in the resource class receiving special education, primarily in reading; other subjects are covered in the regular classroom. He has received special education services since the end of third grade, when his teacher referred him

because of his poor academic performance, especially in reading. After 3 years in special education, his reading achievement improved by 2 years and math by 1.5 years. However, he still lags significantly behind his age-mates.

Gifted and talented students present different challenges for teachers. They may ask difficult questions that teachers do not know how to answer. They may complete work well ahead of other students, posing instructional and management problems. They may get bored easily and act up to make life more interesting. The teacher's job is to provide enrichment work that challenges these students, but does not isolate them from the life of the classroom. Here is what one 9-year-old gifted student had to say about an unenriched regular classroom:

ISSUES EXTRA

The Labeling Controversy

One issue that arises in dealing with exceptional intellectual abilities concerns labeling students. School systems receive special federal funds based on the number and types of exceptional children they serve, so the labeling process looms large in school districts. The greater the number of children identified and labeled as intellectually impaired, the more federal money becomes available to schools.

The Case For

Advocates contend that extra support helps educators meet the needs of special students, bringing additional funding to bear where it is most needed. It costs more to educate a special student, so it is important to know how many special students there are, and who they are, so that the extra monies can be applied precisely where there is the most need.

The Case Against

Opponents counter that labeling creates more problems than it solves. For example, questions about equity arise because of the disproportional placement of boys, lower SES students, and ethnic minorities into special education programs. Further, the incidence of handicap varies wildly from state to state and district to district, because distinctions between labels are quite blurry. For example, it is difficult to distinguish between a mildly retarded student and one labeled learning disabled. In fact, as the reported incidence of learning disabilities has increased in recent decades, the number identified as mentally retarded has correspondingly decreased.

Labels also allow educators to perceive learning problems only as deficiencies inherent in the child, rather than the result of faulty classroom or school processes. Furthermore, labels tend to become permanent; once placed in a special education program, students tend to stay there. Other students may ridicule labeled children, with the result that these children often suffer diminished self-esteem.

Classifying special children is also very time consuming, taking time away from badly needed classroom instruction. Moreover, there exist few

Oh what a bore to sit and listen,
To stuff we already know.
Do everything we've done and done again,
But we still must sit and listen.
Over and over read one more page
Oh bore, oh bore, oh bore.
Sometimes I feel if we do one more page
My head will explode with boreness rage.
I wish I could get up right there and march right out
the door. (Delisle, 1984, p. 72)

Physical

Increasingly, students with a wide variety of physical disabilities are being placed in regular classrooms. Hearing impaired students may attend classes with their sign language translators, and visually im-paired students may substitute large print for regular books. Schools are being equipped with ramps and other structural improvements to accommodate students in wheel chairs. In myriad ways, children formerly educated at home or in special institutional settings are coming to regular public schools.

Students with physical disabilities are a diverse group. In addition to those with visual or auditory disabilities, teachers may find orthopedically impaired students in their classrooms. These difficulties can stem from a number of causes, including traumatic brain injury, cerebral palsy, spina bifida, and spinal cord injuries, among others. With some of these, such as spina bifida, students possess normal intelligence and just need physical adjustments. For others, such as traumatic brain injury,

ISSUES

EXTRA

Continued

well-validated methods of instruction that are tied to the categories. There are no special interventions for the mildly mentally retarded, for instance, that are different from those which might be used with any student experiencing academic difficulty (Reynolds, Wang, & Walberg, 1987). For most teachers, the distinguishing characteristic is that it simply takes longer for these students to learn, which means teachers must devote more time and energy to them.

Here is how one student felt about being labeled learning disabled:

When I was in the third grade, I had no idea what "LD" meant. . . . At the time I didn't think about why I was in these small classes, and I was too young to care . . .

During my junior high school years, I began to realize the consequences of my label, but not really what "LD" meant. I was still in small classes, only now it mattered to me. I compared what I was doing in my English and Social Studies classes to what my friends were doing in the "mainstream" classes. I found that while I was playing in sand trays, my friends were learning useful skills, like writing papers. About this time I began to hear terms like "dummy classes" more often . . . Hearing terms like these relating to yourself shatters your confidence . . . I had a very difficult time making friends and an even harder time trying to accept the fact that I was different . . .

My (high school) counselor and LD teacher advised me not to go to college; in fact they went so far as to tell my parents not to let me go . . . I . . knew I could make it through college, if I got a chance. But that chance was hard to get. (Fairbanks & Hill, 1989, p. 1)

It is difficult to sort out the arguments for and against labeling special needs students. Educators continue to wrestle with the problem of providing additional services to students who need them without stigmatizing or trapping them.

intellectual and social functioning can also be adversely affected.

Health disorders comprise another variety of physical disability. Children who are medically fragile, whether due to diabetes, epilepsy, sickle cell anemia, or another condition experience higher absenteeism, may require medication or other special attention when they are at school, and may be limited in the activities in which they can participate.

Emotional

For many teachers, the most challenging special students are those with **behavioral disorders,** disabilities that adversely affect their social and emotional functioning. Hardman, Drew, Egan, and Wolf (1993) break these down into three primary types:

1. *Conduct disorders* involve overt aggression, both verbal and physical; disruptiveness; negativism; irresponsibility; and defiance.

2. *Anxiety-withdrawal* stands in contrast to conduct disorders, involving . . . overanxiety, social withdrawal, reclusiveness, shyness, sensitivity, and other behaviors implying a retreat from the environment rather than a hostile response to it.

3. *Immaturity* involves preoccupation, short attention span, passivity, daydreaming, sluggishness, and other behavior not in accord with developmental expectations. (p. 138)

These behaviors can be very trying for classroom teachers and for other students. A prerequisite for learning in the classroom is a basic stability and order, in which students are willing to cooperate with the teacher and each other to accomplish learning goals. Behavior disordered (BD) children disrupt this, interfering with not only their own learning but that of other students as well. Teachers often find that one or two BD students can take up a very large percentage of their time, attention, and energy.

Teachers' Responsibilities

Teachers must shoulder several responsibilities for assisting exceptional students, but many of these overlap with their regular duties. Teachers need to be able to identify potentially handicapped or gifted children and make referrals for them. They need to be able to work in a team with other professionals to serve the needs of special students. They may also need to assist handicapped children with special equipment. As always, they must accommodate individual differences in their instructional program and maintain communication with parents. And they must help exceptional and regular students work and play together. Virtually all teacher preparation programs require course work and field experiences in special education, so you will have the opportunity to learn a great deal more about how to assist special needs students.

Demographic Trends

We discussed the importance of demographics to schooling in Chapter 1. To recap, demographic characteristics greatly influence education policies, practices, and finances. Consider a growing community whose child population is projected to double within a 5-year period. If the community did not pay attention to demographic projections and trends, needed new schools would not be built and there would be tremendous crowding and diminishing of educational quality. It is important, then, for societies to attend to demographic trends, and our nation is no exception.

We have noted that ethnic and linguistic diversity are on the rise among America's students. But while student diversity is increasing, diversity in the teaching force is decreasing. Most teachers continue to be white and female. For example, 71 percent of all teachers in 1988 were female; the same year, 87 percent of female teachers and 90 percent of male teachers were non-Hispanic whites (Choy, et al., 1993). The number of young teachers representing ethnic minority groups is also down.

Educational leaders are actively recruiting people from minority groups into the teaching profession to offset this trend. Likewise, those who design teacher education programs are incorporating additional coursework and field experiences that deal with the educational needs of cultural minorities, language minorities, and the physically, emotionally, and learning disabled. As a new teacher, you can expect to study long and hard in order to prepare yourself to meet these new challenges.

At Risk versus Resilient Kids

We have focused on problems students have with school, either because of poverty, disability, or other characteristics that put them at risk for school failure. But the problems students have are only part of the story. Perhaps you have noticed people who grew up in very adverse circumstances yet somehow managed to triumph over their difficulties and develop into happy, capable adults. What is it that allows these people to "get a lemon, and make lemonade," while others disintegrate into despair? The ability to survive and prosper despite adversity has been termed **resilience,** and psychologists and educators alike have been investigating the factors that help children develop this important trait. This research has produced several recommendations for parents and teachers. As a teacher, it will be critical to apprise yourself of this research and to gain the knowledge and skills necessary to help your students develop resiliency.

In a nutshell, adults need to foster four attributes in young people to help them become resilient: social competence, problem-solving skills, autonomy, and a sense of purpose and future (Benard, 1993). *Social competence* means the ability to make friends, to cooperate and share, and to interact effectively with others. *Problem-solving skills* include conflict resolution and decision making. *Autonomy* means the ability to work independently and to participate in decisions that affect one's life. Finally, a *sense of purpose and future* means just that, that there is hope for the future.

To develop these attributes, teachers must create classrooms that:

- Are caring and supportive, in which adults and students trust and value each other. Teachers need to build warm relationships with students, to know them by name, and to make a point to connect with them.

- Convey high expectations, whereby teachers believe in the ability of all students to learn and the school supports high levels of learning. Teachers who craft complex, meaningful learning experiences for students both convey those expectations and provide an environment in which these expectations can be achieved.

- Encourage student participation, whereby students are involved in decisions about rules, curriculum, and instruction. Teachers who engage students in discussions about how classroom life is to be conducted foster commitment to the classroom community.

STUDENT DEVELOPMENT

Student differences are not the whole picture. We all may be unique, but within that uniqueness we share many qualities. All humans progress through stages of development, for example. Babies turn into children who turn into teenagers who turn into adults. For teachers, however, with the responsibility for helping learners of any age acquire new knowledge,

this commonsense idea is not adequate. Developmental level matters when it comes to what humans can learn and to how they learn. What can you expect, then, from students at various ages? How will student development affect your life as a teacher? In this section, we present an overview of the processes of cognitive and affective development, and discuss some of the implications for classroom teaching.

Cognitive Domain

Intellectual Development

Read about novice teacher Mark Hatfield.

> Mark is a new, enthusiastic first-grade teacher trained through an alternative teacher preparation program. It is the first week of class, and he launches eagerly into his first lecture of the day. He firmly believes in challenging students, in setting high expectations, and in thoroughly preparing them for our scientific, technological society. Therefore his talk today is on atomic structure. He displays his carefully constructed chart on the atom, and points in turn to the particles labeled *nucleus, electron, proton,* defining each and describing its motion, charge, and mass. He notices that the children are fidgeting and talking with each other, so he talks louder and more forcefully. He is pleased at the end of the hour that he covered his whole lesson plan before dismissing the children to recess.

What do you think are the strengths and weaknesses of Mark's lesson? You probably noticed that Mark's choice of content, teaching strategy, visual aid, and management techniques were inappropriate for first graders. You may even feel the mismatch was ludicrous. But many beginning teachers fail to grasp that kindergarten through twelfth-grade students are not little college kids and often use texts and techniques from their college courses in their own teaching (Darling-Hammond, 1994). We need reminding sometimes that children and teenagers are different from adults in the ways they think, reason, and learn.

One of the first to realize this was Swiss psychologist Jean Piaget. He intensively studied children's reasoning processes and found some unexpected consistencies in how children of similar age think. Based on years of close observation, Piaget proposed that people progress through four predictable stages of cognitive development: *sensorimotor, pre-operations, concrete operations,* and *formal operations.* Everyone passes through each of these four stages in order, but the rate at which people move differs.

Sensorimotor Stage (0–2 years)   The **sensorimotor** stage covers approximately the first 2 years of life. Here children focus on developing their sensory apparatus and large motor skills. The capacity to represent objects in memory gradually develops during this stage as does the ability to imitate behavior.

Preoperations Stage (2–7 years)   Next is the **preoperations** stage. In preoperations, children's thinking is characterized by the inability to think logically about concrete objects. In one of Piaget's most famous tests for this stage of development, the tester lays out two rows of coins, each with five coins lined up opposite each other. A child at this stage will be able to correctly say that there are the same number of coins in each row. But if the tester then spreads one row out, the child will say that the longer row has more coins in it, even if they were spread right in front of him.

It is easy to see how the first graders in Mark's class, who are likely preoperational, have difficulty with his lecture on the atom. Their perceptual and logical limitations severely limit their comprehension of such an abstract topic. Consider also how difficult it would be to teach preoperational children a fundamental mathematical concept, such as place value. It takes much more than simple rote learning of math facts. Children of this age can be taught to memorize a great deal of seemingly complex material, but their conceptual understanding of this information is quite superficial.

Concrete Operations Stage (7 to 11 years)   During this stage, children acquire the ability to determine when the amount of a substance stays the same independent of its shape. Piaget's coin exercise is one way of testing for this mental ability known as **conservation.** Piaget invented many conservation tasks. In one of these, two balls of clay are presented to the child, and then one is flattened within the child's view. Preoperational children will say that the flat one has more clay, even though no clay has been added, whereas children well into concrete operations will be able to conclude that the amount of clay has not changed, only its shape.

Formal Operations Stage (11 years to adult)   Finally, at about the age of 11, children advance to the stage of **formal operations.** During this stage, adolescent children develop the ability to think logically about abstractions as well as concrete objects. They can examine abstract problems systematically and generalize about the results; they can sort out variables and use proportional reasoning. Under-standing topics as diverse as algebra, representational government, and atomic motion requires thinking at the formal operations level. Studies have shown that many junior high students have not yet attained formal operations (Lawson & Snitgren, 1982), and that college students only function at formal operations about half the time in subjects outside their major (DeLisi & Staudt, 1980).

What does this pattern of cognitive development mean for teachers? Obviously, your teaching must roughly match the developmental level of your students. You need to be tuned into developmental level and design lessons accordingly. Further, it appears that if you are going to err, you should do so on the side of being more concrete. Learning built around the observation and manipulation of physical objects, whenever possible, can be helpful at virtually any age. It is also important to emphasize that *age does not determine developmental stage.* Everyone develops at a different rate, so just because one child is 7-years-old and another is 15, you should not automatically assume that one is at the concrete operation level and the other at the formal operation stage.

Although it is important that teachers be sensitive to their students' developmental levels, it is impractical to test every student in your classroom and to gauge your teaching precisely to each individual's level. As a teacher, you should assume that there will be a range of levels in every group of students you teach, and that you'll need to vary instruction accordingly. You will need to create learning opportunities that make sense to students on their terms. You will find that as you progress through your teaching career, you will continually be on the lookout for alternate ways of presenting content, so that your instruction matches the diversity of your students' needs. The accompanying Research Box explores a related aspect of cognitive development, **subject specific knowledge development,** that is, the way learning proceeds in different subject areas such as social studies and science.

Multiple Intelligences

We have been treating students' intellectual development as if everyone possessed an undifferentiated faculty called "intelligence." In fact, this appears not to be the case. People differ quantitatively in their mental functioning, that is, some are smarter than others. People also differ qualitatively in their mental functioning, that is, they possess different kinds of cognitive aptitudes. For example, you probably have known someone who was very bright in school but who lacked "savvy" and could never quite accomplish anything despite possessing high aca-

Subject Specific Knowledge Development

In addition to being sensitive to students' overall patterns of cognitive development, teachers need to know how children develop knowledge in particular subject areas. When teachers can diagnose children's existing knowledge, they can do a better job of matching their instruction to students' current understanding, thereby increasing the likelihood that their instruction will be meaningful and remembered. Sampled here is research from social studies and science to give you a taste of children's knowledge.

Social Studies Knowledge Development

Social studies researchers have found that young children's views of their government tend to be high in affect (emotionally charged) but low in knowledge. That is, they have strong, positive feelings for their political leaders and government, but do not really understand how government functions or the role of citizens in this process. For example, in one study, 80 percent of fourth-graders reported that the most important role for an adult is that of president, but fewer than 25 percent of them could say anything about what the president actually does (Greenstein, 1965). Children view the government in a very personal way, literally as a benevolent man who looks over and protects them. As students get older, they move from this simplistic, personalized view to a more institutional conception (Hess & Torney, 1967). By the time they reach young adulthood, some degree of cynicism has emerged, although minority children exhibit cynicism at an earlier age than whites.

Oddly, at no point does the idea of voting seem preeminent in their minds. Hess and Torney (1967) reported that only 4 percent of second-graders and 47 percent of eighth-graders thought voting was important. It appears that knowledge growth in this complex domain is quite slow and uneven. For example, Sinatra, Beck, and McKeown (1992) studied the progress of elementary and middle school children in understanding key concepts in American government. They interviewed 26 children before and after instruction on government, first in fifth grade and again in eighth grade. Their findings showed little growth in understanding of the importance of representation in American democracy. The authors noted that the texts used in these grades emphasized how government is structured, rather than how voters voice themselves through their representatives. Confirming findings in other studies, these students also exhibited a strong tendency to think about government in very black-and-white terms and to characterize other countries as exclusively negative and their own as exclusively positive.

Social studies knowledge appears to be spotty even for older students and adults. One study of students in advanced placement American history classes, for example, found that at the beginning of the school year, college-bound juniors and seniors had difficulty correctly placing events like the Civil War, the Great Depression, and World War II in chronological order, scoring on average only 12 out of a possible 20 points. By the end of the year, they had increased their scores to only 15.5 (Henderson, Winitzky,

RESEARCH

Continued

& Kauchak, 1996). Teachers can use information from these and related studies to generate a starting point for their own curricula.

Science Knowledge Development

Children's knowledge of science has also been extensively studied (Glynn, Yeany, & Britton, 1991). Vosniadou (1991) and her colleagues interviewed students at all levels and conducted cross-national studies seeking to understand how knowledge of astronomy develops. They probed understanding of topics like the size, shape, and motion of the earth, sun, and moon; they also examined understanding of the day and night cycle, the seasons, the phases of the moon, and eclipses (Vosniadou & Brewer, 1990). For example, one question they asked had to do with what would happen to someone standing on the "bottom" side of the earth. Look at the diagrams in Figure 5.5. Interviewers asked first-, third-, and fifth-graders, "Suppose there were a little girl here at the bottom of the earth; would she fall off?" Next they asked, "Now suppose this little girl on the bottom of the earth had a ball in her hand. If she dropped the ball where would the ball go?"

Figure 5.5   Questions Used to Investigate Elementary-Age Children's Understanding of Gravity

Question 1: Imagine there's a little girl here on the bottom of the earth. Will she fall off?

Question 2: Now imagine she has a ball in her hand. If she drops it, where will it go?

Source: After Vosniadou, 1991.

Now refer to Table 5.1 to see how children responded to these questions. We can see that most first-graders incorrectly apply their everyday concepts of up and down to the gravity problem and that, as children mature, they more often perceive that gravity pulls objects toward the center of the earth. However, we can also see again that progress is slow and uneven, because even at fifth grade, many children are still confused about the direction the ball would go if the little girl dropped it.

Continued

Table 5.1   How Children Responded to Gravity Questions in Figure 5.5

Question 1: Will she fall off?

	Percentage Responding	
Response	First-Graders	Fifth-Graders
Fall off/down/away from earth	30	0
She will, but not us, because we're inside earth	25	20
Not fall off	25	75
Don't know	20	5

Question 2: Where will the ball go?

	Percentage Responding	
Response	First-Graders	Fifth-Graders
Fall down/away/off earth	75	30
Towards center of earth	20	55
Float in space	5	15

Source: After Vosniadou, 1991.

   Similar patterns have been found for the shape of the earth and other concepts. Of special importance to teachers is the persistence of these misconceptions. For example, young children's initial picture of the shape of the earth is that it is a flat, square object with edges. This mental model is based on their everyday experiences. When they are taught by their parents and teachers that the earth is round, most of them revise their conception in a way that both fits their everyday experience and accommodates what adults say. That is, they picture the earth as a flat disk rather than as a rectangle. They cannot doubt their day-to-day experience of the earth as flat, but neither do they want to disbelieve the adults who care for them. Even when the instruction they receive is quite concrete, using models and pictures, these misconceptions persist. As they mature, their misconceptions gradually become more complex and often very creative: Some children picture a truncated sphere; some think that there are two earths, a flat one that we live on and a round one up in the sky; some say that the earth is a hollow sphere and people live on a flat part on the inside. Note that in every case, if their teacher asked them what shape the earth was, they could say quite handily that it is round. Teachers beware: Students can often give what appears to be the right answer without really understanding the underlying concept.

   There are cultural differences in the predominant answers. Many young children in India believed the earth to be a flat disk floating on a sea of water, but few American children thought of that. An interesting model unique to Samoan children was that the earth is shaped like a ring, with people living along its rim.

demic intelligence. As a teacher, it is important to recognize the variety of ways in which your students can be intelligent.

Harvard theorist Howard Gardner proposed a system for classifying different types of intelligence based on an extensive review of the psychological literature. In Gardner's **theory of multiple intelligences,** there are posited seven basic forms of intelligence (Gardner, 1983; Gardner & Hatch, 1989). These seven types of intelligence are described in Table 5.2.

As a teacher with responsibilities for creating learning experiences and evaluating performance for all students, sensitivity to students' intellectual styles and strengths is critical. Teachers should respond to multiple intelligences in the same way they respond to developmental level and the other forms of diversity discussed: teach in a variety of ways.

Affective Domain

Attending to students' affective, or social and emotional, life is also part of a teacher's professional life. Students bring their emotional as well as intellectual needs with them to school, and the more effective teachers are those who factor these needs into their teaching. Highlighted in this section are aspects of affect that are key to creating productive, humane classrooms. You will have the opportunity to delve into these topics in much greater depth in your educational psychology coursework.

Social-Emotional Development

Like cognitive development, social and emotional development are influenced by learning, maturation, and experience. Social development refers to the ways children learn to interact with others, whereas emotional or personal development refers to the ways they view themselves. One of the most prominent theorists in this area was Erik Erikson, who proposed a stage theory for social-emotional development that, like Piaget, roughly matches certain age spans. Erikson believed that at critical times of life, people confront predictable emotional crises. If the individual successfully navigates the crisis, psychological and interpersonal health are attained, and the individual can move on to the next stage. Erikson believed all humans pass through crises involving trust, autonomy, guilt, mastery, identity, and intimacy as they progress from infancy to young adulthood. Understanding the types of emotional concerns that are most salient for your students will enable you to more effectively manage and instruct. As you study emotional development later in your preparation program, give thought to how you will tailor your practices to your students' emerging social needs.

Emotional Needs

All humans experience at least three basic needs at every stage of life: affiliation, influence, and achievement. **Affiliation** refers to the desire for close relationships with others, the need to give and receive affection. **Influence** has to do with wanting to have some say in the conduct of your life. **Achievement** involves the need to accomplish something and to feel competent. Everywhere we go, we strive to meet these needs, and students are no exception. They do not leave their emotions behind them at the schoolhouse door! If teachers do not provide mechanisms for students to meet these needs in the classroom,

Table 5.2   **Gardner's Seven Types of Intelligence**

Type	Description
Logical-mathematical	Ability to discern logical and numerical patterns and to manage long chains of reasoning
Linguistic	Sensitivity to the sounds, rhythms, and meanings of words and to the different functions of language
Musical	Ability to produce and appreciate pitch, timbre, rhythm, and the different forms of musical expression
Spatial	Ability to perceive the visual-spatial world accurately and to perform transformations on one's perceptions, both mentally and in the world
Bodily-kinesthetic	Ability to exert great control over physical movements and to handle objects skillfully
Interpersonal	Capacity to discern and respond appropriately to the moods, temperaments, motivations, and desires of others
Intrapersonal	Perceptiveness about one's own emotional state and knowledge of one's own strengths and weaknesses

student engagement and learning suffer (Schmuck & Schmuck, 1997).

It is not really very difficult to organize classrooms to support emotional needs as well as academic ones. When teachers use cooperative learning and other interactive teaching methods (see Chapter 6), they are supporting students' affiliation needs. When they provide opportunities for students to have input into classroom procedures, they help students meet their influence needs. And when students are successful learners, their achievement needs are met. The more teachers can dovetail classroom activities to meet multiple needs and goals, the better their students will learn and grow.

Motivation

A final affective concern is **motivation,** the willingness to engage and persist in learning tasks. Motivation, of course, looms large for teachers. Researchers have found that students display certain classroom motivation patterns (Ames, 1992). A **mastery orientation** involves the belief that effort is linked to successful learning, and learning in turn provides an inherently satisfying sense of mastery. A **performance orientation,** in contrast, focuses on affirming one's self-worth by competing with and surpassing others. Students with a mastery orientation are more likely to engage and persist in academic work, especially when the work is challenging. Furthermore, they are more likely to learn material in depth. Performance-oriented students, however, will disengage and take short cuts when that is expedient. They fail to involve themselves very deeply in the subject matter.

When teachers use competitive grading and public displays of grades and focus learning activities on a narrow range of academic outcomes, they promote a performance orientation in their students. However, when teachers use a variety of classroom learning activities, when they minimize public comparison of students, and when they share influence with students, they help them develop a mastery orientation to motivation. The motivation literature is further evidence of the need for teachers to establish democratic communities in their classrooms.

Development and Culture

Astute readers have probably noticed that the theories of development discussed were generated by theorists from Europe and North America. Are all peoples just like Westerners? Do all children everywhere develop exactly the same way? As you might suspect, culture does make a difference. Consider the case of Japan. Here is a description of a Japanese elementary school lesson:

> The *sticky-probing* approach . . . is to select a seemingly small problem that most of the children would not otherwise notice, probe into it through deliberative group discussion and teacher-pupil exchange, and thus spend considerable time on reflecting, examining, and digesting the problem. . . . A fourth-grade teacher spent two class hours discussing only two *haiku,* that is, two short 17-syllable poems. (Hess & Azuma, 1991, p. 6)

Japanese children present a great contrast to American children. As Americans, we believe that fourth-graders (9- to 10-year olds) have neither the emotional maturity nor the physical stamina to sit still for 2 hours for a discussion of poetry that is alien to their lives. This belief is supported by prestigious thinkers like Piaget. It is also supported by our everyday experiences with young American children, who really cannot sit still for very long. But the case of Japan strikingly illustrates that children may be able to do more. Our beliefs about the nature of children, then, influence our classroom practices, the theories that support those practices, and the children themselves.

SCHOOLS' RESPONSE TO DIVERSITY

We have seen that even universal human experiences, like cognitive development, unfold differently depending on culture, ability level, physical factors, social class, gender, and language. We have also seen in the historical sections of this text how the old "factory" model of schooling, in which students are considered raw material to be uniformly processed toward standardized goals, is now thought to be counterproductive to the educational needs of our society and its many individual students. Schools today are trying to replace this mass-production model of education with more flexible and student-centered programs. As a prospective new teacher, you need to be aware of the ways schools have approached this issue.

Pull-Out Programs

The most obvious way to deal with educational problems is to pull individuals out of their regular classrooms for special instruction. In secondary schools, tracking students into special classes is the counterpart to the elementary schools' pull-out programs. Gifted students take time out of the regular curriculum to pursue advanced enrichment activities; students who are floundering academically go to resource room classes for remedial work; and students who do not speak English take special ESL classes.

One of the major federal programs funding such pull-out programs for students in academic difficulty has been Chapter 1, recently overhauled and renamed *Title I.* The new Title I program differs in substantial ways from Chapter 1. Title I mandates states to develop high, challenging standards and to make substantial progress every year in bringing low-achieving students up to those standards. Ultimately, all Title I students are to achieve at these high levels. New assessments are to be developed to test whether students are making sufficient progress. These new programs focus on schoolwide efforts rather than on individual students. They also focus on schoolwide teacher development, relying on team-based approaches rather than a few special education teachers (Juffras & Rose, 1995).

There are several reasons behind these changes. One, in the urban schools that have received the bulk of these funds, most students are low achievers, not a few. It does not make much sense to pull out 60 percent of the students for special instruction. It does make sense to target the educational environment of the whole school and to help all teachers improve their skills in dealing with students in difficulty. Finally educators are beginning to realize that students have academic difficulty for a variety of reasons, and that cooperation between a variety of professionals—teachers, social workers, special educators, parents, and others—is the best strategy for resolving students' academic problems.

Another reason for moving away from pull-out programs and tracking is that their effectiveness has been spotty. We already discussed the ways that tracking in secondary schools disadvantages minorities. It is also unclear whether pulling elementary-age children out of regular classes for special work is helpful. Researchers have found little evidence to support this practice.

Mainstreaming and Inclusion

Another way to deal with diversity is through **mainstreaming.** Mainstreaming was originally developed as a response to the inadequacies of pull-out and other separate education programs for disabled students. The essence of mainstreaming is to educate students with disabilities in regular classrooms to the greatest extent possible. Currently, educators use a broader term, **inclusion,** to describe practices that will facilitate the integration of an even greater number of students with disabilities and other differences into regular classrooms. The two terms can be loosely distinguished in that inclusion tends to rely more on infusing specialists into the regular class-

room, whereas mainstreaming relies more on pulling special needs students out of the regular classroom for short periods. The inclusion movement grew in reaction to years of discrimination and neglect of special needs students.

Mainstreaming involves a couple of key features, both growing out of federal legislation. One feature is termed **least restrictive environment;** this refers to the obligation to serve disabled students as much as possible in the regular classroom. The regular classroom should adjust as much as possible to the needs of the special student in lieu of removing that student from "normal" surroundings.

Another important part of mainstreaming is the **individualized educational plan (IEP).** Each disabled student is to have a special plan drawn up by all interested parties to tailor education to the student's own needs. Serving on IEP committees may be regular teachers, special educators, speech therapists, counselors, parents, or anyone who has an interest in the child and who has expertise that might be brought to bear.

The inclusion movement has many educational benefits besides alleviating discrimination. For example, disabled students have the opportunity to learn appropriate social and academic behavior from observing the behavior of nonhandicapped children. As for the nonhandicapped students, they are able to see firsthand the strengths, limitations, and potential contributions of their handicapped peers. Both the school environment and society at large are thereby enriched.

Multicultural Education

Multicultural education is an umbrella term covering a broad array of programs whose goals may involve any of the following: equalizing the educational and life chances of minority students; promoting understanding and appreciation of cultural diversity; developing students' skills in handling cross-cultural situations; and taking political action to correct social and economic injustice. As James Banks (1993), a prominent multicultural educator asserted:

> The major theorists and researchers in multicultural education agree that the movement is designed to restructure educational institutions so that all students . . . will acquire the knowledge, skills, and attitudes needed to function effectively in a culturally and ethnically diverse world. . . . [It] is not an ethnic- or gender-specific movement. It is a movement designed to empower all students to become knowledgeable, caring, and active citizens in a deeply troubled and ethnically polarized nation and world. (p. 23)

Multicultural programs can include several features whose relevance varies depending on the particular grade level or subject matter. In a history class, for example, the contributions of women can be woven into the story. An English class can include works by authors such as Richard Wright, Amy Tan, and Isabel Allende. A geometry lesson on tessellation (repeating geometric patterns) can draw exemplars from Native American folk art. The possibilities for such curricular integration are endless.

Another important part of multicultural education is prejudice reduction. Educators agree that all teachers must strive to reduce mistrust between Americans. A final component is **equity pedagogy.** When teachers employ strategies to help all students learn, no matter what their cultural or linguistic background, they are utilizing equity pedagogy.

Multicultural education has not been without its critics. Some contend that the movement weakens Western cultural traditions. Banks argues, however, that the purpose of multicultural education is not to exclude the West, but rather to include previously disregarded groups. The focus is on inclusion and equity, not on promoting one group at another's expense (Banks, 1993).

Others fear that multicultural education will have a divisive effect on our national culture. Arthur Schlesinger has been a leading critic on this point, arguing that the study of cultural differences will break our society down along racial lines. Multiculturalists counter that this view presumes we were united in the first place, likely an inaccurate assumption. Further, as we described previously, the aims of multicultural education center overwhelmingly on inclusion, not on factionalizing groups. For example, most multicultural educators advocate an integrated curriculum, not an Afrocentric one.

Another faulty conception is that multicultural education is meant only for African Americans, Hispanics, or other traditionally disadvantaged minorities. Sometimes teachers in all-white settings believe that because they do not have to deal with diversity, they do not have to think about multicultural issues. Nothing could be further from the case. The world is multicultural, and teachers who work in homogeneous settings need to be even more creative in developing multicultural awareness because they do not have natural diversity to draw on. People living in homogeneous communities have a greater need for someone to draw their attention to these issues and to render other groups' views and perspectives sensible to them. The natural person to tap for this role is the teacher.

What skills, knowledge, and dispositions will you need to help you become a multicultural teacher?

The most important skill is the ability to learn about the cultural backgrounds of your students, and to use that knowledge to inform your teaching.

THE PROBLEM AND OPPORTUNITY OF DIVERSITY

At the beginning of this chapter, we showed you different ways that teachers can react to student diversity. Some found it problematic, others found in diversity an opportunity to advance learning for their students. Here are a few more examples showing how teachers and schools have responded to diversity.

Kou was a thirteen-year old, small but very sturdy, Laotian boy assigned to Virginia Nolan's special education class in suburban Santa Barbara, California. Kou was dynamite on the playground; he could throw farther and run faster than anyone. He was tops at soccer. But in the classroom, the English and math he learned one week seemed to disappear the next. Nolan tried every trick to help him acquire English—writing in colored chalk, making clay letters, drawing on the playground—but nothing seemed to work. He was always very willing to tackle any activity Nolan set for him, but it didn't help him learn the language.

Nolan noticed after a time that Kou often sang to himself, and she asked him one day to tell about his song. As he told the song's story, another Laotian student suggested that Nolan write it down. As she did so, other students joined in to debate the proper translation. They ended up singing the song with Kou. The next day, other children brought their own native songs to share and discuss. This launched a song translation and publication activity that developed into a major, long-term language experience project for the whole class.

Kou now had reason to communicate in relating the stories of his Hmong people, and although his written work was laden with errors, these stories became the basis for his language arts education. He began to learn quickly and retain what he had learned. He left Nolan's class at 15, with third-grade reading skills and math basics. Nolan said she was much wiser about capitalizing on what students know and are interested in, and using these as a basis for her teaching. (Sadker & Sadker, 1994, p. 91)

It is the middle of fifth period, and Sabrina Smith, a student who has cerebral palsy, needs to go to the bathroom. She interrupts Carol Masterson, her teacher, who is giving instructions for a writing assignment to her seventh-grade reading class . . . (at a Texas middle school). "Ms Masterson, I need to go now," Sabrina Smith says haltingly, as her right hand operates the control to direct her wheelchair to the hallway door.

"Okay, Sabrina," Masterson says. She knows Sabrina is physically unable to wait until later to go to the bathroom. She tells the other 35 students in class to begin writing on the assignment and walks quickly down the hall in pursuit of Sabrina.

"We don't even know what we're supposed to write about yet!" says Sal Rio. . . .

"Just write, Sal," Masterson responds. "Just write" . . .

The bathroom procedure requires the teacher to open the cubicle door, to lift the 70-pound Sabrina and hold her up while simultaneously taking off her panties, to lower her onto the toilet seat, to wait for her to go to the bathroom, and then to lift her up off the toilet seat, hold her up while simultaneously pulling up her panties, carry her back onto the wheelchair, help her wash her hands at the sink, and then escort her back to class. The routine usually took between 10 and 12 minutes. (Baines, Baines, & Masterson, 1994, p. 40, 57)

As these stories attest, teachers' attitudes, skills, and creativity, as well as the resources provided them by schools, districts, and communities, make an enormous difference in students' educational outcomes. Knowing that you will likely have to confront diversity in your classrooms, you need to think ahead about what skills, knowledge, and dispositions you will need to effectively handle those situations. Be on the lookout in your teacher preparation program for ways you can capitalize on diversity. Prepare yourself by mastering the skills of equity pedagogy, curriculum integration, and of eliciting parental and administrative support. In addition, prepare yourself psychologically for maintaining a constructive attitude when faced with possible inadequate resources and a student population whose culture differs from your own. As the professional, it is your responsibility to cover the most distance in bridging that gap. How will you inform yourself about the cultural differences of your students? How will you recognize and deal with the culture shock that you will likely experience? This job is a big one, and you will spend much of your professional life honing these skills.

SUMMARY

- Cultural and ethnic diversity are growing in the United States. Students' cultural differences (not deficits!) can result in academic difficulty. Increasingly, teachers will be expected to master culturally responsive teaching.

- Language diversity in classrooms is also increasing rapidly. In managing this diversity, a teacher's job is to preserve and respect students' native language or dialect while at the same time helping them acquire standard English.

- Low-income students experience depressed academic success. Teachers must be sensitive to the added burdens of poverty, and exercise flexibility in helping students overcome these burdens.

- Gender discrimination in school adversely affects both boys and girls. Biological explanations for achievement differences do not hold up under close scrutiny. Teachers need to vigilantly monitor their interaction patterns with boys and girls and adjust to make them more equitable.

- Increasingly students with special physical, intellectual, and emotional needs are being placed in regular classrooms. Teachers of the twenty-first century will be expected to manage this diversity efficiently and productively. To facilitate, teacher education programs are increasing coursework in special education and interprofessional collaboration.

- Although student diversity is increasing, the diversity of the teaching force is declining. Increasing numbers of students whose cultures differ from teachers' make teaching a more complex job.

- Emotional resilience helps young people succeed in the face of adversity. Teachers can enhance students' resilience by helping them develop social skills, problem-solving skills, autonomy, and a sense of purpose and hope for the future.

- Humans progress through stages of intellectual development, gaining proficiency in abstract reasoning and learning as they mature. Teachers need to consider students' levels of cognitive development as they instruct.

- Scholars now believe that intelligence is not a unitary factor but that it exists in multiple forms. Among these are linguistic, mathematical, musical, spatial, kinesthetic, interpersonal, and intrapersonal intelligence.

- Just as individuals progress through predictable stages of cognitive development, so too do they progress through stages of social-emotional development. Teachers can positively influence students' development by providing challenging school work within a supportive environment.

- All humans experience needs for affiliation, influence, and achievement.

- Teachers can help students develop a mastery orientation to motivation by providing a variety of learning activities and goals and by encouraging student input into classroom decisions.

- Culture influences developmental processes, and children usually exhibit the age-appropriate behavior their culture expects of them.

- Schools have attempted to meet the individual needs of the diverse student

population through pull-out programs, inclusion, and multicultural education.

READINGS FOR THE PROFESSIONAL

Banks, J. A. *Multiethnic Education: Theory and Practice* (3rd. ed.). Boston: Allyn & Bacon, 1994.
This book is an excellent overview of the burgeoning field of multicultural education.

Means, B.; C. Chelemer; & M. Knapp. *Teaching Advanced Skills to At-Risk Students*. San Francisco: Jossey-Bass, 1991.
Solidly research-based and practical, this book provides a wealth of suggestions for moving beyond the "pedagogy of poverty" and helping at-risk students attain high achievement.

Ogbu, J. U. "Understanding Cultural Diversity and Learning." *Educational Researcher,* 21 no. 8 (1992), pp. 5–14, 24.
This article is a detailed, extended discussion on involuntary minorities, and how teachers can be helpful.

Takaki, R. *A Different Mirror: A History of Multicultural America.* Boston: Little, Brown, 1993.
This book examines history of several ethnic groups in the United States, including Africans, Jews, Japanese, and Irish.

CHAPTER 6

Instruction and Management

The heart of a teacher's job is instruction. When most people think about being a teacher, this is what they usually think about—helping young people learn. As you may have surmised by now, though, just as classrooms and students have changed, so too have the demands of instruction and classroom management. What can you expect to *do* as a teacher? Parts of the job will be familiar to you, but others will be new. This chapter gives you the opportunity to explore what it is like to teach and manage large groups of students in today's schools.

The chapter is organized around the instructional cycle, that is, around the sequence of events teachers typically experience during the school day and school year. First, a teacher has to *organize the classroom,* set up materials, get the physical space ready for students, and formulate some long-range plans. Next, she must develop more specific *plans*

for each day and unit of study. Of course, the heart of the job is *instruction,* and that comes next. Invariably though, some students will be off task, so the teacher needs to consider appropriate *management and discipline* activities in order to maintain a positive learning environment. Finally, she must *assess* what her students have learned and use that information to plan for subsequent lessons.

Central to this chapter are the twin concepts of repertoire and purpose. Like a musician's repertoire, **repertoire** in teaching refers to the variety of techniques and methods teachers have at their disposal for organizing, instructing, managing, and assessing students. The notion of repertoire is meaningless, however, without the corresponding concept of purpose. Just as a musical selection must match an event (a musician would not likely play a Sousa march at a funeral, for example), teachers need to

Organizing the Classroom
  Long-Range Planning
  Physical Arrangement of Classroom
  Rules and Procedures
  Organization and Classroom Management
  Beyond the Classroom

Planning
  Teachers' Thought Processes
  Cycles of Planning
  Use of Time

Instructing
  Repertoire
    Direct Instruction
    Lecture
    Cooperative Learning
    Problem-Based Instruction
  Classroom Discourse
    Questioning
    Recitation
    Discussion
    Informal Interaction Patterns

Managing and Disciplining Students
  Student Cooperation and Classroom
    Management
  Communication and Management
  Discipline
    Jones Model
    Dreikurs Model
    Assertive Discipline
  Classroom Meeting

Assessing
  Purposes
    Sizing-Up Assessment
    Instructional Assessment
    Official Assessment
  Alternatives
    Authentic Assessment
    Portfolios

Summary

Readings for the Professional

Figure 6.1 **The Instructional Cycle**

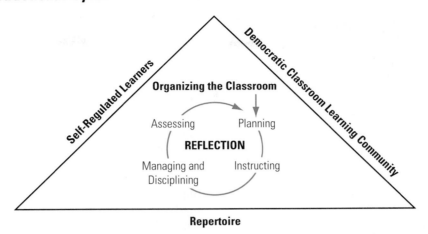

match their instructional, managerial, and assessment methods to particular purposes. We believe every teacher's ultimate **purpose** is to help students become self-regulated learners within a democratic classroom learning community. All techniques, strategies, and methods should be in service to that overarching goal. Over time, working towards this goal will result in an increase in cooperative and helpful behavior among students, an increase in their ability to solve both interpersonal and intellectual problems on their own, more self-initiated learning, fewer instances of teacher-imposed penalties, and greater student achievement.

Matching repertoire with purpose requires teachers to think deeply and make decisions about which strategy is appropriate at any given time. Therefore, another important concept to keep in mind is **reflection,** the ability and disposition to continually reevaluate one's instructional decisions. As noted, we see the reflective process aimed at the goal of producing self-regulated learners within a democratic classroom learning community. The relationship between the instructional cycle and the concepts of repertoire, purpose, and reflection are illustrated in Figure 6.1.

ORGANIZING THE CLASSROOM

Akeisha Jones surveyed her classroom. It was her first day back to work after the summer break. She had 1 hour before district meetings began to work on her classroom set-up. That was okay, though, because as a 5-year veteran of seventh- and eighth-

grade science teaching, much of it was already in place.

For example, she already had the furniture organized so that students could sit in groups of four for frequent small-group and lab activities. She knew where she would place learning centers and the computer center. She also knew how she would organize her bulletin board space for all the upcoming instructional units. Her classroom rules were already posted, also the daily schedule and fire drill procedures. Space was set aside for the display of student work, for highlighting the contributions of famous scientists and mathematicians, and for noting career opportunities that required science and math preparation. Her grade book and computer spread sheets were organized. Experimentation and reflection in previous years had helped her determine the most efficient procedures for picking up seatwork; collecting, correcting, and recording homework; taking attendance; and moving students through learning centers, among other routines.

Akeisha's focus in her science teaching was on conceptual understanding and scientific reasoning, not merely on science vocabulary. For example, rather than just lecturing and drilling on the scientific names and characteristics of the different classifications of plants and animals, she emphasized using data to find patterns and to relate those patterns to biological theories like evolution. Without concrete and analytical thinking experiences, Akeisha knew from both research and her own experience that students never really grasp the purpose, methods, or terminology of biology. They would never be able to apply new skills and knowledge in their own lives, in making career, consumer, and public policy decisions.

Right now she was playing with some new ideas about integrating videodisk technology into her overall plans. She'd explored a few pieces over the summer and was now putting together a proposal for her principal. This was going to require purchasing new hardware and software, training herself on how to operate the machinery, and learning how to integrate it most effectively in her teaching. She was excited about the potential videodisk offered. For example, dissections could be demonstrated and simulated on disk rather than having to cut up a bunch of dead animals. That made a persuasive argument for her principal: no more dead frogs and cats lying about the building or reappearing on each year's budget requests! But she hadn't figured out where she was going to get the time to teach basic videodisk technology to the kids or how she would weave the videodisk lessons smoothly into her existing curriculum. Well, budget first, she thought, and then on to the larger issues. She began drafting her budget plan, and hoped to have it finished before the meetings started. Let's see, today she had to help with the orientation for new faculty, attend the AIDS workshop, and meet with other faculty in her building to develop plans for a new curriculum integration project. A busy day!

Teachers face many classroom organizational tasks before students ever walk in the door. This part of teaching is one of several that necessarily has been invisible to you as a student. Students can only observe teachers in front of the class. This limited view has no doubt influenced and likely somewhat distorted your own ideas about the nature of teaching. Working with students takes lots of planning and preparation. Just like lawyers have to prepare their cases for court and actors have to rehearse their scenes, teachers have to prepare their lessons for class. Highlighted here are several key points about organizing classrooms.

Long-Range Planning

Probably the most important planning and organizational decision teachers must make is what they are trying to accomplish over the long term. Contrary to popular belief, teachers, especially new teachers, cannot wing it. They need to think about what their long-term goals are and how they are going to link those goals to classroom organization, daily instruction, management, and assessment. For example, the goal of establishing a classroom learning community requires that students spend part of their day working with each other in groups, so as to learn the democratic skills of group discussion, decision making, and problem solving. That in turn necessitates a

portion of instructional time being devoted to cooperative learning, which requires that desks are arranged in groups so that students can work together. In a similar vein, the goal of developing self-regulated learners is not compatible with a classroom in which desks are always organized in rows and all class time is spent listening to lectures and filling out worksheets. Because the goal of self-regulated learning requires giving students frequent opportunities to solve open-ended problems, students need some time to work independently, move freely about the classroom, and interact with other students. In short, there is a connection between the big goals and everyday practices. Take a moment to read the accompanying Research Box to see how long-range planning can contribute significantly to the goals of an entire school.

In addition to these broad aims, teachers have other, more specific, objectives appropriate to their particular grade levels and subject areas. For example, a first-grade teacher might have as a goal that students learn the basics of reading, including the acquisition of letter-sound correspondences and some comprehension skills. An eighth-grade social studies teacher, on the other hand, might want his students to learn the chronology of major events in American history, and an eleventh-grade chemistry teacher might want her students to understand the rudiments of quantum mechanics. As teachers set up their classrooms and teach their lessons over the course of the year, they need to keep all their goals firmly in mind.

Before school begins, teachers need to draft an overall plan for the year, mapping out starting and ending dates for the major units of study. In doing so, they need to take into consideration such things as parent-teacher conferences, holidays, schoolwide testing schedules, assembly schedules, and many other events. Many teachers place advance orders to their district for special materials like videos, posters, models, or other realia to make sure they can get the materials when they need them.

Physical Arrangement of the Classroom

How should the classroom be arranged to advance goals for content learning, self-regulated learning, and a democratic learning community? Here's one example, taken from a primary elementary classroom.

When the students entered the room, they saw it as divided into . . . parts. The front part of the room contained a desk for each student, the "teacher's desk" (which was to be frequently used by students during the year), a two-story loft, a seven-foot bench, a chalkboard, a bulletin board, and a cubby box or shelf for each student's personal things. The other . . . parts of the room were set up with round tables and chairs for small-group work. (Putnam & Burke, 1992, p. 121)

Figures 6.2 and 6.3 provide additional examples from other grade levels.

What can be inferred about these teachers' approaches and goals from the way they have organized their rooms? It is immediately apparent that the elementary classroom must support more diverse activities than the secondary one. There are more different kinds of spaces for individual, small-group, and whole-class work. This is to be expected, since elementary teachers spend the whole day with their students and are responsible for teaching every subject. The elementary classroom also houses more concrete materials: pets, games, books, art supplies, and math manipulatives. We can infer from this that the elementary teacher realizes that hands-on experiences and interaction promote learning. It is also clear that the secondary math teacher has integrated cooperative learning methods into his teaching, because we can see that the

desks are organized in groups of four, an arrangement conducive to small-group work. All three teachers have also arranged the layout to minimize congestion and promote easy access to needed materials.

Another consideration concerning the physical layout of classrooms is their decor. Before the year starts, teachers need to think about what basic information to display on walls (or suspend from the ceiling), about three-dimensional display materials, and about how they might use the space to maximize motivation, engagement, and learning. As an experienced teacher, Akeisha had all her materials in place; if she changed grade level or subject area, however, she would need to retool and obtain materials appropriate for a different context. Teachers need to constantly be on the lookout for posters, models, and other "stuff" that will help them create a lively and efficient learning environment. Of course, as the year progresses, teachers can use one of the best decorating materials of all, student work.

A final task in preparing classroom space involves how to store books and other materials. Science classes and lessons may require microscopes,

Figure 6.2   A Secondary Math Teacher's Classroom

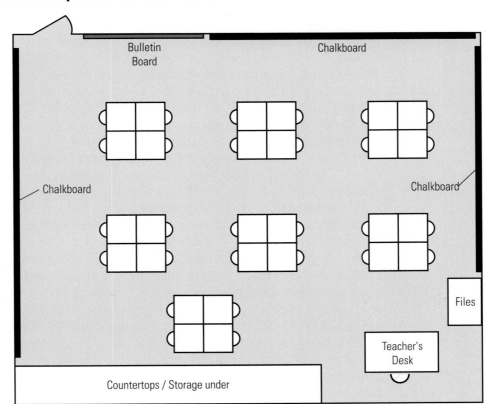

Success for All

Success for All (SFA) is the brainchild of Robert Slavin and his colleagues at Johns Hopkins University in Baltimore. In 1986, Baltimore's superintendent and school board challenged the Johns Hopkins group to specify what it would take to guarantee academic success for every child attending disadvantaged schools. They wanted to reduce the number of students retained in grade, referred to special education, and who experienced school failure. The Johns Hopkins' response was Success For All, launched in 1987 at an all-black school in inner-city Baltimore. After one year, students in the program had achieved much higher reading levels and much reduced special education referrals than comparable students at other schools.

Since implemented in over 300 schools in 70 districts throughout the United States, Success For All was designed to maximize achievement for all students and to intervene in the primary grades to prevent young children from ever experiencing academic failure. Slavin refers to this as "neverstreaming." If you can nip reading problems in the bud, you can reduce the need for remedial education later on. SFA is most often adopted in Title 1 schools, those schools serving large numbers of low-income students at risk for academic failure.

Success for All has several components: classroom learning activities, regular testing, and tutoring. Every day in every reading class, teachers begin their 90-minute lessons by reading children's literature aloud. Students then discuss the story and learn more about story structure and vocabulary. Following the discussion, children in kindergarten and first grade study a curriculum called *Reading Roots.* Reading Roots provides basic knowledge of phonics through a series of specially designed books that pair student and teacher taking turns reading aloud. Further instruction is provided in letter-sound correspondences, story structure, comprehension strategies, metacognition, and writing.

Once students have mastered Roots, they move on to *Reading Wings.* Wings is organized around cooperative learning teams. Story structure, prediction, summarization, vocabulary building, decoding practice, and story-related writing comprise its learning goals. Students also read a book of their choice for 20 minutes each night as homework. Classroom reading curriculum materials are available in both English and Spanish.

Reading classes are organized differently from conventional elementary schools. Students spend most of their day in their own age-graded classrooms. For reading lessons, however, students from different classes are mixed according to their current reading skill level. This means that, for example, high-level first graders might be working with middle-level second graders. In addition, all professional staff are utilized for reading instruction, including counselors, librarians, special educators, and administrators. This feature allows reading classes to be smaller, giving each student correspondingly more attention from the teacher. An additional benefit of this structure (termed the *Joplin plan*) is that the need

RESEARCH

Continued

for multiple classroom reading groups disappears. Typically teachers divide their students into three reading groups of upper, middle, and lower abilities. Teachers instruct only one group at a time, so the students in the other two groups must be kept busy doing worksheets. Worksheet time is not quality instructional time. The teacher is not available to assist them when they run into difficulties. With a Joplin plan, everyone is maximally engaged in productive learning activities.

A key feature of Success for All is regular assessment. Every 8 weeks, student progress is evaluated. The information is used to adjust student placement in reading classes, to determine who needs tutoring, and to identify students who may have special needs, such as for vision or hearing problems, or for family intervention. The assessments are based on teacher judgments as well as on formal testing.

Perhaps the most important component of the program is individual tutoring for students experiencing difficulty keeping up in their reading classes. Tutoring sessions are conducted by certified teachers, special educators, or certified tutors for 20 minutes daily in addition to the regular reading class. Tutors work closely with the reading class instructor, employing the same books and stories and emphasizing the same skills and vocabulary as the regular teacher. However, tutors try to identify learning problems and to use different strategies to teach the same content. They also emphasize metacognitive skills. Based on the concept of neverstreaming, first graders are given priority for tutoring. Success for All aims to help all students learn to read the first time.

Another key feature is family support. A family support team works in each school to enhance participation by parents in the educational process. The team may visit families, organize parenting skills workshops, and train parents to serve as volunteers in the school. The team also solves problems, tracking down why one student is frequently absent, assisting another who may not be receiving adequate nutrition, or helping a child with vision problems obtain glasses.

Evidence of efficacy for Success for All is strong. SFA students have outperformed matched controls on several measures of reading achievement at every grade level ($p < .05$). The longer a school participates in SFA, the higher student achievement becomes. For example, first graders at a school in its third year of implementation of SFA outperform first graders during a school's first year in the program. Another plus is that the costs of running the program come out of federal monies Title 1 schools already receive, necessitating no additional expenditures.

Success for All has grown rapidly in recent years. A new curricula, called *Roots and Wings,* has been developed to teach math, science, and social studies. Given the solid research base of the curricula, teachers can expect to see more schools adopting these programs in the years to come.

Source: After Slavin, 1996.

Figure 6.3   **A Fourth-Grade Classroom**

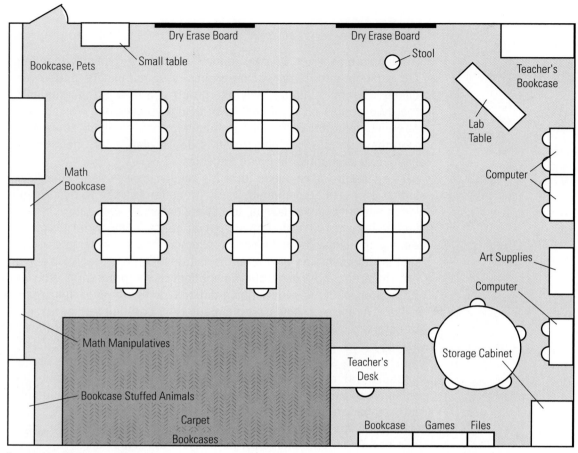

Source: After Weinstein, 1993, p. 41.

electrical circuits, or chemicals; social studies classes may require maps, documents, or cultural artifacts; and English or reading lessons will require books, paper, and pens. Any subject can involve computers. How can such items be stored so they are out of the way, yet easily accessible when needed? As you visit classrooms, look for efficient ways to organize supplies and materials.

Rules and Procedures

Akeisha did not need to give advance thought to classroom rules and procedures, because she had already done that. Beginning teachers, though, need to think these through. **Rules** are principles governing action, and in classrooms are the fundamental guidelines for student behavior. **Procedures** or routines are the means for carrying out everyday tasks in the classroom.

You are probably very familiar with rules from your years as a student. Rules told you to raise your hand before you spoke, to come to class prepared,

and not to chew gum. Look at the following list of typical classroom rules, and decide which ones fit with the goals of self-regulated learning and a democratic classroom learning community.

1. Keep your hands to yourself
2. Do your best
3. One instance of failure to bring a pencil to class will result in five demerits; the second instance will result in a call to your parents; the third instance will result in a one-hour detention
4. No running
5. Respect the property of others

If you selected the second and fifth rules, you are on the right track in aligning rules with long-term goals. Rules that are consistent with self-regulated learning and classroom democracy are principles for guiding action, not detailed prescriptions for behavior. Self-regulated learning implies that students can think for themselves, or at least have the potential to do so. If teachers over-prescribe behavior, they remove an opportunity for self-regulated learning. An important part of a teacher's job is to guide students in applying general principles (rules) in their daily school life.

There are many other factors and issues that teachers take into consideration in designing classroom rules. One of these is students' developmental level. The age and maturity of children necessarily plays a big role in the number and kinds of rules teachers use and in how they communicate them to students. Teachers must decide how many rules to have (four to six is a good range), how to communicate them to students, and how much student input is appropriate. These decisions and the plans for carrying them out need to be developed before the first day of classes.

You may be less familiar with the idea of procedures. Recall how you used to line up to go to recess as an elementary student, and the systems your high school teachers used for collecting homework. These are examples of procedures, or routines, that teachers employ to make classroom housekeeping tasks move along efficiently. They are distinct from rules because they prescribe specific steps students are to follow in certain situations, and because they are merely procedural, they lack the moral tone that rules convey. Before school starts, teachers need to think about those tasks or situations that require procedures, to develop the procedures, and to plan how to teach them. Issues of student developmental level, student input, and alignment with long-term goals must once again be considered.

Organization and Classroom Management

Many of these organizational tasks—setting rules and procedures, arranging the physical space, and so on—are a part of **classroom management.** Most people think of classroom management as equivalent to discipline, that is, reprimanding children who are off task and bringing their behavior back into alignment with expectations. But management is actually much more. Good teachers are proficient at *preventing* management problems through carefully planning their rules, procedures, and the physical layout and decor of their classroom as well as by carefully preparing interesting and appropriate lessons. Plan to devote much time and attention in your teacher education program to issues of classroom organization. Learning how to create and maintain a smoothly operating classroom will pay big dividends in the long run by reducing the level of off-task

behavior and increasing student engagement and learning.

Beyond the Classroom

Perhaps you noticed that Akeisha faced a full day of meetings. Meetings are a fact of life in today's schools, and although they can sometimes feel like a burden, they actually represent a great step forward on the road to teacher empowerment. Teachers are becoming more and more involved in important school decisions about curriculum, textbooks, school policies, school improvement efforts, and much more. This democratization process requires broadly based agreements in which teachers, administrators, parents, and other stakeholders, jointly discuss issues and reach decisions. That means more meetings.

Another factor contributing to the increase in school meetings is that schools and districts are often rather large bureaucratic organizations. The most efficient way for such organizations to transmit important information to large groups of employees—information such as district attendance policies, how to handle first aid emergencies in light of the AIDS epidemic, and how state-mandated testing will be implemented—is through meetings.

Finally, the problems of many students, such as poverty, limited-English proficiency, substance abuse, and disability, are often beyond the expertise of the teacher alone. Meetings involving teachers, parents, special education teachers, speech therapists, social workers, and a host of others, are often needed to develop special programs for students at risk for school failure.

The upshot of all this is that teachers can no longer expect to close their classroom door and teach in isolation. Increasingly, teachers can expect to spend a good portion of their professional life working in collaboration with other adults.

PLANNING

Vera Mendez used the 5 remaining minutes of recess to put the finishing touches on her regular afternoon math lesson for her fifth-graders. They had just completed a unit on fractions, and Vera planned to spend the first 10 minutes of the lesson passing back their unit tests and having them correct their errors in small groups. The students were well versed in this routine, so it wouldn't take very long. Next she planned to introduce the unit on decimals. She had already thought through how she would relate the new symbols to students' prior knowledge about fractions. She selected a group problem-solving activity that she had used last year as a way to activate students' relevant prior knowledge. She quickly scanned last year's notes and began writing problems on the overhead. She wanted to be ready to go as soon as the test-correcting segment was done. The problems she used were derived from stories the students had just read, so this would give everyone a common ground. She also planned to use their new learning about fractions and decimals in a class research project in social studies that would be coming up soon. As the students boisterously entered the classroom from the playground, she greeted them in a warm, businesslike way and instructed each group leader to pick up the tests for their group and to begin helping each other to correct their errors. By the time the bell rang, students were busily engaged.

Teachers' Thought Processes

Planning is clearly an internal, mental activity. As such, it is difficult for beginning teachers to see, to understand, and to model what experienced, expert teachers like Vera do when they plan. How do experienced teachers handle planning tasks? Research has given us some insights into the planning process. Of particular importance for beginning teachers are the differences in planning between expert and novice teachers.

In her approach to planning, Vera exhibited characteristic expert thinking. She had routinized important segments of her lessons, she used available snippets of time as the opportunity arose, she had notes from previous years to guide her, she focused on student learning and prior knowledge, she tied the current lesson to previous content and to what would be coming up, and she prepared materials ahead of time to minimize downtime with students.

Beginners, on the other hand, require a great deal more time to plan, are less sensitive to students' motivation and learning needs, focus more on students' interest level rather than on their learning, and have only a hazy view of how a particular topic fits in with the overall curriculum.

These expert-novice differences have been observed by researchers. Leinhardt and Greeno (1986), for example, found that experienced math teachers had well-organized scripts for important lesson segments that recurred each day, such as homework checks. Teachers had developed routines that allowed for rapid, accurate correction of homework, while also providing absentee information and information on student understanding. In contrast, begin-

ners floundered, wasting much time on routine tasks like absentee and lunch counts, and missing important cues on student understanding of the material. Beginners also had to spend more time planning for these activities, whereas experienced teachers could focus their planning time on substantive matters. In another study of teaching expertise, Berliner (1988) found that expert teachers kept notes, lesson analyses, and learning materials on file from previous years to guide their decisions on matters such as how long an activity would take and about unforeseen obstacles to student understanding and how to circumvent them.

Another key expert-novice difference is the amount of attention given to students. Notice that Vera spent most of her limited planning time thinking about what prior knowledge students possessed, how to link new material to that knowledge, and how to connect it to what they would be learning in the future. She had a grasp of the curriculum for the whole year and of how daily lessons connected to each other and her overall goals. Beginning teachers, on the other hand, are less organized and less oriented to student understanding. They attend to superficial cues about whether students are interested or not, not whether they understand the lesson. In an interesting series of studies, Morine-Dershimer and her colleagues documented that attending to students was a key factor in discriminating between teachers who effectively promoted learning and those who did not (Artiles, Mostert, & Tankersley, 1994; Morine-Dershimer, 1992). They found that beginning teachers who considered students' prior knowledge and motivation in their planning demonstrated more effective teaching behaviors than beginners who did not think about such matters. In turn, the students of these superior planners scored higher on tests on the material.

Cycles of Planning

There are several planning cycles that teachers must consider (Yinger, 1980). As you can see from the vignette, and as we discussed in the previous section, it is important to have an overall plan for the year and to have a strong sense of what you are trying to accomplish academically, socially, and attitudinally. Formulating detailed lesson and unit plans comes more easily when teachers know what the major goals are and where the everyday details fit in the overall scheme of things. Yearly plans are composed of the broad units to be covered, rough starting and ending dates, and testing dates. They take into consideration holidays, vacations, grading periods, and the cycles of the school year. As a general rule, considerable time is spent establishing rules and procedures at the beginning of the year, so less academic work happens then than later. Another rule of thumb is that it is unwise to launch a major new unit just before a big holiday, like winter break.

The next largest planning cycle teachers consider is the grading period. Again, the school's cycles must be taken into consideration when setting important due dates and determining what kind of assignments are needed to produce a fair picture of student achievement. Another important practical question is how many assignments can the students handle and the teacher grade. Further, grades for individual assignments must be easily and efficiently translated into a term grade, because teachers are not given much time to prepare report cards. For example, having to make a lot of judgments on rather subjective factors such as student participation makes assigning term grades take much longer.

Next, teachers create unit plans. In unit planning, teachers consider the major subdivisions in the content to be taught during the grading period. Often a unit is based on a chapter or set of related chapters in a textbook or on major sections in a curriculum guide. The goal of unit planning is to develop a coherent sequence of learning activities that will accomplish the aims of the unit, which, in turn, contributes to the goals for the year. When teachers devise unit plans, they consider student interests and abilities, district and national objectives, available facilities, and logistical matters, such as the amount of time and support materials available. Usually teachers keep records of unit plans in the form of activity outlines, lists of needed materials, lists of objectives, and miscellaneous notes about time needed, management concerns, and what has and has not worked well in the past.

Daily lesson plans come next. Planning for daily lessons is what most people think of first when they think about teacher planning. As you can see, however, daily planning is only one part of the overall planning process. Typically, an experienced teacher does not write down very much, but beginners write down a great deal. The experienced teacher in the vignette, Vera, has her experience and previous notes to guide her, but beginners must still create these, a time-consuming process. When teachers make daily plans, either written or memorized, they specify each activity step by step and they fit the daily schedule to any last-minute intrusions. They also need to set up and arrange the classroom for that particular activity. Many beginners find that lesson plan formats, such as the one in Figure 6.4, are very helpful in getting them started.

Use of Time

An important element that bears emphasis in any discussion of planning is time: how much time to give each activity, to devote to review versus new material, to housekeeping chores like lunch counts and transitions between activities. As we saw in Chapter 4, researchers have found that teachers vary widely in their use of time and that these time differences seriously affect students' opportunities to learn.

Look at the diagram in Figure 6.5. Researchers have conceptualized time in classrooms as planned time, allocated time, engaged time, and academic learning time. **Planned time** is the amount of time teachers set aside to cover a given topic. **Allocated time** is the time actually devoted to the topic after unanticipated interruptions. **Engaged time** is the amount of time students are paying attention during the lesson. **Academic learning time** is the amount of time students are actually learning the material.

Here is an example. Let's say you plan to spend an entire 50-minute period on the major geographical features of Africa. (Planned time equals 50 minutes.) In the middle of a lesson, one of your students rushes in and announces excitedly that there is a big fight in the lunch room. By the time you get him and the rest of the class settled down, you have lost 10 minutes. (Allocated time now equals 40 minutes.) Students' attention wanders in and out during the lesson causing a further loss of 10 minutes. (Engaged time now equals 30 minutes.) Finally, many students falter during your discussion of "sub-Saharan Africa." Confused about the meaning of sub-Saharan, they lose the thread of the lesson and struggle to stay "with it." They are paying attention, but they are not learning, and another 10 minutes is lost. (Academic learning time now equals 20 minutes.) In this example, in only 20 of the planned 50 minutes were students actually learning about Africa. Given the commonsense and research-validated relationship between time and learning—that is, the more time spent learning, the more is learned—it is obvious that time is a precious commodity in the classroom. Good planning, along with good instruction, management, and assessment, will reduce the gap between planned time and academic learning time.

The implication of the research on teacher planning is clear: It takes a while to learn how to plan effectively. Furthermore, planning is intricately bound up with instruction itself. How well you plan affects the success of your teaching, and the success of your teaching affects your planning. Earlier in your teaching career you will need to budget more time for planning, reflect carefully on ways to improve

Figure 6.4   **Sample Lesson Plan**

Lesson topic/subject _____ Grade level _____

PREINSTRUCTIONAL PLANNING

Objectives: Domains:
_____   Cognitive
_____   Affective
_____   Motor/Skill
_____

Materials/special arrangements/individual modifications:

DURING INSTRUCTION

Introduction/establishing set:

Sequence (syntax) of learning activities:

Closure:

Assignment:

POSTINSTRUCTIONAL

Evaluation of student learning:

   Formal:

   Informal:

Evaluation of the lesson (How did the lesson go? Revisions needed?)

Source: After Arends, 1994, p. 53.

Figure 6.5   **How Much Time For Learning?**

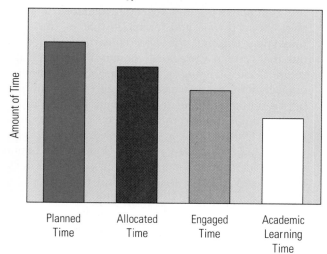

Types of Classroom Time

your planning abilities, and give thought to efficient ways of organizing your teaching materials to make them easily accessible for future lessons. Your teacher education program will give you many opportunities to hone your planning skills and to observe and interact with experienced teachers about their planning practices.

INSTRUCTING

Miryam Narath has been teaching French at Westland High for several years. Her goals are to develop students' ability to speak, listen, read, and write, as well as to increase their knowledge and appreciation of French culture, history, and geography. To accomplish these goals, she uses a variety of strategies. As students enter the room each day, she greets them warmly in French and uses vocabulary they have mastered to banter with them briefly as they take their seats. On the overhead projector, she has already displayed the answers to the previous day's homework assignment, and students immediately set to work in their cooperative learning groups to correct their homework. Most groups are nearly finished when the tardy bell rings. As students complete this task, Miryam quickly takes roll. About 3 minutes into the start of the period, Miryam greets the class and goes through the daily opening ritual, in which students take turns leading the rest of the class in choral response to repeat the month, day, and year, as well as learn a French proverb. During this activity, Miryam collects the homework that each group has stacked in the middle of their desks, glancing through the papers briefly to get a sense of how well students understood the material. Next she announces the agenda for the day and reviews important upcoming dates and assignments. If she has determined that many students did not understand the homework, she will summarize and review the material. If students seemed to understand the homework, she will move directly into the day's lesson, which can take a variety of forms.

When introducing a new grammatical concept, Miryam will often use a concept teaching method or direct instruction. If she is trying to develop conversational skill, she will provide opportunities for interaction in cooperative learning teams. If she is working on vocabulary building, she will employ a variety of mnemonic techniques. If her goal is to impart information on French culture, history, or geography, she normally uses the lecture method coupled with discussion, always careful to reiterate important ideas and to provide examples and analogies that link the new information with students' prior knowledge to help them to make sense of it. To maintain student engagement, check for understanding, and extend thinking, she frequently asks questions. She closes each day by summing up key points, giving students one more opportunity to ask questions, reviewing the homework assignment for the next day, and highlighting topics that are coming up.

Repertoire

The first thing that should jump out at you from this vignette is the number of instructional strategies Miryam used, and used strategically, to accomplish particular learning goals. As we noted at the outset of this chapter, we cannot overemphasize the importance of mastering a repertoire of instructional strategies. These strategies are the fundamental tools of the profession, and the more tools you can use well,

the more effective you will be in helping students learn. Next we highlight those strategies that are taught in most teacher education programs, which many educators agree comprise the essential "starter's kit" for good teaching.

Direct Instruction

Direct instruction is geared toward helping students acquire skills of all kinds. A **skill** is knowing *how* to do something; examples include computing math problems, matching letters with their corresponding sounds, writing summaries of expository text, weighing chemicals on a two-pan balance, determining latitude and longitude from a map, and monitoring one's comprehension while reading. There are four basic steps to teaching skills through direct instruction: explaining, modeling, guided practice, and independent practice.

- *Explaining* is quite straightforward, simply telling students about the skill, describing it, detailing any underlying theory, and making vivid the importance and relevance of the skill.
- *Modeling* is the heart of direct instruction, in which teachers demonstrate how to do the skill.
- *Guided practice* gives students an opportunity to try the skill in the teacher's presence so that corrective feedback and support can be provided.
- *Independent practice* gives students an opportunity to practice on their own, without assistance from teacher or peers.

Refer to Table 6.1 to see an abbreviated example of how direct instruction might be implemented in an elementary mathematics lesson.

Direct instruction is a **teacher-centered strategy.** *Teacher centered* means that the teacher holds the reins of the lesson, determining topic, pace, and learning activities. This high degree of teacher control makes for a very structured learning experience. There is not much room for individual variation in approaching how to perform the skill, how to practice it, or how much time to devote to learning it. Neither does direct instruction develop much depth of understanding. These drawbacks are balanced, however, by the efficiency of direct instruction in accomplishing very focused goals. Direct instruction can be used to efficiently teach how to install a computer, but the student would not gain much understanding of how computers work.

Many teachers and students enjoy the highly structured nature of direct instruction. It is very predictable. From the students' perspective, the

Table 6.1   An Illustration of Direct Instruction: Long Division

Step	Teacher Actions
Explaining	Today we're going to learn a way to do long division. Division is something you'll need to do almost every day of your life as an adult, managing your money and doing your job. You will find that division has some similarities to multiplication, which you've all mastered quite well. Basically, division just breaks numbers down into groups, while multiplication combines groups.
Modeling	Let me show you what I mean. First I'll demonstrate with cookies, then I'll show you how to do it with arithmetic. (*Teacher lays out 12 small cookies on the overhead projector so that all students can see.*) Let's say we have 12 cookies, and you have three friends visiting. You want everyone to have an equal number of cookies. What do you have to do? You have to break down the total number of cookies into four groups, one set for you and one for each of your friends. What happens when you break 12 down into four groups? (*Teacher spreads the cookies out into four distinct groups.*) You end up with three cookies in each group, so each of the four kids gets three cookies. (*Teacher questions students to ensure they understand, then demonstrates how to do the same example using numbers and the symbols of division. Teacher carries out a few more demonstrations, linking each example with the arithmetic symbols, and showing clearly how to do each step of the division algorithm. Teacher has class repeat the steps aloud.*)
Guided Practice	Now I want you guys to try it. I want you to help me solve a new problem. (*Teacher writes a division problem on the overhead.*) What should I do first? (*Teacher takes callouts as, step by step, teacher works through the problem with the class telling what to do.*) Now I want you to try a few problems in your groups. Work on these new problems together (*teacher displays new overhead with four new problems*), and make sure everyone in your group understands how to do it. If you have a question, look first at the steps that you should follow that I've listed on the board. If no one in your group can figure out what to do, raise your hand and I'll come help you. (*Teacher circulates, helping groups who are having difficulty. When groups finish, teacher reviews how to do each problem and responds to student questions. Teacher repeats this sequence of activities, i.e., group practice followed by teacher review, until everyone can do the division algorithm.*)
Independent Practice	Now it's time to do it on your own! Look at the board; you will see the problems I've assigned for homework. You have 10 more minutes to get started on your homework now. This is time to work on your own, but raise your hand if you run into a question, and I'll come assist you.

teachers' expectations are clear and unambiguous. From the teacher's vantage point, it is quite helpful to know step by step exactly what to do next. Planning and preparing for direct instruction are relatively simple. It meshes quite well with performance-for-grade expectations that most students hold. Perhaps not surprisingly, however, many others dislike direct instruction. They feel that it is too confining and too boring, that the complexity of learning is given short shrift, and that it does not work for the really important learning goals.

This variation in personal preferences for learning in certain ways is another reason teachers should master a repertoire of teaching strategies. Because students vary so widely in their learning preferences, it is important for teachers to go beyond what they are personally comfortable with in order to meet the learning needs of all students. Every teacher, too, likes teaching in certain ways better than others. Whether an individual teacher likes direct instruction or any other strategy, however, is not the key factor. Direct instruction works for many students and for many learning goals. Therefore, it should be part of every teacher's repertoire. By the same token, it is equally important to expect students to stretch their own "comfort zones" and to learn how to learn in new ways. When teachers use a variety of teaching methods, they help students learn new ways of thinking and approaching learning problems, thereby enhancing students' skills in self-regulated learning.

Lecture

Another teacher-centered strategy is **lecture,** a method designed for conveying large amounts of factual information. As we saw in Chapter 4, it is one of the most widely used teaching strategies in the country (and probably in the world). At the secondary level, it is practically the only strategy that most teachers use. Often reviled by reformers as ineffective and soporific, lecture can still be useful when applied appropriately and skillfully.

One problem with lecture is that it is greatly overused. Just as a carpenter would be hard pressed to construct a house with only a hammer, teachers are hard pressed to help students construct knowledge with lecture as their only tool. This does not mean that lecture is in and of itself a bad strategy. It just means that it can not accomplish everything that needs to be accomplished. A hammer is a great tool when you want to join two pieces of wood together with a nail, but it is a lousy tool if you want to cut a piece of wood in half. By the same token, lecture can be an efficient way to impart factual information, but it is a lousy way to teach a skill or a concept or develop deep understanding.

This highlights again a key reason for teachers to acquire a teaching repertoire. Different strategies accomplish different learning objectives. Lecture is designed to convey objective information like names, dates, and facts, and when it is done well, lecture is quite effective at transmitting such information. Appropriate lecture topics include the sequence of events of the Civil War, the life of Monet, and the structure of DNA. Lecture is not as useful, however, in helping students to understand the causes of the Civil War, to paint in the impressionist style, or to generate hypotheses about the relationship between genes and cancer. Teachers who attempt to teach inappropriate topics through lecture will find diminished success.

Another problem with the lecture method is that it is often implemented in an ineffective way. The steps in doing effective lectures are:

- Advance organizer
- Clear presentation
- Review and questioning

We will elaborate on each. Effective lecturers begin with an **advance organizer,** an analogy or metaphor that provides a link between the information to be learned and students' prior knowledge. For example, in a lecture on the human immune system, a biology teacher might introduce the topic by drawing an analogy with a military defense system. As he proceeds through the lecture, he would highlight how the immune system is like military defense. Lymph glands are like forts, white blood cells are like soldiers, T-cells are like radar, and so

on. For lectures to succeed, they must serve as a bridge between what is unfamiliar and familiar to students.

After the advance organizer, lecturers present factual information as clearly as possible. Good lectures are high in *clarity,* that is, the structure of the lecture is obvious, little extraneous information is introduced, there are few dangling or run-on sentences, and transitions from one point to the next are clear. Visual aids like overheads and charts boost clarity a great deal.

Another important element is *redundancy.* In everyday life, people consider redundancy a bad thing, but as teachers, it is important to remember that beginners always need to hear new information more than once before they can really understand or remember it. Good lecturers repeat important information and frequently summarize key points. Novice teachers often feel awkward doing this, but with practice it comes naturally.

In the final step, good lecturers review key points and ask questions, creating ample opportunities for students to ask questions as well. We have more to say on the topic of questioning further on.

Cooperative Learning

Cooperative learning is actually a family of related strategies that can accomplish a variety of purposes. Depending on the strategy selected, teachers can impart factual material, basic skills, conceptual understanding, or problem solving. Cooperative learning strategies vary in how teacher centered they are, but since they all involve student-student interaction, they are as a group considered much less teacher centered than lecture or direct instruction. All cooperative learning strategies develop communication and group interaction skills. The key aspects of cooperative learning that distinguish it from other strategies are its use of student-student interaction, purposeful grouping of students, and structures and tactics to enhance individual accountability and to promote academic helpfulness. Refer to Tables 6.2 and 6.3 to see illustrations of the use of cooperative learning.

Cooperative learning is a bit more complex than either direct instruction or lecture, so it is difficult to specify a set of steps. In general, though, in implementing cooperative learning, teachers need to:

- Divide students into groups, attending to purpose for grouping.
- Set the group learning task, attending to individual accountability and positive interdependence.

Table 6.2 A Simple Cooperative Learning Strategy Illustrated: Art History

"Good morning all," Susan Mendon greeted her first-period art class. "Today will be devoted to art history. We'll discuss changes in architecture in the several centuries after the fall of Rome. We'll trace development from Romanesque to Gothic to Baroque, plus look at Byzantine."

Susan provided an advance organizer that linked architectural changes to changing conceptions of the deity and religious priorities. Next she explained the distinguishing features of each architectural style. For example, Romanesque churches have rounded arches, thick walls, few windows, and convey a rooted, down-to-earth feeling. Next she explained the engineering advances of each style and elaborated on the architecture-theology connection. She was careful to use many illustrations of representative cathedrals and to periodically summarize the information. Finally, she reviewed the material using *think-pair-share.*

"Now, let's review. We first talked about Romanesque architecture. How can you recognize a Romanesque church? Don't raise your hand; just think about it a minute. You may review your notes if you like, and you may also jot down a few ideas." She paused for 1 minute to allow all the students a chance to formulate a response. Then she said, "Okay, now tell the person sitting next to you what your answer is." She paused again for 3 minutes as students turned to each other and discussed their answers. As the hubbub died down, she regained the class' attention by signaling with a small bell. "So what did you come up with? How do you know a Romanesque church when you see one?" She took responses from several volunteers and made sure each important point was noted before she moved to the next question.

Table 6.3 A Complex Cooperative Learning Strategy Illustrated: Geography

Nelson Gonzalez was on day 3 of his 5-day unit on the geographic features of Africa. On Monday, he gave his sixth-graders a brief overview of the major landforms of the continent and showed a video that contained dramatic footage of its deserts, mountains, and coastlines. On Tuesday, he provided more detailed information, color-coding a map and explaining the significance of each geographic feature. Students followed along and color-coded maps of their own. Today is the first day of team study. Students worked in groups of four to complete worksheets on the material covered Monday and Tuesday. Each foursome contained a mixture of ability levels and ethnicities. Each group was only allowed two worksheets, and when they had completed those, Gonzalez gave them two answer sheets to check their work. He circulated and assisted groups having difficulty. Students would also spend Thursday studying in teams, completing the worksheets, checking their work, and testing each other, and then Friday he would give them a quiz on the material. In addition to the grade each student received based on his or her quiz score, each team would receive a score based on how much each team member had improved from the last quiz.

Structures to ensure **individual accountability** can be critical to the success of cooperative learning. Individual accountability means that each student is held responsible for personally learning the material. Students may help each other in the learning process, but in the final analysis, each student must demonstrate that he or she can reason, understand, remember, analyze, solve, evaluate, whatever the learning goal has been.

Just as with grouping, individual accountability can assume a variety of forms. Look at the different techniques that the teachers in Table 6.2 and Table 6.3 employed. Susan could enforce individual accountability by merely requiring the sharing of pairs' discussions and her own listening in on pairs as they talked. Nelson used a very structured method, in which team scores depended on how much each individual in the group improved their own performance. This strategy, termed **improvement scoring,** virtually eliminates a common problem in unstructured group work, the "workhorse-deadbeat" syndrome. When a few students do not work, there is usually one very responsible student who will do the work of all. Improvement scoring greatly reduces

One of the first decisions teachers must make in implementing cooperative learning is how to group students. Cooperative learning necessitates **purposeful grouping,** in which teachers match a grouping pattern to their instructional purpose. If the goal is to maximize test scores, students are mixed by their ability levels. When teachers place high, middle, and low achievers in cooperative learning teams, academic achievement is increased. Other goals, such as developing social skills, broadening student friendships, and promoting cross-racial understanding, can be maximized by different grouping patterns.

this unfair and counterproductive distribution of labor.

Promoting academic helpfulness is the final and perhaps most important concern teachers have when implementing cooperative learning. To achieve this type of cooperation, teachers must structure groups for **positive interdependence.** Positive interdependence means that for one person in a group to succeed, the whole group must succeed. Athletic teams are organized for positive interdependence; when the team wins, each member wins. In classrooms, this can happen in a variety of ways. Nelson accomplished it by recognizing high-performing teams, by arranging his seating pattern to facilitate group interaction, and by limiting the number of materials allotted each group so that they would have to share. As you proceed through your teacher education program, be on the lookout for further ways to foster positive interdependence and individual accountability.

Problem-Based Instruction

Another less structured strategy is **problem-based instruction.** Variously labeled student-centered instruction, group investigation, theme cycle, and project-based instruction, this strategy accomplishes several important goals. In addition to acquiring information and developing understanding about the topics under study, students learn how to frame problems, to organize and investigate problems, to collect and analyze data, to marshal evidence, to weigh arguments for and against particular solutions, and to work both independently and with others to solve problems. They also come to understand how knowledge is connected to the real world, how the various disciplines relate to each other, and how to apply knowledge in solving novel, complex problems. Finally, in conducting their investigations and presenting their solutions to others, they engage in reading, writing, and mathematics, strengthening their skills in these basic areas. Problem-based instruction is the best overall strategy for developing self-regulated learning and creating a democratic classroom learning environment.

Because it is highly student-centered, problem-based instruction does not easily lend itself to a simple step-by-step recipe for teachers to follow. Students' work can take them in unanticipated directions, so teachers are not able to plot everything out beforehand, as they are able to do with lecture and direct instruction. However, broad outlines can be sketched. Teachers must:

- Define a problem area.
- Assist students in clarifying a problem topic

and determining how the problem will be investigated.

- Assist students in creating the means by which the problem solution will be reported to others.
- Organize reporting back.

The teacher's initial task is to present a general problem area or issue that students will explore. Next, the teacher assists students in focusing on a particular aspect of the problem and in organizing how they will go about studying the problem. To give you a better idea about how to initiate a problem-based unit, refer to the example in Figure 6.6, in which a group of Australian elementary teachers launched a unit on time.

Once problems and how to research them have been specified, the students conduct their investigations. They may do so in groups or by themselves or in some combination of the two. Investigations involve reading from a variety of reference sources, but they also involve other data sources. Students may get information from government agencies or private organizations, or they may actively collect their own data, conducting community surveys, measuring the acidity of a local stream, monitoring television violence. As a result of their research, they create a product that depicts what they have learned, how they have solved the problem, and their rationale for this solution. The product can be a written paper, an oral report, a video, or a model; they may take the class on a field trip, exhibit works of art, or organize a reforestation project. Whatever the form, the product should be shared with the class, and preferably, other students, teachers, administrators, and community members.

Unlike lecture and direct instruction, problem-based instruction goes beyond a single lesson. Units may last weeks or even the entire academic year. Problems for study may come from the teacher or from students. The Australian math teachers whose time unit was described in Figure 6.6 organize their studies into 5-week blocks. Look at Figure 6.7 for an overview of their approach.

Classroom Discourse

Classroom discourse refers to the ways interaction occurs in classrooms. Interaction can be formal, as when teachers are conducting lectures, or informal, as when students work together at learning centers. Interaction can also be between teacher and students, or among students themselves. Discourse is an important topic for teachers because, as we discussed in Chapters 4 and 5, learning happens primarily through the medium of communication.

Figure 6.6   **Introducing a Problem-Based Unit**

Day 1 – Introduction of Topic

We chose to introduce the topic by posing 3 questions for the children to solve individually or in small groups. These questions were based on issues that were of particular interest to the children at this time.

1   Dave is going home to England via Perth. He wants his friends to meet him at the airport. His plane leaves Melbourne at 2:00 p.m. on Monday 19 December. What time should his friends meet him at the airport?

2   Maria's grandmother lives in Italy. Maria wants to phone her, but wants to make sure that she phones during the day. What time should Maria phone her grandmother?

3   Cheryl wants to phone her friend Marie in Norway. Marie is always home at 5:00 p.m. What time should Cheryl phone Marie?

We gave the children 10 minutes to explore the problems, telling them that we would then gather together to discuss their findings. Some children went straight to atlases, others to dictionaries, and some began to flick through encyclopedias . . . a few children had no idea where to start and just wrote the first thing that popped into their head . . . others had relations in Italy and knew that there was a substantial time difference but didn't know what it was.

On calling the children back together one group explained that they'd found out about time zones in the encyclopedia . . . we talked briefly about how this had helped them to find a solution. We used the telephone book (demonstrating its potential as a resource) to question their solution.

As we discussed the children's answers to the problems it became evident that some of them had a great deal of knowledge about world time but that there were gaps in their knowledge. For instance, some children did not know whether noon was a.m. or p.m. and what these symbols meant. One group attempting to solve problem one worked out that it would take three-and-a-half hours to fly to Perth. They calculated the distance from Perth to Melbourne (using the atlas), asked the speed of jets and then, using the calculator, worked out the time for the trip.

Source: After Baker, Semple, & Stead, 1990, p. 13.

Faulty discourse means learning suffers. Classroom interaction patterns have been extensively researched, and we discuss here salient aspects of that research.

Questioning

Questioning is omnipresent in classrooms. All teachers ask questions. Asking questions can accomplish a wide variety of goals: reinforcing the content, developing critical thinking, and enhancing communication skills. Furthermore, student responses allow the teacher a window into students' thinking, and let the teacher know whether they understand the material, and if not, why not.

Teachers must make a number of decisions when they question students. First, teachers must decide what level of question to ask. *Question level* has to do with the type of thinking needed in order to answer the question. Options range from simple recall or basic comprehension questions to analytical or judgment questions. If the goal is factual review, then a factual question is appropriate. On the other hand, if critical thinking is the desired outcome, then a more open-ended or analytical question is called for.

A second task is to set question difficulty. *Difficulty level* is determined by the percentage of questions the class answers appropriately. If the goal is review, the questions should be easy, and the percentage correct should be very high, at least 90 percent. If the goal is to challenge students and to promote critical thinking, the percentage of questions answered appropriately will be lower.

Third, teachers need to consider *pacing*, how quickly the lesson moves along. Pace influences student engagement: If the pace is too fast, students will be confused, whereas if it is too slow, they will be bored. In either case, they will likely disengage from the lesson.

Wait time is another key consideration in questioning and is intimately bound up with pacing. Wait time has to do with how much time teachers give students to respond to a question—*wait time 1*—and how much time elapses before the teacher responds

Figure 6.7   **Overview of a Five-Week Problem-Based Unit**

Overview of a Five Week Unit Program		
Part 1 (1 week)	Whole-Grade exploration • Teacher selected • Based on children's needs	Teacher demonstrates • Collecting resources • Gathering and recording information • Presenting information • Specific skills • Representing and interpreting data • Processing
Part 2 (3 weeks)	Individual/small group explorations • Child selected • Based on children's interests	Children • Develop and extend their understandings • Take responsibility for their own learning • Develop their ability to work cooperatively
Part 3 (1 week)	Investigations, games, and puzzles • Teacher and child selected • Based on children's interests and needs	Children • Develop their use and understanding of math processes and investigational strategies • Develop work habits of reflection and perseverance • Develop their awareness of the abstract nature of math

Source: After Baker, Semple, & Stead, 1990, p. 11.

to the student or asks another question—*wait time 2.* Surprisingly, researchers have found that teachers on average provide a wait time 1 of only 1 second, and a wait time 2 of only 0.9 seconds (Rowe, 1974). When teachers increase their wait times to 3 seconds, student achievement goes up, as does the quality of their responses.

After a teacher asks a question, students respond to it. How student response is structured can also take a variety of forms. *Gaining the floor,* that is, being the one who gets to talk, is the first step, and teachers have to decide how to organize this. One option is to call only on the volunteer who raises his or her hand first. The benefit of this is that the class is orderly and everyone will be able to hear. On the other hand, not all students raise their hand, especially secondary girls and minority students, thus putting them at a disadvantage. Further, students who never raise their hand and never get called on are more likely to tune the lesson out. For these reasons, many teachers call on nonvolunteers. The benefit here is that participation and thus engagement are increased. The downside is that some minorities, shy students, or those slower to compre-

hend the material may experience embarrassment. One way to balance this dilemma is to use a variety of strategies.

Participation, or the percentage of students involved in responding to questions, is also a very important aspect of questioning. The greater the number of students participating, the greater is the class' achievement. There are a variety of strategies to increase participation. Calling on nonvolunteers, using *think-pair-share,* and choral response are just a few of the options. Related to participation is the concept of *action zone.* Many teachers conduct questioning sessions from the front of the room, and a common side effect is that only those students seated in the front and center of the room are called on to respond to questions. To offset this, teachers should move about and make a point to call on students all over the room.

After a student has responded to a question, the teacher has one major decision: how to give feedback. *Feedback* is information provided the student on the correctness and quality of the response. Feedback is important for several reasons. It lets the particular student and the rest of the class know

Table 6.4 **Basic Feedback Options**

When Student Response Is	Teacher may	Definition
Appropriate	Praise	Recognize good response; should be immediate and specific, e.g., "I like how you gave evidence for your point of view."
	Elaborate	Connect response to other content or student comments.
Inappropriate	Dignify error	Tell what was right about response; give correct answer; indicate that student will be accountable for right answer in future.

what is correct and how to judge response quality, and it can contribute to student motivation. Table 6.4 displays basic techniques for supplying feedback.

Recitation

Another common classroom discourse pattern is *recitation*. Here, the teacher asks a question, calls on a volunteer to respond to the question, and provides an evaluative comment on the student's answer. This pattern is abbreviated **IRE,** for teacher **i**nitiation, student **r**esponse, and teacher **e**valuation (Cazden, 1986). The goal is to review and reinforce the content. The teacher works with the class as a whole, and the pace moves along quite quickly. Usually recitation is used in conjunction with lecture or direct instruction as a means of review and checking for understanding.

When teachers use this simple pattern, they need to tailor their questioning for it. For the initiation phase of recitation, questions should be at the factual and comprehension level, not at higher levels. The difficulty level should be easy, with 80 percent to 90 percent of questions answered correctly. Responses in this range are associated with increased achievement. The pace should be rapid-fire. Remember, the goal is review and reinforcement, so the material should be familiar. A fast pace is more likely to keep students engaged.

During the response phase of recitation, teachers attend to the same factors that were discussed under questioning. Procedures for gaining the floor must be efficient so the pace remains quick, but they must ensure high participation rates. Teachers should avoid an action zone by moving about the room and asking questions from different locations.

When evaluating student responses during recitation, teachers should primarily be praising correct answers and moving quickly on to the next question. Brief elaboration is still helpful, though, as is dignifying error.

Discussion

Discussion is a discourse pattern that is related to cooperative learning, questioning, and recitation. Usually *Discussion* refers to a whole-class discussion, whereas discussion in small groups is referred to as *small-group work* or *cooperative learning*. Discussions that are rapidly paced and focused on review are recitations, but those that are directed at critical thinking are called discussion. Cooperative learning, recitation, and discussion all involve questioning.

In *discussion* the teacher prompts student talk about a topic or issue through a series of questions or other stimuli. The goal is to move students beyond factual learning, although that is reinforced too, to higher-order thinking, such as analysis and evaluation. Discussion also helps students attain important communication and interpersonal skills.

It is helpful when organizing for discussion to arrange seating in a circle or a U-shape. When students can see each other, communication is enhanced. This is not always feasible, however, and good discussions can still take place with the traditional row arrangement. Once the classroom is set up, the purpose of the discussion should be made clear, as should the procedures for participation. Ground rules may need to be established, such as prohibiting derogatory comments. The teacher's first task is to focus the discussion. This can be done by posing a series of questions, raising an issue and inviting comments, presenting a puzzle or problem of some kind and inviting solutions, or presenting a conflict and inviting students to take sides and justify their position. The ways to launch discussion are limited only by teachers' creativity.

Throughout the discussion, the teacher needs to monitor for participation, check for understanding, enforce rules and procedures, and refocus the discussion as necessary. Just as with questioning, teachers will find such concepts as the action zone and effective feedback important in guiding their actions. Most important for discussion is elaboration, making connections between the topic under discussion, the rest of the curriculum, and students' lives. Elaboration is especially useful in closing and concluding discussion.

Informal Interaction

Refer again to the vignette featuring Miryam Narath. In addition to using different teaching methods, Miryam interacted with students in distinct ways. In most classrooms, teacher talk dominates the classroom and is usually focused exclusively on the subject matter. Miryam, on the other hand, used talk to further her relationships with students as well as to further their learning of French, and encouraged student talk in a variety of ways. Promoting positive interaction is a critical teaching skill, because, as we have stressed before, students learn primarily through language; speaking, listening, reading, and writing are the means by which knowledge is acquired. Furthermore, interaction is the means through which relationships are established and nurtured, and without positive relationships, student learning is hampered.

As Chapter 4 emphasized, the social and emotional environment of the classroom plays a vital role in student learning. Students learn more when they feel the adults and peers who surround them know and care about them. A study of at-risk high school students and their teachers illustrates this point. Schlosser (1992) interviewed at-risk high school students about their experiences at school to find out which teachers were most successful with them. Students reported that their best teachers were those who took the trouble to get to know them, who asked how they were doing, who listened to them without "jumping" on them, and who invited them to come and talk further after class.

Schlosser also talked to teachers about their attitudes and practices with at-risk youth. Those teachers who reported they were most successful with these students

> believed that creating warm, personal learning environments in which students were well-known and accepted by teachers could make a difference in the achievement of marginal students . . . that to know students well and let them know you was important. (p. 136)

One teacher said:

> I tell them about things that are going on in my life. . . . You know, [what is important] is interpersonal relationships between people, not necessarily teachers and students, and they respond to that. I tell them about my children, and I ask them about

their brothers and sisters. That's how you get along. (p. 136)

These teachers also believed it was important to help students get to know and to develop relationships with each other. Without these relationships, at-risk students lost interest and ceased paying attention to the academic material in class. Again we see that academic learning happens within a social and emotional milieu that teachers cannot afford to ignore. The accompanying Multicultural Box illustrates this point well.

MANAGING AND DISCIPLINING STUDENTS

Father O'Connell greeted his twelfth-grade social justice students on the first day of class at St. Ambrose Catholic High School. "Welcome," he said, "Our first order of business today is to introduce the class and develop a set of classroom rules. And since this class is about justice and democracy, I think it's only fair that all of you help determine the rules together." He explained that he would only provide them with a few overall principles and that they would develop rules from there. His principles were that students had to learn and that they had to help others learn. To formulate specific rules, he asked each student to complete two sentences, and to write these on large index cards. The sentences were: I can learn when _____ ; I can't learn when _____ . Father O'Connell asked students to post these on the blackboard with masking tape. "I'd like everyone to read what has been posted on the board," he said, "Look for ideas that seem to fit together." As students read the index cards, O'Connell numbered the cards 1 through 40. "Now," he said, "we want to form groups of like ideas. We're going to discuss which cards go together, and from there, we'll use the categories to form classroom rules. So, for example, if we got a lot of cards that say something like, "I can't learn when it's noisy," we'd probably make a rule about limiting talking. So, which cards fit together? Tell me the numbers of the cards you think go together, and I'll put them in a category. We'll fiddle around with the groupings until everyone is satisfied they make sense."

Student Cooperation and Classroom Management

When you think about becoming a teacher, do you worry about classroom management? If so, you are

Central Park East Secondary School, Manhattan, NY

Two high school boys, both African American, sit across a small table from two younger boys. A teacher looks on. One of the older boys, Marcus, begins.

"You two been fighting a lot lately. The principal has had to speak with you both many times. We are here to resolve the conflict between you. Do you agree to participate honestly in this resolution?"

The younger boys, Jude and Aaron, both nod and mumble yes.

"Okay. I want you to start, Jude. Tell us all about what happened. What started this dispute? And then how did it get worse?"

First Jude tells his side of the story. Marcus intervenes occasionally to prevent Aaron from interrupting and to ask clarifying questions. Then Aaron gets his turn. Marcus probes to uncover the roots of the conflict, to find the early warning signals that a fight is about to erupt. He asks the younger boys whether they agree that they committed the provocation the other accuses them of perpetrating. They work until Aaron and Jude agree on the basic facts of the story and on the underlying causes of their hostility. Marcus continues to work with them until they agree on how they can prevent future fights.

A group of English teachers sit in a circle at student desks in a classroom for a subject-area faculty meeting. These teachers are responsible for the entire English curriculum, seventh through twelfth grades. The issues they discuss range widely.

"Based on student portfolios, our students are certainly doing much better writing than they used to."

"I can see the improvement, and I think that giving them choices in what they read and write about has contributed to that greatly."

"I agree. But you know, what they want to read and what is assessed on the college board exam are two different things. Are we shortchanging our students, decreasing their chances of getting into college, by giving them these kinds of choices?"

"That is a problem. I've seen average test scores from other schools, and theirs are higher than ours. But what will happen to students' investment in learning if we limit their curriculum choices?"

"What will happen to them if they don't make it into college?"

"This raises a related concern of mine. We ask them to write and write in our classes, and we can see their writing get better. But on these college entrance exams, they have to answer different kinds of questions, multiple-choice type. Should we be giving them more tests like the SAT so that they have a better shot at doing well? But if we do that, will their actual writing skills decline?"

It's math-science block. Several students are dispersed around the room, hunched over papers, pencils in hand, talking softly. The teacher is circulating around the room, looking over students' shoulders. One group seems stymied and she stops to talk with them.

"So what's going on?"

"We finished."

Continued

"Did you? Let me see your paper. Okay, so you think that the ozone layer is this thick?" She pointed to the illustration on their paper. "You haven't gotten very detailed about that. Exactly how thick is it? Is it the same all over? You need to be more specific."

"But we got the answer."

"You have the beginnings of an answer. Tell me more about how you got there."

The students explain how they arrived at their calculation. The teacher makes a few more suggestions, requests that they provide more convincing evidence for their answer, and then moves on to interact with another group.

Welcome to Central Park East Secondary School (CPESS), located in an impoverished neighborhood in New York City. These vignettes were adapted from actual events and conversations in the school and are representative of the kinds of teaching, learning, and interpersonal interaction that occur there. In this predominantly black and Hispanic East Harlem school, in a city where typically 40 percent of students drop out, over 97 percent of CPESS students graduate and about 90 percent of these go on to college. CPESS is also free of the violence that many urban schools suffer. These facts fly in the face of the conventional view that says minority youth don't care about learning, that they're unmotivated, and that they're so ill-prepared academically by the time they get to high school that it's pointless to expect high achievement from them.

Central Park East, launched in 1985, has a student body of about 450 students, seventh through twelfth grades. Students are organized into grade level divisions—seventh and eighth grades comprise division 1, ninth and tenth are division 2, and eleventh and twelfth grades are division 3, more frequently referred to as senior institute. Divisions are further split into houses with interdisciplinary teams of teachers responsible for the entire curriculum for the same group of students during their 2 years in the division.

English and history are taught in a block, as are math and science. Instruction frequently takes the form of cooperative learning and problem-based learning. Students are assessed through portfolios, exhibitions of their work, and oral exams. Every senior is required to participate in an internship in a workplace to explore possible career paths.

One of the most important aspects of CPESS is its focus on "habits of mind." These habits form the basis for curriculum and instructional decisions and are routinely referred to by teachers and students alike. The habits are: (1) *About perspective:* From whose perspective is this presented? (2) *About evidence:* How do you know what you know? (3) *About connection:* How is the thing that is being considered connected to other things? (4) *About supposition:* What if things were different? (5) *About significance:* Why do these ideas matter?

Source: After Krupnick, 1995.

not alone. Management and discipline are typically the top concerns for beginning teachers (Veenman, 1984). New teachers realize that students can refuse to cooperate at any time. There are many ways to gain and hold students' cooperation, as Father O'Connell demonstrated, and many constructive ways to respond to off-task or disruptive behavior. In this section we provide a brief overview of the techniques you will be learning more thoroughly in a teacher preparation program.

Communication and Management

As we stressed at the beginning of this chapter, an important key to successful management lies in effectively organizing the classroom and planning for instruction. But no matter how excellent an organizer and planner you are, some of your students will at some point fail to engage in classroom work or will disrupt others. One of the first researchers in the area of classroom management studied how teachers managed groups of students moment to moment so as to minimize these disruptions (Kounin, 1970). He found that what distinguished good managers from poor ones was not so much how they coped with off-task behavior but rather how they kept the lesson flowing. He noted several teacher behaviors, especially ways of communicating with students, that contributed to students' work involvement and reduced student misbehavior. The most important of these are defined next.

- **Withitness:** Teachers' ability to spot problem behavior early.
- **Momentum:** Absence of teacher behaviors that slow down pace of lesson.
- **Smoothness:** Absence of teacher behaviors that interrupt the flow of activities.

Withitness refers to the teachers' proverbial eyes-in-the-back-of-the-head, and the ability to nip problem behavior in the bud before it gets out of hand. "With it" teachers frequently scan the class and move around quite often; these behaviors allow them to spot an off-task student (passing a note or talking out of turn), which in turn allows them to inconspicuously redirect the students' behavior. Momentum can be disturbed when, for example, teachers go on and on giving directions and thereby lose the class, known as **overdwelling;** or when they fragment their sentences and make instruction too choppy, referred to as **fragmentation.** Smoothness is diminished by **dangles** and **flip-flops.** Teachers dangle when they start one activity and interrupt it in the middle to start a different one. Flip-flops occur when teachers interrupt one activity, go to a second

one, and then suddenly revert to the original activity. You will recall from Chapter 4 the attributes of simultaneity, immediacy, and unpredictability that characterize classrooms. Given the messy, busy world of classrooms, it is easy to see how teachers can be drawn off-course, but it is important to learn how to maintain lesson momentum and smoothness.

Discipline

Let's say you have planned and organized your classroom perfectly, and you have mastered withitness, momentum, and smoothness. (No mean feats!) You turn around from the chalkboard one day, and there is Susie passing a note to Tyrone. How do you respond to this lack of engagement? This aspect of classroom management, responding to off-task behavior and regaining students' attention and engagement, is referred to as **discipline.** There are innumerable discipline models that teachers can choose from as they design their classroom management program. Here is just a sampling. Rest assured that you will learn several models as you progress through your professional training.

Jones Model

Jones' technique relies primarily on nonverbal cues to bring students' attention back to the lesson, so it is most useful for minor incidents of off-task behavior. Since most misbehavior is minor, Jones' suggestions are very useful. When you first notice a student's attention wandering, you can keep up the pace and momentum of the lesson while simultaneously moving closer to where the student is sitting. This **proximity control** is often all that is needed to regain students' attention. Sometimes a gentle pat on the shoulder will draw a student back in. Alternatively, teachers can make eye contact with students; usually when students realize that the teacher is looking right at them, they shape up.

Dreikurs Model

Dreikurs' system is predicated on the idea that human beings are social animals, and that one of our most basic needs is to feel that we are a part of the social group. If students fail to gain acceptance from teacher and classmates through constructive means, they will revert to antisocial methods; they will make themselves feel a part of the group by defining themselves as its deviant members. Dreikurs maintained that when students misbehave, they are using the only way they know to get the group to recognize them.

According to Dreikurs, there are four basic goals that motivate these students. These goals are misguided in that they do not really result in acceptance by the group. Students may misbehave because:

1. *They want attention.* If no one is paying attention to you, one course of action is to act up, and then people will notice you again.

2. *They seek power.* Students who feel excluded feel they need to force the group to recognize them; they will test limits.

3. *They want revenge.* If a student feels the group has rejected her, she might feel hurt and decide that she wants others to feel as bad as she does. She will then verbally or physically hurt others.

4. *They have given up and feel helpless and hopeless.* If the student has tried everything, he may just give up. These students are withdrawn, quietly refusing to engage with others.

In each case, a different response from the teacher is required. If the student's goal is attention getting, for example, the best response is to ignore the behavior, and to recognize the student at some other time when the behavior is appropriate ("catch 'em in the act of doing something right"). On the other hand, if the student's goal is power, the teacher should decline to get involved in power struggles with the student ("take the sail out of her wind"), and find a way to give the student more responsibility at times when the behavior is appropriate. Students seeking revenge are the most difficult to deal with emotionally, whereas students who have given up are the hardest to reach.

In responding to misbehavior, Dreikurs recommends the use of **natural or logical consequences,** that is, whatever consequences follow naturally from misbehavior should apply, rather than artificial punishment. For example, a student who failed to complete an assignment because she was fooling around obviously needs to take extra time to finish her work, probably during lunch. This is more likely to be effective than a scolding or some other punitive measure.

Assertive Discipline

One of the most popular discipline programs, *assertive discipline* is based on behaviorist principles of learning. In this aggressively marketed approach to classroom management, students are systematically rewarded and punished into the behavior teachers want. You will no doubt have ample opportunity to observe assertive discipline in action as you pursue your professional studies, so we will not cover it here. We caution, however, that assertive discipline is not compatible with the goals of self-regulated learning and democratic classrooms. In addition, the

research base underlying it is not persuasive (Render, Padilla, & Krank, 1989). Do be skeptical and ask lots of questions when you study classroom management strategies.

Classroom Meeting

Another important component of your classroom management program will be the classroom meeting, a strategy developed by William Glasser (1986). Essential to developing a well-functioning democratic learning community, classroom meetings allow students to have input and influence about what happens in the classroom. This gives them concrete experiences with democracy, increases their communication and group decision-making skills, and increases their ownership and commitment to classroom rules and learning activities. Classroom meetings are conducted weekly as follows.

1. *Establish the climate.* The teacher establishes a climate in which all students feel free to participate and share opinions.

2. *Identify problems.* Students sit in a circle. Either the teacher or students can bring up problems for discussion. The teacher makes sure that problems are described fully and nonjudgmentally.

3. *Make value judgments.* After a specific problem has been identified, the teacher asks students to express their own views about the problem and the behaviors associated with it.

4. *Identify courses of action.* The teacher asks students to suggest alternative behaviors or procedures that might help solve the problem. Teacher and students discuss and select one solution to try out.

5. *Make a public commitment.* The teacher asks students to make a public commitment to try out the new behaviors or procedures.

6. *Provide follow-up and assessment:* At a later meeting, the problem is again discussed to see how effectively it is being solved and whether commitments have been kept.

In the vignette that opened this section, Father O'Connell laid the groundwork for effective classroom meetings by involving students in initial rule setting and by grounding this rule setting on the central principles by which the classroom would be guided. As you develop your professional repertoire and refine your teaching philosophy, pay close attention to the links between your own values and professional goals and your classroom management practices. How teachers conduct management and discipline can make or break self-regulated learning and democratic classroom communities.

ASSESSING

Laikwan Baly was lecturing his music appreciation class on the life of Beethoven. "We believe his deafness may have come about as a result of brutal beatings he received as a child at the hands of his father," he said, "so it's even more amazing that at the end of his life he could create something as astounding as the 'Ode to Joy'." As he spoke, he walked about the room. He noticed Tuan staring vacantly out the window, so Laikwan casually walked by his desk, never missing a beat of the lecture. Tuan was mildly startled, then went back to note taking. As he continued to circulate and lecture, Laikwan looked over the students' shoulders at the notes they were taking. Most were rather anemic, so to help them organize their notes, he moved to the front of the room and reemphasized key ideas by pointing to the headings of his outline on the overhead transparency. After finishing, he felt the energy in the room subside a little, so he began to ask questions in a cooperative learning format to review the facts he'd presented, to elicit some analytical thinking by comparing Beethoven's life to twentieth century jazz composer Miles Davis, and to boost engagement. Based on students' halting responses to his questions, he decided they needed further review. He had already prepared a worksheet for this contingency, so he passed this out, instructing students to work on it quietly in pairs. While they did so, he played the "Ode to Joy" in the background, followed by the Miles Davis standard, "So What," and continued to circulate, interacting with students one on one.

Purposes

Assessment brings the instructional cycle to full circle. Assessing students occupies a large part of the instructional process. First, teachers must decide what to teach next based on their sense of what students have learned to date. Second, teachers often have to adjust their lessons in midstream based on student cues as to how well they are "getting it." Third, teachers have to communicate to parents and others what their students have learned. This need to make judgments about what students know and do not know is never far beneath the surface in teachers' minds. These three main purposes of assessment—sizing up, instructional, and official—are detailed here.

Sizing Up Assessment

Sizing-up assessment involves those informal data collection activities that teachers conduct early in the school year to ascertain their students' prior knowledge. The objectives are to get to know their students as individuals and the personality of the class as a whole. Sizing-up assessments rely heavily on teacher observations as they try to profile the cognitive, affective, and psychomotor characteristics of their students. For example, teachers overhear conversations before and after class, at lunch, in the bus line, and at recess. They watch students' body language, and listen carefully when students talk to them. They observe whether a student volunteers questions or comments or waits to be called on, whether they complete homework, whether they are punctual. They evaluate the quality of the work students submit. Sometimes teachers also read students' files, especially if there is a special disability or learning need. Occasionally teachers give diagnostic tests. They then use all this information to help forge a new, diverse group of students into a classroom learning community and to set an appropriate difficulty level for initial assignments.

Instructional Assessment

Instructional assessment occurs every day. Its purpose is twofold: to plan for instruction and to monitor the success of instruction. We have already discussed instructional planning and the importance of accurately assessing students' prior knowledge and capacities. The monitoring aspect of instructional assessment is quite different from planning. Planning usually takes place away from the hubbub of classroom life, but assessment *during* instruction happens in the midst of classroom life. Laikwan, the music appreciation teacher, was conducting instructional assessment during his Beethoven lesson. Airasian (1991) described instructional assessment as follows:

> For many reasons, things do not always go as planned in classrooms. Interruptions, misjudgments about readiness and attention, shifts in interest, and various spontaneous digressions all operate to alter one's instruction. Such factors influence the flow and success of instruction. The teacher must be reading the classroom society minute by minute, sensing its mood, and making decisions about what to do next. (p. 123)

What do teachers pay attention to during instruction? Researchers have found that experienced teachers focus on the adequacy of their instruction, not surprisingly, and on evidence of student understanding (Clark & Peterson, 1986). In studies of instructional assessment, researchers videotaped teachers during instruction, played the videos back to them, and asked them what they were thinking about during the lesson. Here are some examples:

- I was thinking about the fact that they needed another example of this concept.

- I was trying to get him to see the relationship between the Treaty of Versailles and Hitler's rise to power without actually telling him.

- I realized that they didn't understand the concept at all.

- I figured I'd better call on Larry, just to make sure he was with us on the idea of the lesson. (p. 269)

These ongoing assessments about the success of instruction are called **formative evaluations.** They provide feedback to teachers and allow them to take corrective action. They are called *formative* because they influence the form subsequent lessons are to take. Sizing-up assessment is another type of formative evaluation. Formative evaluations are the "meat-and-potatoes" of teachers' assessment work.

Official Assessment

Finally, teachers are responsible for reporting student progress to students, themselves, to their parents, and to the school system. Official assessments include such things as report card grades and the information reported to parents at conferences. They are also used to make a variety of important decisions such as ability group placements, special education placements, and scholarship and other awards.

Official assessments are based on **summative evaluation** of students. In contrast to formative evaluations, a summative evaluation, which "sums up" what a student has learned, derives primarily from formal testing, either standardized or teacher-made tests, rather than from teachers' informal observations. Unlike formative evaluation, summative evaluations are not useful for revising instruction, because the assessment happens at the end of a unit, grading period, or academic year. Report card grades, which are the most common and important type of summative evaluation, are largely separate from the instructional process. Consequently, summative, official evaluations tend to be quite important to students and parents because of their impact on students' lives, whereas formative evaluation tends to be more important to teachers because of its impact on instruction. Summative testing is involved in the difficult process of determining whether a student will benefit from being retained to redo a grade level. You can read more about grade retention in the accompanying Issue Box.

Many teachers are uncomfortable with the process of testing and grading students and most are aware that testing has its limitations. Examples of test limitations include: the match (or lack thereof) between what is tested and what is taught, which is termed **curriculum alignment;** poor test performance due to student fatigue, illness, or anxiety; the relative clarity of test items; and the reliability of the grading process. All these factors can result in student knowledge being underestimated. As we saw in Chapter 5's Research Box on children's development of science knowledge, formal testing can also overestimate what students understand. The school's requirement, therefore, that permanent grades be assigned is not always welcome. Here are some comments by teachers on testing and grading:

- I need to use tests in my algebra class for grading my students and having objective information I can show parents when they complain about their child's grade. With so much emphasis on grades, I'm sure my students work mostly for a test grade and not for their enjoyment or understanding of the subject matter.

- The pressure to perform is too great for anyone, let alone a seven-year old who's still trying to figure out what in the world he needs education for. Because the school system requires it, I test my students once a week in math and vocabulary and about once every two weeks in science, social studies, and religion. The only advantage I see in testing is that it gives the teacher a number on which to base the student's academic progress. (Airasian, 1991, pp. 151–152)

Standardized tests are another form of summative evaluation. Standardized tests, such as the Scholastic Aptitude Test (SAT) used for college entrance and the Iowa Test of Basic Skills (ITBS) used to assess elementary students' understanding in core subjects, are an entrenched part of the American educational landscape. Bracey (1992) reported that American students "bubble-in 100 million answer sheets a year" (p. 108). Such tests are thought to be an efficient, objective means to assess the relative achievement of students and schools.

Despite their universal presence, standardized tests pose several problems. As we discussed in Chapter 5, such tests are often biased against female, minority, and low-income students. The Educational Testing Service, the publisher of the SAT college entrance exam, was even sued by a consortium of legal and women's groups in New York State, charging that sex bias in the SAT had negative financial consequences for young women. The plaintiffs showed that the SAT consistently underpredicted female performance in school and that, because the biased SATs were used in making scholarship awards, girls wrongly received only half the number of scholarships as boys. The judge ruled in favor of the plaintiffs, and New York State was directed to find another means for awarding scholarships.

ISSUES

EXTRA

Student Retention

Many parents have to face the decision about whether to acquiesce to retaining their child. Retention rates have been rising in the last decade, returning to the high rates of the early 1900s, after a mid-century lull. Educators, school board officials, state legislators, and parents argue the issue passionately. At stake are both what is best for individual kids and the integrity of the educational system, two goals that may conflict.

The practice of retention and research on the practice go back at least 100 years. One of the first published pieces on the effects of retention was *Laggards in Our Schools* by Leonard Ayres, which came out in 1909. Hundreds of studies have been conducted since then.

What have these studies showed? As you might expect, obtaining clear findings has been a bit tricky. Consider the problem. How can you tell how retention has affected a student? One strategy might be to follow the student after retention and track his progress. But how much progress do we expect for a student in difficulty? To answer that question, you can compare the retained student's progress with another student from the same grade who was promoted. But there are preexisting differences between these students that would contaminate the results. After all, the retained student was already having difficulty. Such a comparison gives promotion an unfair advantage. Or retained students can be compared with their new grade-mates, but again, poorer performance by the retained students could just be because they are not very able students, so the comparison is not a good indicator of the efficacy of retention. A more appropriate comparison is between two similar students who were both having difficulty and were both being considered for retention, one of whom was retained and the other promoted. Very nice on paper, but in practice, this kind of comparison is very difficult to arrange. These logistical problems have created methodological headaches that in turn have resulted in conflicting findings.

Pro

The basic case for retention is quite simple and straightforward, appealing to many people's common sense. If a child cannot do the work, hold him or her back a year and let the child take longer to master it. With another pass at it, the child will get it easily. Other presumed advantages include decreasing the range of ability levels in the classroom, which ought to make it easier for the teacher to provide appropriate instruction. Upper-grade teachers will know exactly what their incoming students can and cannot do, and they will be able to execute their jobs more efficiently. Furthermore, with firm grade-level standards, it will be easier to spot students in difficulty sooner, and assistance can be given before small learning problems turn into insurmountable hurdles. Some also argue that

Another problem with standardized tests is their heavy reliance on multiple-choice items. These items are better suited to assessing factual knowledge than to assessing more complex cognitive skills, such as problem solving or creativity. Standardized tests thus portray quite an incomplete picture of student achievement. Unfortunately, this fact often gets lost in the competition between students, schools, and districts for high test scores.

Interestingly, although many teachers assume that parents are most interested in their student's performance on standardized tests, recent research

ISSUES

EXTRA

Continued

the clear application of consequences will serve a motivating function for many students.

There is some research that supports this view. For example, Gottfredson, Fink, and Graham (1994) explored the relationship between retention and problem behavior in 401 African American sixth- and seventh-graders. To deal with the problem of the equivalence between the retained and promoted students, the researchers selected both groups from the same pool of low-achieving students. However, the groups still differed significantly on important factors. Data were collected on students' educational expectations, positive peer associations, attachment to school, rebellious behavior, and classroom disruptiveness. Eleven months later, both groups were assessed again. Researchers found that the promoted group's attachment to school decreased, but their rebellious behavior and classroom disruptiveness increased. The retained group, on the other hand, decreased their classroom disruptiveness and increased their educational expectations and positive peer associations. Gottfredson and colleagues concluded that retention had a positive impact.

Another study revealed a similar pattern for academic progress. Alexander, Entwisle, and Dauber (1994) studied a large representative sample ($N = 800$) of urban children beginning in 1982, when they entered first grade, and concluding in 1990 when they finished eighth grade. Academic performance in the first year after retention was poor, but as students returned to the normal promotion cycle, their grades, test scores, and self-concepts improved. This was especially true for students held back only once, in second or third grade.

Finally, in a review of the literature, Karweit (1992) found that retention programs that included a remediation plan were more likely to result in positive outcomes.

Con

The literature supporting the practice of retention appears persuasive. The bulk of the evidence during the last 20 years, though, has shown consistently that retention does more harm than good. Beginning in 1975, literature reviews began to conclude that retention did not work. Jackson (1975), for example, reviewed the available studies and concluded that there was no evidence in the literature that retention was a helpful practice. In 1984, Holmes and Matthews applied the technique of meta-analysis (a technique for statistically averaging the results of many studies) to 44 studies that met their stringent selection criteria. They found retention had deleterious effects on students' academic performance, personal adjustment, self-concept, and attitudes toward school.

has illustrated that parents may be much more interested in other sources, such as discussing their student's progress with the teacher (Shepard & Bliem, 1995). Table 6.5 shows the sources of information on student progress that are most useful to parents.

Alternatives

Given the problems with standardized tests and with formal testing and grading in general, what alternatives are available for assessing students? Fortunately, new options are developing in many districts

ISSUES

Continued

The arguments against retention were eloquently assembled in 1989 by R. Doyle. He cited research dating back to 1900 showing a strong relationship between retention and dropping out of school. He also challenged one of the underlying assumptions of the advocates of retention that children of the same age are at the same level of intellectual development. The whole reason for age grading in the first place was the belief that teachers can more efficiently instruct same-age students. But research on IQ and other intellectual measures over the last 80 years has shown that children of the same age vary widely, as we discussed in Chapter 5. And in fact, according to Doyle, it appears that retention increases rather than decreases the heterogeneity of classrooms. In addition, Doyle vigorously disputed the notion of strict grade-level standards for achievement, arguing that we all need to assume that each classroom will contain a great variety of abilities and interests. Teachers need to work with the diversity present in their classrooms, not sort students based on a preconceived set of standards. Doyle also questioned the argument that retention motivates students.

New studies also have shown negative effects for retention. For example, Roderick (1994) found that repeating a year anywhere between kindergarten and sixth grade was strongly associated with dropping out later on. In this large-scale study ($N = 707$) in a northeast city, among students who were never retained, 27 percent dropped out of high school. But 69 percent of those held back for one year did so, and a disturbing 94 percent of those retained twice.

Alternatives

How can professionals use the literature to guide decisions when the research conflicts? Actually this is not such an unusual situation. In medicine, for example, studies are often contradictory, and advice to patients can change. The research on breast cancer conflicts as to whether a woman should have a mastectomy or a lumpectomy. Twenty years ago, mastectomy was by far the most common practice, 10 years ago, opinion shifted in favor of lumpectomy, and now mastectomy is again coming back into favor.

One way to cope with conflicting findings is to examine the literature with an eye toward the circumstances under which an action should be taken. When research findings are in disagreement, it usually means that some important factor we are unaware of is operating. Based on the studies reviewed here, it may be that retention that occurs only once in a nondisadvantaged setting in second or third grade that is accompanied by a remediation program is more likely to help students than just passing them on.

Table 6.5 **Parent Questionnaire Ratings of the Usefulness of Different Types of Information for Learning about Their Child's Progress in School (in percentages) (n = 105)**

	How Useful					
	Not at all				**Very**	**Blank/Missing**
Type of Information	**1**	**2**	**3**	**4**	**5**	
Report cards	2	2	20	33	43	
My child's teacher talking about his or her progress	0	2	4	17	77	
Standardized tests	6	15	41	22	14	2
Seeing graded samples of my child's work	0	0	10	30	60	

After Shepard & Bliem, 1995, p. 27.

and universities around the country and the world. We will discuss two here, authentic assessment and portfolio assessment.

Authentic Assessment

Sometimes referred to as **performance assessment,** **authentic assessment** involves measuring more directly the outcomes students are to achieve. This means assessing students' ability to perform the desired skill by having them actually perform that skill, rather than taking a paper-and-pencil test about it. For example, consider the laudable goal of writing an effective expository essay. Often, to test attainment of this goal, students will take a test that asks them to correct an ungrammatical sentence, to identify the topic sentence in a paragraph, or to select an appropriate title for a piece of text. Proponents of authentic assessment argue that if the goal is good writing, students should be evaluated by their writing, not by answering multiple-choice questions that bear only a thin connection to the real goal. A good analogy is a piano recital; piano students demonstrate what they have learned about playing the piano by actually playing the piano, not by bubbling in answer sheets. A good performance assessment, then, asks students to clearly demonstrate the skill they have been taught. Teachers then rate performance based on a set of standards agreed on beforehand. Here are further examples of authentic assessments that have been used in schools across the country (Sizer, 1992):

- Completing a federal Internal Revenue Service Form 1040 for a family whose records you receive, working with other students in a group to ensure that everyone's IRS forms are correct, and auditing a return filed by a student in a different group.
- Designing a nutritious and attractive lunch menu for the cafeteria within a specified budget and defending your definitions of *nutritious* and *attractive.*

- Designing and building a wind instrument from metal pipes, then composing and performing a piece of music for that instrument.

Portfolios

Another new approach to evaluating student learning is **portfolio assessment.** Like authentic assessment, the idea behind portfolio assessment is to bring the assessment process into alignment with instructional goals by testing these goals more directly. Academic portfolios are like artists' portfolios; students compile samples of their work to give evidence of their learning, just like artists' portfolios give evidence of their artistry. In addition, portfolios generally contain multiple examples of a student's work over a period of time, which gives them the capacity to demonstrate improvements in performance.

Portfolios, like authentic assessment, are rapidly gaining popularity in educational circles. You may be asked to create a portfolio to document your teaching proficiency as you progress through your teacher education program. Frequently, principals wish to see a teaching portfolio when hiring new teachers. Many logistical problems remain to be worked out, like ensuring that grades are applied consistently among students when the contents of their portfolios differ, but the advantages of portfolios seem to greatly outweigh their drawbacks. Educators will almost certainly be increasing their use of portfolios in the coming years.

SUMMARY

- The instructional cycle is the sequence of activities that comprise the heart of the teacher's job: organizing the classroom, planning, instructing, managing, and assessing.

- Every teacher's central purpose is to help students become self-regulated learners within a democratic classroom learning community.

- Teachers need to master a repertoire of instructional strategies and to match the appropriate strategy to a particular learning goal.

- Making wise and skillful instructional decisions requires teachers to reflect deeply about teaching, learning, goals, values, beliefs, and the larger societal context.

- Long-range planning gives coherence and direction to classroom life, a supportive structure for learning.

- The physical layout of the classroom should provide for the orderly and efficient use of materials and a variety of teaching methods.

- Rules and procedures help establish an orderly and safe classroom and prevent many discipline problems from ever arising.

- In addition to their instructional duties, teachers participate in a variety of groups with other adults in the school: textbook committees, faculty meetings, family support teams, and so on.

- Expert and novice teachers express characteristic differences in their planning: Experts have routinized recurring lesson segments, they focus on students' learning needs, and they have a clear view of how each lesson fits into the overall flow of curriculum across the year.

- Teachers must attend to several levels of planning: annual, grading period, unit, and daily lessons.

- Planned time is generally much greater than actual academic learning time, and teachers need to vigilantly strive to reduce the gap between them.

- A beginning teacher's repertoire of instructional strategies should include at least direct instruction (for skill learning), lecture (for factual learning), cooperative learning (for academic and interpersonal learning), and problem-based instruction (for critical thinking and problem solving).

- Classroom discourse patterns have a great impact on the social, emotional, and academic climate of the classroom. Teachers should master a variety of patterns including questioning, discussion, and recitation. They

also need to be cognizant of informal interactions and their impact on students.

- Good classroom managers use a variety of organizational and communication strategies to create and sustain student cooperation. Among these are clear rules and procedures, withitness, smoothness, and momentum.

- There are a variety of ways to respond to students' inappropriate behavior including Jones' body language techniques and Dreikurs' social goals methods.

- The three main purposes of assessment are sizing up, instructional, and official.

- Authentic assessment and portfolio assessment are alternatives to traditional testing that are gaining in popularity, because they assess actual learning outcomes more directly than paper-and-pencil tests.

READINGS FOR THE PROFESSIONAL

Baker, D.; C. Semple; & T. Stead. *How Big Is the Moon? Whole Maths in Action.* Portsmouth, NH: Heinemann Educational Books, 1990.
Three Australian elementary teachers describe how they implemented a problem-centered approach to mathematics instruction. The book makes the big ideas around student-centered learning, problem-based instruction, and constructivism very concrete and understandable, giving valuable details of classroom set up, planning, instructing, assessing, and record keeping.

Putnam, J. & J. B. Burke. *Organizing and Managing Classroom Learning Communities.* New York: McGraw-Hill, 1992.
An excellent text on classroom management that shows in great detail and with many real classroom examples how to set up and run a democratic classroom learning community that is orderly, respectful of students and their needs, and produces much learning. Included are examples from both elementary and secondary settings.

Weinstein, C.S. & A.J. Mignano, Jr. *Elementary Classroom Management: Lessons from Research and Practice.* New York: McGraw-Hill, 1993.
A terrific text that is clearly written and contains a wealth of suggestions to reduce the terrors of classroom management. It is directed at elementary teachers, but secondary teachers will also find it useful.

Teachers and Their Work

Application and Portfolio Activities

Self-Assessments

Managing the Classroom Context 182

Teacher Candidates' Expectations 183

What Are Your Teaching Goals? 184

Observations

Classroom Climate and Socioeconomic Status 186

Classroom Interaction 188

Asking Questions 190

Interviews

What Is Hard and What Is Easy in
Preservice Teacher Education? 193

Learning about Students from Different Cultures .. 194

How Students Make Sense of School 195

Managing the Classroom Context

Purpose The purpose of this self-assessment is to explore your own strengths and weaknesses in managing some of the complexities of classroom life, such as multidimensionality, immediacy, simultaneity, and unpredictability. If you uncover weaknesses, it certainly does not mean that you should abandon any plans for a teaching career. It just means that you will need to consider how to redress those weaknesses.

Directions For each of the statements below, give the number that best corresponds to your own attitude: 1 = Strongly disagree, 2 = Disagree, 3 = Neither, 4 = Agree, 5 = Strongly agree. The higher your score, the stronger your skills and dispositions are for managing classroom complexity. Possible scores range from 16 to 80.

Statement	Number
I can handle a lot of things at once.	_____
I enjoy managing multiple demands on my time.	_____
I am capable of managing conflicting job expectations.	_____
I can handle ambiguous situations.	_____
I have a lot of initiative.	_____
I'm very patient.	_____
I enjoy people.	_____
I enjoy meeting lots of different kinds of people.	_____
I like kids.	_____
I don't mind it when people criticize me.	_____
I can think fast on my feet.	_____
I can handle making rapid decisions, even with inadequate information.	_____
I can pay attention to more than one thing at once.	_____
I don't get easily shaken when unexpected things happen.	_____
I can adapt to shifting circumstances.	_____
Change doesn't bother me.	_____
TOTAL	_____

Reflection Review your responses to each statement. Are you good at dealing with unpredictability and change? Simultaneity? Immediacy? Multidimensionality? Are you good at some of these and not others? How can you use this to inform your decision about whether to take up teaching as a career? If you do decide to teach, how might you improve your areas of weakness?

Teacher Candidates' Expectations

Purpose

Expectations exert powerful emotional effects and affect both one's own learning and the learning of one's future students. Understanding assumptions and beliefs facilitates learning to teach. The purpose of this exercise is to develop greater understanding of beginning teachers' expectations and beliefs.

Directions

Following is a survey with items relating to beginning teachers' expectations. Circle the response that best fits your attitude. Fill out this survey yourself, then give it to five teacher education students who are in preprofessional classes, methods classes, or student teaching. Compile your results with other students in your class.

Your age _____   Currently enrolled in what courses? _____

In what grade level/subject matter do you intend to teach? _____

1. My teaching potential relative to other students in this program is:

    Below Average   Average   Above Average

2. I pretty much know now what I need to know in order to be an outstanding teacher.

    Disagree   No Opinion   Agree

3. The best teachers are those who: (Circle only one response.)
    (A)   Really love their students.
    (B)   Really know their subject.
    (C)   Set high, demanding academic standards.
    (D)   Nurture and encourage their students.
    (E)   Enthusiastically present interesting lessons.

4. When students have difficulty learning, they most often just need to work harder.

    Disagree   No Opinion   Agree

5. Kids who don't try to learn don't want to learn.

    Disagree   No Opinion   Agree

6. In contemplating a teaching career, what gives me the most anxiety is:
    (A)   Not knowing enough about my subject.
    (B)   Not knowing enough about how people learn.
    (C)   Not being able to maintain order in my classroom.
    (D)   Not having enough time for planning lessons.
    (E)   Not knowing how to deal with student diversity.

Reflection

Compile your responses with other students in your class. What patterns do you notice? Any responses characteristic of elementary versus secondary teacher education students? Of students in preprofessional courses versus student teaching? What effect do these students' expectations have on their teaching effectiveness? How do your responses compare with students you surveyed and with what researchers have found about beginning teachers' expectations? Write a paragraph comparing/contrasting your own responses with the information on expectations contained in Chapter 4 and with your survey results.

What Are Your Teaching Goals?

Purpose You can not teach everything that is worth teaching. You must prioritize learning goals so that you can ensure that you teach the most important things first. Every student outcome in the following list is important but not every one can be the top priority. The purpose of this self-assessment is to uncover and clarify the learning goals you hold for students. It is important to be aware of your goals so that you can consciously examine them. You can check to see that your goals are congruent with your philosophy of education. Also, you may decide you need to revise your goals to bring them into alignment with professional standards for teaching. Further, when you have field experiences, you will want to compare how well your goals align with your actual teaching practice.

Directions Look at each of the five broad goals listed below. Distribute 100 points among these goals, giving more points to the goals you consider more important. If there are other goals that are important to you which are not listed, use the blank spaces to add these. Under each broad outcome, list a few examples. What are some examples of what students would learn under Cognitive Knowledge, say, or Social Interaction?

Points	Student Learning Outcomes
_____	Cognitive Knowledge and Academic Skills
	_____
	_____
_____	Problem Solving and Critical Thinking
	_____
	_____
_____	Self-Esteem and Positive Self-Concept
	_____
	_____
_____	Social Interaction and Conflict Resolution Skills
	_____
	_____
_____	Cultural Values and Attitudes
	_____
	_____
_____	Other? Specify
	_____
	_____

Reflection   In what order did you rank these important student outcomes? Discuss what your ranking means for the way you would structure a classroom. How congruent are your responses with your educational philosophy? How deeply do you believe in your own ranking? How might you respond if the teacher education program you entered, or the school district you worked in, advanced a set of priorities radically different from your own?

Compare your ranking with that of another university student, of a parent, of a university teacher educator, and of a public school teacher. Examine the examples you listed for each goal, and compare these as well. Discuss the similarities and differences with another teacher candidate. Are the differences significant? Does each goal signify the same thing to each person? How might you resolve differences if, say, you served on the same standards committee?

Classroom Climate and Socioeconomic Status

Purpose

One of the most crucial problems in American education today is the disparity between schools in rich and poor neighborhoods. There is some evidence that teaching in low-income neighborhoods tends to be less democratic and more focused on rote learning. The purpose of this observation is to familiarize you with classrooms in a variety of settings, to assess the accuracy of this generalization in your own region, and to explore implications for your potential teaching career.

Directions

Obtain permission to observe in three different classrooms, one each in a low-income, a middle-class, and a wealthy neighborhood. If you are considering an elementary career, visit only elementary schools; if you are thinking about secondary education, visit only secondary schools. Sit discreetly in the back of the classroom, positioning yourself so that you can see and hear most everything in the room. First, write a brief description of the classroom. How many students? What are they like? What furniture is there, and what condition is it in? What is the decor like? Now watch for a few minutes to get a feel for what is going on, then begin your formal observation. Watch for 5 minutes, then make a tally for each of the activities listed below that happened during that 5 minutes. Wait a few minutes, then begin another 5-minute observation period. Repeat this cycle another two or three times. Count totals for each category.

Description

Low-income classroom: _____

_____

_____

_____

_____

Middle-class classroom: _____

_____

_____

_____

_____

_____

_____

Wealthy classroom: _____

_____

_____

_____

_____

_____

Observation

Action	Low-Income	Middle-Class	Wealthy
Teacher Actions			
Gives information	_____	_____	_____
Gives directions	_____	_____	_____
Asks questions	_____	_____	_____
Elaborates on students' comments	_____	_____	_____
Praises or encourages	_____	_____	_____
Reprimands	_____	_____	_____
Observes/listens	_____	_____	_____
Student Actions			
On task			
Listening	_____	_____	_____
Doing drill	_____	_____	_____
Writing	_____	_____	_____
Reading	_____	_____	_____
Discussing	_____	_____	_____
Creating	_____	_____	_____
Problem solving	_____	_____	_____
Off task, nondisruptive	_____	_____	_____
Off task, disruptive	_____	_____	_____
Asking questions	_____	_____	_____
Helping others	_____	_____	_____

Reflection Compile your responses with other teacher candidates. What patterns do you see? Are there differences between classrooms in low-income, middle-class, and wealthy neighborhoods? If so, describe these differences. What seem to be the different challenges faced by teachers in these different schools? How would you handle these challenges yourself? Would you accept a teaching job in any of these schools, or would you limit yourself to certain neighborhoods? Why or why not?

Classroom Interaction

Purpose   Communication is the medium of learning in classrooms. And to optimize student learning, teachers need to create broad interaction patterns, ensuring participation of minority, female, and low-ability students. In this exercise, you will have the opportunity to examine one teacher's interaction patterns.

Directions   Make a seating chart of the classroom. Note the demographic characteristics of each student to the best of your ability: gender, ethnicity, class, and ability level if known. Observe the class for at least 1 half-hour. Every time the teacher calls on or interacts with a student, make a tally mark. Every time the student asks a question of or makes a comment to the teacher, make a tally mark. Then compile your data in a matrix to show frequency patterns of interaction by gender, ethnicity, class, and ability. Study the following example before you begin.

Observation Example

Classroom grade level   _____

Subject area   _____

Date   _____

Time start   _____

Time finish   _____

M = male   F = female

B = Black   W = White   H = Hispanic   A = Asian   NA = Native American

T = Teacher-initiated interactions   S = Student-initiated interactions

Front of Room

FB T II S IIII	MNA T I S	FH T III S	FW T IIII S III
FA	MH	FNA	FNA
MW	MW	MW	FB

188

Analysis Matrix Example			
	Teacher-Initiated	Student-Initiated	Total
Male			
Black			
White			
Hispanic			
Asian			
Native American	1		1
Subtotal	1		1
Female			
Black	11	1111	6
White	1111	111	7
Hispanic	111		3
Asian			
Native American			
Subtotal	9	7	16
TOTAL	10	7	17

Reflection What patterns did you observe in the classroom you studied? Did teacher-student interactions vary by gender? By ethnicity? What appeared to be the effect of the teacher's interaction style on students' engagement, emotional response to the class, and learning? What could the teacher have done to include more students in classroom interactions?

Asking Questions

Purpose   Questioning may be the backbone of instruction. Good questioning skills are critical to effective teaching, and teachers who ask many good questions produce higher achievement in their students than teachers who don't. The purpose of this exercise is to sensitize you to the complexities of asking questions, and to provide you with background knowledge on which your own questioning skills can be built.

Directions   Look at the categories below. Within each are several specific behaviors. Code each question with one of the specific behaviors within each category. In other words, as you observe a teacher, code each question he asks for type of question, wait time, difficulty level, and teacher reaction to student response in the appropriate column.

Code

A. Question Type	B. Wait Time	C. Difficulty Level	D. Teacher Reaction
1. Factual recall	1. Teacher gave at least 3-second wait time	1. Response accepted by teacher	1. Teacher gave specific acknowledgment
2. Cause-effect		2. Response was not accepted	2. Teacher made no acknowledgment
3. Compare or contrast	2. Teacher did not give wait time		3. Teacher elaborated on student comment
4. Give example			4. Student error was "dignified"
5. Give opinion			5. Student error handled inappropriately
6. Solve problem			

Question Number	A	B	C	D
1	_____	_____	_____	_____
2	_____	_____	_____	_____
3	_____	_____	_____	_____
4	_____	_____	_____	_____
5	_____	_____	_____	_____
6	_____	_____	_____	_____
7	_____	_____	_____	_____
8	_____	_____	_____	_____
9	_____	_____	_____	_____

10 _____ _____ _____ _____
11 _____ _____ _____ _____
12 _____ _____ _____ _____
13 _____ _____ _____ _____
14 _____ _____ _____ _____
15 _____ _____ _____ _____
16 _____ _____ _____ _____
17 _____ _____ _____ _____
18 _____ _____ _____ _____
19 _____ _____ _____ _____
20 _____ _____ _____ _____
21 _____ _____ _____ _____
22 _____ _____ _____ _____
23 _____ _____ _____ _____
24 _____ _____ _____ _____
25 _____ _____ _____ _____
26 _____ _____ _____ _____
27 _____ _____ _____ _____
28 _____ _____ _____ _____
29 _____ _____ _____ _____
30 _____ _____ _____ _____

Tally the number of times the teacher:

Repeats or rephrases questions before calling on someone _____

Asks two or more questions at the same time _____

_____

Dangles or flip-flops _____

Uses think-pair-share or other student-student interaction _____

Uses group response _____

Were questions integrated into a coherent sequence, or were they random and unrelated? _____

_____

Did teacher ask students to evaluate their own responses? _____

Reflection   Total your tally marks. What patterns do you see? If possible, repeat this observation in other subjects or grade levels. What differences do you notice? How do these teachers deal with students who are less willing to participate in class discussions? What are the strengths and weaknesses of the teachers you observed in their questioning practices? What do you think you will find difficult to learn about effective questioning?

What Is Hard and What Is Easy in Preservice Teacher Education?

Purpose   What you expect to learn in teacher education will have a great impact on what you do in fact learn. For this reason, it is important to have realistic, accurate expectations. In this exercise, you will have an opportunity to compare your own expectations about learning to teach with what experienced teacher educators have to say about beginning teachers.

Directions   Using the questions below as a guide, interview at least three people directly involved in preservice teacher education: university methods or foundations professors, university supervisors, or cooperating teachers. Summarize their responses.

1. Tell me a bit about your role in teacher education. What do you do? How long have you served in this capacity?

2. What do you think are the important things for beginners to learn about teaching?

3. In your experience, what do beginners find easy to learn? What do you find easy to teach beginners?

4. In your experience, what do beginners find hard to learn? What do you find difficult to teach beginners?

5. Why do you think beginners find these particular topics easy or difficult?

Reflection   What surprised you about these teacher educators' perceptions about beginning teachers? How does this knowledge affect your career decision? Are you now more or less likely to choose teaching? Why? If you do choose to teach, how can you use this information to improve your learning from a teacher education program?

Learning about Students from Different Cultures

Purpose

Part of being an effective teacher is understanding culturally different students, and using that knowledge to facilitate learning. The purpose of this exercise is to help you gain greater understanding of a particular culture and the interaction of that culture with the culture of the school.

Directions

Use the following questions as a guide in interviewing a student from a different culture. Choose a student in the upper-elementary through high school grades.

1. What similarities have you noticed between your own culture and the mainstream culture?

2. What differences have you noticed between your own culture and the mainstream culture?

3. What do you especially like about school?

4. What problems have you run into at school?

5. How did you deal with those problems?

6. What have your teachers done that helped you learn? That helped you make friends with other students?

7. What else could teachers do to help you learn and make friends?

Reflection

Make a list of actions teachers can take to facilitate learning for culturally diverse students based on the information you gleaned from your interview. Compare your list with those generated by others in your class who interviewed students from other cultures. What is the same? What is different? Discuss the pros and cons of each suggestion with an experienced teacher or with a university supervisor.

How Students Make Sense of School

Purpose
A characteristic of effective teachers is that they are student focused. That is, effective teachers pay attention to student interests, socioemotional needs, developmental level, and of course, learning. A lesson that makes sense to adults may not make sense to young people, and many students report that they frequently do not understand their assignments. For these reasons, learning to attend to students is an important part of learning to teach. The purpose of this interview is to help you grow in your ability to understand students' perspectives about classroom learning.

Directions
Observe a complete lesson in any grade level or subject. Write down the teacher's learning goal and the strategies used to accomplish that goal. Then use the following questions as a guide to interviewing a student present at that lesson. Conduct the interview as soon as possible after the lesson. Before you get into the interview proper, spend a few moments getting to know the student and establishing rapport with him or her. Adjust the tone of the questions appropriately depending on his or her age.

1. Tell me a bit about the lesson that just finished. What happened? (Probe for the sequence of events in the lesson.)

2. What was this lesson about? What did your teacher want you to learn in this lesson?

3. What did your teacher do to help you learn in this lesson?

4. What did you do to help yourself learn during this lesson?

5. What did you enjoy about this lesson? What did you dislike about this lesson?

6. How does what you studied today connect with what you studied yesterday?

7. Why did your teacher want you to learn this information?

Reflection
How well did your interviewee understand the lesson? Compare your responses with those from other student interviews. Do students in general seem to understand what is going on? What seems to interfere with understanding? What seems to promote understanding? As you observed the lesson, was it your impression that your interviewee was paying attention and "getting it"? Was your impression congruent with what you later found out in the interview? What can teachers do to get accurate information about what students are comprehending or not during the course of a lesson? What other conclusions do you draw from this interview?

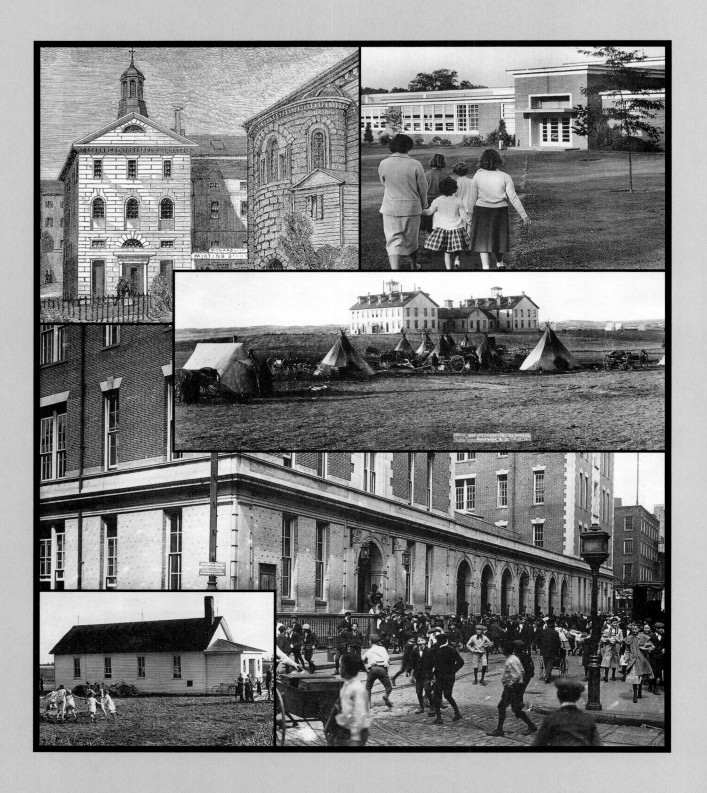

American Schools
and Their Curricula

Part II focused on the classroom and on teachers' instructional practices. In Part III, we shift our attention to the school and its curriculum. The chapters in Part III are concerned with how schools and curricula have changed and expanded over time to reflect changing social conditions and needs. We show how schools moved from the periphery of society, where they served specific groups of children, to the center of local and national life, where they serve everyone. Also, we introduce several issues that constitute the contemporary debate about schooling and curriculum, which are described in more detail in Chapters 7 and 8.

COLONIAL ROOTS

In the Part I and Part II introductions, you read how parents and the church were largely responsible for the education of children during the colonial period. At that time, the primary purpose of schooling was to teach basic literacy skills, so that people could read the Bible and maintain their European-styled civilization. Although schools varied widely from colony to colony, the most common were dame schools, reading and writing schools, Latin grammar schools, and academies.

Dame Schools and Reading and Writing Schools

The colonial era, particularly in New England, saw the beginnings of our present-day system of public schooling. In 1647, Massachusetts passed a law that required towns of 100 or more families to establish schools and to employ a teacher. Called the Old Deluder Satan Act, this law reflected the Puritans' belief that education—to their mind, ability to read the scriptures—was a key to salvation. Dame schools, run by housewives out of their homes, were established for the children of working-class families and emphasized the most basic of aspects of reading, writing, and arithmetic. They were supported for the most part through fees paid by parents. Children generally attended these first schools for very short periods of time, usually no longer than 1 year.

Reading and writing schools were slightly more advanced than dame schools. Attended mainly by boys and supported by parents and the community, the curriculum focused on reading, spelling, and arithmetic. Some of these schools, particularly in the northern colonies, also provided a strong dose of religious doctrine. Many teachers were barely more educated than their students and considered teaching a temporary occupation. The curriculum and the teaching methods used were intended to encourage conformity and self-restraint rather than creativity and self-expression. The following is a description of the curriculum in a colonial reading and writing school as described by Connecticut educator William Woodridge in the late 1700s.

> In the morning, the Bible may be delivered to the head of each class, and by them to the scholars capable of reading decently or looking over. This reading with some short remarks, or questions, with the morning prayer, may occupy the first half hour. The second, may be employed in hearing morning lessons, while the younger classes are preparing to spell and read. The third in attention to the writers. The fourth in hearing the under classes read and spell. The fifth in looking over and assisting the writers and cipherers. The sixth in hearing the under classes spell and read the second time; and receiving and depositing pens, writing and reading books . . .
>
> In the afternoon one half hour may be employed in spelling together, repeating grammar, rules of arithmetic, and useful tables, with a clear, and full, but soft voice, while the instructor prepares pens, writing books, &c. The second and third half hours in hearing the under classes and assisting the writers and cypherers. The fourth in hearing the upper classes read. The fifth to hearing the under classes read, and spell the second time. The sixth in receiving and depositing the books, etc. (Edwards & Richey, 1963, p. 347)

Latin Grammar Schools

The colonial era also saw the development of a two-tiered system of education. Children of wealthier families attended Latin grammar schools, an early form of secondary education. There they received a classical education centered around Latin, Greek, Hebrew, and religion, the prerequisites needed for admission to Harvard College and preparation for the ministry. Students entered Latin grammar schools already able to read and write and normally spent 7 years there, graduating in their early to mid-teens. The teaching in Latin grammar schools was generally considered to be stronger than in the reading and writing or dame schools. A description of the curriculum of the Boston Latin School in 1712 follows:

> The three first years were spent in learning by heart an "Accidence" or Beginning Latin Book, together with the *Nomenclator,* a Latin-English phrasebook and vocabulary called *Sententiae Pueriles,* and for constructing and parsing the *Distichia* attributed to Dionysius Cato, a collection of maxims popular since the early Christian era. Corderius's Colloquies and Aesop's Fables were also read in Latin. The fourth year began Erasmus's Colloquies, continued Aesop, studied Latin Grammar, and read Ovid *de Tristibus.* The fifth continued Erasmus and Ovid, including the *Metamorphoses,* and began Cicero's *Epistolae,* Latin prosody, and Latin composition with Garretson's "English Exercises for School-Boys to Translate." The sixth year began Cicero *de Officiis,* Lucius Florus, the Aeneid, and Thomas Godwyn's excellent English treatise on Roman history and antiquities, which had been used at the University of Cambridge in John Harvard's day; they continued the *Metamorphoses,* made Latin verse, dialogues, and letters, and began Greek and Rhetoric. The seventh and last year, boys of fourteen to sixteen began Cicero's Orations, Justin, Virgil, Horace, Juvenal, and Persius, made Latin dialogues, and turned "a Psalm or something Divine" into Latin verse, with a Latin theme every fortnight. In Greek, they read Homer, Isocrates, Hesiod, and the New Testament. And from Cotton Mather's statements, it seems probable that infant prodigies like himself (who finished school at the age of eleven) began Hebrew as well. (Edwards & Richey, 1963, p. 65)

The heavy reliance on the classics permitted little if any attention to more contemporary or practical subjects such as mathematics, history, and geography. All Latin grammar schools, however, did not have a curriculum like the one just described. In fact, the curriculum of many Latin grammar schools probably did not differ significantly from that of the reading and writing schools.

Academies

In 1753, Benjamin Franklin created an alternative to the Latin grammar school for middle-class youngsters. Franklin's *academy* differed dramatically from the Latin grammar schools of the day in that the curriculum emphasized the more useful and practical subjects that would prepare middle-class youngsters for the commercial jobs available at that time. The academies' curriculum included subjects such as English grammar (instead of Latin grammar) composition, literature, modern foreign languages (instead of Greek), science, writing, drawing, rhetoric and oratory, geography, history, agriculture and gardening, arithmetic and accounting, and mechanics (Urban & Wagoner, 1996). A justification for this curriculum was provided by one writer at the time:

As to their Studies, it would be well if they could be taught every thing that is useful, and every thing that is ornamental: but Art is long, and their Time is short. It is therefore proposed that they learn those things that are likely to be most useful and most ornamental. (Labaree & Whitfield, 1961)

Although the public provided some support for academies, they were mostly financed through fees. Nonetheless, they experienced rapid growth. By the end of the eighteenth century, academies had replaced Latin grammar schools in many communities, and by 1850, there were over 6,000 academies in the United States (Tyack, 1967). Franklin's more practical, nonreligious form of secondary education was a precursor of the secondary schools that evolved in the United States over a century later. His vision was the precursor to a continuing debate about the relative importance of academic versus practical subjects in secondary schools.

The number of reading and writing schools and academies increased rapidly during the eighteenth and early nineteenth centuries, but this expansion did not represent a system of public education. Schools were generally simple organizations, often headed by one person who taught in his or her home or in a church. The curriculum from school to school varied considerably, often depending on the teacher's own educational background and preference rather than on community agreement. Education remained a fragmented and mostly private endeavor financed by the wealthier members of a community.

CREATION OF THE COMMON SCHOOL: 1825–1865

The school-establishment laws passed in New England in the seventeenth and eighteenth centuries signified the importance of teaching children to read and write and set a precedent for some form of public education, but communities did not deem it their responsibility to pay for such schools or to make them available to everyone. However, in the period following the Revolutionary War, public sentiment about who should have access to education and who should pay for it changed dramatically. It was during this time that national leaders began to look to schools to develop an educated citizenry capable of understanding and implementing the Constitution and the Bill of Rights. Soon this faith in public education was expressed in both state and federal legislation, actions that are discussed in more detail in the following chapters.

It was during this time that Thomas Jefferson introduced legislation to establish a system of public education in Virginia. He proposed that taxes be used to provide 3 years of free elementary education for all white children and to establish grammar schools for boys whose parents could pay the tuition. Jefferson's plan was not enacted when it was introduced in 1779, but it set the stage for the common school movement 3 decades later.

The desire for political socialization following the Revolutionary War was not the only factor leading to a broader vision of public education. As we mentioned earlier, economics also played an important role, as the industrial revolution brought large numbers of immigrants to the United States in the first half of the nineteenth century and created a demand for a system of public schools.

The aim of the common school movement was to establish a system of free public schooling that allowed children from average families to receive a common education. Advocates argued that a system of public education should have three features: everyone would have access to schools, schools would be paid for with taxes, and schools would be nonsectarian, that is, separated from a particular religion. These three features of American education persist to the present day.

Two men, James Carter and Horace Mann, both from Massachusetts, provided critical leadership for the common school movement. A Harvard graduate, Carter wrote a series of essays arguing for free schools. Several of these essays were published in 1826, under the title "Essays upon Popular Education," and were widely read throughout New England. Under Carter's leadership, Massachusetts passed a law in 1827 that gave towns the power to tax its citizens to support public schools and to hire teachers. Later, as a member of the Massachusetts Legislature, he served as the chair of the Committee on Education and drafted the bill that created the nation's first state board of education.

Horace Mann, however, is the person most closely identified with the common school movement. Trained as a lawyer, Mann was elected to the Massachusetts Legislature in 1827 and soon became a strong advocate for educational reform. He worked endlessly to abolish the type of corporal punishment that was then used in schools and to make school buildings safer and more sanitary. In 1837, Mann became the first secretary for Massachusetts' newly created state board of education, and through his *Annual Reports* he became a champion for a free school system run by the state rather than by local communities. Mann believed education was a prerequisite for a democratic social order and a vehicle for the poor to better themselves. Mann, also held the firm belief that public schools should be kept separated from religion, an issue the introduction to Part V explores more fully.

Free, public education was not won quickly; opposition to the idea of common schools was considerable. Some citizens clung to the belief that education was a family and religious matter and that governments should not be involved. Others argued that educated workers were not essential, given the rote nature of factory work. Further, some wealthy landowners questioned the value of educating other people's children, particularly children of the poor. In their view, if poor children spent their days in school, they would not be available to work in the factories. Despite such opposition, by 1850, every northern and western state had passed legislation that provided some form of free public education.

As organizations, most schools in the early part of the nineteenth century, as in the colonial era, remained quite simple. Most often, one teacher taught all subjects to all students under the loose oversight of a town school committee. Supervisory roles, such as those of superintendent and principal, had yet to be developed. However, several features of the schools' curriculum that are familiar to us today began to evolve during this time. These included enlarging and enriching the elementary curriculum of the previous century and developing the first features of a comprehensive high school.

Expansion of the Elementary School Curriculum

The forces of industrialization and democratization demanded an extension of the meager curriculum that characterized schools of the colonial era. Between 1820 and 1860, the old elementary curriculum that included reading, writing, spelling, grammar, and arithmetic was expanded to include history, geography, civics, physiology, music, and drawing. Thus, by the time of the Civil War, most subjects taught in elementary school for the remainder of the century had been introduced, particularly in the better and larger urban schools. Two nineteenth century developments made curriculum expansion possible: the development of textbooks and the introduction of the age-graded classroom.

Development of Textbooks

In 1783, Noah Webster published a textbook in spelling, titled *The First Part of a Grammatical Institute of the English Language,* also known as the *American*

Spelling Book. Designed to teach children to read as well as spell, Webster's speller contained lists of words with syllabic guides to pronunciation along with a number of fables and moral stories. The speller has been one of the most popular books ever written, with over 75 million copies sold (Urban & Wagoner, 1996). It popularized spelling and spelling bees in the nineteenth century and is credited with establishing most of the differences that exist today between American and British spelling (e.g., *center* instead of *centre; labor* instead of *labour; organization* instead of *organisation*). More important for our purposes, Webster's speller helped standardize the curriculum around American English, which helped develop a sense of national identity. In the early nineteenth century, it made it possible for teachers to do a better job of teaching reading, writing, and spelling in the crowded one-room schools of that day.

Warren Colburn's *First Lessons in Arithmetic* was published in 1821 and, along with its many imitators, did for the teaching of arithmetic what Webster's speller had done for language instruction. With an emphasis on addition, subtraction, multiplication, and division and with some work in fractions, these arithmetic texts provided much needed assistance to poorly trained teachers and allowed expansion of arithmetic into the curriculum. (See Edwards & Richey, 1963; Johnson, 1904.)

In 1836, the first of several McGuffey readers was published, and by the 1840s these readers had been made into a set of six. The McGuffey readers introduced students to the American version of English grammar by having them read the writings of famous American statesmen, poets, and religious leaders. Through these readers, students received a heavy dose of morality and national pride. Teachers used the McGuffey readers, like Webster's speller, extensively until the turn of the twentieth century. The readers were also popular with adults who wanted to learn to read. Figure P3.1 is an illustration of a McGuffey reader.

Textbooks helped to expand and to unify the elementary curriculum in the first half of the nineteenth century. At the same time, however, the wide use of textbooks created problems for schools that persist to this day. For example, textbooks varied significantly and often were selected without much attention to their quality. Furthermore, although textbooks held the potential for unifying the curriculum, it was not uncommon to have children within a single school using many different textbooks. Edwards and Richey (1963) reported that in Massachusetts during the 1850s, there were at least 100 different books in use, often in the same school: "28

Figure P3.1   **Illustration from a McGuffey Reader**

The Story of "The Wolf" Taken from McGuffey's *Third Reader*

42 *ECLECTIC SERIES.*	*THIRD READER.* 43

42   *ECLECTIC SERIES.*

LESSON XIII.

wolf	grīēved	sleeve	neigh'bors	ēar'nest
ăx'es	elŭbs	ôr'der	sĭn'ğle	de stroy'

THE WOLF.

1. A boy was once taking care of some sheep, not far from a forest. Near by was a village, and he was told to call for help if there was any danger.

2. One day, in order to have some fun, he cried out, with all his might, "The wolf is coming! the wolf is coming!"

3. The men came running with clubs and axes to destroy the wolf. As they saw nothing they went home again, and left John laughing in his sleeve.

4. As he had had so much fun this time, John cried out again, the next day, "The wolf! the wolf!"

5. The men came again, but not so many as the first time. Again they saw no trace of the wolf; so they shook their heads, and went back.

6. On the third day, the wolf came in earnest. John cried in dismay, "Help! help!

***THIRD READER.*   43**

the wolf! the wolf!" But not a single man came to help him.

7. The wolf broke into the flock, and killed

a great many sheep. Among them was a beautiful lamb, which belonged to John.

8. Then he felt very sorry that he had deceived his friends and neighbors, and grieved over the loss of his pet lamb.

The truth itself is not believed,

From one who often has deceived.

Source: Illustration from McGuffey's Third Eclectic Readers, Revised Edition published ca. 1879, © The Newberry Library/Stock Montage, Inc.

Grammars, 24 Histories, 22 Arithmetic's, 20 Geographies, 9 Dictionaries, 4 Natural philosophies, 4 Astronomies, 3 Chemistries, 5 Geometries, and 2 Compositions" (p. 350–351). As you might suspect, in that time as today, it was easy for teachers to become overly dependent on textbooks at the expense of other teaching methods.

Age-Graded Classrooms

The proliferation of subjects and textbooks in elementary schools raised concern about schools' nongraded organizational structure. Teachers complained that they could not teach so many subjects, particularly when their classrooms were overcrowded with children of various ages as they often were in immigrant urban neighborhoods. The initial response to this situation was to begin classifying students according to their level of educational development. The single elementary school was gradually replaced by primary schools for beginning students and advanced schools for older students. This practice was soon followed by age-grading, that is,

classifying pupils into grades—usually from two to five per school—each with its own curriculum, textbooks, and teacher, and requiring students to pass from one grade or division to another.

Historians believe the first fully graded elementary school was the Quincy Grammar School of Boston, which was reorganized into grades in 1847. Soon, many other schools adopted this organizational structure (Edwards & Richey, 1963; Tyack, 1967). However, it was not until well into the twentieth century that this organizational arrangement reached the rural one-room schools that many American children attended.

Creation of Secondary Schools

Democratization, industrialization, and the belief that children from modest backgrounds were worthy of an education were the forces that expanded elementary education during the first half of the nineteenth century. These same forces were largely responsible for extending educational opportunities for older students. The limited purpose of the Latin grammar schools with their narrow focus on Greek and Latin did not address the growing student population in need of a broader, more practical curriculum. And, although the eighteenth century academies expanded rapidly during the first half of the nineteenth century, they remained small and independent and were neither supported nor supervised by the states or local communities. This educational gap was filled by the emergence of the American high school.

The Boston English High School is generally credited as being the first truly American high school. It was created in 1824 because the Boston Local School Committee wanted a school to prepare boys (not girls) to become merchants or artisans rather than to go to the university and enter the professions. This action was soon copied by communities throughout the Northeast and in the newer states in the West. In 1827, the Massachusetts legislature passed a law requiring the establishment of high schools in all communities of over 500 families. By the time of the Civil War, more than 300 high schools were in existence. Close inspection of the curriculum in these high schools reveals several courses and course sequences that can be found in modified form in most modern high schools. For instance:

- High school generally consisted of 4 years.
- Mathematics was organized into the following sequence: algebra, geometry, advanced algebra, and trigonometry
- Two years of modern foreign languages (French & German) was offered.
- Chemistry was taught in year 3; geology and astronomy in year 4.

As with many other aspects of education, public acceptance of high schools did not come easily or quickly. For example, in 1831, groups were organized to oppose the English High School proposed for Salem, Massachusetts (Edwards & Richey, 1963; Perkinson, 1991). They argued that it was proper to support elementary schools because "all classes in the community must proceed together," but further schooling should not be public because "it could be of advantage only to a few but was paid for by the many" (Edwards & Richey, 1963, p. 335). This attitude also slowed proposals to provide educational opportunities for girls, African slaves, and Native Americans as well. Many people simply did not believe that money spent on educating these groups was a wise use of resources.

Public Support for Education

Although the principle of public support for education had been established, it is a mistake to believe that every community had a school or that a large proportion of school-age children attended school. In fact, in 1860 only a small percentage of children attended a school and an even smaller percentage attended schools with extended curricula. It was especially difficult to introduce the newer type of elementary school with its expanded curricula into the rural areas of the country; resources simply did not exist. Also, high schools did not exist in many communities, and most teenagers were still taught by their parents or their employers.

CREATION OF MODERN SCHOOLS: 1865–1940

Between the end of the Civil War and the beginning of the twentieth century, school curriculum and organization took on the forms that are familiar to us today. During this time, the 8-4-4 system of public education—the 8-year elementary school, the 4-year high school, and the 4-year college—gained wide acceptance. Ungraded classrooms of the eighteenth and early nineteenth century rapidly gave away to age-graded classrooms.

High schools experienced a dramatic change between the end of the Civil War and the early part of the twentieth century. In the *Kalamazoo* case of 1874, the Michigan Supreme Court ruled that local school authorities—school districts—could tax citizens to support public high schools, an event that made possible the wide expansion of high schools that Americans saw during the last quarter of the nineteenth century.

Once the issue of financing high schools was resolved, debate over the American comprehensive high school, as it came to be known, shifted to the purposes and curriculum of secondary education. This debate centered around three major dilemmas: (1) how to prepare some students for college and others for vocations within the same institution, (2) how to provide unique experiences for secondary students while simultaneously meeting the standardized entrance requirements of post-secondary institutions, and (3) how to design a curriculum around socially prescribed academic subjects and make it relevant to youth. In reality, these issues have never been resolved and remain with us in discussions of American high schools today.

The Comprehensive High School

In the late nineteenth century, European schools separated students at age 11 or 12, moving some into academic high schools in preparation for college and others into technical schools in preparation for a vocation. Some Americans at the time agreed with this practice, seeing high school's primary responsibility as preparation for college and professional study. Others, particularly those in organized labor, wanted high schools to be places in which students were provided specialized vocational, commercial, and technical education to prepare them for the world of work. Most Americans, however, believed that all students, regardless of their backgrounds, talents, or career aspirations, should attend secondary schools that offered a common curriculum. From this common experience, they argued, the nation's diverse ethnic and social classes would develop a common identity.

Out of this debate, the American comprehensive high school evolved, a unique institution that provided a terminal education for some students and college preparation for others. Parallel curricula were designed so that within academic areas, students could choose between college or technical courses. Thus, the comprehensive high school, with its dual-track curriculum, was a compromise to satisfy competing demands on secondary schools. Although it has been the target of constant criticism for over a century, the comprehensive high school has remained the predominant form of secondary education in the United States. Chapters 7 and 8 discuss further the contemporary debate over its organization and curriculum.

Standardization and Reform

By the 1890s, there were thousands of high schools in the United States. However, there was little standardization among them, and schools varied greatly in their quality and in the variety of course offerings. In many communities, high schools consisted only of a room or two attached to the local elementary school, and as late as the turn of the century, Tennessee still defined secondary education as grades 6 through 8 (Tyack, 1967). Many school reformers of the day and most colleges believed that "high schools needed to be brought to common and higher standards, so that colleges may find in the school courses a firm, broad and reasonably homogeneous foundation for higher work" (p. 374).

In 1892, the National Council on Education appointed the Committee of Ten, whose members were charged with the job of developing a blueprint to bring "order out of the chaos that was the American high school." (Tyack, 1967, p. 356) They asked the committee to study how high schools should select and arrange academic content and to recommend how colleges could modify their admissions policies and requirements. Headed by Harvard University president Charles Eliot, the committee's membership included six college presidents, the U.S. Com-

missioner of Education, two public high school principals, and a private school headmaster. After months of study and debate, the Committee of Ten issued its report in 1893.

In general, the committee affirmed that American secondary education should provide practical experiences that prepared students for life, recognizing that high school for a large majority of students would be their terminal educational experience. The report also outlined a college preparatory curriculum that included study in one of four curriculum areas: the classics, Latin-scientific, modern languages, or English. The committee recommended that students who planned to attend college take only a few subjects and study each thoroughly for 4 years, a recommendation familiar to high school reformers today.

The Committee of Ten's report also highlighted the need for a standard measure for *units of instruction.* This led in 1909 to a system of academic bookkeeping known as the *Carnegie unit.* Under this system, a standard unit of instruction was defined as a course offered for five, 1-hour periods a week for the length of an academic year. This measure was rapidly accepted by state boards of education and accrediting agencies across the country. Colleges liked the Carnegie unit because it brought a measure of uniformity to the high school curriculum and provided a means for more accurate judgments about a student's high school work. However, the Carnegie unit also helped institute a degree of standardization that has prevented high schools to this day from experimenting with flexible curricula and scheduling formats.

The Committee of Ten's report was widely distributed and sparked considerable debate for several years. Some of the report's recommendations were followed; many were not. Most important, though, the report confirmed that high schools should offer more than preparation for college and that the curriculum should include modern subjects and be designed to give students some measure of choice. Drawbacks of the recommended curriculum were that it remained abstract and verbal. It was not until several years later that reforms were proposed to broaden the purposes of high schools and to make the curriculum more relevant and practical.

Broadening Curricula and Making It Relevant

In the years between 1890 and 1920, enrollments in secondary school soared, from 360,000 to 2,500,000 (Tyack, 1967). By 1904, there were over 7,000 high schools, some of which met the recommendations of the Committee of Ten. Most, however, were not organized into the four categories recommended by the committee but, instead, into a dual-track system that offered college preparatory and vocational courses side by side.

In 1916, another committee was appointed to study high schools and their curricula, this time by the National Education Association (NEA). Unlike the Committee of Ten, the NEA's committee had only one college president; other members were from the growing professional education establishment: three education professors, one normal school principal, two state supervisors, one high school principal, and a YMCA secretary. That no teachers were on the committee is illustrative of the low status of the teaching profession at that time. Unlike the earlier committee, the NEA committee spent little time discussing academic content, focusing instead on the nature of students, the social purposes of schooling, and new theories of teaching and learning.

In 1918, the NEA-sponsored committee issued its report, *The Cardinal Principles of Secondary Education*. The report tackled every aspect of secondary education. It argued that both classic and modern subjects needed to be reformed. It stated that the curriculum should be determined by the needs of society and by the nature of students, not by academic disciplines. The main purposes of education in a democracy with a diverse student population, members argued, should consist of the following: health, command of fundamental processes, worthy home membership, vocation, citizenship, worthy use of leisure, and ethical character.

This report challenged much of the academic curriculum of the time, claiming it was too abstract and removed from students' real-life experiences. The report proposed several new subjects, such as business education, household arts, agriculture, art, music, industrial arts, and physical education. It also expanded the idea of universal secondary education and recommended that all boys and girls should attend school full time until they reached the age of 18.

Like the Committee of Ten's recommendations, the *Cardinal Principles* were widely applauded but only partially implemented. Ten years after the report, fewer than half the 1,200 high school principals surveyed had put some of the principles into practice, and over one-fifth had never heard of the report (Tyack, 1967). Nevertheless, the report was historically significant, because it reflected a growing consensus about the broad purposes of secondary schools, reconfirmed the idea of a comprehensive curriculum within a single school, and emphasized the importance of making the curriculum and school experiences relevant to the lives of students.

Thus, by the 1920s, several features of today's schools were firmly in place. All youth were expected to attend elementary and secondary schools for a good portion of their early lives; the elementary curriculum adopted the age-graded organizational structure and expanded its curriculum to include most of the subjects taught today; and the comprehensive high school was firmly established.

THE CONTEMPORARY DEBATE

The second half of the twentieth century has been a time of both constancy and change in America's schools. On one hand, educational opportunities have extended to an ever-increasing and more diverse student population. On the other hand, except for the introduction of middle schools, no dramatic changes in the overall purposes, organizational structures, or curriculum have occurred. That does not mean, however, that Americans have been satisfied with their schools. Recurring reform movements have characterized the last fifty years, in which major changes have been proposed even though few have been fully implemented. Indeed, the United States is currently in the throes of educational reform the outcomes and significance of which remain unknown.

In the 1950s, the so-called life-adjustment curricula of the progressive era and other attempts to make curriculum more relevant for students came under rather severe attack. Critics, many of whom were university academicians, argued for a return to more traditional subjects in elementary schools and more emphasis on an academic curriculum in high schools. Russia's 1957 launching of Sputnik, the first space satellite, further convinced critics that American education was not competitive and that American students were not being challenged. This criticism brought forth a number of national curriculum projects aimed at improving the teaching of mathematics, science, and the social sciences in the elementary grades. It also caused the development of special programs for gifted students, those expected to provide leadership for America's competition with other countries.

High schools again came under scrutiny during this period. In 1959 Harvard President James Conant, issued a report entitled *The American High School Today*. In it, Conant sided with those critics who contended that the high school's curriculum did not challenge students, particularly in the areas of mathematics and science. He recommended more emphasis on mathematics, science, and foreign languages. However, like those reports of earlier eras, Conant's did not challenge America's basic faith in a comprehensive curriculum that allows students to pursue different career paths within a single school. As with earlier report recommendations, many of Conant's recommendations were debated but never implemented.

During the 1950s and 1960s, university scholars, heavily funded with federal monies, developed new courses of study in most of the academic disciplines taught in the secondary schools. Working from the premise that watered-down courses were being taught in lock-step fashion, they designed new courses that used inquiry-oriented teaching methods to discover core concepts and principles of the various academic disciplines. This attempt to reform the secondary school's curriculum reflected the debates of the 1890s and the Committee of Ten.

Efforts at curriculum reform were short lived, however, as educators turned their attention to the civil rights movement that was the center of national debate in the late 1960s and early 1970s. Even the university-based curriculum reforms were not taking hold, because many teachers did not understand or simply ignored the new curricula and teaching methods. By the 1970s, achievement test scores started to decline, which brought criticism that schools were trying to accomplish too much and that they should return to teaching the basics, a charge that continues through the 1990s.

The criticism that American schools lacked standards continued into the 1980s as efforts were begun to develop national standards and a standards-based curriculum. In 1990, the National Governor's Association, chaired by then Arkansas governor William Clinton, published a report that became the basis of national goals for education. These goals, discussed in the chapters that follow, outlined what schools are expected to accomplish by the year 2000. The goals were embraced by the administrations of both President George Bush and President William Clinton. Standards-based reform has led the major

subject-matter organizations, such as the National Council for the Teachers of Mathematics and the National Council for the Social Studies, to develop elaborate documents that define what students at every level of education should know and be able to do as a result of instruction in particular subject areas.

Reforms of the last decade have also focused on the way schools are organized and governed. As Chapter 7 shows, schools across the country are currently experimenting with new scheduling patterns and more flexible ways to organize students for instruction. Many schools are also exploring ways to empower teachers and parents. Involved with site-based management, these schools have created local school councils composed of teachers, parents, and, in some instances, students, all of whom are involved in making decisions about how to run their schools.

It is too early to predict the success of the reform initiatives of the 1980s and 1990s. On one hand, we can view standards-based curriculum and the empowerment of teachers and parents as bold steps toward creating schools that are more responsive to societal needs of the twenty-first century. On the other hand, we know that one of the most remarkable things about American schools is how little they have changed since the late nineteenth century. Elementary schools continue to be organized around age-graded, self-contained classrooms taught by teachers who emphasize the basics of reading, writing, spelling, and mathematics. These schools are similar to those your parents and grandparents attended. Similarly, the comprehensive high school has changed little since its inception. The basic unit of instruction continues to be courses taught in 40- to 60-minute periods, five times a week. A dual-track curriculum, college preparatory and vocational, continues to exist side by side, and much of what is taught in both tracks remains abstract and removed from the day-to-day lives of students.

CHAPTER 7

Schools: Organization, Culture, and Effectiveness

Previous chapters described how teaching is tied to students and classrooms. Classrooms, however, exist within the context of a place we call *school,* and a big part of a teacher's job is providing leadership and being "stewards of good schools." The school-wide aspect of a teacher's job includes working in collaborative ways with colleagues and parents, as well as with nonteaching school personnel. What happens in the school as a whole influences greatly how much students learn and the satisfaction teachers have with their careers. To be effective in their school-leadership role, teachers must understand how schools work and what constitutes good schooling.

This chapter describes the school as a social organization with a unique culture that has an impact on teachers' work environment and students' learning environment. The chapter first explores schools from the three different but complementary

frameworks of culture, organization, and community. An analysis of the effectiveness of American schools follows. The final sections describe what constitutes "good" schooling in today's world and explore the hopes and aspirations many Americans have for schools of the future—the schools in which you will teach and your children will learn.

HOW SCHOOLS WORK

Everyone knows what a school is. It is that red brick building down the street where children go every morning. It has a principal's office inside the front door and a large sign telling trespassers and visitors to check in at the office. It is divided into several rectangular rooms large enough to hold 25 to 30 students. Long halls, often lined with lockers for

How Schools Work
The Culture of Schools
Components of Culture
Subculture in Schools
Effects of School Culture
Schools as Social Organizations
Common Organizational Features
Unique Organizational Features
Schools as Communities

How Good Are Today's Schools?
Cycles of Criticism and Reform
Sputnik Reforms
A Nation at Risk
A More Positive View of Schools
Student Achievement
Citizen Satisfaction with Schools
Are Schools Good or Bad?

Good Schools for the Future
Making Traditional Schools Work Better
Experimenting with Innovative Schools
John Goodlad's Better Teachers,
Better Schools
Sizer's Coalition of Essential Schools
Berliner and Biddle's School Improvement
Principles
Boyer's Basic School
Prototype of the Twenty-First Century School
A Curriculum with Coherence
New Roles and Relationships for Teachers
and Students
New Roles and Choices for Parents
New Grouping Patterns and Reduced Size
Changes in Leadership
Will We Get the Schools We Want?

Summary

Readings for the Professional

storing students' coats and books, connect these rooms. Each room has a chalkboard and a teacher's desk. Most have an American flag and perhaps a picture of the president mounted in a prominent position. Schools also have a cafeteria, a gym, a library, and a multipurpose room. Newer schools have computer laboratories.

As familiar as most people are with these physical aspects of schools, very few have thought much about a school as a complex **social organization** with a distinct history and culture. And, although most people think of school as a place to which children go to learn, few think about it as a

place to which teachers go to work. The sections that follow explore the cultural, organizational, and community aspects of the place we call *school* and, in the process, give us new perspectives for interpreting the behaviors of teachers, students, and others who spend a large portion of their lives there. Figure 7.1 illustrates three ways of viewing schools.

The Culture of Schools

If you have studied anthropology, you probably were introduced to the concept of **culture.** This term, you will remember, is used to define the patterns of

Figure 7.1 **Three Ways of Viewing Schools**

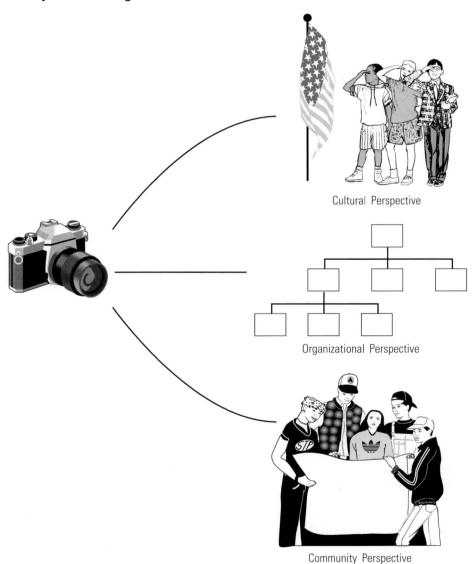

Cultural Perspective

Organizational Perspective

Community Perspective

behavior and the belief systems of particular groups of people. Much of peoples' patterned behavior and thought processes, along with the history and tradition that hold groups together over time, can be attributed to cultural norms. An individual's cultural heritage can provide a sense of security and belonging by showing him or her what is expected and how to act. In anthropology and the social sciences, the term *culture* is used to describe the deeper patterns and beliefs found in larger societies, both preliterate and modern. For example, when we refer to Western culture, we describe particular beliefs and institutions that emerged mainly in Europe over a period of several centuries. We refer to African culture or Chinese culture to identify other patterns of behavior and other belief systems that evolved with different groups in different settings.[1]

As with these larger societies, schools have their own unique cultures consisting of values, beliefs, and expectations that have developed over time. Lortie (1975) referred to school culture as the "way members . . . think about social action; culture encompasses alternatives for resolving problems in collective life" (p. 216). Others have provided similar observations about school culture, although they may have used different labels. For example, Rutter et al. (1979) referred to the common set of values, beliefs, and ways of doing things as a school's *ethos*; Glass (1981) called it *tone*; Joyce and his colleagues (1991) prefer the word *community*. Regardless of the label, the culture of a school greatly influences what goes on there and determines expectations and roles for teachers, students, parents, and others who are involved in them.

Components of Culture

The culture concept is important for understanding schools, but it is somewhat elusive and fuzzy. To help make it more concrete and understandable, Terrance Deal (1985, 1990) separated the concept into components that help us use it more precisely. He thought of schools as places that have shared values and beliefs, heroes and heroines, rituals and ceremonies, and culture carriers.

Shared Values and Beliefs   All interdependent groups of people have *shared values and beliefs.* Freedom and individual rights are examples of shared American values as are beliefs that individuals should work hard and be rewarded on the merits of their work. Many corporations have core values as well. The "customer is always right" or "stay

close to the customer" are examples of these. All schools also have shared values and beliefs that influence the behaviors of teachers and students. Values found in most schools include orderliness, that children are subservient to adults, and the importance of academic learning. Sometimes conflicts arise over core values and beliefs, or the adults in a school adhere to a different set of values than the students. These issues are discussed later.

Heroes and Heroines   Societies and the organizations within them often make their core values visible by identifying *heroes* and *heroines,* prominent persons who embody the society's most important values and beliefs. People such as Martin Luther King, Eleanor Roosevelt, and John Fitzgerald Kennedy are examples of heroes and heroines who embody key American values. In schools the heroes or heroines might be prominent teachers such as Christa McAullife, the New Hampshire school teacher who died in the 1986 Challenger space shuttle explosion, and Jaime Escalante, the high school teacher who dramatically raised the mathematics scores of minority students in East Los Angeles. However, the heroes and heroines of school culture are more likely to be students. If student heroes or heroines value school learning and the educational goals esteemed by the adult community, their popularity serves as a very positive influence. On the other hand, if student heroes or heroines come from subcultures (athletes, greasers, druggies) that hold values contrary to studying hard, getting good grades, or going to college, the situation can have a negative effect on the school as a whole and perhaps on the community as well.

Rituals and Ceremonies   One important way that individuals within groups experience shared beliefs is through *rituals and ceremonies.* Americans share these in many different ways. We sing the national anthem before sporting events; many of us eat turkey on Thanksgiving Day, and we celebrate the birthdays of presidents with official holidays. Hanukkah and Christmas are examples of important American holidays that have many rituals celebrated by Jews and Christians.

Life in schools also is filled with ritual and ceremony. Students are sometimes asked to pledge allegiance to the flag, and they regularly attend pep assemblies and other schoolwide events during which they sing the national anthem or the school fight song. Parents join teachers and students at music concerts and recitals, sporting events, and convocations and graduations. The marching band, senior skip day, and wearing caps and gowns are a few more school ceremonial examples. These rituals

---

1. This section draws from the work of Lee Bolman and Terrance Deal (Deal & Kennedy, 1982; Bolman & Deal, 1991.)

and ceremonies provide settings for teachers, students, and parents to display publicly their shared beliefs and to honor and celebrate members who best embody those beliefs. Once started, school ceremonies and rituals are very difficult to change, even when a ritual has a negative effect. The difficulty many communities have in containing senior skip day or in getting students to agree to a no drinking policy at the junior-senior prom are examples. The attempt to restrict athletic participation by students with poor grades or behavioral infractions is another example of traditions difficult to modify.

Culture Carriers   Culture is preserved over time and transmitted from one generation of organizational members to the next through a network of informal players or *culture carriers* (Deal, 1994; Deal & Kennedy, 1982). In schools, these carriers can be veteran teachers who take beginning teachers aside and explain how "things are done around here." It can be a sophomore telling freshmen "the ropes," or an older sibling explaining what to expect in middle school or high school. The transmission of cultural expectations happens mainly in informal ways and is very effective in providing continuity for societies and their organizations. As we mentioned previously, this can have positive or negative effects depending on the culture carriers.

Subculture in Schools

Numerous subcultures, each with its own particular set of **norms** and beliefs, exist within the larger school culture. Two that are particularly important in understanding how schools work are the subcultures of teachers and students.

Teacher Subculture   In schools, many formal and informal norms and routines affect teacher behavior. Some of these are associated with a particular school, and others derive from the professional **subculture of teaching.** Three aspects of teachers' subculture need highlighting, because they affect the lives of beginning teachers in important ways.

First, teachers in American schools are often perceived as powerless, as having little influence on what goes on in their schools. In some ways this is true. As you read in this section's part opener, historically most schools have been structured in a way that equates teachers with industrial workers supervised by administrators or bosses. However, in their own classrooms, teachers have a great deal of influence, supported by the **autonomy norm.** Once the classroom door is closed, they can do pretty much what they want. Teachers, including beginning

teachers, are responsible for their day-to-day curricula and make almost all instructional decisions by themselves.

Closely paralleling the autonomy norm is a second one known as the **hands-off norm.** The hands-off norm supports the autonomy norm by providing strong sanctions against those who might interfere with teachers in any but the most superficial way. According to Lortie, a sociologist who studies the culture of teaching (1975), it is inappropriate for teachers either to ask for or to offer help to their colleagues. This is not to suggest that teachers are unfriendly to one another or that they do not support one another emotionally. It means that in most schools, teachers avoid such "professional" topics as curriculum and teaching methods and restrict their talk to school politics, student backgrounds, and the like.

A third aspect of teachers' subculture is **role contradictions.** One of the most basic of these stems from society's virtually universal belief in treating each child as an individual, even though schools are organized to teach students in groups. This contradiction is particularly acute for high school teachers, who are expected to teach as many as 150 to 200 students every day, seeing them only for brief periods of time. It is a feature of the teachers' role that is particularly troublesome to student teachers. Each teacher develops his or her own way of dealing with this dilemma, and no teacher is ever completely satisfied with the compromises that are required.

Another contradiction in teaching involves the degree of "social distance" teachers maintain from their students. In many schools, teachers are expected to keep a certain social distance from students in order to maintain their authority. Wearing appropriate clothing, requiring students to address them with a fitting title, and having special faculty lounges are all measures intended to keep distance between teachers and students. However, most teachers know that in order to motivate students and help them learn requires some form of bonding and emotional closeness. Favorite teachers are normally those who have found a strong middle ground where they have earned students' respect but at the same time communicate an emotional closeness and caring about students' well being. Working out the distance contradiction can be troublesome for beginning teachers. They worry about what to wear, whether or not to allow students to call them by their first name, and how friendly to become with favorite students.

Student Subculture   Just as teachers' subculture affects teachers' behavior, so too does **student**

subculture affect what students do and learn in schools. Some studies suggest that by second grade many students start breaking away from their dependence on the teacher and other adults and begin seeking direction, friendship, and support from their peer group. This can be good if friendship patterns are a positive force in the classroom learning environment. Unfortunately, some children are unsuccessful in forming friendships, and as many as 20 percent are friendless; others become victims of peer hostility. Obviously, a teacher's ability to develop a positive learning environment depends, in part, on his or her ability to persuade students to accept school norms into their student subculture.

There is considerable research to show that students in most high schools tend to conform more to the norms of their peer subculture than they do to adult norms. Unfortunately, high school peer group leaders' values often contradict those of many parents and teachers. For example, as far back as 1961, James Coleman found many instances in which adolescent peer leaders supported norms of popularity and athleticism rather than academic achievement. This finding has been replicated many times since Coleman's original study. Fordham and Ogbu (1986) reported that many African American students purposely try *not* to excel in their studies for fear that black peer-group leaders will accuse them of "acting white." In the schools Fordham and Ogbu studied, peer leaders actively discouraged African Americans from studying hard, using standard English, and listening to classical music radio stations run by whites. Many factors contribute to this situation, and there appears to be no easy solutions for getting students to deny the strong influences of the peer group. Some educators and others believe that making schools smaller so that teacher-student relationships and the learning environment can become more personalized is one way to counteract these subculture norms. We discuss this in more detail further on. You can also reread the sections in Chapter 5 on student subcultures.

Effects of School Culture

Cultural perspectives help us understand not only how schools work but why some schools are more effective than others and why it is so difficult to change teacher behavior and school patterns.

Effects on School Effectiveness   Effective schools' cultures differ significantly from those of ineffective schools. In effective schools, for instance, teachers and parents have deeply shared values and beliefs, and they provide clear expectations for students both in and outside the classroom. Student heroes and heroines in effective schools embrace goals for studying hard and deferring immediate gratification to achieve longer-range goals, such as going to college. Peer group norms in effective schools call for students to respect and to help each other rather than to be mean and rejecting. Values and beliefs are publicly shared, and ceremonies ranging from open houses to pep rallies are well planned and attended.

Effects on New Teachers   School culture also has as a significant influence on beginning teachers. Albert Shanker, the recent president of the American Federation of Teachers, remarked that every year literally thousands of new teachers begin their careers in the New York City schools. And even though they come from many different backgrounds and many different teacher education programs, he maintained that after 3 weeks in the classroom, you cannot tell them apart from the teachers they replaced. Shanker described the force with which a school's culture *socializes* new teachers into its prevailing belief system and behavior patterns. In subtle, and not so subtle ways, the cultures of a school and of the teaching profession mold newcomers. There often are wide discrepancies between the professional ideals taught to teachers in their preparation programs and the reality of the school culture in which they begin their careers. Sometimes labeled *reality shock,* this situation can be confusing to a beginner and can sometimes lead to a rapid sense of defeat. With appropriate insight, however, beginning teachers learn to recognize this socialization process as part of their indoctrination into teaching, and they do not let it demoralize them or discourage their impulses toward helping students and school improvement.

Effects on School Change   A school's culture is obviously a major factor in its desire to and its ability to change. Because culture provides stability and continuity, it inherently thwarts departures from conventional practice. Deal and Nolan (1978) reported that many alternative schools in the United States have failed because they were unable to develop a new set of shared values and beliefs to replace the conventional system. Nearly 3 decades ago, Sarason (1971) concluded that the so-called new math curriculum of the 1960s was rejected because it was created by university reformers, and as such, it reflected the culture of the university, not the culture of the school. University reformers, according to Sarason, completely underestimated the strength and complexity of school culture. Even though millions of dollars were spent developing the new mathematics curriculum, it was really never fully implemented, because the people who were trying to change the schools were ignorant about school culture and unwittingly worked in self-defeating ways. Sarason's overall conclusion was that regardless of how effective certain proposals for change and reform may be, they can only be implemented if school routines and school culture can be altered to support new routines and behaviors.

In summary, the culture of a school exists within a larger societal culture and is shaped by that larger culture. At the same time, school culture is influenced by internal factors, such as teacher and student subcultures. Cultural norms, in turn, influence greatly how teachers within particular schools view their work, the kinds of learning environments they choose to create, and ultimately, what students take away from their school experiences. As you consider a career in teaching, think about how you relate to the cultural aspects of schools. How will they influence your work? What parts of this influence do you like? Dislike? Do you think you will be the kind of teacher described by Shanker who, after 3 weeks, will act like every other teacher in the school?

Schools as Social Organizations

Whereas a cultural perspective provides a way to observe and interpret the larger, more global aspects of schools, an **organizational perspective** provides a more precise way to look at schools as social organizations and as workplaces for teachers. Viewing schools as social organizations allows us to compare schools with other organizations in our society and to identify their unique and common features.

Common Organizational Features

In some ways schools are very similar to other social organizations in contemporary society. For instance, the beliefs and actions of teachers and others who work in schools are directed toward the accomplishment of important organizational goals. In a textile plant, the goal may be to produce high-quality, affordable fabrics; Microsoft is committed to developing state-of-the-art computer software. The overriding goal for schools is to provide purposeful learning experiences to help students become the self-regulated learners described in Chapter 1. Those who work in schools, just as those who work at Microsoft, are rewarded when they accomplish important organizational goals and are punished when they fail. The organizational structures and processes that have been developed over time to accomplish these goals gradually lead to natural and accepted ways of behaving.

As with most other organizations today, the work of schools is divided and specialized. Schools are simply too complex for one person or even a few people to know how to do everything. For instance, some teachers are prepared to teach mathematics and others specialize in English. Some have licenses to teach young children, others to work only in high schools. In addition, most schools have specially trained professional personnel in positions of principal, guidance counselor, and special educator. These individuals, each of whom has professional status, are supported by many others, such as janitors, secretaries, teacher assistants, cafeteria workers, and bus drivers. Most people in schools, however, are students, and we can think of them as organizational members whose work is the completion of teacher-assigned tasks.

The fact that school roles are divided and specialized means that its members must behave in more or less interdependent ways. Each member of the school—teacher, student, administrator, parent—must chart his or her course in relation to other members rather than behave independently. We show in the following sections how these interdependent patterns of action have important consequences for student learning.

Unique Organizational Features

Schools have much in common with other organizations, but they also have their own unique organizational features, as you can see in Figure 7.2. These differences, which are often misunderstood by teachers and policy makers, are important because they may be the key to changing schools in desired ways.

Captive Clientele   Except for prisons, schools are the only organizations in our society that compel the clientele attend. All states since the beginning of the twentieth century have had compulsory attendance laws that require parents to send their children to school, generally until age 16. These laws were passed initially to keep children out of the labor force, to end child labor abuses, and to guarantee a minimum education. Over the years, however, these laws have proved troublesome for two reasons. First, they keep unmotivated students in school against their will. Schools with large numbers of these students are the most difficult ones for teachers to work in. Second, compulsory attendance laws have in some instances become unenforceable. For example, a large school district on the east coast had fewer than one-half its students in school on opening day and over one-third were still missing a month later (personal communication). Truant officers, who

Figure 7.2   Unique Organizational Features of Schools

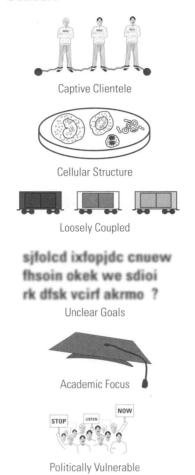

Captive Clientele

Cellular Structure

Loosely Coupled

sjfolcd ixfopjdc cnuew
fhsoin okek we sdioi
rk dfsk vcirf akrmo ?

Unclear Goals

Academic Focus

Politically Vulnerable

in earlier times would chase down a few truant students, today make little effort to enforce attendance in districts with high drop-out rates.

Cellular Structure   Lortie (1975) described the school's organizational structure as **cellular,** that is, each classroom can be regarded as a cell within which a teacher is responsible for organizing and managing a particular group of students. This organizational arrangement, along with the hands-off norm described earlier, has created an isolated work situation for teachers. Unlike most other professionals who work together in teams, teachers usually work alone and make independent decisions about when and how to teach various aspects of the curriculum. This has encouraged principals and others in the school to relate to teachers on a one-to-one basis rather than as an organized faculty unit. The cellular structure and its corresponding isolation fosters the image of teaching as a lonely profes-

sion. It also contributes to teachers' inability to take collective action in improving their schools.

Grade and Age-Level Organization   The cells referred to by Lortie (1975) are defined by the age level of students, a rather recent invention. Throughout much of the nineteenth century, you will recall, teachers were generalists who taught a variety of subjects to students of all ages in one-room schoolhouses. Modern elementary schools, however, place all 6-year-olds in the first grade, all the 10-year olds in the fifth grade, and so on. Although middle school and high school students are organized into separate subject matter classes, such as mathematics or English, they still remain with age-level peers for most of their instruction, for example, tenth-grade English, ninth-grade geography, twelfth-grade world history. Age-level organization is beneficial in that it reduces the developmental differences found within a particular class and thus provides a degree of efficiency. However, even grade-level organization does not preclude wide developmental differences within a particular age range within the charge of a lone teacher.

Loosely Coupled   Schools' cellular structure and grade-level organization cause a condition that Weick (1976) labeled **loosely coupled.** This term refers to the fact that what goes on in any one classroom is not very tightly connected to or coupled with that which goes on in other parts of the school. Teachers can and do carry out their instructional activities independently of administrators and policy makers. The school board or the central office may initiate new curricula or new teaching approaches, but if teachers choose to ignore these initiatives, they can. In a similar way, this structure leaves teachers only loosely connected to each other. These organizational constraints provide few opportunities, according to Rosenholtz (1989), for teachers to establish common goals or to work together. Instead, teachers adopt a view of their work in which their success depends on their own self-reliance without assistance from colleagues. On the positive side, however, loose coupling does allow teachers considerable room for exercising creativity and decision making in complex situations that may resist standardized answers.

Lack of Shared Goals   Throughout history, American schools have been presented with a variety of unclear, often conflicting goals. Most people tend to support broad school goals such as preparing citizens for a democracy or facilitating purposeful thinking. However, when various groups within a community seek more specific goals, conflict usually results. To avoid such conflict, schools often develop goals that are purposely unclear and ambiguous (Rosenholtz, 1989). Consider, for instance, the goal of protecting democracy by teaching its core values—individual freedom, the right to pursue a livelihood as one sees fit, and providing equal opportunities for everyone. Although most Americans embrace these general goals, when schools try to promote them, conflict often arises. What constitutes freedom? What constitutes equality? What constitutes a good citizen? Is a good citizen one who accepts the definitions of freedom and equality that now exist? Or, is a good citizen one who criticizes current definitions and practices, questions existing values, and attempts to modify them?

Academic Focus In addition to organizing students by age, educators have also chosen to organize the curriculum around academic subjects. For example, the core curriculum taught from first grade through high school consists of language, mathematics, science, history, and geography, and in some schools includes foreign language, physical education, and health. The norm is to teach these subjects independently of one another in a sequential fashion, focusing on basic concepts in the earlier grades and more complex concepts and topics in the later grades. The school's schedule is organized around these core subjects, and teachers at the middle school and high school levels are certified to teach some subjects but not others.

As with age-level organization, emphasis on academics has advantages and disadvantages. Requiring all students to pursue an academic core until completion of high school prevents premature sorting into vocational or academic paths. Also, an academic curriculum gives all students exposure to content that many Americans value. On the other hand, a large proportion of youth find many academic subjects irrelevant, and consequently, their motivation to learn is minimal. An academic focus favors students who have particular abilities and backgrounds and prevents others from developing other talents, such those required for success in the creative and performing arts or in technology. An additional drawback to the wide array of required academics is that having to cover so many subjects in such short time periods leads to superficial, vocabulary-focused teaching and learning rather than active, in-depth processing of key material.

Politically Vulnerable Finally, schools differ from many other organizations because they are *politically vulnerable* and resource poor. Pick up any local newspaper and it is apparent that many people take an active interest in their schools. Indeed, some have observed that the local school is one of the few places in complex societies in which citizens can make their voices heard. It is easy for people to attend local school board meetings and speak their minds. It is easy to walk into a school without an appointment and expect to visit with the principal and teachers, something that is nearly impossible to do in most contemporary organizations.

In some ways, such easy access is positive. Open participation helps build support for schools and commitment from parents and other citizens. At the same time, this situation leaves schools and those who work in them vulnerable to unfair political influences and unwarranted attacks, as Cuban (1993) described:

> The unique organizational characteristics of this taxpayer supported public bureaucracy (schools) governed by lay policymakers merge with the imperative to retain the loyalty of the system's constituencies. Both help to explain schools' obvious vulnerability to pressures for change from external groups. When value conflicts arise and external pressure accelerates, both get wedded to an organizational drive for retaining support of critical supporters; such conditions push school districts to try novel programs, join regional and national efforts to improve curriculum, and adopt innovative technologies so as to be viewed as worthy of continued endorsement. (p. 10)

Schools' unique features are not always well understood by people in our society, including many teachers and policymakers. This misunderstanding leads to inappropriate proposals for reform and failure to develop the schools we say we want, a topic we return to later in the chapter. Some of these features can also be frustrating to beginning teachers who are unaware of them. How do you relate to the unique features of schools? Do you look forward to working in an organization that lacks shared goals? Do you agree with today's age-grade organizational arrangement and academic focus? What might you try to change if you decide to become a teacher?

Schools as Communities

Thomas Sergiovanni (1996), a well known scholar in the field of school leadership, agrees that cultural and organizational perspectives help us understand how schools work. He argues, however, that they also limit our vision and prevent us from thinking about what schools could be in the future. Preferring to view schools as *communities,* Sergiovanni explained:

Communities are collections of individuals who are bonded together by natural will and who are together bound to a set of shared ideas and ideals. This bonding and binding is tight enough to transform them from a collections of "I's" into a collective "we." As a "we," members are part of a tightly knit web of meaningful relationships. This "we" usually shares a common place and over time comes to share common sentiments and traditions that are sustaining. (p. 48)

He also said:

When the term *community* is used, the first notion that typically comes to mind is a place in which people know and care for one another—the kind of place in which people do not merely ask, "How are you?" as a formality, but care about the answer. This "weness" . . . is indeed part of its essence. Our focus here, though, is on another element of community, crucial for the issues at hand: *Communities speak to us in moral voices. They lay claims on their members. Indeed, they are the most important sustaining source of moral voices other than the inner self.* (p. 31)

Notice some ideas Sergiovanni put forth: *bonded individuals, shared ideas and values, collective we, moral voice, tightly knit web.* These words describe a

social arrangement very much different from those that can be found in either traditional or contemporary organizations. Communities are caring, intimate places built on shared purpose and mutual respect. They are places in which informal connections, collegiality, and natural interdependence coordinate activities. This arrangement contrasts sharply with the use of hierarchical control structures and formal systems of supervision and evaluation found in contemporary business organizations.

Sergiovanni (1996) used two concepts from sociology—*gemeinschaft* and *gesellschaft*—to expand his theory that schools are more like communities than formal organizations (see Figure 7.3). The German term *gemeinschaft* translates to *community* and its intimate relationships and *gesellschaft* to *society* and its more formal relationships. Together they represent two different ways of thinking and living.

Over time humans have moved from hunting and agricultural communities to industrial societies. This evolution represents a shift from *gemeinschaft* toward *gesellschafte.* The most important aspect of this transformation is the replacement of community values with formal contractual ones. Early agricultural communities were bound together by common beliefs and values. Their closeness to natural disaster required interdependent and reciprocal behavior.

Figure 7.3   **Two Ways of Thinking About Schools**

Gemeinschaft

Gesellschaft

Neighbors pitched in to rebuild a barn after it was devastated by fire, for example.

Over time communities were replaced by more complex societies, with organizational arrangements built on new conditions and assumptions. Most modern organizations are constructed on contractual arrangements rather than on conditions of shared values. Roles within them are prescribed by contracts, workers are evaluated by standardized criteria, and behavior is governed by organizational policies and union contracts and rules.

Schools, according to Sergiovanni (1996), have adopted the same worldview (*gesellschaft*) as corporations. Schools are hierarchical organizations like most modern corporations, with school boards modeled after a corporation's board of directors. The superintendent is often referred to as the school's chief executive officer, whose responsibilities are similar to that of a corporation president. A principal has a middle-management position; he or she is in charge of a particular school building and has responsibility for supervising the work of the teachers there. Teachers are evaluated by standard criteria (teaching competencies) and in most instances by a very formal process defined by a teachers' union contract. During the past 2 decades, both major teacher unions, the AFT and the NEA, have negotiated contractual arrangements with school boards that describe in some detail teachers' obligations, including the time they must arrive at the building, when they may go home, and how many faculty meetings they are required to attend.

According to Sergiovanni (1996), however, when *gesellschaft* values and arrangements are applied to schools, they do not work very well and are the source of many of the school's current problems. This is because schools are more similar in character to a family, a neighborhood, or the myriad voluntary social groups that exist in American society, places that have a special sense of belonging and strong common meaning for participants, than they are to formal business organizations.

The community metaphor is provocative, but it may be more useful in planning future schools than in understanding them as they are today. We come back to this topic in the final section of this chapter, but spend a moment now thinking about the implications to you as a prospective teacher. Would you find satisfaction working in a school characterized by a sense of belonging and with strong bonds among all participants? Or, do you prefer the more formal relationships found in most schools today? Which do you think would be best for students? For their parents?

HOW GOOD ARE TODAY'S SCHOOLS?

We move now from discussing how schools work to consider how *well* they work. First we attend to criticisms and then to some of the successes of contemporary schooling.

Cycles of Criticism and Reform

Curiously, most Americans are ambivalent about their schools. They appear to be comfortable with the familiar patterns of schooling they experienced as children, and they get upset when plans for significant change challenge these patterns. At the same time, Americans are quick to find fault with schools and to support many of the political initiatives aimed at reform. This situation was accurately captured by Bruce Joyce (1983) who wrote, "People like the familiar old schoolhouse as much as they like to criticize it" (p. 4).

Since World War II, schools have taken on added importance as society has sought increasingly to use them for economic as well as civic development. During the past 50 years, educational opportunities have expanded rapidly and far surpass those offered in earlier eras. Yet regardless of schools' growing importance, many believe that our system of public education is failing us. Consider, for example, the analysis provided recently by noted educational historian Lawrence Cremin (1990):

> The (growth) and popularization of American schools and colleges since the end of World War II has been nothing short of phenomenal, involving an unprecedented broadening of access, an unprecedented diversification of curricula, and an unprecedented extension of public control. In 1950, 34 percent of the American population twenty-five years of age or older had completed at least four years of high school, while 6 percent of that population had completed at least four years of college. By 1985, 74 percent of the American population twenty-five years of age or older had completed at least four years of high school, while 19 percent had completed at least four years of college. [In 1995 over 80 percent of the population had a high school diploma and almost a fourth completed college.] It was in many ways a remarkable achievement, of which Americans could be justifiably proud. *Yet it seemed to bring with it a pervasive sense of failure.* (pp. 1–2)

Sputnik Reforms

In the 1950s, American schools experienced the first wave of post-World-War II sense of failure that

Cremin described. Critics claimed that the curriculum contained too many soft, life-adjustment courses and not enough core academic subjects, such as mathematics, science, foreign languages, history, and geography. The Soviet's success in launching Sputnik in 1957 reinforced the view that American students were not being academically challenged. In response to this criticism, the decade following Sputnik saw immense efforts to rewrite curricula and redesign schools.

Critics, mainly conservative intellectuals and university academicians, thought that the existing elementary and high school curricula were outdated, too easy, and irrelevant. They also argued that existing teaching methods failed to stimulate students' natural desire to explore the world. Reformers spent massive funds developing new math and science and, later, social science curricula. Their aim was to teach these disciplines' basic concepts in some rudimentary form in the early grades and then develop them more fully in the upper grades and high school. Their preferred pedagogy involved discovery-oriented teaching methods. Funds were also expended to upgrade the academic preparation of teachers and to help them understand how to teach the new curricula.

Along with criticizing the curricula and teaching methods, critics scrutinized the organizational patterns of American elementary and secondary schools. The cellular, age-level pattern of elementary school was often replaced with flexible open-space classrooms organized around multi-aged teams of students and teachers. At the high school level, the standard six-period day came under attack, and school districts in every state developed alternative schedules aimed at providing more opportunities for students to learn independently and to experience more curriculum.

But the innumerable curricular and organizational experiments of the 1950s and 1960s were not sustained into the next decade. Indeed, they disappeared quickly when schools became influenced by the civil rights movement and the Vietnam War and parents and citizens demanded a return to a basic skills curriculum and more traditional organizational structures. The 1970s thus saw a return to the basic academic curriculum of earlier decades, but this still did not result in schools that satisfied many Americans, and the perception remained that American education was in need of repair.

A Nation at Risk

The second cycle of post World War II educational reform began in the 1980s and continues to the present. Many attribute its beginning to a 1983 report entitled *A Nation at Risk* that began with these words:

> Our nation is at risk. Our once unchallenged preeminence in commerce, industry, science and technological innovation is being overtaken by competitors throughout the world. . . . The educational foundations of our society are presently being eroded by a rising tide of mediocrity that threatens our very future as a nation and a people. . . . If an unfriendly foreign power had attempted to impose on America the mediocre educational performance that exists today, we might well have viewed it as an act of war. As it stands, we have allowed this to happen to ourselves. . . . We have, in effect, been committing an act of unthinking, unilateral educational disarmament. (p. 5)

Publication of *A Nation at Risk* had an effect on education similar to the one caused by the launching of Sputnik 25 years earlier. It produced immediate proposals for reform as well as a spate of reports (well over 300) issued by governors, state education departments, and professional societies all claiming that the schools were failing and all calling for reform. Not unlike the reforms of the 1950s and 1960s, reforms over the past decade have been aimed at raising standards and requirements perceived to have slipped and at making greater demands on students. By 1995, 45 states had increased high school graduation requirements and set minimum requirements in math and science (Carlson, 1995). The school day was extended in many communities, and higher standards were established for teachers. Most of the reforms during this period, as with the post-Sputnik era, have been imposed on schools and teachers by governing agencies.

Despite a half-century of almost continuous reform, many citizens and educators still believe that American schools are failing. The perception persists that academic standards have declined, students' test scores are dropping, and students are less well educated than students in other countries. Americans also believe that schools in many communities are unsafe and dropout rates have reached an unacceptable level. Increasingly, vocal groups trumpet the opinion that public schools, as we know them, have failed completely and must be replaced by radically different educational vehicles. Do you think the critics are right? How accurate are their criticisms of schools? Have standards slipped? Are American schools no longer appropriate places to send our youth?

A More Positive View of Schools

David Berliner and Bruce Biddle, two noted educators, recently challenged the critics of the public schools. They argued that distorted evidence has misled the American public and created a number of myths about the deficiencies and failures of public schools that are not true. They wrote that Americans have come to believe the schools have failed because:

> for more than a dozen years ... a groundless and damaging message has been proclaimed by major leaders of our *government* and *industry* and has been repeated endlessly by a compliant *press*. Good-hearted Americans have come to believe that the public schools of their nation are in a crisis state because they have so often been given this false message by supposedly credible sources. (p. 3)

In their book, *The Manufactured Crisis,* Berliner and Biddle (1995) questioned the widespread view that schools have failed, and they provide evidence and a point of view that contradicts critics' views. They make two important assertions:

- On the whole, the American school system is in far better shape than the critics would have us believe.

- Where American schools fail, those failures are largely caused by problems imposed on those schools, problems that the critics ... ignore. (p. 13)

Let's take a look at some of the evidence and arguments they present.

Student Achievement

Berliner and Biddle countered the often-cited claim that student achievement has declined, particularly as measured by the Scholastic Aptitude Test (SAT). The SAT attempts to predict the likelihood of academic success in college, and critics, including the authors of *A Nation at Risk,* perceive that achievement on the SAT has declined significantly over the past 30 years. This perception has been reported widely by the media. Berliner and Biddle pointed out, however, that it is inappropriate to use the SAT as a measure of school performance for several reasons. First, the test measures only students' knowledge of verbal materials and mathematics, less than a third of the school's curricula. It does not test other important topics taught in schools such as history, science, foreign language, or citizenship. Second, the SAT standards were established in 1941, a time when students taking the test represented a much narrower band of the youth population than is the case today. Most important, however, the SAT was designed to predict the success of individuals to do college freshman work. Its scores were never intended to be aggregated into a group measure of academic performance.

Let's look more closely at what has happened to SAT scores during the past 40 years to see how a cursory glance at these scores can lead to erroneous conclusions about schools. Figure 7.4 presents aggregate scores for verbal and mathematics achievement between 1955 and 1993. As you can see, aggregate scores for verbal and mathematics fell steadily during this period. These are the data used by critics who believe that achievement has declined.

These aggregate scores, however, can be very misleading. Over the years, a larger and larger proportion of American high school seniors have chosen to take the SAT. When in the 1940s and 1950s only a few students with strong high school records took the test, the scores were predictably higher than they are today, because now a larger proportion of students with weak high school records take

Figure 7.4 **Average SAT Scores 1955–1993**

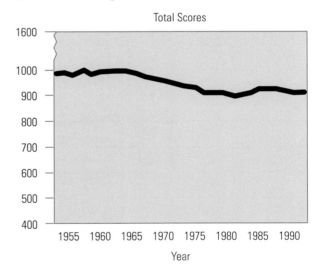

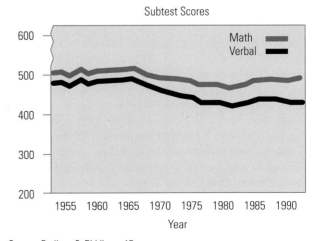

Source: Berliner & Biddle, p. 15.

Figure 7.5　**Average SAT Scores for Verbal and Mathematics by High School Rank**

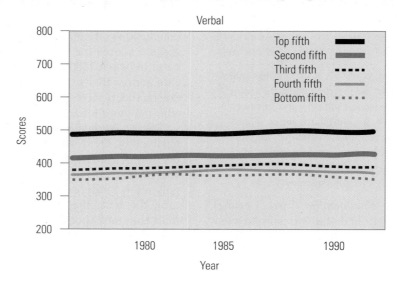

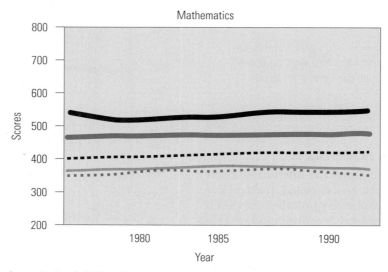

Source: Berliner & Biddle, p. 21

the test. Figure 7.5 divides SAT verbal and mathematics scores according to each high-school rank between 1976 and 1993.[2] These *disaggregated SAT scores* illustrate that student achievement has not declined but has held steady and even climbed at a modest rate since the 1970s. For instance, scores in mathematics for the top ranked high school students increased 10 points between 1976 and 1993.

Mathematics scores for all other ranks also improved, while verbal achievement scores remained steady. What this means is that SAT scores for each

rank of high-school students have not declined but instead have increased slightly over time. It is only when the scores are aggregated that we observe decline, a situation caused by a larger proportion of low-ranking students taking the test.

Over the past several years, the International Association for the Evaluation of Educational Achievement has tested students from selected countries to provide international comparisons of achievement in science and mathematics. Critics use the results of these tests in the same way they do the SAT, that is, to show the shortcomings of American schools. Indeed, at first glance it appears that American students do not compare well to students from selected European countries, Japan, and Korea.

2. This analysis was done only from the 1970s to the present because the class ranking of students was not available in the early years of the test's administration.

For example, *A Nation at Risk* reported that "international comparisons of student achievement . . . revealed that on 19 academic tests American students were never first or second and, in comparison with other industrialized nations, were last seven times" (p. 8). Berliner and Biddle (1995) challenged these conclusions just as they did the negative conclusions based on SAT scores. They said the assertion that American students do poorly in international comparisons is simply not true and critics who have made such generalizations have not bothered "to think about the assumptions involved when one compares aggregate achievement scores among countries" (p. 52).

For instance, different countries have different visions about how to raise children and how to conduct education. Many European and Asian countries sort students at an early age into academic and vocational tracks. Those who proceed into academic schools are expected to concentrate on mathematics and science and to limit their extracurricula activities. Americans, on the other hand, believe their youth should remain together in comprehensive schools and have access to a wide variety of experiences, including clubs and after school sports. Many American parents believe that work experiences for young people are worthwhile, and they do not want these experiences or extracurricular activities interrupted with too much homework. Comparative achievement studies naturally favor schools in countries that focus on academics and do not measure the broader curricular goals of American schools.

Berliner and Biddle (1995) also pointed out, as they did with data from the SATs, that aggregate data on achievement tests can produce misleading conclusions. Westbury (1989) analyzed the educational backgrounds of the 13-year-old American and Japanese students from one international comparison and found that all Japanese students in the sample had been required to take algebra in the eighth grade. American students who took the test came from four different types of eighth-grade mathematics classes: remedial classes (30 cases), typical eighth grade nonalgebra classes (174 cases), enriched prealgebra classes (31 cases), and algebra classes (38 cases). Figure 7.6 shows the results when Westbury compared aggregated scores (part A of the figure) with disaggregated scores (part B of the figure). As you can see, the achievement of American students who had taken algebra exceeded the achievement of Japanese students, and students in the American prealgebra classes came very close to matching the achievement of their Japanese counterparts. When American students' scores were lumped together however, Japanese students' scores appear higher. Berliner and Biddle point out that international comparisons do not necessarily reveal deficits in a particular country's system of schooling but instead illustrate how different countries choose to structure curricula and experiences in different ways.

Citizen Satisfaction with Schools

Critics cite citizen dissatisfaction with schools as another source of evidence that American schools are failing. One regularly cited study conducted by the National Opinion Research Center at the University of Chicago (1993) reported that confidence in the schools had declined significantly between 1973 and 1990. However, when Berliner and Biddle (1995) analyzed these data more closely, they found that public confidence had declined in *all* major American institutions during that time frame: medicine was down 9 percent; religion was down 12 percent; banking was down 15 percent. We seem to be living in a time of eroding confidence, according to Berliner and Biddle, and this erosion seems to be reported more widely for schools than it is for other institutions.

Are Schools Good or Bad?

The truthful answer to this question is probably a little of both. For instance, Lawrence Stedman (1996) argued that parts of Berliner and Biddle's critique is flawed and although test scores have not declined, neither have they increased. Essentially they have remained unchanged in the past 30 years. Stedman goes on to argue that "a steady state" is not enough, particularly when large numbers of students perform below acceptable standards.

On the other hand, the most recently reported SAT scores show that math scores increased between 1992 and 1996 (*Phi Delta Kappan,* 1996). Also, the 1996 report of The Third International Mathematics and Science Study puts the scores of American students slightly below the worldwide average in math and slightly above in science. Students in several countries (mainly Asian) scored better than American students, but American students were on par with Germany, England, and Canada, among others.

Literacy scores for American students are also encouraging. The most recent study of the the International Association for the Evaluation of Educational Achievement (IEA) examined the reading proficiency of 9- and 14-year-olds in 31 countries. For younger students, Finland finished in first place, but Americans came in second (Bracey, 1996). The mean score for the American youngsters was 22 points

Figure 7.6   **American and Japanese Achievement Scores in Mathematics for Age 13 Students**

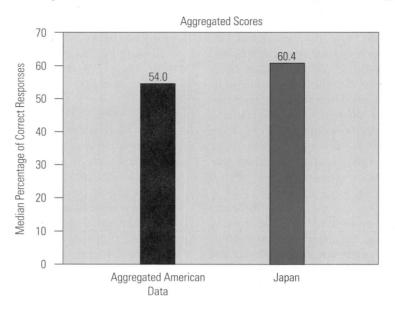

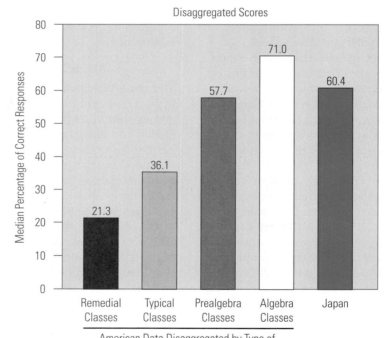

Source: Berliner & Biddle, p. 57.

behind that of the Finnish on a 600-point scale similar to the one used for SAT. American 14-year olds fared a little worse; they scored 25 points behind the first place nation (only 3 points lower than the 9-year-olds), but this gave them only an eighth-place ranking. The top-scoring countries were clustered closely together. Further analysis showed that there were no statistically significant differences between second-place (France) and eleventh-place (Switzerland) (NCES, 1994). This lesser showing, then, is roughly equivalent to second place ranking, an excellent performance, notwithstanding the diversity and economic resources of American students, which were not taken into consideration.

The public has been particularly concerned with the science achievement of American students. Many press reports have charged that American schools lag behind other countries in teaching science. Recently, scholars have challenged these purported learning gaps, as they have challenged alleged gaps in math and literacy. The bad news is that American 13-year-olds finished thirteenth out of 15 nations, and nine-year-olds ranked third on the Second International Assessment of Educational Progress, which examined science knowledge (Bracey, 1996). Keep in mind, however, that American 13-year olds scored above average in the more recent Third International Study. As with literacy achievement, though, rankings for science obscure true relative performance. When actual scores are examined, American students' achievement is actually very close to that of students in other countries.

Some media reports and school critics (e.g., Ravitch & Finn, 1987) have said students do poorly in history and social studies. The test items used to support this conclusion are like the following: What made Samuel Gompers, Andrew Carnegie, and Jane Addams famous? What did the Seneca Falls declaration concern? What does the *nullification* issue refer to? Berliner and Biddle (1995) argued that many people (including themselves) would have difficulty with these items, but their qualifications as citizens would probably not be adversely affected. As with most standardized tests, history tests assess the isolated bits of information that are most easily tested and fail to test for other knowledge, skills, or dispositions that we consider important but cannot readily assess. Thus, drawing conclusions about students' knowledge of history and generating new policies or reforms based on these conclusions seems, at best, unwise.

Citizens' opinions about schools is an additional factor to consider in the determination of how good schools are. Every year for the past 25, a Gallup poll has been conducted on citizen perceptions of the public schools. The results are published in the *Phi Delta Kappan,* a widely read education journal. The journal asks a representative sample of Americans to give the schools a letter grade A, B, C, D, or F. The Gallup poll makes two important distinctions in this opinion survey. First, it distinguishes between public opinion about "school in general" and about one's local school. Second, it distinguishes between two types of respondents: parents with children in school and the rest of the citizenry. Figure 7.7 presents the results of the Gallop Poll over the 10-year period from 1986 to 1996.

Figure 7.7, shows that when respondents were asked to grade the nation's schools in general, they

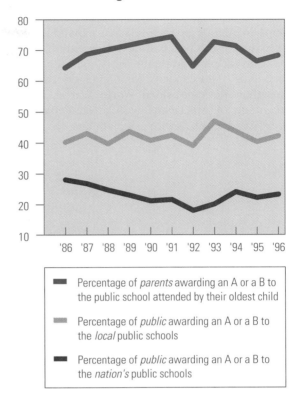

Figure 7.7   **Public School Ratings: Percentage Awarding Schools A or B Grades**

- Percentage of *parents* awarding an A or a B to the public school attended by their oldest child
- Percentage of *public* awarding an A or a B to the *local* public schools
- Percentage of *public* awarding an A or a B to the *nation's* public schools

gave schools a somewhat negative grade. Over time, only 20 percent gave the schools an A or B grade. However, when the same respondents were asked to grade their local schools, a quite different picture emerged. Almost half, for most years, gave their local schools an A or B. These responses change even more drastically when parents' grades are compared with the grades given by nonparent citizens. Two-thirds to three-quarters of parents (except in 1992) gave their child's school an A or B. Note that public satisfaction remained pretty steady between 1986 and 1996. Take a minute to read the accompanying Issue Box that discusses the related question of whose responsibility successful schools really are.

So what do you think about the quality of American schools? Can hundreds of reports issued by blue-ribbon task forces and commissions for over a half century, most of which have been critical of the schools, be wrong? Or are there powerful groups in the United States who would benefit from a failed public school system? What about Berliner and Biddle's optimism and their attempt to debunk the critics? Do they represent special interest groups who might benefit from successful public schools? Are schools as bad as they are made out to be? Are they better?

GOOD SCHOOLS FOR THE FUTURE

You just read that educational opportunities for all groups in American society have expanded significantly during the last half of the twentieth century. More 25-year-olds graduate from high school than ever before. The capacity for higher education has more than doubled since World War II, and the percentage of Americans who attend college has never been higher. Severe criticism has been leveled at American schools since the 1950s. Critics argue that academic achievement has declined, that American students compare poorly with students from other countries, and that the public has lost confidence in pubic education. But public education also has its defenders and, despite serious challenges, today's schools are not failing, as the critics would have us believe.

If we assume that the truth about the quality of American schools is somewhere between the extremes of complete failure and total success, and if

ISSUES

Success for All: Whose Job Is It?

Position 1. Educators should be held accountable for the success of all students.

Sam Stringfield (1995), a researcher at John Hopkins University, recently wrote an article in which he argued that schools should become high reliability organizations. He defined a highly reliable organization as one that "work[s] right the first time . . . and every time." (p. 16) Examples of high-reliability organizations in modern societies include, according to Stringfield, regional electrical grids, which guarantees electricity all the time, and our air traffic control system, which monitors millions of air space events yearly without a major mid-air collision. Stringfield went on to compare this 100-percent reliable organization to schools in which only about 85 percent of the overall student population graduates from high school and this percentage drops as low as 45 percent to 50 percent in some cities. He made an important observation about this situation: "If air travelers were told that their plane had an 85 percent chance of getting safely to their destination, and an 85 percent chance of returning home safely, the great majority of otherwise eager passengers would decline the opportunity to fly" (p. 16).

Stringfield argues that schools should become high reliability organizations, and that success should be guaranteed for all. Education is simply too important to accept anything less. For schools to become this way would require the following:

1. Change the public's perception from toleration of failure to one that perceives failure as disastrous.
2. Develop a clear sense of mission and goal clarity.
3. Pay more attention to existing knowledge. Use what we know about good schools.
4. Extensively recruit and train high-quality teachers.
5. Have standard operating procedures for identifying flaws before disaster occurs.

Stringfield clearly put the responsibility on the shoulders of educators (administrators, teachers, policy makers) to use their knowledge about effective schools to turn schools into high-reliability organizations in which every student, even those at risk, experiences success. He defines success as graduation from a high school that holds students to very high standards.

we accept that many of the reform proposals over the past half-century point toward schools of the future, what can we then predict about schools in the twenty-first century? This final section explores what might constitute good schools of the future and how we can go about creating them.

Making Traditional Schools Work Better

Since the mid-1970s, a number of researchers in the United States and elsewhere identified features of good schools as we know them today. This particu-lar line of inquiry is called **school-effectiveness re-search.** In the tradition of the process-product re-search described in Chapter 2, school-effectiveness researchers study traditional schools and observe two sets of variables—*student behaviors,* such as academic achievement and attendance, and *school processes,* such as academic emphasis, curriculum alignment, and clarity of goals. School processes are correlated with student behaviors to see if relation-ships exist between particular processes and stu-dent behavior, primarily academic achievement.

ISSUES

Continued

Position 2. **This is an impossible goal for educators to accomplish alone. Primary responsibility for school success and failure has to rest with parents or guardians.**
About the same time that Stringfield's article appeared, John Rosemond, a columnist on parenting and a family psychologist in North Carolina, wrote an article that appeared in newspapers around the country. Here are the strong words Rosemond has for parents:

> *The problems crippling American schools are not going to be solved until every adult in this country realizes that "lack of discipline" is the crux of the matter, and further realizes that the problem doesn't rest with administrators, teachers, or school boards, but with parents ... problems come primarily from American's homes. They are a matter of parents who send children to school without the discipline it takes to dig in and get an education; parents who overindulge and undercorrect; parents who neither indulge nor correct; parents who let TV sets run day and night and rarely read anything more than the morning paper; parents who will not give total, 100 percent support to teachers' disciplinary efforts; parents who expect schools to do what they themselves have been too lazy or busy to do. (Hartford Courant, 1995, p. H9)*

What is interesting about Stringfield's and Rosemond's positions is that both are worried about the effectiveness of American schools and both call for 100 percent efforts but differ significantly about who should perform at the 100 percent level. Stringfield's solution is for educators to make schools into high reliability organizations in which things will work the first time and all the time. Rosemond, on the other hand, puts the solution squarely on parents' shoulders, saying that they must take responsibility for motivating and disciplining their children and for being highly reliable themselves in giving 100 percent to their childrens' teachers and schools.

What do you think about this issue? Is it possible to create schools with high standards in which all students are always successful? What would such a school look like? Or, is it the responsibility of parents to motivate their children and to instill the discipline to stick with learning even though the going might be tough?

Two classic studies in this tradition were conducted by Rutter (1979) and his colleagues in London secondary schools and by Brookover (1979) and his colleagues in a group of midwestern elementary schools. These studies, along with many others completed over the past 2 decades, demonstrate that strong relationships do exist between certain features of schools and student achievement. Reviews of school-effectiveness research identified attributes believed to characterize the most effective schools. Table 7.1 contains a list of effective school attributes assembled by Bruce Joyce (1993) and his colleagues.

Notice that these attributes are divided into two categories—those having to do with the social organization of the school and those with the school's instructional programs and curriculum patterns. On the organizational side, effective schools constantly emphasize academic achievement, and teachers, parents, and students share a common vision about the school's academic goals. These schools are also safe and orderly places in which there is agreement about the basic rules of conduct, and teachers are consistent in the way they enforce rules in their classrooms and throughout the school. Teachers in effective schools hold high expectations for students and for themselves, and they communicate "I care" and "you can do" attitudes. Teachers and other adults in these schools have developed a caring atmosphere and have found ways to publicly reward students' successes and achievements, such as publishing honor rolls, sending positive notes home to parents, and displaying student work. Notice here the similarities between these attributes and Sergiovanni's vision of good schools having a community-like organizational structure.

An effective school's curriculum and its instructional methods also have recognizable attributes. Teachers in effective schools have found ways to maximize the time devoted to academic learning. They start classes quickly and move smoothly through their lessons. They require their students to do homework, check it, and provide prompt feedback. Through a variety of evaluation devices (tests, quizzes, work products, and exhibits) teachers keep track of student progress and give parents feedback about their children's progress. The curriculum in effective schools is coherent and tightly connected to the academic goals of the school. Teachers plan the curriculum jointly and know what other teachers are doing in other subjects and at other grade levels. They make schoolwide agreements about what is to be taught and how it is to be taught. Teachers have broad repertories of teaching strategies and use these effectively and appropriately. The adults in effective schools find ways to engage students in helping to run their school and encourage their leadership in and outside the classroom.

Although effective schools research certainly highlights what happens in good schools, it does not provide a complete road map to the future. Indeed, this research has received the same criticism as the process-product research described in Chapter 2. It has studied schools as they *currently exist* and thus provides little insight into *what could be*. Also, the relationships found between school processes and student achievement cannot guarantee the direction of causation. For instance, is it possible that a school with lots of good students and high-achievement scores cause the positive school processes associated with effective schools and not vice versa? Fortunately, there is another body of knowledge that informs our search for good schools of the future.

Experimenting with Innovative Schools

During the past decade, a number of reform-minded educators provided their own critique of the schools and have experimented with several innovative models of schooling. Unlike many of the reform proposals made in the political arena, such as greater academic requirements or longer school days, the

Table 7.1   Attributes of Good Schools According to School Effectiveness Research

Social Organization	Instruction and Curriculum
Clear academic and social behavior goals	High academic learning time
Order and discipline	Frequent and monitored homework
High expectations	Frequent monitoring of student progress
Teacher efficacy	Coherently organized curriculum
Pervasive caring	Variety of teaching strategies
Public rewards and incentives	Opportunities for student responsibility
Administrative leadership	
Community support	

Source: Joyce et al., 1993, p. 25.

experimenters have emphasized the need for a complete overhaul of existing structures. Also, they have solicited grassroot support from teachers and parents for their reform efforts rather than top-down political support. The most noted contemporary reformers include the following people.

- *John Goodlad,* who tied the improvement of schools to the improvement of the teachers who work there.
- *Theodore Sizer,* who leads a nationwide coalition aimed at reforming secondary schools and argues that "teaching less is teaching more."
- *Howard Gardner* and his colleagues, who discovered a different way of viewing intelligence that leads to a different conception of schooling.
- *Henry Levin,* who turned upside down the views about how to work with at-risk kids by proposing to speed up instruction for these students rather than slow it down.
- *Robert Slavin* and his colleagues, who developed an elementary school program whose aim is "success for all students."
- *James Comer,* who found ways for parents to be active participants in their children's education.
- *Ernest Boyer,* who wrote widely about schooling and proposed a restructured, *basic* school.
- *David Berliner* and *Bruce Biddle,* who studied many school-reform efforts and synthesized their own effective schooling principles.

Although these innovative school projects receive support from government and private foundations, they are not part of official reform policy. They gain most of their support from teachers and parents in particular schools across the United States. Four of these projects are described here briefly and the major features summarized in Table 7.2.

John Goodlad's Better Teachers, Better Schools

In the early 1980s, John Goodlad and a team of researchers, studied schooling in the United States. They visited schools from all parts of the country and observed 1,016 classrooms. *A Place Called School,* published in 1984, provided a comprehensive view of schools at that time and began Goodlad's central thesis that the schools we have can be improved if we do the right things. In 1994, Goodlad wrote a second book entitled *Educational Renewal: Better Teachers, Better Schools.* This work incorpo-

rated what he learned in his previous study with his work on improving teacher preparation in the United States. Goodlad's major premise was that school improvement will come mainly from within and, consequently, must be tied to the improvement of teaching. From this work and the case literature on innovative schools, Goodlad found that certain generalizations about good schools have stood up over time, and he translated these into his characteristics of good schools that you find in Table 7.2. In general, Goodlad argued that for schools to become effective they must become overtly conscious of their culture and what they are trying to accomplish and they must spend most of their time building positive relationships with students and parents and figuring out how to help students succeed.

Sizer's Coalition of Essential Schools

Another major study of American schools also appeared in 1984. Theodore Sizer's *Horace's Compromise* studied comprehensive high schools in the United States and revealed several structural weaknesses. He proposed a number of strategies for combating these weaknesses, and following the study's publication, the Coalition for Essential Schools was formed to work on Sizer's reform agenda. The coalition is a voluntary association of teachers and educators from all over the country. Currently, the coalition network has grown to more than 900 schools in 32 states. Teachers and other educators in coalition schools agreed to work toward reforming their schools by following the nine principles listed in Table 7.2. Coalition schools strive to keep goals simple and straightforward. Teachers believe that teaching less is more, that depth is more important than breadth. These schools are also characterized by a personalized teaching and learning environment in which teachers take responsibility for the full range of student growth, not just academics.

Berliner & Biddle's School Improvement Principles

Recall Berliner and Biddle's belief that schools are not as bad as critics claim. Having said this, they go on to say that, nevertheless, American schools face daunting dilemmas and challenges. They believe firmly that we can create the schools we want, and current experiments provide principles on which to build good schools for the future (see Table 7.2). Mainly they believe that schools can be improved: by giving parents and their children more dignity and hope; by enlarging and adjusting curriculum goals with an emphasis on skills needed for membership in a democratic society; by abandoning age-grade group patterns; and by using more innovative

Table 7.2 Characteristics of Good Schools

Goodlad's Good Schools Principles	Sizer's Essential Schools Principles	Berliner & Biddle's Principles	Boyer's Vision
1. A good school is like a complex ecosystem in which all parts are mostly good.	1. Schools focus on helping students use their minds well.	1. Good schools accord parents and children dignity and hope.	1. The basic school is a community with a clear and vital mission.
2. Good schools tend to be found in good school districts. Goodness exists throughout the system.	2. School goals are kept simple—master a limited number of essential skills and areas of knowledge; "less is more" should dominate.	2. Good schools have fairness in funding.	2. The basic school has a clear and coherent curriculum with literacy goals at the core.
3. Good schools are self-conscious of their culture, and they figure out how to help students succeed.	3. School goals apply to all students.	3. Good schools should enlarge their curriculum with emphasis on skills needed for living in a democratic society.	3. The basic school has a climate for learning and is characterized by small classes, rich resources, and commitment to children's learning.
4. Good schools take care of business—they have orderly ways of handling routines, making decisions, taking actions.	4. Teaching and learning are personalized; decisions are placed in the hands of teachers and the principal; small class size is maintained.	4. Good schools are reduced in size.	4. The basic school is concerned with the ethical and moral dimensions of a child's life.
5. Good schools come to terms with external standards . . . teachers are conscious of the importance of quality learning time.	5. A student-worker metaphor replaces a teacher-as-deliverer metaphor—pedagogy emphasizes coaching and learning how to learn.	5. Good schools use innovative teaching methods: cooperative learning, peer tutoring, project-based instruction.	
6. Good schools have an array of positive connections: students are treated equally, teachers value their peers, and principals value their teachers.	6. Schools have no strict age grading or systems of credits earned . . . diplomas are awarded on demonstration of mastery through an "exhibition."	6. Good schools use innovative evaluation techniques: portfolios, exhibitions, performances.	
7. Good schools are connected to home and parents in positive ways . . . parents support teachers . . . parents feel welcome.	7. School tone stresses the value of unanxious expectation.	7. Good schools abandon age-graded classrooms, ability grouping, and tracking.	
	8. Principals and teachers perceive themselves as generalists first and specialists second . . . staff expects multiple roles: teacher-counselor-manager.	8. Good schools have strong ties with community and parents.	
	9. Schools provide for collective planning on part of teachers, professional salaries, and status for teachers.	9. Good schools provide professional status for teachers and other educators.	

teaching methods, such as cooperative learning, cross-age and peer tutoring, and project-based methods.

Boyer's Basic School

Ernest Boyer, one of America's foremost educators, wrote a book under the auspices of the Carnegie Foundation that described how formal schooling in the United States needed to be restructured so a *basic school* could emerge. Boyer did not advocate returning to a basic academic curriculum like the reformers in the 1970s, but argued instead for the creation of a school that had a common core of learning essential for an educated person in contemporary society. The school he proposed has four priorities. The school is a community of learners in which teachers, students, and parents share a vision about what the school should accomplish. The school has a modest, but coherent curriculum, in which literacy is the first and essential goal. His basic school has a positive learning climate characterized by small class size, flexible schedules, and commitment to the whole child. Beyond the academic dimension, his basic school makes a commitment to the ethical and moral dimensions of children.

Prototype of the Twenty-First Century School

It is obvious that schools of the future will serve students who live in a world very different from the one today's schools were designed for. What will these schools look like? Next we synthesize what is currently known about good schools and attempt to create a prototype for twenty-first-century schools.

A Curriculum with Coherence

Almost every study and experiment on effective schooling shows that today's fragmented academic curriculum, delivered in assembly-line fashion, simply does not work. Further, there is a growing consensus that being able to recall important historical facts, perform mathematical operations, or recognize quotations from famous literary figures is insufficient education for a productive worker and citizen of the twenty-first century. The effective-schools research provides clear evidence that students learn more in schools that have clear goals and a focused curriculum than they do in schools where many goals and many subjects compete for precious time. Sizer's curriculum focuses on a few essential topics that force students to use their minds. He argued that the aphorism less is more should characterize future curriculum decisions. Berliner and Biddle (1995) and Boyer asserted that we must replace and refocus the current curriculum, constructed around

specific academic disciplines, so that students learn the skills essential for moral and ethical citizenship in a democratic society. They defined such citizens as those who "are flexible, who embrace new ideas, who can reason well when faced with complex ideas, and who are capable of self-directed learning" (p. 300). In short, our schools of the future will be characterized by a focused curriculum aimed at developing flexible, reflective thinkers who can perform important roles in a democratic society.

New Roles and Relationships for Teachers and Students

Traditional schools are characterized by fixed roles for teachers and students. We know that teachers are expected to be authority figures, responsible for expertly transmitting a predetermined body of knowledge. Students are expected to be subservient listeners, processing knowledge into memory for later recall and use. In future schools, these roles and relationships will be different. Sizer envisions students as workers whose job is to acquire meaningful knowledge and develop learning skills deemed essential to independent living. He sees teachers as facilitators and coaches whose job it is to help students learn how to learn. Sizer, Goodlad, Berliner and Biddle, and Boyer all believe that teaching and learning must become more personalized. Such teaching necessitates that teachers really know their students and assume responsibility for all aspects of their education. Thus, teachers' roles will shift in the direction of generalists rather than as specialists. They will be experts in subject matter and counselors, helpers, and group leaders for young people and their parents as well.

Our twenty-first century schools will also require teachers who have mastered a rich repertoire of teaching methods, in particular cooperative learning and project-based instruction, that stimulate problem solving and creative thinking. According to Berliner and Biddle (1995), certification to teach in schools of the future will require teacher candidates to demonstrate their ability to:

- Sustain an involvement with a few topics rather than superficially cover many topics.
- Conduct classroom lessons that exhibit coherence, continuity, and a logical progression of ideas.
- Pace lessons so students have time to think about topics of interest.
- Ask questions and assign activities that are genuinely challenging.
- Model effective thinking behavior for students.

- Treat students' ideas and contributions with respect.
- Encourage students to justify their contributions.

New Roles and Choices for Parents

Twenty-first century schools will recognize the importance of parents in their child's education, provide expanded roles for them, and afford them more dignity and choice. Many of the problems faced by schools, particularly in poorer communities, stem from the dysfunctional nature of family life. Schools of the future will work more closely with families and communities and involve them more fully in the process of educating their children. The goal is to improve not only the students' in-school education but, as a by-product, the parenting skills of parents and the overall quality of community life.

Throughout American history there has been a single public school system and, despite some regional variations, schools in one community have closely resembled schools in most other communities. Commercially produced textbooks and standardized tests have contributed to the sameness of what is taught. Likewise, structural characteristics, such as subject- and grade-level organization have standardized the way students are treated and taught, whether in Maine or California. Moreover, because of strong beliefs about separation of church and state, religious schools in the United States have been less pervasive than in many other countries, and nonreligious, private schools have drawn mainly the wealthy upper class.

This situation may be changing, as citizens and parents from many political persuasions begin demanding that more school options be more available to them. Many blame lack of choice for the schools' poor performance and inability to change. Many believe that schools would improve significantly if alternatives existed and if parents were given more choice. Numerous choice proposals are currently being considered and others have been already implemented across the country. These include:

1. **Educational vouchers,** a form of currency that can be used to pay tuition either in a public school of the parent's choice or in nonreligious private schools approved by the state.
2. **Magnet schools,** wherein a specific curriculum area, such as mathematics and technology or the visual and performing arts, is emphasized.
3. **Charter schools,** publicly funded schools conceived and started by parents, citizens, or teachers operating in some ways like private schools in that they are independent of the local districts and exempt from many local and state regulations imposed on public schools.
4. **For-profit schools,** in which private companies contract directly with school districts for the purpose of operating charterlike schools.

Two of the most active private companies have been Education Alternative Incorporated (EAI) and the Edison Corporation. Started as a subsidiary of Whittle Enterprises, a communication conglomerate based in Tennessee, the Edison Corporation contracts with school districts for the purpose of operating selected schools. Edison has its own approach to teaching and has spent over 2 million dollars developing a state-of-the art curriculum. Edison schools are also characterized by a longer school day and an extended school year. Some of the initial Edison schools have been in states that allow charter schools and, consequently, Edison has obtained significant independence from local and state regulations. Unlike EAI, which uses the existing faculty in their contract schools, Edison chooses its own teachers and principals.

School choice remains very controversial, and evaluation results are mixed. Some argue that providing choice will nurture competition and will challenge the bureaucratically entrenched school establishment. Others, however, believe that it is impossible to make a satisfactory profit running schools unless the education of children is neglected. Whatever one's view, it is likely that private, for-profit schools, like charter schools, will continue and flourish in the years ahead, because they provide the choice that so many parents and citizens seem to want. Chapter 10 discusses this topic in more detail under school governance. The accompanying Multicultural Box examines the value of single-gender and single-race schools.

New Grouping Patterns and Reduced Size

Studies of good schools provide strong evidence that age-graded classrooms and ability grouping have had negative effects on students, particularly those who end up in the lower tracks. The dilemma of whether to promote or retain those who are not making normal progress in an age-graded school has never been resolved. Also, it is well documented that newer and less able teachers are usually assigned to low-ability groups in age-graded schools. As you read in Chapter 2 evidence also exists that teachers have lower expectations for students in low–ability groups and use drill-and-practice teaching methods with these students more often than they do with students in high-ability groups. Innovative schools are currently finding ways to replace age and ability grouping with nongraded and flexible grouping patterns.

In the United States the trend for most of the last century has been to close small schools, to consolidate school districts, and to build larger and more comprehensive schools. Such schools, people thought, were more efficient economically and offered students more choices. Only large schools, it has been argued, can support specialized teachers (for physics and Japanese, for example) or offer

MULTICULTURAL

Are Single-Gender and Single-Race Programs the Answer?

Large numbers of poor African American and Hispanic students do not do well in school. Often these groups constitute the majority of a schools' discipline problems; are at the top in suspensions, expulsions, and placement in special education classes; and are at the bottom in academic achievement and high school completion. There is also considerable evidence that girls do not do as well in school as boys, particularly in math and science. Most educators believe this situation is not the result of biology or intelligence but is caused by programs that are mismatched for girls and students of non-European backgrounds.

The response by some school districts around the country—Chicago, Illinois, Detroit, Michigan, and Prince George's County, Maryland, for instance—was to start single-race or single-gender schools. Some of these are charter or magnet schools supported by public monies; others are private schools. Joan Ratteray (1996) reported that today there are over 400 African American community-based schools in the United States. Some of these schools date back a good many years. However, efforts to extend single-race or single-gender schools using public monies has been very controversial.

On one side of the issue are those who argue that many students fail in school becasue they lack self-esteem and pride of their gender or cultural heritage. Proponents of these schools believed that programs, or whole schools, that are dedicated to the unique learning styles and needs of minority students or a single gender build cultural pride, enhance identity, and produce positive results. Ratteray (1996), for instance, reported that over 60 percent of the students in private African American schools score above the national average in reading and mathematics even though these schools spend less than half what neighboring public schools spend.

On the the other hand, single-race or single-gender schools and programs have their critics. William Rasberry (1996) an African American columnist, wrote that he supported Prince George's County Black Male Achievement Initiative, but lamented that it is not available to all students who are academically injured. Newsweek columnist, John Leo (1997) criticized these programs in another way. He argued that schools which pay too much attention to identity concerns and politics stress our cultural differences rather than our similarities. In his opinion, identity enhancement does nothing to help students learn how to behave or to speak within the larger society of the dominant culture.

What do you think? Are single-race or single-gender schools helpful to some students? What about identity enhancement? Does it benefit students or harm them? Is it appropriate to use public monies to support single-race or single-sex schools?

advanced courses in mathematics, the sciences, and foreign languages. Large schools can also field stronger athletic teams than smaller schools.

Despite their strengths, however, large schools have not carried the day. Many European countries—Great Britain, Finland, and Italy, for example—have neighborhood elementary schools with only a few classrooms, and their high schools are organized on a much smaller scale. Neither has the research evidence supported the superiority of larger schools. Over 30 years ago, Barker and Gump (1964) provided convincing evidence in favor of smaller schools. In an extensive study of both large and small schools, they found that, despite the resources of large schools, students actually got a better education in small schools, because they were compelled by necessity to assume more responsibility

for their own education. Barker and Gump found that in larger schools, few students were known well by their teachers and few had strong bonds with their classmates. Only a small proportion of students participated in extracurricular activities, played on athletic teams, or were selected for important leadership positions. On the other hand, students in smaller schools experienced more personalized learning environments in which teacher-student and student-student relationships were stronger and more meaningful.

Recent trends in the United States have been toward reducing the size of schools. For instance, the Coalition of Essential Schools has organized students into teams of no more than 80. Likewise, Edward Cortines launched a drive to start 100 small high schools during his tenure as superintendent of

RESEARCH

Why Most School Reform Fails and What We Can Do About It

Some researchers study what makes schools effective, whereas other researchers are more interested in the complex and complicated question, How can ineffective schools be made better? Three decades of research have provided some useful answers for teachers and policy makers alike. Most of this research shows that many school reforms efforts over the past 30 years have failed because we have been going about it all wrong (Sarason, 1971; Berman & McLaughlin, 1975; Goodlad, 1984; Fullan, 1982, 1991, 1993; and Berliner & Biddle, 1995). For instance, it is well documented that *externally imposed changes* (such as new state or federal regulations) alone do little to make schools better (Sarason, 1971; Fullan, 1993). Also, efforts to bypass teachers seldom work (Berman & McLaughlin, 1975; Berliner & Biddle, 1995). School-change researchers have found that most reformers underestimate the complexity of their job and the time span needed for successful change to occur.

On the other hand, there are numerous instances of successful changes in schools. Canadian educator and researcher Michael Fullan studied some successful school innovations for a 30-year period. Fullan (1993) offers the following research-based lessons for would-be change agents.

Lesson 1. You cannot mandate change. The more complex the change, the less you can force it.

Lesson 2. Change is a journey, not a blueprint. Change is never a straight line between point A and point B. It winds around and is filled with uncertainty.

Lesson 3. Problems are our friends. Whenever you try to change something, you will run into problems. Embrace problems and learn from them.

Lesson 4. Planning and goalsetting are often more effective after action has been taken. Planning school reform too carefully can blind us to the possibilities. Use the *ready-fire-aim* principle.

the New York Public Schools. Many school districts have recently created schools-within-schools, or "cohorts of students" in order to provide smaller administrative and instructional units in which special themes and methods can be tried and education can be made more personal. Interestingly, most magnet and charter schools are characterized by their limited size.

Changes in Leadership

Changed conceptions of leadership also will characterize schools of the future. During the course of the twentieth century, as you read earlier, school management followed the model of business and industry in which professionally trained managers at the top of the organizational pyramid guided their organizations with top-down supervisory techniques. This management model led to the following assumptions about school leadership:

- Leadership should be centered in certain high-level positions, primarily the superintendent and the principal.
- Such centralized leadership produces effective schools, with the principal assuming the roll of instructional leader of the school.
- A primary role of centralized leadership is the appropriate use of managerial controls (teacher appraisal systems, standardized tests) to overcome the shortcomings of the teachers and students who work in the schools.

RESEARCH

Continued

Lesson 5. Collectivisim and individualism have equal power. Problems can be better solved working with others, but we have to be careful of groupthink.

Lesson 6. Neither centralization nor decentralization works. Successful change requires top-down *and* bottom-up strategies.

Lesson 7. Connection with the wider environment and community is critical for successful change. Involve students and their parents.

Lesson 8. Every person is a change agent. Change in schools is too important to leave to experts and administrators. Everyone (teachers, parents, and students) must take responsibility.

This is an interesting list, is it not? Yet, many lessons recommended by Fullan have been and continue to be ignored by those who want to reform American schools. Often changes are imposed by state legislatures or local school boards without consultation with teachers and parents. The recommendations of experts are often given more accord than those from citizens or students. Improvement is not viewed as a collaborative effort.

Perhaps in the future, policy makers will better understand the nature of school change, and instead of embracing efforts to impose and regulate, they will reach out to involve teachers and parents in the process. This approach, of course, will demand greater teacher participation than currently exists in many schools. It will also create new professional expectations and responsibilities.

What do you think about school reform? Are the lessons described by Fullan consistent with your experiences or with what you have read about school reform? What do you think about teacher participation and responsibilities in change efforts? Should teachers be expected to take responsibility for making their schools better? Would working toward school improvement take away from or support teachers' responsibilities to their students?

During the past 2 decades a conception of decentralized leadership has emerged in which leadership belongs to everyone. Rather than using top-down control mechanisms that direct and constrain those who work in schools, the leader's job is to cultivate the leadership potential in others. Effective schools are increasingly thought of as learning communities, as with Sergiovanni's vision in which teachers, students, administrators, and parents share in an ongoing dialogue about teaching and learning. The principal's role is to help organize and energize such learning communities. The transformational conception of leadership reduces the principal's formal authority and extends leadership expectations to teachers.

Will We Get the Schools We Want?

Will we be able to get the schools we want for the twenty-first century? Many critics point out that 50 years of reform have left us with a public school system characterized by student failure and parental dissatisfaction. Why would anyone believe future reform efforts will make any difference? Read the accompanying Research Box for an in-depth look at this question.

Many educators and others (Goodlad, Sizer, and Berliner and Biddle, for example) are optimistic and believe it is possible to get the schools we want. They argue that past reforms failed because they were based on poor ideas and that the real problems of education have yet to be addressed. For instance, many of the failed reforms were based on the premises listed here.

1. The schools we now have provide the model we need for the future.

2. Schools can be made better simply by insisting on higher standards, more testing, and more stress on the hard academic subjects such as mathematics and science.

3. Students will learn more if programs are intensified and the school day and year are extended.

4. Classrooms will work better if they are equipped with the latest materials and computers and poor students are dismissed.

With careful analysis you can see that none of these reform items paid much attention to basic organizational patterns or operating procedures. Perhaps reform during the next 50 years will be more successful if reformers tackle the institutions of age-graded classrooms, ability grouping, the different needs of a changing student population, the training needs of teachers, and other fundamental conceptions about what schools and leadership in schools should be.

SUMMARY

- Classrooms and teaching exist within the larger social context of the school, so what happens in the school as a whole influences greatly how much students learn and how satisfied teachers are with their careers.

- We can think of schools as social organizations from at least three perspetives: cultural, organizational, and communitarian.

- The term *culture* is used to define patterns of thinking and behaving within particular groups of people, and like larger societies, schools have their own unique cultures consisting of values, beliefs, and expectations.

- School culture can be considered in terms of its shared values and beliefs, its heroes and heroines, its rituals and ceremonies, and the individuals who act as cultural carriers.

- As with larger societies, schools have a number of subcultures. Teacher and student subcultures are the most important of these in most schools.

- The teacher subculture in most American schools is characterized by the autonomy norm, the hands-off norm, and a variety of role contradictions, such as simultaneously getting to know students while maintaining an appropriate social distance.

- Sometime the norms of the student subculture are consistent with the learning goals of schooling; at other times student subculture can work against schools goals.

- The culture in particular schools affects what students learn, how teachers are socialized, and how they teach. Culture also effects how easy or difficult it is for a school to change.

- When viewed as social organizations, schools have many features in common with other organizations in our society. They are goal directed, work is specialized, and they are usually hierarchically arranged.

- Schools also have organizational features that are unique. These include a captive clientele, grade and age-level organization, an academic focus, a loosely coupled structure, ambiguous goals, and political vulnerability. Some apects of these features have a positive impact on teachers' work; others have a negative effect.

- We can think of schools as communities, a collection of individuals bonded together by natural will who share common ideas and values. This view, according to some observers, is more accurate than the formal organizational perspective.

- Almost from the beginning, Americans have been ambivalent about the design of their schools. On one hand, they seem to be comfortable with schools as they have always existed; on the other, they are quick to find fault with the schools.

- The period between the end of World War II and the present has been characterized by cycles of school criticism and school reform. Despite this attention, schools have not changed very much during this period.

- Some critics have complained that schools are soft and do not challenge students; others have argued for more student-centered, flexible forms of schooling.

- Critics involved in the most recent school reform movement, which dates from the early 1980s, argue that schools are failing as evidenced by declining test scores and high drop-out rates. Others say that even though schools can be improved, they are not failing. They argue that schools are in better shape than the critics assert and point to international test scores of American students that compare quite well with students from other countries and by the large proportion of parents who give their child's school a postive grade.

- Regardless of how well or poorly schools are currently doing, they are likely to change in the future to reflect changes going on in the larger society. Schools of the future will be characterized by a narrower, more coherent, and less fragmented curriculum; more personalized relationships between teachers and students; more flexible grouping patterns; reduced class and school size; teachers who assume greater leadership responsibilities; and new roles and more choices for parents.

READINGS FOR THE PROFESSIONAL

Boyer, E. *The Basic School: A Community for Learning.* Princeton, NJ: The Carnegie Foundation for the Advancement of Teaching, 1995.
This book describes the vision that the late Ernest Boyer had for the American school. He described a school that has been transformed into a learning community, that has a coherent curriculum, and one that considers parents partners.

Bruner, J. *The Culture of Education.* Cambridge, MA: Harvard University Press, 1996.
This is an excellent discussion about the possibilities of education and how schools make sense only if they are considered in a broader cultural context.

Goodlad, J. *A Place Called School: Prospects for the Future.* New York: McGraw-Hill, 1984.
This book reports the results of Goodlad's comprehensive study of American schools and describes what we can do to get better schools.

Lieberman, A. *Building a Professional Culture in Schools.* New York: Teachers College Press, 1989.
This is an excellent collection of readings describing how schools can be restructured to enhance student learning and build a new professional culture for teachers.

Perkins, D. *Smart Schools: From Training Memories to Educating Minds.* New York, The Free Press, 1992.
This book describes ideas for making our schools work better and an array of methods that have been shown to increase students' understanding.

CHAPTER 8

Curriculum

Danny Z. lives in east Houston, near the ship channel that leads to the Gulf of Mexico. The Denver Harbor gang and the Magnolia gang fight each other for control of his poor, mostly Hispanic neighborhood. One day Danny asked to speak in private with his English teacher. He said, "Ms. Whitford, it's so easy to kill somebody. I want to be more than that. How can I be more than that?"

Whitford teaches at the poorest and smallest high school in the city. English is not the home language for many of her students. Very few adults have stable jobs; the most affluent are the drug dealers, and, as the students are quick to point out, the dealers' high earnings are frequently offset by the brevity of their careers. Children in this neighborhood who persist in school often do so against the advice of parents, neighbors, and friends. There is little evidence here that something good will come from having a diploma.

Against this backdrop, Whitford must decide what to teach her students about English. She is not without resources for this task. She has the Texas state curriculum, outlining the "essential elements" for each subject. She has the state-adopted textbooks and state-level tests, which each student must pass to graduate. To make sure her teaching is satisfactory, she is checked twice a year against a checklist of good teaching behaviors, and her advancement on the pay scale is tied to her adherence to these behaviors. Basically, she has the state-level equivalent of a national curriculum. Whitford believes that it's fortunate for Danny that she ignores them all.

She does not teach the state-adopted books, or tests, or essential elements. She teaches the kids.

Curriculum Defined

Who Controls the Curriculum?
National Influences
Political Forces
Social Critics
Professional Associations
Publishing Companies
National Testing
State Influences
Local Influences
School Districts
Principals
Parents and Students
Censorship
Teachers
Curriculum Hegemony
Curriculum in Other Countries

The American Curriculum
Literacy, Language Arts, and English
Mathematics

Science
Social Studies
Foreign Language
The Arts
Physical and Health Education
Vocational Education
Curriculum Trends
Integrating across Disciplines
A National Curriculum, a National
Curriculum War

Curriculum Choices
Choosing What to Teach
Selecting Curriculum Materials
Supplementing the Curriculum
Circumventing Bias
Nontraditional Materials

Summary

Readings for the Professional

She resists the top-down imposition of curriculum in favor of her knowledge and experience, her passion for her subject, and her willingness to confront head-on the clash between her hopes for her students and the strong pull of the neighborhood to take them out of the classroom. It is not likely that Danny would have brought the central question of his life to a teacher who was marching through a state or national curriculum. He would not have been likely to see a connection between his personal survival and his performance on a multiple-choice test. Danny has seen Whitford thinking. He has watched her working with the class to find literature meaningful to their culture, supporting a student trying to find his own voice in his writing, exciting students about reading—all in a neighborhood where a guy can get beat up if he is seen on the street carrying a book. Her credibility for Danny and the other students comes from the connections she makes between her knowledge of her subject and her understanding of her students. (after McNeil, 1995, pp. 13–14)

CURRICULUM DEFINED

How does Whitford know what to teach? Why does she dispense with the curriculum that has been provided her? How does she know what to put in its place? **Curriculum** is the content, the *what,* of instruction, and as such it looms large both in teacher preparation programs and in the daily worklives of teachers. This chapter explores the issues, dilemmas, knowledge bases, techniques, and trends associated with curriculum. The simple definition of *curriculum,* that is, the content of instruction, belies an underlying complexity. When educators speak of curriculum, they may be referring to any one of five types of curricula, all concurrently active in schools. The **official curriculum** is the written curriculum, that curriculum for which official documentation, like a curriculum guide, exists. For Whitford, these were the Texas essential elements for her subject, English, and the accompanying standardized tests. Another is the **operational curriculum,** consisting of what is actually taught by teachers. The operational curriculum includes the topics and ideas teachers emphasize day to day in the classroom and those that they test for. As Whitford's teaching demonstrated, the operational curriculum may or may not be in alignment with the official curriculum, and the operational curriculum may or may not be in alignment with what is tested.

A third is the **extracurriculum.** This is composed of all the planned, nonacademic experiences students have. Included here are clubs, sports, service projects, artistic performances, and student government. Danny apparently did not participate in any of these, probably because of strong peer pressure not to.

Next is the **null curriculum,** so designated because it comprises everything that is *not* taught. We may infer from Whitford's decisions that the official curriculum left out significant aspects of Hispanic literature. The absence of this literature renders it a part of the null curriculum. Analyses of the null curriculum can be very revealing of the assumptions underlying curricular choices. For example, the arts receive short shrift in American schools yet are considered basic in Japanese schools. What does this say about differences in the national character of the two countries? Perhaps there is a stronger aesthetic sense and appreciation of beauty in Japanese culture.

The final type of curriculum is termed the **hidden curriculum,** and it may have the most lasting impact of all on students. The hidden curriculum is composed of the norms, values, and attitudes embedded in the other four. Consider, for example, what is communicated to young people about the value of a particular topic when it is excluded from the curriculum. American students typically do not receive formal instruction in psychology, anthropology, and political science. Students may surmise that these topics are less valuable than, say, geography and driver's education. By the same token, what do students learn about the importance of different types of knowledge when they are tested on their ability to memorize facts rather than on their ability to reflect and analyze? The "medium is the message," and as such, the hidden curriculum teaches a great deal about sex roles; appropriate behavior; the meaning of work, play, and citizenship; the legitimacy of those in authority; the definition of success; and the relative worth of different types of knowledge. Whitford's operational curriculum, for example, communicated her belief that all her students could learn and could be successful, whereas the official curriculum, one may surmise, did not.

WHO CONTROLS THE CURRICULUM?

The issue of what curriculum is pales before the issue of curriculum control. Everyone, it seems, wants to influence the content of instruction because this, it is thought, will influence the course that history and culture take in the next generation.

For this reason, many people are passionate about what is taught in schools, and as we will see, curriculum battles occur from Congress on down to local school boards, classrooms, and even living rooms. Curriculum wars get everybody talking. As one scholar put it:

> school knowledge, the knowledge that becomes the official knowledge in a society, becomes a kind of prize that is sought by competing groups with varying ideological convictions. More and more, the curriculum in any time and place is being seen as contested terrain, the battleground where warring parties contend for a kind of official sanctification of their deeply held beliefs. These warring parties may be defined by their race, language, ethnicity, social class, gender, or sexual preference as well as by their cherished political, cultural, religious, or social convictions. Their primary purpose is to have their most sacrosanct beliefs embodied in the knowledge that is deliberately passed on to the young through the curriculum. The outcome of this struggle is rarely if ever a complete victory for any of the contending parties. Rather, the result is sometimes an open and sometimes undeclared detente among the belligerents. (Kliebard, 1995, p. 63)

The following discussion explores who controls the curriculum. You may notice a disproportionate number of examples of curriculum conflict involving the religious right. This is not political bias on our part; rather, it reflects the current state of controversy over curriculum. In past years, those on the left more frequently challenged the status quo. In this chapter, we merely attempt to give you a sample of current curriculum conflicts in the schools.

National Influences

The American system of education, some say, is not really a system at all, but rather a group of "loosely coupled" units. (This concept was discussed in Chapter 7.) Just because someone at the top makes a decision does not mean that the decision will be carried out by those at the bottom. Each part of the whole has some autonomy. Still, each part is not perfectly independent, and the parts do exert some influence on each other.

Political Forces

National politics influence curriculum in indirect but effective ways. President Bush, for example, convened an education summit with the nation's governors in 1989. At that meeting, an agreement was made about the nation's goals for education. Later, when President Clinton took office, he expanded these goals and codified them in the Educate

Table 8.1   National Educational Goals: Goals 2000: Educate America Act

By the year 2000:

1. All children in America will start school ready to learn.

2. The high school graduation rate will increase to at least 90 percent.

3. American students will leave grades 4, 8, and 12 having demonstrated competency in challenging subject matter, including English, mathematics, science, history, geography, civics and government, economics, foreign language, and the arts; and every school in America will ensure that all students learn to use their minds well, so that they may be prepared for responsible citizenship, further learning, and productive employment in our modern economy.

4. U.S. students will be first in the world in science and mathematics achievement.

5. Every adult American will be literate and will possess the knowledge and skills necessary to compete in a global economy and to exercise the rights and responsibilities of citizenship.

6. Every school will be free of drugs and violence and will offer a disciplined environment conducive to learning.

7. The nation's teaching force will have access to programs for the continued improvement of their professional skills and the opportunity to acquire the knowledge and skills needed to instruct and prepare all American students for the next century.

8. Every school will promote partnerships that will increase parental involvement in promoting the social, emotional, and academic growth of children.

America Act, signed into law in 1994. Table 8.1 displays these goals. No one is mandated to act on these goals; however, they do influence the kinds of projects and research that the federal government funds. These are also the goals that the government invests effort in tracking. Statistics are kept on dropout rates, teen-age crime rates, and achievement, for example, but not on the number of school leadership roles held by girls and minorities. Through these relatively subtle means, schools' and teachers' attention has been drawn toward particular issues and away from others.

Other legislation has also had an impact on what teachers teach. Among the most important was PL 94–142 and its heir, Individuals with Disabilities

Education Act, 1990 (IDEA), which mandated appropriate education for handicapped children (see Chapter 5 for more details). This law forced schools to attend more carefully to the special educational needs of these students and provided federal funding to help schools do so. Another example is the National Defense Education Act, which promoted increased emphasis on math, science, and foreign language.

A final way in which the national government influences the curriculum is through commissions established to examine problems and provide suggestions for improvement. One of the most notorious of these was the National Commission on Excellence in Education, which published *A Nation at Risk* in 1983, also discussed in Chapter 7. As you may recall, the commission claimed that America's schools were substandard, that a "rising tide of mediocrity" was seriously damaging our children's education. To remedy this situation, the commission recommended stiffer academic course requirements for high school graduation and college entrance, longer school days and years, and upgraded textbooks. *A Nation at Risk* received a great deal of press coverage, and resulted in many back-to-basics reforms in state legislatures and local school boards. Sometime later, Terence Bell, who was Secretary of Education at the time the commission was convened, said his primary purpose was not to promote back-to-basics curricular reform but rather to demonstrate that the federal government had an important role to play in the educational system. Federal involvement in education was then under attack by President Reagan, and Bell was attempting to counter Reagan's perspective. Interestingly, as we discussed in Chapter 7, the purported decline in educational quality reported by the commission has since been challenged, and many deny that the report represented an accurate assessment of American schools (Berliner & Biddle, 1995).

Social Critics

Not all political influences come from the government. Also important are thinkers and authors who capture the public's attention. In the 1960s, books like *Why Johnny Can't Read* (1955) and *How Children Fail* (1964) prompted a flurry of back-to-basics and open-schooling efforts. More recently, *Savage Inequalities,* by Jonathon Kozol (1991), has dramatically depicted the educational inequities between rich and poor neighborhoods in the United States. E. D. Hirsch's (1987) *Cultural Literacy* has also garnered much interest. Hirsch argued that an important role for schools to play in a democracy is to enculturate the populace so that everyone shares a common set of knowledge, values, skills, and experiences. Hirsch's Core Knowledge Foundation has produced grade-by-grade curriculum guidelines designed to produce students who are culturally literate. This curriculum is organized into lists of important names, events, concepts, artistic productions, and so on. Critics contend that Hirsch's lists overlook too many of the contributions of minorities and women and that it is an overly simplistic way to think about curriculum. Proponents counter that the core represents only half the total curriculum and that there is room to insert other material. Of course, being left off the list in the first place conveys the message that certain material is unimportant. In any case, since parents and teachers buy *Cultural Literacy* and the grade-by-grade guidelines, Hirsch's ideas have an impact on what is taught.

Professional Associations

Another very important national influence on the curriculum comes from professional associations such as the National Council of Teachers of Mathematics (NCTM), the National Council for the Social Studies (NCSS), the American Federation of Teachers (AFT), the American Association for Colleges of Teacher Education (AACTE), and many others. These organizations publish journals, hold annual conferences, and convene their own commissions to study problems and to make recommendations, and these activities influence teachers', administrators', and teacher educators' curricular decisions. For example, NCTM has garnered much acclaim for the standards they established for mathematics education. Many mathematics teachers at all levels, including elementary, are actively engaged in educating themselves about these standards and how to implement them. Similarly, the efforts of AACTE have led to more coursework in multicultural education, authentic assessment, and field activities in teacher education programs.

Publishing Companies

One of the most influential forces on the curriculum is the publishing industry. Since textbook-based learning still dominates the vast majority of classrooms, textbook content has a great impact on student learning. Too often they contain unfamiliar, unelaborated vocabulary; too many facts and insufficient big ideas; and a writing style that is choppy, unorganized, and bland. Here, for example, is a simulated excerpt from a fifth-grade social studies text:

> In 1367 Marain and the settlements ended a seven-year war with the Langurians and Pitoks. As a result

of this war Languria was driven out of East Bacol. Marain would now rule Laman and other lands that had belonged to Languria. This brought peace to the Bacolian settlements. The settlers no longer had to fear attacks from Laman. The Bacolians were happy to be a part of Marain in 1367. Yet a dozen years later, these same people would be fighting the Marish for independence, or freedom from United Marain's rule. (Beck & McKeown, 1993, p. 2)

Here is a "translation" of this passage:

In 1763 Britain and the colonies ended a seven-year war with the French and Indians. As a result of this war France was driven out of North America. Britain would now rule Canada and other lands that had belonged to France. This brought peace to the American colonies. The colonists no longer had to fear attacks from Canada. The Americans were happy to be a part of Britain in 1763. Yet a dozen years later, these same people would be fighting the British for independence, or freedom from Great Britain's rule. (Beck & McKeown, 1993, p. 2)

Of course, not all textbooks are this poorly written, but some are. Teachers should take two lessons from this hard-to-comprehend passage and its translation. One, textbooks should be carefully evaluated for their difficulty level, and if they are too difficult, teachers must compensate in some way. Two, we should never lose sight of the fact that our students have much less background knowledge than we do, and because of this, what seems to us easy to understand may be quite incomprehensible to them.

There are further problems with texts. For example, Mayer, Sims, and Tajika (1995) compared American and Japanese junior high math texts. They found that the Japanese books devoted much more space to explaining solutions to problems, showing worked-out examples, and presenting relevant diagrams and illustrations. In contrast, the U.S. books gave much more space to unsolved exercises and high-interest but irrelevant illustrations. The different texts were about even in the amount of practice exercises provided. In short, the American books spent relatively little space explaining how to actually do the mathematics but did include catchy, irrelevant pictures.

Publishers, in their defense, counter that enormous amounts of money are invested in textbooks and that they are written by subject matter experts and teachers. Authors also spend considerable time and energy to produce good books. Publishers actively seek input from literally thousands of teachers and other experts around the country to ensure that content meets buyers' needs. Given the great efforts that already go into producing textbooks, some wonder what more could possibly be done.

If textbooks are so important to instruction, and if so much effort is put into producing good ones, why aren't they of better quality? The answer lies at least in part in the **adoption process,** the means by which school textbooks are selected in states and districts around the country. In 22 states, mostly in the South and West, districts choose texts from a state-approved list; these states are termed **state adoption states.** The rationale for state adoption at first seems sensible. When a statewide committee examines all available books and selects a limited number for districts to choose from, it serves to even out the curriculum across the state so that when students (or teachers) move, they are less likely to experience disjunctures in schooling. The process also saves time for teachers who do not have to wade through a multitude of materials. The first cut has been done for them. Finally, large-scale adopting can save money, because books can be bought in quantity at negotiated prices.

In practice, however, a number of problems arise with state adoptions that turn out to affect schools everywhere. First of all, the selection committees often lack training. Members may not know, for example, to look for more worked-out sample problems in a math text, a coherent writing style in a history text, or an equitable representation of women and minority authors in a literature anthology. In addition, as with committees everywhere, members often lack sufficient time to carry out their duties. Without enough time, they are reduced to merely flipping through pages and, consequently, may base their evaluations on superficial qualities like zippy illustrations.

Another problem is curriculum overload. Producing textbooks is enormously expensive, and publishers naturally want to make as many sales as possible. They know that their books will not be adopted in a state unless they contain information required in that state. And since states and districts vary somewhat in their requirements, publishers are forced to mention every name, event, or concept required in each state in order to have a chance of being adopted there. This means that, rather than limiting coverage to a few really important topics and covering these coherently and in depth, texts tend to mention everyone and everything. Selection committees too often scan to see if the required information is included, not whether it is included in a quality manner. The result, of course, is writing that is fragmented and loaded with lots of disconnected details.

A final problem with state adoption is that large markets, such as California and Texas, where publishers can make a great deal of money, have a disproportionate degree of influence over the process. Publishers try especially hard to please committees in these states, because they want the big sales there. They produce national texts based on what can get adopted in California and Texas. Thus small but vocal groups, often those on the Christian right, work very hard to get appointed to state selection committees or lobby these committees to get materials they do not like vetoed. In effect, vocal groups in large-adoption states too often control what students in Utah or Vermont will have access to.

National Testing

Publishers of national tests also have a great deal of influence over the curriculum. Popular achievement tests such as the Iowa Test of Basic Skills (ITBS), college entrance exams such as the Scholastic Achievement Test (SAT), government testing such as the National Assessment of Educational Progress (NAEP), and special exams such as Advanced Placement (AP) push teachers to adjust their curricula to match the content of the test. If they do not, their students will not do as well, and, since test scores are frequently published in the press, the reputation of the school or the teachers themselves will suffer. Thus, teachers work hard to ensure students do their best on these tests even if it means narrowing their curriculum to fit the content and format of the tests. Whereas as a nation these tests give us comparative information about how students in different schools and regions are doing, we also experience a loss of the hard-to-test portions of the curriculum, namely critical thinking, creativity, problem solving, and other higher-level cognitive operations.

State Influences

States also influence the content of instruction, often in ways similar to national influence. In addition to the influence of textbook adoption, states often convene their own commissions to examine the state's curriculum, and these groups produce guidelines and standards for what should be taught. These documents, termed **core curricula** or **curriculum frameworks,** are distributed statewide, workshops are conducted to familiarize teachers with them, and teachers are often evaluated on how well they implement the core.

State offices of education, being part of the executive branch of state government, carry out several regulatory functions that influence what gets taught. Approving university teacher certification programs, accrediting secondary schools, overseeing compensatory programs for ethnic and language minorities,

monitoring special education, conducting continuing education for educators, and producing curriculum guides are some of the ways these entities make themselves felt in teachers' curricular decisions.

Another avenue of state influence is legislative. For example, legislatures may modify graduation requirements, thereby creating the need for new or restructured high school courses. A popular addition of late is coursework in technology and computers. Many states also pass laws on what *cannot* be taught. Communism, for example, has been a forbidden topic in many states, and in some areas restrictions have been placed on what teachers can say about AIDS.

Local Influences

School Districts

Nested within constraints from the national and state level are local influences on curriculum, the most important of which is the district. Districts influence curriculum in a variety of ways. Curriculum guides, for example, are often produced by district teachers, administrators, parents, and others working in committees. And, just as at the state level, district committees may also help select texts and other instructional materials. Superintendents and school boards may set curriculum policies and mandate or prohibit the teaching of certain topics.

The impact of school boards is controversial. As a locally elected body, some argue, school boards are most in touch with the needs and values of their community, and thus should have a great deal of input into curricular decisions. Local boards may, for example, insist that earthquake safety be taught in areas at risk for earthquakes, or that sex education is a priority where the teen pregnancy rate is high. On the other hand, school boards are sometimes hampered from making the best decisions precisely because they are local, and, consequently, rather provincial. School board members may be uninformed about national issues or professional perspectives. They may balk, for instance, at the new standards for mathematics or object to inclusiveness in the literature that students are required to read.

Many districts employ curriculum specialists in the subject areas. These individuals work with teachers to help them make wise curriculum decisions and to inform them of district policies and national trends. Finally, many districts also offer workshops (termed **in-service**) to help teachers learn new curricula and teaching methods.

Our dispassionate discussion of the various forces impinging on the curriculum hides the fact that beneath the surface tempers flare and curriculum warfare often erupts. For example, a recent fight broke out in Utah involving a dispute between federal, state, and local school board control over the extracurriculum. A student at East High School in Salt Lake City, Kelli Peterson, wanted to start a club to help homosexual students. The Gay/Straight Alliance was to serve as a support group for these students and their straight friends. She requested permission from her principal to start the alliance. The request went to the board, and this at once launched a statewide uproar.

In making a decision on Kelli's request, the board had to operate within existing law. The relevant statute, the federal Equal Access Act, was passed in 1982. The initial purpose of the bill's sponsor, Utah Senator Orrin Hatch, was to ensure that student Bible study groups would be allowed to use school facilities for their activities. Fearing charges of discrimination and violating separation of church and state, the law mandated that *all* student groups should have equal access to school facilities. If religious groups were to be allowed, then all groups had to be allowed.

Under this law, the Salt Lake School Board had a deceptively simple choice, either allow all noncurricular clubs or ban all noncurricular clubs. They chose the latter. No longer available to students would be activities like Black Students Union, Chess Club, service clubs, the National Honor Society, as well as the Gay/Straight Alliance. The board's argument rested in part on their belief that localities ought to have the right to pick and choose what kinds of activities students would be allowed to participate in, precisely the state of affairs the federal law attempted to prohibit.

Students at another Salt Lake high school had also initiated a Gay/Straight Alliance. Junior and senior high students all over the district were outraged at the school board's action, and staged a protest walkout. Some marched to the state capital, demanding to speak to legislators about their concerns. Another group descended on the school district office, where the president of the school board was called in to parlay with them. When students returned to their schools, lunch time and much class time for several days were devoted to arguing who was right. One group of young men tried to organize opposition to the Gay/Straight Alliance by forming a new group, SAFE (Students Against Faggots Everywhere). Many, but not all, students shunned SAFE.

Meanwhile members of the Utah State Legislature were organizing to exert their influence over the extracurriculum. Legislators believed that they had a right to establish and enforce community standards at the state level. Religious fundamentalists in the legislature lobbied for and passed a law restricting the types of clubs that students could organize. Any club promoting criminal behavior or bigotry or dealing in any way with sexuality was prohibited. The American Civil Liberties Union has initiated a challenge to the law based on constitutional guarantees of freedom of speech and assembly. The challenge is pending.

This episode pitted the federal government's statute protecting individual rights against local and state authorities who wanted to abridge those rights based on deeply, albeit not universally, held community values and standards. This was a complicated situation with many arguments on all sides. What further arguments can you generate for each position? What do you think the correct decision should be in this situation? What do you think a teacher's position should be? Interestingly, both the teachers' and principals' associations favored granting Kelli's request to form a support group for gay and lesbian students.

Principals

Principals also play a role in the curriculum. The best principals act as instructional leaders, and when they do, they can exert much influence on teachers' content choices. When principals attend in-service classes themselves; make frequent visits to classrooms and give teachers feedback; provide curriculum information on a regular basis in faculty meetings and other outlets; and support teachers' efforts in professional development, they help establish a dynamic environment conducive to effective curriculum decision making.

Parents and Students

Parents, students, and community groups can also influence the curriculum. Student activism in the 1960s and 1970s, for example, contributed to an increase in the practicality and relevance of coursework. Parents have a voice in what is taught in schools by talking personally with individual teachers and by organizing into interest groups. Of course, parents are not unified about what they want. Some favor increasing vocational education, some want more information disseminated on drugs, while others consider these frills and lobby for a rigorous academic program.

Some parents launch curriculum battles in the courtroom. Two recent cases demonstrated how the federal courts balanced parental versus school authority in designing curriculum. In *Curtis vs. School Committee of Falmouth,* the school board had permitted the distribution of condoms to high school students by the school nurse and through vending machines in the bathrooms, an activity that could be construed as part of the extracurriculum. A group of parents sued the school alleging that their rights to direct their children's upbringing and to freely exercise their religion had been violated. Both the state courts and the U.S. Supreme Court ruled for the school district. The courts said that students were not compelled to accept condoms, so there was no effect on parents' rights to raise their children as they desired. They could still instruct their children not to request them. The Supreme Judicial Court of Massachusetts declared, "Parents have no right to tailor public school programs to meet their individual religious or moral preferences." (cited in Walsh, 1996, p. 11).

A similar case was also decided in favor of the school. Parents in Chelmsford, Massachusetts, sued the school because they did not have the opportunity, as required by school board policy, to pull their children from an AIDS awareness assembly. The school had hired an outside AIDS educator whose performance was "streetwise ... [and] comedic" and violated parents' sense of propriety (Walsh, 1996, p. 11). The parents lost in the district court, the Court of Appeals, and the U.S. Supreme Court. The Appeals Court argued, "If all parents had a fundamental constitutional right to dictate individually what the schools teach their children, the schools would be forced to cater a curriculum for each student whose parents had genuine moral disagreements with the school's choice of subject matter" (cited in Walsh, 1996, p. 11).

Censorship

There are a few trends in community influences on the curriculum. As we noted early in the chapter, in the 1960s and 1970s, a liberalizing trend dominated, but in the 1980s and 1990s, conservativism has held sway. In particular, Christian fundamentalists aim to increase the teaching and practice of Christianity in the public schools, and to eliminate certain other books and topics from the curriculum. People for the American Way, a censorship watchdog group, reported that of 264 attempts at censorship during 1990-1991, one-third were successful. The books listed below are among those frequently challenged:

- *Of Mice and Men,* John Steinbeck.
- *The Catcher in the Rye,* J.D. Salinger.
- *Forever,* Judy Blume.
- *I Know Why the Caged Bird Sings,* Maya Angelou.
- *Diary of Anne Frank.*

Many curriculum wars, this time secular versus religious, break out in response to literature. In a recent incident in the western United States, Christian parents objected to the use of Isabel Allende's *House of Spirits,* a novel that has received worldwide acclaim, in an advanced world literature class. The class was part of an international curriculum, originally organized for the children of diplomats, terminating in the *International Baccalaureate,* or IB degree. The IB curriculum is set by an international committee of IB teachers, and students are tested on this curriculum in order to be eligible to receive the degree.

The parents, much like the parents in the Massachusetts cases, charged that certain incidents in Allende's book, such as rape and political violence, were offensive and not appropriate for their students. The school's response was to offer students the option to read something else that parents would find acceptable, and to excuse them from the classroom when the book was discussed, with the caveat that students may be at a disadvantage on the international exam. This still posed some problems for the teacher. What if the book is referred to in later discussions? Should students leave the class again? That issue became moot, however, because parents still objected so strenuously that the administration created a special class just for those students, with a book list tailored to their wishes. This special class had 12 students, all white and upper-middle class, whereas the average class size in the school is about 40 students. (About one-third the student population is minority, and many students are low income.) The teacher for this class was hand-picked based on his fundamentalist religious views, not his expertise in the subject matter. Needless to say, serious equity, professional, and legal issues were raised by this solution to the problem.

The teaching of evolution is also controversial for the religious right, which results in many publishers and teachers softpedaling the topic so as not to raise the ire of fundamentalists (Bernstein, 1988). A rather bizarre bete noire of the right is *secular humanism,* a philosophical position that it is possible to live an ethical life without believing in a supreme being. Fundamentalists believe this view constitutes a religion that is unconstitutionally taught in the public schools. In one case brought in Tennessee in 1986, the judge agreed with the plaintiffs' charge that a reading text, which depicted a boy making toast and a girl reading, was promoting secular humanism, because it implied that there were no god-given roles for the sexes. In another case, this time in Alabama, a judge banned more than 40 textbooks because they allegedly promoted the secular humanist belief that people can lead moral lives without relying on a deity. Both cases were reversed on appeal (Sadker & Sadker, 1994).

Most people find the charge that schools are promoting the religion of secular humanism more than a little hard to swallow, but these attempts at censorship still raise several issues. The most important of these is the role of the curriculum in a diverse, multicultural, democratic society like ours. Should schools avoid any topic or instructional materials that might provoke controversy? If a group of parents objects to certain materials or topics, should the school accommodate their objections? Should special classes be set up for every diverging opinion group? Only for a few different opinions? If so, which ones? Should students only be exposed to the ideas their parents agree with? Or should schools purposely introduce students to a variety of beliefs and conflicting ideas? Which approach is more appropriate in our pluralistic democracy? Which demonstrates most respect for differing opinions? Which one is more supportive of families? What is the reasoning behind your views?

Teachers

You may have come to the conclusion by now that everyone *but* teachers controls the curriculum. Nothing could be further from the truth. Teachers are the ones who make the day-by-day decisions about what to teach, what to leave out, and what to emphasize. It is these on-the-spot decisions by teachers that create the official, operational, extra, null, and hidden curricula in schools. As has been noted, teachers often serve on national, state, and local bodies that set curriculum policy and approve instructional materials. The advent of site-based decision making has also placed more power in the hands of teams of teachers within schools. Although decisions at other levels have an impact on teachers, much control remains in their hands. Figure 8.1 displays the percentage of teachers who felt they had considerable control over the choice of materials and topics in their classrooms.

Curriculum wars also rage around teachers' control of classroom content. In the 1980s, for example, Texas faced a set of problems in schools (high drop-out rates, student disengagement with learning, lackluster academic performance) and then-governor Mark White decided that the remedy was to increase state control of schools. It was argued that teachers had too much leeway in setting curriculum and that too many of them were not competent and hard-working enough. If only the state could set and enforce curriculum standards, the reasoning went, then students would learn more. The results, according to McNeil (1995), did not live up to the promise. What exactly happened in Texas?

White named billionaire businessman Ross Perot to head a blue-ribbon commission whose job it was to design reforms. Perot's commission introduced curriculum standards, the "no pass-no play" rule, a one-time basic literacy test that all teachers had to pass to retain certification, and a teacher evaluation checklist linked to pay raises. The checklist, the Texas Teacher Assessment System (TTAS), was designed to be in alignment with the new standard curriculum and was to serve as a means to enforce that curriculum. If a teacher failed to score high on the TTAS, then the teacher failed to receive any pay raise.

From a business perspective, linking job performance to pay makes sense. But the problem, according to McNeil, was that the TTAS was a:

> perfect example of an attempt to impose an across-the-board solution that goes against all our best understandings of teaching and learning. The checklist places the teacher at the center of the room, 19th century style, and assumes that . . . the source of knowledge is . . . the official state list of the essential fact and skill components of the traditional subjects. (1995, p. 21)

Figure 8.1   **Percentage of Teachers Reporting a Great Deal of Control over Curriculum Decisions**

Materials	xxxxxxxxxxxxxxxxxxxxxxxxxxxxxxxxxxxxxxxxxx 44 percent
	ooooooooooooooooooooooooooooooooooooooooooooooooooooooooooo 64 percent
Content	xxxxxxxxxxxxxxxxxxxxxxxxxxxxxxxxxxxxxxxxxxxxxxxx 50 percent
	ooooooooooooooooooooooooooooooooooooooooooooooooooooooooooooo 68 percent

xxxxx Elementary
ooooo Secondary

Source: After National Center for Education Statistics, 1993, p. 128.

The checklist ignored the role of students in the learning process and mandated one way of teaching for every student, subject, grade level, and learning goal. It also failed to consider a teacher's knowledge of subject matter or his or her rationale for teaching a certain lesson a certain way. Mediocre teachers gained greater job security from this system, McNeil (1995) charged, while innovative teachers (like Whitford) or those who used problem-based curricula or cooperative learning were very frustrated. The result was to focus teachers on compliance rather than on what helped students learn. This top-down approach also interfered with the development of collegiality. What works for business, it became clear, does not necessarily work for education.

Why did teachers go along with this? The initial agreement was a package deal: If teachers acquiesced to TTAS evaluation, then the state would reciprocate with large pay raises. Teachers had not received substantial pay increases in a number of years, so they agreed. Unfortunately, the state legislature and subsequent governors failed to keep their end of the deal. Teachers now are evaluated but without any pay incentives. To add insult to injury, the state required all teachers to take a basic literacy test. In a state in which some teachers have to run extension cords across the hallway in order to show a video, laboratory equipment can be scarce, and librarians often scour garage sales to stock their paperback fiction shelves, the state government paid $70 million to a California firm to run the teacher testing operation. In a final slap, the media made a great show of teachers who scored low, further depressing teacher morale.

This unhappy tale reflects fundamental conflicts between teachers and communities. How much influence should the community, represented by business, parents, and political leadership, have in how teachers do their jobs? How much freedom should teachers have to operate classrooms and schools as they see fit? Clearly, education is a community concern, but it is equally clear that teachers have a great deal of specialized knowledge that communities ignore at their peril. Where would you draw the line?

Curriculum Hegemony

Hegemony refers to the domination of one class or group by another. The dominant group strives to make its interests legitimate and to extend its domination of the oppressed group. Why is this concept relevant in a discussion of curriculum? Because many believe that the curriculum serves a hegemonic role in America's schools. At the root of many of the curriculum wars we have discussed is this struggle to maintain hegemony by the dominant group (white, middle class, English-speaking, Christian, male) while weaker groups (ethnic and language minorities, women, working class, religious minorities) strive to restructure the existing power relationships.

Hegemony manifests itself through the official, hidden, and null curricula. Consider a school's official goals and objectives in history, for example. Usually the dominant group's version of history is presented, highlighting its heroism and minimizing its shortcomings. For example, most American texts treat Columbus as a great explorer and hero, failing to mention how he slaughtered and enslaved thousands of indigenous people (Loewen, 1996). We saw the same thing in the opening vignette about the Texas English curriculum that emphasized only the works of mainstream authors. In the accompanying Multicultural Box you can learn about on-going attempts to teach an Afrocentric curriculum in special schools in the United States.

By the same token, the null curriculum, that is, what is not taught, can enforce hegemony. Just as the official curriculum legitimizes the dominant group's perspective, the null curriculum delegitimizes the perspective of other groups: If the lives and accomplishments of women and minorities are not included in the history curriculum, for example, then they must not be important. Arguments over the literary canon and over standards for history, which we discuss later, represent hegemonic conflicts between dominant and minority groups.

The hidden curriculum is another vehicle for hegemony. As noted educator and scholar George Posner (1992) said:

> I know the schools I went to taught me a number of powerful lessons through their hidden curriculum: that individual competition is the fairest and most effective way to run an institution like a school; that whether I succeeded or failed in school, I got what I deserved—that is, that school is basically meritocratic; that males are inherently better at science and math than females; that punctuality, neatness, and effort are often more important than achievement; that following instructions, i.e., compliance, is often more important than learning; and that intellectual skills like the ability to manipulate symbols are more important than other characteristics like business acumen, leadership, and creativity. It wasn't until I had experiences after and outside of school that I realized both the impact of these unofficial lessons and their limited validity. . . . (T)hese lessons of the hidden curriculum created or reinforced myths that are still difficult for me to forget. (p. 121)

The values of the hidden curriculum are the values of the dominant group, and by absorbing them, young people are preparing for the adult roles they will fulfill in society. Those who adhere to a different set of values and who are members of nondominant groups will have difficulty finding success in school and in society at large. Critics on the political left charge that schools reproduce an inequitable social order, that is, they perpetuate the disadvantaged economic and political status of women, minorities, and the poor, in part through using the curriculum to further the hegemony of the white middle and upper classes.

Curriculum in Other Countries

As we have noted before, it is often instructive to examine the ways of other countries and cultures to gain a deeper insight into our own. Germany and Japan, for example, provide more opportunities for business to become intimately involved with stu-dents and schools than is typical in America. In Japan, schools have established agreements with local businesses to hire a set number of noncollege-bound graduates every year, no matter what economic conditions happen to prevail at the moment. In turn, schools nominate those students they consider best for particular businesses, based on students' academic performance; the better students have done in school, the better the job they are nominated for. Not surprisingly, students are highly motivated to succeed in school.

Germany, in contrast, has long followed an apprentice system. Over half the country's high school juniors and seniors attend school 1 day per week for academics and spend 4 days per week learning a trade on site at a local business. A uniform curriculum has been developed collaboratively by educators and business representatives as a means of quality control.

MULTICULTURAL

Afrocentric Curriculum

Many scholars have criticized the Eurocentric nature of the American curriculum. The history, literature, arts, sciences, and perspectives of Europeans and their descendants permeate American schooling. Several reforms have attempted to adjust the curriculum to make it more inclusive, such as the new history standards project. Another reform with similar goals has centered around developing an **Afrocentric curriculum.** Such a curriculum would be organized around African themes and perspectives rather than European.

The rationale for an Afrocentric curriculum is very like the rationale for instituting multicultural curricula in general. As Vann and Kunjufu (1993) pointed out:

> *Was America discovered by Columbus or was it invaded? Is Thanksgiving a day to give thanks or a day of sadness for Native Americans? Why should African Americans celebrate the Fourth of July?... Native Americans were already living on this continent when Columbus arrived... To Native Americans, Thanksgiving is a day of mourning because the kindness of their ancestors was ultimately rewarded with the loss of their lands and the near-extinction of their people... When America's first Independence Day was celebrated in 1776, African Americans were not independent; they were not even citizens ... (p. 490)*

The curriculum of the dominant group ill serves students of minority backgrounds, critics argue, because it alienates them and presents them with a picture of the world that does not include or value them. Afrocentric curricula are designed to counteract these deficiencies.

What does such a curriculum look like in practice? Several schools around the country are experimenting with Afrocentrism, among them the Paul Robeson Academy in New York, the Marcus Garvey School in Los Angeles, and Victor Berger Elementary School in Milwaukee. Most Afrocentric schools enforce strict dress codes, maintain high academic

The German and Japanese systems are not unusual in their close working relationships between schools and businesses and in the greater uniformity of their curricula. Most countries have a more intentionally centralized curriculum than the United States. In the Canadian province of Alberta, for example, a new curriculum has been instituted that integrates career studies with technology and the traditional academic curriculum from grades 7 to 12 throughout the province. Rather than separating vocational education from academics, the new system links the two across 22 strands. The strands, which include a range of career areas like agriculture, design studies, energy and mines, and tourism studies, are composed of modules. Students pursue a set of activities within each module and are required to demonstrate specific competencies associated with the module. No longer do they earn credits for seat time; credit is earned when competency is demonstrated, and that can take different amounts of time for different students. Each module requires work that integrates academics and practical skills, as well as solitary and group work. For example:

> a learner expectation in the Management and Marketing strand requires students to apply management systems and strategies by completing a management analysis report. Students must identify a system that needs improvement, such as increasing attendance at sporting events or improving efficiency in the cafeteria line. Students define the problem, offer a rationale for changing the system, develop and implement a plan for change, and monitor the changes. The final report format can be as creative as students wish, including written, oral, video, and other multimedia formats. (deWijk, 1996, p. 51)

MULTICULTURAL

Continued

expectations, and mandate parent involvement, in addition to orienting the curriculum toward Africa. At Victor Berger (Scherer, 1992), students learn to count to 10 in Swahili, read African folktales, and study the black history alphabet—A is for Armstrong, B is for Banneker, C is for Carver. Further, Victor Berger students pursue an integrated curriculum. When they study George Washington Carver, for example, they also study peanuts, learning about their origin and uses, and bake peanut butter cookies learning about recipes and measurement.

A typical day at Victor Berger starts with a period of self-esteem building and instruction in conflict resolution. Students then spend 2-hour blocks of time studying language arts in the morning and a like period studying math, science, and social studies in the afternoon. Students do much memorization and reciting in an effort to capitalize on the African oral tradition. Students' emotional and social needs are also attended to through "school families." These consist of three or four multiage classrooms that meet together every 2 weeks.

Teachers at Victor Berger receive special training. They are required to take several university courses in topics like black American history and culture and racism in America, as well as special courses in pedagogy. They plan together each day, utilizing the help of specialists in art, physical education, and music to free their time to do so. They also make many home visits each year.

It is premature to tell whether such schools will be successful in their goal of increasing African American children's achievement. They are highly controversial, and many parents, teachers, and scholars argue about whether an Afrocentric curriculum really serves students. Will these schools further estrange Americans of different races? Will black children grow up so unfamiliar with the dominant culture that they will have an even harder time being successful within it? Or will they, on the other hand, be more empowered to accomplish great things? Time will tell.

In this project-based program, students have the opportunity to develop advanced academic skills in English and mathematics in the context of solving complex, real-life business problems.

Interestingly, Americans are not the only ones who engage in curriculum wars. Debate has seethed in China, for example, for many years about the appropriate course of study for rural Chinese students. On one hand, the Chinese Communist Party decreed that vocational education for secondary students should be developed rapidly. But some want vocational education that meets current economic needs, training students for jobs currently available in their own communities, whereas others advocate a future focus, arguing that students should be prepared for jobs yet to be developed. Still others, mostly teachers, want to eliminate all vocational education for rural Chinese students and put in place the same academic curriculum that urban students receive. These teachers fear that the rural students will be limited in their choices if they are given only vocational training (Lo & Lee, 1996, p. 60).

Note certain trends on the international scene: interdisciplinary curricula, critical thinking, problem solving, questioning the relative importance of an economic rationale for curriculum decisions versus a civic or personal development rationale. Many of these concerns are mirrored in American curriculum discussions.

THE AMERICAN CURRICULUM

We have emphasized that the American system of education is loosely coupled, that is, unclear and conflicting lines of authority run through the various levels of the system. Although local entities exert much curricular control, we saw that larger forces—textbooks, national testing, professional associations, and so forth—produce considerable curriculum similarity across the country. We turn now to an overview of these similarities in the American curriculum.

Literacy, Language Arts, and English

Fundamental to any curriculum is **literacy**, that is, the ability to read, write, speak, listen, and, most recently, to communicate visually. The reasons are obvious. Literacy is not only essential to success as a citizen, an employee, a parent, and a consumer but is also the primary means by which the rest of the school curriculum is taught. Failure to acquire literacy is a serious problem for anyone. Because of its centrality to the curriculum, much research has been conducted in this area.

In the past, reading was taught exclusively through *phonics,* or letter-sound correspondences. Children memorized which sound went with which symbol, and then step by step built these sounds into words and the words into sentences. This bottom-up, skills-based method had problems, though, because only about 50 percent of the time do English words follow the symbol-sound rules.

Because of this problem with phonics, another system to teach reading was developed, the sight method. In the sight method, children simply memorize what a particular word looks like. This solved the problem of inconsistent phonics rules, but it created an enormous memorization problem. Another problem with both the phonics approach and the sight method was that many children failed to perceive reading as an activity to obtain meaning from text; they thought reading meant only "pronouncing the words correctly." As a result, an exclusive emphasis on phonics and sight reading often led to comprehension failures.

To solve the comprehension problem, teachers and researchers developed literature-based and whole-language approaches to the teaching of reading. These methods maintain a focus on getting meaning from the page, encourage students to use a variety of techniques to figure out a word, and link the teaching of reading to the teaching of writing. Some whole-language teachers, though, in reaction to the excesses of phonics, refuse to teach any phonics at all. Research has shown, though, that their students also experience reading problems. A dogmatic reliance on one method alone, whether phonics or whole language, is doomed to fail some children.

What are recommendations from research at the present time for curriculum in reading and language arts instruction? Current research supports an eclectic approach. The findings were summed up in the report *Becoming a Nation of Readers* (Commission on Reading, 1985). Of special note to teachers was the finding that teachers' skill is more important for student learning than any particular reading program or set of materials.

That news is both invigorating and sobering, placing an enormous responsibility on teachers. How can teachers best exercise that responsibility? *Becoming a Nation of Readers* advocates that teachers create a **literate environment,** one in which reading and writing take place routinely and often, and for a variety of purposes. Current views of reading instruction link learning to read with learning to write and suggest that the two should not and cannot be separated. Each facilitates the development of the other. Further, teachers are encouraged to directly teach **comprehension strategies,** those learning strategies that help students understand what they are reading. Finally, the report chides teachers for allotting too much time to worksheets and drill; more time should be given to actual reading, including independent reading, and less time to meaningless drill work. This does not mean, however, that phonics should be abandoned. Although it is not effective as a stand-alone strategy, it does have a place in an effective reader's repertoire of comprehension strategies and thus merits a place in the reading curriculum. Figure 8.2 displays selected standards for literacy as promulgated by the National Council of Teachers of English (NCTE) and the International Reading Association (IRA).

It is important to note that it is incumbent on all teachers, not just primary grade educators, to work to create a meaningful literate environment that is appropriate to their grade level and subject area. Students often need help in learning how to learn from complex textbooks, and upper-grade teachers have a responsibility to assist students in developing these high-level literacy skills.

Not everyone is happy with the new standards released by NCTE and the IRA. For example, Al Shanker, former president of the American Federation of Teachers (AFT), lambasted the standards as vague, weak, and unhelpful as a guide to teachers of English. Shanker (1996) complained that the standards do not specify what students ought to know and be able to do. What would a good piece of writing by a fourth-grader look like? What methods of analysis ought an eighth grader know when critically examining a story or a TV show? What should we expect of graduating seniors? Shanker charges that none of these questions is answered by the standards.

Proponents of the standards countered that teachers need to be student centered, that overly narrow standards can blind teachers to what students can actually do and can result in premature labels of low ability. Such standards can also militate against problem-based or project-based curricula, the type of curriculum more likely to meaningfully engage students in learning.

Figure 8.2   Selected Standards for the English Language Arts

IRA/NCTE STANDARDS
FOR THE ENGLISH LANGUAGE ARTS

The vision guiding these standards is that all students must have the opportunities and resources to develop the language skills they need to pursue life's goals and to participate fully as informed, productive members of society. These standards assume that literacy growth begins before children enter school as they experience and experiment with literacy activities--reading and writing, and associating spoken words with their graphic representations. Recognizing this fact, these standards encourage the development of curriculum and instruction that make productive use of the emerging literacy abilities that children bring to school. Furthermore, the standards provide ample room for the innovation and creativity essential to teaching and learning. They are not prescriptions for particular curriculum or instruction.

Although we present these standards as a list, we want to emphasize that they are not distinct and separable; they are, in fact, interrelated and should be considered as a whole.

1. Students read a wide range of print and nonprint texts to build an understanding of texts, of themselves, and of the cultures of the United States and the world; to acquire new information; to respond to the needs and demands of society and the workplace; and for personal fulfillment. Among these texts are fiction and nonfiction, classic and contemporary works.

2. Students read a wide range of literature from many periods in many genres to build an understanding of the many dimensions (e.g., philosophical, ethical, aesthetic) of human experience.

3. Students apply a wide range of strategies to comprehend, interpret, evaluate, and appreciate texts. They draw on their prior experience, their interactions with other readers and writers, their knowledge of word meaning and of other texts, their word identification strategies, and their understanding of textual features (e.g., sound-letter correspondence, sentence structure, context, graphics).

4. Students adjust their use of spoken, written, and visual language (e.g., conventions, style, vocabulary) to communicate effectively with a variety of audiences and for different purposes.

5. Students employ a wide range of strategies as they write and use different writing process elements appropriately to communicate with different audiences for a variety of purposes.

Source: Adapted from International Reading Association/National Council of Teachers of English, 1996, p. 3.

Shanker and other critics replied that without some sense of what our expectations are for each grade level, low-achieving students will fall through the cracks. No one will take responsibility for ensuring that these students attain high levels of achievement. Such a system, they argued, will fail to promote excellence. Both sides make a strong case in this debate. What is your view?

Literacy is important at any level of school, but gaining prominence in the higher grades is the study of literature. This area has become increasingly controversial, as the dispute over Allende's *House of Spirits* illustrates. Other controversy reigns regarding the literary canon. For example, some contend that all American students need to read and appreciate the same set of books and stories—those of the standard, traditional curriculum. The rationale behind this thinking is that this shared experience and uniformity exerts a uniting force on the vast diversity that characterizes the American student population and citizenry. Without this shared experience, some fear, we may fracture into quarrelsome ethnic polities (Schlesinger, 1992). Others counter that attention to stories and myths from other cultures, like African folktales, Native American cosmologies, or novels by female authors, honor the perspectives of all cultures and promote democratic values like tolerance and understanding of diverse views (Banks, 1992). Without learning about others' perspectives, we may never learn to enter into civil, democratic discourse with each other. Take a minute to read the accompanying Issue Box about a serious curricular concern—the best approach to bilingual education.

Mathematics

Mathematics educators should take the prize for being the first to create theoretically sound and pragmatically feasible curriculum standards in their area. Their *Curriculum and Evaluation Standards for School Mathematics* (1989) started the latest wave of curriculum reform among professional associations. Mathematics educators have identified five broad goals for math instruction. They want to educate students to:

- Value mathematics
- Reason mathematically
- Communicate mathematics
- Solve problems
- Have mathematical confidence

Valuing mathematics means that students realize the many roles mathematics serves in our society and that they believe in its value for them personally.

Mathematical reasoning is construed as a habit of mind that includes gathering evidence, making conjectures, formulating models, inventing counterexamples, and building sound arguments for one's ideas. The standards also assert that learning mathematics requires working in groups, tutoring each other in math, and arguing about which is the preferred solution method in both verbal and written form. In short, communicating about mathematics is essential to learning mathematics. Further, the point of learning math is to be able to solve problems involving numbers; therefore, the focal point of mathematical studies should be problem solving, not merely speed of computation. Finally, math educators advocate enhancing students' confidence in doing math. Attitudes about mathematics have a great deal to do with one's use of mathematics and one's persistence at mathematical tasks, so math self-confidence is an important learning goal.

Math education goals were not always like this. In years past, the goal was speed. The faster a student could compute math facts, the better. Students completed worksheet after worksheet and timed test after timed test in order to up their computational speed and accuracy. Teachers drilled students in algorithms without much attention to building underlying conceptual understanding. Although many math teachers today still operate under the old assumptions, many others are changing to the current, problem-centered approach.

Science

As in the area of mathematics, scientists and science educators have been active in national curriculum reform in recent years. In 1990, the Association for the Advancement of Science, under the aegis of a reform effort termed Project 2061 (the year Halley's Comet will return), published *Science for All Americans,* an overview of the knowledge all Americans need in order to be scientifically literate. A follow-up book, *Benchmarks for Scientific Literacy,* was published in 1993 and provides more specific guidelines for science education.

The point of view of these important documents is not that schools need to teach more and more science, math, and technology but rather that schools need "to focus on what is essential to scientific literacy . . . the ideas and skills having the greatest scientific and educational significance" (Rutherford & Ahlgren, 1990, p. ix). The reformers desire to implement a more integrated and scientifically defensible curriculum. Specifically, they advocate teaching science, mathematics, and technology together and seek to limit what is taught to the central ideas in those fields. The goal is to develop scientific literacy. They criticize current science textbooks and teaching because these emphasize:

> learning answers more than the exploration of questions, memory at the expense of critical thought, bits and pieces of information instead of understandings in context, recitation over argument, reading in lieu of doing. They fail to encourage students to work together, to share ideas and information freely with each other, or to use modern instruments to extend their intellectual capacities. (p. viii)

They also criticize the current curriculum on the grounds that it is simply jammed with too much stuff, resulting in teachers and students being overwhelmed with information, none of which is tied together in anything resembling a coherent form.

What might this new curriculum look like? *Benchmarks for Science Literacy* specifies in a bit more detail how science literacy can be developed over the course of a student's school career. Rather than providing long lists of topics that should be taught at each grade level, *Benchmarks* discusses guidelines for the kinds of knowledge and skills that should be nurtured during certain grade levels, K through 2, 3 through 5, 6 through 8, and 9 through 12. Figure 8.3 shows a sample section from *Benchmarks,* a piece concerning processes that shape the earth.

ISSUES EXTRA

Bilingual Education

Debate is currently raging about the best approach to use in bilingual education. In dispute is the extent to which limited English proficiency (LEP) students should be taught in their native languages. Practitioners, researchers, and policy makers are divided on this issue. We describe here what bilingual programs look like and then present arguments on each side of the issue.

Teaching English to LEP students can take a variety of forms. At one extreme are **immersion programs** in which students are totally immersed in the English language and participate with age-mates in regular classrooms; no instruction in the native language is provided. **ESL programs** provide English-as-a-second language classes. In these programs, LEP students participate in regular classes most of the time but are pulled out to attend separate classes in English. Some instruction may be provided in the student's native language during the transition to English. If this is the case, the program is termed **transitional bilingual. Full bilingual programs** offer a fourth alternative in which content instruction in various subjects is provided in both the native language and English on a permanent basis. All four types of programs are called bilingual, but this is a bit of a misnomer. The intent in all cases is to help LEP students master English but the programs differ in their emphasis on maintaining and strengthening students' native language skill.

Let's examine research on what works best. Ramirez (1991) conducted a longitudinal study of elementary programs for Spanish-speaking students, which he broke down into three groups. **Early-exit programs** involved using Spanish about 20 percent to 30 percent of the time, usually for reading instruction; children stayed in the program through second grade. In **late-exit programs,** at least 40 percent of instruction was in Spanish, and students transferred to regular classes in seventh grade. (Both the early-exit and late-exit programs constitute transitional bilingual programs.) Finally, in immersion programs, all instruction was in English, with Spanish used only when clarification was needed.

Ramirez found that the late-exit transitional bilingual program did the best job in helping language minority students keep up with their age-mates in mathematics and English language arts performance. According to some scholars, Ramirez' work is in keeping with:

Social Studies

Social studies is no doubt the most nebulous of school subjects. To clarify what social studies is, the National Council for the Social Studies (NCSS) developed this definition:

> Social studies is the integrated study of the social sciences and humanities to promote civic competence. Within the school program, social studies provides coordinated, systematic study drawing upon such disciplines as anthropology, archaeology, economics, geography, history, law, philosophy, political science, psychology, religion, and sociology, as well as appropriate content from the humanities, mathematics, and natural sciences. The primary purpose of social studies is to help young people develop the ability to make informed and reasoned decisions for the public good as citizens of a culturally diverse, democratic society in an interdependent world. (1994, p. 3)

Unlike the goals in other disciplines, in which students learn mathematics, say, in order to become more proficient mathematics problem solvers, or they learn science to become better scientific rea-

ISSUES

Continued

nearly all the research . . . over the last four years . . . [which] shows that the more native-language instructional support LEP students receive (if combined with balanced English support), the higher they are able to achieve in each succeeding academic year, relative to matched groups being schooled solely in English. Students who do not receive native-language instruction appear to do well in the early grades, but their performance fails to match that of the norm group and gains go down as they reach upper elementary and especially secondary school. (Willis, 1994, p. 4)

Other support for this view comes from reading researchers, who have found that students can transfer reading strategies acquired from their first language to reading in English (Allen, 1991). They also contend that trying to simultaneously teach English and reading to first graders is an overwhelming cognitive load. Further, it appears that it takes quite a few years to develop academic competence in a new language, so many argue that it is unfair to ask LEP students to compete academically with native English speakers. This body of research and reasoning lead one to conclude that full bilingual programs, or at least late-exit transitional programs, do the best job developing English skills, advancing LEP students at the appropriate pace through the curriculum, and enhancing their native language literacy.

Others vigorously dispute this conclusion, and cite other research and experience to support their views. For example, Rosalie Pedalino Porter (cited in Willis, 1994) of the Research in English Acquisition and Development (READ) Institute described a study conducted by her organization in El Paso, Texas, schools. The effects of a transitional bilingual versus an immersion program were compared over time, and immersion students outperformed their bilingual peers in every subject up until the seventh grade, when the bilingual students caught up.

Pedalino initially became disenchanted with bilingual programs as a result of her own experience as a bilingual teacher. She found that the program did not help students acquire English, that students in bilingual programs were not being transferred into regular classrooms on schedule, and that first language instruction isolated students from native English speakers, removing an important incentive for learning English. As late as sixth grade, students still could not function academically in English.

soners, the key in social studies is to learn to become a better citizen in a democracy. It is also arguably the most integrative of school subjects, and as such, it impinges on all others.

Like other disciplines, curriculum in social studies used to be centered around memorizing facts. Students learned by rote locations of countries and their capitals, how a bill becomes a law, dates of wars and other major political upheavals, and so on. But now, as in many other disciplines, social studies educators have recently produced new national standards. The new standards emphasize critical thinking and conceptual understanding instead of rote memorization. Social studies learning is now to be active, integrative, and to fully treat issues involving ethical conflicts. The standards are organized into several themes, and each theme is broken down into general performance expectations for the early grades, middle grades, and high school. The themes include such broad concepts as culture, power and authority, production and consumption, and global connections. Table 8.2 displays the full set of performance expectations for the "culture" theme.

ISSUES
EXTRA

Continued

What are we to make of these opposing views? It may be that program quality, whether immersion or bilingual, varies widely from one program to another, making it difficult to generalize about which one works better. There are also definitional problems; that is, what one researcher calls an immersion program, another one calls a transitional bilingual program. Without clear definitions and quality controls, practitioners and policy makers are hard pressed to make wise decisions.

Given the current state of our knowledge on the subject, an intermediate stance that captures the best of both positions seems most sensible. Too much emphasis on instruction in the native language risks diminishing English competence and isolates language minority students from the mainstream. On the other hand, offering no instruction in the native language can hamper the development of reading skills and the acquisition of academic content. Learning English does require using English, but simple conversation with English speakers will not develop *academic* competence. Programs for LEP students, then, should immediately begin developing academic language competence through direct teaching of English and as much interaction with native English speakers as possible. However, instruction should also be maintained in the home language, decreasing each year, so that students can acquire literacy in their own language and gain content knowledge in the disciplines.

Astute readers will recognize this recommendation as falling into the transitional bilingual category. Of course, if there is a wide variety of languages spoken in the classroom or school, pull-out ESL classes are the only alternative; a critical mass of speakers of a single non-English language is needed before transitional bilingual programs become feasible.

An interesting new development are two-way bilingual programs, which are gaining popularity across the country. In these programs, students of two different languages participate in coursework that is offered in both languages. The goal is complete bilingualism for each group, not just for the language minority students. Students receive half their instruction in English and half in the other language. Schools use either one bilingual teacher or two monolingual teachers for each grade level or subject. On a regular basis, the language of instruction in a particular area is alternated; for example, history will be taught in English for one lesson, unit, or year, but will be taught in the other language for the next lesson, unit, or year.

Figure 8.3   Sample Section from *Benchmarks for Science Literacy*

Kindergarten through Grade 2

Teaching geological facts about how the face of the earth changes serves little purpose in these early years. Students should start becoming familiar with all aspects of their immediate surroundings, including what things change and what seems to cause change. Perhaps "changing things" can be a category in a class portfolio of things students observe and read about. At some point, students can start thinking up and trying out safe and helpful ways to change parts of their environment.

By the end of the 2nd grade, students should know that

▶ Chunks of rocks come in many sizes and shapes, from boulders to grains of sand and even smaller.

▶ Change is something that happens to many things.

▶ Animals and plants sometimes cause changes in their surroundings. ■

Grades 3 through 5

In these years, students should accumulate more information about the physical environment, becoming familiar with the details of geological features, observing and mapping locations of hills, valleys, rivers, etc., but without elaborate classification. Students should also become adept at using magnifiers to inspect a variety of rocks and soils. The point is not to classify rigorously but to notice the variety of components.

Students should now observe elementary processes of the rock cycle--erosion, transport, and deposit. Water and sand boxes and rock tumblers can provide them with some first-hand examples. Later, they can connect the features to the processes and follow explanations of how the features came to be and still are changing. Students can build devices for demonstrating how wind and water shape the land and how forces on materials can make wrinkles, folds, and faults. Films of volcanic magma and ash ejection dramatize another source of buildup.

By the end of the 5th grade, students should know that

▶ Waves, wind, water, and ice shape and reshape the earth's land surface by eroding rock and soil in some areas and depositing them in other areas, sometimes in seasonal layers.

▶ Rock is composed of different combinations of minerals. Smaller rocks come from the breakage and weathering of bedrock and larger rocks. Soil is made partly from weathered rock, partly from plant remains—and also contains many living organisms. ■

Grades 6 through 8

At this level, students are able to complete most of their understanding of the main features of the physical and biological factors that shape the face of the earth. This understanding will still be descriptive because the theory of plate tectonics will not be encountered formally until high school. Of course, students should see as great a variety of landforms and soils as possible.

It is especially important that students come to understand how sedimentary rock is formed periodically, embedding plant and animal remains and leaving a record of the sequence in which the plants and animals appeared and disappeared. Besides the relative age of the rock layers, the absolute age of those remains is central to the argument that there has been enough time for evolution of species. The process of sedimentation is understandable and observable. But imagining the span of geologic time will be difficult for students.

By the end of the 8th grade, students should know that

▶ The interior of the earth is hot. Heat flow and movement of material within the earth cause earthquakes and volcanic eruptions and create mountains and ocean basins. Gas and dust from large volcanoes can change the atmosphere.

▶ Some changes in the earth's surface are abrupt (such as earthquakes and volcanic eruptions) while other changes happen very slowly (such as uplift and wearing down of mountains). The earth's surface is shaped in part by the motion of water and wind over very long times, which act to level mountain ranges.

▶ Sediments of sand and smaller particles (sometimes containing the remains of organisms) are gradually buried and are cemented together by dissolved minerals to form solid rock again.

▶ Sedimentary rock buried deep enough may be reformed by pressure and heat, perhaps melting and recrystallizing into different kinds of rock. These re-formed rock layers may be forced up again to become land surface and even mountains. Subsequently, this new rock too will erode. Rock bears evidence of the minerals, temperatures, and forces that created it.

▶ Thousands of layers of sedimentary rock confirm the long history of the changing surface of the earth and the changing life forms whose remains are found in successive layers. The youngest layers are not always found on top, because of folding, breaking, and uplift of layers.

▶ Although weathered rock is the basic component of soil, the composition and texture of soil and its fertility and resistance to erosion are greatly influenced by plant roots and debris, bacteria, fungi, worms, insects, rodents, and other organisms.

▶ Human activities, such as reducing the amount of forest cover, increasing the amount and variety of chemicals released into the atmosphere, and intensive farming, have changed the earth's land, oceans, and atmosphere. Some of these changes have decreased the capacity of the environment to support some life forms. ■

Grades 9 through 12

The thrust of study should now turn to modern explanations for the phenomena the students have learned descriptively and to consideration of the effects that human activities have on the earth's surface. Knowledge of radioactivity helps them understand how rocks can be dated, which helps them appreciate the scale of geologic time.

By the end of the 12th grade, students should know that

▶ Plants alter the earth's atmosphere by removing carbon dioxide from it, using the carbon to make sugars and releasing oxygen. This process is responsible for the oxygen content of the air.

▶ The formation, weathering, sedimentation, and reformation of rock constitute a continuing "rock cycle" in which the total amount of material stays the same as its forms change.

▶ The slow movement of material within the earth results from heat flowing out from the deep interior and the action of gravitational forces on regions of different density.

▶ The solid crust of the earth--including both the continents and the ocean basins--consists of separate plates that ride on a denser, hot, gradually deformable layer of the earth. The crust sections move very slowly, pressing against one another in some places, pulling apart in other places. Ocean-floor plates may slide under continental plates, sinking deep into the earth. The surface layers of these plates may fold, forming mountain ranges.

▶ Earthquakes often occur along the boundaries between colliding plates, and molten rock from below creates pressure that is released by volcanic eruptions, helping to build up mountains. Under the ocean basins, molten rock may well up between separating plates to create new ocean floor. Volcanic activity along the ocean floor may form undersea mountains, which can thrust above the ocean's surface to become islands. ■

Standards for history have generated much controversy. Liberals battle conservatives over what is important about the past. During the Reagan-Bush era, conservative Diane Ravitch, then assistant U.S. Secretary of Education, funded a project to set history standards. She later became a vocal critic of those standards when they were first released in 1994. Ravitch and others charged that the standards were anti-American, that important figures like George Washington were given short shrift, and that too much attention was given to America's sins against minorities (Diegmuller, 1996).

Liberals responded that previous views of history had whitewashed American treatment of African-

Table 8.2   Sample Section from *Expectations of Excellence: Curriculum Standards for the Social Studies*

Social studies programs should include experiences that provide for the study of *culture and cultural diversity*, so that the learner can:

Early Grades	Middle Grades	High School
a. Explore and describe similarities and differences in the ways groups, societies, and cultures address similar human needs and concerns.	a. Compare similarities and differences in the ways groups, societies, and cultures meet human needs and concerns.	a. Analyze and explain the ways groups, societies, and cultures address human needs and concerns.
b. Give examples of how experiences may be interpreted differently by people from diverse cultural perspectives and frames of references.	b. Explain how information and experiences may be interpreted by people from diverse cultural perspectives and frames of reference.	b. Predict how data and experiences may be interpreted by people from diverse cultural perspectives and frames of reference.
c. Describe ways in which language, stories, folktales, music, and artistic creations serve as expressions of culture and influence behavior of people living in a particular culture.	c. Explain and give examples of how language, literature, the arts, architecture, other artifacts, traditions, beliefs, values, and behaviors contribute to the development and transmission of culture.	c. Apply an understanding of culture as an integrated whole that explains the functions and interactions of language, literature, the arts, traditions, beliefs and values, and behavior patterns.
d. Compare ways in which people from different cultures think about and deal with their physical environment and social conditions.	d. Explain why individuals and groups respond differently to their physical and social environments and/or changes to them on the basis of shared assumptions, values, and beliefs.	d. Compare and analyze societal patterns for preserving and transmitting culture while adapting to environmental or social change.
e. Give examples and describe the importance of cultural unity and diversity within and across groups.	e. Articulate the implications of cultural diversity, as well as cohesion, within and across groups.	e. Demonstrate the value of cultural diversity, as well as cohesion, within and across groups.
		f. Interpret patterns of behavior reflecting values and attitudes that contribute or pose obstacles to cross-cultural understanding.
		g. Construct reasoned judgments about specific cultural responses to persistent human issues.
		h. Explain and apply ideas, theories, and modes of inquiry drawn from anthropology and sociology in the examination of persistent issues and social problems.

Source: From National Council for the Social Studies, 1994, p. 33

Americans, Native Americans, Japanese-Americans, and others and that it was time to face the truth about ourselves. They argued that in order to forge a more inclusive and genuine democracy, we need to learn from our past mistakes. If we do not understand what really happened in history, we are less able to make wise decisions today.

The University of California at Los Angeles' National Center for History in the Schools, the group overseeing the standards process, came under heated and prolonged attack by conservatives wishing to maintain their hegemony over the history curriculum. So intense was the criticism that the center agreed to revise the standards once more. The new revised standards, released in 1996, scaled back the attention given to minorities and women and reinstated parts of the traditional curriculum. George Washington, for example, is back. Refer to Table 8.3 for a sample comparison of the two sets of standards.

Table 8.3   **National History Standards, Round Two**

The Standard: Massive immigration after 1870 and how new social patterns, conflicts, and ideas of national unity developed amid growing cultural diversity.

Original Version	Revised Version
Students should be able to demonstrate understanding of the sources and experiences of the new immigrants by:	*The student understands the sources and experiences of the new immigrants. Therefore, the student is able to:*
• Distinguishing between the "old" and "new" immigration in terms of its volume and the newcomers' ethnicity, religion, language, and place of origin. (Analyze multiple causation)	• Distinguish between the "old" and the "new" immigration in terms of its volume and the immigrants' ethnicity, religion, language, place of origin, and motives for emigrating from their homelands. (Analyze multiple causation)
• Tracing the patterns of immigrant settlements in different regions of the country. (Reconstruct patterns of historical succession and duration)	• Trace patterns of immigrant settlement in different regions of the country and how new immigrants helped produce a composite American culture that transcended group boundaries. (Reconstruct patterns of historical succession and duration)
• Analyzing the obstacles, opportunities, and contributions of different immigrant groups. (Evidence historical perspectives)	• Assess the challenges, opportunities, and contributions of different immigrant groups. (Examine historical perspectives)
• Evaluating how Catholic and Jewish newcomers responded to discrimination and internal divisions in their new surroundings. (Obtain historical data)	• Evaluate how Catholic and Jewish immigrants responded to religious discrimination. (Obtain historical data)
	• Evaluate the role of public and parochial schools in integrating immigrants into the American mainstream (Analyze cause-and-effect relationships)

Source: After Diegmuller, 1996, p. 14.

Ravitch and other critics applauded the changes. Gary Nash, the UCLA history professor in charge of the project, declared himself pleased with the outcome and pleased with the broader consensus behind the revisions. However, as minority groups continue to increase their power within the American political system, we are likely to engage in continued contentious debates about whose history should be taught in the public schools.

Foreign Language

As the world increasingly evolves into a "global village," the study of foreign language is gaining greater importance. Foreign language teaching has waxed and waned in popularity over this century, with a peak just before the 1920s and a trough in the 1970s. Currently, approximately 66 percent of American high school students enroll in at least one foreign language course, according to a U.S. Department of Education transcript study. It is likely that as corporations become ever more multinational and as more immigrants move into the United States, the

study of foreign language will continue to increase in importance.

Until the 1960s, the dominant goal in foreign language classes was to develop the ability to read the language, and speaking and listening were almost totally disregarded. With the advent at that time of the *audiolingual method,* in which students listened and responded to audiotaped conversations, conversational fluency developed into an important goal and language labs sprang up all over the country. The audiolingual method has faded from view in recent years, but current thinking on foreign languages still emphasizes reading, writing, speaking, and listening and focuses more on what learners can do with the language than on what they know about the language. In addition to the usual lessons on grammar and pronunciation, more emphasis is being placed today on cultural awareness.

Most districts offer language study beginning in the junior high years, with most serious study occurring in high school. The trend, however, is to begin the study of a second language earlier in the elementary grades. The most common languages studied are Spanish, French, and German, but many schools are expanding their offerings to include Russian, Chinese, and Japanese.

The Arts

Arts education, including visual arts, dance, drama, and music, has always taken a back seat to the more "rigorous" academic disciplines. Because of its stepchild status, funding for art in schools has consistently been unreliable: the last to be included and the first to go when funding cuts must be made. In the face of this uncertainty, arts educators have gone on the offensive to make the case that art is vital to educating American students.

They advance several arguments. First, arts educators assert that art is important in and of itself. After all, the achievement and impact of the arts throughout history is undeniable. Further, the arts link imagination with life's most profound questions: Who am I? What should I do? Where am I going? Learning how human beings have responded to those questions artistically over time and across cultures, and gaining proficiency in the artistic tools needed to answer those questions oneself, are necessary to understanding life and to living it fully. In addition, the arts are used for multiple purposes in our society, including presenting issues, persuading, entertaining, decorating, and designing. Becoming literate in the arts helps young people better understand and execute these activities (National Committee for Standards in the Arts, 1994). Interestingly, the new English language arts standards now include communication in the visual arts as a fundamental goal.

For many people, arts advocates' final claim is the clincher: Evidence is mounting that artistic experience helps boost academic achievement and other important school outcomes (Hanna, 1992). For example, an elementary school in a very low-income area in the Bronx emphasizes the arts throughout its curriculum and has seen attendance and achievement shoot up way beyond other schools in the neighborhood. Students participating in a special program at Los Angeles' Music Center "improved their written and oral communication, their grades in academic subjects, and their problem-solving skills" (Hanna, 1992, p. 603). Sampson County, North Carolina, injected a strong arts emphasis into its curriculum and saw test scores rise 2 years in a row. Finally, the arts appear to contribute to desegregation efforts in positive ways, fostering increased cross-racial interaction and friendship.

Although offering intriguing possibilities, these arts-intensive programs are rare. More typically, elementary teachers are responsible for infusing some visual arts and music into their curriculum, such as singing holiday songs, drawing a picture based on a story that has just been read, or working in clay. Art training becomes more specialized, more rigorous, and available to fewer students in secondary schools. Students who sing or play musical instruments can participate in an *a cappella* choir or marching band, those who can draw take art classes and present student exhibitions, those with a dramatic flair get involved in producing and acting in plays.

Even the arts can generate political controversy. Several Jewish students around the country have challenged school choirs for an overemphasis on Christian music. Most schools have Christmas programs each December, and Christian music figures prominently, but even in spring concerts, religious music often predominates. Jewish and other non-Christian students charge that this practice violates their religious beliefs and argue that all music performed in public schools should be secular in order to protect everyone's religious freedom. Christian groups and others, on the other hand, maintain that most choral music is Christian and that it is very difficult to create a nonsectarian repertoire. To date, most courts have agreed with the Christian argument that since most choral music comes out of a Christian tradition, a preponderance of Christian music in public school choirs does not violate the rights of minority religious groups. The only caveat has been to make students aware of this before they enroll in choir.

Arts educators have also recently published new standards for dance, theater, music, and visual arts education (National Committee for Standards in the Arts, 1994). These standards spell out what all students ought to know and be able to do at various grade levels. Figure 8.4 displays the five basic standards for arts education.

Physical and Health Education

Surveys show that American students' fitness is subpar. For example, according to the National Center for Health Statistics, 11 percent of young people (ages 6 to 17) are overweight, whereas only 5 percent were overweight in 1960. Not only are children heavier than in past years, their percentage of body fat is higher (Ross & Pate, 1987). Further, half of all children have at least one cardiovascular disease risk factor (Wheeler, Marcus, Cullen, & Konugres, 1983). Increasing numbers of children are choosing a sedentary lifestyle, and experts blame this trend for the decline in fitness.

Despite these alarming figures, physical education gets little attention in most schools. In many

Figure 8.4 **Standards for Arts Education**

- *Communicate at a basic level in the four arts disciplines*
  Dance, music, theater, and visual arts, including knowledge and skills in the basic vocabularies, materials, tools, and techniques of each discipline.

- *Communicate proficiently in at least one art form*
  The ability to define and solve artistic problems with insight, reason, and technical proficiency.

- *Develop and present basic analyses of works of art*
  Using structural, historical, and cultural perspectives. . .

- *Informed acquaintance with exemplary works of art from a variety of cultures and historical periods*
  Basic understanding of historical development in the arts disciplines, across the arts as a whole, and within cultures.

- *Relate various types of arts knowledge and skills within and across the arts disciplines.*
  Includes mixing and matching competencies and understandings in art-making, history and culture, and analysis.

Source: After The National Committee for Standards in the Arts, 1994, p. 1.

parts of the country, recess time in elementary schools is very brief, and daily physical exercise is not universally available at the secondary level. The PE curriculum at the elementary level may consist simply of letting children play at recess, or it may be more formalized and provide instruction in games and specific physical skills. At the secondary level, the traditional competitive sports like football, baseball, and basketball are available only for a gifted minority of boys and girls. In some high schools, lifelong activities like swimming, biking, aerobics, and golf are offered.

Goals of physical education programs include cardiovascular fitness, abdominal strength, optimizing the proportion of body fat, and overall strength. In addition, social and emotional goals, like cooperation and teamwork, comprise important aspects of the PE curriculum. The current political climate in the United States, which emphasizes academics and economic competitiveness, leads most people to overlook health and fitness issues.

Health topics are often taught in conjunction with PE classes. Health education addresses important issues like nutrition, human anatomy, mental health, substance abuse, sexuality and family life, and disease prevention, including AIDS prevention. The aim of health educators, more than teachers in other subjects, is to change students' attitudes and actively encourage them to adopt more healthy lifestyles. Because of their more action-oriented goals, and because their content can be controversial, health educators often run into political opposition, especially from conservative religious groups. American students' lack of knowledge about sex, AIDS, and other health-related topics may be related to our country's relatively high rates of teen pregnancy, abortion, and venereal disease in comparison with other developed nations. In contrast, Sweden has a compulsory program of sex education, and enjoys the lowest incidence of these problems among industrialized countries (Ryan & Cooper, 1995).

Vocational Education

Primarily associated with high schools, vocational education coursework includes home economics, auto mechanics, word processing, meal management, computer technology, and a host of others. Vocational and career education suffer low status in our educational system and in the larger community. Voc ed has been criticized as being outdated, irrelevant, and a poor way to prepare students for the world of work. Two out of three high school dropouts come from the vocational track, and elementary teachers complain that career awareness takes precious time away from their more central academic lessons. Critics also charge that at the high school level, the quality of teaching is low, as are academic expectations of students. As a further sign of its decline, enrollment in vocational education has slipped in the last decade.

Faced with these criticisms, vocational educators and labor leaders released the report *What Work Requires of Schools* as a way to begin reinvigorating education for the workplace (U.S. Department of Labor, 1991). This report identified competencies and foundational knowledge needed for effective job performance that schools should develop. Effective workers, the report maintained, need to be able to productively use resources like money, time, and staff. They also need interpersonal skills to enable them to participate in workplace teams, to serve customers, and to work well with people from different cultural backgrounds. In addition, they need a firm foundation in basic academic skills like reading, writing, speaking, listening, and mathematics as well as thinking skills like creativity, decision making, and problem solving. Finally, effective workers need personal qualities like responsibility, sociability, self-management, and integrity.

A promising new development is to link high school vocational classes with postsecondary coursework at community colleges. It is hoped that students' academic performance as well as their specific vocational skills, will be enhanced by this collaboration. Another frequent collaboration is between high schools and businesses offering *cooperative education* programs. Similar to apprenticeship programs in Germany, students in cooperative education go to school part time and work at a job part time. The goal is to help students realize how important academic competence is to job success, and in turn to gain practical job skills that will help them after graduation.

Curriculum Trends

Alert readers will likely have noticed certain patterns in this brief treatment of the American curriculum. Most of the new standards released by professional associations are calling for more depth and less breadth, more active engagement by students in their own learning, more interaction, more focus on the unifying principles that give a discipline coherence rather than rote memorization of isolated facts, more student input into the learning process, more emphasis on critical thinking and problem solving, more integration of subject areas, and more attention to diversity as a resource rather than a problem. These principles of teaching, learning, and schooling should by now be familiar to you: They flow from the goals of developing self-regulated learners within a democratic classroom learning community. They are also consistent with the methods of classroom instruction, organization, and management that we discussed in Chapter 6. We outline additional trends here.

Integrating across Disciplines

A continuing debate in American education is between disciplinary specialization (English, mathematics, science, etc.) and interdisciplinary instruction. Proponents of specialization argue that only through years of carefully sequenced instruction can students fully comprehend and master the basic knowledge of any discipline. On the side of specialization are our departmentalized high schools that perpetuate disciplinary boundaries and allegiances. The egg-crate structure and inflexible time schedule of schools also support specialization. Advocates of integration counter that the real world is not divided up into neat disciplinary bundles and that the false borders of the traditional subject areas render them dry, lifeless, and irrelevant to most students. Methods of integrating the curriculum, like problem-based instruction, project-based instruction, thematic instruction, and team teaching have all been proposed as ways to enliven school subjects, make them more coherent and meaningful to students, and better reveal the connections among the disciplines themselves and between the disciplines and real-life problems.

We already described project-based and problem-based instruction, but a brief recap may be in order. While project-based instruction is organized around a particular topic, say Costa Rica, problem-based teaching is organized around a problem. Examples of problems include: What is the relationship between culture and climate? Should wolves be purposely reintroduced into Yellowstone National Park? Should Congress prohibit cigarette smoking? In each case, students need to draw on knowledge from many disciplines in order to develop a solution to the problem. Teachers from different disciplines might alternate teaching lessons designed to provide information helpful in solving the problem. Students then construct solutions to the problem—using reading, writing, scientific, mathematical, and artistic skills—and share these solutions in a variety of media with others.

Thematic instruction is similar to problem- and project-based teaching in that there is a central focus. It differs in that the focus is usually broader and sustained over a longer period of time. For example, a team of high school teachers may use the theme of "war" to organize instruction during a whole year or semester. Students might study the technology of war in physics and chemistry, the mathematics of trajectory and cartography in math, martial music and paintings like Picasso's "Guernica" in art classes, literature with military themes like *The Red Badge of Courage,* and the history of war and peace. Students might run obstacle courses, practice military calisthenics, and develop martial arts skills in PE, and learn gun safety and first aid in vocational education. Young children, in contrast, might study thematic units like "apples" over just a few weeks, making apple sauce, visiting apple orchards, drawing pictures of apples, and reading stories about Johnny Appleseed. The advantage of thematic instruction is the connection that students can make between the different content areas. The disadvantage is that not everything worth teaching fits easily into any given theme.

Finally, simple **team teaching** is the easiest way for teachers to move toward integrating disciplines. If you are a high school English teacher, for example, who plans to teach *All Quiet on the Western Front,* you can consult with the history teacher and

Table 8.4　**National Curriculum Pro and Con**

Pro	Con
There are common areas of knowledge, skills, and values that all citizens should possess.	Unlikely to serve the needs of all students, because they vary in their interests and aptitudes and live in very different localities.
Because all children should have equal chances in life, they should have access to the same educational diet.	May give the impression that other needs of children (emotional and social) do not merit same attention as intellectual needs.
Can set clear objectives for what all students should be able to do . . .	Reinforces a transmission model of teaching and a passive mode of learning.
Enables students to move from one area to another with minimal disruption.	Serves to legitimize certain kinds of knowledge, usually associated with the dominant groups in society, with result that knowledge and values of minority groups are further marginalized.
Helps to promote cultural cohesion . . .	Fosters a top-down approach to decision making antithetical to participatory democracy.
Makes it possible to check on students' progress.	Reduces the professionalism of teachers, because it removes from them many decisions.
Provides state authorities with control over private schools . . .	
Provides a mechanism for making schools more accountable.	

Source: After Kellaghan & Madaus, 1995, pp. 93–94.

coordinate your reading of the novel with her schedule for covering World War I. Or if you are a biology teacher planning to do a unit on genetics, you can coordinate with the math teacher's unit on probability. Team teaching is not restricted to this simple form, but it can certainly start there.

Elementary teachers are at the greatest advantage in their ability to integrate the subject areas, and many resources exist to help them do so. Many authors, for example, have produced lists of children's literature that have to do with particular concepts in mathematics, science, and social studies. Since most elementary teachers are in charge of one group of children for the entire school day, it is a relatively simple matter to link the academic subjects.

A National Curriculum, a National Curriculum War

Another trend is the push for a more unified national curriculum, one driven by standardized national exams. This trend has been fueled in part by the purported low achievement of American students compared with students in other countries, whose curricula are mandated at the national level. We

have seen that these supposed achievement failures are questionable, but many leaders are still persuaded that they are real and that a national curriculum will cure our educational ills. This trend is countered, however, by a strong bias toward local control of schools by boards of education, parents, and teachers. Arguments for and against a national curriculum are summarized in Table 8.4.

Many of the arguments supporting a national curriculum were made at an education summit convened in the spring of 1996 by the governor of Wisconsin. The by-invitation-only meeting, held at a facility owned by IBM, included governors and CEO's of major corporations. A few educators attended as observers. These business and political leaders saw a strong national curriculum as a key part of their educational reform agenda. Much as the Perot commission in Texas, summit participants viewed the nation's educational system as ineffective and believed that imposing and enforcing standards at the national level would boost student achievement. In a speech to the group, President Clinton endorsed the concept of national standards and advocated a system of testing at each of the transition points, that is, from elementary to junior high, and from junior to senior high. Students would be required to pass these tests before they could move on.

Although there was some haggling over the details, everyone at the summit agreed with the notion that a national curriculum was the obvious cure for our educational ills. But outside the summit, this reasoning was vigorously disputed. The Family Research Council, a conservative religious organization, had this to say:

> "The time for debate is over," declared IBM CEO Lou Gerstner at the opening of last week's education summit. Over? Since when? Look at any state in the union and you'll find heated debates over government standards, top-down education policy and—most of all—who controls the children. But parents' side of the debate was not well-represented at the summit, which closed with the passage of a document stating: "The primary purpose of education is to prepare students to flourish in a democratic society and to work successfully in a global economy." Education is no longer for the individual's "good life," as Aristotle put it, but to serve the interests of the Nation and its employers. (cited in Pipho, 1996, p. 701)

As we saw in the Chapter 4 Issue Box on home schooling, members of conservative religious groups want schools to promote students' moral and religious development and view the economic and civic aims of education as base materialism.

Can research shed any light on the effects of a centralized curriculum? Although studies are sparse, there are some indicators. Evidence is mixed regarding the effect of increased academic rigor on student achievement. The American Federation of Teachers (1996) noted that more, stiffer high school graduation requirements implemented in the 1980s resulted in higher percentages of minority students enrolling in advanced courses. Further, students who take a rigorous curriculum are more likely to score higher on the SAT and to go to college.

On the other hand, the Texas experience shows that the curriculum can constrict in response to centralized standards, that content can be reduced to easily tested material, that is, isolated facts and figures rather than conceptual understanding and critical thinking. In addition, evidence from Europe indicates that teachers under a centralized system are more likely to teach the same material, but they are less likely to be student oriented, that is, to be aware of developmental and other individual differences and of the level of student understanding (Stevenson & Baker, 1991). When the United Kingdom made the change from a locally controlled to nationally controlled curriculum, British teachers reported

that bureaucratic demands on their time and their overall workload increased markedly (Osborn, 1991; Silcock, 1992). Teachers found they had to spend more time in planning and record keeping for the system and had correspondingly less time available for lesson preparation. Finally, in a comparison of British teachers before the national system to French teachers who have worked under centralized control for a number of years, researchers found that the French teachers used a much smaller repertoire of strategies and did less to meet individual student needs (Osborn & Broadfoot, 1992).

Battles over a national curriculum in America will continue to rage, pitting advocates of local versus national control, professional versus community control, liberal versus conservative, and secular versus religious perspectives. The national curriculum debate inflames passions around the fundamental question: Who will control the children? Where do you stand on this issue? How will this controversy affect your life in the classroom?

CURRICULUM CHOICES

Teachers participate in curriculum decision making in several ways. First, of course, they select the curriculum for their own classrooms. They also serve on school grade-level or subject-matter teams that collaborate on curriculum for their school. They may also serve on district or statewide committees that develop curriculum frameworks, specify core curricula, or select textbooks, videos, and other materials. As the current trend to integrate disciplines gains strength, teachers will have even more say about designing curriculum for their own schools. Finally, they may also work with professional organizations at the national level to reform and update curriculum within their own specialty areas. Understanding how to evaluate curricular options, then, is a critical teaching skill.

Choosing What to Teach

As we discussed, teachers have many resources to draw on as they make curriculum decisions. The nation's educational goals, standards set by professional associations, state and district curriculum guides, and textbooks help create a basic framework for decision making. In addition, teachers' knowledge of students, that is, students' background knowledge, developmental level, interests, and needs, is another key consideration. Further, in developing students' abilities to regulate their own learning and to build a democratic classroom community, teachers must negotiate content decisions appropriately with students. Teachers need to continuously reflect on the amount and kind of input that students are asked to make and to revise these upward as students mature. Of course, teachers' own knowledge of the subjects under study cannot be underestimated.

Finally, many teachers mentally test their learning goals as they plan their curriculum. They imagine what their response would be if a student asked, as they so often do, "Why do we have to learn this?" If the only answer teachers can come up with is that it's on the test, or that you need to know it to get into college, then the intrinsic value of the material is immediately suspect. Any topic worth studying should be connected to important long-term goals, such as effective citizenship, workplace success, inter- or intrapersonal efficacy, personal fulfillment, ethical development, wise parenting, or the public good.

Selecting Curriculum Materials

We have referred a number of times to the important role that materials—texts, videos, posters, realia, and so forth—play in establishing the curriculum. We have also criticized the frequent lack of training of those responsible for selecting these materials. What should you look for when choosing curriculum materials? Although this important job will receive more attention later in your teacher education program, Figure 8.5 offers an overview of the criteria for making choices about curriculum materials.

Supplementing the Curriculum

No matter how carefully textbooks have been chosen or how precisely the core curriculum is followed, there will be a need to supplement the curriculum. Curriculum frameworks are simply guidelines and will always require fleshing out to put them into practice. In particular, teachers need to pay special attention to circumventing bias and to integrating nontraditional materials in their classrooms.

Circumventing Bias

What can teachers do to ameliorate the problem of bias in texts? One very important step is to supplement the curriculum with unbiased materials. If the adopted textbook does not include people of color or women, then teachers need to find additional materials that do. Further, when teachers make presentations, they need to supply examples and illustrations from a variety of cultures. Finding such materials and examples often demands great initiative. One resource is practitioner journals, such as *Instructor, Arithmetic Teacher, Art Education,* and *So-*

Figure 8.5   **Curriculum Materials Evaluation Criteria**

- *Publication and cost.*
  Were the materials field tested? Is the cost reasonable?

- *Physical properties.*
  Are the materials aesthetically pleasing? Are they durable?

- *Content.*
  Is the approach used consistent with the district's curriculum? Are the materials free of bias and reflect contributions of diverse groups? Do the materials teach to multiple goals?

- *Instructional properties.*
  Will the materials be clearly understood by the students who will be using them? Does publisher provide any data attesting to materials' instructional effectiveness? Is the writing clear? Are examples used appropriately? Are pictures and diagrams used in appropriate ways to support learning?

Source: After Gall, 1981, pp. 118–129.

cial Studies. These provide much helpful information. For example, the February 1991 issue of *Arithmetic Teacher* described a unit on the geometry concept "tesselation" taught through Native American art forms. Associations devoted to multicultural education are also good sources of information for redressing bias in the curriculum. For example, Interracial Books for Children, based in New York, regularly publishes bulletins about multicultural resources in literature and history for elementary through adult education.

Another way teachers can address bias in the curriculum is to raise the issue directly with students. Students themselves can analyze materials for bias and share their findings with peers. Class discussions can focus on the emotional impact of various forms of bias, on the political conditions that give rise to bias, or on action that can be taken to correct it.

You may discover other ways to circumvent bias as you assume classroom responsibilities. Table 8.5 lists the forms curriculum bias can take. It is important to remember that whatever means you choose, circumventing bias is a critical teaching skill. From the eyes of young black students, a curriculum lacking black faces tells them that they do not count, and it conveys the same message to students of other groups. As teachers in a pluralistic democracy,

Table 8.5 **Forms of Curriculum Bias**

Invisibility	Groups excluded from the curricula become invisible to students.
Stereotyping	Groups are portrayed in traditional, limited ways. For example, texts that depict African Americans only as servants, Asians as laundry workers, Chicanos as migrant workers, women as passive and dependent, or men in terms only of their careers.
Imbalance and selectivity	Only one aspect of a complex situation is portrayed. Often "dirty laundry" is left out: female suffrage is mentioned without reference to the preceding years of struggle, or treaties with and protection of Native Americans without reference to broken treaties and misappropriated lands.
Unreality	Presenting unrealistic picture of society.
Fragmentation	A box is inserted here or a bulletin board there, rather than integrating information in a coherent way. When material about disadvantaged groups is isolated like this, it conveys the impression that their experiences are a mere sidelight to the "real" story, i.e., that of the dominant group.
Linguistic bias	Language is used in ways that stereotype. For example, Native Americans may *roam* and *wander* whereas Europeans *explore* and *settle;* immigrants groups may be *hordes* or *swarms.*

Source: After Sadker & Sadker, 1995, p. 195.

we cannot send such a message to any group of students. You can read more about curriculum bias in the accompanying Research Box.

Nontraditional Materials

Even if all your textbooks were free of bias, you would still need to supplement them with additional types of materials. As we discussed in Chapter 6, textbook-based, teacher-directed forms of instruction are inadequate by themselves. Teachers need a repertoire of teaching strategies in order to effectively help students learn. By the same token, teachers need a variety of materials in order to effectively help students learn. Manipulatives in math, rock samples and drosophila in science, political documents and cultural artifacts in social studies—these

are all examples of materials teachers can and should take advantage of as they instruct students. As you think through the materials you can use to augment your teaching, be sure to think broadly. Are there people and places within the community, for instance, which can be utilized? Grandparents make great resources for oral history projects, and the vacant lot next to the high school could become a terrific ecology lab.

Of special importance are technological tools. Teachers can use the internet to gain access to a new world of materials. Students can use email to query students in other parts of the world about their country and culture; they can access government and university databases to download information about the weather or the environment; they can use telnet to explore documents at the Library of Congress. A special bonus for teachers is *AskERIC,* a question-and-answer service accessed through email on the internet. ERIC is a national educational information and research database, and teachers can email AskERIC with questions about learning, teaching strategies, management, and other concerns. AskERIC's email address is: askeric@ericir.syr.edu.

You can also use technology to assist students with disabilities. For example, a new set of computer games have been developed that help young children overcome dyslexia and other language impairments. The computer slows the speed of ordinary speech to help the student discriminate sounds. Using colorful and whimsical animation, the game requires students to release a button when they hear a change in sound. As they get better, the speed increases until it approaches normal speech. Evaluation of the games at Rutgers University found that after one month, students advanced 2 years in language development and later had fewer difficulties in learning to read.

SUMMARY

- Curriculum constitutes the content of teaching. Curricula can be classified as official, operational, extra, null, and hidden.
- National influences on the curriculum come from the federal government, professional associations, social and political movements, publishing companies, and national testing.
- State departments of education and legislatures exert curriculum influence at the state level.

Bias in Curriculum Materials

As we continue to emphasize, it is important for teachers to believe in the potential of all students and to create a classroom environment conducive to learning for all students. One task teachers must execute in constructing such a classroom is to reduce bias in curriculum materials.

Researchers have examined bias for many years, primarily tracing changes in stereotyping and other expressions of racism in textbooks. Garcia (1993), for example, reviewed a number of studies that showed how the portrayal of African Americans and other minority groups in school texts has changed since the nineteenth century. Two hundred years ago, if texts mentioned black people at all, it was to show them as gay and foolish, in need of protection by whites. African Americans were presented as useful servants. Later, as the Ku Klux Klan came into power, blacks were seen as menacing and dangerous. Similarly, the portrayal of Native Americans and Latin Americans was disdainful. Native Americans were sometimes described as brave but more often as cruel, vengeful, and barbarous. One author said:

> The creoles have all the bad qualities of the Spaniards from whom they descended, without the courage, firmness, and patience which makes the praiseworthy part of the Spanish character. Naturally weak and effeminate, they dedicate the greatest part of their lives to loitering and inactive pleasures. (Elson, 1964, p. 156)

Nineteenth century authors also made distinctions among the various European ethnic groups, favoring those from northern Europe. A typical geography book published in 1844 had this to say about different nationalities:

> The Dutch are honest, patient, and persevering; and remarkable for their industry, frugality, and neatness... The Irish in general are quick of apprehension, brave, and hospitable; but passionate, ignorant, vain and superstitious... The Italians are affable and polite; and excel in music, painting, sculpture; but they are effeminate, superstitious, slavish and revengeful... The English are intelligent, brave, industrious and enterprising ... (cited in Garcia, 1993, p. 30)

Such racism and ethnic stereotyping continued into the twentieth century. Even in the 1940s, the American Council on Education found textbooks harmful to positive relations between different groups.

Things began to change with the advent of the civil rights movement. Beginning in the 1960s, authors and publishers started inserting more information, both in text and visuals, about minority groups and women. Progress, however, was uneven. Marcus (1961), for example, studied the treatment of Jews and African Americans in 48 books used in the 1950s and 1960s. He found that some, but not all, publishers had reduced stereotyping and increased coverage of minorities. Kane replicated Marcus' study in 1970 and concluded that books had improved but that relatively few gains had been made by Asians, Chicanos, Puerto Ricans, and Native Americans.

RESEARCH

Continued

The picture has continued to improve, albeit slowly, through the 1980s and 1990s. A vexing problem has been how much to say about which groups. Many groups have contributed to America, and as we have noted, making decisions about which groups to cover, which events, and in how much depth is not easy. In his review, Garcia concluded that overall breadth of treatment has improved, but depth is sorely lacking.

Some educators question whether such changes are a good thing. If authors add content about Native Americans, say, then the coverage of something else will have to decline proportionately. We described the recent attempt to adjust the history curriculum to make it more inclusive and the resulting storm of controversy. Sure, the critics seemed to say, put more stuff in the book about Frederick Douglass, but do not touch George Washington, Thomas Edison, or any of the other figures traditionally included in American history courses. Teachers realize, however, that time is a limited commodity, and the decision to include one topic means that another must go. If Americans are to change their treatment of history, then, to include more of the experiences of minorities and less of the experiences of the majority, they must have good reason to do so. What are those reasons?

First, of course, are simply our values. As a pluralistic nation, and in the interests of historical accuracy, we must give credit to all the peoples who have forged our nation. As one nation within a diverse world, we must also recognize the achievements as well as the problems of other groups. As a society that values democracy, we have an obligation to give voice to all members of the polity. We do young people a disservice if we convey the impression that the only ones who count in this world are members of the wealthy white male elite. Further, a biased curriculum alienates marginalized groups and fractures the cohesiveness and shared values needed to maintain democracy.

As important as our guiding principles are as a nation, also important is the impact curriculum materials have on students' attitudes. There is evidence that multicultural curricula can reduce racism and sexism (Banks, 1995). For example, Katz and Zalk (1978) employed a 15-minute intervention involving stories about African Americans and found the prejudice of second- and fourth-grade white students was reduced. Surprisingly, this reduced prejudice was sustained for at least 6 months. Research spanning from the 1940s through the 1970s has shown that reading stories, viewing films, or learning the history of minorities can result in prejudice reduction. By the same token, curricula that ignore or stereotype minorities, or portray nondemocratic values, tend to sustain prejudice. The evidence for gender bias is much the same. Exposure in school to nonstereotypical roles for women and men can expand students' sense of what both males and females can accomplish; this effect is stronger for girls than it is for boys (Banks, 1995).

What does curriculum bias look like? Table 8.5 (p. 261) summarized the different forms of bias. Be on the lookout for these as you review texts and other materials.

- Local curriculum control is exercised by districts, administrators, parents, students, and most important, teachers.

- Hegemony refers to the domination of one group by another. Many charge that the U.S. curriculum is a vehicle for hegemonic control and serves to sustain the power of a white, male, Christian, economic elite.

- Most other nations have a more centralized curriculum than the United States. Several have stronger working relationships with business. International curriculum trends include a greater emphasis on integrating disciplines and problem-based curricula.

- Fundamental to the acquisition of literacy is the creation of a literate environment within the classroom, one that links reading and writing, develops comprehension strategies, balances skill-based with meaning-based approaches, and utilizes a variety of texts.

- Basic goals in math are to educate students to value math, reason mathematically, communicate about math, solve problems, and develop a sense of mathematical competence.

- Science educators believe that science teaching should focus on the central ideas within each discipline, scientific reasoning and problem-solving processes, and integrating science with math and technology.

- The primary purpose of social studies is to help young people develop the ability to make informed and reasoned decisions for the public good as citizens of a culturally diverse, democratic society in an interdependent world.

- The importance of foreign language is likely to increase as we move into the twenty-first century. Current thinking on foreign language learning emphasizes the ability to speak and listen as well as to read the new language.

- New arts standards mandate that all students acquire basic proficiency in visual arts, music, dance, and drama and, in addition, develop advanced proficiency in one of these four areas.

- American children's health and fitness appear to be on the decline, but this issue has taken a back seat to academics. PE goals include strength, cardiovascular fitness, cooperation, and teamwork.

- Trends in curriculum include increasing the emphasis on student-centered instruction, problem-based learning, and interdisciplinary teaching. Counterposed to these trends is the highly controversial push to establish and test for attainment of a national curriculum.

- Teachers rely on a variety of resources to help them make curriculum choices. Among these are their own knowledge of their subjects and of their students, curriculum guides, and student input.

- Teachers need to supplement the curriculum for at least two reasons: to reduce bias and to augment instruction with nontraditional materials.

Readings for the Professional

Hollins, E.R. *Transforming Curriculum for a Culturally Diverse Society.* Mahwah, NJ: Lawrence Erlbaum Associates, Inc., 1996.
This book is a compilation of essays by many authors who discuss curriculum and diversity from many perspectives. It will give you a thorough grounding in multicultural approaches to thinking about curriculum issues.

Maurer, R.E., and A.M. Dorner. *Designing Interdisciplinary Curriculum in Middle, Junior High, and High Schools.* Needham Heights, MA: Allyn & Bacon, 1994.
This is a practical guide for developing integrated curriculum in secondary education. Included are several successful interdisciplinary curricula currently in use at many schools around the United States.

Posner, G.J. *Course Design: A Guide to Curriculum Development for Teachers.* New York: Longman, 1997.
This is the basic book for curriculum development, a must for your professional library. Takes you through the basics of curriculum development.

PART III

Teachers and Their Work

Application and Portfolio Activities

Self-Assessments

You and the Standards 266

Assessing Your Workplace Skills 267

Observations

Making Textbook Selections 268

Observing for School Effectiveness 269

Interviews

Teachers' Curriculum Decisions 271

Perceptions about the Effectiveness of Schools ... 272

You and the Standards

Purpose What are the cutting-edge goals in your intended teaching field? How well will you be able to teach to those standards? The purpose of this exercise is to help you find out.

Directions Obtain the current goals and standards published by the professional association in your subject area. If you are a prospective elementary teacher, obtain standards for either mathematics or language arts. Your college's curriculum library will likely stock these documents, or you can contact the relevant association directly. (Names and numbers are in Appendix D.) Read the standards carefully. Write a page summarizing the standards and assessing their strengths and weaknesses.

Reflection How do you feel about the standards in your area? Are they good? Why or why not? Do you feel comfortable with the prospect of teaching to these standards? Why or why not? Are there particular standards you strongly agree or disagree with? If you do have any strong negative feelings, how will you manage these feelings in the classroom? Is it more ethical to violate your personal feelings and teach the standards, or the other way around? How has this exercise informed your decision about whether to pursue a teaching career?

Assessing Your Workplace Skills

Purpose   We stressed in Chapter 7 that new conceptions of schools as organizations focus on their communitylike characteristics. Workplace skills in such settings center on abilities to foster a community atmosphere. The purpose of this self-assessment is to gauge your current level of such workplace skills.

Directions   Mark the response that you think best estimates your skill level in each area below.

Skill	Level of Competence		
	High	**Medium**	**Low**
Developing cooperative interaction with colleagues			
Observing fellow teachers	_____	_____	_____
Discussing educational issues	_____	_____	_____
Working in teams	_____	_____	_____
Developing collegiality with administrators			
Meeting with principal	_____	_____	_____
Informing principal of classroom work	_____	_____	_____
Inviting principal to observe class	_____	_____	_____
Developing collegiality with parents			
Reporting class activities to them	_____	_____	_____
Holding conferences	_____	_____	_____
Using parents as helpers	_____	_____	_____
Developing rapport with students			
Involving students as appropriate in class decisions	_____	_____	_____
Establishing warm relations with them	_____	_____	_____

Reflection   What do you consider your areas of strength and weakness? Should you decide to pursue teaching, how might you go about improving your weak areas?

Making Textbook Selections

Purpose Teachers and many others are involved in selecting materials in the classroom. What does this process look like in action? How do these decisions affect teachers' daily working lives? The purpose of this activity is to help illuminate these issues.

Directions Find out from the local school or district when a textbook selection committee is to meet. Obtain permission to attend as an onlooker. Take notes on the discussion and decisions. What issues do they discuss? Who seems to wield the most influence? What is their rationale for the decisions they make?

Reflection How well did the committee's discussion reflect best practice? (Refer to the guidelines in Chapter 8.) If you had been a member of this committee, what would you change about their discussion? If you were a teacher in this school or district, how would their decisions have affected your professional life?

Observing for School Effectiveness

Purpose   How does one recognize an effective school? Chapter 7 presented research that has shed some light on this important question. As you interview for a job or as you select a school for your own children, it will be important for you to be able to gauge a school's effectiveness. This exercise gives you the opportunity to develop that skill.

Directions   Spend a half day visiting a school. Observe in several classrooms, the library, cafeteria, outdoor areas, teachers' lounge, and any others that pique your interest. Read flyers posted on bulletin boards and newsletters sent home to parents. Peek over students' shoulders and observe the work they are doing. Make a check below for each of the characteristics of effective schools that you observe, and then make a note about what you saw that led you to this conclusion under the column "Evidence." For example, if you see student work displayed, then you would check "Public rewards and incentives," and write under "Evidence" that student work was displayed.

Attribute	Present	Evidence
Social Organization		
Clear academic goals	_____	_____
Clear behavioral goals	_____	_____
Order and discipline	_____	_____
Teacher efficacy	_____	_____
Pervasive caring	_____	_____
Public rewards and incentives	_____	_____
Administrative leadership	_____	_____
Community support	_____	_____
Instruction and Curriculum		
High academic learning time	_____	_____
Homework monitored	_____	_____
Student progress monitored	_____	_____

Attribute	Present	Evidence
Coherently organized curriculum	_____	_____
Variety of teaching strategies	_____	_____
Opportunities for student responsibility	_____	_____

Reflection Although research shows the above characteristics to be associated with effective schools, they are still controversial. What is your impression of the validity of these attributes? Did you think that what you observed at this school was contributing to student achievement? Think back to your own schooling—to what extent were such characteristics present, and did they contribute to student learning? How intent do you think you will be to find a job only in a school that demonstrates these attributes?

Teachers' Curriculum Decisions

Purpose   As we emphasized in Chapter 8, making decisions about curriculum is an enormously important part of a teacher's job. How do teachers really go about this task? Gaining insight into this process will help you become more skillful when you become a teacher.

Directions   Interview a teacher at the grade level or in the subject area you plan to teach. How does he or she go about making curriculum choices? What does he or she think about? Does he or she consider the textbook? Students' knowledge or interests? Curriculum guides? Professional association standards? What resources does he or she find most useful in making decisions about the content of instruction?

Reflection   What resources do you imagine you will find most useful in making curriculum decisions? You can start now to build your professional library to include such resources. Speculate on how your curriculum decision-making process might change as you develop from novice to expert.

Perceptions about the Effectiveness of Schools

Purpose

How accurate are the general public's understandings about the strengths and weaknesses of our nation's schools? Community attitudes affect not only teacher morale but also decisions made by schools boards, state governments and beyond. The purpose of this exercise is to help you become more familiar with how the average person views schools.

Directions

Interview two or three people using the questions below as a guide. Try to vary the kind of people you interview—by age, gender, occupation, socioeconomic status, race, neighborhood of residence. After the interview, share with them the information from the text to correct any misapprehensions they may harbor.

1. What is your sense of the level of achievement of American students?

2. What do you think are American schools' biggest problems?

3. What do you think American schools are especially good at?

4. Do you have children in school yourself? When was the last time you visited a school?

Reflection

How accurate were your interviewees in their assessment of the quality of American schools? Compare your responses with other teacher candidates'. Do you notice any patterns based on age, gender, parental status, or other factors? How do you think the educational community should respond to misconceptions? How do you think these attitudes will affect your professional life?

Relationships between Schools and Society

This book looked first at you as a person, at your needs, goals, and motivations and how these relate to the world and work of teaching. It extended this view outward and examined in some depth the classrooms and schools in which you will be working. Part IV expands this framework further still to examine the larger social, legal, and governmental contexts surrounding schools and classrooms and to consider the impact of these larger social forces on teaching. We begin with a brief look at the school-society bond and at five unique features of American education that characterize this 350-year relationship. Following this overview is a more detailed look at how these five features evolved into today's modern school system.

FEATURES OF AMERICAN EDUCATION

Schools rest on societal beliefs about what learning is most important, who should be educated, and how education should be conducted. The introduction to Part II discussed the influence of society's purposes and values on American classrooms and the teaching practices therein. The introduction to Part III used this same school-society connection to analyze how the school and its curriculum have been organized and how these have changed over time to reflect changing societal conditions and values. This introduction shows once again that much of what goes on in classrooms and schools is the result of the larger social, economic, and political forces in our society. These invisible forces both surround and penetrate schools and classrooms, shaping the perceptions, goals, and behaviors of everyone connected to them. Specifically, they have created a unique system of schooling characterized by five features: local control of education, public education, a secular orientation to education, a comprehensive school system with competing purposes, and universal education. A word about each of these features follows.

Local Control of Education   Unlike many countries, such as Great Britain, France, and China, which have national and unified educational systems, the American system of education has rested on the premise that schools should be controlled and directed mainly by local communities. This idea emerged in the colonies and resulted in quite different systems of education in the northern, middle, and southern colonies. The idea of local control was subsequently extended into the nineteenth and twentieth centuries and remains an important if sometimes debatable feature of today's system.

Public Education   The colonists brought with them from Europe the concept of private education and a belief that education was mainly the province of society's elite. This view changed dramatically in the years following the American Revolution. The common school movement in the early nineteenth century advocated a system of public schools, paid for by local and state governments. As with local control of schools, debates about the benefits of public versus private education remain active as we approach the twenty-first century.

A Secular Orientation to Education   The colonists, particularly the Puritan communities of New England, viewed education as a religious tool. Salvation depended on one's ability to read the Bible. However, in its attempt to ensure individual liberty, the Constitution established political mechanisms that separated most church and government functions. Subsequently, schools in the United States, more than in other Western European countries, took on a secular orientation. This secularism, first articulated in the late eighteenth and early nineteenth centuries, has continued to the present day. However, debates still occur regarding such issues as how to deal with religious holidays, when to allow prayer in schools, and whether or not to use public monies to support religiously affiliated schools.

A Comprehensive School System with Competing Purposes   Many countries have multitrack educational systems. Students who are preparing for college go to one type of school, and students preparing for vocations go to another type. Issues related to a multitrack system of education were heatedly debated during the late nineteenth and early twentieth centuries. From this debate grew a uniquely American creation—comprehensive schools—in which chil-

Table P4.1 **Features of American Education and When Each Emerged**

Educational Feature	Historical Period
Public education with local control	Early Republic Era
Free education with secular orientation	Common School Era
Multiple purposes within a single institution	Progressive Era
Universal education with equity	Post-World War II Era

dren and youth prepare for both college and the vocations under the same roof.

Universal Education   In the nineteenth century, common school reformers began the debate in support of universal education, but it has taken almost 2 centuries for that goal to be achieved. By the end of the nineteenth century, elementary education was available to everyone, and most states had passed compulsory attendance laws requiring parents to send their children to elementary school. However, universal secondary education was not realized until the end of World War II. As the twentieth century draws to a close, some form of post-secondary schooling is becoming commonplace. However, in the nineteenth and the first half of the twentieth centuries, education in the United States was not characterized by its universality. It was not until well into the second half of the twentieth century that a serious, nationwide effort was made to provide equal educational opportunities for minorities, the handicapped, and women.

The major features of American education and the historical era in which each emerged are summarized in Table P4.1.

MAJOR PERIODS IN AMERICAN EDUCATION

Many historians identify at least six periods in American history that have had a profound impact on the schools we have today (see Tozer, Violas, & Senese, 1995). These periods include: (1) the colonial era, 1620 to 1780; (2) the early republic era, 1780 to 1820; (3) the common school era, 1820 to 1870; (4) the progressive era, 1870 to 1920; (5) the post-World War II era, 1950 to 1980; and (6) the contemporary era, 1980 to the present. Highlights of the larger social, economic, and political forces of these periods and their impact on schools are described in the sections that follow.

Colonial Roots: 1620–1780

This is the time when laws were passed in the early American colonies, particularly in Massachusetts, that required towns with a specific number of families to establish schools and to employ teachers. Although these early schools were open to the public, they were not public schools as we know them today. Some community support was provided, but parents were generally expected to pay fees to support the education of their children. Teachers, who often ran the schools on a day-to-day basis, rarely had complete autonomy. Instead, early schools usually were controlled and supervised by local school committees, a situation that led ultimately to the present day system of local control.

The Early Republic: 1780–1820

Public sentiment about who should have access to education and who should pay for it changed dramatically in the period following the Revolutionary War, mainly in response to significant economic and social changes of the time. Before the war, over 90 percent of the population, most of whom were of English and Northern European descent, made their livelihood from farming and were widely scattered in sparsely settled areas. The prevailing political theories were built around the "progressive" views of the enlightenment. The progressives believed that human reason, when combined with a virtuous outlook and freedom from outside interference by church or state, would ultimately allow mankind to progress to a perfect understanding of God and nature. These principles were central to the formation of the Constitution and Bill of Rights.

In the years following independence, national leaders worried a great deal about how to maintain social cohesion and how to create a unique American identity. They began looking to the schools to perform this important political function. Leaders of the day also believed that understanding the sophisticated features of the Constitution and the Bill of Rights required an educated citizenry. Soon these beliefs were expressed in state and federal legislation. For instance, the Northwest Ordinance, passed in 1787 for the purpose of regulating settlement into the western territories, required each township to set aside a mile square section of land for local educational purposes. It also required each state to set aside two townships to support institutions of higher education. The writers of the ordinance justified their support of schooling with these words:

> Religion, morality, and knowledge being necessary to good government and the happiness of mankind, schools and the means of education should forever be encouraged. (Perkinson, 1991, p. 9)

The most prominent political and educational figure of the time was Thomas Jefferson. As you read earlier, he believed strongly that a free, democratic society was possible only through education. It was at this time, Jefferson introduced his "Bill for the More General Diffusion of Knowledge" into the Virginia Legislature in 1789 and proposed a system of free elementary and secondary education for all free boys and girls (not slaves). They were to receive free schooling for 3 years and could stay longer if their parents paid a small fee. Jefferson believed that 3 years of schooling provided the minimal education required of citizens in a free and democratic society. Although not enacted, Jefferson's bill anticipated a system of public education that received wider support in the common school movement 3 decades later.

The Common School Era: 1820–1870

Major economic and social forces changed the nature of American society in the first half of the nineteenth century and led to a different and broader vision of public education. The beginnings of the industrial revolution created thousands of new jobs and brought large numbers of immigrants to the United States. Many of these immigrants had large families, and they sought "equality of opportunities for their children" (Tyack, 1967, p. 123). Industrialization also brought with it poor working conditions in the emerging factory system, from which arose the need for labor unions. These newly organized unions made free, public education one of their early causes. So did humanitarian social reformers of the day, who believed that social institutions in the United States should be made more livable. And like many social reformers today, they believed in the power of education to remedy society's ills.

The educational reform movement of this era is commonly referred to as the *common school movement.* The aim of common school reformers was to establish a system of publicly financed schooling so that children from average families could receive a decent education. Advocates argued that such schools should be accessible to everyone, supported with taxes, and outside religious influence. These three features, first enunciated by nineteenth century common school reformers, persist to the present day.

James Carter and Horace Mann were the most visible leaders of the common school movement, as you read earlier. Due to Carter's persistence,

Massachusetts passed a law in 1827 that gave towns the power to tax local citizens to support public schools and to hire teachers. In 1837, Mann, as the first secretary of Massachusetts' newly created state board of education, became the champion of common schools everywhere with his belief that schools should be free and run by the state. Like Jefferson, Mann believed education was prerequisite for a democratic social order and a vehicle through which the poor could better themselves. He also argued, as did others of the day, that education had economic value:

> Those who have been blessed with a good common school education, rise to a higher and higher point, in the kinds of labor performed, and also in the rate of wages paid, while the ignorant sink like dregs and are always found at the bottom. (Tozer, et al., 1995, p. 69)

The common school movement and the writings of Horace Mann began the debate about what level of government—local, state, or federal—should control schools, an issue that remains controversial today. Since the Constitution and the Bill of Rights are pointedly silent about education, we rely on the following clause of the Tenth Amendment, which states that "the powers not delegated to the United States by the Constitution, nor prohibited by it to the states, are reserved to the states respectively, or to the people." This clause leaves it open for both the states and the people (which can be interpreted as local communities) to take responsibility for education. Indeed, by 1789, Massachusetts had already passed a law that legalized the concepts of school districts and local governance. Horace Mann, however, was an advocate for a more centralized system of education, one headed by a strong state board of education. As Secretary of the Massachusetts Board of Education, he believed that achieving high standards of education would be impossible if control was given to local communities. Many at the time, however, did not agree with Mann on this issue. For instance, the Boston Board of Education wrote in its second annual report (1839) that:

> experience proves that when the powers of the school district were greater, and the interference of the state . . . less . . . the common school was altogether better than it is at present. . . . We regard the board of education as an unwise establishment. It is a measure to reduce yet lower the power and responsibilities of the school districts. . . . They are removed to a great distance . . . and to confide our common schools to the board is like taking the children from their parents, and entrusting them to strangers. (p. 5)

Chapters 10 and 11 explore the contemporary debate about who should control and finance public schools.

Free, public, universal education did not become a reality overnight. Many citizens in the nineteenth century believed that education should be left up to the family and religious institutions. Others, although they believed that children should be educated, did not like providing taxes to educate other people's children. Nevertheless, by the Civil War, every northern and western state had passed legislation that provided some form of free, public education, and many states followed Massachusetts' lead in passing compulsory attendance laws.

The Progressive Era: 1870–1920

Steven Tozer (1995) wrote that "the fifty year period from the 1870s to the 1920s represented nothing short of a revolution in American schooling, with the most fundamental changes taking place in the fifteen years on either side of 1900" (p. 86). That "revolution" gave us today's public school system. Fueling this change were the dramatic occurrences in American society between the Civil War and World War I—urbanization, immigration, and industrialization. In 1870, only 25 percent of the population lived in cities. By 1920, this percentage had doubled, making the nation primarily an urban rather than a rural society for the first time. The number of cities with a population of 500,000 or more grew from 2 to 12, growth that brought a series of problems familiar to us today: crime, poverty, corruption, and family pathologies. It also brought progressive reformers who, like their common-school predecessors, believed education could remedy many of society's ills.

Part of this urban growth resulted from the migration of rural people, namely poor whites and African Americans from the South to the industrial cities of the North. Most of the growth, however, resulted from massive immigration of peoples from eastern and southern Europe. Unlike earlier immigrants, who came primarily from northern and western Europe, these new immigrants came from poorer economic circumstances and they brought with them values, customs, and religious beliefs that were new to Americans. This new cultural diversity brought out hostile and racist attitudes shared by many Americans already here. It also presented schools with circumstances and problems not previously experienced, such as how to socialize children from many backgrounds in American values.

The industrial revolution, which had its beginning in the early part of the nineteenth century, reached its zenith between 1870 and 1920. The percentage of workers involved in manufacturing during this era doubled, and the work they performed changed drastically. Although mass production and scientific management techniques pushed America into worldwide leadership in the production of goods, it also produced dangerous repetitive work, in which workers had virtually no control over their working conditions. This situation led to increased activism on the part of workers' unions and to an increase in child-labor laws that prohibited children from working in the factories. All these factors led to greater demands on the public school system.

Schools created between 1870 and 1920 reflected these changes in the larger society in three important ways. First, the large, bureaucratic forms of organization that grew from scientifically managed factories, where work became increasingly specialized, soon found its way into schools. Educators of the day created large schools characterized by standardization, specialization, and differentiated roles for teachers and administrators. Second, the waves of immigrant children flocking to the schools led school leaders to seek ways to efficiently educate large numbers of students. Third, the industrial age embraced science, including the emerging field of psychology, the science of how people learn and behave. New, scientifically oriented methods of teaching and learning emerged and were used by educators to defend the educational system they were creating. These schools had lasting effects on our schools today.

During the late nineteenth century, according to David Tyack (1974), most school systems, particularly those in the urban areas, became bureaucracies. Although superintendents and educators of the time did not use that term, they developed educational organizations that were different from those of earlier eras and similar to those that had evolved in business and industry. For most of history, business organizations had been owned by individuals or by families, and the behavior of individuals who worked in these privately owned businesses was governed by the dictates of the owner. Although schools in early times were public institutions and not subject to the dictates of a single individual, they were, nonetheless, operated according to the desires of local community leaders. This individualistic mode of operation in both the private and public sectors was considered chaotic in an age that was striving to convert itself to the mass production of standardized goods and services. The bureaucratic form of organization evolved as part of this conversion process and was characterized by elaborate rules of behavior that were tailored to the standardization and specialization that characterized factory pro-

duction. Hierarchical arrangements suited factories, because organizational behavior could be controlled and coordinated.

Educators followed suit. Early twentieth century educators reflected the establishment's desire to make schools like factories. They saw children as the raw materials to be manufactured into various products to meet life's demands, as dictated by twentieth century civilization. Achieving efficiency of production required specialized machinery, quality control, precise measurement of output, and the elimination of waste.

The age-graded classroom and the standardized curriculum as we know them today came into being. Textbooks were widely used, and teachers used only officially approved teaching methods. This standardization was deemed beneficial for students as well. Pedagogy emphasized punctuality, regularity, and paying attention to teachers, who lectured, gave directions, and conducted recitations. The superintendent in Portland, Oregon, bragged that he could sit in his office and know on what page in each book work was going on at the same time in every school in the city.

Educators embraced the emerging discipline of psychology and used it as a means for understanding and defending the developing educational system. Psychology provided the foundation for new standardized testing procedures that were being used to measure student achievement and intelligence and, thereby, to segregate students into different academic tracks. Learning theories were based on the social philosophy of John Locke and the behavioral school of psychology then emerging. Locke's philosophy conceived of children's minds as empty vessels waiting to be filled, and their motivation to act, or to learn, arising primarily from a system of externally imposed rewards and punishments. This view of children and of the learning process led to a system of teacher-centered instruction that is still dominant in most contemporary classrooms.

The Post-World War II Era: 1945–1980

The period following World War II was characterized by tremendous economic growth, a sustained cold war with the Soviet Union, and a baby boom that resulted in an explosion of school construction. Although few modifications in the kindergarten through twelfth-grade school configuration were actually accomplished, we remember this period for two important reforms. The first was making higher education universally available. The second was making significant strides in achieving equal educational opportunities for previously excluded groups.

Figure P4.1   U.S. Higher Education Enrollments, 1940–1980

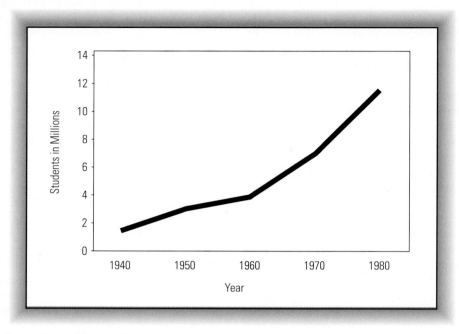

Source: Bureau of Census, 1982–83, p. 135.

Extending Higher Education

There was much discussion in the postwar period about who should receive a college education. On one side of the debate were those who worried that colleges would have to lower their standards if too many students were allowed to attend and that serious social consequences would result from providing large numbers of people with an advanced education they would not be able to use. On the other side of this debate were the majority of Americans who believed that a college education should be available to everyone who had the ability to do college-level work.

In 1944, the GI Bill of Rights, which provided full college scholarships to all veterans, was passed. Although many colleges feared the influx of veterans, these fears proved to be unwarranted. Veterans, many of whom had not done well in high school or had low SAT scores, flourished in college. Professors found them to be responsible and highly motivated students. They excelled in class discussions, and they earned better grades than their younger counterparts did. This success story, along with the rise of the community colleges in the postwar era, tended to discredit those who wanted to keep colleges more selective, and it opened the doors for many other students who would have been denied higher education in previous eras. Figure P4.1 shows the dramatic increase in the number of individuals attending college in the 40 year period between 1940 and 1980. Note in particular the steep rise between 1960 and 1980.

Expanding higher educational opportunities also had important consequences for the lower levels of schooling. For the first time, a majority of kindergarten through twelfth-graders were there to prepare for college. Also, as demand for higher education increased so did the competition for grades and high test scores. This created new conditions in schools, such as more competition among students, unknown when few students aspired to a college education.

Extending Educational Opportunities to Women and Minorities

In many ways, the history of American education is a proud one. Before most other countries contemplated universal education, the United States provided widespread opportunity through a system of education that became the envy of the world. The public school system that was created in the common school era and extended by progressive reformers embraced the belief that it was important to educate poor and immigrant children in order to maintain a unified and democratic nation. Unfortunately, this belief did not always extend to non-European ethnic minorities, such as African Americans, Native Americans, and children with an Asian or Hispanic heritage. Neither did it extend to women or to children who were handicapped. It took longer for these groups to gain reasonably equal educational opportunity.

Prior to the Civil War, few educational opportunities existed for African American slaves. The Puritans, motivated by religious reasons, sometimes had evening schools for slaves. Likewise, the Quakers in New York and Pennsylvania opened part-time schools for the children of African Americans. These efforts, however, were not substantial. In the South, a few slaves were taught to read by their owners. However, most owners were afraid that literacy for slaves would lead to a dangerous desire for freedom and perhaps even rebellion. Several southern states in the early 1800s passed laws expressly prohibiting the education of African Americans.

Following the Civil War, reconstruction forces and northern religious groups attempted to establish southern schools for African American children. For the most part, these efforts were unsuccessful. The South at that time, unlike the North, did not have a system of common schools, so no infrastructure existed on which to build schools for a new and different population of students. More important, throughout the region, southerners were starting to develop racially separate institutions in all aspects of life. Soon separate schools for African Americans, both at the elementary through high school and the university levels, were created. The Supreme Court deemed the "separate but equal" doctrine constitutional in 1896 in *Plessy* v. *Ferguson,* where the court upheld a Louisiana law requiring railroads to provide equal accommodations for African Americans. This, of course, provided federal support to local segregationists. It also set the stage for the civil rights actions that struck down the "separate but equal" institutions 50 years later.

In 1954 in *Brown* v. *Board of Education of Topeka,* the Supreme Court ruled that separate schools for African Americans and whites were inherently unequal, and school districts were ordered to begin the process of school desegregation. This court decision did little to stimulate immediate change, however, and most local communities continued their past practices. The 1964 Civil Rights Act went a step further. It not only prohibited discrimination based on color, race, religion, or national origin, it also ordered school districts to take steps to integrate schools, a form of **affirmative action,** or risk losing federal financial support.

What the *Brown* decision ruled unconstitutional was **de jure segregation,** that is, segregation resulting from laws, governmental actions, or school policies specifically designed to keep the races separate. As school boards and other governmental bodies took actions to eliminate or reduce de jure segregation, **de facto segregation,** which results from housing patterns, persisted. Throughout the 1960s and 1970s, many schools districts tried to end de facto

segregation by busing students from one area of a city to another. However, in cities such as Washington, DC, New York, Philadelphia, Chicago, and Detroit, where over 75 percent of the school population were minority students, it was difficult to accomplish any meaningful form of integration through busing. As a result, integration plans in some cities began to focus on busing across traditional city boundaries, called **metropolitan desegregation.**

A number of court cases in the 1970s addressed the legality of forced busing of all kinds. In *Swann* v. *Charlotte Mecklenberg* (1971), the U.S. Supreme Court ruled that busing was an acceptable means of integrating schools. However, in 1974 the U.S. Supreme Court ruled in *Bradley* v. *Miliiken* that metropolitan desegregation could not be used unless it could be shown that severe violations in one district exacerbated segregation in another district. The impact of busing has never been completely documented. Some argue that it drove white parents from the cities, making city schools even more segregated; others argue that it has helped the situation. It remains controversial to this day, a topic that we return to in Chapter 9.

Extending Education to Women and to Children with Handicaps

The civil rights movement initially focused on the unequal treatment of African Americans. However, it was soon extended to other disenfranchised groups, such as women and the handicapped. We touch on the educational history of these groups only briefly here, because extended discussions were provided in Chapters 4 and 6 and are discussed again in Chapters 9 and 11.

Originally, women in our society were denied equal educational opportunities because their social roles were confined largely to family matters. Supporting this restricted view of their social functions was the underlying assumption that women and girls were inherently less rational but more nurturing than men and boys. Consequently, as schools developed in the nineteenth and early twentieth centuries, they were organized with boys rather than girls in mind. And, even though the large majority of teachers since the middle part of the nineteenth century have been women, teachers have consistently communicated a different set of expectations to boys than to girls. Traditionally, girls were not expected to do well in math and science; they were not expected to prepare for college; and they were not allowed to participate in competitive sports.

This all changed after World War II. In 1972, Congress passed Title IX of the Educational Amendment Act. Title IX said that individuals could not be excluded from participation in any school program on the basis of sex. This act, along with later interpretations and extensions, had the effect of legally ending gender discrimination and opening up new opportunities for girls, particularly in physical education and athletics. It also heightened awareness of the subtle ways in which teachers and textbooks among other influences unintentionally discriminated against girls and thereby perpetuated harmful stereotypes.

In the reform minded 1960s, society began raising concerns about the type of education afforded physically, mentally, or psychologically handicapped students. Until that time, the common approach had been to design special schools or classes for these students. In 1975, Congress passed the Education for All Handicapped Children Act, designed to assure all children, regardless of the severity of their handicap, the same educational rights and privileges as their nonhandicapped peers. The law prescribed that handicapped children, to the extent possible, should be educated in regular classrooms along with nonhandicapped children. It also established a legal review process to assure that handicapped children and their parents were given the special help and educational experiences they needed to become productive adults.

Affirmative Action

The idea of affirmative action, which also grew out of the civil rights movement, has had an important impact on education. The underlying rationale was that merely outlawing discrimination was not enough to create a level playing field for groups who have endured generations of discrimination. As a society we should take affirmative steps to correct past discriminatory practices and to assure racial and gender balance in all aspects of our society. The results of affirmative action in education have been most pronounced in the areas of school hirings and student admissions. Affirmative action policies have been controversial from the start, being viewed by some as a form of reverse discrimination, in which women and minorities are given preferential treatment in hiring and admission practices.

In 1978, the United States Supreme Court ruled on the issue of reverse discrimination in the *Regents of the University of California* v. *Bakke* case. In 1973 and 1974, Allan Bakke, a white male, was rejected by the University of California medical school, while minority candidates with lower grade averages and test scores were admitted. Bakke brought suit, arguing that he was discriminated against because he was white and that the medical school's two-track system violated the equal protection clause of the Fourteenth Amendment and Title VI of the Civil

Rights Act. Both the state court and the California Supreme Court concurred. The U.S. Supreme Court, in a very complicated 5 to 4 decision, ruled that the admission procedures at the medical school were unconstitutional and ordered the medical school to accept Bakke, at the same time ruling that some forms of race-conscious admission procedures were constitutional.

The legislative and court decisions stemming from the civil rights movement have had a significant impact on our society and its system of education. Never in the nation's history has so much effort been directed at the issue of equality of opportunity. As with other matters of social concern, society sees schools as one of the primary vehicles for solving inequality. However, despite over 3 decades of legislative and judicial action, inequality, segregation, and discrimination remain with us. It is true that many of the historical and legal barriers denying equality for minorities, women, and the handicapped have been removed, but there is still much to accomplish in regard to equal educational opportunities. Schools in many cities are more segregated today than they were in 1954; complete elimination of gender bias and sex-role stereotyping has not been accomplished; and not all handicapped children are provided the educational experiences they require. As a society, we all too often treat people as members of a group rather than as individuals. Chapters 9, 10, and 11 explore contemporary challenges and the schools' response to them in more depth.

The Contemporary Era: 1980 to the Present

Our educational system is currently in transition and is beginning to take on the organizational features of the emerging information age. Organizational arrangements in the larger society are evolving from fixed, bureaucratic structures to ones characterized by flexibility and diversity. The hierarchical boss-worker relationship is being replaced by self-governing teams working together in cooperative rather than competitive ways.

Many hope that our educational system will be transformed over the 2 decades to mirror these changes going on in the larger society. We do not detail these changes here, because they form the content of the next three chapters. These chapters explore the complex relationships between schools and the larger society, the legal system and its impact on the ways schools are financed and governed and, finally, how all of this influences the lives and work of teachers.

CHAPTER 9

Schools and Society

Chapter 7 looked at schools as a unique type of social organization. We saw that each school has an individual history and develops a culture and a community that affects what teachers and students do. Schools, however, are not isolated organizations whose patterns are influenced only by the students and teachers who populate them. Like churches, families, and other social institutions, schools are specifically designed by the larger society to perform vital social functions from generation to generation. Because schools are so much a part of our lives, it rarely occurs to most people to question why they exist or what their proper role is, or if we even need them. These issues, which often evoke heated debate, are the focus of this chapter.

Giving thought to what schools are for is an essential aspect of developing your own philosophy of teaching. As we saw in Chapter 3, there is a link between what you consider the purpose of schooling and how your teaching is conducted. It is also important for each citizen to consider the purposes of schools. Whether you decide to become a teacher or not, thoughtful reflection on the purposes of education in a democracy will aid you in future policy deliberations and decisions.

To consider the proper role of schools, let's begin by eavesdropping on two meetings. One is a formal school board meeting in Circleville, Ohio; the other is an informal discussion between two inner city teachers in a Columbus, Ohio high school.

The Circleville School Board is holding that portion of its monthly meeting where members discuss personnel matters. This evening the topic is a controversial high school teacher, Anthony Digilio, who is finishing his third year and is being evaluated for tenure.

"I simply don't understand Anthony Digilio or his teaching methods," barked board member Ellen Crassnew. "However, I'm sure of one thing, we shouldn't renew his contract." Her words spark a heated and long standing debate among board members about the purposes of schools in their community and the proper role of Circleville teachers.

"What are you talking about, Ellen," asked Roger Zaconi, even though he already knows her views on this topic. "My son Mark is in Tony's class, and this is the first time Mark has truly enjoyed history. As I understand it, Tony is extremely popular with all the students. In fact, last year the senior class voted him their favorite history teacher."

"Well," replied Ellen, "I, for one, do not consider what goes on in that class history. What does having homeless people visit class or arguing about the

Why We Have Schools

Purposes of Schooling
   Transmitting the Culture
     Political Socialization
     Cultural Socialization
   Developing Human Potential
   Reconstructing Society

Social Problems Come to School
   Social Class and Poverty
   Family Configurations and Distress
   Child Abuse
   Drug and Alcohol Abuse

Teen Pregnancy
Crime, Violence, and Social Tensions
Kids and Television
Other Social Problems
Perspective on School Problems

Schools, Social Reform, and the Next Millennium
   Schools and Social Reform
   Schools, Society, and the Third Millennium

Summary

Readings for the Professional

county's environmental policies have to do with helping students develop an appreciation of American institutions and our way of life?"

Mr. Zaconi, continuing in Mr. Digilio's defense, replied, "I think Tony is one of the most innovative and effective teachers in the school. His students always seem to be intellectually engaged rather than bored. They do a lot of small-group work—like role playing, simulations, and provocative debates. He even invited me to one of his classes to talk about my experiences during the Vietnam War. The discussions that followed my talk were lively and respectful, even though it was clear that many of the students thought our involvement was wrong."

"I know Mr. Digilio quite well," chimed in Marsha Diel. "He goes to my church and we cochaired last year's Run for Cancer Committee. While we were working on that project, we talked a lot about education and his views on teaching. He's a very serious, devoted young man. He believes that one of the most important things a teacher can do is raise students' awareness of the injustices and inequalities that exist in our society. He wants to motivate them to help solve the problems facing our society. I can see absolutely nothing wrong with this. It's consistent with the teachings of all of our great spiritual leaders, from Jesus to Martin Luther King."

Ellen Cressnew replied, "He may be a nice young man, even a good Christian, but he wasn't hired to be a spiritual leader. He shouldn't be using his classroom as a soapbox to brainwash students to his own views. A teacher's values and personal social agenda should be left at home."

"I agree with Ellen", said John Scannell, a local stockbroker who has been on the board for a number of years. "I want our young people to get an education that will prepare them for college and a career. That is not happening in Digilio's classes. He spends all his time getting them to be social activists, not learning how to be producers. All this talk about American errors in Vietnam or the plight of the homeless is not what our teachers should be doing. And why, please tell me, did he take his students to the antiwar rally during the Persian Gulf War? To me that's being unpatriotic, perhaps even un-American. This has to stop! Our young people should be learning how our economic system operates and acquiring the knowledge they'll need to get high SAT scores."

After a long period of strained silence, Marsha Diel decided to make her point one more time. "Those of you who are opposed to Mr. Digilio and his teaching methods just don't understand. For our kids to gain an appreciation of American history and our cultural heritage, they have to deal in concrete ways with things like equality, freedom, and respon-

sibility. They learn about equality when they study the homeless, and they learn about freedom and responsibility by exercising free speech at an antigovernment rally. Without such first-hand experiences, the ideals of a participatory democracy, on which our country has been built, will remain only an academic abstraction. The real-life experiences that Tony gives them will take them much further in life than making high marks on their SATs." Marsha stopped and sighed. She knew that she wasn't going to convince her fellow board members of her point of view. She was saddened that a dedicated teacher like Tony would not be teaching in Circleville next year.

A few miles from Circleville in the largest city in the state, Luther Sparks and Elma Ridinger, two teachers in a high school with many African American, Hispanic, and Southeast Asian students are talking over lunch about the new core curriculum adopted by their school district.

Luther began, "What, may I ask, are they trying to do to these kids? Teaching the so-called cultural literacy curriculum to our students is ridiculous. It will absolutely kill their desire to learn."

Elma asked him, "Luther, you seem so angry. What are you talking about?"

Luther continued in a heated voice, "I'm talking about the new curriculum framework the school district has adopted, with its emphasis on a long list of facts and ideas recommended by the Core Knowledge Foundation. You know the foundation, started by E.D. Hirsch, to rescue the world from all us cultural illiterates."

Elma responded, "Oh, sure, I heard about that idea, but I really haven't paid much attention to what's been going on in the district."

Luther sounded annoyed, "Well, you should! The new guidelines require that all the kids learn a prescribed set of ideas in science, history, and literature along with the biographies of selected leaders in all these fields. This "core curriculum" is supposed to be taught at least 60 percent of the time. What's so ridiculous is that most of the ideas and the people in this curriculum represent Western culture and traditions and won't mean a thing to most of these African American and Hispanic students, not to mention our kids from Southeast Asia.

Elma frowned and said, "You sound overly upset about this, Luther. There's another point of view, you know. Some people say our schools are putting so much emphasis on diversity and pluralism that we aren't helping our kids develop a shared sense of national identity."

Kurt, who had been listening intently, entered the discussion, "I disagree with them totally and absolutely! Some of the things on the list—Benjamin Franklin, the League of Nations, John Cotton—will make no sense to my students. They've got to learn to appreciate their own culture and its history before they'll feel positive about themselves and become productive citizens. The core curriculum will only be a turnoff for our students; it will give them one more reason to drop out.

Elma shook her head and said, "You might be right, but I read in *Newsweek* that over 100 schools, including several in inner cities like ours, have been using a curriculum similar to the one you are talking about, and teachers report that their kids are enthusiastic and are learning a lot."

Kurt thought a minute and said with a shrug, "Well, maybe, but I still don't want it to happen here. We've worked too hard over the past 20 years getting a curriculum where kids read African American authors, study the discoveries of Hispanic scientists, and are proud of the successes of female athletes. Our national identity doesn't rest on the ideas of a bunch of DWMs [dead white men]. It comes from our diversity and the contributions of all, not just the few who are idolized by a few same-culture elitists."

These discussions are similar to real ones that citizens and teachers have every day about the purposes of schools. They occur because most people in our society realize that their future and the nation's is inextricably bound to our children's education. And, as with any public issue that really matters, people have different opinions about what constitutes the good society and how to get there. In this chapter, we position ourselves outside the school, so we can get a panoramic view of how schools and their surrounding societies interact with one another.

WHY WE HAVE SCHOOLS

Education, in its broader sense, is an ongoing process that takes place in all settings: while reading books, watching television, attending movies, and simply talking with and observing other people. From this perspective education happens everywhere and is a life-long process. Schooling, on the other hand, refers to those educational experiences, both planned and unplanned, that take place within a setting specifically designed for learning, a place called school.

In simpler societies, those characterized by hunting or agrarian economies, children were educated mainly by observing and imitating adults. Boys learned how to hunt or to farm by watching their elders, joining a hunting party, or working beside their fathers. Girls learned the skills required of women by helping their mothers and watching other women in the community as they performed day-to-day work. Most of these educational activities were informal and unplanned. In slightly more complex societies, those where many individuals were skilled workers or artisans, the education of the young became increasingly formal. Apprenticeship systems were devised to help the young learn important adult roles. Youth in these societies are required to spend specified amounts of time working under the tutelage of adults who are considered experts and are willing to "sign off" when the young person has acquired journeyman status. Watching and imitating adults, however, remains the primary method of learning. Simpler societies also use its other institutions (family, church, and work organizations) to assist with child rearing and to help youth make the transition from family to work.

While imitative learning and informal teaching fit the needs of small, traditional societies, they do not suit the needs of more complicated societies, especially those with technologically advanced economies and culturally diverse populations. Many of the understandings and skills required in economically and culturally complex societies cannot be left to chance or whim. It is not enough to be "street smart" in complex societies, nor is it sufficient to know only the science and technology of one's parents. Thus, as far back as the early Greeks, complex societies have created specialized institutions (schools) to provide their young with educational experiences considered vital to the continuation of their society. By now you are familiar with the evolution of schools in the United States from rather simple institutions with a narrow focus on basic literacy skills into an institution with broad academic goals and a variety of nonacademic functions ranging from day care to mental health. The process of schooling also has become much more formal. Desired learning experiences are now organized into a formal, tightly sequenced curriculum taught in a certain place (a school building), for a certain amount of time (9:00 A.M. to 3:30 P.M.), for a specified number of years (12 plus).

On the surface, it may appear that formal schooling is a rather straightforward and simple matter. As the vignettes at the beginning of the chapter illustrate, though, it is exceedingly difficult in complex and culturally diverse societies, such as the United States, to reach agreement on what types of learning experiences are best for children and youth.

Throughout history, people have held widely different opinions on the primary purposes of education. The section that follows gives you the opportunity to look at some of the traditional purposes of schools and to begin reflecting on what seems to you an appropriate mix among them.

PURPOSES OF SCHOOLING

Nearly everyone who has ever been to school has thought about the many purposes and functions of schools. The following list provides only a few of the school goals that have appeared in the popular press from time to time.

1. To teach basic academic skills.
2. To build student self-esteem.
3. To promote critical thinking skills.
4. To teach cooperative, prosocial behaviors.
5. To promote equality of opportunity.
6. To prepare students for college.
7. To prepare students for the world of work.
8. To transmit our cultural heritage.
9. To preserve our cultural richness and diversity.
10. To promote national unity and patriotism.
11. To build and maintain a strong economy.
12. To promote social justice.
13. To promote global understanding.
14. To combat social problems (discrimination, AIDS, drugs, etc.).
15. To provide social services (child care, health services, etc.).

These and other school goals periodically gain national attention, because they are perennial concerns of a democratic society. Very often they appear in public in small clusters of three or four at a time, because increased attention to one or two related purposes often means less attention to one or two others. For example, the civil rights movement in the 1960s brought a renewed concern for social justice, social problems, and student self-esteem into our nations' schools. However, by giving increased attention to these issues, it was almost inevitable that less attention was paid to the equally legitimate goals of teaching basic academic skills and preparing students for college and the world of work. In short, it is impossible to focus on everything at once.

Although this list of school purposes may seem a bit overwhelming at first, a closer examination reveals that many of the items overlap. For example, items 1 through 7 all have something to do with helping students reach their full human potential. Likewise, items 8 through 10 have to do with maintaining our society by socializing students into its cultural heritage. Finally, items 3 through 5 and 12 through 15 have something to do with the ongoing goal of social renewal. That is, they all deal in one way or another with replacing outdated norms, attitudes, skills, and programs with newer ones better adapted to an ever-changing world.

Rather than examining an extended list of school purposes, such as ours, this section organizes its discussion around the three overarching goals just mentioned: transmitting the culture, developing human potential, and reconstructing society. Even when reduced to these three general purposes, it is easy to see why any discussion of schools can quickly fall into the heated debates you read at the beginning of the chapter. The following sections examine each of these perennial school purposes individually. Before you proceed, take a moment to reflect. Which purposes of schooling do you believe are the most important? Least important?

Transmitting the Culture

It should be no surprise that one important purpose of schools is to transmit the culture and institutions that support a particular society. In American society, this means socializing (educating) students into a democratic political system that operates around a common set of cultural tools. To that end, we next look at the school's role in transmitting our unique political systems and the cultural tools that sustain it.

Political Socialization

It is critical for every society to transmit understanding about power relationships among its members. In the introduction to Part IV, you read how Thomas Jefferson and other early political leaders saw schooling as a means for socializing citizens into the constitutionally based system of democratic government they had recently created. You also read how nineteenth century common school reformers, such as Horace Mann, believed schools would create a sense of cohesion and national identity among its citizens. Indeed, every society with a formal system of schooling uses its schools to politically socialize its young. Without a shared understanding of some agreed on political process, a community simply could not function or perpetuate itself.

Societies define and politically socialize their citizenry in various ways. In some, especially those with totalitarian forms of government, schools give students selected information that supports the society's dominant ideology. Information that might be critical of existing ideas or institutions is censored. In open, democratic societies characterized by a measure of political freedom, political socialization is approached quite differently. Although students are taught to value and respect the society's social arrangements and institutions (e.g., the Constitution, the Bill of Rights, trial by jury, a free enterprise system), they also are taught how to critically examine these arrangements and institutions.

The way schools teach citizenship skills also differ from one society to another. Totalitarian societies provide few opportunities for citizens to participate, so there is little need to teach young people citizen participation skills. In fact, schools in authoritarian societies are likely to teach the young that it is inappropriate to participate, to criticize, or to make demands on the government. Democratic societies, on the other hand, can only survive if citizens are capable of making informed judgment about complex issues and if they are willing to act on these judgments by participating in the electoral process. This, you may remember, was Tony Digilio's reason for taking his students to an antiwar rally. Schools, thus, spend time teaching children how to express and to support their opinions, how to keep abreast of current affairs, how to write a letter to a member of congress, and how to vote. Some believe schools do not spend enough time on this aspect of a student's education, and some neglect the social studies altogether.

It would be incorrect to conclude from this discussion that democratic societies are not biased in their approach to political socialization, because they are. The political and social ideas taught in schools are mainly those of the dominant class and are taught in order to justify existing social arrangements. Ideas and values of other cultures, of minority groups, or of the poorer economic classes, are not as a rule given much attention. For instance, few schools in the United States during the 1950s and 1960s taught very much about socialism or communism, even though a large portion of the world's population lived under these systems. Women's views and the views of American minorities have likewise been excluded from the school's curriculum until recently. Nonetheless, American students receive a great deal of information about diversity and controversial issues, and this information is more freely discussed than it would be in closed societies. Read the accompanying Global Box to get an idea of

what a school system based on a church, rather than a state-operated system would be like.

Cultural Socialization

Every culture has a set of beliefs, skills, feelings, and ways of interpreting the world. Jerome Bruner (1996) referred to this as a culture's tool kit. A society's cultural tool kit includes just about everything: physical artifacts, such as tools, houses, and means of transportation; beliefs about time and space; views about right and wrong; and norms that define acceptable and unacceptable behavior. The language system within which people think and communicate is particularly important, since it is the basic transmission tool. The culture's tool kit is also cumulative, that is, it is built on what has come before. Bruner provides the observation, for example, that any math major in college today can do more advanced mathematics than Leibniz, who invented calculus. Likewise, most children today know more about computers than their parents do.

The tool kit in culturally diverse and technologically advanced societies is incredibly vast, which means that schools must be selective in what they choose to transmit. For instance, in contemporary American society, Native Americans, Hispanics, and people from European backgrounds vary significantly not only in their languages but in such basic things as their concepts of time and beauty. Faced with such diversity, schools must decide what to include and what to leave out. Controversy develops when people strive to answer such questions as, What is basic and required versus what is secondary and optional? and What represents commonality and what diversity? All great curriculum debates center on these types of questions. Let's explore how this works by examining a contemporary debate between an educational traditionalist and an educational progressive about which items in our own cultural tool kit should be considered basic and how schools should go about transmitting these items to the young.

On one side is educational traditionalist E.D. Hirsch, whom we mentioned in Chapter 8. In 1986, Hirsch, an English professor at the University of Virginia, wrote a book, *Cultural Literacy: What Every American Needs to Know*. Hirsch defined *cultural literacy* as core topics in history, literature, science, and mathematics taken from the Western intellectual tradition. He argued that democratic institutions are threatened if every citizen does not share a common cultural vocabulary. He advocated national standards and a curriculum that prescribes what students should learn each year they are in school. Table 9.1 shows some of the items on Hirsch's list of

GLOBAL

Newfoundland's Church-based School System

Almost every technologically advanced society in the world has a public, state-operated school system. In some instances, this system is centralized, such as in France and Japan, and major decisions about the schools' operations are made by the national governments. In others, the society provides considerable autonomy to local political jurisdictions, as we do in the United States. Regardless of the degree of centralization or autonomy, these school systems are governed by political bodies—legislatures or boards of education—whose members decide on the purposes of schooling and how the schools should go about socializing children and transmitting the society's culture. The Newfoundland schools in Canada are an exception.

Instead of a public school system, the province of Newfoundland has a church-based system that has existed since 1722, when the first school was started by the Church of England. Currently, seven churches—Roman Catholic, Anglican, United Church of Canada, Salvation Army, Presbyterian, Seventh-Day Adventist, and the Pentecostal Assembly—are guaranteed under the constitution the right to operate schools and a promise that "the legislature will not have the authority to make laws prejudicially affecting any right or privilege of church-controlled schools" (McConaghy, 1996, p. 173).

Currently, according to McConaghy, there are 27 members from separate denominational groups who comprise the school board. The province is responsible for funding education, determining some aspects of the curriculum, and training teachers. The churches, however, recommend certification of teachers, hire teachers, run the schools, and determine the school's religious program. Students attend the school of their choice and faith, sometimes hours away from their homes. Transportation costs are paid by the province.

Many attempts have been made to reform this system of education, but as of 1996, all efforts have been successfully blocked by the churches. Those who want change, according to McConaghy (1996), believe that having so many schools and having them so spread out is costly. Newfoundland, for instance, spends 11.3 percent of its gross domestic product on education compared to less than 7 percent in other Canadian provinces. Others argue that there is no school for Newfoundlanders who are not Christians and that it is not right to hire teachers on the basis of their religious affiliation rather than their ability to teach.

Most people in the United States, with our tradition of separation of church and state, tend to agree with these arguments. But it seems that Newfoundland has created a school system that is the product of the society and culture in which it is embedded. Over 95 percent of Newfoundlanders are Christians, and most people live in small, scattered fishing and farming villages. The church-based system, at least in its early days, was a way to provide education for the province's children and to allow parents (rather than the state) to decide the type of education their children should receive. It is interesting to speculate what the results will be if this system is ever changed.

Table 9.1 **Examples of Items for Cultural Literacy**

Names	Dates	Places	Concepts
John Adams	1066	Adirondack Mts.	amoeba
Adam and Eve	1492	American Stock Exchange	genre
William Pitt	1861–1865	Philippines	quorum
Puccini	1914–1918	Yucatan	trench warfare
Uncle Tom	1939–1945	Dien Bien Phu	lesbian

Source: From E. D. Hirsch, 1986, pp. 152–215.

what a culturally literate American should know. In his book and in subsequent publications, thousands of items were identified and categorized by subject and grade level at which they should be taught.

For Hirsch, core knowledge in the form of facts, principles, and cultural vocabulary should form the cornerstone of students' education. As he put it, "this knowledge . . . serves as a kind of intellectual Velcro to which all new learning can cling" (p. 32). Finally, Hirsch's book advocated teacher-centered methods of instruction, such as lecture and recitation, and he criticized progressive or child-centered teaching methods, wherein students are permitted some voice in determining their curriculum.

Brown University's Theodore Sizer (1992) had a different vision of what should be taught in schools. In his book *Horace's Hope: What Works for American Schools,* Sizer argued that traditional academic curricula, which march students in lockstep fashion through a broad, prescribed curriculum, are basically boring to most students and contribute to low motivation and high drop-out rates. Sizer believed that schools should teach a few subjects in greater depth, and that students should be taught to see the interdisciplinary nature of subjects. Unlike Hirsch, he opposed national standards and curricula, believing instead that local communities should provide general guidelines, and that most topics should be dictated by student interests.

Sizer, as you read in Chapter 7, wants schools to become more personal places, and his book called for student-centered, rather than teacher-centered, instructional practices. To Sizer, learning to think critically and to solve problems of all kinds is more

important than learning a common cultural vocabulary. It is likely that the debate between these two opposing viewpoints will go on for some time. We use the debate to illustrate how people in a diverse society can hold different views about the appropriate role for schools. Although such debates can become very heated, it is important to recognize that both sides agree that schools should reproduce the culture. Their disagreement centers on what tools should be stocked in the cultural tool kit.

Developing Human Potential

In addition to transmitting the surrounding culture, schools are also expected to help individual students develop to their fullest potential. This is especially true in our society in which the worth and dignity of each individual is highly valued. This purpose puts the spotlight on the individual student rather than on the entire society. In this view, the school's job is to identify each child's interests, needs, and talents and then to make sure that these are realized.

In some instances, developing human potential in schools is quite straightforward. For example, most schools have music programs and students with musical talents are sought out and urged to participate in them. Students with athletic talents are nurtured (some would say coddled) so they will be successful at current and future levels of competition. Most professional football, basketball, and baseball players' talents were discovered and developed while the athletes were in school, as were many exceptional musicians, actors, and scientists.

Generally, however, trying to develop human potential in a public institution with limited resources is not a simple and straightforward matter. Americans can quickly get into heated discussions about how best to develop an individual's various talents. For instance, is talent best developed by holding individuals to high standards and recognizing only those who reach these standards? Or, is human potential more likely to be realized if schools focus on helping students acquire positive self-concepts and high self-esteem? Should we spend more resources developing potential in the academic subjects, such as mathematics and science, or in the aesthetic subjects, such as the arts, music, or dance? If all students' talents cannot be developed equally, who should come first, the gifted, who have potential for greatness, possibly advancing the good of society as a whole, or the handicapped, whose limited potential requires extraordinary support? How would you answer these questions? Obviously, these are not easy questions, and they illustrate the complexity of educational aims in a diverse society.

Reconstructing Society

The third overarching purpose of formal schooling is to assist in the ongoing process of social renewal. This purpose rests on the assumption that a society never lives up to its noble intents. Societies like our own, for instance, may embrace the ideal of social justice, yet discriminate against minority groups. We may embrace values of equity and equality, yet allow hunger and homelessness to exist within our midst. Given this situation, some people believe that schools should be a vehicle for teaching the young to be effective change agents who will seek to improve society. As with the other purposes of schooling, the reconstructionist purpose is complex and contains many subgoals and nuances.

To some social reconstructionists, the primary purpose of schooling can be viewed as reform-minded political socialization. Schools should not only help students acquire a deep appreciation of basic democratic processes but also motivate them to help solve contemporary social problems, such as poverty, racism, environmental destruction, and child abuse. Schools with this perspective encourage students to study problems in their own communities and to plan reforms that will make things better. Project-based and group investigation teaching methods, described in Chapter 6, facilitate this type of study and social action. Sometimes a school, such as Gonzaga High School in Washington, DC, builds its whole curriculum around reconstructionist principles. Gonzaga students are required to participate in "service learning" and to work toward improving the social conditions they find in their community. Gonzaga wants their students to graduate not only with in-depth understanding and appreciation of democratic institutions but also with a commitment to join with others to help eliminate some of the ills of the world.

Other reconstructionists take a more critical view of society and advocate more radical teaching methods and projects. They argue that the dominant culture, in creating schools that will serve their needs, inevitably creates schools that keep members of minority cultures passive and subservient. Consequently, students should be taught not only to understand the injustices that confront them but also how to take action, even radical action, to correct such injustices.

Movement toward school reconstructionism is generally motivated by unrest and upheaval in the larger society. For instance, U.S. racism and participation in the Vietnam War during the 1960s led many teachers and students to become involved with various components of the civil rights and anti-Vietnam movements. Today, teacher and student activists work to improve conditions of the poor and homeless and to promote better environmental policies. For the most part, however, Americans have not embraced the reconstructionist purposes of schooling as much as they have those that transmit the culture and develop human potential. Most communities will not tolerate teachers or students who question or show grave disregard for the fundamental social or economic arrangements of American society. One highly publicized example of this was the teacher a few years ago who was summarily fired after tearing the flag off the wall and stomping on it in front the class. As the next section shows, many Americans want to use their schools to remediate particular social ills. However, most do not want their young to become active participants in the reform process, particularly if that means criticizing existing social arrangements.

What beliefs do you hold about the reconstructionist purposes of schooling? As a teacher, should you be expected to criticize existing social arrangements? Should you help students work toward improvements? If you think this is part of a teacher's job, what will you do if you work in a community in which citizens want teachers to stay away from controversial issues?

In summary, schools in the United States are responsible for accomplishing three overarching goals: transmitting the culture, developing human potential, and improving society. Unlike other, more tightly focused institutions, schools have multiple, often competing, purposes that make them a unique, complex, and conflict-prone institution. For example, choosing to develop a child-centered school risks neglecting the transmission of our cultural heritage, or preparing students for college and the world of work. On the other hand, transmitting the dominant culture often neglects other ways of viewing the world. Similarly, working toward social reconstruction often puts schools in conflict with the dominant social groups in a community, a condition that can lead to withdrawal of resources and support.

Trying to balance competing school purposes can be one of the most interesting and challenging aspects of a teacher's job. It is a struggle that never ends. As you progress through your teacher preparation program, you should periodically revisit the basic question, *What do I consider to be the fundamental purposes of my profession?* Unless your thoughts are clear about this question, your teaching will never be as purposeful or as fulfilling as it might be. Take a moment now, at the outset of what we hope will be a lifelong journey into teaching, and ask yourself the following questions:

- Which of the three school purposes that we have discussed is most and least important to me?

- How much and in what way will I embed each of these purposes in my curriculum?

- Will I make cultural commonality or diversity a focus of my teaching?

- Will I attempt to develop politically active students with a strong sense of social responsibility and activism, or will I focus mostly on academic goals and leave the ills of the larger society to other institutions such as the family, government, and church?

If you want to be a purposeful and reflective teacher, start the dialogue now, and never let it slip too far from view. Take a moment to read the accompanying Issue Box, which questions the validity of schools in their present state.

SOCIAL PROBLEMS COME TO SCHOOL

The purposes of schools are tightly connected to the needs of the parent society as you just read. Consequently, educators must strive to fit school practices to the social problems that come to school with students. This section helps you examine some contemporary social problems and how they affect schools and teachers. It is not our contention that teachers can or should cure the larger social problems facing youth. They should, however, be sensitive to these problems and know how they affect teaching and student performance.

Social Class and Poverty

Most Americans do not think about social problems in terms of social class or socioeconomic status (SES). We think of ourselves as having a relatively classless society. However, a number of disturbing statistics might lead us to question that assumption. First, the nation's poverty rate has been increasing over the last decade while its middle class has been shrinking. Census Bureau estimates of poverty indicate that 35.7 million Americans now live below the poverty line, a 28-year high. Sadly, most of them are children. Six times more children than elderly Americans are in poverty. Reed and Sautter (1990) reported that the United States has the highest rate of childhood poverty (21.2 percent in 1994) among industrial nations. Since the poverty level in 1975 was 16 percent and is expected to reach 27 percent by 2020, it is clear that childhood poverty is an increasing problem (Pallas, Natriello, & McDill, 1989; Coontz, 1995). Figure 9.1 shows the percentage of children under 18 living in poverty between 1960 and 1994. Note that in 1994, black and Hispanic children were more than twice as likely as white children to live in poverty. To be more positive, also note that the percentage of children from all groups living in poverty has decreased when compared to the early 1960s.

Social class is an educational problem because there is a reciprocal relationship between economic status and educational achievement. That is, if you do not make it in school, you are likely to earn less money as an adult. Likewise, if you come from a poor family, you are less likely to make it in school. The bottom line is that if you are poor, the economic and educational deck is stacked against you. This does not mean that it is impossible to succeed without money, since many people obviously make it out of poverty, but it does mean that getting into the middle class is much more difficult than staying there.

There is also a troubling relationship between poverty, ethnicity and gender. Look at the graph in Figure 9.2, which shows how poverty is disproportionately a problem of minority groups and women. Median income is higher for whites and, predictably, poverty rates are lower. Unemployment rates for minority groups are also higher than for whites. For example, male unemployment among Native Americans living on reservations ranges from 58 percent to 80 percent, and for Latinos unemployment is 60 percent higher than for whites.

What happens to the children of the poor when they go to school? Attendance, achievement, and participation in extracurricular activities are all lower, while drop-out rates and suspension for misbehavior are higher. Drop-out and employment rates are illustrated in Figure 9.3. Low-income students also lose more ground academically over the summer than middle-class students do. (Heyns, 1978).

Two research studies show vividly how SES can affect school learning. Cazden (1972) examined speech patterns under differing contexts for a low-income child and a middle-income child. She found that each student gave their shortest comments in the same context, an arithmetic game. They differed, however, in the circumstances in which they talked the most. For the middle-income child, it happened during a formal story-retelling situation, whereas for the low-income child, it occurred during an informal out-of-school conversation. In another study, Heider, Cazden, and Brown (1968) found that children's descriptions of animal pictures were equally detailed but that low-income students required more prompts from the adult interviewer to create their descriptions than the middle-income students did. If the interviewer had not persisted in requesting more information, the knowledge and language ability of the low-income students would have been underestimated. These findings suggest that low-SES stu-

dents have verbal abilities that may not be accessed by typical classroom tasks.

Interaction patterns in low-SES homes may account for these differences in verbal performance. Hess and McDevitt (1984) found that low-SES parents were more likely to *tell* rather than to *explain*

ISSUES

EXTRA

Is Formal Schooling the Answer for the Twenty-First Century?

Over the past 30 years, several observers have argued that formal schooling, as currently conceived and practiced, is as out-of-date in the enterprise of learning as the horse and buggy is to our modern transportation system. Two books that are particularly provocative in this area are *Deschooling Society* and *School's Out: Hyperlearning, the New Technology and the End of Education.*

In 1970, Ivan Illich wrote *Deschooling Society,* a little book that shocked the educational establishment at that time. The primary thesis developed by Illich was that formal universal education does more harm than good and that we should do away with our schools. Let's look at what Illich proposed and the pros and cons of his ideas.

On one side is the point of view outlined in this chapter, that schools are created by society to achieve certain purposes deemed important by that society. As societies become more complex and diverse, schools do as well, assuming important functions not provided by other institutions in the society. Over a period of time, the schools' curriculum and routines became more bureaucratized, and children's education became less self-regulated. Eventually, compulsory attendance laws required all children to attend schools for specified periods of time and diplomas and licenses were awarded to show who was and was not qualified to perform certain societal roles.

Illich, on the other side, said that all this is wrong and that a formal system of schooling is not needed. In his view schools actually harm children as well as the larger society. The present system, according to Illich, favors the privileged at the expense of the disadvantaged. Poor children come to school without the advantages of middle-class children, that is, with fewer parent-child conversations, fewer books, less travel, and fewer family activities. Since schools are designed to fit the developmental levels of middle- and upper-class children, poor children will only fall behind if they depend on the schools for their advancement and learning.

Further, argued Illich, the idea that most learning results from school-based teaching is an illusion. School he said, "confuses teaching with learning, grade advancement with education, and a diploma with competence" (p. 1). Although school-based teaching can contribute in minor ways to learning, most knowledge is acquired through informal activity that occurs outside of school.

So what should we do? Illich believed that schools could not be reformed, as many were trying to do in the 1960s and 1970s. Education will gain only if we deschool society and replace the schools we now have with more informal learning webs and networks aimed at accomplishing three purposes:

things to their children. Their language was less elaborate and their directions less clear. High-SES parents talk more with their children, explain ideas, discuss the causes of events, ask more questions, and encourage more independent problem solving. These verbal behaviors of high-SES parents are quite congruent with school practices.

Here we find another variation of the cultural difference theory described in Chapter 5, this time applied to differences between social classes. As with any cultural group, people of each socioeconomic group behave and talk in ways appropriate to their subcultures. Middle-class teachers unconsciously expect middle-class verbal behavior, and

ISSUES

Continued

1. Provide all who want to learn access to available resources at any time in their lives.

2. Help all who want to share what they know to find those who want to learn it from them.

3. Furnish all who want to present issues to the public with the opportunity to make their challenges known.

Illich's highly informal structures would not be under the control of professional educators. Teachers would come not from those who have a certificate but from those called "natural educator", that is, those who have practical wisdom they are willing to share with others.

Two decades later, L. Perelman (1992) wrote *School's Out: Hyperlearning, the New Technology and the End of Education*. The term *hyperlearning* in his title refers to the speed and connectedness of learning. He developed the thesis that new technology (computers, information networks, multimedia) gives everyone access to learning, something not possible when the schools we now have were created. Instead of learning occurring within the "classroom box," now learning permeates every form of social activity. Instead of learning being confined to children, it is now everyone's province.

Like Illich, Perelman argues that it makes no sense to reform schools and that reform efforts such as "school choice" and "higher standards" are only diversion from the main principles of reform, which include:

- Completely privatizing education.
- Replacing school buildings with learning channels and the information superhighway.
- Abolishing all credential systems, which choke progress.
- Creating national technological schools that would exist without campuses or faculty.

What do you think of Illich's and Perelman's ideas? Will the future produce a deschooled society in which most learning occurs informally through families, peer groups, work organizations, and computer networks? What will deschooling mean to learners? Can they obtain through informal means the type of education required in a technologically advanced society? What will it mean to teachers? Will teaching careers any longer exist? If we do away with credentials, how will quality control be provided for consumers of medical, legal, or education services? What will it mean to the social class structure that currently exists? Will deschooling society be beneficial to the poor? To the middle class?

Figure 9.1   **Percentage of Children under 18 Who Live in Families below the Poverty Level, 1960–1994**

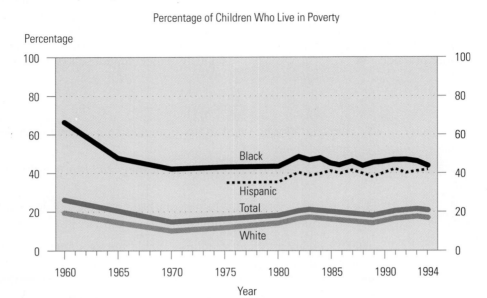

Percentage of Children Who Live in Poverty

Source: National Center for Education Statistics, 1996, p. 143.

Figure 9.2   **1990 Median Income in the United States by Race and Gender**

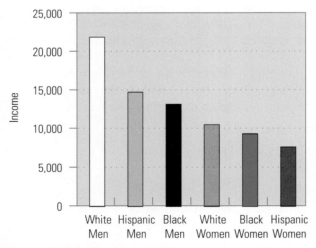

Source: U.S. Department of Commerce, 1992, p. 435.

when low-income students behave differently, teachers' expectations about their abilities diminish. Lowered expectations result in fewer and more abbreviated student-teacher interactions, which leads to poorer academic performance and, eventually, to harmful responses such as tracking and ability grouping. These, in turn, further exacerbate the situation, because instructional quality in lower tracks is generally poorer. Thus, another mismatch

between student and school culture—this one based on socioeconomic differences—sets in motion a predictable cycle of school failure.

Teachers, however, should not bear all the blame for this situation. Schools are supported and financed by middle-class parents who demand they support middle-class values. This is not surprising or necessarily wrong. However, it does present many low-SES students with learning conditions that may not be aligned with their families' backgrounds. For instance, middle-class parents generally support the norms of hard work, obedience to school authority, taking on difficult tasks, and delaying immediate gratification so that long-term goals such as college can be achieved. Lower-class parents, on the other hand, though wanting their children to work hard and to get a good education, often can not support some norms like middle class parents do. For instance, lower-class parents may be working multiple jobs and thus are less available than middle-class parents to direct their children's after-school time or to supervise their homework. As a result, lower-class students may not seriously perceive school as an escape from poverty only as an institution that reinforces that they are failures and losers.

While the problems of students in poverty are profound, there are positive actions teachers can and should take to help these students. Most important, teachers need to be alert to differences in language use. Low-SES students' communicative

Figure 9.3   **Dropout and Employment Rates in the United States**

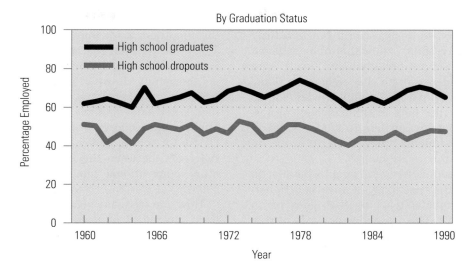

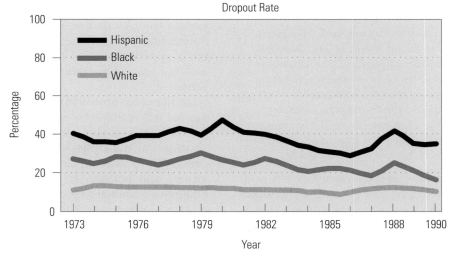

Source: National Center for Education Statistics, 1995, p. 5.

style may be different from that of middle-class students, and teachers need to account for this as they assess and instruct these students. Teachers also need to be sensitive to the following problems created by these students' difficult life circumstances:

• Parents may be working more than one job and may be working for inflexible employers, thus making it difficult to get to school for conferences or other activities.

• In families experiencing the stresses of economic hardship, parental warmth can be diminished.

• Transportation is often difficult, so poor students tend to be tardy more often.

• Adequate food, clothing, and shelter may not be available, thus increasing the frequency of illnesses and absences.

• Poor children are often stigmatized by both peers and adults, which leads to a diminished sense of self-esteem and lower achievement.

• The poor often need to move frequently, so transience rates will be higher.

• Living quarters are likely to be more cramped and noisy, thus making a poor environment for homework assignments.

• Older students may need to work to supplement the family income, so time to do homework or to participate in extracurricular activities may be unavailable.

Homeless families experience the same kinds of problems, only more acutely. Teachers need to be flexible and creative in assisting these students. For example, they need to design a firm but fair tardy and absence policy, and to know that non-academic services such as school breakfast and health care can help poor students attain academic goals. They need to work around parents' complex work schedules and to enlist the help of other school professionals in removing any barriers to students' learning. As with all students, they need to work on building warm, caring relationships.

Finally, teachers must strive to avoid what Martin Haberman called the "pedagogy of poverty" (Haberman, 1991), the typical teaching that goes on in low-income schools. This pedagogy consists of rote learning, based on drill and practice. Teachers command and students comply. There is nothing wrong with drill and practice in and of itself, but when it becomes the exclusive teaching behavior, Haberman argues that it becomes problematic:

> The pedagogy of poverty does not work. Youngsters achieve neither minimum levels of life skills nor what they are capable of learning. The classroom atmosphere created by constant teacher direction and student compliance seethes with passive resentment that sometimes bubbles up into overt resistance. Teachers burn out because of the emotional and physical energy they must expend to maintain their authority every hour of every day. (p. 291)

As a teacher you will need to move beyond such simple, directive teaching and develop a repertoire of instructional and management strategies that is adaptable to a wide variety of students and teaching situations.

Family Configurations and Distress

Families have changed dramatically over the last several decades. In 1955, a large proportion of families included a mother, a father, and one or more children; nowadays, less than 50 percent of all youth live with both biological parents (Coontz, 1995). Today, the divorce rate for first marriages is over 50 percent, and in 60 percent of American households, both parents work. Many children come to school from single-parent families, with the rate for one-parent families varying by race: 17 percent white, 28 percent Hispanic, 54 percent black (Educational Testing Service, 1992).

Although most people assume that these shifting patterns are bad for children, research on the effects of these changes on student performance in school is actually mixed. For example, working mothers' self-esteem and family financial security is enhanced by their employment, both of which contribute to a positive environment for children (Hoffman, 1986). On the other hand, children can become insecure if their mothers work when they are very young. One study showed that the achievement of children left alone by working parents may decline. However, another study showed that girls and adolescents of working mothers have higher achievement and higher self-esteem. Some studies find that latch-key children and children from single-parent families are at risk for school failure, but several others find no difference between these children and those from more conventional family arrangements (Coontz, 1995).

How can we make sense of these conflicting findings? Overall, it appears that the particular family configuration is less important than quality of family life and the economic status of the family. If parents can provide a decent standard of living and good day care, then the actual family structure diminishes in importance (Coontz, 1995). At the same time, if certain family activities, such as reading to children, monitoring their television watching, or participating in special traditions or events are missing, then children have more difficulty both at home and in school.

At the same time, Stephanie Coontz (1995) warns against falling into a "nostalgia trap" in regard to the American family. She reminds us that only for a few short years (the 1950s) did large numbers of Americans identify the "nuclear family as the fount of virtue" and parents as fully responsible for their children's personal adjustment" (p. K7). Throughout most of American history, according to Coontz, parenting was treated in a casual fashion and children were seldom carefully supervised.

Child Abuse

You may know, or you certainly have read about, children who have been abused by their parents or by other adults. Virtually every classroom today has students who have been the victims of this abuse. Abuse includes physical attack, sexual molestation, and psychological abuse. In 1993, the U.S. Department of Health and Human Services published statistics on the increase in child abuse during the past two decades, which Figure 9.4 illustrates.

Experts believe this problem is even more widespread than we think, because many cases of child abuse go unreported. Obviously teachers have the responsibility to teach these children, but as with children of poverty, their emotional and physical scars can make this a difficult goal. Teachers also have a responsibility to deal with known child abuse situations by helping children seek protection and

Figure 9.4 Rise in Child Abuse in the United States: 1976–1993

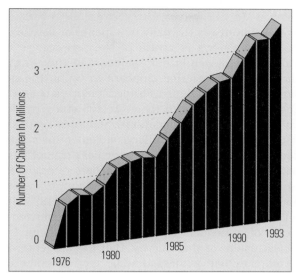

Rise in the reported victims of child abuse and neglect, 1976–1993. Of the cases officially confirmed in 1993, an estimated 14% involved children who had been sexually abused.

Source: U.S. Department of Health and Human Services, 1994, p. 14.

treatment. Indeed, in some states, teachers are required by law to report suspected cases of child abuse. This too is a difficult responsibility, an aspect of the teacher's work that creates much heartache and anger. Are you aware of these dramatically rising child abuse figures? Do you think people really abused children less in the past than they do today? Or, is the rise we see in statistics due to greater awareness and higher reporting?

Drug and Alcohol Abuse

Another social problem that youth bring to school, drug and alcohol abuse, actually dates back to the early twentieth century. While use of drugs such as marijuana and cocaine has mostly been decreasing in recent years, alcohol use by teens has remained steady over the past 20 years. In a recent survey, 76 percent of adolescents reported that they consumed alcohol during the previous year whereas 90 percent reported trying it at one time or another (National Educational Goals Panel, 1995). Alcohol use was highest for whites (80 percent) followed by Hispanics (77 percent), and was lowest for blacks (64 percent). The same ethnic pattern, but with much lower percentages (about 25 percent) was found for marijuana use. A few students (about 7 percent) reported using drugs at school, with little variation by race. There are recent indications that marijuana

use may be increasing among teens of all racial groups.

There is a correlation between drug use and poor performance in school. For example, marijuana users are more likely to receive failing grades than nonusers, and most drop-outs are users. Of course, it may be that drug use is an effect of poor grades and school failure (an escape device) rather than a cause of them.

Just about everyone believes that drug use is a serious problem that schools have a responsibility to help solve. The schools' response has been mainly to provide students with information about the negative consequences of substance abuse. The best programs seem to be large-scale to involve entire schools, the parents, and the larger community. One example of such a program is D.A.R.E. (Drug Abuse Resistance Education). Targeted for upper-elementary students, D.A.R.E. brings local law enforcement officers to school on a regular basis where they conduct motivational workshops on the dangers of drugs. At the secondary level, one of the most promising antidrug programs has been peer counseling. Unfortunately, these programs have not been well researched, and their efficacy has recently been called into question (Rich, 1997).

Teachers have an important role to play in regard to drug education. In addition to being role models for students, they can support schoolwide and community drug resistance programs. Teachers can also conduct frank and open discussions with young students as they approach the age when they may want to experiment with drugs and alcohol. However, teachers have to be careful not to preach or moralize. If they exaggerate the harmful effects of drugs, they are likely to lose their credibility and be ignored by today's informed and sophisticated youth.

Teen Pregnancy

Another long-standing youth problem is teen pregnancy, one that affects not only the education and achievement of pregnant teens but their children as well. This problem is particularly acute in the United States, which has the highest adolescent birth rate of all Western industrialized countries and where teenagers account for about three quarters of out-of-wedlock births. These statistics seem to reflect a higher rate of sexual activity among teenagers and less adult condemnation of early sexuality and out-of-wedlock births.

Teen mothers and their children are likely to live in low-income areas with poorer funded schools and higher exposure to crime, alcohol, and drugs. Pregnant teens are more likely to miss school and to have low performance than other teens. When coupled with health and nutrition problems, this inevitably leads to higher drop-out rates. As a result, the children of teenage mothers face disadvantages that are likely to keep them from academic success when they start school. Thus, the cycle is perpetuated.

As with other social problems, schools are expected to do something about teen pregnancy. The statistics illustrate, however, that most past efforts have not been very successful. Some proposals have focused on the prevention of teenage pregnancy; others have sought benefits for the children. Examples of pregnancy prevention include sex-education programs and school-based programs aimed at raising students' self-esteem and self-control. These programs are nearly always controversial, since many citizens and parents believe that matters of human sexuality are the responsibility of the family or the church, not the school.

Another approach to pregnancy prevention is teaching youth about birth control. Some programs examine the moral and practical implications of early sexual activity and provide admonitions to young people to abstain from sex until they are older and married. In other instances, teachers give students information about how to use various birth control methods. Free condoms are available in some schools. Jocelyn Elders, Surgeon General during the first 2 years of Bill Clinton's presidency, was a well-known advocate of school-based health clinics which would make contraceptives available to high school students who wanted them. Her policies were highly controversial and eventually led to her being fired, another example of the difficulty of dealing with this problem.

In the past, girls who got pregnant during high school were expected to drop out. That trend has been dramatically reversed, as seen by the many school-support services offered in an attempt to keep pregnant teens in school. These services include flexible schedules, individual tutoring, home-based instruction, and school-based child care. Schools have also introduced programs that teach about nutrition and parenting.

There is little doubt that teenage pregnancy is a serious problem, particularly among disadvantaged youth, and that it clearly perpetuates the other social problems discussed in this section. As with drug abuse, teachers must be prepared to have frank and honest discussions, in this case about human sexuality and reproduction and their consequences. Once again, moralizing is less effective than honest discussion, but keep in mind that teachers who choose to take independent action, such as distributing condoms on their own, can soon find themselves in trouble.

Crime, Violence, and Social Tensions

Anyone who reads the daily newspaper or listens to the evening news is aware of the seriousness of crime and violence in our society. And though the amount of violent crime appears to be on the decline, students continue to bring violence and social tensions to school with them. A 1995 study by the National Center for Educational Statistics reported that "an estimated 2.7 million violent crimes take place annually either at school or near school [and that] one in four public school teachers rated physical conflicts among students as being a serious or moderately serious problem in schools." In 1993, the National Center for Education Statistics conducted a survey of students in grades 6 through 12. Figure 9.5 shows results of that survey. Half the students reported they had witnessed some type of crime or victimization and one out of eight reported they had been directly victimized at school.

Social tension among students is closely connected to violence, indeed is often the cause of violence. A survey conducted by the Metropolitan Life Insurance Company (1996) collected information from students in Grades 7 through 12 regarding their perceptions of violence and social tension. Table 9.2 summarizes student responses to the question about how serious they believe violence and social tensions are in their school. As you can see, nonwhite and urban students perceive social tension and violence to be of greater importance. On the average, however, 20 to 25 percent of students living in suburban areas identify threatening remarks, destructive acts, turf battles, physical fights, and gang violence as very serious problems in their schools.

This situation is serious, and it means that tomorrow's teachers must be prepared to confront and stop violence when they see it occurring and to protect victims when they can. Many schools have introduced violence prevention programs aimed at providing students with skills for dealing with disagreements and conflict situations. Findings from most studies, according to Metropolitan Life, indicate that these programs work, and they underscore the critical role teachers play in promoting positive social relations among students. Two important teacher behaviors have been identified: the overall quality of teachers' relationships with students, and the social skills teachers impart to students. When teachers support and treat students with respect, students are more likely to respect and get along

Figure 9.5 **Violence in Schools Reported by Youth**

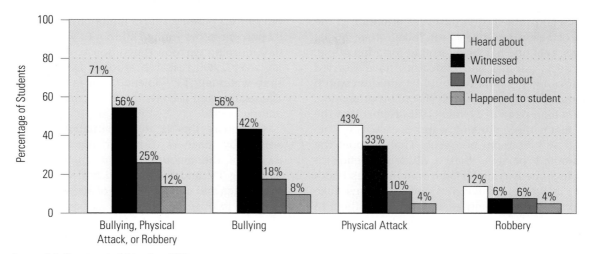

Source: U.S. Department of Education, 1993.

Table 9.2 **Social Tensions in School**

Thinking about your school, do you think each of these issues is a very serious problem, somewhat serious, not very serious, or not at all a serious problem?

| | **SUMMARY OF VERY SERIOUS (in percentages)** | | | | | | |
| | | **White** | | **African American** | | **Hispanic** | |
	Total	**Urban**	**Suburban/ Rural**	**Urban**	**Suburban/ Rural**	**Urban**	**Suburban/Rural**
Tight groups of friends that do not talk to one another	10	11	9	12	14	12	15
Hostile or threatening remarks between different groups of students	26	29	19	38	33	36	31
Threats or destructive acts, other than physical fights	25	31	17	35	28	33	31
Turf battles between different groups of students	22	25	13	36	23	33	34
Physical fights between members of different groups of friends	27	29	20	39	34	35	35
Gang violence	26	28	16	42	35	46	37

SOURCE: After Metropolitan Life Insurance Co., 1996, p. 34

with one another. When teachers show students that there are alternatives to violence and actively teach social skills, students are better able to deal with conflict situations and to be more tolerant of others. The Metropolitan Life study (1996) concludes on an optimistic note regarding schools' ability to do something about violence and social tensions.

One important implication of these findings is that students can and do learn from teachers how to get along better with their fellow students. This message is an important one for educators who feel discouraged by the many factors that contribute to social problems at school that lie outside their control. When these factors are present in the school environment, students are also less likely to perceive social problems in their school as very serious, and they express greater levels of confidence that young people from different backgrounds are treated equally by adults in their community. (p. 37)

Kids and Television

A final social problem that deserves attention is the impact of television on youth. Like other social problems, this one has been around for a long time. For decades, parents and educators have worried about how much TV they should let children watch and about the content of television programming. Studies summarized by Levine (1996) report that the typical elementary student watches television between 25 and 30 hours per week. That is about the same amount of time that a student spends in school. In some ways television watching has had a positive effect on children. Good programs take children into other countries and introduce them to other cultures in ways that cannot be done with books. They give children an awareness of contemporary affairs that their pretelevision peers did not have. Likewise, programs like Sesame Street help teach emerging literacy and numeracy skills.

At the same time, TV has had some decidedly negative effects on children and their education. It competes with time for homework and family activities and too often reinforces prejudice and stereotyping. Most important, however, are the effects of TV violence. As early as 1962, a surgeon general's report called for a curb on television violence because of its effect on children. During that same decade, Albert Bandura, a well known psychologist at Stanford University, conducted a series of studies called the Bobo Doll experiments. In these experiments, Bandura had one group of preschool children watch a simulated TV show with an aggressive scene. The scene consisted of a man approaching a stuffed clown named Bobo. After a brief verbal altercation, the man threw Bobo on the floor and hit him, saying, "Pow, right in the nose, boom, boom." The man also hit the clown with a mallet and kicked it. Bandura had another group of children watch a live performance of the same scene. Children in a control group were not exposed to either live or simulated violence. Later all children were observed playing in an area that had toy guns and mallets. Children in both experimental groups displayed much more aggressive behavior than children in the control group. Although Bandura's' study was criticized at the time for methodological flaws, later studies have continued to demonstrate that children who observe violence on TV and in real life are more likely to be violent.

A recent literature review and study by Madeline Levine (1996) supports earlier studies and reveals some rather startling findings about children's TV watching. Levine reports that TV today is filled with violence, hardly a surprising conclusion. However, she also reports that young children usually witness this violence in unsupervised situations. Three out of four parents set no limits on TV viewing, and 92 percent allow young children to watch any Saturday morning cartoon they choose. After summarizing over 1,000 research studies, Levine concluded that watching TV violence makes children more aggressive, and it contributes to crime and violence among youth.

Obviously this is not a situation that can be solved by teachers. However, teachers should be aware of the amount of time their students are watching TV, and they should find ways to discuss the causes and consequences of aggressive behavior when it is observed in their classrooms. Teachers also can help their students become more selective in the television programs they watch.

Other Social Problems

As a teacher, you may encounter a number of other societal problems, ranging from poor health care and poor nutrition to teen suicide. Because all these problems affect student achievement, many schools have special programs to help young people cope with these situations. Obviously, teachers can expect to be deeply involved in these programs. In some cases, such as suspected child abuse, teachers have a legal responsibility to report the situation. In all cases, teachers have a *moral obligation* and responsibility to care.

Perspective on Social Problems

Although it is important for teachers to be aware of social problems and the effects they have on students, it is equally important that they maintain a sense of healthy skepticism about media treatment of these problems. For example, media portrayals of schools lead one to believe that school violence is a widespread and rapidly increasing problem. Whereas violence certainly is a problem, it is a localized problem. Recent surveys, for example, show that only 5 percent of high school seniors (most in high-poverty areas) reported being injured by a weapon at school (National Educational Goals Panel, 1995). Schoolyard fights are a problem, but they have been for a century. The fact is that most teachers and students work in safe environments, clearly not the impression one gets from TV news or news magazines.

To illustrate this situation further, pollsters recently conducted a survey of 750 sixth- to twelfth-graders in New York City public schools, a system that serves a million students, many of whom represent the urban poor. Certainly most people perceive New York City as a district with serious problems.

But the survey found that 91 percent of the students felt safe coming to school, 88 percent said their teachers were good or excellent, 86 percent use computers in school, 81 percent like living in New York, and 86 percent plan to attend college (Tomasky, 1996). The current drop-out rate is a troubling 30 percent, but in the 1950s it was 50 percent. To be sure, New York City schools struggle with guns, violence, drugs, and teen pregnancy, but for the vast majority of students, these problems are less likely to affect their lives than is the less sensational but more important disparity in funding between rich and poor districts.

SCHOOLS, SOCIAL REFORM, AND THE NEXT MILLENNIUM

Most social problems described in this chapter have existed for generations, and it is unrealistic to expect them to disappear during the coming decades. Therefore, we conclude this chapter with a discussion about the school's role in social reform and a glimpse of those forces in the larger society that may have a rather dramatic impact on the purposes and operations of twenty-first century schools.

Schools and Social Reform

Let's begin by pondering the question, Should schools be expected to solve society's ills and to create a new social order? This is a complex and provocative question, and it returns us to the purposes of schooling introduced at the beginning of this chapter and discussed at some length in Chapter 3.

You remember that one of the three dominant purposes of schools is social renewal and improvement. Social activists in every era, from the reformers of the early nineteenth century until now, have looked to the schools to help cure society's ills. Educator George Counts provided one of the most eloquent statements of this perspective at the height of the Great Depression. In a series of speeches later published as a pamphlet, *Dare the School Build a New Social Order* (1932), Counts argued that the United States, indeed the whole world, was in serious danger because of the social and economic dislocation brought about by the Great Depression. As illustrated in the following passage, Counts believed that the schools could help fashion a new social order:

> We can view a world order rushing toward collapse with no more concern than the outcome of a horse

race; we can see injustice, crime and misery in their most terrible forms all about us . . .

> . . .

> If . . . education is to be genuinely progressive, it must emancipate itself from the influence of the . . . (liberal minded, upper middle class) . . . face squarely and courageously every social issue, come to grips with life and all of its stark realties; establish an organic relationship with the community, develop a realistic and comprehensive theory of welfare, fashion a compelling and challenging vision of human destiny, and become less frightened than it is today at the bogies of imposition and indoctrination. (as cited in Urban & Wagoner, 1996, pp. 249–250)

Today, those who argue that schools should address such issues as drugs and violence, racism and segregation, and poverty and despair, use essentially the same arguments that Counts used in the 1930s. To them, schools are remiss if they teach children only about academic subjects and basic skills. Instead, they purport, schools should challenge existing social arrangements, and teachers should plunge into the social arena and help create a fairer and more just social order.

On the other hand, many people believe that it is naive to think that schools can fix problems they did not cause and over which they have little control. If schools try, they are doomed to failure said social critic, Neil Postman (1995):

> If you heap upon the schools all of the problems that the family, the church, the political systems and the economy cannot solve, the school becomes a kind of well-financed garbage dump, from which very little can be expected except the unsweet odor of failure. (p. 3)

Individuals such as Postman point to several contemporary social problems to buttress their arguments. Desegregation is one. The expectations that school desegregation after the *Brown* decision in 1954 would fuel harmonious race relationships was unrealistic. In retrospect, the schools by themselves could not accomplish school integration in the face of entrenched racial attitudes of many whites, who moved to the suburbs or sent their children to private schools. Drug use and violence also are pervasive social problems that are neither caused by schools nor predominantly connected to schools. Though schools can play an important role in providing information about drugs and preventing criminals from entering school buildings, it is unlikely that schools can solve the fundamental drug problem. Poverty is yet another social problem that schools have only limited power to address. Most people

Table 9.3 **Assigning Blame: Schools or Society**

In your opinion, which is more at fault for the problems currently facing public education in this community—the performance of the local public schools or the effect of societal problems? [in percentages]

	National Totals	No Children in School	Public School Parents	Nonpublic School Parents
Performance of schools	16	14	18	26
Effect of societal problems	73	73	75	63
Don't know	11	13	7	11

Source: After S. Elam, 1990, p. 54.

agree that it is important for schools to educate poor children, but there are many aspects of poverty, such as job availability and adequate housing, that are beyond the school's immediate control.

It is likely that the debate about the school's role in addressing social problems will be an ongoing one. It is also likely that the controversy surrounding this debate will wax and wane as one or another social problem becomes more and less contentious. In short, schools will always exist within a social context, and students will always bring society's problems to school with them. As a teacher, you will be faced with troubled students in your classroom, and you will need to be clear about your own views and responsibilities. At the same time, you might be encouraged to find that many citizens do not assign blame to schools for society's problems, as Table 9.3 shows.

Do you think schools should be blamed for society's problems? Should schools and teachers be expected to build a new social order? Should schools teach about social problems? Should they be held responsible for solving society's problems? If schools are responsible, which social problems deserve priority? Which are beyond the scope of school intervention?

Schools, Society, and the Third Millennium

This chapter began with the statement that the school is a social institution created by the larger society to achieve important social goals and that schools inevitably change in response to changing social forces. Let's think for a moment about changes currently going on in our society that will likely affect the schools where you will spend a large portion of your teaching career.

We have no crystal ball that gives us clairvoyance about the future. However, futurists such as Kennedy (1993), Naisbitt and Aburdene (1990), and Toffler (1980), describe current trends and forces that are

Table 9.4 **Major Forces Shaping Twenty-First Century Society and Schools**

1. A postindustrial economy based on information, knowledge, education, and service.
2. Globalization of business and culture.
3. Explosive technological change.
4. A labor force consisting primarily of highly skilled knowledge workers.
5. Major demographic shifts toward more diversity.

likely to continue shaping twenty-first century society and schools, a few of which are listed in Table 9.4.

The economies of the United States and most other developed countries are in the process of dramatic transformation. We are moving rapidly from an industrial age based on manufacturing to an information age based on knowledge. Rail, coal, steel, rubber, and textiles no longer dominate the economic scene. Instead IBM, Intel, and Microsoft represent the global economic leadership of the future. California's Silicon Valley replaced New England's Merrimack Valley as the place where society's important work is done, and Microsoft's Bill Gates replaced Andrew Carnegie as the richest man in the United States.

Information-age economies and cultures are no longer national in scope. Instead, the production of goods and information and their distribution and consumption are global. For instance, over a dozen countries manufacture the parts needed to assemble the new Boeing 777; doors for the plane are made in Japan, engines in England, and the rudder comes from Canada. Most of the customers for the 777 are not United States airlines but instead are from Great Britain, China, Saudi Arabia, and Kuwait. Nike running shoes, which are sold throughout the world, are made in Mexico with materials from Thailand. Toyotas are assembled in the United States under the supervision of Japanese managers working with parts manufactured in Central America.

Information-age economies are technologically driven, and these technologies change quickly. This is particularly true for the technologies used to create, store, and disseminate information. As one new type of hardware or software is introduced, work on its successor is already underway. Within our immediate lifetimes, our computers, fax machines, cellular phones, and internet accesses have all changed more quickly than we can keep abreast of.

The information-age labor force is also significantly different from that of the industrial age. Instead of factory workers, the information age requires a labor force of intellectual and technical workers. Instead of spending a lifetime working at the same job or for the same company, information-age workers have to prepare for changing jobs and retraining several times during a career. The question we need to ask is, so what impact will all this have on schools?

Schools as we know them today have maintained their dominant characteristics since the height of the industrial age, between 1870 and 1950, and they are organized for industrial-age learning. The larger social forces now in play will affect schools in many important ways. For instance, the definition of what should go into our cultural tool kit will change. International information-age companies will look for individuals who are multilingual and multicultural. Twenty-first century schools and students will not have the luxury of making second-language acquisition an elective, or a requirement only for those who pursue scholarly or diplomatic careers. In a global community, all Americans will need to know other people's languages as well as their own. They are well advised to acquire an in-depth understanding of the norms and values of other cultures as well. The ethnocentrism characteristic of American business and education for the past 100 years will no longer suffice in communities that cross national boundaries and merge with other cultures.

The larger social forces will also necessitate new and different perspectives about what it means to develop human potential. The economic, social, and political institutions of the future will want workers who are more than simple technicians able only to follow directions and perform routine tasks. Schools will be expected to prepare leaders and workers who are capable of creativity and resourcefulness and who have advanced problem-solving skills. Society will also expect people to work from their homes, using technological networks rather than a central office as their operating base. It is interesting that futurists such as Toffler (1980) predict that schools

of the future may resemble those of the past more than those of the present. For example, it is likely that tomorrow's students will spend more time learning outside rather than inside the classroom. Also, education may be interspersed with work and spread throughout a lifetime rather than be crammed into one's early years.

The factory organization model, which has dominated the twentieth century, will be reshaped to address the problems and values of the information-age society. Already, organizational modes in the larger society are changing from fixed, bureaucratic structures to flexible and diverse structures. Self-governing teams working together in cooperative rather than competitive ways are replacing the hierarchical, boss-worker relationships of the past. Schools will change to mirror these organizational patterns. The schools-as-factory metaphor will be replaced by a vision of schools and classrooms as learning communities. Leadership and authority, traditionally given to the principal, will rest in the hands of school councils made up of teachers, parents, and community members. Collegial supervision among teachers will replace the traditional top-down supervision by administrators.

It is probably not an exaggeration to say that we will need to rethink every aspect of schooling, ranging from its overarching social purposes to its relationship with specific social problems to stay abreast of future social change. The resulting changes should make teaching one of the most interesting and challenging careers of the twenty-first century.

SUMMARY

- There are tight connections between schools and society. Society designs schools to perform vital social functions.

- In societies characterized by hunting and agrarian economies, children learned from observing and imitating adults.

- Imitative and informal learning fit simpler societies; however, contemporary, complex societies require formal educational systems.

- Many purposes have been proposed for schools. All of these can be divided into three main categories: transmitting the culture, developing human potential, and reconstructing society.

- While transmitting the culture, schools provide political socialization for the young and instruction on the culture's tool kit, which includes the culture's beliefs, skills, and symbolic systems.

- Schools help individuals develop their own unique potential through preparation for college, work, parenting, and citizenship.

- Reform-minded individuals believe that schools have responsibilities not only to transmit the culture but also to motivate students and to give them the skills to make society better.

- Unlike some of society's institutions, schools have competing purposes, which can produce conflict. Trying to balance competing purposes is one of the most challenging aspects of a teacher's job.

- Because schools are so tightly connected to the needs of society, the problems of society come to school with the students.

- Social class, poverty, and their effects become educational problems, because students' social and economic backgrounds affect school learning. In general, middle-class teachers expect middle-class behavior from all their students, a situation that can create a mismatch between some students and the school's culture.

- There are positive actions teachers can take to address the problems of social class and poverty. They can be alert to their students' communicative styles and to their home situations.

- Family configurations affect students and student learning. These configurations have changed dramatically over the past several decades. Today many students come to school from single-parent families. Teachers, however, should not jump to the conclusion that this situation is always bad for children.

- Child abuse is another problem children bring to school. Teachers have responsibilities to be alert to potential child abuse situations and to help victims receive available counseling and services.

- Some older students do poorly in school because they abuse drugs and alcohol. Teachers can help this situation by being role models for their students and by having frank, honest discussions about drug and alcohol abuse.

- Many schools today have programs to deal with the problem of teen pregnancy. As with drug abuse, teachers can help out by having frank and open discussions with their students and by supporting schoolwide and communitywide pregnancy prevention programs.

- Today's students spend a large proportion of their time watching television, and some aspects of TV have negative effects on children. Although teachers cannot stop students from watching television, they can help them to become more selective viewers.

- Although it is important for teachers to be aware of the social problems children bring to school, it is equally as important that they maintain a healthy perspective about the scope of these problems. Often, media attention to problems makes them seem more pervasive than they actually are.

- The next millennium is likely to have a rather dramatic impact on the purposes and operation of schools. Schools of the twenty-first century will prepare students to live in an information-based society rather than the industrial society they served in the past. Thus schools will need to change.

- Schools of the future are likely to be characterized by greater flexibility. They will use new and different means to help students realize their potential and prepare for life in a different society.

Readings for the Professional

Bruner, J. *The Culture of Education.* Cambridge, MA: Harvard University Press, 1996.
This is an excellent book for helping to rethink the purposes of schooling from the emerging perspective of cultural psychology.

Kennedy, P. *Preparing for the Twenty-First Century.* New York: Random House, 1993.
This book provides a provocative analysis of what the twenty-first century will be like and how we can prepare to live in this different world.

Postman, N. *The End of Education: Redefining the Value of School.* New York: Alfred A. Knopf, 1995.
This book is an insightful analysis of how we have lost sight of the true purposes of schools and how these purposes can be restored.

CHAPTER 10

School Governance and Finance

The governance and finance of American public education is a multitiered system, with state government having the primary legal responsibility to educate its citizens. However, both historically and presently, local and federal levels of government have figured prominently in the control and finance of schooling. Traditionally, the primary source of funding has come from local property taxes, and local school boards have had wide discretionary powers over educational policies and practices. In the last third of the twentieth century, however, this picture steadily changed, with state governments assuming an increasing responsibility for funding schools and for control over local curriculum and school activities. During this same period, the federal government first increased then decreased both its funding and control of local education.

The control and financing of America's schools is a dynamic process that varies from state to state and is constantly changing as a result of shifting socioeconomic and political conditions. In addition, there is a close relationship between funding and control. As funding for schools shifts from one level of government to another, control over what goes on

Background

Role of State Government
Legislature
  State Boards of Education
  State Departments of Education
  Chief State School Officer
Governors
State Courts

Role of Local Government
School Boards
  Finances
  Personnel
  Curriculum
  Students
  Maintaining the Infrastructure
Superintendents and Central Administration
Principals
Policy Development and Implementation
School District Organization
  Traditional
  Site-Based Management
  Schools of Choice
  Charter Schools
  Privatization

Role of Federal Government
Legislative Influence
Executive Influence

Judicial Influence
Other Federal Education Agencies

Nongovernmental Influences on School Governance
Teachers' Organizations
School Boards' Associations
Professional Educational Organizations
Parent Organizations
Business Organizations

Funding of Public Education
Collection of Revenues
  Federal Revenues
  State and Local Revenues
  Collection Inequities
Distribution of Funds
Funding Reform
Other Financial Concerns
  Graying of America
  Accountability
  Increasing Enrollments
  Inadequate Infrastructure
New Funding Practices

New Approaches for the Twenty-First Century

Summary

Readings for the Professional

in schools—how the money is used—also shifts from one level to another.

You may be wondering how much school government and funding issues affect you, a prospective classroom teacher. The answer, of course, is that they have a tremendous impact, not only on the salaries you are able to command, but on such issues as class size, classroom supplies, extracurricular activities, and teacher accountability for learning outcomes.

In addition, as control of education continues to be decentralized, that is, pushed down to the building level, teachers are being asked increasingly to share in matters of school leadership. The concept of the school as a learning community, in which all stakeholders—teachers, students, administration, parents—share in school decision making and accountability, is currently emerging. And with this new perspective comes the need for teachers to be knowledgeable about matters of school funding and governance.

BACKGROUND

You may recall from our discussion in Chapter 7 that there is wide variation in the public's perception of how America's schools are performing. There are almost as many people who believe they are failing or close to failing as there are people who believe they are excellent. Although such variation might be expected when rating any public institution, there are several reasons why the evaluations of our public schools vary so widely. First, there is no central education agency or authority in this country, as there is in many European countries. This means there is no government-sponsored nationwide consensus on what students should learn, the levels of proficiency they should achieve, how they should be taught, the length of the school year, graduation requirements, and teacher certification requirements. In America, such matters have always been established, implemented, and enforced at the state level. As a result, although there is great similarity among states, there are 50 different sets of education codes in this country.

Another factor contributing to the wide disparity among individual school districts is the fact that until the 1970s, most state governments exercised only minimum control over local education. Thus, state legislatures have always been legally responsible for what takes place in schools, but in practice, individual districts have had almost complete control over school operation.

This picture changed dramatically during the latter third of the twentieth century. As issues of equality, especially in terms of student performance on standardized tests, came increasingly into the public's attention, a growing number of states moved to establish both curriculum standards and test-based graduation requirements for high schools. This means that local districts have increasingly less control over curriculum. For example, in 1995, New Jersey mandated that all high schools in the state must develop course content dealing with the Holocaust and other instances of genocide, a growing trend nationally.

Additionally, much of the school variation in this country can be traced to the fact that financial support for the school comes primarily from local *real estate taxes.* Thus, the quality of education within each district depends on a community's wealth. Under this arrangement, children living in affluent suburbs in the Northeast are far more likely to have small classes, adequate laboratory equipment, access to computers, and a wide variety of cocurricular and extracurricular activities than are those living in the deep South or in many inner-city areas. The courts in a number of states have attempted to remedy this situation by shifting the balance of school funding from the local to the state level. Under court mandates, many states use state tax monies to supplement inadequate local funding in poor districts, hoping thereby to lessen the gap in student performance outcomes.

In order to understand the changing roles of local, state, and federal governments in the control and funding of education, we will need to look first at how each of these levels is organized, then at their traditional educational responsibilities. It is important to note that all three levels of government are divided into the same three branches: *legislative, executive,* and *judicial.* Although local courts do not generally deal with educational matters, the role of the courts at the state and federal levels has been substantial, as we see in Chapter 11. In this chapter, however, we focus on legislative and executive influences on education, beginning with the state, the unit that is legally responsible for education.

ROLE OF STATE GOVERNMENT

Legislatures

The state legislature is the primary source of educational policy and has broad powers to enact legislation. Not only do legislatures determine the selection and operating procedures of the state board of education, the state department of education, and the chief state school officer, they also have control over the following:

- Structure of local school districts and method of selecting of board members.
- Level of financial support for education and methods of taxation.
- Personnel policies, including tenure and certification.
- Curriculum requirements.
- Student policies including testing and graduation requirements.
- Length of school year and school day.
- Building and construction policies.

Until fairly recently state legislatures did little more than establish broad policies in the above areas. In most states they left the actual governance of schools to local school districts. However, as issues dealing with student performance standards and inequality in school funding have emerged, state legislatures have enacted an increasing number of statutes extending their control over local schools. In addition to determining the structure of the educational establishment at the state level, state legislatures are also the source of empowerment for local school boards.

State Boards of Education

All states except Wisconsin have **state boards of education,** the majority of which are appointed by the governors. The primary role of state boards of education is to develop, implement, and regulate state codes that carry out legislative acts related to education. They also appoint personnel to state departments of education, manage state educational funds, collect data and keep records, appoint advisory bodies, hear disputes, and advise the legislature and governor on educational matters. In many states, there are separate boards for higher education. Boards range in size from as few as 7 to as many as 17 members (State Education, 1995). Members usually serve without pay.

State Departments of Education

The **state departments of education** are the agencies charged with implementing and regulating educational legislation and codes. They are the agencies schools deal with on a day-to-day basis and are often organized into several divisions with staffs that sometimes number in the thousands. In recent decades, as both state and federal regulations dealing with education have expanded, so too have state departments of education.

Chief State School Officer

The state department of education is directed by a **chief state school officer,** often referred to as the *state superintendent* or *commissioner of education.* In the majority of states this individual is appointed by either the governor or the state board of education; in the remaining states he or she is elected. Many maintain that election to the post makes the office more responsive to the people, others argue it entails too much involvement in partisan politics. Historically chief state school officers have been primarily male, but there is a growing number of females who occupy the office (The Council, 1995).

Governors

Although governors' responsibilities extend far beyond schools and education, in recent years school issues, particularly equalizing school funding between rich and poor districts, have become a top priority for many governors. As a result, they have become far more involved both in making recommendations for educational legislation and in allocating tax monies to address educational problems. Also, in every state except North Carolina, the governor has the power to veto educational legislation and funding.

Not only do governors have a great deal of power over educational policy and practice within their own states, but in recent years, the National Governors' Association (NGA) has become increasingly influential regarding national education policy. President Bill Clinton, then Governor of Arkansas, was chair of the NGA when it developed the list of national education goals that eventually became Goals 2000, establishing the national agenda for education.

State Courts

Legislatures enact the laws that establish educational policy, but it is the courts that interpret these laws when disputes arise. The courts must first make sure that laws do not violate either state or federal constitutions and then must apply these laws in specific cases. These activities have resulted in a body of *case law,* which is discussed in detail in Chapter 11. Here it is important to note that the role of the courts in shaping educational policy and practice grew considerably during the 1970s and 1980s, especially in the areas of teacher and student rights and school finance. In fact, entire state school systems, such as Kentucky's, were restructured as the result of state courts' rulings regarding inequities in school funding.

ROLE OF LOCAL GOVERNMENT

Although state legislatures are legally responsible for enacting the laws that determine school policies, the basic unit of school governance has historically been the local school district. Throughout this country, school districts vary enormously in size, from those with only one school and a few students to the New York City school system, which has approximately 1 million students, 1,000 schools, over 53,000 teachers, and annual expenditures of over 4.5 billion dollars. The number of school districts within states varies widely also. For example, the entire state of Hawaii is a single school district, whereas Maryland has 24 districts and New Jersey over 600. Some districts contain only elementary schools, some secondary, and some both. There is also great variation in the types of students served, per capita expenditure, and the quantity and quality of programs provided. Some affluent suburban districts serve predominantly white, middle-class students, have annual expenditures approaching $10,000 per student, and provide excellent programs, facilities, and equipment. Others, such as those in most inner-city areas, work mainly with minority students and those in lower socioeconomic levels, spend less than half as much as wealthier districts, and are unable to provide such essentials as new books and computer labs.

School Boards

Local school boards are the basic governing unit for education. In the United States, there are over 15,000 local school boards responsible for 42 million students in over 84,000 schools. Eighty-five percent to 90 percent of local school board members are elected. The remaining members, mostly in large urban districts, are appointed.

As with state school boards, many believe that election rather than appointment of school board members leads to greater accountability to the people. However, others have questioned this because of the relatively low number of people who vote in school board elections, in some cases fewer than 7 percent. In fact, a 20 percent voter turnout for a school board election is considered an overwhelming success. In light of the fact that school boards spend more money than any other single public service at any level of government, this has increasingly become a cause for alarm among those looking to reform the structure of educational governance. Many argue that school boards reflect the composition and values of the local power structure rather than of the whole community.

Joel Spring (1993) developed a model to analyze four general types of communities and the school boards which reflect them. They are:

- **Dominated communities,** in which majority power is exercised by a few persons or one person. Such communities generally produce *dominated school boards* representing the community elite.

- **Factional communities,** in which two factions having different values (particularly religious values) compete for power. In such communities, *factional school boards,* with members who have won hotly contested elections and rarely agree on any agenda items, are the norm.

- **Pluralistic communities,** in which competition exists between a variety of community interest groups with no single group dominating school policies. *Status congruent school boards,* which represent a wide variety of community groups and encourage open debate in hopes of reaching a consensus, are prevalent here.

- **Inert communities,** in which there is no visible power structure and there is little competition for positions on the school board and little display of public interest in the schools. Such communities tend to produce *sanctioning school boards,* which are relatively inactive, do not represent any factions within the community, and tend to approve the recommendations of the school administrative staff.

Certainly political activity in each type of school district varies widely, but in one important way the outcome is very similar: Between five and nine people generally make decisions that affect the lives of virtually all citizens in the community. All citizens are required to attend school for a minimum number of years, and the majority are required to pay taxes to support their schools. School board decisions include not only the rate at which the community will be taxed to support schools but the amount and quality of schooling students will receive.

What types of people usually make up school boards? They are predominantly male, white, well educated, older, affluent, conservative, and in professional or managerial occupations. The number of women on local school boards has increased from just under 33 percent in 1981 to slightly over 40 percent in 1995. During the same period, minority representation has declined from 8.5 percent to 7.1 percent (Education Vital Signs, 1994).

It is important to realize that, as individuals, school board members have no more authority in school matters than the average citizen. They have power to make decisions and to implement policies only as members of a legally constituted school board. Individual board members cannot act on behalf of the board unless they have been directed by the entire board in a legally held board meeting, which is usually open to the public. All final decisions in school matters must be approved by the entire board.

School boards' responsibilities fall into five main areas: finances, personnel, curriculum, students, and maintaining the infrastructure of the school system. We briefly describe their role in each of these areas.

Finances

School boards must develop budgets, obtain revenue, and determine the disbursement of monies. Of all the topics discussed at school board meetings, financial matters occupy the greatest amount of time, over 25 percent (School Boards, 1992). Budgets are developed annually. They usually begin with the articulated needs of the classroom teacher, are then integrated into the broader school-level budget, and finally are submitted to the superintendent. The superintendent then merges school-level budgets into districtwide budgets that are taken before the school board for review and approval. A board may add to or subtract from the budget presented by the superintendent. In some states, the budget must then be voted on by the taxpayers. This budgeting process usually begins in the fall of each year for the upcoming academic year. This means that when you begin your first year of teaching, your classroom supplies will have been ordered under a budget approved the previous spring.

Personnel

All school personnel, from janitors and aides to the superintendent, are appointed by the school board. Although principals and the superintendent usually interview new teachers and other personnel, it is the board who hires them. The board is also responsible for determining how many employees are needed in the various positions within the district and for approving additional positions and job descriptions when necessary. Finally, if an employee is to be terminated, the board is responsible for carrying out this action.

Curriculum

One of the most important responsibilities of school boards is to provide a curriculum that will prepare a wide variety of students for success in college or in the world of work. Although all states stipulate minimum curricular requirements, it is local school boards that approve the actual courses of study, textbooks (if not selected by the state), and other curricular materials. If students do poorly on standardized tests, it is the school board that is generally held responsible by the public.

Students

In addition to curricular and academic standards, school boards are also responsible for policies that govern other areas of school life: cocurricular and extracurricular activities, transportation, out-of-school trips, attendance, dress and grooming, coordination with social services, and most important, conduct and discipline. Boards establish policies in all these areas and serve as the ultimate courts of appeal regarding all disciplinary matters. Although principals and superintendents can suspend students, such suspensions can be appealed to the board. Only school boards can expel students.

Maintaining the Infrastructure

The buildings and grounds of any school district have much to do with the public perception of its schools. Although we all know that high-quality teaching and learning can take place in a log cabin, in today's world, run-down buildings and poorly kept grounds are usually equated in the public's eye with poor education. In addition to routine maintenance, school boards are responsible for determining the need for capital improvements, such as a new roof, larger grounds, and new schools.

Superintendents and Central Administration

By far the most important person the board hires is the **superintendent,** who advises the board and provides the vision, leadership, and challenge for the district's other employees. If the superintendent is weak, lazy, or uncaring, not much can be expected from those who are working under him or her. On the other hand, a superintendent who is intelligent and has a clear vision of public education can gain community support and inspire the district's teachers to provide a high quality education that is recognized and appreciated by parents and other citizens.

The superintendent is the chief executive officer of a school district, with the responsibility for carrying out the policies of the school board and seeing to the day-to-day operations of the district. Depending on a district's size, the superintendent may be assisted by a number of assistant superintendents, responsible for such areas as curriculum, personnel, transportation, and buildings and grounds. Therefore, the superintendent is required to have extensive training and experience in both supervision and administration. Increasingly, superintendents are expected to have doctoral degrees, and most have come through the ranks as teachers, principals, and assistant superintendents.

The responsibilities of and demands on superintendents are great and growing. The superintendent must interact with and respond to substantial numbers of staff and students whose needs and problems often cannot be predicted on a day-by-day basis. This includes carrying out the statutes of the state and federal governments as well as those policies and directives put in place by the local school board. Additionally, superintendents must be constantly prepared to address the many demands of parents, both individually and as representative groups, in the form of parent and civic organizations. Since few institutions in our society are as visible and vulnerable to criticism as the public schools, the position of superintendent is highly vulnerable. Various studies have reported that the average tenure of a superintendent is 3 to 4 years, with turnover in urban areas occurring even more frequently.

In most states, superintendents and other central office administrators do not receive tenure. Therefore, their ongoing employment and annual salary increases, unlike those of teachers, are dependent on regular evaluations, which are done by boards of education. As those boards change, goals and directions for school districts can also change, sometimes dramatically, and this often leads to a search for a new superintendent. On the other hand, when a school board becomes entrenched, which frequently happens in dominated communities, a mediocre superintendent can remain in charge of a mediocre school district with little hope of change for many years. Many proposals for school reform focus on local school governance levels and the intractability of the traditional structures.

Some districts, especially in urban areas, are taking what can be described as a "management team" approach to the role of the superintendency. In 1995, the Illinois state legislature abolished the superintendent's position in Chicago and gave the mayor sole control over who runs the schools. The mayor appointed the former city budget director as superintendent, who immediately appointed a five-member board, which gained strong media support for its frugal approach to addressing school budget concerns. In Seattle an ex-Army general with a background as a Pentagon financial expert was hired as superintendent. Although this raises questions about who will provide academic leadership in school districts, many predict that with increasing social problems and public demand for fiscal accountability, this trend will continue.

Principals

For most students, especially young ones, the most daunting school figure is the principal. Most students who have frequent contact with this individual do so for disciplinary reasons. This reality reflects an important issue concerning how schools should be structured. Although "being sent to the principal's office" has historically been a primary component of a school's disciplinary system, many argue that the principal's primary role should be that of instructional leader. Others maintain that, in reality, the primary responsibility of principals is managerial and those trained as managers can do the job better than those prepared as educators. New Jersey legitimized this perspective in 1994 when they made it possible for those with degrees in management but not education to receive administrative certification after serving a school internship.

Regardless of one's perspective on the principal's role, there is near unanimity that the principal is extremely important, not only in establishing the overall culture of the school, but in its day-to-day operations. Much of the effective schools research of the 1980s focused on the importance of the principal in creating a climate of academic success for students. The superintendent is ultimately responsible to the school board for the successful operation of the entire district, but wide variations in the performance of principals sometimes results in similar wide differences between schools in a district.

Policy Development and Implementation

Let's now look at how school governance affects teachers' daily activities. Having read this far, you know the educational system is structured from the top down. State legislatures pass laws establishing general educational policy, which state departments of education, led by state superintendents of schools, are expected to implement and monitor across all districts. Local school boards, although generally elected by the citizens within a municipality, receive their authorization from the state legislature to develop policies at the local level. Those policies, along with state mandates, are then implemented within the district by the superintendent, who holds principals responsible for implementation within their individual schools. And, of course, it is teachers within individual classrooms who are ultimately responsible for carrying out most of these mandates. (See figure 10.1.)

Conversely, if problems develop within the educational system, the chain of command is reversed. If a parent is concerned about a classroom practice and goes directly to the superintendent or a board member, it is appropriate for those individuals to send the parent back to the individual teacher to try to resolve the situation. If that does not work out, or if a teacher has a problem, the next step is the building principal. Failing success there, individuals with school problems—including all parents, district employees, and students—have access to the superintendent of schools. If an individual is not satisfied with the superintendent's decision, that individual can then appeal to the entire board of education, which also does not have the final say. Whether it is a disagreement about a disciplinary matter on the part of a parent or an objection to not being recontracted on the part of an employee, individuals can then appeal to the state superintendent of instruction and the state board of education. The final court of appeal in any disputed matter is, indeed, the courts. We consider the results of many such cases in Chapter 11.

School District Organization

Traditional

The pattern and number of school districts varies widely throughout the United States, with Hawaii having only a single district and Texas having 1,048, as you can see in Table 10.1. One of the smallest states geographically is New Jersey, but it has the seventh highest number of school districts. The number of school districts within a state becomes especially important when discussing administrative

Figure 10.1 **Typical State and Local Educational Governance Structure**

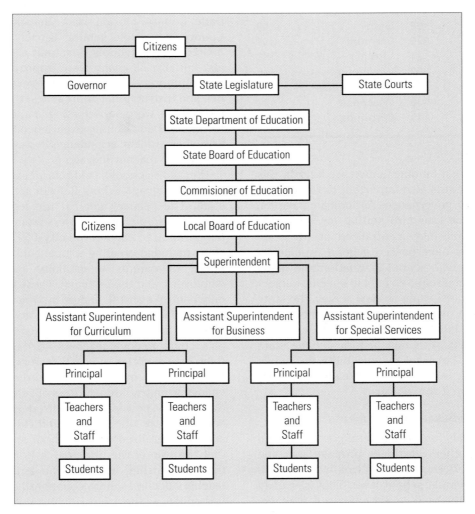

Table 10.1 Number of School Districts by State, School Year 1993–1994

50 states and DC	14,523	Missouri	534
Alabama	127	Montana	486
Alaska	56	Nebraska	676
Arizona	217	Nevada	17
Arkansas	315	New Hampshire	164
California	1,002	New Jersey	583
Colorado	176	New Mexico	88
Connecticut	166	New York	714
Delaware	19	North Carolina	121
District of Columbia	1	North Dakota	251
Florida	67	Ohio	611
Georgia	181	Oklahoma	554
Hawaii	1	Oregon	271
Idaho	113	Pennsylvania	500
Illinois	922	Rhode Island	36
Indiana	292	South Carolina	95
Iowa	396	South Dakota	173
Kansas	304	Tennessee	138
Kentucky	176	Texas	1,046
Louisiana	66	Utah	40
Maine	226	Vermont	251
Maryland	24	Virginia	133
Massachusetts	262	Washington	296
Michigan	556	West Virginia	55
Minnesota	400	Wisconsin	427
Mississippi	149	Wyoming	49

Source: U.S. Department of Education, 1995, p. 9.

costs and education funding, as we see later in this chapter. However, it is also important to the consideration of school governance. As indicated earlier, policy making and standard setting for education has become increasingly centralized at the state level. Most states have passed general proficiency requirements for high school graduation and many are developing such requirements in specific subject areas. In some states, such as New Jersey, the state can actually take over the operation of the school district from the local government if low scores on these tests persist. Although historically the state government has had legal responsibility for public schools, it is only in the last few decades that they have truly exercised this power.

Site-Based Management

Although proposals for more federal control of education persist, other reformers propose just the opposite, that is, decentralize control and responsibility to the individual school level. This is usually referred to as **site-based** or **school-based management.** The rationale for moving in this direction is that those most directly affected by decisions ought to have some say in those decisions. After all, the argument goes, those closest to the situation are most likely to have the knowledge needed to make good decisions. In addition, when individuals are directly involved in making decisions, rather than having them handed down from above, they are more likely to take responsibility for making them work.

Much has been written about site-based management, and a wide variety of practices currently exist. In some schools, site-based management consists of a teacher and parent committee that provides advice to the principal. In other schools a central committee, composed of teachers, parents, the principal, and sometimes students determines the policies of the school, including budget allocations and the hiring and firing of personnel. In some instances, the principal has only one vote, just like everyone else. As you may expect, this more democratic form of site-based management is less frequently encountered.

Two places where major experiments in site-based management have been undertaken are in Dade County, Florida, and Chicago, Illinois. Dade County is a single school district, and in 1987, it invited its 297 schools to submit site-based proposals. Initially, 32 plans were approved, giving each school unprecedented control over budget, personnel, and instructional approaches. By 1992, over half the schools were participating in site-based management, and Dade County experienced such outcomes as higher student attendance, lower drop-out rates, and higher teacher morale.

Chicago's school-based reform came as a result of the 1989 Chicago School Reform Act enacted by the state. The primary goal of the legislation was to move decision-making powers from the central administration to each of the city's 597 schools. Provisions included creating a local school council composed of parents, community members, school employees, and the principal. These councils had not only control over the budget but the authority to hire and fire the principal. In addition, teachers were to be hired on the basis of merit, not seniority, and principals could remove teachers 45 days after serving them official notice of unsatisfactory performance.

Site-based management represents a major change from traditional forms of school governance. Not only is power decentralized from the central administrative office to the individual school, it is also decentralized at the school level. This means that the role of the principal is less dominant, and the relationship between the principal and the teachers becomes more collaborative. In many ways this enhances the professionalism of teachers, but at the same time does not diminish the importance of a strong leader in the principal's position. In addition, parents, students, and other citizens can have a say in school policies and practices.

Although the underlying premises of site-based management make good sense, successful implementation requires a principal who is willing to share power. In addition, collaborative decision-making is time consuming. Unless teachers and parents are committed to providing the extra time and energy necessary to get a site-based plan in operation, frustration and failure will be common experiences. Estimates are that more than one-third of all school districts in the United States experimented with some form of site-based management between 1986 and 1990, and since then at least five states have jumped on the bandwagon. It remains to be seen whether or not this reform will make a permanent impact on the structure of schooling in the United States. You can read more about site-based management in the accompanying Research Box. In addition, you can read about New Zealand's commitment to site-based management in the Global Box later in the chapter.

Schools of Choice

Another form of school organization that has gained popularity since the late 1980s is referred to as **schools of choice.** Rather than students' being assigned to specific schools based on the geographic location of their residences, students and their parents are able to select schools of their choice within a district, county, or state depending on the structure of their school system. Some school choice proposals have included private schools, but most existing programs permit choice only within the public sector.

One example of choice within a district is Montclair, New Jersey. Each of the elementary and middle schools throughout the district has a specific theme around which the program is organized. The schools are referred to as **magnet schools,** because they draw students on the basis of these themes. Another example is Montgomery County, Maryland, where parents can choose from among 14 elementary, 2 middle, and 1 secondary magnet schools. In Minnesota, public school choice is available statewide. It is the only state that currently provides this opportunity.

Proponents of school choice argue that such programs give parents the opportunity to select the best possible schooling for their children, rather than forcing them to accept schools, irrespective of their quality or the types of programs they offer. They also contend that parents are likely to be more

involved with and more supportive of the schools they choose for their children. In addition to individual benefits, proponents argue that competition will force all public schools to improve in order to attract clients. This, of course, is the basic premise behind our free-market economic system.

Opponents of school choice argue that it will not benefit those most in need of a good education—disadvantaged students—because their parents and guardians are least likely to have the knowledge and motivation needed to select better schools. Nor, they argue, would better schools be likely to accept disadvantaged students. Thus, most low-achieving and unmotivated students will be left in schools, often in the inner cities, with little support from middle-class taxpayers. Such a system, opponents contend, will not bring about the competition needed to improve all schools; rather, it will result in the poorest performing schools falling even further behind as their better students and more active parents disappear.

The argument over school choice becomes even more intense when the question is raised of including nonpublic schools, through the use of an **educational voucher.** A *voucher* is a promissory note provided by the government that can be redeemed by parents for a stipulated amount at the school of their choice. Currently, only the Milwaukee Public Schools provide such vouchers. The Wisconsin legislature approved a plan that allows for the transfer of low-income students to nonsectarian nonpublic schools. A 1993 report on the program after 3 years of operation indicated the following:

- Academic outcomes varied considerably over the 3-year period with reading scores initially improving, then declining, and math scores not improving until the third year, but then significantly.

- Parental attitudes toward choice schools and involvement were very positive over the first 3 years. Parents were much more positive about their choice schools than they were about their previous public schools. This change happened in every category (teachers, principals, instruction, discipline, etc.). Parental involvement was much more frequent than for the average Milwaukee public school parent. In all years, parents expressed approval of the program and strong belief the program should continue.

- Attrition was initially high but declined over the 3-year period. Approximately half the students appeared to be returning to the

Milwaukee Public School System, with most of the rest going to other private schools. The reasons given for leaving included complaints about the choice program, especially the limitation on religious instruction and problems with transportation. They also included complaints about staff, general educational quality, and the lack of specialized programs in the private schools. (Witte, 1993)

The authors of the evaluation study also recommended changes in the transportation reimbursement system that would give more options, make reimbursement payments more timely, and provide additional school-supported busing. Following this report, legislation was passed to include religious private schools as eligible recipients of vouchers for Milwaukee public school students, but this was immediately taken into the courts and not implemented.

In 1993, the National Center for Education Statistics conducted the National Household Education Survey, which provides national data on school choice. The survey asked parents of children in Grades 3 through 12 who were over 8-years-old whether their children attended a private school or a public school that was their "regularly assigned"

RESEARCH

Site-Based Management

During the 1989–1990 and 1990–1991 school years, a RAND research team studied five major urban and suburban school systems that had adopted site-based management: Columbus, Ohio; Dade County, Florida; Edmonton, Alberta (Canada); Jefferson County (Louisville), Kentucky; and Prince William County, Virginia. They also tracked newspaper and scholarly accounts of site-based management in other communities, including Los Angeles, Chicago, New York City, Montgomery County (Maryland), Salt Lake City, Tampa, and Indianapolis.

The report concluded:

1. Though site-based management focuses on individual schools, it is actually a reform of the entire school system.

Schools cannot change their established modes of operation if all the controls of a centralized system remain intact. School boards, superintendents, and central office staffs must commit themselves to long-term decentralization.

2. Site-based management is successful only if it is a school system's basic reform strategy, not just one among several reform projects.

Site-based management is the basic process whereby a school staff and community define needs and coordinate efforts to meet them. It cannot be just one of several uncoordinated projects operating in the school or in the school system.

3. Site-managed schools evolve over time and develop distinctive characters, goals, and operating styles.

After an initial period of floundering, in which many school staffs concern themselves with labor-management and budget issues, schools that are free to solve their own problems develop specific and well-defined missions, climates, and methods of instruction. Schools become less and less alike. The challenge for school boards and superintendents is how to assist schools and guarantee quality in a system whose basic premise is variety, not uniformity.

4. A system of distinctive, site-managed schools requires a rethinking of accountability.

school or a "chosen" school. A small number of parents volunteered that their assigned schools were their schools of choice (1.2 percent). Thus, these parents, as well as those whose children attended private schools or chose public schools, were considered to have chosen their children's schools. In addition, it is interesting to note that, in a separate question on the survey, 47 percent of parents responded that their choice of where they live was now influenced by where their children would go to school.

As you can see from Table 10.2, views from both proponents and opponents of schools of choice are supported by these data. In 1993, 19 percent of chil-

dren attended schools their families selected—11 percent in chosen public schools and 8 percent in private schools. Although black students (23 percent) were more likely than white students (19 percent) to be in schools their families chose, black and Hispanic students were more likely to be in chosen *public* schools, whereas white students were more likely to be in chosen *private* schools. Families in urbanized areas were twice as likely as those not in urbanized areas to choose schools for their children (25 percent to 12 percent). However, these children were more likely to be in public than private schools. In addition, parents with higher incomes (over $50,000) and higher levels of education were

RESEARCH

Continued

Though state legislatures and school boards remain ultimately responsible for the schools, they must find ways of holding them accountable without dominating local decisions or standardizing practice. The basis of a site-managed school's accountability must be its ability to define and meet its own goals, not compliance with procedural requirements.

5. The ultimate accountability mechanism for a system of distinctive site-managed schools is parental choice.

Choice underlines the need for each school to offer a coherent social and instructional climate and to prove that it can deliver on promises.

Like many other ideas that call for a change in organizational and human behavior, the decentralization of school systems has progressed slowly and with difficulty. This is not to say that site-based management has failed. Rather, school boards and central offices have failed to recognize that their structures, operations, and cultures must change along with those of the schools if site-based management is to improve students' education. But the difficulty of decentralizing is not an argument for rejecting the concept.

The situation that motivated site-based management in the first place still obtains. Past efforts to control schools in detail from the outside, by contract, court decree, regulation, and financial incentives, have made schools more responsive to higher authorities than to the students and parents they are supposed to serve. Many principals and teachers, because they do not feel free to make full use of their professional judgment, have come to concentrate on tasks that are discrete, bounded, and noncontroversial—that is, the implementation of programs and the imparting of specific facts and skills—rather than on cognitive development, the integration of ideas, and students' personal growth. If site-based management is to work, school staff must come to take more initiative and responsibility in serving their students.

Table 10.2 **Students in Grades 3 to 12 Attending a Chosen or Assigned School, by Family Characteristics, 1993**

| | Total Number of Students | Percent Distribution | | |
		Public, Assigned (in percentages)	Public, Chosen	Private
Total Students	59,004,955	81	11	8
Race/Ethnicity				
White	41,039,023	82	8	10
Black	9,332,499	76	20	4
Hispanic	6,557,854	80	14	6
Type of area				
Inside urban area	35,080,073	75	14	11
Outside urban area	8,692,522	88	7	5
Rural	15,232,361	88	6	6
Parent Education				
<H.S.	5,549,763	85	13	2
H.S. grad	19,196,779	84	11	5
Vo-Tech	18,536,028	81	11	8
College grad	6,940,164	77	10	13
Gradute School	8,578,628	75	9	16
Parent Income				
< $15,000	12,848,325	82	15	3
$15–30,000	15,108,627	82	12	6
$30–50,000	15,915,309	82	10	9
$50,000 +	15,132,694	77	8	15

Source: U.S. Department of Education, 1995.

more likely to place their children in chosen schools than those with lower incomes and less education. As income and amount of education rose, so also did the likelihood that schools chosen would be private.

The three primary reasons parents gave for choosing public schools for their children are a better academic environment (26 percent), special academic courses (23 percent), and school convenience (23 percent). It is important to note, however, that although families with lower socioeconomic status were more likely to select schools for convenience than families with higher socioeconomic status (28 percent compared to 16 percent), similar proportions of both populations chose schools for the two academic reasons. The top two reasons given by all population groups for enrolling their children in private schools were a better academic program (37 percent) and religious or moral reasons (30 percent).

As you can see in Figure 10.2 and Table 10.3, parents' perceptions of schools differed when they chose schools for their children. Parents who chose schools were more likely to be "very satisfied" with the schools their children attended than those who did not (Figure 10.2); parents who chose private

schools were even more satisfied than those who chose public schools. This is also true for parents' degree of satisfaction with their children's teachers, the schools' academic standards, and the schools' disciplinary policies. This same pattern emerges (Table 10.3) when considering levels of parent satisfaction with specific aspects of public-assigned, public-chosen, and private schools. Parents who chose schools for their children were more likely to agree or strongly agree that their children were challenged at school, their children enjoyed school, the teachers maintained discipline, the students and teachers respected each other, and the principal maintained discipline than were parents of children in assigned public schools. Once again, those who chose private schools had higher levels of agreement than those who chose public schools.

The right of parents to select the schools their children attend promises to be one of the major education issues facing this country in the foreseeable future. Both presidents Bush and Clinton pledged their support for school choice, although for very different reasons. As the quality of public education, especially in urban areas, continues to come under attack, increasing numbers of families

Figure 10.2   **Percentage of Parents of Students in Grades 3 to 12 Who Are "Very Satisfied" with Aspects of Their Child's School, by School Type: 1993**

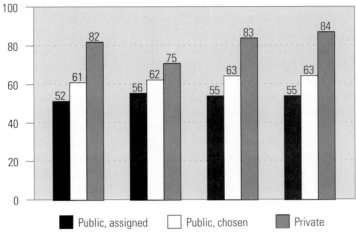

■ Public, assigned   □ Public, chosen   ■ Private

Source: U. S. Department of Education, 1995, p. 2.

Table 10.3   **Parents' Perceptions of the Schools Their Children Attend by Type of School, 1993 (Children in Grades 3 to 12)**

	(in percentage)		
Agree or Strongly Agree That:	**Public, Assigned**	**Public, Chosen**	**Private**
Child challenged at school	83	85	97
Child enjoys school	87	91	94
Teachers maintain discipline	89	92	98
Students and teachers respect each other	86	90	98
Principal maintains discipline	91	93	98

Source: U.S. Department of Education, 1995.

are abandoning either the inner city or the public schools, thus eroding their tax base and hastening their deterioration. Although the American Federation of Teachers (AFT) endorses choice among public schools, the National Education Association (NEA) remains adamantly opposed to it. Both organizations oppose choice plans that would include the use of vouchers for nonpublic schools, arguing that schools would be divided along socioeconomic lines, segregation would increase, and financial support of public schools would decrease.

Since there has never been a full school-choice program that includes nonpublic schools, arguments have taken place without the benefit of hard data about the outcomes of such programs. Thus, the first step in determining the success or failure of such a proposal is to establish a system in which all families are free to choose any public or private school within a designated geographic area. This experiment can be taken a step further by providing

all parents with vouchers and requiring them to select their children's schools. This would, of course, require the collection and dissemination of information about schools, an approval process for nonpublic schools that wished to participate, and establishment of information centers to counsel parents about their children's needs and available schools. One of the major arguments against a system of school choice is that the most knowledgeable and privileged families would benefit most, and the disadvantaged would become even more so. This is undoubtedly true currently, because any existing or proposed programs have *limited* choice, that is, only *some* get to choose. A system in which *all* get to choose would be very different from any we have experienced up to this point.

Charter Schools

Another innovation in the organization of public schools at the local level is **charter schools.** A *charter school* is one that a group of individuals designs from the ground up in order to meet a specific purpose with clearly delineated outcome objectives for students. These individuals can be teachers, parents, community or corporate members, or any combination of these. Once the plan for the school is developed, it is submitted to the state. If the plan is approved, the individuals who developed it are then given a charter to operate the school for a specified length of time. Renewal of the charter is dependent on achievement of the stated objectives. Funding for the school is provided through the same sources as other public schools. By mid-1997, 27 states had authorized roughly 400 charter schools (O'Neill, 1997), and the U. S. Department of Education had awarded its first grants for charter demonstrations and research, provided for in the reauthorization of the Elementary and Secondary Education Act in 1994 (Lewis, 1996).

One major variation in the governance structures of charter schools is how accountable they are to the local school board. This can vary from complete autonomy to total accountability. As Anne C. Lewis (1996), a columnist for *Phi Delta Kappan,* commented,

> In a surprisingly short amount of time, the questions raised by the spread of charter schools have moved from "if" and "why" questions to "how" questions. The debate is no longer about whether or not to have charter schools, but about how autonomous these schools should be. Where charter laws have been "strong"—i.e., where they have granted a great deal of independence to the schools, interest in charter schools and in actual "start-ups" has been vigorous. Opponents of charter schools are no longer trying to defeat the laws and are instead supporting the "passage of weak laws," according to the Education Commission of the States. (p. 267)

As with other proposed changes in the organization of public schools, charter schools have both supporters and opponents. Many see them as a way to provide parents with choice within the public system and teachers with the opportunity to innovate. Critics, however, feel that they will drain revenues as well as the most motivated students, parents, and teachers away from public schools that are in need of help.

Privatization

Even more controversial than charter schools is the movement to privatize the management of schools. Although school districts have used private contractors for cafeteria, cleaning, and transportation services for a number of years, the move to turn the management of entire schools over to private con-

tractors has provoked the opposition of many observers, especially teachers' unions. The most well know private contractor, Educational Alternatives, Inc., was awarded contracts to manage selected schools in Miami, Baltimore, and Hartford. The American Federation of Teachers has waged a no-holds-barred media campaign against the company, and the National Education Association has filed suit against another private contractor, the Alternative Public Schools of Nashville.

Despite such resistance on the part of these teacher organizations, firms that run preschools, alternative schools, Title I programs, charter schools, and other private schools are part of a $600 billion a year market, according to EduVentures, a consulting firm that specializes in investments in the "education industry." Moreover, the market for private education is predicted to grow as the numbers of people who graduate from college increases. The more educated parents are, the more likely they are to enroll their children in private schools; according to the National Center for Education Statistics, parents with graduate degrees enroll their children in private schools at twice the national average—16 percent versus 8 percent (Lewis, 1996).

ROLE OF FEDERAL GOVERNMENT

The United States, unlike most developed countries, has never had a national office of education that determines nationwide curriculum. As indicated earlier, the Tenth Amendment reserved all the powers not specifically mentioned in the Constitution to the individual states. Education was one of these non-specified powers. However, as McCarthy and Cambron-McCabe (1992) noted,

> Congress and federal administrative agencies have exerted considerable influence in shaping public school policies and practices through categorical funding laws and their accompanying administrative regulations. Individual states or school districts have the option of accepting or rejecting such federal assistance, but if categorical aid is accepted, the federal government has the authority to prescribe guidelines for its use and to monitor state and local education agencies to ensure fiscal accountability. (p. 12)

Legislative Influence

Legislative influence on public education at the federal level has generally been through acts of Congress that address national needs, often supplying accompanying funding to accomplish the identified legislative goals.

Before the twentieth century, there were two major pieces of federal legislation that affected education. In 1785 and 1787, the federal government passed the Northwest Ordinances, which required that settlements in the Northwest Territories be surveyed and 1 section out of 36 be dedicated to education. This form of federal land grant support for education was followed up in 1862 by a second bill, the Morrill Land Grant Act. Through this act, Congress granted every state 30,000 acres of land for each senator and representative it had. The land was to be sold and the proceeds invested and used to establish and maintain colleges for agriculture, the mechanical arts, and military science and tactics. Congress added money to the grants through the Second Morrill Act in 1890 and an amendment in 1907. The purpose of the Morrill Acts was to extend higher educational opportunity to ordinary people.

Following the Morrill Acts, the federal government turned its attention to specific components of the public school curriculum. The Smith-Hughes Act of 1917 provided federal appropriations to secondary schools for practical programs in agriculture, home economics, and vocational education, to be matched by funds from local and state education agencies. The original Smith-Hughes Act was periodically extended by various acts over the next several decades, culminating in the 1984 Perkins Vocational Education Act. This broad-reaching legislation extended funding to programs for people with handicaps, single parents, homemakers, and the incarcerated. Its vocational focus was consistent with the growing influence of the progressive education movement initiated by John Dewey and others in the beginning of the twentieth century.

Although this federal emphasis on vocational education continued into the 1960s, there was a brief change of focus as a result of the 1957 Soviet launching of the spaceship Sputnik. Fearing that the Russians would win the "space race," thus jeopardizing our national defense, then President Kennedy promised Americans that we would put a man on the moon before the Russians. In order to do so, it was necessary to pour enormous resources into American public schools. Funding was provided, among other things, for the improvement of instruction in science, mathematics, and foreign languages. This represented a swing of the educational pendulum toward those students who were most likely to be academically advanced.

However, the pendulum swing toward academic rigor was short lived as our society got caught up in the civil rights movement and other efforts to address the glaring needs of those who had suffered various forms of discrimination throughout our history. In 1954, the Supreme Court ruled in the *Brown* v. *Topeka, Kansas Board of Education* case that segregated schools were inherently unequal, an event that sparked the civil rights movement in the United States. However, little was actually done to eliminate segregation until a decade later. In 1964 the federal government passed the Civil Rights Act, which mandated, among other things, that school districts that discriminated against individuals on the basis of race, color, or national origin would not receive federal educational funds. Although the amount of those funds had been steadily growing throughout the twentieth century, their absence had little impact on the day-to-day operations of most school districts. In 1965, the federal government passed three major acts that dramatically increased these funds. One was the Economic Opportunity Act, which established Head Start, providing compensatory preschool education, and extended educational opportunities for adults through Adult Basic Education programs. The second was the Elementary and Secondary Education Act (ESEA), the most comprehensive and costly educational legislation in the history of the federal government. Its purpose was the development of compensatory kindergarten through twelfth-grade programs for minority and low-income children. With the passage of this act, federal aid to education doubled. It provided $1 billion in its first year, and by 1980, $30 billion had been appropriated. Finally, the Higher Education Act provided direct assistance to institutes of higher education and loans and scholarships to students who otherwise would not have been able to attend college.

In the next few decades the federal government passed several key pieces of legislation, often with funding attached, which provided assistance to students in specific categories. For example, the Bilingual Education Act of 1968 and the Education for All Handicapped Children Act of 1975 (which became the Individuals with Disabilities Education Act of 1990) provided funding to assist schools in developing and implementing services for students with special needs. Although many forms of federal funding shifted during the 1980s from being categorical in nature to block grants to states to distribute at their own discretion, aid for economically disadvantaged and other special needs students has remained primarily categorical.

In addition to providing regulated financial aid to schools, the federal government has passed legislation that affects schools in a variety of other ways. Some examples are:

- Title VII of the Civil Rights Act of 1964, which prohibits employment discrimination on the basis of race, color, gender, religion, or national origin.
- The Age Discrimination in Employment Act of 1967.
- Title IX of the Education Amendments Act of 1972, which bars gender discrimination against participants in education programs.
- The Rehabilitation Act of 1973, which prohibits discrimination against otherwise qualified handicapped persons.
- The Family Educational Rights and Privacy Act of 1974 (FERPA, also known as the Buckley Amendment), which controls access of both school personnel and outsiders to students' records.

All the legislation cited in the foregoing paragraphs is discussed in detail in Chapter 11, as well as its impact on teachers' professional lives.

Executive Influence

In addition to federal legislative and judicial influence on education, the executive branch of the federal government increasingly has exercised a leadership role. The federal Office of Education was formed in 1867, and Henry Barnard was appointed its first commissioner. Sometimes residing in the Department of the Interior, sometimes in the Federal Security Agency, it became a branch of Department of Health, Education, and Human Services from 1953 to 1979. Its original purpose was to collect statistics and facts to show the condition and progress of education in the states and territories, and to distribute information to improve the organization and management of schools, school systems, and methods of teaching, and otherwise promote the cause of education throughout the country.

In 1979, a separate *Department of Education* was established by President Jimmy Carter in response to the National Education Association's endorsement of his presidential candidacy. After decades of trying, the education community finally was represented by a cabinet-level officer. Although Ronald Reagan promised to disband the department during his presidential campaign, various political forces prevented its dissolution, and its future now appears reasonably secure. Those who have headed this office have had varying levels of visibility and national recognition, including William Bennett, one of the most conservative and outspoken, and Lamar Alexander, former governor of Tennessee and 1996 candidate for the Republican presidential nomina-

tion. Although the secretary of education has no direct control over what takes place in schools, the individual who fills this cabinet-level post is recognized as the national spokesperson for education and can have a substantial impact on the national dialogue about educational reform goals and policies as well as set educational funding priorities.

Since Carter's presidential campaign in 1976, all presidential candidates have presented educational reform as an important part of their platforms, many presenting themselves as "education presidents." This is not surprising in light of the growing importance of education in the modern world. During Reagan's term as president, the National Commission on Excellence in Education published the now-famous report entitled *Nation at Risk,* which decried the rising tide of mediocrity in American schools that it claimed was putting the nation at risk of losing its "once unchallenged preeminence in commerce, industry, service, and technological innovation" (National Commission, 1983, p. 5). The report cited several areas of educational decline and made a number of recommendations that focused on increasing and tightening educational standards.

In 1990, the National Governor's Association, chaired by then Arkansas Governor Clinton, published *Educating America,* which became the basis for President Bush's *National Goals for Education.* This report, which outlined six specific goals to be reached by the year 2000, subsequently became known as *Goals 2000.*

The influence of the executive branch of our national government on education in the closing decades of the twentieth century has been unprecedented. Although federal spending for education has declined from its all time high of 9.8 percent in 1989, there is little doubt that future presidents will continue to address the crucial role that education plays in dealing with society's problems. Take a minute to read the accompanying Global Box about New Zealand's decentralized education governance in light of what you have just read about bold recommendations for change.

Judicial Influence

The other major area of federal influence on education comes from federal district courts and the United States Supreme Court. Most court cases affecting educational policy have taken place in the latter half of the twentieth century and have had an impact on a wide range of school practices, as you will read in Chapter 11.

Other Federal Influences on Education

In addition to funding programs for disadvantaged children, the 1965 Elementary and Secondary Educa-

Site-Based Management in New Zealand

The movement toward school autonomy and site-based management is not unique to the United States. Many countries are experimenting with forms of decentralized governance.

Site-based management was introduced in New Zealand in the early 1990s, and all its 2,666 schools have become stand-alone units (Wylie, 1995). There are no districts, education boards, or county bodies governing how schools operate. Every school has a board composed of five parent trustees (elected by parents), the principal, one staff representative, and, in secondary schools, a student representative. The board is responsible for all staff appointments and dismissals, managing the budget, maintaining the buildings and grounds, staff development, and performance.

The Ministry of Education provides the funding and broad curriculum guidelines for all state schools and standardized assessment tasks for all elementary schools. Every 2 or 3 years the Education Review Office inspects schools for compliance with regulations.

In assessing the impact of site-based management, researchers found there were no radical changes from existing curriculum and instructional methods (Wylie, 1995). Both teachers and parents were satisfied with the activity-centered learning approaches that already existed. However, by 1993, 41 percent of elementary teachers reported that the switch to school-based management had a positive effect on children's learning. Elementary teachers also reported doing more assessment, using a wide assortment ranging from work samples to spelling tests, and increasing the use of profiles, which describe children's social skills as well as their academic progress. Teachers attended more to reporting to parents. Although school boards were originally expected to focus on learning, property and finance decisions dominated.

By 1993, 27 percent of elementary teachers felt they did not have an adequate opportunity to share ideas and experiences with teachers in other local schools. But significantly more elementary teachers were receiving training on their own time, up from 42 percent in 1989 to 70 percent in 1993. Elementary principals, teachers, and trustees also identified workload as the least-satisfying aspect of their work. Elementary principals' average workload increased from 48 hours a week in 1989 to 60 hours a week in 1993. Teachers' workloads increased from an average 46-hour week in 1989 to 48 hours in 1993, and teacher morale declined during the same period. The involvement of parents in school life did not increase, and the number running for school board declined. Most school boards experienced tension at some point—either within their own ranks, with school staff, or with parents.

Funding was the major issue facing school boards during the period of time under study. School operational grants from the government were lower in 1993 than they were in 1989 and most schools increased fundraising activities. School boards were active in bringing funding issues to the attention of the media and politicians. As a result, one major achievement of the site-based reforms was the growth of an education lobby, which included parents as well as teachers seeking a role in the national policy-making process.

What do you see as the similarities and differences in American versus New Zealand style site-based management? What might American educators learn about site-based management from the New Zealand experience?

tion Act established two kinds of agencies dedicated to carrying out and disseminating the results of educational research. Regional education laboratories, which serve from three to seven states, try to link educational personnel in school districts and state agencies with the latest research findings. They conduct their own research, engage in curriculum development, provide training sessions, and organize regional conferences. In addition, national research and development centers are based at major universities and receive multiyear funding to carry out research in education.

In 1985, the Office of Educational Research and Improvement was established to replace the National Institute of Education, formed in 1972. Its purpose is to conduct educational research and disseminate programs to improve educational practice. However, it is neither well funded nor very successful in overcoming the long-standing gap between educational researchers and practitioners.

NONGOVERNMENTAL INFLUENCES ON SCHOOL GOVERNANCE

The executive and legislative branches of government at the local, state, and federal levels formally establish policies for public schools, but a variety of interest groups influence the development of these policies and their implementation. James Guthrie, Walter Garms, and Lawrence Pierce (1988) proposed the concept of an "iron triangle"—composed of the executive and legislative branches of government and educational interest groups outside of government—to describe the forces that shape the education agenda for this country. Some of these interest groups are composed of educators and others of laypersons. A look at some of these interest groups and how they influence the daily lives of teachers follows.

Teachers' Organizations

Often referred to as *unions,* the National Education Association, with over 2,000,000 members, and the American Federation of Teachers, with approximately 800,000 members, have exerted substantial influence in the development of educational policies throughout history but especially in the closing decades of the twentieth century. They have exerted the most influence on teachers' salaries, which constitute the largest portion of educational expenditure, and working conditions. Since the 1960s, when the AFT won the right to bargain collectively for the

public school teachers in New York City, both organizations used the tools of collective bargaining and teachers' strikes to substantially increase teachers' salaries (see Chapter 1). Throughout the 1990s, teachers' associations have continued to win multiyear contracts for their members that exceed not only the cost of living, but also the settlements won by many other unions.

In addition to salary gains, teachers' associations are often able to influence the outcomes of both state and local elections. Recognizing the importance of electing strong proeducation candidates, their national and state political action committees (PACs) spend millions of dollars annually on lobbying activities and political campaigns. Many credit the 1978 endorsement of President Carter by the NEA as the key to his victory over former President Ford. In contrast, the lack of support from New Jersey's teachers' associations was considered to be a major reason why Governor Jim Florio did not win reelection as governor in 1994.

Both the NEA and AFT have taken strong stands, but not always the same stand, on a number of volatile issues, such as school choice, affirmative action, and standardized testing. They encourage their members to be politically active, especially in getting themselves elected to local school boards. There is little doubt that these activities, along with political action committees and extensive use of the media, have enabled these organizations to have a great deal of influence on educational policy and practice.

School Boards' Associations

Just as teachers have formed associations at the local, state, and national levels, so too school boards have joined together to influence the political process. The National School Boards' Association (NSBA) has affiliates at the state and county levels that not only provide information and services for their constituent members but solicit input from them and lobby legislators at the state and national levels. Although their concerns are frequently the same as teachers, in some areas, such as salaries, benefits, and contracts, their interests differ. For example, an ongoing area of conflict between school boards and teachers' associations is that of tenure. School boards want to provide taxpayers with the highest quality education at the lowest possible cost, a goal that is difficult to achieve because of tenure laws and collective bargaining. Teachers, on the other hand, want contracts that guarantee automatic increments irrespective of their performance. Boards often feel unable either to improve education or lower costs in their communities because they have a large number of older, tenured teachers who are resistant to change. Consequently, boards frequently lobby at the state level for repeal or weakening of tenure laws. Of course, teachers do not share this view.

Professional Educational Organizations

Professional societies also influence educational policies and practices. The two largest educational organizations devoted to educational research and curriculum development are the American Educational Research Association (AERA) and the Association for Supervision and Curriculum Development (ASCD). Both have national, regional, and/or state affiliates and both publish monthly journals. They are committed to researching and disseminating information about the most appropriate and successful educational practices. Similarly, national specialty organizations in subject areas exert a major influence on school curriculum. In 1989, the National Council of Teachers of Mathematics (NCTM) published mathematics curriculum standards for each level of schooling, as well as the methods for teaching that curriculum, as described in Chapter 8. Not only did school districts move to adopt these standards, they also began retraining teachers to implement them. As a result, other subject-area organizations soon began to develop their own standards. Such activities can have a major impact on what gets taught in schools.

Parent Organizations

The largest, oldest, and probably most influential nongovernmental, noneducator organization is the National Congress of Parents and Teachers, commonly know as the PTA. Founded in 1897, its membership is open to anyone interested in working to advance the welfare of children and youth. Although teachers in many schools do belong to the organization, it is composed primarily of parents (mostly mothers) who are organized into over 27,000 local units in all 50 states and the District of Columbia. The influence of local PTA units varies according to the activism of the members and leadership in any one school. However, the organization wields considerable influence at the national level, where it lobbies for programs relating to sex education, reading, nutrition and safety education, and drug abuse prevention.

Although the PTA is the only nationally affiliated organization for parents, other local organizations do exist. Parent-Teacher Organizations (PTOs) are frequently formed in communities that do not agree with the politics of the PTA or want to keep monies in the local organization and avoid paying national dues. These organizations sometimes have substantial influence at the local level, but they have little political impact at the national level.

Business Organizations

A nongovernmental influence on education that frequently receives little attention is that of business and industry. In 1895, the National Association of Manufacturers (NAM) was founded as a policy-making body for the manufacturing industry. Its concern with industrial and economic matters has led it into a number of related public policy areas such as education. One public issue on which it spoke out loudly during its early years was the growing system of common schools. Charging them with "gross inefficiency," the NAM president declared in his 1898 annual report that "we expend very large sums of money in city and county for public education that is for the most part of such a character that it avails the people little in their practical affairs" (Rippa, 1984, p. 162).

One proposal put forth by the NAM and endorsed by business leaders in general was the development of vocational education in the public schools. With the rise of factories and the disappearance of the apprenticeship training system, there was no reliable means of preparing young people for skilled labor jobs at a time when large numbers of barely literate students were leaving school at an early age. The combination of funds provided through the Smith Hughes Act in 1914, the increased number of young people remaining in school as a result of the Depression, and the labor demands of business and industry all contributed to the rapid growth of vocational education during the 1920s and 1930s.

By the end of World War II, membership in the NAM had grown to more than 20,000 companies, located in every state. Its membership included every major company and most of the smaller ones in the United States. Its constitution listed as one of its general objectives "the education of the public in the principles of individual liberty and ownership of property" (Rippa, 1984, p. 307). Rippa further points out that:

> During the early decades of the twentieth century, the schools slowly adopted a business ideology that stressed the need for efficient workers and citizens. School administrators, in particular, applied the values and techniques of an industrial order to public schooling in a democracy... By introducing new administrative techniques and devising all sorts of tests and evaluative instruments, educators sought to eliminate "waste," accelerate "promotions," and increase "efficiency" in the public schools. This

development had profound consequences: it narrowed the function of the public school by teaching specific skills and attitudes that mirrored the business world and molded the individual to fit into an industrial society. (p. 166)

Following the stock market crash in 1929 and the ensuing Great Depression, many began questioning the leadership role of business in American life. To combat their tarnished image, the NAM, along with the National Chamber of Commerce, launched a campaign to increase the public's appreciation for the importance of business and industry. Rippa describes this campaign as "the most elaborate and costly public-relations project in American history" (p. 306). The organization used a wide variety of mass media to disperse its views about the importance of the free enterprise system to the success of America and the major role education plays in preparing citizens to participate in that system. These media efforts included films, booklets, brochures, billboards, and mass mailings to businessmen, educators, students, and the general public.

As the twentieth century concludes, no one can doubt the role that business and industry continue to play in shaping educational policy and practice. Today there are entire high schools dedicated to training young people for specific vocations, and both individual business people and large corporations make substantial contributions to education at all levels to support programs in which they are interested. One interesting example is that of the industrialist Henry Rowan who, in the summer of 1992, contributed $100 million to Glassboro State College in New Jersey to establish a school of engineering. The college reciprocated by changing its name to Rowan College of New Jersey.

FUNDING OF PUBLIC EDUCATION

In the 1990s, perhaps the most controversial issue regarding public education is how schools are financed, that is, how funds are raised and how they are distributed. In this section, we first examine how monies for education are collected, then look at their distribution.

Collection of Revenues

Just as education has governance structures at the local, state, and federal levels, it also has funding mechanisms at these three levels. Figure 10.3 shows the proportion of revenues from these various sources for the 1992–1993 school year.

Figure 10.3   The Public Education Dollar: Revenues from Various Sources, School Year 1992–1993

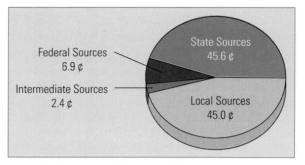

Source: U.S. Department of Education, 1995, p. 3.

Federal revenues include direct grants-in-aid to schools or agencies, funds distributed through a state or intermediate agency, and revenues in lieu of taxes to compensate a school district for nontaxable federal institutions within a district's boundary. For instance, wherever military bases, which do not pay real estate taxes, are located, the federal government provides such revenues in lieu of taxes. *Local revenues* include revenues from such sources as local property, income, and sales taxes, investments and revenues from student activities, textbook sales, transportation and tuition fees, and food service revenues. *State revenues* include both direct funds from state governments and revenues in lieu of taxation. Revenues in lieu of taxes are paid to compensate a school district for nontaxable state institutions or facilities within the district's boundary. One example of such a state institution is a state college.

Over time, the proportion of revenues collected from the three levels of government has varied considerably, as can be seen in Table 10.4, which shows the percentage of revenues for elementary and secondary schools from local, state, and federal sources for selected years from 1919–1920 to 1992–1993.

Federal Revenues

A brief examination of the figures in Table 10.4 shows that the proportion of funding coming from the federal government increased dramatically between the early part of the twentieth century and 1980. The reason for this increase was the enactment of major education bills with categorical funding, such as the Elementary and Secondary Education Act in 1965 and the Education for All Handicapped Children Act in 1975. With the 1980 election of Reagan as president, the involvement of

Table 10.4   **Percentage of Revenues for Elementary and Secondary Schools from Local, State, and Federal Sources for Selected Years, 1919–1920 to 1992–1993.**

School Year	Federal	State	Local
1919–1920	0.3	16.5	83.2
1959–1960	4.4	39.1	56.5
1970–1971	8.4	39.1	52.5
1980–1981	9.2	47.4	43.4
1984–1985	6.6	48.9	44.4
1991–1992	6.6	46.4	47.0
1992–1993	6.9	45.6	47.4

Source: U.S. Department of Education, 1995, p. 3.

the federal government in all aspects of society, including education, diminished. Federal revenues decreased by 30 percent between 1980 and 1984. Since then, the federal contribution to education has remained fairly steady, with a slight increase in 1992–1993, the last year for which statistics are available.

State and Local Revenues

Funding from these sources must be studied together, because as Table 10.4 shows, when one increases the other decreases, and vice versa. Historically the primary funding source for education has been taxes on property owned by the residents of a community. Taxes are assessed on the basis of *mills,* i.e., one mill represents one-thousandth of a dollar. If the tax rate is 30 mills, a property owner will pay $30 for each $1,000 of assessed property value. When a school board prepares a budget, in conjunction with the municipal budget, the tax assessor determines the entire worth of property in the community and indicates what the tax rate must be in order to raise the necessary funds for the upcoming year. Most frequently property taxes go up; occasionally they remain the same or actually go down.

Collection Inequities

There are a number of problems with this system of taxation. One problem is the lack of uniform assessment practices and formulas in different areas within the same state. The assessed value of a property is based on how much it would sell for in that area. Two physically comparable properties may sell for very different amounts, depending on their location, for instance, on whether they were in an urban or suburban area. In addition, different assessors working in different municipalities may use different methods of assessing market values. The result can sometimes lead to widely varying valuations on comparable properties.

Such variations lead to the problem of *inequitable impact* on residents of different communities. If one considers two comparable properties, one in the inner city and one in a surrounding suburb, it is likely that the suburban property will sell for many thousands of dollars more than the one in the city, maybe even for twice as much. In that case, the rate at which the city taxed itself would have to be twice as high as the suburb in order to raise the same number of dollars to educate its children. This problem is compounded by the fact that families in the inner city are likely to be in lower socioeconomic groups. In addition, if the community averages more children per household, it must tax itself at an even higher rate in order to achieve the same per capita spending for education as the suburb. And, of course, when this happens, more and more middle- and higher-income families move from the cities to the suburbs, thereby further reducing property values in the inner city. Furthermore, in terms of family income, property taxes take a higher proportion of the income of poorer families than of more affluent families. Thus property taxes, because they have an inequitable impact on both families and communities, are considered to be *regressive.*

One additional problem with property taxes is that they frequently *no longer represent the real income or value* of individuals or families. For instance, a retired couple with no school-aged children may have a home with a high market value that they purchased and paid for during their income-productive years but now maintain on a limited fixed income. Or a higher income individual with school-aged children may own little or no real property but have a great deal of wealth in stocks, bonds, or other intangible sources. This produces a situation in which the retired couple are subsidizing the schools for the higher-income family, who are using but not contributing to the financial support of the schools.

Other possible sources of income for public schools are sales taxes and income taxes. Of these two, income taxes are considered the more *progressive* because they require individuals to pay proportionate to their income, or their ability to pay. Some large cities have both sales and income taxes, but it is primarily states that assess sales taxes and the federal government that collects income taxes. Although the state share of education revenues increased gradually from about 16 percent to about 39 percent in the 50-year period from 1920 to 1970, it increased dramatically to over 47 percent in the next 10 years. This was due primarily to several court cases that were heard in various states, one of which eventually went to the U.S. Supreme Court.

In 1971 the California Supreme Court issued a landmark ruling in the *Serrano* v. *Priest* case that the school funding scheme employed by the state "invidiously discriminates against the poor because it makes the quality of a child's education a function of the wealth of his parents and neighbors." Elaborating, the ruling continued,

> This public school system is maintained throughout California by a financing plan or scheme which relies heavily on local property taxes and causes substantial disparities among individual school districts in the amount of revenue available per pupil for the districts' educational programs. Consequently, districts with smaller tax bases are not able to spend as much money per child for education as districts with larger assessed valuations.

Following Serrano, over 30 similar cases were filed in various states. The most significant of these was *San Antonio Independent School District* v. *Rodriguez*. After a federal circuit court issued a similar ruling as that in Serrano, the state of Texas took the case to the U.S. Supreme Court. In 1973, the Court held in a 5 to 4 decision that "a funding system based on the local property tax that provides a minimum educational offering to all students is constitutional." The rationale for this decision included the claim that "there is no loss of a fundamental right since education, in itself, is not constitutionally protected and since the minimum education guaranteed to every student is sufficient for the exercise of protected political (voting) and First Amendment (expression) rights." The Court further indicated, however, that disparities in educational expenditure might be unconstitutional under individual state constitutions.

Despite the ruling in Rodriguez, a substantial number of states had begun to revise their educational funding formulas, with an increasing amount of fiscal responsibility going to the state level, as reflected in Table 10.4. As revenues for education collected at both the state and federal levels increased in the decade of the 1970s, revenues collected at the local level decreased. One example of this occurred as a result of the *Robinson* v. *Cahill* case heard in 1972 by the New Jersey Supreme Court. The ruling was similar to that in Serrano, and

the legislature was charged with finding a more equitable system for funding public schools than real estate taxes. After over 2 years of deliberation without a new plan, the Court ordered the schools shut down until a plan was devised. At that point, a state income tax was enacted and a system of property tax rebate was put into place. It was anticipated that increased state funding would narrow the gap in per capita expenditures between wealthier and poorer districts, but over the next decade the opposite happened. Even though total spending in all districts increased, the difference in spending between wealthier and poorer districts also increased. A follow-up case, *Abbott* v. *Burke* (1990), was filed on behalf of five of the poorest districts in the state. Once again, the Court found the system of funding education unconstitutional and ordered that spending be equalized at the level of the highest-spending districts. After several years of refining the system, which included moving over $100 million annually from the richest to the poorest districts, equity was still not achieved. By the end of 1996, the state legislature had barely met a court-ordered deadline to enact new funding legislation. But as soon as it was, advocates for less affluent districts had filed in the courts, charging that it would not achieve the court-ordered levels of equity.

One other major case that struck down property taxes as the means to fund schools was the *Rose* v. *Council for Better Education* (1989), in which the Kentucky Supreme Court declared the entire state system of education unconstitutional, because it failed to provide an "efficient system" of schooling. The court ordered the legislature to create a new and more efficient system to address the problems of the property tax. By adding corporate and sales taxes and developing new local taxes, Kentucky was able to increase average education spending approximately 30 percent. The issue of irregular funding for schools is brought into clear focus in the accompanying Issue Box.

Distribution of Funds

We can look at distribution of funds in terms of both what they are spent on and how they are distributed to various school districts. Figure 10.4 shows the expenditure of the public education dollar by function.

How funds are distributed by function causes little controversy in the discussion of educational funding. However, the same cannot be said for how they are distributed to various school districts. Although collection and distribution of educational funds can be considered separately, understanding funding inequities requires understanding their interrelationship. When taxes for education are col-

Figure 10.4   **The Public Education Dollar: Expenditures by Function, School Year 1992–1993**

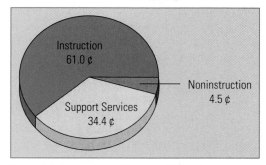

Source: U.S. Department of Education, 1995, p. 3.

lected *primarily at the local level,* usually through real estate taxes, it is extremely difficult to persuade individuals living in more affluent areas to release some of their tax money for the support of poorer schools. In many cases, people have bought homes in a specific community because of the perceived quality of the schools in that community. It seems unfair to these residents that they would be taxed at an even higher rate to support both their own schools and those of other communities. However, as can be seen from Table 10.5, variations in per capita expenditure for education can be enormous, with Mississippi spending only $3,159 per student in the 1992–1993 school year while New Jersey spent $8,770. Variations within individual states can be nearly as great. As unfair as it may seem to expect some to support the education of other people's children, it seems equally unfair that privileged children should have so much spent on their education and underprivileged children so little.

As you just read, the primary means by which states raise school funds is through sales and income taxes, both of which are considered more progressive than real estate taxes. In some states, revenues from lotteries are also designated for education. As for distributing funds, states have three general means. The first and simplest is a specified amount per child *on the basis of average daily enrollment or attendance.* This explains why keeping an accurate attendance book is required. The larger the district, the more money it receives from the state, even though per capita receipts are the same. Thus, if the state provides $2,000 per child, a district with 3,000 students will receive $6,000,000 and one with 30,000 will receive $60,000,000. This method, which is employed in some form in most states, does not take into account the extra cost of educating students with special needs.

The second method does. It establishes a formula that *weights those characteristics known to increase the cost of schooling,* such as being handicapped, disadvantaged, or in a special program of some kind. Districts with high concentrations of such special-needs students receive more money per capita from the state than those with lower numbers. Thus a district with 20 percent of its student population identified as special needs will receive more funds from the state than a comparably sized district in which only 6 percent of its student population is so classified.

The final form of state support is referred to as a *foundation plan.* Under this formula the state determines the cost of providing a basic level of education to all children, assesses how much the local district can raise toward this amount, and provides the difference. As a result, poorer districts get substantially more from the state than wealthier districts. For example, if the state determines that $8,000 per child must be spent and one community can tax itself to raise $5,000 whereas another can raise only $3,000, the state will provide far more to the second than the first.

The major problem with all three formulas is that none results in equalization of expenditure per pupil. Even if money is taken from wealthier districts and given to poorer districts, as formulas 2 and 3 provide for, nothing prevents wealthier districts from taxing themselves at an even higher rate in order to raise additional funds for more and better equipment, facilities, and teachers. Thus, poorer districts are never able to catch up.

Funding Reform

If we are to achieve equality in educational funding, we must be prepared to reform both how monies are collected and how they are distributed. This will require first that most or all of the funds for education be collected at the state level. Centralizing collection to the state will increase the dependence on income and sales taxes, both based on ability to pay, and decrease dependence on real estate taxes, which are increasingly less reflective of wealth and ability to pay.

Reducing inequity in educational expenditure (i.e., equalizing distribution of funds) will necessitate that the state fund education almost completely through a weighted formula, such as formulas 2 and 3 mentioned here. Remember that *equity* in expenditure does not necessarily mean that an equal amount is spent on each student. Recognizing that some children (e.g., poorer, handicapped, non-English speaking) are more difficult to educate than others, spending the same amount on each would clearly result in unequal outcomes. Rather, equity requires that we spend enough on each child for him or her to reach some acceptable level of educational performance. States must find a way to separate the *distribution* of educational funds from their *collection* if such equity is to be achieved. Currently, those children who have the greatest needs live in areas least able to raise the funds necessary to educate them to the same levels as more affluent children. As discussed, one possible way to separate the distribution of funds from their collection and to make the distribution more equitable is through the use of a voucher system that requires every parent to select schools for their children. Even if such a system included only public schools, the state could require that those schools accept the voucher as full pay-

ISSUES EXTRA

Savage Inequalities

Many contend that the worst problem facing public schools is not poorer math achievement than Singapore or lower reading scores than Finland. The biggest problem is the differential in educational funding between rich and poor. For example, Dave Hornbeck, Superintendent of Philadelphia public schools, calculated that if he had the same per pupil funding that the surrounding suburban districts had, he could maintain current services, fully implement his reform agenda, and still have $150 million left over. But given current constraints, he has found it necessary to cut after-school athletics, instrumental music, and summer school, programs taken for granted in suburban districts. One of Hornbeck's goals was to establish full-day kindergartens in all Philadelphia elementary schools, but he had to cut back on this program, so critical to the success of low-income children. He has been forced to slash the budget every year since assuming the superintendency, some $300 million over four years, due to stagnant state and local revenues coupled with surging enrollment.

Districts in other major cities face similar problems. The Washington, D.C., district suffered a deficit of $378.5 million in spring 1996 after already cutting its budget from $512 million in 1991 to $491 million in 1996. Cuts came through closing schools, eliminating summer school, firing teacher aides, and freezing the hiring of substitutes. Many schools are also in great need of repair, with serious leaks causing water and mildew damage to libraries and classrooms. There aren't enough textbooks, and many that are available are out of date.

The East St. Louis, Illinois, district is also in dire straits (Kozol, 1991). It spends half of what the state's wealthiest districts spend per pupil, yet its problems, and thus its needs, are much greater. For example, the infrastructure of schools is crumbling, requiring much higher costs for upkeep. More spent on maintenance means less can be spent on educational programs. But strong programs are more needed here because of the acute educational and health needs of the children, children who must walk to school past piles of smoldering garbage, who must play on industrially contaminated land, and who must live in substandard housing.

Chicago is another district with serious money problems. It has about one-third less to spend on its secondary students than do the surrounding suburban districts (Kozol, 1991). This means that each high school class of 30 students in Chicago receives $90,000 less than those in suburban Winnetka or Glenview. On some days, as many as 18,000 students in Chicago are assigned to classes with no teacher. In light of this teacher shortage problem, some see the city's 50 percent dropout as a boon. If all 440,000 eligible high school students showed up, who would teach them?

ment of "tuition." Any additional funds received would then be based on the two criteria we mentioned: degree of difficulty of educating the children accepted and the cost of programs.

In addition to equity issues, there are a number of other financial concerns facing our public schools, a few of which we examine here.

Other Financial Concerns

Graying of America

The increase in per capita expenditure for education that has occurred over recent decades has been accompanied by growing resistance on the part of the public. Many communities that vote on their

ISSUES

Continued

New York City also confronts money and infrastructure problems. The money available to the district is a half to a third of what wealthier districts in the state can spend (Kozol, 1991). Many blackboards are so badly cracked that teachers will not allow students to write on them for fear they will be cut. Paint is so chipped that furniture is often covered with a snow-like layer of dust. After heavy rains, small waterfalls course down flights of stairs. Floors have gaping holes in them, and acoustic tiles fall off the ceiling.

Poor districts in Texas share similar problems. The system of funding schools in Texas was found by state courts to be unconstitutional in 1989. Wealthier districts at that time spent as much as $19,000 per student, whereas poorer districts like San Antonio spent just over $2,000. The richest district drew on property wealth of $14 million per student, but the poorest had property worth of only $20,000 per student. The 100 wealthiest districts provided on average $7,000 per student, whereas the 100 poorest had to tax themselves at a rate 50 percent higher in order to garner enough to spend only $3,000 per student on average.

San Antonio, New York, East St. Louis, Philadelphia—these are some of the most economically disadvantaged cities in the country. They share these money problems, critics like Kozol say, because of the way education is financed in the United States. But do we know that if we equalized funding these problems would disappear? Some evidence is emerging that fairer funding does improve educational outcomes for the children of the poor.

Like Texas, state courts in Kentucky found the state's system of funding schools unconstitutional in 1989 after suit was brought by 66 poor Kentucky districts (Galuszka, 1997). The courts ordered the legislature to plan a total remake of the system. The legislature's plan for reform, the Kentucky Education Reform Act (KERA), mandated several changes, among them equalizing funding between rich and poor districts. In the seven years since the plan was implemented, the achievement of students in poor districts now matches that of students in wealthy districts, good evidence that equitable funding leads to improved performance.

If you lived or taught in a wealthy district, how would you feel about sending some of your funds to poorer districts? If you lived or taught in a poor district, how would you feel about not having the wherewithal to give your students the education they need? What constitutes fairness in this situation? What is the appropriate way to fund schools in a democratic society?

Table 10.5 Student Membership and Current Expenditures per Pupil in Membership for Public Elementary and Secondary Schools, by Function and State, School Year 1993–1994

State	Fall 1993 Student Membership	Current Expenditures per Pupil in Membership			
		Total	Instruction	Support Services	Noninstruction
United States	43,476,268	5,325	3,257	1,826	242
Alabama	734,469	3,826	2,392	1,131	302
Alaska	125,948	7,960	4,106	3,607	246
Arizona	709,453	4,104	2,369	1,467	268
Arkansas	444,271	4,013	2,514	1,226	273
California	5,328,558	4,718	2,820	1,701	197
Colorado	625,062	4,727	2,904	1,645	178
Connecticut	496,298	7,947	5,039	2,525	383
Delaware	105,547	6,101	3,782	2,062	257
District of Columbia	80,678	8,843	4,351	4,127	365
Florida	2,040,763	5,063	2,926	1,890	247
Georgia	1,235,304	4,569	2,812	1,476	281
Hawaii	180,430	5,532	3,410	1,789	333
Idaho	236,774	3,628	2,295	1,156	177
Illinois	1,893,078	5,323	3,204	1,939	181
Indiana	965,599	5,245	3,232	1,783	230
Iowa	498,519	5,070	3,126	1,717	227
Kansas	457,614	5,081	2,939	1,892	249
Kentucky	655,265	4,505	2,699	1,571	235
Louisiana	800,560	4,133	2,457	1,305	371
Maine	216,995	5,569	3,726	1,639	203
Maryland	772,638	6,191	3,742	2,135	314
Massachusetts	877,726	6,423	3,872	2,327	224
Michigan	1,599,377	6,138	3,559	2,401	178
Minnesota	810,233	5,342	3,403	1,722	216
Mississippi	505,907	3,410	2,107	1,030	273
Missouri	875,639	4,547	2,759	1,587	201
Montana	163,009	5,043	3,153	1,675	215
Nebraska	285,097	5,310	3,302	1,557	452
Nevada	235,800	4,661	2,775	1,727	159
New Hampshire	185,360	5,433	3,489	1,753	192
New Jersey	1,151,307	9,075	5,438	3,346	291
New Mexico	322,292	4,106	2,405	1,464	237
New York	2,733,813	8,069	5,445	2,396	229
North Carolina	1,133,231	4,540	2,789	1,405	346
North Dakota	119,127	4,385	2,689	1,319	378
Ohio	1,807,319	5,319	3,163	1,959	196
Oklahoma	604,076	4,403	2,569	1,464	370
Oregon	516,611	5,522	3,307	2,027	188
Pennsylvania	1,744,082	6,443	4,097	2,101	245
Rhode Island	145,676	6,797	4,529	2,094	174
South Carolina	643,859	4,335	2,566	1,496	273
South Dakota	142,825	4,095	2,525	1,344	226
Tennessee	866,991	3,813	2,451	1,152	210
Texas	3,608,262	4,488	2,661	1,558	269
Utah	471,365	3,206	2,150	860	196
Vermont	102,755	6,266	4,087	1,972	207
Virginia	1,045,471	5,205	3,133	1,802	270
Washington	915,952	5,342	3,189	1,906	247
West Virginia	314,383	5,292	3,292	1,701	300
Wisconsin	844,001	6,126	3,892	2,050	183
Wyoming	100,899	5,534	3,420	1,919	195

Source: U.S. Department of Education, 1996, p. 17.

school budgets are voting them down, which in turn causes school boards to attempt to reduce costs. One of the reasons for this growing taxpayer resistance is the increasing number of older adults whose children have already passed through the schools. Many of these citizens are reaching retirement age and will soon be living on fixed incomes. Although many of these individuals have grandchildren of school age and are concerned about the quality of their education, they are unable to pay the ever-increasing property taxes required to support our schools. A similar resistance is seen in young people who decide to delay marriage and children or even decide to forego families completely. They too are disinclined to support an educational system from which they are receiving no immediate benefit.

Accountability

Taxpayer resistance is further fueled by growing demands for accountability from schools and teachers. Whether it is true or not, many believe the schools are less academically successful than they were in the past and that discipline and drop-out problems are increasing. In both 1994 and 1995, respondents to the Phi Delta Kappa/Gallup Poll of the Public's Attitudes toward the Public Schools indicated that they thought lack of discipline was the major problem with which public schools of their communities had to deal. Respondents were also concerned about the lack of high academic standards in public schools and by the lack of proper financial support.

Many critics of the public schools argue that the combination of decreasing academic achievement and growing discipline problems are the two major factors driving parents to nonpublic schools. They propose that unless accountability for outcomes is increased, this trend will continue until the public school system is virtually destroyed. We discuss the issue of teacher accountability at greater length in Chapter 12.

Increasing Enrollments

At the same time that support for public education is decreasing, the number of children to be educated is increasing. Although there was a steady decline in enrollments throughout the 1970s, 1980s, and early 1990s, this trend has reversed as the result of both heavy immigration and what is being called the "post WWII grandbaby boom," the children of the baby boomers coming of school age. It is clear that as the number of children to be educated increases, so does the cost of educating them. This is especially true if we want to maintain the decreased class sizes public schools have gradually achieved over

the last several decades, an achievement that calls for more teachers. The problem of increasing enrollments is exacerbated by the fact that, primarily as the result of a variety of societal problems, a greater number of children now come to the public schools with special needs. And, as we have discussed elsewhere, both law and public sentiment demand that we raise the money to address these needs.

Inadequate Infrastructure

Still another major problem facing America's public schools is the condition of their buildings and facilities. An overwhelming number of schools were built in the 1950s and 1960s in response to the post-World War II baby boom, and many have received inadequate levels of maintenance since then. This has led to serious infrastructure problems that are now making major financial demands on local school boards. Deferring repairs to such items as roofs and heating units results in further deterioration and far more costly repairs later. According to the General Accounting Office (GAO), it would take about $112 billion to make our schools minimally habitable, approximately $3,000 per student (School Facilities, 1995). The GAO estimates that about one-third (14 million) of American students attend "inadequate" schools.

In addition to problems with the physical infrastructure of schools, there is also the question of the technological infrastructure. This refers to what needs to be installed in schools to make data, voice, and video technology effective, including conduits, cables, and electrical wiring for computers and other communications technology. Although these can be fairly easily and inexpensively installed in new schools, retrofitting existing schools is extremely costly. Numerous reports have indicated that infusion of information technology into instruction lags far behind the levels at which students will be expected to use such technology in college and in the business world.

New Funding Practices

Few knowledgeable observers of American education would deny that finding an equitable way to fund the education of *all* our children is one of the most pressing social problems we face. Everyone realizes that our government must address this issue, and many states are in the process of reforming their systems of educational funding. At the same time, educational professionals are taking the initiative to seek resources beyond the routine system of funding.

A growing trend in public school funding has been the practice of **user fees.** These are fees for a variety of what are considered nonessential school services such as athletic equipment, driver's education, summer school programs, and transportation. For example, in many cases the state will subsidize local district busing only within a specified radius from the school. If districts choose to bus other children, they must either absorb the costs in their budgets or charge parents for this service. As more budgets are defeated at the polls, more districts have begun to charge for these items.

Another resource that is being increasingly tapped to reduce costs is the use of parent and citizen volunteers. Although there has been a long tradition of "room mothers" in most elementary schools, the idea that unpaid individuals could provide services that districts have historically paid for is becoming more and more popular. In fact, some districts have developed an extensive system of recruiting and training volunteers, much like that of hospitals. And, of course, these districts generally provide extensive, low-cost reward systems, such as public recognition ceremonies, receptions, and special school privileges.

Many schools are also seeking money from the business sector. By 1989, the U.S. Department of Education estimated that there were approximately 140,000 school-business partnerships in operation, and it is estimated that corporate gifts to kindergarten through twelfth-grade education in 1992 totaled about $364 million (Sommerfield, 1992, p. 10). Business support for education takes a variety of forms. Sometimes a local McDonalds or Burger King provides food vouchers for students who get good grades or read a certain number of books; in other cases a corporation may underwrite extensive purchases of equipment, often in the area of emerging technologies. Many companies provide programs and materials for students and teachers. Although educators are grateful for such support from business and industry, the question of business control of the educational agenda invariably accompanies such school-business partnerships.

An increasingly popular form of outside support for public schools is the use of educational foundations. Although these have long existed in higher education, their emergence at the public school level is fairly recent. An educational foundation is established as a private, non-profit entity that solicits funds to support specific educational endeavors. Such foundations have their own decision-making boards that determine how these funds will be spent. In addition to seeking funds from corporations and wealthy individuals, foundations often contact alumni for small gifts, encourage them to remember the foundation in their wills, and request donations in the memory of loved ones.

NEW APPROACHES FOR THE TWENTY-FIRST CENTURY

Allan Odden, who has published extensively on the topic of educational finance, summarized the major issues facing us as we enter the twenty-first century. He also suggested some possible solutions.

Of course, the first order of business . . . is for the country to deal with the widely varying revenues per pupil that are provided across states and districts; this thorny problem must be remedied to some degree if all schools and districts are to be accountable for results.

Then the American system of public education will need to reorganize for high performance from top to bottom. Such reorganizing is critical in determining whether the money currently in the system and the new money likely to be provided to the system will be used effectively. One approach might be devolving much more authority, responsibility, and accountability to local schools. Such a strategy entails decentralizing power over the budget and personnel system, providing a comprehensive array of fiscal and student information, developing the knowledge and skills of school work teams, and changing the reward and compensation structure. It also entails developing high-quality curriculum standards, goals for student achievement, and measures of progress toward those goals. The system could also include more public school choice, more charter schools, and more deregulation. . . .

The hope is that such new approaches will allow schools to focus intently on the goal of student achievement, to dispense with current regularities of both program and finances, to redesign themselves and redeploy resources to take advantage of effective programs and strategies, and to use the nation's considerable investments in public education to place student achievement on a rapidly rising upward track. Thus, within the first years of the 21st century, all children might be achieving at the high levels that only a small portion attain today (Odden, 1995, p. 167–168).

SUMMARY

- The governance and finance of American public education takes place at the local, state, and federal levels, with state government having primary legal responsibility to educate its citizenry.

- Components of state government that affect public education include the legislature, state boards of education, state departments of education, the chief state school officer, governors, and state courts. Of these, the legislature has primary power to establish educational policy through the enactment of laws.

- The primary source of educational policy at the local level is the school board, which has control over finances, personnel, curriculum, students, and the physical infrastructure.

- Types of communities and school boards vary. These include dominated communities with school boards that represent the power elite, factional communities with divided school boards, pluralistic communities with status congruent school boards that strive for consensus, and inert communities with sanctioning school boards that tend to approve the recommendations of the administrative staff.

- Local school personnel in policy-making positions include superintendents, who are the chief executive officers for school districts, and principals, who are in charge of what goes on in individual school buildings. Individuals in these positions are crucial in determining vision, challenge, and achievement in school districts.

- There is a hierarchy of command in public schooling, with the state legislature at the top and students at the bottom. Anyone who has a problem within the system is expected to deal with it at the level at which it occurs before taking it to the next higher level.

- Several new forms of educational organization and control are currently being proposed. These include site-based management, which decentralizes control and responsibility to the individual school level; schools of choice, which give students and parents the right to select their schools within a district, county, or state; charter schools, which are set up by a group of individuals with clearly delineated outcome objectives for students, then approved by the state to operate with public funds; and privatization of school services.

- At the federal level, educational policy and practice are affected by the legislative, executive, and judicial branches of government. Increasing amounts of legislation during the 1960s and 1970s increased both the funding and control of the federal government in education. In 1979, a separate Department of Education was established, which extended the influence of the executive branch of federal government on educational policy.

- Nongovernmental influences on education include organizations of teachers, school boards, professional educators, parents, and businesses.

- Funds for education are collected at the local, state, and federal levels, with the local and state levels each contributing about 45 percent. Federal funds are usually provided through legislation to support education in a specific category, such as basic skills.

- Historically, local government, through property taxes, has had the primary responsibility for funding schools. Problems with this system of funding include the lack of uniform assessment practices that result in inequitable impact on residents of different communities and the fact that property taxes frequently do not represent the real income or value of individuals or families. In an effort to reduce these inequities, several court cases since the 1970s required state governments to assume increased responsibility for providing funds for education.

- The primary means by which state governments raise money for schools is through income and sales taxes and, in some states, lotteries. There are three formulas by which states distribute education funds: a specified amount per child on the basis of average daily enrollment; a formula that weights those characteristics known to increase the cost of schooling; and a foundation plan through which the state determines the cost of providing a basic level of education to all children, assesses the amount the local district can raise, and provides the difference.

- Funding reform in education must focus on reducing inequity in both the collecting and distribution of monies.

- Other financial concerns that face our public schools include the graying of America, resulting in an increased number of taxpayers living on fixed incomes and resistant to paying higher taxes; growing demands for accountability from schools and teachers;

increasing enrollments; and inadequate infrastructures.

- New sources of financial support for schools include user fees, volunteers, school-business partnerships, and educational foundations.

READINGS FOR THE PROFESSIONAL

Callahan, R. *Education and the Cult of Efficiency.* Chicago: University of Chicago Press. (1962).
This work examines the origin and development of the adoption of business values and practices in educational administration, highlighting not only the strength of the business ideology in the American culture, but the weaknesses and vulnerability of school administrators to public criticism. Callahan proposes ways to change these conditions.

Kozol, J. *Savage Inequalities: Children in Americas Schools.* New York: Crown, (1991).
Kozol examines schools in the cities of East St. Louis, New York, San Antonio, Chicago, Washington, and Camden to demonstrate that schools in most of the United States remain segregated and unequal. The book is a plea for fairness and decency in the way we pay for education of all children in this country.

Spring, J. *The Sorting Machine.* New York: David McKay. (1976).
This book is a classic examination of the role of the federal government in establishing educational policy. It examines the Cold War and the Civil Rights Movement in an attempt to consider whether the primary purpose of schooling should be individual fulfillment or preparing young people to meet the needs of society.

Tannenbaum, M. *Concepts and Issues in School Choice.* Lewiston, NY: The Edwin Mellen Press. (1995).
This book examines the history and conceptual development of school choice, including vouchers, magnets, and current forms of public school choice. It brings together works of major educational theorists and policymakers to examine key issues in the school choice movement.

CHAPTER 11

Legal Foundations of Education and Teaching

The bell for the opening of school rings, and you are in the school office, leaving the students in your classroom unsupervised. Before you get back to the room, a fight breaks out between students, and one is seriously injured when he falls and hits his head after being pushed by another. Are you legally liable for what took place during your brief absence?

You are not happy with your school district's policy of requiring school faculty to convert time previously spent on academic planning over to school supervision and security duties. You have

Historical Perspective
  Early Legislation
  Constitutional Basis for Education
    Tenth Amendment
    First Amendment
    Fourth Amendment
    Eighth Amendment
    Fourteenth Amendment

How Will the Law Affect Your Life As a Teacher?
  Certification Requirements
  The Interview Process
  Acquiring Tenure
  Grounds for Dismissal
    Incompetence
    Insubordination
    Immoral Conduct
    Conduct Unbecoming a Teacher
    Good and Just Cause
    Reduction in Force (Riffing)
  Collective Bargaining

Teachers' and Students' Legal Rights
  Freedom of Expression
    Teachers' Free Speech Rights
      Freedom of Expression beyond the Classroom
      Academic Freedom in the Classroom
    Students' Free Speech Rights
  Religious Freedom
  Freedom of Association
    Teachers
    Students

Personal Freedom
Freedom from Discrimination
  Racial Discrimination
    Students
    Teachers
  Gender Discrimination
    Sports
    Administration
    Pregnancy
  Age Discrimination
  Discrimination Based on Disability
Due Process Rights
  Students' Due Process Rights
    Corporal Punishment
    Academic Sanction
    Search and Seizure
    Remedies
  Teachers' Due Process Rights

Legal Bases for Curriculum and Teaching Issues
  Curriculum
  Student Testing
  Copyright Laws
  Access to Student Records
  Liability
    Negligence
    Abuse
    Malpractice

Summary

Readings for the Professional

tried to address the problem through channels—principal, superintendent, school board—but have gotten no response. You decide that if the taxpayers in the community knew what was going on, they would be outraged and demand change. After giving it a great deal of thought, you decide there is only one way to let the taxpayers know—a letter to the editor. In the letter, you identify your efforts to solve the problem within the system, criticizing your superiors' failure to respond. Are you within your First Amendment rights to speak out in this way?

One of the realities of modern life that makes this topic so important to you as a prospective educational professional is the increasing litigiousness of our society. It is extremely important that you know your own legal rights and responsibilities as well as those of your students if you are going to successfully navigate the shark-infested waters of educational policies and practices.

Many volumes have been written regarding teachers' and students' legal rights, mostly because these have been defined through the process of case law rather than legislation. **Case law** consists of the results of court cases heard at both the state and federal levels. Similar cases brought in different parts of the country through different courts may result in different outcomes. The study of case law attempts to abstract from these cases common grounds from which guidelines for professional practice can be established.

The legal foundations of education and teaching are deeply rooted in historical tradition and Constitutional law. Since there were no public school systems in place at the time of the ratification of the Constitution and Bill of Rights, responsibility for education became one of the powers "reserved" to the individual states. The courts have subsequently defined education as a property right assured to all citizens by the Fourteenth Amendment. State constitutions have stipulations that public schools will serve all students within specified age ranges and for a specified number of days per year.

Understanding the profession of teaching and your role as a teacher within a legal context necessitates a consideration of the relationship between the schools and the state, teachers' legal rights and responsibilities, and students' legal rights and responsibilities. This chapter examines educational legislation and case law from historical and contemporary perspectives so you understand both how and why things came to be as they presently are as well as the directions things appear to be going in the future.

HISTORICAL PERSPECTIVE

Early Legislation

As we described earlier, twenty-three years after their arrival on the New England shores, the Puritans of the Massachusetts Bay colony passed The School Law of 1642, the first educational legislation to be enacted in the colonies, requiring parents and guardians to make certain their children could read and understand the Bible and the laws of the commonwealth. Five years later they passed the Old Deluder Satan Act, which required all towns with 50 or more families to hire a teacher and those with 100 or more to also build a school. With the exception of Rhode Island, the other New England colonies passed similar laws, primarily to ensure that children would be able to read and to become imbued with the principles of the Puritan religion.

It is important to emphasize that the Puritans' primary motive for making sure that children could read was religious, not secular. Although they had fled England to escape religious persecution from a government that endorsed a single religion, they had no desire to separate church and state. They simply wanted to substitute their own brand of Christianity for that of the Church of England and to ensure that their own religious beliefs became the foundation for political and social life in Massachusetts.

The ratification of the Constitution in 1788 made the establishment and conduct of education a state matter. Beforehand, in 1785, however, the federal government made clear the extent of its interest in education with the passage of the Northwest Ordinances, which required each of the townships in the Northwest Territories to set aside a specific section of the township to be used for education. These practices illustrate the first step that government took to ensure an educated citizenry—mandating that schooling be provided. It was not, however, until much later that state governments began to pass legislation which mandated that parents and guardians actually send their children to school, beginning in 1852 with Massachusetts. By 1918, all states had similar laws.

Constitutional Bases for Education

Despite America's strong faith that an educated populace was the backbone of democracy, the Constitution was conspicuously silent regarding the federal government's role in matters of education. Consequently, without *explicit* guidance regarding matters of educational control and policy making, national and state leaders were forced to seek whatever *implicit* guidance was available in the various amendments to the Constitution. This section briefly examines those amendments that have been used most frequently in charting the course of educational development in this county. We begin with the one that results in state control of education, the Tenth Amendment.

Tenth Amendment

This amendment, ratified as part of the Bill of Rights along with the Constitution, states that "the powers not delegated to the United States by the Constitution, nor prohibited by it to the states, are reserved to the states respectively, or to the people." As explained in the introduction to this section, the Constitution was silent on education, and thus it became one of the powers "reserved to the states respectively." As you read in the previous chapter, it is primarily the legislature in each state that has responsibility for making laws which control education. Legislatures then authorize local school boards, both elected and appointed, to carry out the legal provisions enacted by the state. Interestingly, because the federal Constitution says nothing regarding education, "individuals do not have an inherently federally protected right to an education. The federal Constitution does, however, confer basic rights on individuals, and these rights must be respected by school personnel" (McCarthy & Cambron-McCabe, 1992, p. 7).

First Amendment

The Bill of Rights, consisting of the first ten amendments to the Constitution, were enacted by the early patriots who had just fought for freedom from the overpowering mother country, to protect the rights of individuals from encroachment by the state or federal government. The most important of these rights were described in the First Amendment.

> Congress shall make no law respecting an establishment of religion, or prohibiting the free exercise thereof; or abridging the freedom of speech, or of the press; or the right of the people peaceably to assemble, and to petition the government for a redress of grievances.

We look at public school policies and practices affected by this amendment in the following three categories:

- Religious freedoms involving teachers' and students' behavior.
- Students' and teachers' rights to express themselves in speech and the press.
- Students' and teachers' rights to get together on school property for various purposes.

All three of these protections, but especially the third one, remain the object of heated debate today and are examined later in this chapter.

Fourth Amendment

This amendment establishes the right of citizens "to be secure in their persons, houses, papers, and effects against unreasonable searches and seizures," referring to potential actions by governmental officials. In recent years, this amendment has been particularly relevant to the right of school officials to search students' personal belongings and lockers for such things as cigarettes, drugs, and weapons.

Eighth Amendment

This amendment prohibits the use of "cruel and unusual punishment" with incarcerated criminals. Corporal punishment cases in the public schools have been taken to the Supreme Court under this amendment.

Fourteenth Amendment

This amendment provides that no state shall "deny to any person within its jurisdiction, the equal protection of the laws." It has been the basis for cases involving alleged discrimination as well as those involving school finance. The due process clause of this amendment prohibits states from depriving citizens of life, liberty, or property without due process of law and has played a role in cases involving compulsory attendance, tenure, and privacy. Finally, the Supreme Court has interpreted the Fourteenth Amendment as incorporating the personal freedoms contained in the Bill of Rights. It has also mandated that these rights extend to state governments as well.

HOW WILL THE LAW AFFECT YOUR LIFE AS A TEACHER?

We answer this question by examining the ways in which legislation and rulings from court cases will impact your professional life in three different categories. The first area regards your preparing for and acquiring a teaching position and the political dimensions of remaining in that position, including tenure and collective bargaining. Following that, we examine those legal rights and responsibilities teachers and students share as they go about their daily lives in schools. Finally, we look at certain curriculum and teaching responsibilities with which teachers, unlike students, must deal. The information contained in this chapter can be thought of as a minimum compendium of legal understandings that every teacher needs in order to avoid stressful, costly, and time-consuming interruptions to the business of teaching.

Certification Requirements

The first way in which legal considerations affect your life as a teacher is through the state requirements established for you to become certified. This certification or licensing process is similar to that required in other professions, such as law, medicine, and architecture. Although certification requirements vary from state to state, they generally include knowledge of content and how to teach and such personal items as good moral character, age, good health, and U.S. citizenship. Part V discusses these more closely.

The Interview Process

The state establishes certification requirements, but local school boards have the legal authority to hire teachers, and most school boards have written contracts with the teachers they hire. Some time shortly before or after completing your certification program, you will prepare a resumé and send it to several school districts in which you want to teach, requesting an interview. Do you know what your legal rights are as school officials ask you questions that will help them decide whether or not they want to hire you?

Until the last few decades, almost no one questioned the right of school officials to ask women about their marital status and family plans during a job interview, since these would obviously affect the district in the ensuing years. However, both Title IX of the Education Amendments Act of 1972 and Title VII of the Civil Rights Act prohibit asking questions about race, creed, sex, religion, marital status, handicaps, or national origin. Also, districts may not request pictures of candidates with job applications.

If you find yourself in a job interview in which such questions are asked, you may politely refuse to answer them. If they are asked by a building principal, you may want to inform the superintendent of schools. Of course, this could mean you will not be offered a job in this district. If such practices are condoned, you may want to give a second thought to whether you want a job in the district. One further step you can take if your reception by the superintendent is cool is to inform the U.S. Office of Civil Rights.

Once you complete the interview process and are offered a teaching position by a principal or superintendent, you may think that your acceptance of the position means that you have a job. It does not, and anyone offering you a job should let you know that it is not official until it is approved in a public meeting by the school board. Along the way, the recommending supervisor may change his or her mind, or the school board may not vote to approve you. Such a circumstance took place in the *Board of Education of D.C.* v. *Wilson* case in 1972. Jessie Wilson applied for a job in the District of Columbia summer school program. She was informed that she had been selected for the position contingent on the district's receiving funding for the summer school and was asked to return an acceptance form, which indicated that her appointment was not official until approved by the school board. However, the board changed the requirements for the position and decided that Wilson no longer met them. She sued for loss of income in the District of Columbia Court of Appeals. She lost on the basis that she never had a valid contract, because the board had never given its approval.

Acquiring Tenure

Once you obtain a teaching position, your next concern, if you want to remain in the position indefinitely, is acquiring tenure. Tenure is a legal right that provides teachers with a continuing contract in a school district. That contract can only be terminated on the basis of causes set out by law. A tenured teacher is entitled to notice of charges from a school board as to why he or she is not fit to teach and must also be given a hearing in which the board has the responsibility of proving its case. Most states have laws that outline the requirements a teacher must fulfill to become tenured. These generally include a probationary period (usually of 3 years) during which the teacher must have a specified number of satisfactory observations by a supervisor. In some states, teachers automatically become tenured on the first day of the school year following the probationary period, whereas other states require specific action on the part of the school board.

It is important to note that once a teacher receives tenure, there are two major differences in his or her relationship to the school board. Prior to acquiring tenure, it is the teacher's responsibility to prove that he or she is *competent* and worthy of being rehired. After acquiring tenure, the first change is that the responsibility shifts to the school board, and the second change is that what must be proven is *incompetence*. Many critics of tenure argue that herein lies one of its major problems: It is much more difficult to prove incompetence than it is to demonstrate minimal competence. Thus, they claim, some teachers may go through the probationary period not doing anything grossly wrong, acquire tenure, then never get any better. In fact, some teachers get worse over time.

We emphasize here that before receiving tenure, teachers are *not* typically entitled to a hearing prior to dismissal. Only a few states give nontenured teachers minimal procedural rights. Illinois requires that a second-year teacher be provided with notice of the reasons for nonrenewal. In Connecticut, teachers receive a statement of the reasons for nonrenewal only if they request it in writing.

As a tenured teacher, you have the legal right to continued employment unless dismissed "for cause." This does not mean, however, that you are guaranteed employment in any particular position. In fact, school boards have the right to reassign tenured teachers as long as their decisions are in the best interest of the school district and are not arbitrary or unreasonable (*Proviso,* 1987). In particular, courts have ruled that tenured teachers can be reassigned as part of a school desegregation plan. One other guarantee that you do *not* have as a tenured teacher is that your salary will never be reduced. School boards' legal right to determine teachers' salaries includes reducing them, as long as a reduction is applied to all teachers uniformly and is not in the middle of a school year.

If, as a tenured teacher, you are faced with dismissal charges, you also have certain rights guaranteed to you. As indicated you must be given notice of the charges against you and an opportunity for a hearing. In some states, a tenured teacher cannot be dismissed without an opportunity to remediate deficiencies. The notice of charges against you must be clear and specific enough that you can answer them directly. You have a right to be present at a dismissal hearing, to bring counsel, to present a defense against charges, and to subpoena witnesses.

Grounds for Dismissal

In most states, legitimate grounds for dismissal of a tenured teacher include incompetence, insubordination, immorality, unprofessional conduct (or conduct *unbecoming a teacher*), and "other just cause." In addition, school boards may dismiss tenured teachers because of reduction in force. Let's look at each of these individually in order to understand how the courts have defined them.

Incompetence

The most straightforward form of incompetence is demonstrated by a teacher's lack of knowledge in the subject area he or she is expected to teach, but cases often involve issues relating to teaching methods, grading procedures, classroom management, and professional relationships. Incompetence is legally defined as "lack of ability, legal qualifications, or fitness to discharge the required duty" (Black, 1990, p. 765). Table 11.1 shows some of the many forms of incompetence for which teachers have been dismissed.

It is important to note that a teacher cannot be dismissed for incompetence on the basis of one or two "bad days" of teaching. A school board must prove that a teacher continually fails to carry out contracted responsibilities before such a dismissal case will hold up in court.

Insubordination

Insubordination is defined as willful disregard for or refusal to follow reasonable school regulations or administrative orders. Insubordination charges can be brought as the result of a single incident if the circumstances are serious enough. The courts upheld a Missouri teacher's termination after she refused to teach an assigned course (*McGlaughlin,* 1983) and a Colorado teacher's dismissal for using offensive language toward a student after being instructed not to use profanity when dealing with students (*Ware,* 1988). Many states, however, require that acts be "persistent" over a period of time to be considered insubordination.

Many cases of insubordination arise as the result of inappropriate use of corporal punishment, with teachers either using it when it is prohibited by the school board or failing to follow guidelines established by the board. Another frequent area of insubordination is that of conflicts arising out of teacher-administrator relationships. However, in order for a rule or administrative order to be reasonable, it must be clear and specific enough for a teacher to understand. For example, a Kentucky court did not uphold a teacher's dismissal for refusal to "cooperate" with the principal because the teacher had neither violated any specific school rules nor refused to obey any administrative directives (*Osborne,* 1967).

Examples of reasons for dismissals for insubordination that have been upheld by the courts are failure to inform administrators of absences; abusing sick leave; taking personal leave without permission; refusal to sign an attachment to a contract; refusal to accept a transfer to another school; violating a

Table 11.1   Examples of Reasons for Dismissal of Tenured Teachers for Incompetence

Area of Evaluation			
Academic	Students scoring poorly on standardized basic skills tests (*Scheelhaase* v. *Woodbury Cent. Community School Dist,* 1974)	Mistakes in grammar and punctuation (*Singleton* v. *Iberville Parish School Board,* 1961)	Poor spoken English, mispronounced words and errors in a geography lesson (Appeal of *Mulbollen,* 1944; *Beck* v. *James,* 1990)
Classroom Management	Inappropriate use of class time, irrational grading of students (*Whaley* v. *Anoka-Hennepin Indep. School Dist. No. 11,* 1982)	Inability to control a class and to plan and teach lessons effectively (*Mongitore* v. *Regan,* 1987)	Displaying a starter pistol in an attempt to gain control of a group of students (*Myres* v. *Orleans Parish School Board,* 1983)
Personal	Deficiencies in personality, composure, judgment, and attitude that have a detrimental effect on a teacher's performance (*Hamburg* v. *North Penn School Dist.,* 1984)	Smoking in front of students, leaving the classroom unattended, and making sexual remarks to both students and teachers (*Bradshaw* v. *Alabama State Tenure Commission,* 1988)	Poor rapport with students (*Whaley* v. *Anoka-Hennepin Indep. School Dist.,* 1982)

school directive to retain final examination papers; failure to follow directives designed to improve instruction; failure to acquire board approval to use supplementary materials in the classroom; refusal to cease religious exercises in the classroom; and refusal to cease residing with a 16-year-old student.

The key to insubordination cases is that the rules or directives the teacher is required to follow must be reasonable, clear, and not in violation of the teacher's constitutional rights. In addition, for these cases to be upheld it is usually necessary that the school district demonstrate willful or *deliberate* disregard of the rule or directive on the part of the teacher. And, except in extreme instances, it is usually required that there be a *pattern* of insubordinate behavior on the part of the teacher for the courts to uphold dismissal. On the other hand, there is generally no requirement that the teacher's insubordination be in any way connected to classroom effectiveness; the two are seen as independent, and a teacher who is considered effective in the classroom can, nonetheless, be dismissed for insubordination.

Immoral Conduct

Immorality, which is the most frequently cited cause for dismissal, generally is not defined in the statutes of most states (McCarthy & Cambron-McCabe, 1992). However, the courts have held immorality to be unacceptable behavior that affects a teacher's "fitness" to teach. Until fairly recently, teachers were viewed as moral exemplars and in their private lives were expected to be role models for students. In the past, teachers were dismissed for such reasons as obesity, public drinking, drug use, cheating, lying, using obscene language, expressing disbelief in God, heterosexual or homosexual behavior, and talking about sex.

Today, dismissal cases for immoral conduct must generally be related to a teacher's classroom effectiveness, one exception being in the area of sexually related conduct between a student and a teacher. Courts in Washington, Michigan, Alabama, Minnesota, Pennsylvania, and Missouri have held that sexual contact between a teacher and a minor, including sexual harassment, was sufficient grounds for dismissal.

In addition to in-school behavior involving students, teachers' out-of-school behavior and lifestyle have been the subject of many cases taken before the courts under the "role-model" standard. Community disapproval of a teacher's lifestyle has not usually been considered sufficient grounds for upholding dismissal charges. Generally, it must be shown that a particular lifestyle has an adverse effect on a teacher's classroom effectiveness. One particularly controversial area is teacher homosexuality, and the courts have rendered diverse opinions in this area. We look at this topic more fully when we discuss teachers' and students' legal rights.

Although a large number of immorality cases involve sexual conduct, such things as dishonesty, criminal behavior, and drug-related conduct have been the basis of court-upheld dismissals. Some examples include misrepresenting absences from school as an illness when a teacher was actually attending a conference unrelated to work, submitting false tax documents, taking school property without permission, and instructing a student to lie and cheat during a wrestling tournament. On the other hand, some state courts have held that conviction for a crime or misdemeanor in and of itself was not sufficient grounds for dismissal.

Conduct Unbecoming A Teacher

This is often referred to as *unprofessional conduct* and covers a wide latitude of possible misdeeds on the part of teachers that could become the basis for dismissal. In fact, what is considered unprofessional conduct in one state may be considered neglect of duty in another state. For example, a teacher being absent after having been denied permission for a leave was dismissed on the basis of unprofessional conduct in New York (*Pell,* 1974), neglect of duty in Colorado (*School Dist. No. 11,* 1973), and unfitness to teach in Maine (*Fernald,* 1975). In general, conduct unbecoming a teacher, or unprofessional conduct, refers to any violation of the rules or the ethical code of the teaching profession, and it may include actions inside or outside the classroom. Dismissals on the grounds of unprofessional conduct were upheld in the courts in one case in which a teacher campaigned in his classroom for a superintendent running for election and in another case in which a teacher smoked marijuana with students in his apartment. In both New Jersey (*State* v. *Parker,* 1991) and Connecticut (*Rado,* 1990), the courts ruled that teachers can be dismissed for unprofessional conduct even when they were acquitted of criminal charges on which the conduct allegedly was based.

Good and Just Cause

Although this is an even more vague and ambiguous term than *conduct unbecoming a teacher,* the courts frequently have upheld dismissals brought under this category, arguing that it is not possible for state tenure laws to specify in advance all the possible circumstances under which teachers might legitimately be dismissed. However, the charges brought forward by a school board must be reasonable and rational and not arbitrary or irrelevant.

Reduction in Force (Riffing)

When school districts experience such circumstances as decline in student enrollment, reconfiguration or consolidation, or financial problems, they can dismiss tenured and untenured teachers because of a reduction in force, commonly referred to as *riffing.* State legislation, board policies, and collective bargaining contracts form the basis for guidelines for riffing teachers. Generally speaking, probationary teachers are dismissed before tenured teachers, but in the case of reconfiguration of teaching responsibilities, if a tenured teacher is not qualified for a new position, that individual can be dismissed rather than a qualified probationary teacher. Many state laws also incorporate seniority as a basis for dismissal of tenured teachers. Pennsylvania permits merit ratings to be used to determine which teachers will be dismissed, and Nebraska has permitted the use of such noneducational factors as contribution to the school activity program. It is important to note that school boards may not use the riffing process to bypass tenure laws or to avoid teachers' due process rights. In the absence of state statutes or collective bargaining agreements, for the courts to uphold dismissal decisions because of reduction in force, boards must develop consistent policies and apply them to all teachers in a nondiscriminatory fashion.

Collective Bargaining

Until the early 1960s, when the AFT won the right to represent the teachers of New York City in the bargaining process, school boards had a great deal of power to determine teachers' salaries, both individually and collectively. Since that time, the two major teachers' unions, the AFT and the NEA, have consistently increased their membership and bargaining power throughout the country. This means that you are not able to negotiate individually with a school board regarding your salary or other terms of employment. Rather, the union that represents the teachers in your district negotiates a contract for everyone in the bargaining unit. We look at this process more thoroughly and critically in Chapter 12. For now you need to be aware of how it will affect your professional life.

In the first place, many states permit the bargaining agent—the union elected to do the bargaining—to require that all teachers pay for its services. Although it is impermissible to mandate that teachers join a union, the courts have upheld the concept of an agency shop, which requires that employees pay at least a portion of union dues to support collective bargaining activities from which they will benefit. The U.S. Supreme Court ruled that laws at the state level permitting agency shop arrangements are constitutional, but states are still free to prohibit such arrangements, as has happened in Vermont. On the other hand some states, such as Hawaii and Rhode Island, have passed legislation mandating that teachers pay agency fees. In many cases, the bargaining agent also negotiates the process of paying dues or agency fees through the means of dues checkoff, whereby equal amounts of dues are deducted from each pay check.

Another important dimension of the collective bargaining process is what is described as the *scope* of bargaining—the areas about which bargaining takes place. There are three classifications of topics: mandatory, permissive, and prohibited. Although there is wide variation throughout the states regarding the topics that fall in each of these categories, those that are generally mandatory are wages, hours, and fringe benefits. Other items that courts in some states have found to be mandatory are formulations of an agreement; binding arbitration; interpretation of existing agreement; amount of leave time; length of the school calendar; safety; vacations; in-service training; jury duty; and disciplinary procedures. One of the most controversial items in the negotiating process is class size, with the majority of state courts finding it to be in the permissive rather than in the mandatory category.

One area of the collective bargaining process that you may find it necessary to use in the course of your career is the grievance procedure. A *grievance* may be defined as *a claim by a teacher or by the union that there has been a violation, a misapplication, or a misinterpretation of the agreement*. A grievance may also be defined more broadly to mean *a claim by a teacher or the union that there has been a violation, a misapplication, or a misinterpretation of any policy or administrative decision affecting employees of the school district*. The procedure usually defines the steps that must be taken and the time limits that apply. It may include provisions for arbitration. There is generally a subcommittee of the union designated to handle grievances and a representative of that committee meets the teacher to determine the basis of the grievance and, once determined, to help carry the grievance forward. If the grievance cannot be resolved at the district level, it may go forward to binding arbitration.

Another area of the collective bargaining process that can have an enormous impact on your life as a teacher is strikes. Teachers do not have a constitutional right to strike, and most teachers are prohibited from striking by state statute or common law, but some states have now passed laws that give teachers a limited right to strike.

When does a strike occur and what is its relationship to collective bargaining? Typically, a teachers' union will negotiate a contract that is in effect for 2 or 3 years. Toward the end of that period, the negotiating committees of the union and the school board begin to meet to discuss agreed upon items.

Once a contract has expired, if agreement cannot be reached on any part of the contract, the union may take a vote of its membership to see if they are willing to strike in order to pressure the board to reach agreement on the unresolved items. Typically contracts run out after the end of the school year, and it is rare for teachers to strike before a new school year begins. However, it is also rare for much to get accomplished over the summer.

One important thing you need to know in relation to teachers' strikes is the possible penalties for striking illegally. If it is in violation of state law, or if teachers refuse to return to work after a court has issued a back-to-work order, a strike is illegal. Teachers engaged in an illegal strike can be fined or imprisoned and the U.S. Supreme Court ruled that school boards can validly conduct a hearing to terminate illegally striking teachers even though the board is negotiating labor questions with the teachers (*Hortonville*, 1976).

Once you have acquired a teaching position, then tenure, it is likely that you will not only have been involved in one way or another with the union but also probably have encountered some areas in which your rights or responsibilities as a teacher or the rights of students were in some way challenged. The next section examines primarily case law that has attempted to hammer out these very complicated constitutional questions.

TEACHERS' AND STUDENTS' LEGAL RIGHTS

It may appear that teachers and students have very different roles to play in the schooling process, but closer examination reveals that they share many common activities, especially as schools increasingly attempt to operate as integrated learning communities in which students have a role in constructing their own educational environment. The legal rights that teachers and students share in the educational world include freedom of expression; religious freedom; freedom of association; personal freedoms; freedom from discrimination; and due process rights. Next we examine the ways in which these rights are similar for both teachers and students as well as ways in which they differ.

Freedom of Expression

Until the middle of the twentieth century, school boards had a great deal of control over what both teachers and students could say in school and, in some cases, out of school. This was especially so regarding political matters. Little attention was paid to First Amendment rights of free speech, and courts generally used the "reasonableness" test to judge school policies.

> If there was any reasonable relationship between the rule and some educational purpose, the rule would be upheld even if most judges believed it was unwise, was unnecessary, or restricted constitutional rights. Courts felt that school boards should have discretion and that judges should not substitute their judgment for that of school officials, who were presumed to be experts in educational matters (Fischer, Schimmel, & Kelly, 1995, p. 151).

Two major cases occurred within a short time of each other that had a dramatic impact on changing this picture in regard to both teachers and students. In 1968, the U.S. Supreme Court ruled on a teacher's right to air his political views, and in 1969 the Court handed down a ruling that neither teachers nor students lose their rights to freedom of expression when they enter the doors of the public schools. We will look at each of these cases in some detail.

Teachers' Free Speech Rights

Teachers' freedom of expression has been tested both as it relates to matters of concern beyond the classroom and to academic freedom within the classroom. Because nearly all the cases that have addressed teachers' academic freedom within the classroom have arisen since the 1968 ruling in the *Pickering* v. *Board of Education* decision, we begin with that case.

Freedom of Expression Beyond the Classroom

Marvin Pickering was a secondary teacher in Illinois whose letter to a local newspaper criticizing the school board's expenditure of funds for an athletic program when they were allegedly unable to pay teachers' salaries was published. Pickering charged that "taxpayers were really taken to the cleaners" by the construction company that built one of the district schools, and he cited the "totalitarianism teachers live in" at the high school. Pickering was dismissed because, the school board argued, his statements were false and damaging to the reputations of the administrators and board members and impeded the efficient operation of the district. The Illinois court upheld his dismissal, and Pickering appealed to the U.S. Supreme Court on the basis that the statements in his letter were protected by the First Amendment. Justice Thurgood Marshall wrote that the issue in this case was "to arrive at a balance between the interests of the teacher, as citizen, in commenting upon matters of public concern, and the interests of the state, as an employer, in promoting the efficiency of the public services it performs through its employees." The Supreme Court reversed the lower court's decision, arguing that Pickering's statements did not have a detrimental effect on his relationship with his supervisor or coworkers, on his classroom performance, or on the school's operations. Furthermore, the Court argued that because Pickering spoke out on a matter of public interest, he was protected by the First Amendment.

Teachers' freedom of expression outside the classroom is one of the most complicated areas of teachers' legal rights. The courts generally have focused on whether a teacher's criticism addressed matters of public concern, not simply personal interest. Teachers' right to speak out publicly is usually upheld by the courts if the contents of the expression meet this requirement, even if the consequences are disruptive of the operation of the school or if some component of the statements is unintentionally false. Interestingly, in matters of public concern, teachers may not even be required to go through the chain of command in speaking out. In Oregon, a judge ruled against a school board for suspending a coach who mailed a letter about the athletic program directly to the board instead of sending it through the appropriate steps, barring the enforcement of "any policy which prohibits direct communication by teachers on matters of public concern with the members of the District School Board" (*Anderson,* 1984).

According to Fischer, Schimmel, and Kelly (1995):

> When teachers allege that they are unconstitutionally punished because of their statements, recent court decisions suggest a 4-step analysis. (1) Do the statements involve matters of public concern? If so, (2) does the teacher's right to discuss public matters outweigh the school's interest in promoting efficiency? If the court answers these questions in the affirmative, the teacher's statements would be protected by the First Amendment. But before judges order schools to rescind the punishment, they also ask (3) was the teacher's speech a substantial or motivating factor in the action against him? If so, (4) did the administration prove that it would have taken the same action even in the absence of the protected conduct? If not, courts should find the punishment unconstitutional and perhaps award damages. Since judges have differing notions of what constitutes "a matter of public concern," and since they weigh the rights of the teachers and the interests of the schools differently, the outcome of a close case may vary from one court to another. (pp. 189–190)

Academic Freedom in the Classroom Academic freedom was originally a concept primarily applicable at the post-secondary level, but in our country it has increasingly become the basis of numerous cases coming from public elementary and secondary teachers. Cases taken before the courts involving the right of teachers to select topics, materials, and teaching methodologies have been decided both for and against them. In many situations, two major factors determined the decision. First, if teachers clearly violated a school board's established rules, such as the teacher in Alaska who refused to follow a policy requiring the superintendent's approval to use supplementary material in the classroom, the courts generally ruled in the favor of the school district. Their decisions were based on the idea that it is the school board, not the teacher, who has the right to control the curriculum (*Fischer,* 1985).

The second rule of thumb is whether or not the supplementary material is in line with the prescribed curriculum. In cases in which teachers wanted to emphasize certain topics in the course syllabus while ignoring or only lightly touching on others, the courts have generally ruled against the teachers. More than one teacher has been dismissed, and the courts upheld the dismissals, for showing in class an R-rated, sexually explicit film unrelated to the curriculum. In contrast, courts have overturned disciplinary actions against teachers because materials or topics were just controversial, such as one teacher's use of *Welcome to the Monkey House,* by Kurt Vonnegut, in her eleventh grade English class (*Parducci,* 1970), another teacher's willingness to allow open discussion of interracial marriage in his social studies class (*Sterzing,* 1974); and still another's use of an article from the *Atlantic Monthly* that discussed dissent, protest, and revolt, and used the term *motherfucker* (*Keefe,* 1969). In those cases, the materials and topics were seen as relevant to the school's prescribed curriculum.

To summarize, the courts have given teachers control over the materials to be used in their classes. Although most districts have committees of teachers that review and recommend textbooks and supplementary reading lists, the courts have upheld the right of the school board to both select texts and remove books, including literary classics, from the curriculum.

Students' Free Speech Rights

A case with even more impact on subsequent educational policies and practices than the *Pickering* case was the 1969 landmark Supreme Court decision, *Tinker* v. *Des Moines Independent School District.* During the Vietnam War, the Des Moines school system suspended three students for wearing black armbands to express their antiwar views. Although a federal court ruled that the no-armband policy was reasonable, the Supreme Court reversed that position, concluding that the authorities punished students for an act that caused no disturbance or disruption, pointing out that "undifferentiated fear or apprehension of disturbance is not enough to overcome the right to freedom of expression " and emphasized that "students in school as well as out of school are 'persons' under our Constitution. They are possessed of fundamental rights which the state must respect." The Court went on to say that neither students nor teachers "shed their constitutional rights to freedom of speech or expression at the schoolhouse gate."

This ruling, that students could express their opinions on controversial issues, applied not only to the classroom but to the cafeteria, halls, playing grounds, or any other places where school activities took place. However, such expression must "not materially and substantially interfere with the requirements of appropriate discipline in the operation of the school" or interfere with the rights of others. The Court emphasized that school officials have the responsibility to establish and maintain discipline in the schools, but they must balance their actions in light of students' constitutional rights.

Subsequent to *Tinker,* a number of cases tested the guidelines established in this case, especially in relationship to prohibiting personal student expression *before* it took place. The Sixth Circuit Court of Appeals upheld the rule of a Cleveland high school banning the wearing of freedom buttons, because the wearing of some symbols had led to fighting between black and white students and disruption of the educational process (*Guzick,* 1971). An Indiana federal court also upheld the suspension of several high school students for distributing leaflets calling for a school walkout, in light of the fact that 54 students had walked out the day before causing substantial disruption of the educational process and school officials legitimately anticipated that this would be repeated (*Dodd,* 1981).

In contrast, the courts have ruled that students cannot be disciplined for *nondisruptive* expression just because it is critical of school personnel or policies. The Ninth Circuit Court of Appeals reversed the trial court's support of the suspension of two high school students for wearing anti-scab buttons to protest the hiring of teachers to replace those who were on strike. The court argued that though the message on the buttons was "vigorous," it was not vulgar, and there was no evidence that the buttons caused disruption. In another case, the Seventh Circuit Court of Appeals upheld students' rights to criticize school officials and policies in a mimeographed paper containing various articles and urging students to reject "propaganda" (*Scoville,* 1970). And an Arkansas federal district court ruled that two football players could not be disciplined for their protest against a coach who they claimed had manipulated the election for homecoming queen to prevent a black student from winning (*Boyd,* 1985).

Just as students have certain rights regarding actual speech, they also have a right to remain silent under certain circumstances. As the result of a landmark U.S. Supreme Court decision in the 1940's, *West Virginia* v. *Barnette,* brought on behalf of children of the Jehovah Witnesses faith, students cannot be compelled to participate in the Pledge of Allegiance or be required to salute the flag. In fact, they cannot even be required to stand at attention while the flag is being saluted (*Lipp,* 1978).

One area of student expression that the courts have limited is lewd and offensive speech. In a major decision in 1986, *Bethel School District No. 403* v. *Fraser,* the U.S. Supreme Court, overturning lower courts, upheld the right of school officials to punish a high school senior for giving a nominating speech at a school assembly, despite teachers' admonitions that his planned speech, which described his candidate by using an "elaborate, graphic, and explicit sexual metaphor," was inappropriate. Although the speech was not legally obscene or disruptive, the court maintained that "the school's legitimate interest in protecting the captive student audience from exposure to lewd, vulgar, and offensive speech justified the disciplinary action." (McCarthy & Cambron-McCabe, 1992, p. 112)

An additional area of students' freedom of expression that has increasingly received a great deal of attention has to do with student publications. Whether or not school officials can regulate student publications has been determined by the relationship of the publication to the curriculum. In *Hazelwood School District* v. *Kuhlmeier* (1988), the Supreme Court ruled that school authorities can exercise "editorial control over the style and content of student speech in school-sponsored expressive activities so long as their actions are reasonably related to legitimate pedagogical concerns." If the publication is sponsored by the school as part of the regular curriculum, those in charge have wide discretion over its contents. If, however, it is an underground publication, written and published off campus, students' First Amendment rights enjoy far greater protection.

This form of free speech falls under the guidelines of the *Tinker* case and cannot be restricted unless it is libelous or obscene, likely to cause substantial disruption of the educational process, or interferes with the rights of others. Thus, the following apply to what are generally described as "underground newspapers." They cannot be banned or prohibited for any of the following:

- Discussing controversial or unpopular topics.
- Criticizing school officials or policies.
- Proselytizing for a particular religious belief.
- Containing offensive, vulgar, or "dirty" language.
- Containing material not written by a student or school employee.

The sale of underground newspapers cannot generally be banned on campus, nor can school officials regulate off-campus publications. However, school officials can enforce reasonable regulations concerning the time, place, and manner in which student publications are distributed, but such regulations cannot have the effect of making it impossible for students to distribute their materials. At least two cases have upheld a school district's right to prohibit distribution of such materials in hallways.

In summary, *Tinker* and *Hazelwood* form the parameters for court decisions regarding students' free speech rights. Although *Hazelwood* gives school officials broad discretion in controlling the contents of school-sponsored publications, the guidelines established by *Tinker* are the basis for regulation of "underground" student publication, written and published off campus. School officials may ban distribution of such off-campus publications only if they are libelous, obscene, or likely to create a substantial disorder. Beyond that, they may control only the place and manner in which such publications are distributed.

Religious Freedom

You will recall that the First Amendment begins with, "Congress shall make no laws respecting the establishment of religion or prohibiting the free exercise thereof." Cases brought to the courts in this area examine whether or not school policies and practices have the effect of establishing a single religion or make it difficult or impossible to practice one's own religious beliefs.

There are a number of rights that students and teachers share in this area. As indicated above, students cannot be required to salute the flag; nor can teachers, if their objections are based on either religion or conscience. In fact, in 1977 the Massachusetts

Supreme Court informed the legislature that the recently enacted law requiring teachers to lead a group recitation of the Pledge of Allegiance each morning was a violation of their First Amendment rights.

In regard to religious exemption from participating in portions of the state-prescribed curriculum, the courts have been much less liberal with teachers than they have with students. A case brought from the Chicago public schools taken to the U.S. Supreme Court involved a teacher who, because of her beliefs as a Jehovah's Witness, indicated that she would not be able "to teach any subjects having to do with the love of country, the flag or other patriotic matters in the prescribed curriculum." The Supreme Court upheld the school board, indicating that "the First Amendment was not a teacher license for uncontrolled expression at variance with established curricular content" (*Palmer,* 1980).

The courts are far more likely to support parental requests for student exemptions from specific curricular activities. Instructional areas in which exemptions have been granted on religious grounds include sex education, drug education, dancing in physical education courses, coeducational physical education, watching movies, playing cards, and ROTC training. The court's reasoning is that students, unlike teachers, are compelled to attend schools, which makes them vulnerable to coercive school practices.

Interestingly, parents can remove their children completely from the public schools for religious reasons and place them in private schools. In a 1925 landmark case, *Pierce* v. *Society of Sisters,* a Catholic religious order challenged the Oregon law requiring every child between the ages of 8 and 16 to attend public schools, and the Supreme Court ruled in the order's favor. In a famous quote, the Court clearly expressed the rationale for its ruling:

> The fundamental theory of liberty upon which all governments in this Union repose excludes any general power of the state to standardize its children by forcing them to accept instruction from public teachers only. The child is not the mere creature of the state; those who nurture him and direct his destiny have the right, coupled with the high duty, to recognize and prepare him for additional obligations.

Although parents can remove their children from all public schooling for religious reasons and put them in private schools, with one exception, the courts have not ruled favorably in requests to remove them completely from schooling. In 1972 in *Wisconsin* v. *Yoder,* the Supreme Court ruled that the free exercise rights of the Amish were violated in requiring their children to attend school beyond the eighth grade. Recognizing the legitimacy of the claim of the Amish that requiring their children to acquire secondary schooling threatened the ongoing existence of their community, the Court ruled on the importance of balancing the interests of the state in the education of the child with the Amish interest in practicing and preserving their religion and community. The courts have not, however, extended this protection to other religious groups.

A final area of religious freedom that affects both students and teachers almost equally is that of religious practices in public schools. For most of our history the overwhelming majority of public schools in this country required the practice of morning exercises that included either prayer or Bible reading or both. In 1963, in the landmark *Abington School District* v. *Schempp* decision, the Supreme Court ruled that mandatory prayer and Bible reading in public schools that children were required to attend violated the establishment clause of the First Amendment. The fact that children may have participated voluntarily did not matter inasmuch as these activities were conducted under the auspices of the public schools. On the other hand, students may engage in private prayer, even if it is audible, such as saying grace before lunch, as long as it is nondisruptive.

Although the Supreme Court explicitly indicated in the *Schempp* case that the *practice* of religion in public schools is unconstitutional, studying *about* religion is not. That means that there can be courses or units on the Bible as literature, comparative religion, the history of religion, religious art and music, and other approaches which do not entail religious exercises, rituals, or celebrations. In 1971, the Court further defined the guiding principles to be used in determining whether a school practice was in danger of violating the establishment clause in what has come to be known as the "tripartite test" (*Lemon* v. *Kurtzman,* 1971). In order to pass muster the practice must:

1. Have a secular purpose.
2. Have a primary purpose that neither advances nor impedes religion.
3. Avoid excessive government entanglement with religion.

For the next 2 decades the courts were fairly consistent in applying these guidelines. One of the major areas in which controversy arose had to do with Christmas programs and displays in the schools, which have led to lawsuits in numerous communities. Celebrating Christmas in any way in the schools was ruled unconstitutional, and it is no less so if there is parallel celebration of such holidays as Hanukkah. Furthermore, how many or how few parents object to the practice is irrelevant. The schools may teach *about* religion, but they may not engage in the celebration of a specific religious practice. This separation of religious expression from school activities was extended recently to such noncurricular activities as athletic events and graduation ceremonies.

Conservative political factions are pushing vigorously for an amendment to the Constitution to permit prayer in public education. If this movement receives congressional approval and is ratified by the necessary 38 states, practices in public schools will likely go in a very different direction than they have for the last several decades. Read the accompaning Global Box to learn about the Court's rulings on Bible studies in after-school clubs.

Freedom of Association

Freedom of association refers to the right of teachers and students to join with others to express their views. Although this freedom is not explicitly included in First Amendment protections, the Supreme Court has recognized that associational rights are "implicit in the freedom of speech, assembly, and petition" (*Healy,* 1972, p. 181). This affects teachers in terms of what political and social organizations and activities they can engage in and students in terms of participation in clubs.

Teachers

The courts have ruled that teachers, as a condition of employment, can be required to sign oaths pledging the faithful performance of their duties, support for the federal Constitution and their state's constitution, and opposition to the overthrow of the government by any illegal or unconstitutional method. However, they cannot be required to swear that they are not members of subversive organizations or that they will promote respect for the flag, reverence for law and order, or undivided allegiance to the government. In 1967, in *Keyishian* v. *Board of Regents,* the Supreme Court established that membership in the Communist party cannot be the basis for not hiring or for releasing a teacher, as long as an individual does not engage in any illegal activities. In addition, teachers cannot be dismissed solely for their support or nonsupport of particular candidates in school board elections, for wearing political badges, or for discussing political issues or candidates in class if the discussions are related to the curriculum. On the other hand, teachers cannot advocate for a particular candidate or engage in campaign activities that interfere with school procedures.

The issue of whether or not teachers can participate in partisan political activities is not one with a clear-cut answer. In 1973, the Supreme Court upheld the provisions of the Hatch Act, which prevents federal employees from holding formal positions in political parties, playing substantial roles in partisan campaigns, and running for partisan office (*U.S. Civil Service Commission,* 1973). In addition, some courts have supported restrictions that prevented state and municipal employees from running for public office. It is not clear, however, how this affects public educators. Although educators can be required to take a leave from their positions if campaigning interferes with the performance of their duties, several courts have held that because they are not directly involved in the operation of public agencies, they have the right to run for and hold public office. The Utah Supreme Court upheld teachers' and administrators' rights to serve in the legislature (*Jenkins,* 1978), and Ohio supported a principal's right to serve as a county commissioner (*State* ex rel. *Gretick,* 1984). On the other hand, teachers cannot run for or serve on school boards in the districts in which they are employed inasmuch as it is a clear conflict of interest to vote on policies that directly affect their employment, such as salary schedules.

Examining the social affiliations of teachers, we find that although teachers cannot be dismissed because the people they married are controversial or because of a divorce, a teacher can be dismissed because of the criminal activity of his or her spouse. The state appeals court in Oregon upheld the dismissal of a teacher whose husband used their home for growing and selling marijuana, supporting the superintendent's argument that the circumstances would "significantly diminish [her] ability to effectively teach" and would "damage [her] credibility in the eyes of students and parents" (*Jefferson County,* 1991). Furthermore, a teacher can also be prohibited from marrying an administrator or else either the teacher or the administrator could be transferred if such a marriage took place.

Students

Students' free association rights in schools are far more limited than those of teachers. On one hand, courts have upheld the rights of schools to prohibit the existence of secret societies, fraternities, sororities, or other nonschool clubs that perpetuate themselves by choosing new members rather than being open to all students equally. At least 25 states have laws banning such clubs or prohibiting students from belonging to them.

There is quite a different picture in regard to student-initiated organizations and clubs with open

GLOBAL

Extra-curricular Student Clubs

School district officials often fear that student Bible study meetings and other religious after-school activities on school premises will violate the establishment clause of the First Amendment to the Constitution. However, this is not necessarily true. In fact, if a district has created a limited open forum in its secondary schools, (i.e., has allowed other noncurriculum-related student groups to meet on school premises during noninstructional time), the district is required under the Equal Access Act of 1984 (EAA) 20 U.S.C. Secs. 4071-4074, to permit all noncurriculum related student clubs to meet on school premises.

That would include a Bible reading club. It would also include a meeting wherein students discussed controversial issues that the administration may find repugnant. For once a district creates a limited open forum, it may not deny the right of any club to assemble on the basis of the "religious, political, philosophical or other content of the speech of such meetings" [sec. 4071(a)]. This is not without limitation; a district maintains its ability to exercise discipline and must provide that the meeting "does not materially and substantially interfere with the orderly conduct of educational activities within the school" [sec. 4071(c)(4)]. Nor is the district required to permit meetings in which unlawful conduct occurs.

However, whereas a district that has created a limited open forum must grant equal access to the student Bible club, this must be reconciled with the establishment clause prohibition against state sponsorship of religion. In the U.S. Supreme Court case of *Board of Education of the Westside Community Schools* v. *Mergens, 496 U.S. 226* (1990), the Court held that the EAA did not violate the establishment clause. A school district could not refuse to permit a student Christian club to meet after school hours on school premises on the same basis as it permitted other noncurriculum-related clubs to meet. In so ruling, the justices pointed out numerous requirements of the EAA that served to minimize the risk of official state endorsement of religion. For example, the EAA expressly states that there must be no "sponsorship" of (defined to include promoting, leading, or participating in) the meeting by the school, the government or its agents or employees [Secs. 4071(c)(2); 4072(2)].

The EAA requires that students themselves must voluntarily seek permission for the club, and must direct and control the meeting. It expressly limits participation by school officials at the meetings, and any such meetings must be held during "noninstructional time" defined to mean "time set aside by the school before actual classroom instruction begins or after actual classroom instruction ends" [Sec. 4072(4)]. Neither teachers, other school employees, nor non-school persons may initiate or direct the meetings; employees or agents of the board may be present at student religious meetings only in a "nonparticipatory capacity" such as for custodial purposes or as monitors to maintain order and discipline [sec. 4071(3)(3)].

If the district has a monitor for one noncurriculum-related club, it must have one for each such activity. However, school officials may not require

GLOBAL

Continued

any individual employee to monitor a particular meeting if the content of the speech is contrary to the beliefs of that employee. The act also prohibits teachers or other school officials from influencing the form or content of any prayer or other religious activity, and from requiring any person to participate in prayer or other religious activity.

Further, the district may not spend public funds to support the club "beyond the incidental cost of providing the space for student-initiated meetings" [sec 4071(d)(3)]. Thus, the district should not provide the club with paper or other school supplies, nor allow it access to the school copying machine. The fact that a school pays a teacher for monitoring a student religious club probably does not constitute sponsorship. Congressional debate apparently took for granted that payment of a school-required monitor for any club was an "incidental cost of providing the space for student-initiated meetings." The student group may use the school media (e.g., P.A. system, school newspaper, and bulletin board) to announce its meetings so long as all noncurriculum groups are treated similarly. A district that wishes to make it especially clear that it does not endorse or sponsor noncurriculum-related student groups may issue a disclaimer to that effect, emphasizing that it is merely making its facilities available to these groups.

However, a school district may decline the use of school premises for after-school student religious activities if it has maintained a closed forum, i.e., permitting no "noncurriculum-related student groups" to meet on school premises. The district is then under no obligation to permit a Bible study club or any other noncurriculum-related club to conduct its meetings at the school.

However, districts must be very careful regarding the interpretation of *curriculum-related.* In *Mergens,* the Court gave a very narrow definition to *curriculum-related student group.* A curriculum-related student group only exists if:

- The group's subject matter is actually taught or will soon be taught in a regularly offered course.

- The subject matter of the group concerns the body of courses as a whole.

- Participation in the group is required for a particular course or results in academic credit.

So, for example, a French club would be a curriculum-related club if French were taught, or were soon to be taught, in the school. But groups such as a chess club, a stamp collecting club, or a community-service club would not be curriculum-related clubs unless the district could show that they directly relate to the curriculum.

How would you feel if your school allowed a Bible-study group? How about a Koran-study group? What would your attitude be for a Gay-Straight Alliance or a Young Socialists Club? Would you consider serving as a faculty monitor for any of these clubs? Why or why not?

membership. In 1984, Congress enacted the Equal Access Act, stipulating that if school districts permit *any* noncurricular organizations to use school facilities for their activities, they must do so for *all*. School officials cannot ban a group because they do not agree with their philosophical, political, or religious ideas. This does not mean that the district *must* provide such a forum for student groups; they can limit *all* after-school activities to those that are related to the curriculum, such as drama, language, or science clubs, or athletic teams. However, if they permit some student-initiated groups this forum, they must permit it for all such groups.

One area in which appellate courts have yet to address this issue at the secondary level is the recognition of gay student groups. Although courts have generally ruled in favor of gay college groups that have been denied recognition, some constitutional scholars have suggested that the picture might well be different at the high school level.

> Judges might give high school administrators wider latitude in restricting gay student groups among teenagers in their formative years on the grounds that the Equal Access Act does not apply to groups that "substantially interfere" with the school's responsibility "to protect the well-being of students." (Fischer, Schimmel, & Kelly, 1995, p. 240)

On the other hand, there is some effort among educators to teach tolerance for different lifestyles and demand that schools protect gay students from harassment. In 1993, Massachusetts approved the first state policy prohibiting discrimination against gay and lesbian students and encouraging school districts to set up support groups and to provide counseling for these students. It is expected, then, that students in these organizations have the same right to meet as other student groups.

Personal Freedom

Traditionally, neither teachers nor students challenged school dress and grooming codes, nor is it likely they would have been successful in the courts if they had. However, this picture changed during the 1960s, as both teachers and students became more aware of their individual rights.

There is wide variation in federal courts' interpretation of the Constitution in relationship to student grooming. The U.S. Supreme Court, which usually reviews cases when federal appeals courts differ in their interpretations of the Constitution, declined on at least nine occasions to review cases on this issue, apparently because justices do not believe it deals with constitutional questions of national significance. About half of the U.S. circuit courts of appeal

have ruled that students are free to wear their hair as they wish.

Controversies over hair length are only one part of what is at issue regarding students' appearance; there is also the question of dress codes. Although all courts recognize that schools have the right to establish student dress codes, not all codes are constitutional. A federal court in New Hampshire ruled that a policy prohibiting the wearing of blue jeans was unconstitutional, rejecting the school's position that wearing jeans "detracts from discipline and a proper educational climate" (*Bannister,* 1970). Similarly, a New York state court struck down a secondary school's prohibition against girls wearing slacks on the basis that it applied only to girls and included every kind of slacks (*Scott,* 1969).

In general, dress codes dealing with health, safety, order, and discipline are likely to be held valid. Schools may prohibit students wearing clothing that is dirty, displays obscene messages, is too tight or too revealing, or that would cause safety problems in the shop or gymnasium.

One relatively new area of controversy regards the wearing of jewelry, special colors, or other symbols of gang membership. A federal court in Illinois supported a school's suspension of a senior male student who wore an earring to school in violation of the school's policy banning all gang activities and the wearing of gang symbols such as jewelry, earrings, and badges (*Olesen,* 1987). The student argued that the earring "expressed his individuality" and was "attractive to young women." However, the court supported the school district, maintaining that the earring was not a protected form of expression, because it did not "convey a particularized message" that "would be understood by those who viewed it."

Another recent area of controversy deals with T-shirts with sexual connotations. Courts have upheld suspensions of students wearing T-shirts with the following messages: "Drugs Suck!"; "Co-ed Naked Band: Do It to the Rhythm"; and "See Dick Drink. See Dick Drive. See Dick Die. Don't be a Dick." In each case, the words were seen as potentially vulgar, offensive, or sexually provocative and not forms of protected speech, even if the messages were laudable (*Brousard,* 1992; *Pyle,* 1993).

Questions regarding teachers' appearance have been resolved much more easily by the courts than those about students. Although a few courts have declared a teacher's right to determine appearance a fundamental constitutional right, these rulings have generally come when the policy prohibiting a particular form of grooming or dress was arbitrary or inequitable. A California appeals court overruled the transfer of a high school teacher to home teaching because he refused to obey an administrative order to shave off his beard (*Finot,* 1967). The court maintained that beards on teachers "cannot constitutionally be banned from the classroom" unless school officials can prove that it interfered with instruction.

Since the 1970s, most courts have supported school districts in imposing grooming and dress regulations on teachers. Although recognizing the right to govern personal appearance is a protected interest, the courts have not seen this issue as a fundamental right. As long as such dress and grooming regulations are reasonable and related to carrying out educational responsibilities, most courts have supported them.

Freedom from Discrimination

One of the often-praised goals of American society and education has been to provide equality of opportunity. The equal protection clause of the Fourteenth Amendment specifies that "no state shall . . . deny to any person within its jurisdiction, the equal protection of the laws." This means that schools, as state institutions, cannot discriminate against either teachers or students on the basis of race, color, sex, religion, national origin, age, or handicapping condition. In addition to this constitutional protection, various federal and state laws provide the basis for protecting equal opportunity rights. The most significant federal laws are shown in Table 11.2.

We look briefly at the categories of race, gender, age, and handicapping condition to understand the role of the school and of individual classroom teachers in making sure discrimination does not take place, either for their students or for themselves.

Racial Discrimination

Historically, one of the most complicated and controversial areas of American life has been the area of racial discrimination. A number of court cases and much federal legislation have dealt with racial discrimination in schools, much of which affects both students and teachers. Many of those cases and laws were later extended to include other forms of discrimination. Take a moment to read the accompanying Research Box to learn about some recent actions in the area of desegregation.

Students   In 1849, the Massachusetts State Supreme Court (*Roberts*) endorsed racial segregation in public schools. This case was later cited in the well known *Plessy* v. *Ferguson* case of 1896 involving segregated railroad facilities out of which the "separate but equal" doctrine emerged. This infamous doctrine maintained that separate facilities for

Table 11.2   Legislation Protecting Equal Opportunity Rights

Date	Legislation	Provisions
1964	Title VII of the Civil Rights Act	Prohibits discrimination on the basis of race, color, or national origin in institutions with federally assisted programs.
1972	Title IX of the Educational Amendments	Prohibits gender discrimination in institutions with federally assisted educational programs.
1973	Section 504 of the Vocational Rehabilitation Act	Prohibits discrimination against otherwise qualified handicapped individuals in programs receiving federal financial assistance.
1974	Equal Educational Opportunity Act	Guarantees all children equal educational opportunity without regard to race, color, gender, or national origin.
1990	Individuals with Disabilities Education Act	Ensures a free, appropriate public education for children with disabilities.

blacks and whites did not violate the Constitution as long as those facilities were equal. When applied to public schools, it provided the justification for legally segregated schools throughout the South. In the early 1950s, the Supreme Court ruled in several higher education cases that separate educational programs offered for African American and white students were unequal, thus violating the equal protection clause of the Fourteenth Amendment. This perspective was extended to the public schools in the landmark ruling in 1954 in *Brown* v. *Board of Education of Topeka,* in which the Court declared that racially segregated public schools were inherently unequal. A year later the Court issued an implementation decree requiring school officials to convert segregated, dual school districts into integrated, unitary districts "with all deliberate speed" (*Brown II*).

Little integration was accomplished before the mid-to-late 1960s, however, as the courts provided little guidance regarding what should be done or any mechanism for enforcement. In 1964, the federal government passed the Civil Rights Act barring discrimination on the basis of race, color, or national origin in institutions with federally assisted programs. Initially, that act did not have much effect on public schools, because there was little reward for compliance. However, with the passage of the Elementary and Secondary Education Act in 1965, which provided the most massive influx of federal funds into education in the history of this country, public schools began examining their policies and practices in order to have access to these federal funds.

In addition, in several late 1960s cases, the Supreme Court required school officials to take **affirmative action** to convert segregated school districts into integrated ones. This meant that simply eliminating policies and practices that had resulted in segregated schools was not satisfactory;

RESEARCH

Segregation Revisited

Much has changed in the years since *Brown* v. *Board of Education* outlawed segregated education and ushered in a tumultuous period when school boards tried to balance the new law with community resistance to desegregation—all the while struggling with a flood of lawsuits, citizen protests, and court mandates.

Today, the political climate is improved. In 1954, 40 percent of the population opposed desegregation; today, it's 11 percent. Long past are the ugly protests, where stones and epithets were hurled at black children.

But desegregation remains a battleground. In Topeka, Kansas, for instance, school officials have spent years in court over the issue, and the superintendent has received anonymous letters and phone calls with racial slurs from citizens opposed to a desegregation proposal that would have expanded busing and closed segregated schools.

Adding to the complexity of the issue are changing attitudes about desegregation. For example, many African Americans, disenchanted with busing's impact, now are urging that more resources be put into neighborhood schools, even if that perpetuates segregated schools. This change of heart puts educators squarely in the middle of discord within the minority community, where many still believe desegregation offers the best hope of providing students with a good education. In Darlington, SC, for example, some African Americans wanted to close a predominantly minority high school in favor of an integrated school, while others sought to preserve the school as a symbol of pride for the African American community.

Discord also can break out among various minorities, an increasing likelihood as communities become more racially and ethnically diverse. For example, some Chinese-Americans filed suit in San Francisco challenging a desegregation plan that limits the percentage of any ethnic group that can attend academically prestigious schools, a legal challenge looked upon unfavorably by some Hispanic and African American groups.

Many whites, for example, fled urban centers because of declining academic quality and violence, creating a concentration of largely poor minorities in urban districts. The result is de facto segregation.

For minorities, the consequences have been immense. Almost two-thirds of African American students, three-fourths of Hispanic students, and almost one-half of Asian students now attend schools that are predominantly minority. Isolation is the norm. Very troubling is the fact that today, segregation has resurged. The trends weren't always this way. After *Brown* v. *Board of Education,* the percentage of minority students attending integrated schools rose dramatically during the 1960s and 1970s. In the

school officials had to take positive steps to bring about integration in schools. In *Green* v. *County School Board of New Kent County, Virginia* (1968) the Supreme Court ruled that school officials must eliminate racial segregation in terms of not only students but "every facet of school operations—faculty, staff, transportation, extracurricular activities, and facilities." Three years later, in 1971 in *Swann* v. *Charlotte-Mecklenburg Board of Education,* the Supreme Court attempted to identify the characteristics of an unconstitutional dual school system and to describe the steps necessary to achieve an integrated one. Among the various remedies suggested by the Court was the one that came to be the most widely used and the most controversial, the use of busing.

RESEARCH

Continued

South, the percentage of African American students in white majority schools rose from .001 percent in 1954 to 43.5 percent in 1988.

Many strategies have been tried to reduce segregation; these have had mixed success. In Boston, busing failed. But busing enjoyed greater success in Indianapolis, one of the few instances where the courts, finding that surrounding communities conspired to maintain segregation, approved an interdistrict desegregation plan. Here, students are bused among the city and largely white suburbs, with the result that many of the city's schools are integrated.

Another approach with a mixed record is magnet schools. The strategy has worked well in South Carolina's Charlotte-Mecklenburg district, a county system serving urban, suburban, and rural communities with a diverse racial mix. Serving the entire county has proven a key factor in the district's success, because white flight from Charlotte does not mean white families leave the school district.

However, in Kansas City, a predominantly minority urban district, the city and state have invested $1.2 billion to create 58 magnet schools to attract suburban students to the city. But suburban parents, wary of the city schools' academic quality, have resisted. White enrollment is stagnant at 24 percent.

One of the most recent desegregation plans was announced the summer of 1994 in Topeka, KS, where a federal court approved a strategy that would close several segregated schools, develop magnet schools, and pay transportation costs for students who ask to transfer to schools whose racial mix would improve by the transfer.

Some segregation could probably be eased by metropolitan desegregation plans that incorporate suburban areas into any busing or magnet school program. Indeed, where such plans exist, such as Louisville, KY, and Indianapolis, IN, desegregation is successful.

But this strategy has largely been blocked by the 1973 U.S. Supreme Court *Milliken* v. *Bradley* decision, which essentially ruled that urban-suburban integration requires proof that the suburbs used racial discrimination to help create the segregation problem.

This picture may change, however, if a lawsuit recently filed by several Connecticut students is successful. It argues that the segregation that exists between predominantly minority Hartford and surrounding white suburbs violates students' constitutional rights to an equal education.

How important is desegregation to a good education for all? What kind of school would you prefer to work in, one that is desegregated or one in which one race predominates? Why?

It is interesting that after initial conflict and resistance, school desegregation proceeded more steadily and successfully in the South than it did in the North. Only 1 percent of minority students in 11 southern states attended school with white children in 1964, but by 1972, over half of minority students were in schools that were predominantly white (U.S. Commission on Civil Rights, 1975, pp. 46–47). However, in the North, where schools were not previously segregated by law, which is known as **de jure segregation,** the picture was quite different. Several cases highlighted the difference between de jure segregation and **de facto segregation,** which results from residential patterns, which became increasingly prevalent in the North. The concept of de jure was extended to include those districts in which intentional policies or practices of school officials resulted in segregated schools and many of the courts heard cases that attempted to define and clarify when this had occurred. In some cases they ruled it had and in others that it had not.

Another problem that emerged primarily in the North but also in major urban areas in other parts of the country was **resegregation,** which often stemmed from "white flight" from the urban areas to avoid school integration. Many remedies were proposed to address this problem, including inter- and intradistrict busing, altering attendance zones, reassigning teachers, and magnet schools—all forms of affirmative action. To date, however, predominantly single-race schools have continued to exist, especially in urban areas.

Another problem of major concern to educators is the presence of segregation *within* integrated schools. This has resulted from both academic tracking practices and from social segregation in which students self-segregate for nonacademic activities. Only academic tracking has raised the issue of discrimination, however, because of the high percentage of African American students that are placed in lower tracks with little opportunity to escape. This was addressed in *Hobson* v. *Hansen* (1967) in which the federal court examined the use of standardized test scores used to place students in various tracks in the Washington, DC schools. The court concluded that such tests discriminated against minority children, as mistakes were often made placing them on this basis. This ruling and similar ones following it ruled out the use of ability grouping only if it results in discrimination against identifiable groups of children. However, the high incidence of minority children placed in low-ability tracks or special education classes has not diminished. According to a 1991 study by the General Accounting Office, a disproportionate number of minority students are in these classes in over half the school districts nationally (*School Law News*, 1991, p. 3).

Teachers   In contrast, the use of tests in employment decisions for teachers, even when they eliminated a disproportionate number of minorities from the applicant pool, have not generally been ruled unconstitutional. In most cases, the court's decisions rest on its evaluation of whether or not the test being used is a valid indicator of job performance.

The legal basis for teachers to bring discrimination charges has primarily been Title VII of the Civil Rights Act of 1964. This act prevents employers with 15 or more employees, employment agencies, and labor organizations from discriminating against employees on the basis of race, color, religion, sex, or national origin. It covers hiring, promotion, compensation practices, fringe benefits, and other terms and conditions of employment. It permits employers to impose hiring restrictions based on gender, national origin, or religion (but not race), if such characteristics are genuinely related to job performance. Interestingly, Title VII did not originally apply to educational institutions, but in 1972, this exemption was repealed, with the exception of employment by religious educational institutions.

Discrimination questions in regard to teacher employment are most frequently raised in the context of affirmative action. The United States Commission on Civil Rights has defined affirmative action as "steps taken to remedy the grossly disparate staffing and recruitment patterns that are the present consequences of past discrimination and to prevent the occurrence of employment discrimination in the future" (United States Commission on Civil Rights, 1973). Following passage of the Civil Rights Act, many school districts that were under court-ordered desegregation were also required to take race into consideration when filling teaching vacancies, as in Boston. Beyond this, many more districts also established voluntary affirmative action hiring plans to bring about more racial balance in their teaching staff. Many of these plans have subsequently been challenged under both the equal protection clause of the Fourteenth Amendment and Title VII as bringing about **reverse discrimination,** defined as discrimination against nonminorities, which results from attempting to correct for past discrimination against members of minority groups.

The strong push for affirmative action initiated under presidents Kennedy and Johnson grew unabated until the Reagan and Bush years, when many of the federal funds specified for specific minority populations, especially in education, began to be eliminated. In 1995, a landmark event took place when the board of regents for the university system for the state of California voted to eliminate affirmative action in awarding contracts, hiring, and student admission policies, arguing that paying attention to race in any way was a form of discrimination.

Gender Discrimination

Title IX of the Education Amendments Act of 1972 provides that "no person in the United States shall on the basis of sex be excluded from participation, be denied the benefits of, or be subjected to discrimination under any education program or act or activity receiving federal financial assistance." For a decade there was a lack of agreement over the scope of the act. Then the Supreme Court resolved this issue in 1982, ruling that Congress intended the law to cover employees as well as students (*North Haven,* 1982). In 1984, the Supreme Court found Title IX to be program-specific, applying only to programs or activities receiving direct federal assistance (*Grove City,* 1984). However, in 1988 Congress signed into law the Civil Rights Restoration Act, which nullified the Supreme Court's narrow 1984 interpretation and applied Title IX to the entire institution when any program in the institution received federal funds.

Sports　One area in which gender discrimination has traditionally been most prevalent for both students and teachers is athletics. Historically, females have been denied the same opportunities as males to participate in and coach sports. To date, Title IX has been much more positive for female students than teachers. Courts have generally required school districts to permit female students to participate with males in *noncontact* sports if no comparable programs are available for females. In 1972, in one of the first notable cases in this area, the Eighth Circuit Court of Appeals allowed a female senior student at St. Cloud Technical High School in Minnesota to play on the boys' tennis team when there was no girls' team (*Brendan,* 1972). Other courts supported this position, ruling that in noncontact sports such as golf, swimming, and cross-country skiing, where there are no teams for girls, they must be permitted to compete on boys' teams.

In recent years, controversy over female students' participation in contact sports has increased. Several courts have ruled that school districts must provide female students the opportunity to participate in contact sports, such as football, basketball, and wrestling either through gender-segregated or coeducational teams. Courts in New York and Mississippi have rejected school districts' arguments that regulations barring females from participating in

these sports were necessary to protect their health and safety, especially when females were not given the opportunity to demonstrate their fitness and males were permitted to participate regardless of safety considerations (*Lantz,* 1985; *Force,* 1983). Most courts have ruled that school districts can meet their legal obligations for gender equity in athletics by providing comparable, gender-segregated contact teams, but not all have. Rulings in this area are sure to increase as girls continue to increase their participation in school sports programs.

One last question that arises in the area of athletics in terms of students is whether or not schools must provide equal funds for boys' and girls' sports. Although Title IX prohibits discrimination in financial support for sports in coaching and equipment, it also indicates that unequal expenditure alone does not constitute discrimination. If the sports are comparable, such as tennis or golf teams for boys and girls, equality is easier to determine than it is in such high-cost, high-revenue sports such as football. This is an area that has yet to be fully tested in the courts, especially regarding inequities in travel funds and accommodations provided for male and female college athletes.

In addition to Title IX, the Equal Pay Act of 1963 stipulates that all employees are entitled to equal pay for equal work; jobs performed do not have to be identical but must be substantially equal with regard to skills, effort, and responsibilities. Employers can defend differences in pay for males and females on the basis of "a seniority system, a merit system, a system which measures earnings by quantity or quality of production, or a differential based on any factor other than sex." As a result, courts have invalidated school districts' pay schedules that paid male and female coaches differently if they performed equivalent duties. For example, the Seventh Circuit Court of Appeals ruled in favor of a group of female junior high coaches who brought suit because they were paid less than male coaches in the same sports. The court found there were no significant differences between the male and female teams in terms of number of students, length of the season, or number of practice sessions, except that the female track coach worked longer hours than the male coach. The female coaches were awarded back pay (*EEOC,* 1987). By contrast, an Illinois court found that different pay was not a violation when there were different work hours for male football coaches and female volleyball coaches (*McCullar,* 1987).

One other way in which discrimination may emerge in relationship to coaching is if a school district couples a teaching position with coaching. An appeals court in Arizona ruled in favor of a female applicant who did not even make it into the list of finalists for a position in biology that required applicants to have the ability to coach varsity football, arguing that "there was in fact substantial evidence that hiring alternatives [for the school district] were available and were not used" (*Civil Rights Division,* 1983).

It should be evident from this discussion that in no way can gender be a basis for a difference in compensation. In most school districts, variation in salary schedules are based on amount of education and experience. Merit and additional duties can also be factored in, but they must apply equally to men and women.

Administration   Another area in which sex discrimination is an issue in public schools is in promotion and selection of administrators. Although male administrators predominate in education, as they do in most areas, it is in violation of both the equal protection clause of the Fourteenth Amendment and Title VII of the Civil Rights Act to use gender in administrative hiring decisions. The Alabama Superior Court upheld a female assistant principal's charge of discrimination after she had applied for and been denied 13 administrative positions over a 4-year period. A male was chosen each time, and among the reasons given was that "a woman could not handle the responsibilities, such as sports and cleaning, that went along with a high school principalship" (*Tye,* 1987).

On the other hand, gender may be a relevant consideration in the selection of a school counselor. The Montana Supreme Court upheld a school district's right to exclude male applicants from applying for an advertised position as a counselor because they already had one man and were looking for a woman. The court ruled that this was a legitimate occupational qualification as a female counselor needed to be available to work with female students in sensitive situations (*Stone,* 1984).

Pregnancy   A final area in which issues of discrimination arise in relationship to females, both teachers and students, is pregnancy. Historically, school districts frequently had rules forbidding female teachers to be married, and later when marriage was accepted, requiring women to take an unpaid leave of absence by their fourth or fifth month of pregnancy. This, and other inequitable practices based on pregnancy, are no longer permissible. In 1993, the federal government passed The Family and Medical Leave Act (FMLA) requiring state and local government employers to provide up to 12 work weeks of unpaid leave during any 12-month period for the

birth or adoption of a child. Upon return from such a leave, an employee must be restored to his or her original job, or to an equivalent job with equivalent pay and benefits. The employer may require an employee wishing to use FMLA to provide 30 days notice, if possible, medical certifications, and periodic reports during the leave about when the employee intends to return to work. Employees can report violations to the U.S. Labor Department's Employment Standards Administration, which will investigate, or can bring civil action against an employer to recover damages for lost wages and employment benefits as well as reinstatement and promotion.

Just as school districts cannot discriminate against female teachers on the basis of their pregnant status, neither can they treat pregnant students differently from others unless it is absolutely necessary for health reasons. Although districts may provide an alternative program for pregnant students that they may *choose* to attend, courts in both Massachusetts and Texas have ruled that school authorities may not exclude pregnant students from regular classes, even if they offer to provide evening classes or individual tutoring (*Ordway,* 1971; *Alvin Independent,* 1966).

Just as school authorities may not bar a pregnant student from any regular or extracurricular school activities, neither can they restrict the participation of married students, pregnant or not, from these same activities. Until the 1960s, courts routinely upheld school dismissals of married students accepting the school districts' arguments that married students' presence encouraged "immoral behavior," sex talk, and early marriages. However, in 1967, the U.S. Supreme Court ruled that the right to marry is "one of the vital personal rights"(*Loving,* 1967), and for the last several decades courts have upheld married students' rights to participate equally in all school activities.

Age Discrimination

Issues of age for students and teachers occur at exactly the opposite ends of their school careers— admission to school and specific programs for students and retirement for teachers. The courts have consistently upheld school districts' requirements that students be a certain age before being admitted to school, accepting evidence that there is a substantial correlation between school readiness and chronological age. They have also supported age-related arguments that restrict students from participating in certain activities, such as accelerated programs, even though all academic requirements had been met. Admission of students with disabilities to special programs and services under the Individuals with Disabilities Education Act is also age-related. Districts must provide services for individuals with disabilities between the ages of 3 and 21, with the exception of those younger than the state school starting age unless there are programs for other children in this age group. Similarly, if school districts are providing services for students in general beyond 18 years of age, students with disabilities must also have access to services. However, students cannot generally demand tuition-free services beyond the age of 21.

Regarding teachers, Congress enacted in 1967 the Age Discrimination in Employment Act, prohibiting age-based discrimination against employees 40- to 65-years-old in hiring, promotion, and compensation. In 1978, the upper age limit was extended to 70 and in 1986, it was removed completely. Although employers, including school boards, can terminate employees because of substantiated inability to carry out the responsibilities of a job, they can no longer dismiss them on the basis of age alone. Nor can they demote them or refuse to provide the same retirement benefits to older individuals as an effort to entice them to retire.

Discrimination Based on Disability

There are major federal laws protecting individuals with disabilities from discrimination. Section 504 of the Vocational Rehabilitation Act of 1973 prohibits the recipients of any federal funds from discriminating against an otherwise qualified handicapped person solely because of the handicap. The Americans with Disabilities Act of 1990 extends protection of individuals with physical or mental impairments beyond federally assisted institutions. The law now applies to all employment, public transportation and accommodations, and telecommunications. This, of course, includes handicapped persons wishing to teach. In 1984, the Superior Court in Iowa awarded a disabled applicant who had been rejected for a preschool teaching position attorney's fees and damages for mental anguish and loss of earnings when the school district subsequently hired an individual who was less qualified (*Fitzgerald,* 1984).

Another very controversial situation arises when an individual acquires a handicap, such as AIDS, in the course of employment. Although Section 504 does not include individuals with AIDS as handicapped, many courts have interpreted it as protecting such individuals. In 1988, the Ninth Circuit Court of Appeals ordered a school district to restore teaching duties to an AIDS victim, rejecting the lower court's contention that not enough was known about AIDS to determine if there was a threat of the teacher's spreading the disease (*Chalk,* 1988).

Student discrimination based on disability has a much longer and more detailed legislative and case history than with teachers. Two landmark cases were heard in the superior courts of Pennsylvania and the District of Columbia in 1972. In *Pennsylvania Association for Retarded Children* v. *Commonwealth* (*PARC*), the Association claimed Pennsylvania's state law that allowed school systems to exclude children with disabilities violated the equal protection and due process clauses of the constitution. The case resulted in a consent agreement that mentally retarded children must be placed in a program of free public education appropriate to their capacities and there could be no change in their educational status without procedural due process.

The second case, *Mills* v. *Board of Education of District of Columbia* (*Mills*), extended the right to an appropriate education to all children with mental, behavioral, emotional, or physical deficiencies. In addition, the court ruled that fiscal concerns cannot be the basis for denial of an appropriate education to a handicapped child. Finally, the court indicated that school authorities must adhere to stringent due process procedures in student assignments, stating that any change affecting a student's instructional program for as little as 2 days had to provide some type of hearing to give parents an opportunity to contest the placement.

Close on the heels of these two cases, in 1975, Congress passed the Education for All Handicapped Children Act, usually referred to as PL 94–142. This law required that states provide all handicapped children with "a free appropriate public education and related services designed to meet their unique needs." Crucial to the successful implementation of this law is an understanding of what is a **free appropriate public education** (**FAPE**). As indicated previously, it is one designed to meet the needs of each individual child; it includes special education and related services. According to the Individuals with Disabilities Education Act of 1991, *special education* refers to "specially designed instruction, at no cost to parents or guardians, to meet the unique needs of a handicapped child, including classroom instruction, instruction in physical education, home instruction, and instruction in hospitals and institutions."

Just what counts as an *appropriate* education has been tested many times in the courts. It is not acceptable merely to provide "equal" experiences for all children as those with disabilities may be unable to progress without support services. This is referred to as functional exclusion. For instance, the Superior Court in Pennsylvania ruled that the placement of non-English-speaking students in ordinary classrooms without support services was an inappropriate placement, as the children were "certain to find their classroom experiences wholly incomprehensible and in no way meaningful" (*Fialkowski,* 1975).

In order to satisfy the requirement of an appropriate education and meet the needs of each individual child, an **individual educational program or plan (IEP)** must be drawn up. This plan must identify the child's needs, annual instructional goals and objectives, specific educational services to be provided, and evaluation procedures. It must be jointly prepared by education officials and parents and reviewed annually.

In 1991, Congress reenacted Pl 94–142 as the Individuals with Disabilities Education Act (IDEA). Although states have the option of whether or not to participate in IDEA funding, all currently participate in the IDEA assistance program and must adhere to the following major provisions of the act:

- States must institute a comprehensive program to identify all children with disabilities within the state. Under the act, disabled children include those who are mentally retarded; hard of hearing; deaf; speech impaired; visually impaired; seriously emotionally disturbed; orthopedically impaired; other health impaired or learning disabled; or suffering from autism or traumatic brain injury.

- No child with disabilities can be excluded from an appropriate public education (zero reject).

- Individualized education programs must be developed for all children with disabilities.

- Policies and procedures must be established to safeguard due process rights of parents and children.

- Children with disabilities must be placed in the least restrictive educational setting, which means educating children with disabilities with other children to the maximum extent appropriate.

- Nondiscriminatory tests and other materials must be used in evaluating a child's level of achievement for placement purposes.

- Comprehensive personnel development programs, which include in-service training for regular and special education teachers and ancillary personnel, must be established.

- One state agency must be accountable for ensuring that all provisions of the law are properly implemented by other agencies in the state serving children with disabilities. (McCarthy & Cambron-McCabe, 1992 p. 166–167)

In addition to identifying and selecting children with disabilities for the appropriate programs, developing individualized educational plans, and assuring parents of their due process rights, this act requires placement of disabled children in the least restrictive environment and the provision of necessary services related to the disability.

The key to placement decisions is establishing the least restrictive environment in which an appropriate education can be provided for the child. If there is a conflict between the two concepts of least restrictive environment and appropriateness, various courts have concluded that the intention of the act is for "appropriateness" to be the primary consideration. If a child's needs can be met in the regular classroom, then an alternative, more restrictive, placement would be considered inappropriate. For example, the Ninth Circuit Court of Appeals concluded that a proposed homebound program for a child suffering from cystic fibrosis and tracheomalacia was inappropriate, because the child's previous participation and progress in a regular classroom in a private school, a less restrictive environment than the one proposed, demonstrated that similar services could be provided in the public school (*Department of Education,* 1983). On the other hand, the Fourth Circuit Court of Appeals upheld a school district's decision to place an autistic child in a specialized vocational center rather than the local high school because even with special support services, the mainstreamed program could not accommodate his special needs (*Devries,* 1989).

The other question that arises in providing an appropriate education for disabled children is that of necessary related services. The definition of *related services* in the act is "transportation, and such developmental, corrective, and other support services (including speech pathology and audiology, psychological services, physical and occupational therapy, recreation, and medical and counseling services, except that such medical services shall be for diagnostic and evaluative purposes only) as may be required to assist the handicapped child to benefit from special education, and includes the early identification and assessment of handicapping conditions in children."

In matters of discipline, the courts have held that handicapped students can be disciplined in the same ways that other students are. For example, the Fifth Circuit Court of Appeals held that a principal's use of corporal punishment with a special education child in a Texas school did not violate the child's substantive due process rights (*Fee,* 1990). In addition, children with disabilities whose misbehavior *is not* related to their disabilities can be given such disciplinary actions as detention, isolation, and short-term suspensions. However, long-term suspensions, that is, more than 10 days, constitute a change in placement and appropriate due process procedures must be followed. Furthermore, although both the Fifth and Sixth Circuit Courts of Appeal have agreed that misbehaving students with disabilities can be expelled, and they defined expulsion as removal from the current placement to a more restrictive placement, denying the possibility of termination of all services.

Due Process Rights

The Fourteenth Amendment provides that no "state deprive any person of life, liberty, or property, without due process of the law." Compulsory school attendance laws establish for students a legitimate property right to attend school and tenure arrangements for teachers gives them a property right to continued employment. Both *substantive* and *procedural* due process rights have been identified by the federal judiciary. **Substantive due process** requires that state action depriving an individual of life, liberty, or property rights be based on a valid objective with means reasonably related to attaining the objective. The intent is to shield the individual against *arbitrary* governmental action that impairs life, liberty, or property interests. **Procedural due process** requires *fairness* in procedures if the government (school officials) threaten any actions that would deprive an individual of life, liberty, or property. Minimally this requires notification of charges, opportunity to refute charges, and a fair hearing. We look at how procedural due process requirements affect both students and teachers.

Students' Due Process Rights

Due process issues for students vary with the seriousness of disciplinary infractions. There are two situations in which teachers or school administrators may proceed without engaging in due process procedures. The first involves minor infractions of rules and routine disciplinary measures such as verbal reprimands, extra work, isolation, detention, and being sent to the principal's office. It is expected that school officials will act appropriately based on their understanding of child and adolescent development in these matters. The second type of situation is when quick action is required by educators to protect the safety of persons or property. It is

expected, however, that as soon as the imminent danger is removed, due process procedures will be carried out.

Any time suspension is a possibility, students must be given some kind of notice, even if it is only oral, and be afforded a hearing with an opportunity to refute the charges. The landmark case in this area, *Goss* v. *Lopez,* was heard by the U.S. Supreme Court in 1975. Several students in a high school in Columbus, Ohio, were suspended for up to 10 days without being informed of the charges or a hearing. There were documented acts of violence by some students, but others, Lopez among them, claimed to be innocent bystanders. Both the federal district court and the Supreme Court (in a 5 to 4 decision) ruled in favor of the students, the latter citing the principle of the *Tinker* case that "young people do not shed their constitutional rights at the schoolhouse door."

In serious disciplinary cases, those which might lead to long-term suspension or expulsion, extensive care must be taken to assure students of their due process rights. This includes the following.

- Written description of the charges; the likely disciplinary action; the date, time and place of the hearing; the procedures to be followed including what evidence will be used, the names of witnesses, and the substance of witnesses' testimony; with sufficient time for a defense to be prepared.

- A full and fair hearing before an impartial adjudicator.

- The right to legal counsel or some other adult representation.

- The opportunity to present witnesses or evidence.

- The opportunity to cross examine opposing witnesses.

- A written or taped record of the proceedings with a clear indication of how the decision was based on the evidence presented at the hearing.

- Notice of the right to appeal the decision. (McCarthy & Cambron-McCabe, 1992, pp. 257–258; Fischer, Schimmel, & Kelly, 1995, p. 203)

Corporal Punishment   Although only 1 state prohibited the use of corporal punishment in 1971, by 1991 20 states and the District of Columbia had banned the practice. Those states are: Alaska, California, Connecticut, Hawaii, Iowa, Maine, Massachusetts, Michigan, Minnesota, Nebraska, New Hampshire, New Jersey, New York, North Dakota, Oregon,

Rhode Island, South Dakota, Vermont, Virginia, and Wisconsin.

The Constitution does not prohibit the use of corporal punishment, which was at issue in the *Ingraham* v. *Wright* case heard by the Supreme Court in 1977. Two junior high students in a Dade County, Florida, school were severely paddled, one so badly that he required medical attention and missed 11 days of school and the other lost the use of his arm for a week. Although Florida had a law forbidding punishment that was "degrading or unduly severe," it did not prohibit corporal punishment, and the Dade County school used it. The students filed suit, claiming that the punishment they received was cruel and unusual, violating the Eighth Amendment. Both the lower courts and the Supreme Court disagreed, ruling that although the beatings were excessive and unreasonable, they did not violate the Eighth Amendment, because that was intended to protect incarcerated criminals. Further, the Court indicated that procedural due process requirements were not violated, indicating that the purpose of corporal punishment would be diluted if elaborate procedures had to be followed before its use.

However, cases have been successfully pursued on the basis of violation of students' substantive due process right to be free of brutal and harmful state intrusions into realms of personal privacy and bodily security. The Fourth Circuit Court of Appeals, in a case in which a young girl was so severely paddled in school that she required 10 days' hospitalization, ruled in favor of the student. The court indicated that the standard for determining whether a cruel or excessive corporal punishment may violate students' substantive due process rights is "whether the force applied caused injury so severe, was so disproportionate to the need presented, and was so inspired by malice or sadism rather than a merely careless or unwise excess of zeal that it amounted to a brutal and inhumane abuse of official power literally shocking to the conscience" (*Hall,* 1980).

In another case, the Eighth Circuit Court of Appeals used the following criteria to assess a substantive due process claim (*Wise,* 1988):

1. The need for the application of corporal punishment.
2. The relationship between the need and the amount of punishment administered.
3. The extent of the injury inflicted.
4. Whether the punishment was administered in a good faith effort to maintain discipline or maliciously and sadistically for the very purpose of causing harm.

In this case, the court concluded that "two licks" with a paddle did not violate a student's substantive due process rights.

In states where corporal punishment is permitted, local districts may outlaw its use. Most districts that do permit its use have restrictions, such as that it will only be administered in the presence of another adult or only by a school administrator. Local school boards, however, cannot prohibit the use of corporal punishment if state law specifically authorizes educators to use it. Nor can a supervisor forbid its use by a teacher if school district policy allows it. On the other hand, several courts have upheld the dismissal of tenured teachers for violating school board policy against the use of corporal punishment or not following guidelines. Finally, in states and districts that permit corporal punishment, parental permission is not required. In fact, school boards may permit the use of it even if a parent objects, which was the ruling of the Supreme Court in a 1975 case from North Carolina. In this case, the court ruled that because both professional and popular opinion are split on the use of corporal punishment, it would not allow "the wishes of a parent to restrict school officials' discretion in deciding the methods to be used in . . . maintaining discipline" (*Baker,* 1975).

Academic Sanctions   Another disciplinary measure challenged in the courts is academic sanctions for misconduct, including lowered or failing grades, denial of credit, academic probation, retention, and expulsion from specific programs. Although school authorities have been granted wide discretion in establishing academic standards and requirements, courts have been divided regarding their right to lower grades and/or deny course credit as disciplinary measures. For the most part, reduction of grades because of unexcused absences has been upheld and, in some cases, because of exceeding a stipulated limit in excused absences. However, the courts have been divided on the question of the school's right to reduce students' grades *in addition to* another disciplinary measure, such as suspension. On one hand, a Texas court upheld the 3-day suspension and zeros for missed school work given two boys caught consuming alcohol on school grounds (*New Braunfels,* 1983). On the other hand, a Pennsylvania court struck down an eleventh-grade student's reduction in grades in all classes by two points in addition to a 5-day suspension and expulsion from the cheerleading squad and the National Honor Society because of drinking a glass of wine with friends on a field trip to New York (*Katzman,* 1984).

In general, courts have not upheld the withholding of course credit or the high school diploma solely for disciplinary reasons. A Pennsylvania court ruled that a student who was expelled from school after finishing his courses and final examinations could not be denied his diploma (*Shuman,* 1988). Once again, however, the courts are divided on whether students can be denied the right to participate in graduation ceremonies.

Search and Seizure   An additional area that deals with students' due process rights is that of search and seizure. With cigarette, drug, and alcohol use by students has come an increase in court cases charging school officials with violation of the Fourth Amendment right to be free of unwarranted search and seizure of possessions. The landmark ruling in this regard came in 1985 in *New Jersey* v. *T.L.O.* In this case, T.L.O. was discovered by a teacher in the restroom with other girls holding a lighted cigarette. However, when questioned by the assistant principal she denied not only smoking in the restroom, but that she smoked at all. He asked her to open her purse and found cigarettes and drug paraphernalia. He then called her mother and the police.

The Supreme Court rejected the Fourth Amendment requirement of probable cause to conduct a search, maintaining that school searches are justified "when there are reasonable grounds for suspecting that the search will turn up evidence that the student has violated or is violating either the law or the rules of the school." The Court further indicated that the appropriate standard for searches by school officials is "reasonableness under all circumstances," which "involves a two-fold inquiry: first, one must consider whether the . . . action was justified at its inception; . . . second, one must determine whether the search as actually conducted was reasonable in scope to the circumstances which justified the interference in the first place."

This case resolved the question of whether school officials are considered representatives of the state—they are—in relationship to student searches. It also established the criterion of reasonability as being less strict than that of probable cause. However, school officials were not given unilateral freedom to search students and their possessions. Many questions remain unanswered in terms of just how far school officials can go, but there are several general rules of thumb, as follows:

- Lower courts have generally upheld the search of students' lockers and automobiles on the basis of *reasonable* suspicion. This has included searches in the presence of police officials. However, police themselves cannot search a student's locker without a warrant.

- The search of a student's room for alcohol on a field trip was ruled unconstitutional by a lower court but upheld as reasonable by the Sixth District Court of Appeals, which also applied the *in loco parentis* doctrine (*Webb,* 1987). This means "in place of the parents" and although historically it was widely used to justify school officials' authority over students, some courts no longer apply it.

- School officials can search students' clothing but the two-pronged test of reasonableness must be carefully applied. Going a step further, courts have supported strip searches of students, but substantial evidence must exist to make them reasonable.

- The search for drugs by means of using dogs to sniff for them has generally been limited to objects such as clothing and bags. However, in a well known case in Indiana (*Doe,* 1981) the Seventh District Court did not consider the presence of dogs in classrooms, alerting officials to suspicious students, to constitute a search. When the dogs continued the alert, the students were asked to empty their pockets and purses and some students were subjected to a strip search. The court did not see this to be a satisfactory basis for reasonable suspicion.

- The Supreme Court has held that urinalysis, the most frequent means used for drug testing, is a search under the Fourth Amendment (*Skinner,* 1989). No court has upheld random urinalysis for all students, although some have upheld such tests for members of athletic teams, even without individual suspicion, when there was evidence of widespread drug use among athletes.

In regard to school searches, school officials are well advised to inform students and parents at the beginning of the school year what the policies are regarding locker and personal searches. They should be conducted only when there is reasonable suspicion that contraband is present and in the presence of two adults. Police should never be permitted to search students' lockers or person without a search warrant.

Remedies   Educators need to be aware that students who are unlawfully disciplined by school authorities have several remedies available to them. When students have been suspended or expelled without just cause, they have been reinstated without penalty to grades and have had their school records expunged of any reference to the illegal disciplinary action. When academic sanctions were illegally imposed, grades were restored and transcripts altered. Damages have been awarded in unlawful searches when they have resulted in substantial injury to the students. Furthermore, school officials can be sued for monetary damages if they violated students' federally protected rights in disciplinary hearings, even if the violations resulted from ignorance on the part of those in charge. Figure 11.1 suggests guidelines in the development of school disciplinary policies and procedures.

Teachers' Due Process Rights

These are the very same procedures that must be followed in instances in which teachers are facing termination of employment. You will recall that earlier in this chapter we discussed the reasons for which tenured teachers could face dismissal: incompetence; insubordination; immorality; unprofessional conduct; and other just cause. Notice of deficiencies must always be provided in writing. Whether or not the school board is required to give you a period of time to remediate deficiencies varies by state. Interestingly, various courts have ruled that the school board, although it would seem that it would not be an impartial arbitrator, is a fair tribunal for a teacher dismissal hearing. Furthermore, strict legal procedures are not required, since these are administrative hearings, not court proceedings. Nor

do technical rules of evidence apply, although the proceedings must be orderly.

LEGAL BASIS FOR CURRICULUM AND TEACHING ISSUES

We have examined how the law will affect you as you prepare to be a teacher and as you look for your first job. In addition, we have given extensive consideration to those legal rights that teachers and students hold in common. In this section we look at some additional legal issues that may affect you as a classroom teacher. These include the curriculum, testing of students, copyright laws, access to student records, and personal liability.

Curriculum

The authority and responsibility for determining the public school curriculum lies with each state legislature. All states require instruction in the federal Constitution and most require it in American history. Other subjects frequently required are English, mathematics, drug education, health, and physical education, and many states have detailed requirements pertaining to vocational education, bilingual education, and special services for children with disabilities. State laws generally require local school boards to adopt the state-mandated minimum curriculum, which they may then supplement. In addition, states have the authority to specify textbooks and in many states these are selected at the state level. In other states, school boards can choose from among lists of acceptable books, and in still others, they can select books completely at the local level. With the exception of supplementary reading, public school teachers, unlike college teachers, do not select their own classroom texts, although they may be members of school district textbook selection committees and in that way may have an influence on what texts are selected.

States can also determine standards for pupil performance, and school districts have the right to establish prerequisites and selection standards for admission into courses and programs of study, as long as the criteria are not arbitrary and do not discriminate. The Fifth Circuit Court of Appeals ruled that students have no property right to any specific courses in public schools, other than those mandated by the state (*Arundar*, 1980).

You will recall that earlier in this chapter we discussed the parameters of your right to academic

Figure 11.1   Guidelines for the Development of Disciplinary Policies and Procedures

- Any conduct regulation adopted should be **necessary** in order to carry out the school's educational mission; rules should not be designed merely to satisfy the preferences of school board members, administrators, or teachers.
- The rules should be **publicized** to students and their parents.
- The rules should be **specific** and **clearly stated** so that students know what behaviors are expected and what behaviors are prohibited.
- The regulations should **not impair constitutionally protected rights** unless there is an overriding public interest, such as a threat to the safety of other students.
- A rule should **not be "ex post facto;"** it should not be adopted to prevent a specific activity that school officials know is being planned or has already occurred.
- The regulations should be **consistently enforced** and **uniformly applied** without discrimination to all students.
- Punishments should be **appropriate to the offense**, taking into consideration the child's age, sex, mental condition, and past behavior.
- Some **procedural safeguards** should accompany the administration of all punishments; the formality of the procedures should be in accord with the severity of the punishment.

Figure 11.2   **Proficiency Testing Guidelines**

- School curriculum should adequately prepare students for the test.
- Students should be advised upon entrance into high school of test requirements as a prerequisite to graduation.
- Tests should not be intentionally discriminatory and should not perpetuate the effects of past school segregation.
- Students who fail should be provided remedial opportunities and the chance to retake the examination.
- Appropriate accommodations should be made for children with disabilities.

freedom in the public school classroom regarding topics, subject matter, and methodology. In general, teachers are expected to teach the school-board approved curriculum with the topic emphasis reflected in the state syllabus. They are also expected to abide by established policies for using supplementary material. On the other hand, courts have overturned many cases of teachers being reprimanded or dismissed for teaching unpopular or controversial material or for using an open-classroom forum for discussing these topics.

Student Testing

One area of student testing that has become controversial in recent years is **proficiency testing** for receipt of a high school diploma. In 1976, only four states had legislation mandating such testing. By 1987, 30 states had either legislative or administrative regulations about statewide performance testing and a third of the states required students to pass a test to receive the high school diploma.

The landmark case in this area is *Debra P.* v. *Turlington* (1984), a challenge to Florida's statewide proficiency testing that raised questions of both due process and equal protection. Although the lower courts found that the 13-month notice of the test requirement was inadequate and issued an injunction, the additional challenges that Florida's taught curriculum did not prepare students for the test and that it discriminated against African American students were disproven in the appeals court, and the injunction was lifted. Proficiency testing guidelines emerging from this case are presented in Figure 11.2. Read the accompanying Issue Box to learn about one family's experiences with statewide proficiency testing.

Copyright Laws

Almost any original work, including written, musical, dramatic, pictorial, or graphic work, can be copyrighted. This gives the creator of the work exclusive control over it. However, courts have recognized

exceptions to this control under what is termed the **fair use** doctrine, which is defined as the "privilege in others than the owner of the copyright to use the copyrighted material in a reasonable manner without his consent, notwithstanding the monopoly granted to the owner . . . " (*Marcus,* 1983). Guidelines for educational copying have been developed by the Ad Hoc Committee of Educational Institutions and Organizations on Copyright Law Revision, the Author's League of America, Inc. These guidelines follow (Fischer, Schimmel, & Kelly, 1995, pp. 139–140).

Teachers are permitted to make *single* copies of the following copyrighted works for their own use in scholarly research or classroom preparation:

1. A chapter from a book.
2. An article from a periodical or newspaper.
3. A short story, short essay, or short poem.
4. A chart, graph, diagram, drawing, cartoon, or picture from a book, newspaper, or periodical.

Teachers can make *multiple* copies of the following copyrighted works for use in the classroom (with the number of copies not to exceed one copy per student in the class), provided that copying meets the tests of brevity, spontaneity, and cumulative effect and that each copy includes a notice of copyright.

The definition of *brevity* is as follows:

1. A complete poem, if it is less than 250 words and printed on not more than two pages.
2. An excerpt from a longer poem, if it is not more than 250 words.
3. A complete article, story, or essay if it is less than 2,500 words.
4. An excerpt from a prose work, if it is less than 1,000 words or 10 percent of the work, whichever is less.
5. One chart, diagram, cartoon, or picture per book or periodical.

The definition of *spontaneity* is as follows:

1. The copying is at the instance and inspiration of the individual teacher.
2. The inspiration and decision to use the work and the moment of its use for maximum teaching effectiveness are so close in time that it would be unreasonable to expect a timely reply to a request for permission.

To meet the test of *cumulative effect:*

1. The copying of the material is for only one course in the school in which the copies are made.

2. Not more than one short poem, article, story, essay, or two excerpts are copied from the same author, or more than three from the same collective work or periodical volume during one class term.

3. There are not more than nine instances of such multiple copying for one course during the school year.

(Note: Numbers 2 and 3 do not apply to current news periodicals and newspapers.)

In addition, teachers cannot make copies of "consumable" materials such as workbooks or answer sheets to standardized tests. Finally, teachers are prohibited from making a copy of works to take the place of an anthology.

With the increasing sophistication of technology, two other major educational areas are affected by copyright laws: videotaping and computer software. In 1981, Congress issued guidelines for videotaping (*Guidelines*, 1981). The fair use doctrine permits the videotaping of a television program for noncommercial use in the classroom under the following two conditions: The tape may be shown only once, and it must be within the first 10 consecutive days after making it, after which it may be used only for the purposes of reinforcement or evaluation of its educational effectiveness, and after 45 days, the tape must be erased or destroyed.

The copying of computer software has become a major problem, especially in public schools in which budgets are very limited and software is expensive.

Black Flight

Lester and Coque Gibson, a middle-class black couple from Waco, Texas, had always hoped their children would defy the odds and reach the American dream. They realized education is the key, and were understandably dismayed when their two older children both failed the Texas basic skills test in high school.

Gibson demanded an accounting of the school district's scores. He found the numbers shocking. Seventy-five percent of the black students and 66 percent of the Hispanic students failed the test in 1995, compared to 37 percent of the white students.

The school district, charged Gibson, blames poverty and poor parenting for the failure rates, but Gibson blames institutional racism. He accused teachers of holding low expectations for minority students. His solution? Let black parents control their own schools.

The Waco experience is not uncommon. In many communities around the country, especially inner cities, black parents are deserting a system they say has fostered failure. They are taking their kids out of public schools and putting them in church schools and private black academies. These alternative schools have doubled in number in recent years, according to the Institute for Independent Education in Washington, D.C.

Why the return to segregation? After all, civil rights leaders have for decades pushed for desegregation as a means of equalizing educational opportunity. For the last 25 years in Waco, for example, black students have been bused from their east side neighborhoods to white schools on the west side. Integration was supposed to be good for children, but now some parents and educators believe it has done more harm than good.

Gibson cited two problems with desegregation through busing. When schools in black neighborhoods were shut down, they were no longer maintained. They became vacant eyesores, and ceased serving as community centers. Furthermore, most black children, including his own son, were tracked into remedial classes, and never took the algebra and other advanced courses needed to pass the state exam.

Gibson's plan is to secede from the mother district and create a separate school district in the minority neighborhood. This takes advantage

It is estimated that in 1990, $2.4 billion worth of software, almost half of the total sales of $5.7 billion, was stolen—illegally copied—in the United States and Canada. The federal copyright law was amended in 1980 to include software, stipulating that an owner can make a single copy for back-up purposes. In addition, it appears that the law permits teachers to load a copy on a computer for classroom use by a single student at a time, but not on several computers or a network for simultaneous student use. Many software companies offer site licenses whereby software programs can be made available to a large number of users over a network.

Violations of copyright law are punishable with fines up to $100,000 and as much as 5 years in prison. It is important that school districts develop and

teachers abide by policies for copying material for use in the classroom, not only to avoid penalties, but to convey to students this little known information.

Access to Student Records

In 1974, Congress enacted the Family Education and Privacy Rights Act (FERPA), also referred to as the Buckley Amendment, with the following components.

1. It requires school districts to establish a written policy concerning student records and to inform parents each year of their rights under the act.

2. It guarantees parents the right to inspect and review the educational records of their children.

ISSUES

Continued

of a law passed recently in the Texas legislature that allows neighborhoods to detach from a larger district. It is unclear, however, whether the plan will be allowed. The Waco district barely has the minimum 16,000 students needed in order to be eligible for splitting. In addition, Waco voters must approve the plan. And the courts may not condone a return to segregation.

The community is also divided on the issue. Some blacks, such as the chair of the local NAACP (National Association for the Advancement of Colored People) chapter, oppose resegregation. Others, such as downtown merchant Marilyn Banks, thinks it may not be a bad idea. "With me, it's hard to say segregation is something that would hurt us, because I went to an all-black school and turned out to be okay. Some people see that as a way of hurting us, but sometimes I have to wonder if it was to our benefit to be in integrated schools" (Prodis, 1996, p. D1).

Few whites have taken public positions, fearing they may be branded racist no matter which view they espouse. "They're scared to death," says Waco state senator David Sibley. "If they say it's a good idea, people will call them racist. If they say it's a bad idea, people will say that white folks just want to keep them on the plantation" (Prodis, 1996, p. D1). However, Waco Superintendent Fred Zachary said some white parents have indicated privately, "Don't stand in their way if they're headed to the door" (Prodis, 1996, p. D1).

Gibson has given the district a one-year ultimatum: Improve minority scores by then, or face secession. Zachary says his teachers are working hard to improve the achievement of all Waco students, including minority children. But he doubts that substantial improvement is feasible in such a short time.

What are your views on desegregation? If you were in Lester and Coque Gibson's shoes, what would you decide for your children? Do you see busing as the central problem in this situation? If not, what might the problem be? For example, why does it appear that tracking breaks down along racial lines? What do you think students, minority and majority, gain from an integrated education? What might they gain from a segregated education? Which type of school would you prefer to teach in? Why?

3. It establishes procedures through which parents can challenge the accuracy of student records.

4. It protects the confidentiality of student records by preventing disclosure of personally identifiable information to outsiders without previous parental consent.

5. It entitles parents to file complaints with the FERPA office concerning alleged failures to comply with the act.

After a student reaches 18 years of age or begins attending a post-secondary institution, these rights are accorded only to the student.

The records that are covered by this act include all information compiled in a central location no matter what form it takes. Teachers' individual notes on a student are not covered, as long as they are not shared with anyone else, except a substitute teacher. Parents have a right to be informed about the location of records, to receive an interpretation of them, if necessary, and to be provided with access to the records within 45 days of the request. Noncustodial parents are also entitled to access to the student's records unless there is a court order forbidding it.

Parents also have the right to challenge information contained in students' records if they believe it is "inaccurate or misleading or violates the privacy or other rights of the student." If the school refuses to amend it, they must inform the parents of their decision and of their right to a hearing, which must be conducted by an impartial individual. The school must then notify the parent of their decision in writing, based on the facts presented at the hearing. If the parents still disagree, they must be permitted to place a statement commenting on the contested information in the student's file.

If records are going to be released to outsiders, parental consent is required, unless they are being shared with the following people.

1. Teachers and "other school officials" in the district who have "legitimate educational interests."

2. Officials of another school in which the student seeks to enroll (as long as the parents are notified).

3. Persons for whom the information is necessary "to protect the health or safety of the student or other individual."

4. Financial aid providers to whom the student has applied.

A school can also release what is described as *directory information,* which includes such items as the student's name, address, phone number, date and place of birth, field of study, sports activities, dates of attendance, awards received, and similar information. It must first, however, try to notify parents regarding what they consider to be directory information and provide parents with the opportunity to deny, in writing, its release.

Students can waive their right to read confidential letters of recommendation when they apply for admission to post-secondary institutions, although the institutions may not require such waivers as a condition of admission, only request them. Students, not their parents, are required to sign such waivers.

Special education students have additional rights under the Individuals with Disabilities Education Act. These require that teachers and other school personnel who use identifiable information about students who are in special education receive training on confidentiality. In addition, this act requires that parents be informed when their children's special education records are no longer needed and that they be destroyed at a parent's request.

Before the enactment of the FERPA, there were countless incidents of educational decisions made on the basis of records that were totally inaccessible to parents. Frequently these records contained poorly supported opinions of school personnel that were freely shared with outside agencies and institutions, even while parents and students were being denied access to them. Although many school personnel are still not familiar with the requirements of the act, most educational professionals believe that the situation has improved greatly in the last 2 decades.

Interestingly, FERPA does not apply to teachers' records. Although teachers do have privacy rights, several courts have ruled that when these privacy rights conflict with the appropriateness of public disclosure, the decision should be made in favor of public disclosure. For example, the Supreme Court of Washington required the state superintendent of public instruction to provide a newspaper publisher with records specifying the reasons for teacher certificate revocations (*Brouillet,* 1990). In Texas, in a case in which a teacher's college transcript was sought by a parent concerned about the quality of education under that state's Open Records Act, the Fifth Circuit Court of Appeals ruled that whatever privacy right the teacher had in her transcript, that right "is significantly outweighed by the public's interest in evaluating the competence of its school teachers" (*Klein,* 1987).

Liability

The area of law that deals with liability and negligence is referred to as *tort law.* A *tort* is defined as a civil wrong, other than breach of contract, for which a court will provide relief in the form of damages. The primary area of tort law that affects educational personnel is negligence.

Negligence

There are four major conditions that are necessary to establish an individual's negligence (Prosser, W., Wade, J. & Schwartz, V., 1982, p. 144). We will briefly discuss each of these.

1. The individual must have a **duty** *to protect another from unreasonable risks.* The duty that school personnel have is to protect students from foreseeable injuries during school hours and as part of after-school or extracurricular school-sponsored activities. This does not mean that teachers must have every child under constant surveillance during every school activity. However, when a teacher should reasonably be expected to be present and is not and a child is injured, courts may judge that the duty requirement was violated. For example, the Supreme Court of Minnesota awarded parents damages when their eighth-grade daughter was injured by a pebble thrown by one of the boys playing baseball in the absence of the teacher during morning recess (*Sheehan,* 1971). In other cases, awards have been made to parents when their children were not properly supervised in shop activities.

Teachers can also be held liable for negligence if they make out-of-school assignments that result in injury. Such was the case involving a Louisiana student who was injured making a volcano for a science project, in which the teacher, after demonstrating how to make a volcano in class, allowed the student to take his own volcano project home without determining what chemicals the student had (*Simmons,* 1975).

2. The duty must be breached by the failure to **exercise an appropriate standard of care.** In determining liability, the courts use the reasonableness theory, which is based on a consideration of whether a reasonable and prudent person would act in the same manner under similar circumstances. The degree of care expected is determined by factors such as the age of students, the environment, and the type of instructional activity. Younger students require closer supervision than older ones, and students in riskier activities such as shops, laboratories, and gymnasiums require more careful supervision than those in regular classrooms.

3. There must be a causal connection between the negligent conduct and the resulting injury (referred to as **proximate or legal cause).** An important part of establishing a teacher's negligence

as proximate cause of an injury to a student is *foreseeability.* For instance, an Illinois appeals court did not find two teachers liable for negligence when a 12-year-old boy under their supervision on a field trip to a museum was beat up by several boys not connected with the school (*Mancha,* 1972). On the other hand, a Tennessee appellate court found a shop teacher guilty of negligent conduct when a student's misuse of a drill press resulted in a serious head injury to another student because the teacher had not instructed the students in the use of the drill bit, had not warned of the dangers associated with its improper use, and was absent from the shop during the use of the drill (*Roberts* v. *Robertson,* 1985).

4. There must be physical or mental injury **resulting in actual loss.** Although a teacher's conduct may be considered negligent, there must be verifiable physical or mental injury for legal action to be taken. If more than one individual is involved in causing the injury, damages will be apportioned to all. Compensation may include any direct financial loss such as for medical expenses or loss of income, as well as for pain and suffering.

In summary, although failure to exercise appropriate supervision may be the proximate cause of a student's injury, there are many factors taken into consideration by the courts to establish negligence. A teacher's absence alone is not sufficient; also examined are the reasons for leaving the class unattended, the length of the absence, the age and maturity of the students, what activities were going on at the time, and the history and make-up of the class. Furthermore, if students ignore or go against a teacher's direct instructions and are injured, teachers are not likely to be held liable. There have been a myriad of cases dealing with negligence, and it is difficult to generalize a set of rules other than what has been discussed here.

Abuse

Two areas that have been of increasing concern are whether school districts and officials can be held liable for sexual abuse of students by teachers or other students and the extent of liability for failure to report suspected cases of child abuse. Regarding sexual abuse of students, the majority of courts have ruled that districts and officials cannot be held liable. However, in 1991 the Fifth Circuit Court of Appeals, in a case in which a female high school student was sexually molested by a teacher-coach, about whom numerous complaints had been previously received, ruled that school officials may be sued for failing to protect students from teachers' sexual misconduct (*Doe,* 1991).

By contrast, all 50 states have laws that require educators and others to report child abuse and neglect. Each state has a set of procedures that reporters are to follow, and reporters are always provided immunity from any civil suit or criminal prosecution that may arise as a result of their report. In most states *failure* to report is a criminal liability that is punishable by a jail sentence of from 5 days to 1 year and/or a fine of $10 to $100.

Malpractice

An additional form of liability with which schools have been charged is instructional negligence, also known as educational malpractice. In the most well known case, *Peter W.* v. *San Francisco Unified School District* (1976), a high school graduate brought charges against the school district for not only promoting and graduating him even though he could read only at the fifth-grade level, but for never informing his parents of his lack of progress, which they later discovered through private testing. The case was dismissed for the following reasons: (1) There were no clear standards to determine whether the school had been negligent, (2) there was no way to determine that a teacher's negligence was the proximate cause of the student's injury, and (3) it would impose too great a financial burden on schools to hold them to an actionable duty of care in the discharge of their academic functions.

Even though educational malpractice suits have not yet been successful, courts in at least two states, Maryland and Montana, have indicated in their rulings that both intentional and unintentional acts of negligence could be the grounds for bringing a successful suit. The Supreme Court of Montana ruled that unintentional acts might result in liability where school authorities have violated mandatory statutes pertaining to special education placements (*B. M.* v. *State,* 1982), even though the parents in the case being heard had not proven this. It is certainly conceivable that in the future "schools will be held legally accountable for diagnosing pupils' needs, placing them in appropriate instructional programs, and reporting their progress to parents" (McCarthy & Cambron-McCabe, 1992, pp. 91–92).

SUMMARY

- Being a competent educational professional requires knowing education law and practicing accordingly.

- The Constitutional basis for education includes the following amendments: Tenth, First, Fourth, and Fourteenth.

- Educational laws affect a teacher's life in the areas of certification requirements, job interviews, acquiring tenure, dismissal, and collective bargaining.

- Teachers and students have legal rights in the following areas: freedom of expression; religious freedom; freedom of association; personal freedom; freedom from discrimination; and due process.

- There are legal requirements in the following areas: curriculum; student testing; copyrights; access to student records; and teacher liability.

READINGS FOR THE PROFESSIONAL

Fischer, L., Schimmel, D., Kelly, C. *Teachers and the Law.* White Plains, NY: Longman (1995).
This is a thorough discussion of the legal rights and responsibilities of teachers, including employment contracts, collective bargaining, liability, protected freedoms, due process, discrimination, and student issues. It includes a review of significant United States Supreme Court cases affecting public elementary and secondary education.

Tyack, D., James, T., Banavot, A. *Law and the Shaping of Public Education 1785–1954.* Madison, WI: University of Wisconsin Press. (1987).
The authors explore the relationship between law and public education from several nontraditional perspectives. They employ case studies and a quantitative analysis of appellate decisions in public education and pursue two themes: the use of constitutional and statutory law to build standardized state school systems, and the tension of majority rule and minority rights in education law.

Zirkel, P. A. & Richardson, S. N. *A Digest of Supreme Court Decisions Affecting Education.* Bloomington, IN: Phi Delta Kappa. (1988).
This is a comprehensive and concise set of individual case summaries of United States Supreme Court cases decided by the Court as of March 1988. The cases described in this digest are those that directly affect students and staff in public and private schools from kindergarten through grade twelve.

PART IV

Teachers and Their Work

Application and Portfolio Activities

Self-Assessments

The Purposes of Schooling 370

You and the System 371

Knowing the Law 372

Observations

The Resource Room 373

Site-Based Decision Making 374

Shadowing the Principal 375

Interviews

Programs for At-Risk Kids 376

Getting to Know a School Board Member 377

The Principal on Job Interviewing...................378

The Purposes of Schooling

Purpose   As we discussed in Chapter 9, part of clarifying your own views about teaching is to reflect on your priorities regarding the purposes of schooling. This exercise will aid you in sorting out your thinking about what schools are for.

Directions   Review the list of school purposes that follows. Distribute 100 points among these purposes, giving more points to those that are most important to you. If there are other purposes you deem important that are not listed here, add them and assign the desired number of points to them.

Points	Purposes
_____	Teach basic academic skills.
_____	Build student self-esteem.
_____	Promote critical thinking skills.
_____	Teach cooperative, prosocial behavior.
_____	Promote equality of opportunity.
_____	Prepare students for college.
_____	Prepare students for the world of work.
_____	Transmit our cultural heritage.
_____	Preserve our cultural richness and diversity.
_____	Promote national unity and patriotism.
_____	Build and maintain a strong economy.
_____	Promote social justice.
_____	Promote global understanding.
_____	Combat social problems like AIDS, drugs, etc.
_____	Provide social services like child care.

Reflection   Classify your top purposes under one of these broad categories: Transmitting Culture, Developing Human Potential, Reconstructing Society. In what order did you rank these broad aims? Discuss what your ranking means for the way you would structure a classroom. How congruent are your responses with your educational philosophy and goals? How deeply are you committed to this ranking? Would you be comfortable teaching at a school whose purposes differed markedly from yours? How could you find out what purposes were most important to a particular school staff and community?

You and the System

Purpose   Reading about how the educational system is governed and financed can make it seem rather remote. However, this large, complex system will have a big impact on your professional life, so it is important to understand it. The purpose of this self-assessment is to personalize the information on governance.

Directions   Using a diagram, picture, concept map, or other visual form of representation, depict the American system of education. Make sure every layer of governance and every constituency is represented. Place yourself in this picture. Where do you fit in?

Reflection   Compare your representation with another student's. Give each other feedback on what the other's representation tells you about their understanding of the overall educational system. Based on this conversation, write a page discussing what these representations signify about your views on your place within the educational system.

Knowing the Law

Purpose The purpose of this assessment is to gauge how well you understand the legal foundations of American schooling.

Directions Circle the indicator that best represents your understanding of each concept.

Concept	Level of Understanding		
Early legislation	High	Medium	Low
Constitutional law	High	Medium	Low
Federal involvement	High	Medium	Low
Certification requirements	High	Medium	Low
Interview process	High	Medium	Low
Tenure	High	Medium	Low
Grounds for dismissal	High	Medium	Low
Collective bargaining	High	Medium	Low
Teachers' free speech rights	High	Medium	Low
Students' free speech rights	High	Medium	Low
Religious freedom	High	Medium	Low
Teachers' freedom of association	High	Medium	Low
Students' freedom of association	High	Medium	Low
Freedom from discrimination	High	Medium	Low
Sex/gender discrimination	High	Medium	Low
Due process rights	High	Medium	Low
Curriculum	High	Medium	Low
Student testing	High	Medium	Low
Copyright law	High	Medium	Low
Student records	High	Medium	Low
Liability	High	Medium	Low

Reflection How well do you understand the law as it relates to teaching? What questions remain for you about teachers' legal rights and obligations? Which of the many legal issues surrounding teaching and schools most arouse your ire? Which cause you the most trepidation? Speculate about why you react in these ways, and about how these reactions might affect your professional life.

The Resource Room

Purpose   One way schools deal with students in academic difficulty is to pull them out of their regular classes and put them in special classes where they can get extra help. These special classes are often referred to as "resource rooms." Often the teacher-student ratio is greatly reduced so that the teacher can give more individual attention to these students. For most regular teachers, the resource room is an unknown. In this exercise you'll have the opportunity to familiarize yourself with this aspect of schooling.

Directions   Visit a resource room in an elementary or secondary school. Stay for at least an hour. Keep a running log of what happens. Who talks? How often? What kind of work is going on? How many students are there? What does the teacher do to help them learn? How long do students stay in the special class? Shadow a few students back to class. How do they reintegrate themselves back into the regular classroom? How much time does the resource teacher have between different groups of students?

Reflection   What is similar and what is different between a resource classroom and a regular classroom? Based on what you've seen, what do you think the pros and cons are of pull-out programs aimed at giving extra help to students who are struggling? Compare your field notes with another student's. Did you both see similar patterns?

Site-Based Decision Making

Purpose

A major trend in education today, as we've discussed, is the attempt to democratize the traditionally very hierarchical governance structure of schools. One way to accomplish this is to establish site-based decision making. Many schools now boast site-based teams, school improvement councils, or school-community councils so that more people will have more influence in educational decisions. The purpose of this exercise is to introduce you to the workings of these local decision-making groups.

Directions

Locate a site-based decision-making team at a school in your area and sit in on one of their meetings. Keep a log of what happens. Who is present? Teachers, parents, administrators, students, other community members? Do all have the same role? Who chairs the meeting? What issues are under discussion? What perspectives do the various members hold about these issues? What decisions are made? Who is responsible for implementing the decisions? How long does the meeting last? Where and when is it held? Do teachers serving on this committee receive extra compensation?

Reflection

If you were a teacher at this school, would you want to serve on the site-based committee? Why or why not? How has this experience affected your views on site-based decision making? Do you think it's generally a good idea, or a bad one? Justify your position. How will the committee's decisions affect teachers and students in this school?

Shadowing the Principal

Purpose   Most beginning teachers do not have much personal experience with the legal aspects of schooling. As a result, principles of educational law may appear rather obtuse. The purpose of this exercise is to give you direct experience with the practical aspects of school law as they work out in the day-to-day life of school people.

Directions   Make arrangements to shadow a principal, elementary or secondary, for at least half a day. Follow her to meetings with parents, teachers, and other administrators. Listen to phone conversations. Tag along as she visits classrooms, the library, and the custodian's room. Make note of each time the principal's activity involves a legal issue—discipline, curriculum, free speech, due process, and so on. What is the situation? What aspect of the law is involved? How does the principal handle it?

Reflection   How often did situations in which legal issues had a bearing arise in this principal's day? Write a page analyzing one incident in depth. What happened? What did the principal do? What alternatives did she consider? Why did she make the decision she did?

How many of these incidents involved teachers in some way? What role did teachers play? Did teachers understand the relevant law? Discuss the pros and cons of the way teachers handled these incidents.

Programs for At-Risk Students

Purpose
We've emphasized the difficulties many students have in schools due to limited English proficiency, low income, drug abuse, or other factors. Many programs exist to assist such students, and it is likely you will become involved in them as a teacher. The purpose of this exercise is to familiarize you with programs for at-risk students in your area.

Directions
Visit a principal, school counselor, or school social worker, and interview him or her about programs for at-risk students in the school, using the following questions as a guide.

1. We've been learning about how social problems, like poverty and drugs, can impact schools. Can you tell me a bit about some of the social problems you face at this school?

2. What programs and procedures do you have in place for assisting kids facing these problems? How did these programs get implemented here? How did you hear about them?

3. How are teachers involved in these programs? How about parents? Other members of our community?

4. How effective are these programs? How can you tell?

5. What programs do you wish you had? Why?

Reflection
How well is this school meeting the needs of at-risk populations? Are the school's decisions based on evidence? Are some problems easier to ameliorate than others? To what extent is the school trying to fit itself to its students versus to fit the students to its own traditional ways? How deeply involved are teachers in these programs? How do you feel about participating in these programs as a teacher yourself?

Getting to Know a School Board Member

Purpose

We have emphasized the political nature of schools. Schools are potentially vulnerable to political machinations. A more sophisticated understanding of school and community politics will help you be more successful as a teacher. The purpose of this exercise is to enhance your understanding of local politics and how they affect neighborhood schools.

Directions

Make an appointment with the school board member representing your district. Before you meet, find out how your school district is divided up, how many members there are on the board, and which board member represents which neighborhood. You may also want to familiarize yourself with recent issues the board has faced, perhaps by scanning back issues of the newspaper. Interview him or her, using the questions below as a guide. (If many students live in one district, you may want to collaborate in making up a questionnaire and mailing it instead.)

1. Typically school boards deal with policies and decisions concerning finance, personnel, curriculum, students, and infrastructure. Do you make decisions in all these areas? What percent of time is spent, roughly, in discussing each area over a typical year?

2. Can you give me an example of a recent decision? What was the problem? How was it solved?

3. Usually turnout in school board elections is very low. Is that the case here? Given the great impact school boards have, why do you think these elections generate so little interest? What do you think could be done to improve voter turnout?

4. Describe the political structure of this community. (You may want to explain Joel Spring's (1993) breakdown of different types of communities, in Chapter 10, and ask which one best describes this community.) How does the structure of power within the community affect discussions and decisions on the school board?

5. What do you think the most important problem is facing this district? What do you think should be done about it?

Reflection

Which groups are the most powerful in this community? Is power shared across all groups, or is it concentrated? Speculate on how this power structure affects teachers' lives in this district. Share your results with a student who interviewed a school board member from a different district. If you made a job decision solely on the basis of school politics, which district would you rather work in? Why?

The Principal on Job Interviewing

Purpose   An area of great concern for most new teachers is finding that first job. Most understand very little of school district procedures for hiring teachers, much less their own rights. The purpose of this activity is to familiarize you with one key aspect of job-hunting, the interview with the principal.

Directions   Interview a principal using the questions that follow as a guide.

1. First, please explain how the process of hiring teachers works in this district.

2. What do you look for on paper to help you decide whom to interview?

3. Do you like to use portfolios in your hiring process? At what point do you use portfolios? When reviewing applications? During interviews? What information in portfolios is most useful to you?

4. What questions do you ask in a typical interview? Can you give me an example of a poor answer to that question? An example of a good answer?

5. In what ways does educational legislation and case law affect your interviewing practices?

Reflection   If you were an applicant being interviewed by this principal, how well would you do? What are your own areas of strength and weakness? By the same token, how well did the principal do? Would you want to work in this school? Why or why not?

What if a principal asked you an inappropriate question during an interview? How would you handle it? Role play this situation with another student, then replay after exchanging roles and discuss various strategies for coping with this awkward possibility.

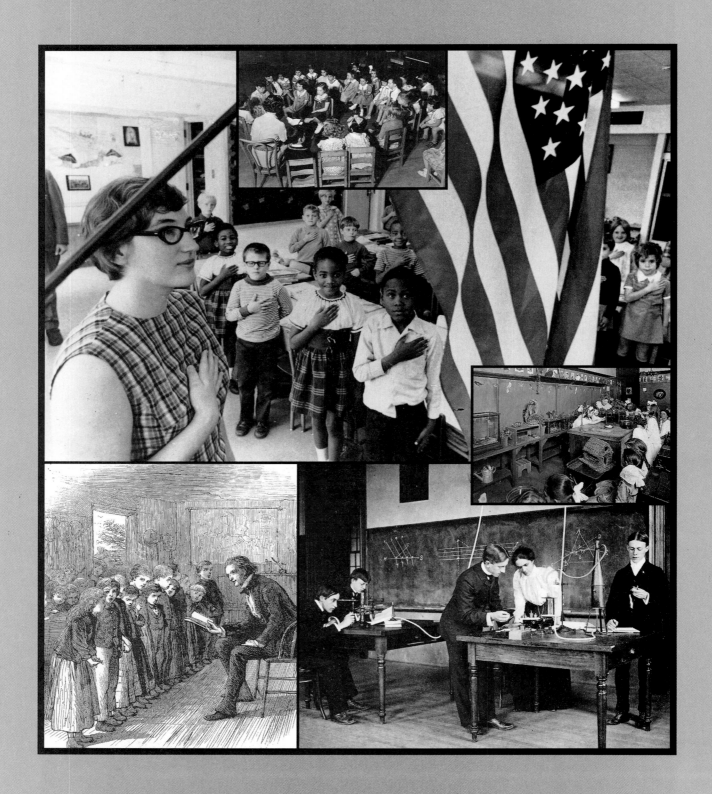

The Professionalization of Teaching

T he final part of this book focuses on one of the most important aspects of teaching—its professional context. In some ways, this is a continuation of the discussion about the conditions of work begun in Part I. However, it extends that discussion by focusing more specifically on what it means to be professional and how teachers have struggled over the years to acquire professional status. It also traces how learning to teach has become an increasingly demanding process and how the ethical and moral dimensions of teaching have become more complex in the last years of the twentieth century.

Like the historical perspectives provided in previous introductions, this one divides its coverage into the following periods: the colonial and early republic eras (1620 to 1820); the common school era (1820 to 1870); the progressive era (1870 to 1920); the post-World War II era (1945 to 1980); and the contemporary period (1980 to the present). The contemporary period is dealt with only briefly, since it provides the content for Chapters 12 and 13.

WHAT DOES PROFESSIONALIZATION OF TEACHING MEAN?

Since the time of Horace Mann, school reformers have centered their school improvement efforts around the professionalization of teaching. They reasoned that for schools to improve, teachers must improve and become more professional. But what does it mean to be a professional? What constitutes a profession? Both historically as well as today, this debate has focused on how teachers can acquire the following conditions of professional status (see Goodlad, 1990; Holmes, 1986; Darling-Hammond, 1996).

- Mastering a reasonably coherent body of *specialized knowledge,* which requires an extended period of training.

- Receiving government *licensure* (a certificate), which legally separates the qualified from the unqualified and provides the holder with special *status* and *income.*

- Practicing *professional autonomy* wherein members regulate themselves, hold each other *accountable* for using best practice, and follow an agreed upon code of ethics.

Throughout history, the teaching profession has had difficulty in attaining these conditions. In the following pages we take a brief historical look at teachers' struggle to attain professional status, a discussion that is continued in Chapters 12 and 13.

THE COLONIAL AND EARLY REPUBLIC ERAS: 1620–1820

The introduction to Part I, outlined the substantive changes that teaching has undergone in the United States in the last 300 years. You learned that teaching in the colonial period was primarily an occupation for middle class, quasi-educated males who took teaching jobs while preparing for other careers, such as the ministry. The major criteria for being a teacher during that period were knowing slightly more than one's students and being of high moral character. Lucrative new jobs during the beginnings of the industrial revolution lured these men away from teaching, and in a few short years, teaching was converted into a primarily female occupation. This conversion was fueled by the fact that state and local boards of education found they could hire women for lower wages than men. Boards also found that women were more compliant about adhering to the social restrictions that accompanied the job. It goes without saying that discussions about teaching as a profession were essentially nonexistent during this period.

THE COMMON SCHOOL ERA: 1820–1870

The first serious efforts to improve the quality of teaching began in New England in the period just prior to the Civil War. Horace Mann, Henry Barnard, and other common school reformers did not speak in terms of the "professionalization of teaching" as reformers do today, but they realized that better trained teachers were necessary if a new and expanded system of public education was to succeed. Several reform initiatives during this era marked the beginnings of the professionalization movement in teaching.

Common school reformers in the early nineteenth century recognized teachers' need for a codified body of specialized knowledge to guide their practice. They also recognized the need to create a new institution, the normal school, in which teachers could receive special training in this knowledge. Modeled after similar schools in Prussia, the first normal school was opened in Lexington, Massachusetts, in 1839. Although this first school was for women only, coeducational normal schools soon followed and became the norm. Spreading quickly throughout New England and the new western states, these schools began the process of organizing a formal teacher-training curriculum. Early courses included study of the academic subjects taught in the common schools (reading, writing, ciphering, history, geography, etc.), the nature of the learner, and how to organize classrooms. For the most part, however, the normal school curriculum was more oriented toward *how* to teach than it was toward *what* to teach. Some normal school observers were critical of this orientation at the time, a criticism that has plagued the preparation of teachers and their professional status to the present day.

Common school reformers, particularly Horace Mann, believed that teachers should be moral examples to their students. A teacher's primary obligation, in his eyes, was to develop loyal, ethical, and patriotic citizens who shared a common set of "American" values. He also believed that teaching was a nurturing process and was very critical of the corporal punishment practices commonly used by teachers in the early nineteenth century. Mann's concerns about the moral character of teachers and their conduct toward students began a long and sustained debate regarding the moral and ethical aspects of the teaching profession.

Finally, common school reformers worked hard to standardize school curricula and the ways schools were operated. Horace Mann wanted the state board of education to define what was taught in schools and to regulate such things as the length of the school day and the school calendar. On the face of it, this type of standardization appeared to be a good thing, and in many ways it was. Under the jurisdiction of hundreds of local districts and one-teacher schools, the curriculum had grown in a haphazard and disjointed fashion. Some standardization was needed. However, as Tozer (1995) observed, moving the control of education to the state level had the effect of diminishing the autonomy of teachers, a condition that greatly affected the way the profession of teaching evolved compared to other professions such as law, medicine, and architecture.

THE PROGRESSIVE ERA: 1870–1920

The explosion of secondary schools between the Civil War and World War I, along with new theories of learning and pedagogy led to demands for better prepared and more committed teachers. Although advances in teaching were made in the common school era, teaching still fell far short of being a true profession. A specialized body of professional knowledge was still not well defined, nor was it codified in any meaningful way. Two years of preparation in a normal school can hardly be considered a lengthy and demanding preparation program. Few states required teachers to have a license, and continuing efforts to standardize the curriculum and to put management of schools in the hands of superintendents and principals served to erode teacher autonomy even more.

However, by the beginning of the twentieth century, conditions were starting to change. The time allotted to teacher preparation was increased, and the curriculum began to reflect modern elements: mastery of subject matter, child and educational psychology, and research-based teaching methods. This period also saw the emergence of professional organizations for teachers, a change that ultimately had great influence on the status of the teaching profession.

Teacher Preparation and Licensure

The years between 1870 and 1920 saw significant advances in the ways teachers were prepared and certified. By the turn of the century, teachers in every state were being prepared in 4-year normal school programs that evolved from the 2-year institutions. The focus also changed from training elementary, rural school teachers to training high school teachers (Johnson, 1989). Led by the University of Michigan, many of the larger universities also began entering the teacher-training field. They pioneered departments and schools of education within the larger university, and they housed the first professors of pedagogy. The curriculum in many of the better preparation programs began to reflect the new field of psychology and progressive ideas about child-centered teaching.

More important, perhaps, this era marked the triumph of formal certification for teachers. In the middle and late nineteenth century, teaching standards were ill defined and almost nonexistent. Many teachers were hired by local authorities as a result of political patronage. This of course undermined the meritocracy goal that was starting to guide the

educational enterprise. State boards of education, distressed by the patronage-based hiring practices used by local school districts, began demanding more control over this situation. Likewise teachers, who were becoming more organized and committed to their profession, also fought against political hiring practices and pressed for standardization and uniformity in teacher licensure and appointment.

Between the 1870s and 1920, state after state strove to reduce the authority of the local boards and superintendents, mainly by moving the certification of teachers to the county or state levels (Sedlak, 1989). By 1900, the authority of most local boards had been substantially reduced, and certification began to be centralized at the state level. State regulations generally required that educational attainment and/or examination be the basis for acquiring a teaching certificate, rather than political connections. By 1925, the process of moving licensure to the state level was complete, as illustrated in Table P5.1.

During this period, states also developed different kinds of teaching certificates, and the concepts of initial and continuing certification as we know them today were introduced. By 1920, most states had over a dozen different certificates, including those for early childhood, elementary, vocational, and each of the subject specialties taught in high school.

Table P5.1   Jurisdiction over Teacher Certification between 1894 and 1926

Jurisdictional Authority	Number of States			
	1894	**1911**	**1919**	**1926**
State systems (states issued all certificates)	3	15	26	36
State-controlled system (state prescribed rules and monitored examinations; counties issued some certificates)	1	2	7	4
Semistate system (state regulations; county issued certificates)	17	18	10	5
State-county system (both issued certificates; county controlled examination for at least one certificate)	18	7	3	2
County system (county issued all certificates)	4	1	0	0

Source: Cook, 1927, p. 19.

Professional Associations

The National Education Association was actually founded in 1857, just before the Civil War. Known first as the National Teachers Association (NTA), its original mission was twofold: to advance teaching and to make schools better. The original mission statement read:

> to elevate the character and advance the interests of the profession of teaching, and to promote the cause of popular education in the United States. (Lieberman, 1956)

In 1870, the NTA merged with the associations representing school superintendents and normal schools. This new, expanded organization became the National Education Association, and throughout most of its history, its membership included both teachers and administrators. In its early years, the NEA was more concerned with the second part of its mission, improving schooling, than with enhancing teaching. It became very interested in efforts to standardize school curricula, particularly that of the emerging comprehensive high school. In 1913, the NEA appointed the Commission on the Reorganization of Secondary Education, the commission that issued the now famous "Cardinal Principles of Secondary Education" described in the introduction to Part III. This report, you may remember, expanded the purposes of secondary education. It placed vocational education more squarely within the educational enterprise and challenged teachers to use newer psychologically based pedagogies and to relate their subjects more closely to the needs and interests of their students. In the 1920s, the NEA established a research department and started to communicate "best practices" to its members through the *NEA Journal.*

All teachers, however, were not satisfied with the focus of the NEA. For example, in the early part of the twentieth century, the NEA had no separate division that represented the interests of classroom teachers. The organization often treated teaching as a "calling," like the ministry, thus making it inappropriate to negotiate for higher salaries or better working conditions. Since the leadership of the organization was generally in the hands of school superintendents and college faculty, its focus often failed to fit the immediate, bread-and-butter concerns of teachers. A speech delivered to the NEA convention in 1904 by Aaron Grove, a superintendent, illustrates this point of view:

> A dangerous tendency exists (today) toward usurpation by teachers of power that should be retained by superintendents. An apparently growing feeling seems to exist ... that the public school system should be a democratic institution, and that the body of teachers constitute the democratic government. This is a false conception of democracy. The truth is that boards of education are the representative bodies of the democracy ... for whom they are making laws, and to whom they are responsible to act. (Eaton, 1975, p. 10)

As a result of such bureaucratic neglect, teachers in the larger cities began organizing into independent teacher associations whose primary focus was their salary and working conditions. One such local organization, the Chicago Teachers Federation, formed in 1897 and eventually combined with other large-city teacher associations to form the American Federation of Teachers in 1916. As conditions in the urban schools deteriorated at the turn of the century and as dissatisfaction with the NEA increased, interest in the AFT grew. As its membership grew, the AFT soon became affiliated with the American Federation of Labor (AFL). Unlike the NEA, the AFT was interested almost exclusively in representing teachers on issues of salary and working conditions through the use of collective bargaining. The teacher was at the center of their concerns as illustrated in the following quote:

> In the structure and successful operation of schools, the teacher is central. Good teachers make good schools. The professional teacher not only knows how to direct the educational and personal development of children in the classroom, he also joins with his colleagues in an effective organization to advance the interest of teachers, pupils, and the schools through collective bargaining. (American Federation of Teachers, n.d., p. 3)

By not allowing administrators to join the organization, the AFT was able to maintain its commitment to both economic gains and professional autonomy for teachers. John Dewey, from the University of Chicago, became an early AFT member and remained active throughout his career. Dewey supported teachers in their efforts to improve their economic benefits, once writing that "teachers have to pay their grocery and meat bills and house rent just the same as everyone else."

THE POST-WORLD WAR II ERA: 1945–1980

By the end of World War II, the vast majority of both elementary and secondary teachers held 4-year degrees, and by 1970, a majority held master's degrees, which had become a requirement for higher salaries and permanent certification in many states (NEA, 1990). Two additional forces that boosted the professionalization movement in this period were: post-World War II criticism of the public schools and teachers and a growing teacher activism.

Postwar Criticism

As described in the introduction to Part II, the years following World War II saw the public schools and their teachers come under attack for being too student centered and nonacademic. Tensions stemming from the cold war and Soviet technological triumphs such as the launching of Sputnik, the first space satellite, led critics to assert that our schools had become academically soft and that teachers were being miseducated. The postwar curriculum was first attacked by Arthur Bestor in a widely read book, *Educational Wasteland* (1953). Severe criticism of teachers and their preparation followed a few years later in James Koerner's *The Mis-education of Teachers* (1963).

The response to this criticism resulted in numerous projects to reshape school curriculums, particularly in math and science. New curricula, developed under the auspices of university-based academics and supported by federal monies, aimed at making school subjects more rigorous and challenging. Many university faculty who developed these new curricula believed that teachers were incapable of dealing with intellectually challenging materials, so they strove to make them "teacher proof." This meant that they wrote instructions on how to use the new curricula in such detail that anyone could use them successfully, regardless of whether or not he or she understood the content. Predictably, teachers resisted such efforts to turn them into instructional automatons. However, the wide publicity given these teacher-proof curricula created a public perception that teachers as a group were not very capable and that they could not be relied on to work in autonomous ways.

In the mid 1960s, James Conant, President of Harvard University, published *The Education of American Teachers* (1963). Conant was also critical of teachers, and he was particularly critical of educa-

tion courses. He recommended that teacher preparation involve more general academic content (like other college majors), fewer teaching methods courses, and more intensive clinical experiences (like the internship required of doctors).

The criticism of schools and teaching unfortunately did little to professionalize teaching during this era as Johnson (1989) observed:

> Teachers came to be seen as less central to the improvement of schools during the early 1960s because, beyond a consensus among lay critics that more intensive academic training was needed, there was no agreement on how to train teachers. This was not a matter of disagreement over which models of professional training ought to be supported. There were no models. Not even imperfect ones which might, through renovation and reform, hold promise for the future (p. 239)

Although the criticism of teachers and the reform efforts they spawned did little to professionalize teaching, the teachers reaction to all of this did. Hurt and offended, teachers in the 1960s instigated a political uprising, not only in their own classrooms but as a professional group.

Postwar Teacher Activism

In the period following World War II, teachers' already low salaries failed to keep up with inflation. At the same time, the postwar baby boom produced a teacher shortage and overcrowded classrooms. As a result, some teachers started to organize and to become more vocal in their demands for higher salaries and better working conditions. They also began using collective bargaining and the strike to secure concessions from state and local school districts. At first, the NEA opposed strikes and euphemistically labeled collective bargaining "professional negotiations." By the late 1960s, however, the NEA became increasingly militant and began standing along side the more militant AFT in fights to increase teacher salaries and to improve their working conditions. During the 1970s, the NEA and AFT supported more than a thousand strikes, which were made possible by legislation passed in most states requiring collective bargaining and making teachers' strikes legal for the first time.

Today, both the NEA and the AFT have strong national organizations and active local and state affiliates. Both have healthy treasuries that they freely use to influence legislation and to elect proeducation candidates. For example, the NEA contributed significantly to Jimmy Carter's campaign in 1976 and, as a consequence, was rewarded when Carter created a cabinet-level U.S. Department of Education in 1979. In both 1992 and 1996, the NEA was among the largest contributors to Bill Clinton's two successful presidential bids. In addition to pursuing their own economic and professional interests, both the NEA and the AFT have worked for legislation to support bilingual education, and they helped secure passage of the Education for All Handicapped Children's Act in 1975.

The AFT has kept its efforts more narrowly focused on teacher salaries and working conditions, although it also has a long history of advocacy for academic freedom and for teachers' and students' political rights. It has also supported disempowered groups such as Jews, African Americans, and Hispanics, against whom the educational system has discriminated.

THE CONTEMPORARY ERA: 1980 TO THE PRESENT

Much of what occurs today in regard to teacher professionalism is the topic of Chapter 12. Here, we outline briefly the events that have occurred since the early 1980s, events some believe are of great significance and that may result in teaching's becoming a true profession for the first time.

Starting with *A Nation at Risk* (1983), education in the United States has experienced many proposals for reform. These calls for reform have been motivated by dissatisfaction with student achievement and a generalized sense that the public education system is failing. Many of the reforms, such as Goals 2000: Educate America Act, aim at improving the academic performance of students. Others, however, believing that schools cannot be improved unless the quality of teachers and teaching are improved, have sought ways of improving the four conditions of a profession described here earlier. We now turn briefly to recent trends in regard to each of these conditions. More thorough discussions are provided in Chapters 12 and 13.

Specialized Knowledge

Most who have studied teaching and schools have observed that teaching is a weak profession because it lacks a strong and coherent knowledge base (Goodlad, 1990). Several initiatives were launched in the past decade to remedy this situation. These include sponsored efforts to begin the long process of codifying the knowledge bases for teaching, adopting standards specifying what beginning teachers should know and be able to do, and developing performance measures on these standards.

Preparation and Accreditation

During the 1970s and 1980s, many teacher educators came to the conclusion that inadequate time was available to prepare teachers. Getting a well-balanced general education, acquiring a command of subject matter, and mastering the knowledge bases on teaching, learning, and pedagogy simply could not be done in the 4-year baccalaureate degree program. As early as 1976, reports appeared that called for improving the preparation of teachers by extending preparation over a 5- or 6-year period (AACTE, 1976). Ten years later, the Holmes Report, *Tomorrow's Teachers* (1986), recommended that all teacher education programs include a bachelor's degree in an academic discipline and a master's degree in teaching. The Carnegie Report, *A Nation Prepared: Teachers for Our Nation's Schools* (1986) reached similar conclusions. Today, over 300 of the 1,200 colleges and universities that prepare teachers have experimented with aspects of the recommendations proposed by the Holmes and Carnegie reports.

Teacher Licensing and Certification

As described earlier, teacher licensing or certification has been centralized at the state level since the early 1920s. This situation is similar to license procedures used in other professions. Unlike other professions, however, the teaching license for most of the twentieth century has been granted after finishing a teacher education program instead of after successfully passing an examination about the profession's specialized knowledge. This has changed quite dramatically in the past decade. Today, teacher candidates in almost all 50 states are required to pass some type of examination before they are issued an initial license to teach, a matter described in more detail in Chapter 12. In addition, the National Board for Professional Teaching Standards, created in 1987, currently offers advanced certification for experienced, accomplished teachers.

Autonomy and Accountability

Finally, during the past decade, many proposals for restructuring schools included provisions for increasing teacher autonomy as a means of increasing student achievement. Several of these reforms are discussed elsewhere in the book and their details do not need to be repeated here. This trend of giving teachers more autonomy from the principal's authority through flattened hierarchies, more say in school management, and participation in site-based councils, seems destined to continue, at least for the next few years. In addition, many districts have restructured the school day so that teachers can have time to work together and be involved in school decision making.

As with other recent efforts to professionalize teaching, the effects of giving teachers more autonomy will only be known in the future. Many believe that the profession will change significantly over the next decade or so; others remain skeptical and argue that many questions remain unanswered. For instance, could it be that site-based councils will cancel out some of the autonomy teachers have won from administrators? Will local councils counteract efforts to increase standards for teachers at the state and national levels? If teachers do acquire more autonomy, what mechanisms will hold them accountable to their students? To the larger profession? To society?

CHAPTER 12

Becoming a Professional Teacher

Most people choose a career in teaching because they have aspirations of working with children and youth. However, as you know by now, there is much more to teaching than this. In the preceding chapters, we showed how the teacher-student relationship is influenced by a variety of contexts—classrooms, schools, and the larger society. In this chapter we examine yet another context that helps shape the work-life of teachers, the professional context. After exploring what it means to be a professional teacher, we examine the process by which one prepares for and acquires a teaching license. The final sections, then, consider issues confronting the teaching profession today and our analysis of what might happen in the years ahead.

WHAT IS A PROFESSIONAL TEACHER?

To begin thinking about this question take a moment and consider two teachers who are about to launch their careers.

Meet Samantha Martin, who is beginning her teaching career in an urban, multiethnic elementary school. Unlike countless new teachers who have preceded her, Samantha is *unlikely* to quit her job in the next 5 years.

Samantha enters the classroom fully armed with the knowledge and skills she needs. She is a graduate of a professionally and nationally accredited

What Is a Professional Teacher?
   Features of a Profession
      Specialized Body of Knowledge
      Respect, Status, and Income
      Autonomy
      Accountability
   Is Teaching a Profession?
      Specialized Knowledge
      Respect and Income
      Autonomy
      Accountability

Becoming a Teacher Today
   Phases of Professional Preparation
   Preservice Preparation and Accreditation
      Teacher Candidate Selection
      Teacher Education Program Accreditation
      Changing Context
         Extending Time
         New Curricula
         Clinical Experiences
   Certification
      Initial Certification
      Alternative Certification

Continuing Education and Advanced and National Certification
      Advanced Certification
      National Certification
      Tenure

Teachers' Organizations and Collective Bargaining
   Teachers' Organizations
   National Education Association
   American Federation of Teachers
   Collective Bargaining

A Look Ahead
   Research and Performance-Based Teacher Education
   Testing to Assure Teacher Quality
   Restructured Schools for Teacher and Student Success

Summary

Readings for the Professional

preparation program from which she received a rigorous liberal arts education, studied research-based pedagogy, and worked with real students in an urban school.

Samantha passed a battery of exams focusing not only on what she knows but also on her ability to put that knowledge into action. This last step involved a yearlong supervised internship in a professional development school—a requirement for licensure in her state. At this point, Samantha has a good understanding of children and how they learn, can tailor lessons to meet their needs, and can justify her decisions on the basis of research and proven practice.

During her first three years of teaching, Samantha will be assigned a mentor who will assist her when she needs help. Her teaching will be observed by experienced teachers in the school, and she will submit a portfolio for evaluation by a statewide panel of peers. Only after satisfying a peer review will she be granted a continuing teaching license.

Teachers work in teams at Samantha's school, and they have considerable autonomy in deciding what should be taught and how to teach it. Decisions that affect everyone in the school are made by a schoolwide council composed mainly of teachers and parents. In short, Samantha is now a professional who works in a professional setting. (after Bradley, 1995)

Now meet Jon Yalung, who is beginning his teaching career in an inner city school in a neighboring state. Unlike Samantha, Jon will not enter the classroom confident that he has the knowledge and skills required to be an effective teacher. Jon's teacher education program was accredited by the state, but it was not professionally and nationally accredited. Instead, it consisted of acquiring a bachelor's degree in history and taking four courses in education required by that state: Introduction to Education, Philosophy of Education, Social Studies Methods, and Special Education. In addition, Jon was required to observe in schools for 30 hours during his social studies methods course, and he completed 10 weeks of student teaching. Jon did his student teaching in his home town, a small community in the northeast corner of his state, which allowed him to save on expenses by living with his parents.

Jon was recommended for certification as a result of having an overall 2.5 GPA and getting all A's and B's in his education courses. Jon got an A in student teaching, and his cooperating teacher emphasized how much Jon liked children and how he developed a very positive relationship with his students.

As Jon approached his first day of class, he was reminded of what his principal said during the interview, "New teachers are expected to sink or swim on their own in this school." Experienced teachers simply have too many problems to help beginners, and the administration has its hands full keeping the school under control. What the principal didn't tell Jon was that fewer than 30 percent of the new teachers in the school returned for a second year.

These two illustrations of beginning teachers, their preparation, and the schools where they are going to teach contrast sharply. Jon entered teaching after completing a minimal amount of approved coursework from a state-approved teacher education institution. He is beginning his career in a school in which teachers are isolated from one another and their work is seldom mentored or reviewed by peers. The portrait of Samantha, on the other hand, has been drawn from standards and guidelines recommended by the National Council for the Accreditation or Teacher Education (NCATE) and the National Board for Professional Teaching Standards (NBPTS), organizations that many believe will reform the teaching profession in the years ahead. Samantha is well prepared for her first teaching assignment, and unlike Jon, she is fortunate to be starting her career in a school in which teachers are respected as professionals. Given this backdrop, let's begin our exploration of what a profession is and what it means to be a professional.

Features of a Profession

Although definitions abound, most people agree that a professional is someone, as described in the part introduction, who has acquired through a fairly long period of training a specialized body of knowledge, who has received a license to practice, who is respected for that knowledge by the larger community, and who is given a degree of autonomy in his or her work. A professional is also held accountable to peers for continued learning and for using best practices. Let's look at each of these criteria and then apply them to teaching to see if teaching should be considered a profession.

Specialized Body of Knowledge

Professionals have mastered a specialized body of knowledge that allows them to deal with their work more effectively than the average person. For instance, we all have some information about the human body, and we know when we are sick. We may also treat some of our illnesses by taking vitamin C or chicken noodle soup. On the other hand, we go to doctors when we are seriously ill, because we have confidence that they have knowledge we do not have about biology, human anatomy, and how to treat disease. Similarly, most individuals can build a small dog house. However, they seek the services of a licensed architect if they want a fashionable home built on a high bluff. In short, the amount of knowledge demanded of professionals, such as doctors and architects, differs significantly from that of a young person who fries hamburgers at McDonald's or carries materials at a construction sight.

Respect, Status, and Income

Most professionals are afforded a high level of respect, status, and income. This is true for several reasons. First, acquiring a specialized body of knowledge requires a more rigorous and extended period of training than most other occupations. Such training is needed because the work that professionals perform is more complex and demanding than that of other occupations. The fact that professionals hold themselves accountable to a code of ethics and high standards of practice also contributes to their high status and income.

Autonomy

Because individuals in a profession command specialized knowledge that others do not have, they are allowed to carry out their responsibilities with minimal supervision. For instance, a hospital administrator would not interfere with a doctor's recommendation for patient care, nor would a carpenter unilaterally change the type of roofing materials prescribed by an architect.

Accountability

Finally, professionals have considerable control over who can enter their profession. Furthermore, they create codes of ethics and professional boards to monitor the practices of peers. These boards have the authority to expel members who violate professional standards of behavior or practice. Figure 12.1 illustrates the four important features of a profession.

Is Teaching a Profession?

Although specialized knowledge, status, autonomy, and accountability are common features of most professions, each profession varies in its mix of these features. We turn now to how teaching mixes these features and speculate on whether or not this mix deserves the label *profession.*

Most observers would agree that the answer to the question of whether teaching is a profession is mixed. A recent report called *What Matters Most,*

issued by the National Commission on Teaching and America's Future (1996), argued that teaching in the United States falls far short of the standards of other professions and of teaching in other countries. On the other hand, the same report believes that current reform efforts have a high likelihood of making teaching a true profession early in the next century. How do teachers stack up against other professions in terms of specialized knowledge, respect, autonomy, and accountability?

Specialized Knowledge

Historically, teachers have *not* had a clearly defined knowledge base that set them apart from the average person. Indeed, early tests for teachers described in the introduction to Part I required teachers to know only slightly more than their students. Remember also, as described in the introduction to Part V, that for most of our history, individuals could get a teaching license with only 2 years of normal-school education. Thus, a thin and disparate knowledge base has led to training programs for teachers described by some as short, fragmented, incoherent, and lacking in vision (Darling-Hammond & Goodwin, 1993). Lack of an agreed upon knowledge base has also led to alternative routes into teaching that require virtually no preparation beyond a bachelor's degree in the liberal arts.

Fortunately, the last decade has seen considerable progress in clarifying and organizing the specialized knowledge base in teaching. In 1989, the American Association of Colleges of Teacher Education (AACTE) commissioned and published a book entitled *The Knowledge Base for Beginning Teachers.* This book along with a later volume, *The Teacher Educator's Handbook* (1996), are serious attempts to clarify and define what beginning teachers should know and be able to do. And, as you will read in the next section, many states now require teachers to demonstrate their command of this knowledge base before they are given a license to teach.

Respect and Income

Compared to professions such as medicine and law, teaching does not command a high level of respect or income. Various reasons have been provided for this situation. Some, as described in the introduction to Part I say that the status and salaries of teachers have remained low because teaching has been mainly a "women's profession." Others believe that the absence of a specialized knowledge base, a relatively brief preparation time, and low entry standards contribute to the low pay and low status of teachers. (Lortie, 1975). Rowan (1994), on the other hand, argues that teachers' work, although complex,

Figure 12.1 **Four Important Features of a Profession**

Specialized Knowledge

Status and Income

Professionals

Autonomy

Accountability

is not so complex as the higher-status professions, and this explains teachers' lower pay and status. We highlight Rowan's research in the accompanying Research Box.

Despite Rowan's or others' assessments, society does entrust its children to teachers, and teachers' work is recognized as difficult and noble. As a result, teachers are afforded considerably more status in our society than are many other occupational groups. Also, as many have observed, teaching in the United States is viewed by the working class as a primary route to upward mobility and, for many years, by society at large as one of the most respectable careers for women (Charters, 1963; Lortie, 1975; Lanier & Little, 1986).

Autonomy

As for autonomy, teachers have considerable freedom in the way they structure their classrooms, the specific content they teach, and the instructional

methods they use. Traditionally, they have only seldom been observed by outsiders and even more rarely by peers. Consequently, the "hands-off" norm has become one of the fixtures of the culture of teaching. Indeed, in many schools, it would be considered professionally inappropriate to criticize the practices of a fellow teacher.

Despite their autonomy, there are constraints on teachers that do not exist for individuals in other professions. For example, schools are governed by local and state bodies that make important decisions about curriculum, school organization, and personnel, often without teacher input. Further, because schools are politically vulnerable, teachers are often constrained by public opinion and parental complaints. Similarly, the client relationship between teachers and students is different from that in other professions: Children are required to attend school, and teachers are required to accept all the students assigned to them.

Comparing Teachers' Work with that of Other Occupations

There are many ways of viewing teachers' work. Compared to many other occupations, teachers perform complex work that requires specialized knowledge. However, different observers see the work that teachers do variously. For instance, Apple (1988), argued that teaching is really just another form of labor. Huberman (1993) emphasized the craft of teaching, whereas Eisner (1978) viewed teaching an artistic endeavor.

To look more closely at the nature of teachers' work, University of Michigan researcher Brian Rowan (1994) systematically compared teaching with other forms of work. He was particularly interested in the complexity of teachers' work compared to other occupations, because this seems to be one of the most important factors in determining the status, respect, and income accruing to an occupation. His analysis relied on data found in *The Dictionary of Occupational Titles,* considered to be the best source for examining the nature of work for many occupations in the United States.

Table 12.1 **The Complexity of Selected Occupations as Reported in the *Dictionary of Occupation Titles,* 4th ed.**

Occupation	Worker Functions[a]			Educational Development[b]		
	Data	People	Things	Reasoning	Math	Language
K-12 education occupations						
Teacher	2	2	7	5	4	5
Principal	1	1	7	5	3	5
Counselor	1	0	7	5	5	5
Selected professional, technical, managerial occupations						
Architect	4	6	1	6	6	6
General doctor	1	0	1	6	5	6
Criminal lawyer	1	0	7	6	4	6
Accountant	1	6	2	5	5	5
Occupations in the arts						
Reporter	2	6	2	5	3	5
Painter	0	6	1	5	2	4
Skilled trade occupations						
Carpenter	3	8	1	4	3	3
Electrician	2	6	1	4	4	4
Clerical and sales occupations						
Secretary	3	6	2	4	3	4
Sales clerk	4	7	7	3	2	2
Unskilled labor occupations						
Waiter	4	7	7	3	2	2
Drill press operator	3	8	3	3	2	2

[a] 0 = most complex; 9 = least complex

[b] 1 = low; 6 = high

Continued

A small sample of Rowan's analysis is found in Table 12.1. You will notice that the table includes ratings on two types of measures.

1. *Measures of a worker's functions.* The complexity of skills needed in relation to data, people, and things. These skills range from 0, most complex, to 9, least complex.

2. *Measures of educational development.* The reasoning, mathematical, and language skills needed to successfully perform the work. These skill ratings are reversed from the ones under worker function—6 indicates the highest level, 1 the lowest level.

We included only a small sample of the occupations compared by Rowan, but the table provides a reasonably good picture regarding the complexity of teaching. Note that teaching receives a 2 on the data and people scales, which means that providing instruction demands the use of complex ideas and a high level of skill in working with people.

From his complete analysis, Rowan drew several conclusions about the complexity of teachers' work and how it affected the professional status of teaching. One conclusion was that teachers' work does appear to be quite complex but not as complex as the most prestigious and highly paid professions. Although teaching is more complex than 75 percent of the occupations surveyed, the work of physicians and lawyers, for example, are more complex in their use of ideas and reasoning skills. Further, the most prestigious occupations require higher levels of educational development and preparation than teaching.

Rowan also concluded that the skilled trades and the arts require functions of greater complexity with "things" than teaching does. Teaching, however, requires greater complexity in working with people.

In Rowan's view, if teaching is to become a more prestigious profession, teachers must seek ways to make their work more complex. This would occur if teachers performed a broader array of functions that include leadership, mentoring, and research in addition to their regular instructional work. He pointed out as we have that many current reform proposals address such new roles for teachers as mentoring, leadership through site-based management, and more personalized relationships with students. The professional status of teaching, according to Rowan, will not change markedly until these role changes become part of the larger system of schooling and education.

What do you think of Rowan's analysis of teachers' work? Will making teachers work more complex enhance the prestige of the profession? As a teacher, do you want your work to be more complex? Do you want to assume schoolwide leadership and coordination functions? Or would you prefer to stay focused on classroom instruction and leave school leadership to others?

To summarize, the issue of professional autonomy for teachers is unique. In a democracy, we believe that citizens and parents should have a say about how their children are educated. To date, this has led to local, state, and federal policies that confine teachers' professional autonomy. This dilemma is one that will not be resolved in the near future.

As for licensure, doctors, lawyers, nurses, and architects must all obtain a state license before they can legally practice in that state. Usually, a professionally controlled and autonomous standards board must recommend issuance of the license. However, this is not the case for teachers. Their recommendation normally comes from the institution at which the applicant has trained or directly from a government agency, such as the state's department of education.

Accountability

Finally teachers, unlike other professionals, have not assumed the responsibility for monitoring professional behavior and holding peers accountable for ethical behavior and best practice. No mechanisms for peer review boards exist for this purpose, and as we have pointed out, it is often considered unprofessional to criticize the practices of a peer, even if those practices are inappropriate or harmful. The teachers' unions and professional organizations until very recently believed their role was to protect and defend teachers rather than to hold them accountable to a code of professional ethics and best practice.

Thus, at the present time, most observers would argue that teaching satisfies only some features of a profession. Although teachers perform important

---

GLOBAL

Perceptions of the American Teaching Profession by Teachers from Five Countries

During the 1991–1992 school year, Richard McAdams (1993) conducted lengthy interviews with over 2 dozen foreign teachers who were in the United States as part of the Fulbright Teacher Exchange Program. These teachers came from five different countries:—Denmark, Germany, England, Canada, and Japan. From extended interviews and conversations with these individuals, McAdams constructed a portrait about how other countries educate their children and what it is like to teach in other countries. He also was able to glean what teachers from other countries thought about teaching in the United States. Following is a summary of these perceptions.

1. *American teachers have more autonomy.* They have more freedom to decide on their curriculum than teachers in other countries do. This is both a positive and a negative. As a teacher from Scotland noted, "Teachers in America are free to be as good or as bad as they wish." The presence of a national curriculum and standards in other countries serves as both a guide and a goal for teachers in planning their instruction.

2. *Teachers in America have heavier teaching loads than teachers in most other countries.* There are few breaks during the day for American teachers, and teachers are assigned more teaching time and supervisory duties than in other nations. A teacher from Germany remarked that in light of the heavy teaching schedule of American teachers, she was "absolutely astonished that many teachers hold second jobs in addition to teaching."

3. *Teachers in American schools plan and teach by themselves.* They are more isolated from one another than teachers in other countries are. This is a result of very full teaching schedules with few breaks, short lunch periods, and no common planning time. American teachers simply have fewer opportunities to meet for either social or professional purposes than their colleagues abroad do.

work, provide a valuable service to the community, and command a degree of respect and autonomy not afforded other job holders in our society, their work does not satisfy all features of a profession. Teaching still does not have a fully defined knowledge base, some teacher preparation programs lack rigorous standards, and teachers' professional judgment is often subject to governmental and parental constraints. However, a decade of reform efforts yields beginning signs that teaching is becoming more of a profession, which we discuss next. First, however, take a minute to read the accompanying Global Box, which reports foreign teachers' views about teaching in the United States versus in their own countries.

BECOMING A TEACHER TODAY

Over the past decade, every aspect of teaching and teacher preparation has been subjected to scrutiny. Out of endless debate, a series of reforms have been initiated that are gradually overhauling the way teachers are prepared, licensed, and treated. Let's consider each stage of these reforms and what it means for those who want to become teachers today.

Phases of Professional Preparation

In all major professions, candidates must go through the following three-phase process before being granted permanent license to practice:

GLOBAL

Continued

4. *Teachers in the United States are more closely supervised.* They are supervised by their principals more closely and more frequently than is common elsewhere. This came as a surprise to teachers from several countries who were more accustomed to a peer review system.

5. *More is expected of American teachers.* Exchange teachers endorsed the comment of a teacher from France that the American definition of a teacher seems to include elements of a "camp counselor and an entertainer," role expectations that were new to his experience.

6. *American teachers are often put on the defensive by students and parents.* "It seems that in conflict situations the onus is always on the teacher rather than on the student," said the teacher from one country. This situation is reversed in most countries represented in the study.

7. *American teachers do not enjoy high status.* Teachers from other countries perceived that American society did not value teachers as much as their own societies did.

It is obvious that teachers from other countries do not see teaching in America as positively as they saw it in their own country. They perceived that American teachers had a heavier work load than they did and that American teachers' work was not as highly valued. The autonomy afforded American teachers and the lack of standardized curriculum were perceived as a mixed blessing. It left American teachers with considerable freedom but also isolated and without direction.

What are your reactions to foreign teachers' perceptions of American teachers? Are they accurate? Are they perhaps colored by the teachers' own cultural blinders? What do their perceptions suggest for strengthening teaching in the United States?

Phase 1. They must be accepted into and successfully complete an accredited preparation program,

Phase 2. They must successfully complete a clinical preparation phase, pass knowledge and performance-based assessments, and be granted an initial certificate.

Phase 3: They must successfully complete ongoing education requirements and demonstrate advanced knowledge and skills.

Figure 12.2 illustrates the continuum formed by these three phases of teacher preparation as described by the National Council for the Accreditation of Teacher Education.

Preservice Preparation and Accreditation

The initial phase of becoming a teacher consists of being accepted into and successfully completing an accredited pre-service teacher preparation program. Until very recently, this process could be a haphazard and fragmented experience. Acceptance into a college or university often meant automatic acceptance into the institution's teacher education programs, some of which lacked high standards and professional accreditation. Recent reforms have focused on changing this situation as the following discussion illustrates.

Teacher Candidate Selection

Over the past decade, many colleges and universities have established entrance criteria for their teacher education programs. Generally, students are required to have a 2.5 to 3.0 GPA in liberal arts coursework and must demonstrate that they have successfully completed some form of volunteer work with children. State legislatures have also initiated entry requirements. Twenty six states now require college students to demonstrate their competence in reading, writing, and mathematics skills before acceptance into a teacher education program. These skills are generally assessed using Praxis I, a test developed and administered by the Educational Testing Service (ETS). Many of you may have already taken this test or may be planning to do so in the near future.

Teacher Education Program Accreditation

Program **accreditation** means that an external accrediting agency examined a college or university's teacher education program and found that it meets some agreed upon standards. In most professions, program accreditation is nationally governed by the

larger profession, and individuals cannot apply for a license until they have graduated from an accredited program. For example, before prospective lawyers can take the bar exam, they must graduate from a law school that is accredited by the American Bar Association. Nurses are required to hold degrees from institutions that have been accredited by the National League for Nursing.

Professional and national accreditation, however, are not required of all programs that prepare teachers. In most states, program approval and accreditation fall under the jurisdiction of governmental agencies, usually the state department of education. Placing accreditation under the auspices of a political rather than a professional group has had important and sometimes negative consequences for the way teachers are prepared. For example, many colleges and universities have alumni who are state legislators and have intervened on the side of their alma maters when threatened with nonaccreditation. This has happened even when all the evidence suggests that the preparation programs do not meet minimum standards.

Current reforms propose to adhere to national accreditation standards and to require all teacher education programs to demonstrate their adherence to these standards to a team of examiners from the National Council for the Accreditation of Teacher Education (NCATE). NCATE is a consortium of representatives from 29 educational organizations. Each subject matter organization, such as the National Council of Teachers of Mathematics, has representation in NCATE, but the three controlling organizations are the National Education Association (NEA); the American Federation of Teachers (AFT); and the association that represents teacher educators, the American Association of Colleges for Teacher Education (AACTE). In 1987, and again in 1994, NCATE raised its standards and instituted performance-based criteria for judging prospective teachers. Here is how the president of NCATE summarized what his organization expected beginning teachers to know and to be able to do.

Teachers should be able to use strategies for developing critical thinking and problem solving. They should be able to use formal and informal evaluation strategies to ensure continuous student learning. They should be versed in educational technology, including use of the computer and other technologies for instruction and student evaluation. Prospective teachers should be skilled in classroom management and be able to collaborate effectively with parents and others in the community. They should know and use research-based principles of practice

Figure 12.2 The Three Phases of Teacher Preparation

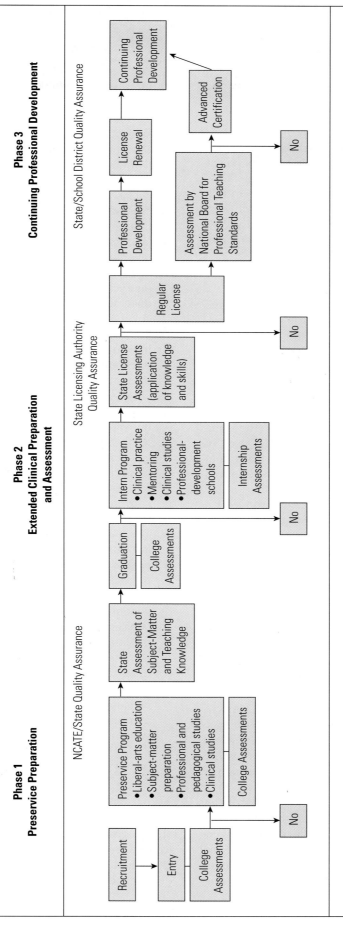

NOTE: This flow chart is derived from a schematic designed by NCATE in an effort to promote discussion about the evolving quality assurance system for the teaching profession.

SOURCE: From Wise, 1995, p. 6–7.

proven to be effective. In other words, teachers should be able to explain why they decide to use a certain strategy or teach a particular idea in a certain way. In short, prospective teachers should demonstrate competence, needed knowledge, and acceptable proficiency. (Wise, 1995, p. 5)

The specialized knowledge NCATE deems essential for beginning teachers comes directly from a list of 10 principles developed by the Interstate New Teachers Assessment and Support Consortium (INTASC). The INTASC principles are the result of work that began in 1987 that has involved 36 states and all the professional associations. Figure 12.3 summarizes their ten guiding principles.

Changing Context

The many shortcomings in teacher education have been thoroughly documented over the past 20 years. Between 1976 and 1996, several major reports were issued. The weaknesses they identified include (1) the lack of depth in liberal arts preparation (Holmes, 1986); (2) lack of depth in pedagogical knowledge (Smith, 1980, Joyce & Clift, 1984); (3) fragmentation and lack of integration across various components of preparation programs (Howsom, 1976; Goodlad, 1990; Holmes, 1990); and (4) lack of alignment between teacher candidates' classroom coursework and their field and clinical experiences (Holmes, 1990; National Commission, 1996).

This intense scrutiny and criticism produced a number of reforms aimed at improving teacher education, some of which you will undoubtedly encounter in your own preservice programs. The principle reforms are (1) to extend the time required for teacher preparation, (2) to provide new, more integrated curricula, and (3) to find ways to make clinical experiences more powerful and more tightly connected to college coursework.

Extending Time A position taken by many reformers is that insufficient preparation time is the albatross that has hung around the neck of teacher education (Howsom et al., 1976; Holmes, 1986). To these critics, improving the quality of new teachers requires extending preparation time beyond the traditional 4-year baccalaureate program. It is simply impossible, critics argue, for students to obtain a broad liberal arts education, a strong major in a subject field, and an in-depth understanding of the knowledge base on teaching and learning in 4 years.

Currently, there are over 300 colleges and universities in the United States that have extended their programs beyond 4 years. The way this is done, however, varies. The most common pattern has

Figure 12.3 **Standards for Beginning Teachers**

1. The teacher understands the central concepts, tools of inquiry, and structures of the discipline(s) he or she teaches and can create learning experiences that make these aspects of subject matter meaningful for students.
2. The teacher understands how children learn and develop and can provide learning opportunities that support their intellectual, social, and personal development.
3. The teacher understands how students differ in their approaches to learning and creates instructional opportunities that are adapted to diverse learners.
4. The teacher understands and uses a variety of instructional strategies to encourage students' development of critical thinking, problem solving, and performance skills.
5. The teacher uses an understanding of individual and group motivation and behavior to create a learning environment that encourages positive social interaction, active engagement in learning, and self-motivation.
6. The teacher uses knowledge of effective verbal, nonverbal, and media communication techniques to foster active inquiry, collaboration, and supportive interaction in the classroom.
7. The teacher plans instruction based on knowledge of subject matter, students, the community, and curriculum goals.
8. The teacher understands and uses formal and informal assessment strategies to evaluate and ensure the continuous intellectual, social, and physical development of the learner.
9. The teacher is a reflective practitioner who continually evaluates the effects of his or her choices and actions on others (students, parents, and other professionals in the learning community) and who actively seeks out opportunities to grow professionally.
10. The teacher fosters relationships with school colleagues, parents, and agencies in the larger community to support students' learning and well-being.

Interstate New Teacher Assessment and Support Consortium, 1993, pp. 1–29.

been to maintain the traditional 4-year baccalaureate program and to add coursework and clinical experiences that extend into a fifth year of study. Other institutions have added coursework and field experiences, but now grant two degrees—a bachelor's degree in a liberal arts subject at the end of the fourth year and a master's degree in teaching at the end of the fifth year. A third alternative for extending preparation time has been to require students to acquire a bachelor's degree before admission into a graduate-level teacher preparation program. Several universities offer more than one type of program and/or combinations of these three configurations.

Many teacher educators believe that extended preparation programs have increased the quality of preparation, which will enhance the status of the profession. New teachers will enter the profession with more knowledge of their subject fields, deeper understanding of pedagogy, and more real-life experiences in schools. Others, however, are critical of extending the time required to prepare teachers (Hawley, 1987; Darrell, 1990). They argue that extended programs do not make efficient use of students' time and that the programs are too costly. Further, they point out that increased educational requirements are unwarranted until the complexity of teachers' work changes and until teachers accept higher standards of accountability.

New Curricula   Insufficient knowledge of subject matter, low standards, and curriculum fragmentation have been criticisms leveled at teacher preparation curricula for many years. Reform initiatives during the past decade have emphasized efforts to require more subject matter preparation and to reduce **curriculum fragmentation.**

To combat insufficient study of subject matter, many colleges and universities and some states (Connecticut and California, for example) now require that all elementary and secondary teachers complete a major in some subject field, such as biology, mathematics, or English, and that they demonstrate their mastery of these subject fields through testing. Many believe that this requirement is producing teachers who have stronger subject matter backgrounds and that the intellectual rigor of teacher education programs is rising.

One solution to curriculum fragmentation has been to design programs with **thematic orientations.** This means that programs are organized around a set of ideas and a view of teaching and learning. An example of a conceptual, or thematic, orientation is the organization of ideas used to write this book; that is, the major job of teaching is to develop self-regulated learners within democratic classrooms. Researchers believe that a thematic approach provides direction to faculty as they decide on the type of experiences to provide for students. It also serves as a roadmap to students as

they proceed through their program, helping them understand the purposes behind the various components therein.

Another solution to fragmentation has been to create student teams, called **cohorts**, in which a group of students proceeds through their training program together. Such long-term sharing of training experiences offers an effective method of socializing students into the culture of teaching. Cohort groups also provide powerful learning communities in which students support and learn from one another.

Clinical Experiences   Researchers such as Evertson, Hawley, and Zlotnik (1985) and Holmes (1990) have documented that once teacher candidates commence their field experiences and student teaching, the influence of cooperating teachers and the culture of their assigned school washes out the influences of university-based coursework. Reasons given for this situation are that teacher preparation programs have been too theoretical and shallow and have lacked strong links between college classrooms and the real world of schools. In the mid-1980s, two major reform groups fostered the creation of professional development schools (PDS) to correct this deficiency (Holmes, 1986; Carnegie, 1986). Modeled after teaching hospitals in medical education, PDSs are settings in which university and school-based faculty meet and experiment with innovative classroom practices. There, professors and classroom teachers work together to provide quality clinical experiences and internships for individuals learning to teach. Hundreds of PDSs have been developed over the past decade, and most observers believe they provide teacher candidates with superior field experiences (Holmes, 1990; National Commission, 1996).

Certification

Graduating from an accredited teacher education program is only the first step toward becoming a teacher. Obtaining a teaching certificate is a crucial second step.

Initial Certification

The certification process is regulated by state governments, and each state has its own certification requirements. A teaching certificate specifies the grade levels and subject areas an individual is qualified to teach. For instance, one might receive a kindergarten through twelfth grade, early childhood, elementary, middle, or secondary level certificate. To teach high school, and sometimes middle school, also requires a certificate in an appropriate subject area, such as English, mathematics, or social studies.

Nonteaching assignments, such as librarian and counseling, also require certificates. Although a teaching certificate is normally good only in the state that issued it, some states have **reciprocity agreements** with other states that allow teachers certified in one state to obtain certification in the other. Appendix B at the back of this text provides addresses of certification offices in each state, where you can get information about certification requirements and reciprocity.

Until recently, prospective teachers acquired certification simply by graduating from a state-accredited teacher education program or by completing a set of courses required for certification. Today, state requirements often extend beyond general courses and require that particular topics be covered in teacher education programs. Table 12.2 shows the broad requirements of the various states for an initial teaching certificate. As you can see, all states require a bachelor's degree and some study in general education, subject matter content, and pedagogy. Many also require study in special education, drug and alcohol abuse, and computers and technology. In addition, most states now require prospective teachers to pass a variety of tests or performance exams before they are issued a teaching certificate. Table 12.3 provides a state-by-state summary of assessment requirements for the initial teaching certificate. Forty-three states expect teacher candidates to demonstrate their command of basic reading, writing, and mathematics skills. Thirty states require a passing score on a subject matter exam, and 20 states require teachers to pass a general knowledge test. Twenty-six states test knowledge of teaching pedagogy, and 12 assess actual teaching performance.

The tests used in most states are those developed by the Educational Testing Service (ETS). Praxis I measures proficiency in reading, mathematics, and writing. Praxis II measures general knowledge, communication skills, and professional knowledge. Specialty tests are used to measure knowledge in most subject matter fields.

The performance assessments used for initial certification are most often developed by particular states and/or universities, and most are in their infancy. Teacher portfolios are also used to assess teaching performance. Although portfolios have long been used in fields such as music and the visual arts, they are relatively new to the field of teaching. Whereas portfolios in other fields may consist of illustrative pieces of an artist's or designer's creative work, a teacher's portfolio consists of selected pieces of work that demonstrate teaching effectiveness. Portfolio items might include a statement of the teacher's philosophy, sample lesson plans, and/or videos of lessons being taught. Most important, portfolios have examples of work performed by the teacher's students. As better evaluation procedures are developed, the use of portfolios to assess a candidate's qualification for certification is sure to spread.

Alternative Certification

Many reforms aim to raise the standards for teacher education and to make certification more performance based and demanding. At the same time, however, a number of states have initiated the practice of **alternative certification.** As the name implies, alternative certification allows college graduates who have not completed an approved teacher preparation program to be certified to teach. Alternative certification programs generally consist of 2 or 3 weeks of training before the start of a school year followed by an internship program that includes full-time work in a school plus a series of after school seminars. Advocates of alternative certification argue that this practice helps deal with anticipated shortages of qualified teachers in science and math and in poor urban and rural schools. They also maintain that it attracts talented young people into the teaching profession who do not want to go through traditional teacher education programs.

Although emergency certification has long been available to handle teacher shortages, using alternative certification to attract more talented people into the teaching profession raises serious concerns about both the expertise of the current teaching force and the quality of teacher preparation programs. If some teachers can be prepared adequately with just a few extra hours of instruction, then why is a multiyear preparation program necessary for others? Would we respond to a shortage of doctors or lawyers by licensing promising individuals for these jobs without appropriate training? The pros and cons of alternative certification are explored in the accompanying Issue Box.

Continuing Education and Advanced and National Certification

An initial teaching certificate is normally good for 2 to 4 years. To continue teaching requires additional education, which leads to an advanced certificate and tenure.

Advanced Certification

Advanced certificates, like initial certificates, are issued by state departments of education, the requirements of which vary from state to state. Tradi-

Table 12.2 Broad Academic Requirements for the Initial Teaching Certificate

	College BA/BS Degree	General Education	Studies of Subject Matter	Pedagogical Studies	Course Work In: Special Education	Course Work In: Computer Education
Alabama	X	X	X	X	X	X
Alaska	X	X	X	X	X	X
Arizona	X	X	X	X	X	X
Arkansas	X	X	X	X		
California	X		X	X	X	X
Colorado (1)	X	X	X	X	X	
Connecticut	X	X	X	X	X	
Delaware	X	X	X	X	X	
D.C.	X	X	X	X	X	X
Florida	X	X	X	X	X	
Georgia (1)	X	X	X	X	X	
Hawaii	X	X	X			
Idaho	X	X	X			
Illinois	X	X	X	X	X	
Indiana	X	X	X	X	X	
Iowa (1)	X	X	X	X		
Kansas	X	X	X	X	X	X
Kentucky	X	X	X	X	X	X
Louisiana	X	X	X	X		
Maine	X	X	X	X	X	X
Maryland	X	X	X	X	X	
Massachusetts	X	X	X	X	X	X
Michigan	X	X	X	X	X	
Minnesota	X	X	X	X		
Mississippi	X	X	X	X	X	
Missouri	X	X	X	X	X	X
Montana	X	X	X	X		
Nebraska (1)	X	X	X	X	X	
Nevada	X	X	X	X		
New Hampshire	X	X	X	X	X	X
New Jersey	X	X	X	X		
New Mexico	X	X	X	X	X	X
New York	X	X	X	X	X	
North Carolina	X	X	X	X	X	X
North Dakota	X	X	X	X	X	
Ohio	X	X	X	X	X	X
Oklahoma	X	X	X	X	X	
Oregon	X		X	X	X	
Pennsylvania	X	X	X	X	X	X
Rhode Island	X	X	X	X	X	
South Carolina	X	X	X	X	X	X
South Dakota	X	X	X	X	X	X
Tennessee	X	X	X	X	X	X
Texas	X	X	X	X	X	X
Utah	X	X	X	X	X	X
Vermont	X	X	X	X	X	X
Virginia	X	X	X	X	X	
Washington	X		X	X	X	X
West Virginia	X	X	X	X	X	X
Wisconsin	X	X	X	X	X	
Wyoming	X	X	X	X	X	X

Source: After National Association of State Directors of Teacher Education and Certification 1996–1997.

Table 12.3 Assessment Requirements for the Initial Teaching Certificate

	Basic Skills Exam:				Subject Matter Exam	General Knowledge Exam	Knowledge of Teaching Exam	Assessment of Teaching Performance
	Reading	Math	Writing	Spelling				
Alabama	X	X	X	X	X		X	X
Alaska								
Arizona	X	X						
Arkansas	X	X	X		X		X	
California	X	X	X		X			X
Colorado	X	X	X		X	X	X	
Connecticut	X	X	X		X			
Delaware	X	X	X					
D.C.	X	X	X		X			X
Florida	X	X	X		X	X	X	X
Georgia					X			
Hawaii	X	X	X		X		X	X
Idaho								
Illinois	X	X	X		X			
Indiana	X		X		X	X	X	
Iowa								
Kansas	X	X	X				X	
Kentucky	X	X	X	X	X	X	X	X
Louisiana	X	X	X		X	X	X	X
Maine						X	X	
Maryland	X		X	X	X		X	
Massachusetts					X			
Michigan	X	X	X		X	X		
Minnesota	X	X	X					
Mississippi	X	X	X		X	X	X	
Missouri	X	X	X	X	X			
Montana	X	X	X			X	X	
Nebraska	X	X	X					
Nevada	X	X	X		X		X	
New Hampshire	X	X	X					
New Jersey					X	X		X
New Mexico	X	X	X			X	X	
New York						X	X	
North Carolina	X	X	X		X		X	
North Dakota	X					X	X	
Ohio	X	X	X		X	X	X	
Oklahoma	X	X	X		X			X
Oregon	X	X	X		X	X	X	X
Pennsylvania	X		X		X	X	X	
Rhode Island	X	X	X	X		X	X	
South Carolina	X	X	X		X		X	
South Dakota	X	X	X		X			X
Tennessee	X	X	X		X	X	X	X
Texas	X	X	X		X		X	
Utah								
Vermont								
Virginia	X	X	X		X	X	X	
Washington	X	X	X					
West Virginia	X	X	X		X			X
Wisconsin	X	X	X					
Wyoming								

Source: After National Association of State Directors of Teacher Education and Certification 1996–1997.

tionally, most states issue a continuing or advanced certificate after teachers have taught successfully for 2 or 3 years and have acquired additional college course work, usually the equivalent of a master's degree. As with initial certification, continuing certification is becoming more demanding as teachers are asked to demonstrate their effectiveness through a variety of assessment devices.

Some states (Connecticut and New Mexico, for example) have mentoring and assessment programs for beginning teachers. In these states, experienced teachers are assigned as mentors who help new teachers develop their teaching skills. Beginning teachers are expected to demonstrate under classroom conditions their knowledge of subject matter and pedagogy. In some states, teams of observers consisting of experienced teachers and college professors periodically visit beginning teachers' classrooms during their first and second years to judge their competence on predetermined criteria.

Most often, the observation instruments used in beginning teacher assessments are developed by state departments of education. Some states, however, use Praxis III, an assessment tool specifically developed by ETS to judge the classroom performance of beginning teachers. Praxis III employs trained local observers who use a common framework of 19 criteria divided into four domains to evaluate the skills of teachers in their own classrooms. The evaluation also includes interviews and analysis of such written documents as lesson plans, curriculum materials, and teacher-made assessment devices. Praxis III is intended for use during a teacher's first year of teaching.

Other states require beginning teachers to develop portfolios during their first and second years of teaching. These portfolios are then judged by a team of assessors at the end of the second or the beginning of a teacher's third year and, if found satisfactory, lead to an advanced teaching certificate and tenure.

National Certification

In 1986, the Carnegie Task Force on Teaching As a Profession recommended establishing a career ladder for teachers and creation of a national board for regulating advanced certification. The National Board for Professional Teaching Standards (NBPTS) was formed the following year and is currently governed by a 63-member board of directors, mostly kindergarten through twelfth grade teachers but also including administrators, curriculum specialists, state and local officials, union and business leaders, and college and university professors. This national board designed procedures to assess the competence of experienced teachers, and it issues a national teaching certificate to those who pass its rigorous standards. National certification is voluntary, and the national certificate is not intended to replace the continuing or advanced certificate offered by the states. Currently, there are no specific extrinsic rewards, such as a higher salary, that accompany national certification. However, some teacher groups argue that for national certification to become wide spread will require a reward system.

When fully realized, the NBPTS will offer certificates in more than 30 fields, categorized by subject matter and developmental level of students. Certification will be available to teachers either as generalists or specialists in subject areas or special education. Currently the board recognizes four developmental levels:

- Early childhood (ages 3 to 8).
- Middle childhood (ages 7 to 12).
- Early adolescence (ages 11 to 15).
- Adolescence and young adulthood (ages 14 to 18+).

Each set of standards is grounded in the NBPTS policy statement, "What Teachers Should Know and Be Able to Do," and is guided by the five general propositions illustrated in Figure 12.4.

Systems of advanced certification are well established in other professions, such as medicine and accounting. Educators anticipate that advanced and national teaching certification will enable schools to develop more appropriate teaching assignments as well as to attract and to retain talented young people with the promise of career advancement, better compensation, more congenial working environments, and higher prestige. The NBPTS certification processes stress portfolio development, collegiality, self-reflection, and intellectual challenge. Some believe that their efforts and approach will gain the teaching profession a new level of professionalism.

Tenure

Chapter 10 defined *tenure* as a legal right that provides teachers with a continuing contract from which they can be terminated only on the basis of specific legal causes. Tenure guarantees threatened teachers with due process rights, including formal notice of charges and a hearing in which they can defend themselves.

The first state to enact tenure was New Jersey, in 1909. At that time, tenure was considered a desirable way to provide more stability in the teaching force. The job security of tenure, educators believed, would offset the low wages most teachers received. Tenure represented a means of protecting teachers from the nepotism and political patronage practiced in many local communities and from arbitrary dismissal on the basis of the religious, political, or moral views of a particular community group.

For most of the twentieth century, tenure was seen in a positive light. However, several developments after World War II changed this situation. Massive teacher shortages during the 1950s and 1960s simultaneously led many poorly prepared teachers to the profession and caused a significant rise in teachers' salaries. During this same time, an increasing number of individuals began to think of teaching as a life-long career rather than an interim job until something else came along. In addition, the women's movement encouraged expanded career expectations for female teachers, and fewer left teaching to raise their families as they had in earlier times. Thus, the percentage of older, higher paid,

and tenured teachers increased substantially between 1950 and 1975.

For a number of reasons, by the 1970s, politicians as well as the general public began questioning the desirability of tenure, and in the 1990s, tenure was formally challenged in many states. Critics of tenure argue that teachers no longer need it, because they are protected by the strength of powerful teachers' unions. They also maintain that too many incompetent teachers are protected under tenure laws thus making it extremely difficult and expensive to remove them from the profession.

Teacher's unions, however, maintain that the protections provided by tenure are as important today as they were at the beginning of the century. They point out that teachers are politically vulnerable and at the mercy of elected school boards. Without tenure, boards could dismiss teachers simply for holding unpopular political views or so that younger, less expensive teachers could take their places.

Alternative Routes to Certification

Throughout American history, the preparation of teachers has been perceived as inadequate. As a result, there have been repeated attempts to extend and enrich teacher preparation programs. In the nineteenth century, for example, 2-year normal schools were created to provide teachers with post-high school preparation in their subject fields and to introduce them to the study of pedagogy. Eventually, people agreed that these 2-year programs were inadequate, and by the middle of the twentieth century, most had given way to four year bachelor's degree programs that included a supervised student teaching experience. This trend to expand and enrich teacher preparation programs still continues, with many states now requiring new teachers to acquire both a bachelor's degree in a subject field and a master's degree in education. This latest extension usually requires a 5-year preparation program. Some reformers even propose that teacher preparation be extended to a 6-year program, but such programs are not yet enacted on a statewide basis.

Some reformers have focused on the need for longer and more rigorous teacher preparation programs, but others have been so critical of these programs that they have been willing, particularly in times of teacher shortages, to admit individuals into teaching who have not completed any formal preparation. Known earlier as *emergency certification* and today as *alternative certification,* this route into teaching allows individuals with liberal arts degrees to begin teaching after a brief summer school orientation program. Following these abbreviated preparation programs, students are usually placed under the supervision of an experienced, mentor teacher. Needless to say, the practice of providing alternative certification is controversial.

On one side of this issue are those who argue that alternative routes into teaching are good because they help break the hold that the educational establishment (teachers' unions and schools of education) has

Although policy makers and legislators continue to talk about eliminating tenure, such actions are currently unlikely given the current power of teachers' unions.

TEACHER ORGANIZATIONS AND COLLECTIVE BARGAINING

Teacher Organizations

Much of the pressure to enhance the status of teaching and to establish it more fully as a profession comes from the many teachers' organizations. Currently, there are over 300 associations organized to help teachers and to improve the quality of education. Some of these professional organizations exist to provide leadership to teachers regardless of their teaching specialties. An example of this type of organization is the Association for Supervision and Curriculum Development (ASCD). ASCD publishes a monthly journal, *Educational Leadership*, that summarizes important research and analyzes policy issues of interest to teachers. It also has local units in every state that produce newsletters and hold regular meetings.

Other teacher organizations focus on the needs of teachers in particular teaching fields or on those who teach at particular grade levels. The National Council of Teachers of Mathematics (NCTM) and the National Council for the Social Studies (NCSS) are examples of subject-specific organizations. Alternatively, the National Association for the Education of Young Children (NAEYC) is an example of an age-related organization that addresses the concerns of teachers of young children. Table 12.4 contains a sample of the most common general and specific teacher organizations.

ISSUES EXTRA

Continued

on the profession. These critics argue that alternative arrangements encourage bright, energetic, liberal arts graduates to enter the field without taking a lot of "mickey mouse" education courses. People who hold this position believe that effective teaching stems mostly from individuals' command of and enthusiasm for their subject matter. They believe that courses in human learning, development, and pedagogy are unnecessary and that they deter many eager young people from becoming teachers. They also believe teaching is best learned on the job, thus negating the need for college-based programs.

On the other side of this issue are those who believe that alternative routes into teaching are shortsighted and harmful. They argue that knowledge and enthusiasm for subject matter, although important, do not provide an adequate basis for teaching, particularly in today's schools that must serve a highly diversified student population. They also point out that most alternative-route teachers secure jobs in the neediest schools, namely those in rural and inner-city areas in which there are large populations of at-risk and immigrant students. Thus, school districts deploy the least prepared teachers in the toughest teaching situations. Conversely, graduates of college-based programs seem to get the jobs in more attractive, affluent suburban school districts. Those who disagree with alternative certification point to evidence suggesting that enthusiastic liberal arts graduates, having acquired easy entry, show less long-term commitment to a teaching career. Within a few years, many go back to graduate school where they prepare for college teaching or for careers in other professions, such as law or medicine.

What do you think? In the long-run do alternative-route programs provide better teachers for children and youth? What about the short term? Would you consider alternative certification? Why or why not?

Figure 12.4 **National Boards Standards**

1. *Teachers are committed to students and their learning.* They understand how students grow and mature within a certain developmental level. They are skilled at coming to know students' interests, views, and communities. They are committed to equitable practice and act accordingly.

2. *Teachers know the subjects they teach and how to teach those subjects to students.* They grasp the major ideas and key facts within their disciplines. They keep up with the emerging theories and debates in their fields. They possess a repertoire of analogies, experiments, tasks, metaphors, and the like, and so can help students recognize key dilemmas and grasp important concepts, events, or phenomena.

3. *Teachers are responsible for managing and monitoring student learning.* They create an environment that encourages risk-taking, inquiry, persistence, and collaboration, and fosters democratic values. They can assess student progress, and they teach students how to evaluate their own progress. They are adept at grouping students and at regulating the pace of instruction. They recognize the teachable moment and know how to seize it.

4. *Teachers think systematically about their practice and learn from experience.* They reflect on their practice to strengthen and improve it. They seek the advice of students, colleagues, administrators, parents, teacher educators, and others to reexamine and rethink their own approaches.

5. *Teachers are members of learning communities.* They work well not only with students but also with adults—both parents and professional colleagues. They contribute to the intellectual life of the school. And they advance the profession in a variety of ways: for example, mentoring, presenting, publishing, serving on task forces and committees at the local, state, or national levels.

Like ASCD, subject and age-specific teacher organizations publish journals and have local affiliates that hold meetings for teachers in particular states or regions. They work to promote their fields and to encourage reform. If you want to grow as a teacher, you will want to join some of these organizations and through them build networks of colleagues in your field.

The two organizations that have the most influence over educational policy, teachers' salaries, and teaching are the National Education Association and

Table 12.4 **Examples of Teacher Organizations**

General Focus	Subject- or Age-Specific Focus
American Education Research Association (AERA)	American Council for Teachers of Foreign Languages (ACTFL)
American Federation of Teachers (AFT)	American Home Economics Association (AHEA)
Association for Supervision and Curriculum Development (ASCD)	Association for Education Communication and Technology (AECT)
National Education Association (NEA)	International Reading Association (IRA)
Phi Delta Kappa (PDK)	Music Teachers National Association (MTNA)
	National Art Education Association (NAEA)
	National Council for Social Studies (NCSS)
	National Council of Teachers of English (NCTE)
	National Council of Teachers of Mathematics (NCTM)
	National Science Teachers Association (NSTA)

the American Federation of Teachers. You read a brief history of these two organizations in the introduction to Part V. Some additional information about each organization follows.

National Education Association

The NEA is the larger of the two associations, with a 1995 membership of 2.2 million. Of these, 1.9 million are classroom teachers, 103,000 are professional support staff (guidance counselors, librarians, and administrators), and the remainder are college professors, auxiliary staff (school secretaries, teacher aides, cafeteria workers, bus drivers, and custodians), retired members, and students. (NEA Handbook, 1994–1995). The NEA was formed in the middle part of the nineteenth century and reflected the needs of teachers and schools of that time, namely to advance the interest of teaching and to promote the cause of public education. Until after World War II, the NEA was dominated by school administrators, and its policies were often consistent with the larger educational establishment such as state departments of education and local school boards. At the same time, the membership of the NEA was primarily classroom teachers, and this constituency has dominated the organization increasingly since the 1960s. Today the NEA has numerous standing committees at both the state and national levels to provide advocacy and support for teachers, to enhance the teaching profession, and to improve education. Member services include the following.

- Publications that provide statistical information to the profession and the public as well as information about NEA's policies and programs.

- Research services for teachers, including publications that synthesize important research information.

- A wide variety of economic services connected to salaries, insurance, retirement, etc.

In addition, the NEA has used its resources to promote innovation in local schools and school districts. Its most important actions, however, remain in the political arena, where the NEA advocates legislation that supports education and the teaching profession and provides considerable financial support to proeducation political candidates.

American Federation of Teachers

In contrast to the NEA, the AFT was organized in the early part of the twentieth century with a single purpose—to improve the working conditions of teachers. School administrators were never permitted membership in the AFT, and early on the organization aligned itself with organized labor. Where the union movement was strong, such as in New England and in the urban areas, the AFT grew rapidly and greatly influenced educational developments. On the other hand, many teachers in small cities and towns without a strong labor movement spurned the AFT. Like the NEA, the AFT offers a variety of publishing and economic services.

To summarize, the NEA gradually moved from an administrator- to a teacher- dominated organization. Inasmuch as the kindergarten through twelfth grade teaching force was overwhelmingly female, so was the membership of the NEA, except for its leadership. Its roots were primarily in suburban and rural areas, and it remained independent of any labor affiliation. The AFT, in contrast, found its primary constituency in urban areas, especially where there were secondary schools with a higher proportion of male faculty. The AFT, affiliated with and supported by the American Federation of Labor (AFL), developed an aggressive, hard bargaining stance on bread-and-butter issues such as salaries and working conditions several years before the NEA did.

Collective Bargaining

From the 1950s to the present, the NEA and AFT competed for members and the right to represent teachers in collective bargaining. Early on, the NEA maintained the position that it was a professional organization and rejected as unprofessional the strike tactics adopted by the AFT. By contrast, the AFT objected to the presence of administrators within the NEA membership, considering them "management" in the traditional sense of that term. The AFT was the first to use striking as a means of gaining economic benefits and better working conditions for teachers, but by the late 1960s, the NEA was similarly involved. Whereas both organizations made extensive use of the strike from the 1960s until the early 1980s, their use of this bargaining tactic has decreased significantly since that time as Table 12.5 shows.

Today, the power of teachers' associations and the contractual work rules they have secured through collective bargaining are controversial. Some teachers in the AFT and the NEA maintain that without continued vigilance and tough bargaining, many of their economic gains over the past 30 years will be lost. Many concerned citizens, school reformers, and some teachers, on the other hand, consider today's teachers' associations large bureaucratic organizations whose agendas focus on their memberships' well being at the expense of providing quality

Table 12.5   Approximate Number of Teacher Strikes from 1966 to 1987

Years	Number
1966	30 per year
1967	76 per year
1968	88 per year
1968–1975	Over 100 per year
1975–1980	Over 200 per year
1981–1987	Fewer than 100 per year (except in 1984)

Source: Margaret Tannenbaum, personal records.

education for young people. This negative perception of teachers and their unions led both Albert Shanker, president of the AFT until his death in 1997, and Bob Chase, president of the NEA to urge their membership to forego "old-style" unionism, which pitted management against rank-and-file teachers, and to adopt new strategies to address the demands of education in the information age. They argue that teachers today have won their voice and that they should now use their collective power to improve the quality of education as well as the teaching profession. Recently Shanker and Chase made major pronouncements about their visions for their organizations' policies in the future (Checkly, 1995; Case, 1997; Mezzacappa, 1997). The new style of unionism they support no longer seeks to separate managers from the rank and file. Instead, it emphasizes the importance of administrators, teachers, and parents working together toward making schools better. Shanker cited due process agreements as a case in point. He said that "although such accords provide for job security, they may also make it far too difficult to fire unfit teachers." "Fairness," Shanker insisted, "should not shield mediocrity. We fought to have due process, to give teachers a fair trial," he said. "We did not fight to protect incompetence" (Checkly, 1995). Chase, on the other hand, said that "our challenge is to break free of the adversarial style and constricted scope that still characterize all too much collective bargaining and move toward a new collaboration that is not sleeping with the enemy . . . [but] is about waking up to our shared stake in reinvigorating public education" (Mezzacappa, 1997, p. R4).

In light of their common purposes, the NEA and the AFT have been discussing merger for the past 2 decades. Talks stopped on more than one occasion because of disagreements regarding policy or practice. However, in 1995, the NEA Representative Assembly voted again to engage in merger discussions. Many believe a common organization could make a major contribution to the enhancement of the teaching profession. Others believe that it would concentrate too much power in a single organization.

A LOOK AHEAD

Over the past decade, every aspect of teaching and the teaching profession has come under intense scrutiny. Reform proposals address the ways teachers are prepared, the procedures used to certify them, and the means for keeping them abreast of best practice throughout their careers. These proposals often detail practices that contrast sharply with those followed for most of the twentieth century, and there are signs that many suggested reforms are taking hold. Teaching appears to be gaining in its mission to become a true profession. Keep in mind, though, that attempts to reform education have faltered in the past, and it is always possible that current efforts will stall or be redirected. In the event that recent trends continue, here is our analysis of what the years ahead may hold for teaching and the teaching profession.

Research and Performance-Based Teacher Education

It is highly likely that current efforts to extend and codify the knowledge base on teaching will continue. Most teacher educators believe that three decades of educational research have produced a substantial body of knowledge that explains learning and informs teaching. There appears to be a strong consensus that the principles found in the INTASC standards and the propositions put forth by National Board for Professional Teaching Standards have helped the profession classify what effective teachers should know and be able to do. Further, these principles and propositions are built into the NCATE standards and will influence curriculum development in those teacher education institutions seeking national accreditation. This knowledge base will thus form the core of teacher preparation programs in the twenty-first century.

As with other professions, teaching is a performance-based occupation that must provide opportunities to link knowledge to practice. This is why professional development schools, similar to teaching hospitals, are likely to continue to spread. PDSs are an excellent vehicle, not available in the past, to expose prospective teachers to the expertise of university professors and practicing teachers simultaneously and to link the expertise of both groups for the purpose of providing high-quality clinical experiences.

The goals of the professional development schools, however, are both difficult to achieve and costly to implement. Building partnerships between colleges and public schools is time consuming and requires coordination and compromise. Currently, there are few incentives to motivate practicing teachers to take time away from their own students to assist with the preparation of new teachers. Similarly, there are few rewards for college professors to spend their days in schools instead of in their university offices.

According to Darling-Hammond and Cobb (1995), of the 1,250 plus institutions that currently prepare teachers, only slightly over 500 are accredited by NCATE. Further, there has been considerable resistance in states such as West Virginia when state agencies have tried to require NCATE accreditation for all teacher preparation institutions. Although the movement toward national professional accreditation is strong at this point, there is no telling how far the movement will spread. Indeed, currently there are counter movements under way arguing against a single set of national standards. Given the history of education in America, this should not be surprising. We are well advised to keep in mind that all innovations are fragile and the reform tasks at hand are great.

Testing to Assure Teacher Quality

Over the past decade, considerable progress has been made in raising standards for teachers. We are much clearer today regarding the work expected of teachers, and we have better ways of assessing the quality of that work. Assessments are now used to make decisions about who should get into teacher education programs, who should receive an initial teaching certificate, and who should continue in the profession. Furthermore, the more sophisticated means of assessments, such as performance tests and portfolios, can measure a wide range of attributes—subject matter expertise, pedagogical knowledge, use of teaching strategies, and teachers' cultural adaptability.

Many of the reforms aimed at increasing the rigor of and strengthening assessment for certification are currently taking hold. As Table 12.4 showed, well over half the states currently require some form of teacher testing before certification and others are in the process of starting this practice. At the same time, many unprepared teachers continue to enter the profession through alternative certification programs, or through programs that are poorly run. For instance, the National Commission on Teaching and America's Future (1996) reported that approximately 25 percent of newly hired teachers lack qualifications for their jobs and that more than 12 percent enter their classrooms through alternative certification that provided no formal training. In short, although progress has been made in upgrading the preparation of teachers, there is still widespread work to be done in devising procedures to assure

that fully trained and qualified teachers are found in every classroom.

Restructured Schools for Student and Teacher Success

A final point to consider is that for teaching to become a true profession, changes must be made in the ways schools are organized. We treated this topic in previous chapters so will only mention it again here. You will remember reading that current trends aim at making schools and classrooms more flexible and more responsive to diverse student populations. These trends focus on more choice for parents and greater authority and autonomy for teachers. Ways are being sought to restructure the school day so that teachers have time to work with one another and parents can be more highly involved in their children's schools. Restructured schools often have flattened hierarchies and changing roles for principals and teachers: Principals are often found teaching, and teachers carrying out leadership responsibilities. School, or site-based, councils already exist in many schools, involving administrators, teachers, and parents in joint decisions about budget expenditures, personnel selection, curriculum, and various daily activities affecting the school.

Many school-restructuring experiments are currently under way, and we expect this trend to increase. For the most part, reforms are supported by teachers' associations as well as school boards and parent groups. As always, any school restructuring runs counter to some very long traditions in American education, such as age-graded classrooms, teacher autonomy, and a hierarchial structure in which principals or other supervisors monitor and evaluate teachers' work. School councils that empower teachers and parents also encroach on the decades-old traditional authority of school boards and state education agencies. Recent studies document how many school restructuring efforts have not been widely implemented, or if they have, how they have had only marginal effects on the ways teachers conduct their work (Lee & Smith, 1996).

We believe, however, that the teacher professionalization reforms you have read about in this book will be around when you begin your teaching career. They will require diligent preparation on your part but should also lead to greater rewards. Implementing and sustaining the reforms currently under way in this field will be hard work but work required of any who want teaching to acquire the status of a true profession in the twenty-first century.

SUMMARY

- Professionals in all fields have acquired and can use a specialized body of knowledge, are respected by the larger community, are allowed autonomy to carry out their work, and hold themselves accountable for ethical behavior and best practice.

- Most observers conclude that teaching in the United States falls short of full professional status when compared to other professions or to teaching in other countries.

- The field of teaching, unlike that of medicine or architecture, does not have a fully defined knowledge base. This has led to fragmented teacher education programs and has allowed individuals to enter teaching with little or no special preparation. However, there have been several efforts over the past decade to clarify and codify the knowledge base on teaching.

- Although society entrusts its children to teachers, the teaching profession does not command as high a level of respect or income as other professions do. Some people say this is true because teaching has traditionally been a woman's profession; others believe it is because teachers' work is not so complex as work performed by other professionals.

- The client relationship for teaching is different from that of most other professions. Children, the clients, have little choice in their teachers, and they are required to attend school. Similarly, teachers have little choice in their clients; they must accept all students assigned to them.

- Teachers have considerable autonomy in deciding what to teach and how. However, our system of democracy and local control serves to confine some aspects of this autonomy.

- Professionals in all fields go through a three-phase process before being granted a permanent license to practice. They must be accepted into and complete an initial training program; they must complete a clinical phase and demonstrate their knowledge and skill through testing; and they must complete continuing education and obtain an advanced certificate.

- During the past decade, colleges and universities established higher standards for admission into teacher education programs. Today, most programs require students to have at least a 2.5 GPA and a command of reading, writing, and mathematics before they are admitted.

- Slightly more than 500 colleges and universities that prepare teachers are accredited by the National Council for the Accreditation of Teacher Education (NCATE). Over 700 do *not* have national accreditation but instead are approved by various state processes. This has led to wide variance in the quality of teacher candidates and in the coherence of teacher preparation programs in the United States.

- Reform initiatives over the past 2 decades focused on correcting many of the identified weaknesses in teacher education. Time to prepare for teaching was extended; more integrated and better articulated curricula were developed; candidates were required to have stronger subject matter and liberal arts backgrounds; and professional development schools were created to afford better clinical experiences.

- The teacher certification process in most states is regulated by state governments. Over the past 2 decades, states have increased the requirements for obtaining a teaching certificate. In many states, candidates must not only complete an accredited teacher education program, they must also demonstrate through testing a mastery of the knowledge and skills required of teachers.

- Although certification requirements have expanded, a large number of individuals still enter teaching through alternative certification programs. In general, these programs provide little formal training and rely on on-the-job assistance for full-time novice teachers.

- An initial teaching certificate is good for only 2 to 4 years. To gain advanced certification, teachers in most states must successfully complete 2 to 3 years of teaching, acquire additional education, and demonstrate their effectiveness through a variety of assessment devices.

- The National Board for Professional Teaching Standards was created in 1987 to provide national certification for teachers. Today, national certification is voluntary and does not replace the advanced certificate offered by the states.

- Tenure is a legal right that provides teachers with a continuing contract and protects them from unfair dismissal. Today, a portion of the general public and some politicians question the desirability of tenure. They believe that it gives teachers too much power and protects incompetent teachers.

- There are over 300 associations organized to help teachers and to improve the quality of education. Some of these are general in focus; others focus on particular grade levels or on teaching specialty fields.

- The two largest and most influential teacher associations are the American Federation of Teachers (AFT) and the National Education Association (NEA). The NEA dates back to the mid-nineteenth century and has had its strength in suburban and rural areas. The AFT dates to the early twentieth century and has found its primary constituency in urban areas.

- Traditionally, the AFT developed an aggressive collective bargaining stance, which included the use of teacher strikes to obtain economic concessions. For the past 20 years, the NEA has used the same collective bargaining tactics. Both organizations are in the process of developing a new style of unionism, partially in reaction to the negative public perception that teachers are more concerned with their own economic well being than they are with trying to provide quality education for children.

- Over the past decade, many reform proposals have addressed the ways teachers are prepared and certified and the nature of the shortcomings of the teaching profession. It is likely that the progress made to improve teaching and the teaching profession will continue in the years ahead. We can expect continued efforts to clarify and codify the knowledge base on teaching, to raise standards for teachers, and to use tests for the purpose of assuring teacher quality.

- All efforts to reform teaching and the teaching profession are difficult and complex

and will require the continued vigilance and work by twenty-first century teachers.

READINGS FOR THE PROFESSIONAL

Eaton. W. H. *The American Federation of Teachers, 1916–1961: A History of the Movement.* Carbondale, IL: Southern Illinois University Press, 1975.
This book provides an interesting historical account of events that shaped teacher activism during the first half of the twentieth century.

Goodlad, J. *Teachers for Our Nation's Schools.* San Francisco: Jossey-Bass, 1991.
This book presents the results of a 5-year study of teacher training programs in the United States. Many contemporary teacher education reform initiatives today stem from the recommendations made in this book.

Murray, F. B. (ed.). *The Teacher Educator's Handbook: Building a Knowledge Base for the Preparation of Teachers.* San Francisco: Jossey-Bass, 1996.
This book is a contemporary explication of what teachers should know and be able to do along with many recommendations about best practice in teacher education.

Purkey, W. W. & J. M. Novak. *Inviting School Success: A Self-Concept Approach to Teaching, Learning, and Democratic Practice.* Belmont, CA:Wadsworth, 1996.
This book presents what has come to be known as invitational theory, based on the idea that education is an imaginative act of hope. It connects educational activities and democratic practices by demonstrating how everyone and everything in and around classrooms, schools, and the larger culture add to or subtract from the educational experiences of individuals and groups.

Sarason, S. *The Case for Change: Rethinking the Preparation of Educators.* San Francisco: Jossey-Bass, 1993.
Sarason advocates a complete conceptual redesign of teacher education programs, arguing that current programs do not prepare educators for what life is really like in schools.

CHAPTER 13

Ethical Dimensions of Teaching

Your school has mandated that all its teachers use direct instruction for all lessons, believing that it represents the single most effective pedagogy available. Being a kindergarten teacher, your knowledge of research together with your own teaching experience lead you to conclude that a constructivist, child-centered pedagogy is more developmentally appropriate for your students. How should you respond to the district's mandate?

Your local school board has approved the establishment of a gay and lesbian student club at the high school where you teach social studies. You and a small group of parents attend a church whose religious values forbid homosexuality. In addition, the local newspaper has recently published a survey indicating that a slim majority of citizens also disapprove of such clubs. How should you respond to the board's decision?

You are a lead teacher in a suburban junior high school. On your way home from a late-night budget committee meeting, you decide to stop off at a neighborhood bar for a nightcap. To your surprise, an eighth-grade English teacher from your school is dancing topless there. Upon investigation, you discover that she is moonlighting to support her sick mother. How should you respond—do you report her, or should you just forget about it?

Giving thought to the ethical dimensions of teaching and schooling is often overlooked amid the press of more immediate curriculum, instruction, and management concerns. However, as the problem situations listed here make clear, moral dilemmas are thrust on teachers daily. Every decision you make, every action you take, has an impact on someone's life and, consequently, takes on moral overtones. Should you rebuke Johnny for side-talking or ignore him? Should you refer Malekia for counseling or wait until you have additional information? Should you hold a classroom meeting today or present a lesson on self-esteem? Decisions such as these about teaching, students, or colleagues are judgment calls, and all judgment involves consideration of values. Teachers, in short, are moral agents. For beginners, this can be a daunting and confusing role.

Because of the centrality of values to teaching, this chapter is about becoming an ethical teacher. We begin by laying the groundwork in highlighting the history of moral education, discuss research on moral development, examine ethics in the classroom, and close with a discussion of the code of ethics for educators.

First, however, let's define a few key terms. We will frequently use the terms *moral, ethical, values,* and *character*. **Moral** refers to commonly accepted standards of right and wrong, whereas **ethical** indi-

History of Moral Education

Research on Moral Development
  Piagetian Perspective
  Kohlberg's Stage Theory
  Kohlberg's Critics

Ethics in the Classroom
  Should Morals Be Taught in the Classroom?
  Teaching Values
    Research-Based Principles
    Social Learning Principles
    Parenting Applied to Teaching

Classroom Research
Moral Discussion
Service Learning
Additional Tools
The Moral Development of Teachers

Professional Ethics
  Codes of Ethics
  Moral Problem Solving
  Becoming an Ethical Teacher

Summary

Readings for the Professional

cates high standards of behavior of a particular group, that is, a group or culture's system of moral principles. **Character** means moral excellence, and **values** are principles or ideals that are intrinsically desirable. There is a lot of overlap here, and in this chapter, we use these terms interchangeably.

HISTORY OF MORAL EDUCATION

Interest in moral education has been increasing since the late 1980s. Many believe that recent social changes in family structures, the status of women, and attitudes about sexuality, coupled with a heightened preoccupation with material gain, represent a fraying of the moral fabric of our society. One response to this perceived social decay has been to promote a return to moral education in our schools.

As we made clear in the introduction to Part V, this is by no means the first time that Americans have looked to the schools for moral leadership. During the eighteenth and nineteenth centuries, you may recall, teachers were expected to promote moral development through both personal example and explicit instruction. The Bible served as the primary vehicle for drumming good behavior and a sense of moral rectitude into children. When Horace Mann and other nineteenth century reformers tried to separate the common school from specific religious doctrines, many religious factions created their own schools in order to inculcate their children with their own moral and religious outlook (Sockett, 1995).

As disputes raged regarding which version of the Bible should guide instruction, a former frontier teacher named William Holmes McGuffey began writing a series of graded readers intended to impart moral values as well as to teach basic reading skills. McGuffey's readers contained some Bible selections but also added poems, epic stories, and exhortations to encourage honesty, love of neighbor, kindness to animals, hard work, thriftiness, patriotism, and courage in young people (Lickona, 1993). First published in 1836, the readers eventually sold approximately 122 million copies. See Figure 13.1 for an excerpt from a reader.

Americans' thinking about moral education began shifting in the early twentieth century (Lickona, 1993). The religious tone of the previous century was gradually replaced by a more secular attitude that arose from the confluence of two important ideas: Darwinism and logical positivism. **Darwinism**, the idea that life is continuously evolving, not static,

Figure 13.1 **Excerpt from a McGuffey Reader**

Lazy Ned

" 'Tis royal fun," cried lazy Ned.
"To coast upon my fine, new sled.
And beat the other boys;
But then, I cannot bear to climb
The tiresome hill, for every time
It more and more annoys."

So, while his schoolmates glided by,
And gladlly tugged uphill, to try
Another merry race,
Too indolent to share their plays,
Ned was compelled to stand and gaze,
While shivering in his place.

Thus, he would never take the pains
To seek the prize that labor gains,
Until the time had passed;
For, all his life, he dreaded still
The silly bugbear of *uphill,*
And died a dunce at last.

Source: From *McGuffey's Fourth Eclectic Reader* (1920).

led people to see both social and biological functioning in evolutionary terms. Rather than viewing morality as an absolute handed down by a creator, people began to see it as situational and changing. **Logical positivism**, a major philosophical thrust of the late nineteenth and early twentieth centuries, made a distinction between objective facts, ideas that could be proven, and values, which were emotionally driven opinions that could not be proven. Only ideas that could be objectively proven were thought to have merit, so the currency of morality based on faith declined in many circles. These two intellectual developments led people to see morality in a more relativistic light.

Still, adults worried about the values of their young. While the religious aspect of moral thinking declined, vigorous efforts were made between 1900 and the 1930s to promote what came to be called character, rather than moral, education. Its advocates hoped that the name change would reduce conflict about the religious aspect of moral education. In an interesting parallel with our own time, social critics in the early twentieth century believed that individual ethics were deteriorating. Pointing to immigration, industrialization, the First World War, revolution in Russia, and the relaxed attitudes of the Roaring Twenties, many concluded that moral standards needed to be strengthened and promulgated in schools (Leming, 1993).

Educators responded enthusiastically to the call for character education. In 1918, for example, the NEA declared that ethical character was a primary objective of schooling. The Children's Morality Code, developed in 1917 by the Character Education Institute of Washington, DC, consisted of 10 "laws of right living," and was used in schools across the country to guide character education. The 10 laws—self-control, good health, kindness, sportsmanship, self-reliance, duty, reliability, truth, good workmanship, and teamwork—were integrated into all aspects of schooling and were actively promoted in school clubs. Children were directly taught the code through a variety of subject matter lessons, and they recited pledges promising to keep the code.

This hortatory style of character education suffered a blow in 1930. After an extensive study involving over 10,000 pupils around the United States, researchers at Teachers College, Columbia University, concluded that character education had no influence on student conduct (Hartshorne & May, 1930).

> In schools where character education was taking place, the researchers created classroom situations that provided students with opportunities to cheat and to voluntarily engage in helping behavior. They found that the incidence of deceit varied widely in classrooms and schools and that deceit was situationally specific; honesty in one situation did not predict well to another ... they found no relationship between membership in organizations that purported to teach honesty and honest behavior. (Leming, 1993, p. 64)

By the 1950s, character education was virtually absent from the public schools. This lull did not last very long, however, as interest in ethics surged again during the 1960s and 1970s. The emphasis this time, though, was very different from previous eras. Rather than indoctrinating students into a particular set of moral standards, the new approaches focused on helping students reflect about ethical decisions. Two major views that gained widespread popularity were Kohlberg's focus on *moral reasoning* and an approach known as *values clarification*. **Values clarification** was a process by which teachers helped students clarify the values they held without making any judgments on the worth of those values (Raths, Harmin, & Simon, 1966). The goal was to illuminate values through asking questions and probing students' thinking, not to impose a set of moral rules on them. Values clarification was enormously popular, but research revealed that it, like the Children's Morality Code, had little effect on student conduct

(Leming, 1993). We discuss the impact of Kohlberg's moral reasoning research in the next section on moral development.

It is interesting to note that, although the details of moral education have changed over the years, several ideals at the heart of these programs, such as honesty, work, duty, and kindness, have remained intact. No doubt many today would interpret these values in different ways, but it is equally likely that most modern Americans subscribe to values like honesty and kindness in some form. The accompanying Global Box describes a school in India which serves students from several major religions and actively promotes values held in common across religions. The school's staff has found ways of teaching mutual understanding and a common moral code despite (or perhaps because of) their great religious diversity.

RESEARCH ON MORAL DEVELOPMENT

Piagetian Perspective

Children's intellectual development, which we discussed in Chapter 5, is paralleled by observable stages of moral development. Jean Piaget delved into both aspects of development. To study children's morality, Piaget observed them at play, noting their behavior in following the rules of the game, changing the rules, and cheating. He also interviewed children, as he did in his studies of their intellectual development, and posed dilemmas for them to solve. In one of these dilemmas, he described a child who was carrying 15 cups and accidentally dropped and broke them all, while another child broke only one cup but with malice aforethought. Piaget asked his respondents which child was naughtier, the child who broke many cups accidentally or the one who broke one cup on purpose.

Some of the children, termed **heteronomously moral**, looked at outcomes only, not intentions, and labeled as naughtier the child who accidentally broke 15 cups. Other children, at the **autonomous** level of moral development, realized that intentions play a key role in ethical behavior and considered the child who purposely broke one cup the naughtier one. Piaget's work was greatly amplified later by Kohlberg, but teachers can begin to gain some insight into how children think about behavior. As with intellectual development, Piaget provided evidence that younger children are much more concrete and may have difficulty with abstract ideas like intention.

Kohlberg's Stage Theory

Building from the early work of Piaget, Lawrence Kohlberg, a Harvard psychologist, devised a more elaborate stage theory for moral development. Kohlberg also relied heavily on dilemma-based interviews, and his initial work was conducted with young boys (Kohlberg, 1966). Kohlberg created a series of moral dilemmas he asked his interviewees to solve. One of the most famous is the Heinz dilemma. Heinz is married to a woman who is terminally ill. She needs a newly invented medication or she will certainly die. The medicine is very expensive, and Heinz asks everyone he knows to help him raise the needed cash. However, he falls short. He goes to the pharmacist, who also happens to be the drug's inventor, and asks him to give him the medicine anyway. The druggist refuses. The dilemma posed is: Should Heinz steal the drug to save his wife's life? Before reading on, think about your own response to this situation, and consider your reasons for the action you deem appropriate.

Kohlberg's interview process focused on the *reasons* respondents gave for a course of action, rather than the particular action itself. Based on the

GLOBAL

City Montessori School, Lucknow, India: Teaching Values in a Multicultural Setting

City Montessori School (CMS) in Lucknow, Uttar Pradesh, India, was established a mere 20 years ago. It now educates 19,000 students at 15 branches around the city. Its mission from the outset was to provide not only an excellent academic education for its kindergarten through twelfth grade student body, but also to provide for students' emotional and spiritual needs.

The curriculum, instruction, and organization of CMS is rooted in what the school terms *the four building blocks.* These building blocks form the basis for guiding and integrating education for the whole child. The first building block is *universal values,* and this is the cornerstone on which the other three are built. The universal values, derived from the world's major religious traditions, are kindness, compassion, cooperation, and responsibility. The other three building blocks, also springing from several religions, are excellence, global understanding, and service. CMS faculty and parents believe that a solid foundation in these values will best equip their students with the skills they will need to deal with the world's complex problems.

Teachers at CMS pursue the building blocks in an almost developmental way. In the primary grades, the main focus is on universal values. Teachers strive to help students develop character. The school believes that all young children can learn fundamental values like honesty and kindness. They also believe that knowledge is not enough, and that ideals must be put into practice. Values education is therefore woven into daily instruction. For example, if students are writing essays, the topic may be peace and unity. An art or drama project may be organized around an environmental theme. Each school day opens with a half-hour assembly run by students on topics linking moral action and civic issues. Teachers also explicitly teach commonalities in the value traditions of the world. Here, for example, is how the golden rule is expressed in a variety of religious traditions:

- Do unto others as you would have them do unto you. (Christianity)

- What is hateful to you, do not to your fellow man. That is the entire Law; all the rest is commentary. (Judaism)

- Hurt not others in ways that you yourself would find hurtful. (Buddhism)

rationales his subjects gave him, Kohlberg posited a 6-stage process for the development of moral reasoning. People advance through the stages in the same order but at different rates. He found that progress is gradual and continuous rather than abrupt and that once a level is attained, people do not regress to lower levels. Following is the list of Kohlberg's six stages:

1. *Punishment-obedience stage.* Children at stage 1 reasoning view moral decisions in terms of

punishment and obedience. Their guiding concern is whether they will be caught. If not, then the action is justified.

2. *Instrumental relativist stage.* In stage 2 thinking, an action is judged right if it meets one's own needs. Often reciprocity is involved. People at this stage consider such adages as "an eye for an eye and a tooth for a tooth" and "you scratch my back I'll scratch yours" to be good guidelines for action.

GLOBAL

Continued

- No one of you is a believer until he desires for his brother that which he desires for himself. (Islam)
- Blessed is he who preferreth his brother before himself. (Baha'i) (Cottom, 1996, p. 56)

Out of these primary grade experiences emerges a focus on excellence; the goal is to inspire intrinsic motivation in students rather than a dependence on external rewards and punishments. The school accomplishes this in a variety of ways. Students engage in solving real-life problems, such as working with the city government on trash collection. These community learning experiences are closely linked with classroom goals and activities. The arts are also fully integrated with academics to provide multiple avenues for understanding the curriculum and encouraging creativity. CMS also supports student-initiated learning projects; for example, when several students became interested in robotics, the school sought out the resources to build a small robotics lab for them. Finally, quality circles are part of the routine at CMS, giving students ongoing input into the functioning of the school.

Global understanding, the third building block, is built on the first two. To support global understanding, students themselves conduct a daily reflection time in which stories from sacred texts are read. Field trips are also regularly taken to holy sites of the Hindu, Sikh, Buddhist, Muslim, Christian, Jewish, and Jain faiths. Another activity promoting understanding is an international student exchange program. Exchange programs and month-long summer camps involve young people from over 20 other countries. Rituals also contribute to the goal of global understanding. For example, students pray for peace in the World Peace Prayer Ceremony. In this ritual, costumes and artwork are created by the students to represent 180 different countries. Then wearing their costumes and displaying their artwork, the students say together, "May peace prevail on earth; may peace prevail in Thailand," continuing on to name all 180 nations. These activities contribute to a world perspective and help students learn tolerance for people who are different from themselves.

Finally, students develop a commitment to make the world a better place through service, and they participate in numerous community service projects. For example, every year they plant trees in conjunction with the government's forestry department. Students are also active in ecology clubs. They may adopt villages and teach literacy and first aid. Making real

3. *Good boy/good girl stage.* The desire to be a good boy or a good girl begins to guide moral reasoning at the third stage. Kohlberg characterized this socially oriented stage as concern with living up to the expectations of others, being nice, and gaining the approval of others.

4. *Law-and-order stage.* At the fourth stage, moral reasoning hinges on law and order. Rules, pure and simple, guide decisions. Rules should always be followed, because the given social order is considered sacrosanct.

5. *Social-contract stage.* Fifth-stage reasoning is based on the idea of a social contract. Rules are important at this stage, but there is recognition that rules are socially agreed upon standards, created in such a way as to promote the greatest social good. It is social-contract reasoning that guides American government and jurisprudence.

GLOBAL

Continued

contributions like these to the vitality of their communities gives students a sense of mastery and empowerment.

CMS teachers also work closely with parents. Parents are expected to actively participate in the life of the school. They are also expected to model and foster at home the values taught at school. To this end, teachers have created a guide for parents to assist them, *How Parents Should Behave with Their Children.* Parents are instructed, for example, to ask themselves the following questions.

1. Do I trust my child?

2. Do I encourage my child's confidence and listen attentively when she talks to me?

3. Do I meet my child's questions frankly, honestly, and without embarrassment?

4. Does my child know that I will do my best never to betray his confidence?

5. Do I build up the positive side of my child by using do's rather than don'ts?

6. Does my child know that she must always accept the consequences of her own actions?

7. Instead of claiming obedience from my child, do I try to earn it and evoke spontaneous obedience and cooperation?

8. Does my child love and appreciate beauty in its every expression?

9. Am I willing to see my child become an adult?

10. Is my child considerate, thoughtful, and tolerant? (Cottom, 1996, p. 57)

Many of the practices at City Montessori are consistent with the recommendations of the western literature on schooling and moral development: Use constructivist teaching practices, foster self-regulation, create a democratic environment, involve parents. The way they go about implementing these ideas may be most suitable to Indian culture, but Westerners can still take some interesting lessons from the Lucknow experience. When people put their minds to it, it appears, they can find shared values. If Indians can accomplish this in a society with a long history of interreligious violence, perhaps Americans, divided as we are by race and class, can, too.

6. *Universal-principles stage.* Finally, stage 6 is termed *universal principles.* At this stage, moral reasoning involves abstract and general principles that go beyond society's rules. Where they conflict, an individual at this stage adheres to his or her own internalized principles of action, not society's rules, in making moral decisions. Moral reformers (Gandhi, Martin Luther King, Jr.) employing civil disobedience tactics exemplify this stage. Very few people attain stage 6.

Because Kohlberg's framework is based on moral reasoning, not moral action, a person advocating that Heinz steal the drug could be at any level of development. Likewise, a person advocating that Heinz *not* steal the drug could also be at any level of moral development. It is the reason people give for the action, not the action itself, that determines which stage of moral development is operating. For example, at stage 1, arguments for or against stealing would be couched in the following terms, revealing the underlying concern with obedience and punishment.

- If you let your wife die, you will get in trouble. You'll be blamed for not spending the money to save her and there'll be an investigation of you and the druggist for your wife's death.
- You shouldn't steal the drug because you'll be caught and sent to jail if you do. If you do get away, your conscience would bother you thinking how the police would catch up with you at any minute. (McCormick & Pressley, 1997, p. 223)

People reasoning at stage 2 are also primarily concerned with self-interest, but more in terms of their own desires rather than punishment. Examples of stage 2 thinking follow.

- If you do happen to get caught, you could give the drug back and wouldn't get much of a sentence. It wouldn't bother you much to serve a little jail term, if you have your wife when you get out.
- He may not get much of a jail term if he steals the drug, but his wife will probably die before he gets out, so it wouldn't do him much good. If his wife dies, he shouldn't blame himself; it isn't his fault she has cancer. (McCormick & Pressley, 1997, p. 224)

At stages 3 and 4, reasoning is based on pleasing and gaining the approval of others and the larger society. A stage 3 thinker, grounded in the desire to conform to others' expectations, might reason in this way about the Heinz dilemma.

- No one will think you're bad if you steal the drug but your family will think you are an inhuman husband if you don't. If you let your wife die, you'll never be able to look anyone in the face again.
- It isn't just the druggist who will think you're a criminal, everyone else will, too. After you steal it, you'll feel bad thinking how you've brought dishonor on your family and yourself; you won't be able to face anyone again. (McCormick & Pressley, 1997, p. 224)

While at stage 3, people are concerned with the immediate reactions of others, those reasoning at the law-and-order level of stage 4 care more about adhering to the rules and conventions of society at large or of some subgroup that they affiliate with. The following rationales illustrate this perspective.

- If you have any sense of honor, you won't let your wife die because you're afraid to do the only thing that will save her. You'll always feel guilty that you caused her death if you don't do your duty to her.
- You're desperate and you may not know you're doing wrong when you steal the drug. But you'll know you did wrong after you're punished and sent to jail. You'll always feel guilty for your dishonesty and lawbreaking. (McCormick & Pressley, 1997, p. 224)

The social contract level of moral reasoning, stage 5, focuses on the purposes of rules as socially agreed upon guidelines for conduct. The following are examples of stage 5 reasoning.

- The law wasn't set up for these cirucumstances. Taking the drug in this situation isn't really right, but it's justified to do it.
- You can't have everyone stealing when they get desperate. The end may be good, but the ends don't justify the means. (McCormick & Pressley, 1997, p. 224)

The following rationale would be categorized at the highest level, stage 6, universal principles.

- Heniz should steal the drug because the sanctity of human life must take precedence over all other considerations. (McCormick & Pressley, 1997, p. 224)

It is difficult to imagine someone advocating that property rights supercede all others, but if so, then they, too, would be operating at the level of universal principles.

Kohlberg's system has some intuitive appeal; it resonates with our assumptions about human development moving from an egocentric focus grounded in a narrow self-interest to a wider societal focus based on enlightened self-interest. But does research support Kohlberg's framework? The answer is yes and no. Follow-up studies on the same cohort of students that Kohlberg initially interviewed showed that as they aged, they proceeded through the hierarchy in anticipated ways. That is, during adolescence, the proportion of the group reasoning at stages 1 and 2 declined, and the number at stage 3 increased. Few were at stage 4 until early adulthood, but by their mid-twenties, the proportion at stage 4 surpassed that at stage 3. Most got to stage 4 and stayed there, with very few ever attaining stage 5; none reached stage 6. Cross-sectional research confirms this progression. One very clear pattern is that moral development happens very slowly over a number of years.

Kohlberg's Critics

Despite this empirical support, Kohlberg's theory has received criticism. Even though some of his data were collected in other cultures, he has been accused of reifying Western culture's notions of what is good at the expense of perhaps equally meritorious moral systems from other cultures. For example, it is clear that Kohlberg valued the individual over the group, a strong tendency in Western culture, whereas many other cultures place a premium on cooperation and the centrality of the group. Kohlberg's highest stage is based on an individual's ability to act in defiance of his society, but in many cultures it is devotion to the needs of the group, not the sensibilities of the individual, that is most cherished.

For example, one respondent in New Guinea, in reacting to the Heinz dilemma, focused on what the group should do. He asserted that the community should collectively shoulder the blame for the problem, because Heinz appealed for help and was refused. In another replication of Kohlberg's work in India, respondents also focused on the social, rather than the individualistic, nature of moral problems. One woman in the study stated:

> The problems that Heinz is up against are not individual problems that are afflicting 1 or 2 Heinzes of the world. These are social problems. Forget Heinz in Europe, just come to India and you are speaking of the same thing with 60 percent of the people living below the poverty line. In fact, Heinz's story is being repeated all around us all the time with wives dying,

with children dying, and there is no money to save them. . . . So Heinz in his individual capacity—yes, okay, steal the drug, but it's not going to make any difference on a larger scale; and if his wife dies it is not going to make any difference on a larger scale. I don't think in the final analysis a solution can be worked out on an individual basis. (Vasudev & Hummel, 1987, p. 110)

Many of the more advanced respondents in India, as well as in communist China, favored this focus on community solutions over private conscience.

Other cross-cultural research, however, appears to substantiate Kohlberg's framework. Members of cultures that are complex, urban, and technological seem to share similar developmental processes. Further, when children are introduced early to concepts of law and government, they move through Kohlberg's stages more quickly. For example, Israeli children raised on *kibbutzim*—small, complex, democratic communities—are more aware of societal rules than other children in either Israel or America. It appears that youth from a variety of cultures do progress through the same lower stages, albeit at different rates, but that the endpoint of an ethical system depends on the culture (Berk, 1994; Snarey, 1985).

Another weakness of Kohlberg's hierarchy is that most of the original subjects were boys. Gilligan (1982), in contrast, collected data indicating that women view moral decisions differently, from a perspective based on caring and responsiblity for others, rather than on rugged individualism and justice. For example, most women would have a hard time rendering moral judgments without considering the concerns of the people around them. According to Kohlberg's framework, their attention to others would locate them at stages 3 and 4, rather than at the highest stages.

Larry Nucci also found flaws with Kohlberg's system. In an interesting series of studies with young children, Nucci explored their understanding of moral principle as opposed to social convention—that is, following the rules for their own sake or for fear of punishment—attitudes that Kohlberg associated with early childhood (Nucci, 1987). Contrary to Kohlberg's findings, Nucci's young subjects were quite capable of making this distinction and of thinking beyond the early stages of moral reasoning. For example, here is a piece of an interview with a 3-year-old girl about events at her preschool.

> Interviewer: Did you see what just happened?
> Child: Yes. They were playing and John hit him too hard.

I: Is that something you are supposed to do or not supposed to do?

C: Not so hard to hurt.

I: Is there a rule about that?

C: Yes.

I: What is the rule?

C: You're not to hit hard.

I: What if there were no rule about hitting hard; would it be all right to do then?

C: No.

I: Why not?

C: Because he could get hurt and start to cry. (p. 87)

This conversation shows that the child understood that causing harm to others was wrong independent of explicit rules, the possibility of punishment, or personal desires. Stage 6 reasoning in a 3-year-old! Here's another excerpt from the same interview contrasting her reasoning about social convention.

I: Did you see what just happened?

C: Yes. They were noisy.

I: Is that something you are supposed to do or not supposed to do?

C: Not do.

I: Is there a rule about that?

C: Yes. We have to be quiet.

I: What if there were no rule; would it be all right to do then?

C: Yes.

I: Why?

C: Because there is no rule. (p. 87)

Contrary to both Kohlberg and Piaget, these findings suggest that young children can use universal principles like justice and human welfare to guide their moral reasoning and actions. This is not to say, however, that young children handle moral issues the same way adults or older children do. For example, a preschooler understands that it would not be fair for her to keep all the classroom toys for herself, but she may believe that it is okay to keep the best toys as long as she shares the rest. Thus, a sense of justice indeed appears to be rather egocentric in its early stages.

Cross-cultural and cross-religious studies have for the most part confirmed Nucci's (1987) findings. Children in the Netherlands, Nigeria, Taiwan, and the Virgin Islands, as well as fundamentalist Christian, Catholic, and Jewish children in the United States, were all able to differentiate basic moral principles from social rules in ways similar to American secular youngsters. Further, they treated moral problems as more serious than breaches of convention, and by the same token, viewed prosocial behavior as more valuable than merely following social mores.

Most agreed that moral transgressions such as stealing, hitting, or slander would still be wrong even if there were no religious rules against them, because they are harmful to others. However, work on the Sabbath, women preaching in church or synagogue, and the use of contraceptives, for instance, would be all right in the children's view if there were no religious rules ... concerning them. This research indicates that conceptions of morality (justice and beneficence) are independent of religion. (p. 88)

The work of Alfie Kohn (1990) also suggests that Kohlberg's framework should be held tentatively. Kohn has compiled evidence showing that even very young children can display prosocial behaviors and that they appear to have the capacity to reason beyond their own needs. For example, young children often respond empathetically to others in distress, spontaneously patting the hand and comforting someone who is crying. This action cannot be interpreted from a punishment-obedience or other low-level, egocentric perspective.

Despite the emergence of criticism and alternative frameworks, Kohlberg's system has received enough empirical validation to remain the dominant perspective for understanding children's moral development today. It may not be perfect, but it does provide teachers with some helpful ways of thinking about children and their ethical decision making. We turn now to the practical issues of dealing with morals in the classroom.

ETHICS IN THE CLASSROOM

Should Morals Be Taught in the Classroom?

This question vexes both expert and novice teachers. On one hand, one of America's core values is a belief in the individual and the individual's right to determine right and wrong for himself or herself. We advocate religious freedom, freedom of speech, freedom of thought, and freedom of individual conscience. Further, we know that different groups pressure schools and teachers in opposite directions. For example, religious fundamentalists want prayer in the schools, but secularly minded citizens vigorously oppose this practice. Given this diversity, how can we ask the public schools to teach a single set of values? And even if we could agree on a set of core values, wouldn't teaching them amount to indoctrination, something antithetical to our central beliefs about self-determination?

On the other hand, without *some* shared values, wouldn't our society become chaotic? How can people function without basic agreements concerning appropriate and inappropriate behavior? Fortunately, evidence from historical, cross-cultural, cross-religious, and survey research point to the existence of universal human values (Rose & Gallup, 1996). Cultures and religions may differ in their emphasis on the group versus the individual, say, or on norms concerning public prayer, and these are by no means trivial, but there is high agreement on other important values, such as not deliberately harming others. Further, to operate a democracy effectively necessitates some specific agreements and values concerning participation in the democratic process and tolerance for differing points of view.

Within school settings, teachers are responsible for maintaining an orderly, safe, and productive learning environment in their classrooms. This means teachers need to establish and enforce rules and procedures that foster a healthy learning climate. In short, teachers are responsible for classroom management and discipline. Implicit in any management system are underlying values about human rights and responsibilities. Teachers have to maintain order, and the way they go about that task sends powerful messages about right and wrong to their students.

The upshot is that teaching values in the classroom is really unavoidable. Although you may not explicitly teach a particular moral precept, the way you relate to your students, the management system you enact, the way you expect students to relate to each other, the curricular and instructional choices you make, all combine to create a de facto moral climate in the classroom. Adults teach children values, good or bad, by the way they interact with them. When parents swat instead of explaining why a consequence is invoked, they fix their children at lower stages of moral reasoning in which external authority and fear of being caught are the only concerns. On the other hand, when teachers involve students in making some classroom decisions, they communicate the importance of democratic process. It is really not a matter of whether to teach values; it is a matter of which values will be taught and how to teach them.

Where does all this leave you? What will schools and society expect of you as you take on classroom responsibilities? We believe, along with the majority of Americans, that part of a public school teacher's job in a democracy is to socialize young people to their roles as citizens (Rose & Gallup, 1996). Democracy requires that its citizens understand that the social order is their own creation and that their active participation is necessary to keep society functioning effectively. Citizens also need to discuss issues in a constructive way with a variety of people. To do so, they need to exercise self-control and self-regulation and to see things from others' points of view. These capacities are strongest at the upper levels of moral reasoning. It is important, then, for teachers to structure their classrooms so as to promote democratic values, and they do this in part by increasing students' level of moral reasoning and action. Helping your students increase their capacity for moral self-regulation, and creating and maintaining a democratic learning community within your classroom will constitute central aims of your professional practice.

Lickona (1988) provided three specific goals for character development in the classroom that most parents and teachers can agree on.

1. To promote development away from egocentrism and excessive individualism and toward cooperative relationships and mutual respect.

2. To foster the growth of moral agency, (that is) the capacity to think, feel, and act morally.

3. To develop in the classroom and school a moral community based on fairness, caring, and participation. Such a community is a moral end in itself, as well as a support system for the character development of each child. (p. 420)

How does an individual become moral? There are many skills and dispositions underlying the ability to think and to behave in an ethical manner that need to be developed as a child grows up. **Perspective taking**, or the ability to see things from someone else's point of view, is one of the most critical. This makes sense, because so much of morality hinges on how actions affect other people. One is kind so others will not be hurt, for example, and one is fair because injustice harms other people. A lack of empathy results in a deficit in compassion and in the ability to think and act ethically. Deficits in empathy are often seen in domestic abusers and others prone to aggression and violence (Baumeister & Smart, 1996).

Related to perspective taking is the ability to read another person's emotional state. If you want to avoid harming someone else, it is helpful to be able to comprehend signs of distress and other emotions. Thus, **emotional insight** is another key skill underlying moral reasoning and action. A common problem in classroom **isolates**, students who have a hard time getting along with others and who are rejected by their peers, is their lack of emotional insight (Goleman, 1995).

A final crucial attribute involves self-control, especially knowing how to **defer gratification**, that is, postpone satisfying some immediate desire. If, for example, being fair means taking turns, then you have to be able to wait your turn. As we discussed in Chapter 4, this is an important skill for students, since so much of a student's life involves waiting—for their turn at the drinking fountain, to be called on by the teacher, to receive feedback on their homework. Students who lack the ability to defer gratification experience many problems in school. There are wide individual and cultural differences in this characteristic.

These three skills, perspective taking, emotional insight, and deferring gratification, are key elements of what researchers have termed **emotional intelligence** (Goleman, 1995). Emotional intelligence is the ability to establish and maintain mutually satisfactory relationships. Interestingly, the skills and dispositions that educators and ethics scholars have designated as moral are the same ones that psychologists have found central to effective social and emotional functioning. Thus, when teachers construct classroom experiences that advance character development, they are simultaneously enhancing students' relationship abilities.

Teaching Values

How can a classroom be structured so as to promote moral development? You will have many opportunities to explore this question in depth as you pursue coursework in educational foundations, classroom management, and other classes. For now, we provide a brief overview of some of the tools that teachers use to facilitate their students' capacities for moral reasoning and action.

Research-Based Principles

Research has supplied us with some general principles about what does and does not work in the field of moral education. Leming (1993) reviewed evaluations of character education and values clarification programs, applications of Kohlberg's ideas, and research on drug and sex education. He drew several conclusions based on this synthesis. The first was that didactic methods alone do not work. Just as Hartshorne and May discovered almost 70 years ago, when teachers lecture, exhort, extract pledges, or impose codes of conduct, they have little effect on students' moral reasoning or behavior. Leming also concluded that advancing ethical reasoning does not necessarily translate into ethical

action. Students' ability to engage in high levels of moral discussion does not mean that they will then act in conjunction with that reasoning. Moral reasoning is a necessary but insufficient basis for moral action. Attention also needs to be placed on encouraging such action in its own right. We discuss how this can be accomplished later in this chapter.

Third, Leming found that:

> Character develops within a social environment. The nature of that environment, the messages it sends, and the behaviors it encourages and discourages are important factors to consider in character education. Clear rules of conduct, student ownership of those rules, a supportive environment, and satisfaction resulting from complying with the norms of the environment shape behavior. (p. 69)

Certain types of social experiences and environments are more effective in promoting character development than others. Moral reasoning appears to be advanced, for example, simply by education. Those with higher levels of education perform at higher levels in tests of moral reasoning. In addition, living in an urban environment and attending school with people of other ethnic groups also seems to help. For example, Kenyan and Nigerian adolescents who attended racially mixed high schools exhibited higher moral reasoning than peers who were schooled in more homogeneous settings (Edwards, 1978).

How can we apply these findings to classrooms? Common to all of the above is the experience of *diversity*. Exposure to different kinds of people, either directly through social contact or indirectly through new ideas encountered in educational experiences, helps youngsters advance in moral thinking. This effect is no doubt due to the opportunity to consider the thoughts and feelings of others, in other words, to the chance to engage in and practice perspective taking. As we saw earlier, perspective taking is a key component of moral development, and exposure to diversity appears to enhance character by enhancing perspective-taking abilities. Teachers can help their students develop this fundamental skill by helping those of different backgrounds get to know each other and by infusing diversity into their curriculum.

Social Learning Principles

One fundamental way that students, especially young children, acquire moral behavior is by modeling the behavior of adults. This sort of learning by imitation is explicated in a view of learning and development termed **social learning theory**. Social learning theory posits that children learn by observing and copying the behavior of respected adults, whose actions are then rewarded in some way. For example, when a preschooler watches an adult share food with someone who then responds with smiles and thank yous, the child learns both how to share and that sharing is a desirable behavior. This learning is further strengthened when the child himself shares and is recognized (rewarded) for doing so. Praising the child's character with comments like, "What a kind and thoughtful boy you are!" is an especially potent form of reward. When teachers model moral actions such as kindness and honesty, when they reinforce those actions in others, and when they in particular reinforce those actions in their students, they are helping to advance children's moral development. Of course, social learning theory predicts that children will emulate *any* respected adult's behavior, so teachers' less than praiseworthy actions will also be copied.

Social learning theory capitalizes on another key skill underlying moral development, that of emotional insight. For observational learning to work, children must be able to accurately read the emotional state of significant others. The better they can do that, the better they can take advantage of social learning opportunities. This may help us explain an additional finding from the research on schooling and moral development, that involvement in leadership and service activities enhance character. Apparently, when students can observe adults at close hand engaged in leadership and service within a supportive environment, they are able to emulate their behavior. There is one important exception to this finding: High school athletes display significantly lower levels of moral development than their peers (Berk, 1994; Manners & Smart, 1995). It is interesting to speculate on why this is so; it may be the emphasis on competition and winning or on the fact that team sports are not usually run on a democratic basis. An implication for teachers is that they should provide opportunities for students to be involved in leadership and service activities more than in athletics.

Parenting Applied to Teaching

To further understand how to promote moral development in the classroom, we can look to research on parenting for helpful guidelines. This research shows that when parents use threats, commands, or physical force, or when their discipline is inconsistent and harsh, their children often behave aggressively toward others and feel little guilt when they cause harm. More effective is a technique called **inductive discipline** in which young people are shown the effects of their actions on others, another

instance of perspective taking. When parents say, for example, "Samantha probably felt hurt when you grabbed her toy away," they are using inductive discipline. Parents who use this technique help their children develop a conscience, which the children can then use to guide their own conduct toward others (Berk, 1994).

Another line of parenting research, also concerned with how parents exert control, is instructive. Baumrind (1987) classed parenting styles into three categories: laissez-faire, authoritarian, and authoritative. **Laissez-faire parents** exert little or no control or guidance over their children, whereas **authoritarian parents**, in contrast, maintain strict control despite their children's emerging maturity. Between these two extremes are **authoritative parents**, those who provide explanations for the limits they set and who enforce these limits fairly and flexibly, according to their children's growing capacities for self-management. "They discuss their standards, teach their child how to meet them, and value behavior that is monitored by self-discipline and self-control" (McCaslin & Good, 1992, p. 11).

How can this research be applied to the classroom? When teachers enforce classroom rules calmly and fairly, when they discipline consistently, when they invoke reasonable consequences rather than harsh punishments, they are utilizing research-validated techniques that will help their students become more ethical people. Further, when they alert students to the effects of their actions on others, they help them develop perspective taking. When they involve students in rule setting, to the degree appropriate for students' developmental level, they are modeling how to create a community predicated on mutual respect and are employing an authoritative leadership style.

Classroom Research

These suggestions are confirmed by classroom research that examined students' evaluations of their teachers. Model teachers, according to sixth- through eighth-grade students across the country, display the following qualities.

- Present clear, consistent, and sincere messages.
- Do not pull rank—are never authoritarian.
- Communicate high expectations.
- Really listen.
- Communicate their commitments through actions (as well as words).
- Are hard-working and really care about student learning. (Williams,1993, p. 22)

Further research has shown that responding to student misbehavior by reasoning can also be effective:

> Students rated highest those teachers who responded to moral transgressions with statements focusing on the effects of the acts ("Joe, that really hurt Mike."). Rated lower were teachers who responded with statements of school rules or normative expectations ("That's not the way for a Hawthorne student to act."). Rated lowest were teachers who used simple commands ("Stop it!" "Don't hit!"). (Nucci, 1987, p. 91)

We see here a convergence of classroom research, basic research in family and educational psychology, and philosophical analyses concerning the place of morality in schools. These separate lines of evidence converge toward a view of teaching that is authoritative. Authoritative teaching means creating a democratic classroom learning community and working to promote students' abilities to self-regulate. As you pursue your studies in education, pay special attention to developing your skills as an authoritative teacher.

In addition to setting the overall moral tone of the classroom through their leadership style and their daily interactions with students, teachers have specific techniques at their disposal for promoting moral thought and behavior. We provide a brief overview of two such techniques here.

Moral Discussion

Moral discussion is a teaching strategy that grew out of the work of Lawrence Kohlberg and focuses on the development of moral reasoning, an important precursor to moral behavior. To conduct a moral discussion, a teacher first sets the class a moral dilemma—a societal problem or controversy, something that arises out of a real classroom situation, or a problem like the Heinz dilemma discussed earlier. The teacher next invites the class to share their reactions, and the students discuss the pros and cons of various ways to resolve the problem.

Berkowitz (1982) identified three characteristics of moral discussions that best facilitated students' moral growth. The first is conflict, but conflict with a caveat. For students older than 8-years old, conflict and disagreement about the resolution of a moral dilemma increase moral reasoning better than placid agreement. In contrast, for students younger than 8-years-old, cooperation and compromise is a more effective environment for growth. For teachers of young children, this means finding moral problems that will likely lead to easy agreement, whereas for

teachers of older students, it means selecting dilemmas likely to provoke argument.

The second characteristic of effective moral discussions is **stage disparity**, or having a range of stages of moral development together in the classroom. To hold a discussion in which there are multiple points of view, it is necessary that participating students exhibit a spread in moral development. This feature is typical even for most single-grade classrooms.

Early proponents of moral discussion wanted teachers to contribute statements during moral discussions that were about a half level above their students' current level of functioning. This not only turned out to be a very difficult assignment for teachers, but one that did not have the desired effect even when done correctly. Much better than teacher talk, it was discovered, is a particular type of interaction known as **transactive discourse**, the final key ingredient of effective moral discussions. Transactive statements are those that incorporate the previous speaker's points in some way, either by extending the argument, refuting it, or locating commonalities between the speaker's and listener's viewpoints. When listeners simply restate what the speaker has said without elaboration, or when they merely tell their own view without any acknowledgment of the speaker's position, moral reasoning is not promoted. Conversely, when students build on each others' contributions, the overall level of moral thinking is raised. Teachers can help students learn to engage in transactive discourse by directly teaching how to do it, by modeling it themselves in their own comments, and by recognizing and reinforcing students for such speech as it happens during discussions.

Service Learning

A teaching strategy to develop students' capacities for moral action is **service learning**, and it is currently gaining much ground. Some states, districts, and programs have mandated student service as a high school graduation requirement. It is also becoming very common at the university level. Service learning engages students in performing acts of school and community service and, in contrast to moral discussions, focuses on moral action as much as it does on moral reasoning.

Typically, service learning projects take two forms (Kahne & Westheimer, 1996). In one, students in a class may be assigned a service project, but the students are left to work out the logistics on their own without much connection with the actual course. For example, a twelfth-grade unit on city government may involve students variously in helping out at a clinic for crack babies, assisting patients with their appointments at a hospital, or handing out survival kits for the homeless. In these activities, students have the chance to interact with people in difficulty and to experience the satisfaction of helping others. Though laudable, such independent projects may not be well monitored, and the quality of the experiences can be very uneven. Further, such projects are often not integrated in a meaningful way with the objectives of the class, so students may fail to see the connections between what they are doing in the community, what they are learning in the classroom, and larger social issues.

The other type of service learning aims at change rather than charity, and integrates service activities more coherently into classroom learning goals. For example, in a social studies class on community problems, students begin with a discussion of issues they are concerned about. From this discussion, students may identify homelessness as a problem they all wish to address. The teacher then facilitates the study of the social, economic, legal, and political aspects of homelessness, and the class agrees on actions they can take to ameliorate the problem. They might raise funds for the local homeless shelter, volunteer to serve meals at the soup kitchen, or devise other ways to improve relief efforts in their community. This more ambitious form of service learning engages students in moral discussions, provides multiple opportunities for perspective taking, provides vehicles for moral action, and supports content learning goals.

Additional Tools

Lickona (1993) supplies several suggestions that both summarize our discussion and offer additional tools by which teachers can affect students' character.

- Act as a caregiver and model, one who treats students with love and respect.

- Create a moral community in which students know and care about each other.

- Practice moral discipline. Conduct moral discussions when enforcing rules.

- Create a democratic classroom in which students are involved in decision making.

- Use the curriculum constructively by selecting materials that communicate values, examine moral questions, and provide multiple perspectives.

- Make frequent use of cooperative learning strategies.

- Encourage moral reflection through discussion and writing.

- Teach conflict resolution.

- Foster a climate of caring in the school as a whole, not just in your own classroom.

The Moral Development of Teachers

One implication of these recommendations is that teachers themselves need to attain high levels of moral development. Teachers cannot promote something in students that they themselves do not possess. Interestingly, teachers who score at the higher levels of Kohlberg's framework do tend to implement a more democratic classroom organization and to give students more opportunities to make decisions, just the sort of actions that help students advance. An unavoidable conclusion is that teachers need to work on moving themselves to higher levels of moral development.

As you reflect on your prospective career, give thought to your own level of moral development. Look for moral dilemmas in your own life (workplace, family, friends), in the news, or wherever you can find them. Reflect on how you would resolve these dilemmas, but equally important, reflect on the moral reasoning behind your decisions. Compare your reasoning with Kohlberg's scale; where do you fit? Should you be at a higher stage? How might you go about raising your own level of moral reasoning and your own capacities for moral action?

PROFESSIONAL ETHICS

Elevating your own level of moral functioning, creating democratic classrooms, and acting as an ethical model for students are all ways to advance moral education. Another important aspect of ethical teaching is conducting oneself in alignment with professional ethical standards. Teachers' associations have established codes of ethics for educators, and in this section, we discuss the NEA code, AFT guidelines, and other ethical guidelines for professionals.

Codes of Ethics

All professions establish codes of conduct for themselves, and teaching is no different. Just as members of other helping professions, such as psychology and nursing, have agreed upon standards of professionalism, so teachers have devised their own code of ethical behavior. These codes are not legally binding, but they do represent the profession's expectations for itself. Figure 13.2 offers you the American Federation of Teachers' Bill of Rights and Responsibilities for Learning.

The AFT took an interesting approach in designing its professional standards. Rather than state the expectations for teachers' behavior, they laid out expectations for the community and students. Arguing that it takes all parties pulling together to make the educational system work, the AFT created community standards for education, not standards for teachers.

Figure 13.3 displays the National Education Association's Code of Ethics of the Education Profession. In contrast to the AFT, the NEA focused on a more traditional outline of teachers' responsibilities. Note that the NEA categorizes teachers' duties into two aspects, commitment to students and commitment to the profession.

It is interesting to compare codes for other helping professions with those for education. Examine Figure 13.4 for excerpts from the codes for social workers, counselors, and psychologists. What similarities and differences do you notice between their ethical standards and educators'?

This comparison is revealing. Look, for example, in Figure 13.4 at the excerpt from the standards for counselors. It specifies that counselors should strive to improve the profession and their own practice through continuing education and research. Neither the NEA nor the AFT calls its members to lifelong professional learning for themselves or commitment to advancing the professional knowledge base. Both education associations also fail to address problems of conflict of interest, an issue addressed in detail in the excerpt from the American Psychological Association's code for psychologists. Five of the eight NEA standards relating to commitment to the profession deal with false statements on job applications; the social work code simply states categorically that professionals should not engage in deceit under any circumstances. The full standards for social work, counseling, and psychology reveal even more instances of the failure of the education associations' codes to measure up.

It is more than a little troubling that the major teacher associations have produced ethical standards that are so deficient in comparison to those of other helping professions. The NEA code, with a few exceptions, reads like a job contract, while the AFT's Bill of Rights sounds like political diatribe. Given the current call for a greater emphasis on teaching as moral action from such educational leaders as John Goodlad, Thomas Sergiovanni, Nel Noddings, and Philip Jackson, professional associations should

Figure 13.2 A Bill of Rights and Responsibilities for Learning

Standards of Conduct, Standards for Achievement

The traditional mission of our public schools has been to prepare our nation's young people for equal and responsible citizenship and productive adulthood. Today, we reaffirm that mission by remembering that democratic citizenship and productive adulthood begin with standards of conduct and standards for achievement in our schools. Other education reforms *may* work; high standards of conduct and achievement *do* work—and nothing else can work without them.

Recognizing that rights carry responsibilities, we declare that:

1. All students and school staff have a right to schools that are safe, orderly, and drug free.

2. All students and school staff have a right to learn and work in school districts and schools that have clear discipline codes with fair and consistently enforced consequences for misbehavior.

3. All students and school staff have a right to learn and work in school districts that have alternative educational placements for violent or chronically disruptive students.

4. All students and school staff have a right to be treated with courtesy and respect.

5. All students and school staff have a right to learn and work in school districts, schools and classrooms that have clearly stated and rigorous academic standards.

6. All students and school staff have a right to learn and work in well-equipped schools that have the instructional materials needed to carry out a rigorous academic program.

7. All students and school staff have a right to learn and work in schools where teachers know their subject matter and how to teach it.

8. All students and school staff have a right to learn and work in school districts, schools and classrooms where high grades stand for high achievement and promotion is earned.

9. All students and school staff have a right to learn and work in school districts and schools where getting a high school diploma means having the knowledge and skills essential for college or a good job.

10. All students and school staff have a right to be supported by parents, the community, public officials and business in their efforts to uphold high standards of conduct and achievement.

Source: From American Federation of Teachers, 1995.

Figure 13.3 **NEA Code of Ethics**

Preamble

The educator, believing in the worth and dignity of each human being, recognizes the supreme importance of the pursuit of truth, devotion to excellence, and the nurture of democratic principles. Essential to these goals is the protection of freedom to learn and to teach and the guarantee of equal educational opportunity for all. The educator accepts the responsibility to adhere to the highest ethical standards.

The educator recognizes the magnitude of the responsibility inherent in the teaching process. The desire for the respect and confidence of one's colleagues, of students, of parents, and of the members of the community provides the incentive to attain and maintain the highest possible degree of ethical conduct. The Code of Ethics of the Education Profession indicates the aspiration of all educators and provides standards by which to judge conduct.

The remedies specified by the NEA and/or its affiliates for the violation of any provision of this Code shall be exclusive and no such provision shall be enforceable in any form other than one specifically designated by the NEA or its affiliates.

Principle I—Commitment to the Student

The educator strives to help each student realize his or her potential as a worthy and effective member of society. The educator therefore works to stimulate the spirit of inquiry, the acquisition of knowledge and understanding, and the thoughtful formulation of worthy goals.

In fulfillment of the obligation to the student, the educator—

1. Shall not unreasonably restrain the student from independent action in the pursuit of learning.
2. Shall not unreasonably deny the student access to varying points of view.
3. Shall not deliberately suppress or distort subject matter relevant to the student's progress.
4. Shall make reasonable effort to protect the student from conditions harmful to learning or to health and safety.
5. Shall not intentionally expose the student to embarrassment or disparagement.
6. Shall not on the basis of race, color, creed, sex, national origin, marital status, political or religious beliefs, family, social or cultural background, or sexual orientation, unfairly:

   a. Exclude any student from participation in any program;
   b. Deny benefits to any student;
   c. Grant any advantage to any student.

7. Shall not use professional relationships with students for private advantage.
8. Shall not disclose information about students obtained in the course of professional service, unless disclosure serves a compelling professional purpose or is required by law.

Principle II—Commitment to the Profession

The education profession is vested by the public with a trust and responsibility requiring the highest ideals of professional service.

In the belief that the quality of the services of the education profession directly influences the nation and its citizens, the educator shall exert every effort to raise professional standards, to promote a climate that encourages the exercise of professional judgment, to achieve conditions which attract persons worthy of the trust to careers in education, and to assist in preventing the practice of the profession by unqualified persons.

In fulfillment of the obligation of the profession the educator—

1. Shall not in an application for a professional position deliberately make a false statement or fail to disclose a material fact related to competency and qualifications.
2. Shall not misrepresent his/her professional qualifications.
3. Shall not assist entry into the profession of a person known to be unqualified in respect to character, education, or other relevant attribute.
4. Shall not knowingly make a false statement concerning the qualifications of a candidate for a professional position.
5. Shall not assist a noneducator in the unauthorized practice of teaching.
6. Shall not disclose information about colleagues obtained in the course of professional service unless disclosure serves a compelling professional purpose or is required by law.
7. Shall not knowingly make false or malicious statements about a colleague.
8. Shall not accept any gratuity, gift, or favor that might impair or appear to influence professional decisions or actions.

Source: From National Education Association, 1976.

Figure 13.4   **Excerpts from Ethical Codes of Other Helping Professions**

1. The member influences the development of the profession by continuous efforts to improve professional practices, teaching services, and research. Professional growth is continuous throughout the member's career and is exemplified by the development of a philosophy that explains why and how a member functions in the helping relationship. Members must gather data on their effectiveness and be guided by the findings. Members recognize the need for continuing education to ensure competent service.

Source: From American Association for Counseling and Development, 1988.

Principle 6: Welfare of the Consumer
Psychologists respect the integrity and protect the welfare of people and groups with whom they work. When conflicts of interest arise between clients and psychologists' employing institutions, psychologists clarify the nature and direction of their loyalties and responsibilities and keep all parties informed of their commitments. Psychologists fully inform consumers as to the purpose and nature of an evaluative, treatment, educational, or training procedure, and they freely acknowledge that clients, students, or participants in research have freedom of choice with regard to participation.

Source: From Ethical Principles of Pschologists, American Psychological Association, 1989.

I. The Social Worker's Conduct and Comportment as a Social Worker.

A. *Propriety.* The social worker should maintain high standards of personal conduct in the capacity or identity as a social worker.

   1. The private conduct of the social worker is a personal matter to the same degree as is any other person's, except when such conduct compromises the fulfillment of professional responsibilities.
   2. The social worker should not participate in, condone, or be associated with dishonesty, fraud, deceit, or misrepresentation.
   3. The social worker should distinguish clearly between statements and actions made as a private individual and as a representative of the social work profession or an organization or group.

Source: From National Association of Social Workers Code of Ethics, 1990.

take heed, and as a minimal first step, revisit and revise the standards they uphold for the teaching profession.

Moral Problem Solving

Refer to the dilemmas we posed at the beginning of the chapter. Even with the best professional standards to guide you, it may be difficult to decide on a course of action that is ethical. How can one be sure all important factors have been considered? How can one distinguish between competing interests? There are a number of ways these issues can be approached. Here we present two methods of moral problem solving, Kitchener's critical-evaluation model and Corey and colleagues' step-by-step procedure.

Kitchener (1984) developed the *critical-evaluation model for ethical decision making.* Her model, originally developed for counselors, is grounded on four basic principles: autonomy, beneficence, nonmaleficence, and justice. When reflecting on your teaching practice, or on how to handle a troubling situation, consider these principles.

Autonomy.   Fostering self-determination. Which course of action will lead to increased capacities for independence and self-regulation in your students?

Beneficence.   Promoting good. The question, "What's best for students?" should be a central one whenever you are considering what action to take.

Nonmaleficence.   Avoiding harm. Just as physicians must "at least do no harm," so should teachers avoid taking actions that might harm students.

Justice.   Fairness; provision of equal treatment for all students. Equal treatment, though, does not mean "same" treatment. For example, the same lesson taught twelfth graders and first graders would not provide equal opportunities for learning. When considering the principle of justice, it is more helpful to think in terms of equal opportunity or equal access rather than treating everyone the same.

Take a moment to consider the dilemma presented in the accompanying Issue Box. See if anything you have read so far in this chapter helps you think about this controversy.

Applying a set of general principles is one way to think through moral problems. But sometimes their application can raise more issues than they resolve. Another method you may find helpful is the step-by-step procedure devised by Corey, Corey, and Callanan (1993). Their series of questions helps break moral problem solving down into a manageable process. When confronted with a moral problem, think about the following questions:

1. *What is the problem?* Gather as much information as possible about the problem, and examine it from multiple perspectives. Are there legal as well as ethical issues involved? Are there particular facts that change the situation? Like the lead teacher who discovered a colleague was working in a strip joint, also learning that she was earning extra money for her sick mother may have been an important factor in deciding what to do. Find out as much as you reasonably can about a situation before you leap to a decision.

2. *What are the issues involved?* After collecting background information, list the key issues. Analyze the rights, duties, and welfare of the parties involved. Identify competing moral principles. For example, the teacher ordered to implement instruction she believed harmful to her students was faced with competing duties to her employer and to her students. If you applied the principle of autonomy to this moral dilemma, what would the appropriate decision be? Would the decision be different if the principle of beneficence was taken as primary? It may be helpful to prioritize the four principles.

3. *What do professional codes of ethics say?* Do existing professional standards offer a solution? The NEA code may not be perfect, but it does offer some guidance. For example, it states that teachers may not exclude students from school activities based on, among other things, sexual orientation. Therefore the code may help resolve the high school teacher's conflict between his religion and his civic duties as a public school teacher. In addition to national codes, states often create more detailed codes of ethical conduct and professional competence; these may also provide guidance.

4. *What do colleagues have to say?* Consult with teachers, administrators, school counselors, or other school professionals. You need to be able to justify whatever action you ultimately take, and sharing your reasoning with others can provide a check to ensure that it is sound. It may also alert you to factors you have overlooked. In addition, if your decision is later challenged, demonstrating that there was professional consensus may be helpful.

5. *What courses of action are possible?* Brainstorm and make a list of possible actions to resolve the situation.

6. *What are the consequences of different decisions?* For each possible decision, list the likely consequences. What will happen to students? To the image of the school? To your own career?

7. *What appears to be the best course of action?* Make a decision and try to avoid second-guessing yourself later on. Professionals never have all the information they might desire, but following this problem-solving format will most often result in the best decision possible given the information available at the time.

As a teacher, you will not always have time to follow this elaborate problem-solving process, so it should be reserved for the major dilemmas you face. With experience, you will become more efficient with it.

Becoming an Ethical Teacher

Teaching, like life itself, is an unavoidably complex and value-laden enterprise. Becoming an ethical teacher is a lifelong journey that should begin now. As we have emphasized throughout this text, in considering whether to pursue teaching as your career, you need to examine your own values thoroughly and to determine the match between yourself and the demands of the profession. Following are some specific questions you need to ask yourself as you explore this issue.

First of all, what is your motivation for teaching? First raised in Chapter 1, we believe this crucial question is a good way to end this text. What personal rewards do you expect to get out of teaching young people? Are you trying to relive your high school days and do it right this time? Do you seek the adulation of small children? Do you need to be in charge? Do you need to be the one with all the right answers? Are you depending on students to tell you what a good person you are? In moderation these are normal feelings, but taken to extreme, they are not appropriate motivators for a professional teacher. Such feelings could interfere with the quality of your relationships with students and hamper your growth as a teacher. Probe your own attitudes honestly, and if teaching interests you because of your own unresolved emotional needs, be sure to get those needs addressed before you become a teacher.

We also hope that we have impressed on you by now the rigors of a teaching career. Teaching can be enormously satisfying, but it can also be very demanding. If teaching interests you because of short work days and extended winter and summer vacations, reconsider.

Continuous reflection needs to be given to what your values and beliefs are. What do you consider right and wrong, proper and improper? As you contemplate your values, think about how you came to adopt them. Where did you develop your views?

There is some evidence, for example, that there are subject matter differences in value orientations (Pintrich & Schunk, 1996). People who are drawn to mathematics tend to be higher in **restrictive control values**; that is, they place importance on cleanliness, obedience, politeness, responsibility, and self-control. On the other hand, those who love English tend to be high in **prosocial concern**; that is, they

Channel One in the Classroom

Channel One is a TV news show produced for high school students. Its founder, Chris Whittle, provided free TV sets to schools in exchange for broadcasting the show. In addition to news, Channel One also airs commercials. The program now reaches 40 percent of American secondary classrooms, or an audience of 8 million students every day. Each year, students see more than 700 commercials in addition to the news.

From its inception, Channel One has generated controversy and has thrown educators into a moral dilemma. Schools need equipment, but this equipment comes with strings attached. Is it right to accept televisons when it means students will be forced to watch a commercially produced news show in school? Is it right to refuse needed equipment just because students will have to watch 15 more minutes of something they already watch hours of at home?

The arguments for Channel One are straightforward and have been persuasive for many American educators. Teenagers do not watch the news very often, and Channel One is a way to encourage that important habit. Many schools desperately need equipment, and it would be a disservice to students to turn a gift like this down. Most political leaders enthusiastically support business-school partnerships, and many such programs are currently in operation, so what is one more? Many corporations, for example, provide curriculum materials with their own company name and logo displayed prominently. Schools sell advertising space at football games and other athletic events to support these programs. Channel One is simply another link between the educational and corporate communities.

Roy Fox (1995), however, sees it differently. He interviewed 200 high school students in rural Missouri about their perceptions of Channel One and commercials. What he found was rather startling. Most teens had a difficult time telling the difference between commercials, news stories, and public service ads. The style in which commercials are shot mimics news and public service messages, blurring the distinction for the students. Fox asked 29 students in particular about one Pepsi ad; only 12 were aware that it was a commercial.

These high schoolers also failed to realize that the young people portrayed in the ads were paid actors; they felt like they were kids just like them, kids that they could be friends with. One girl commented:

> *Well ... I know that I'd be terribly disappointed if the kids in that commercial turned out to be paid actors—they're just real kids off the street, like us. They just* couldn't *be actors, ya know? (p. 77)*

place importance on forgiveness, helpfulness, and caring. Do these patterns hold in your case? If so, you may need to actively work on stretching yourself. Prospective math teachers, or elementary teachers who love math, may need to consider developing the caring aspects of their value system. Prospective English teachers, or elementary teachers who love language arts, may need to consider developing greater emphasis on responsibility. In many teacher education programs, students write autobiographies (also termed **personal life histories**) to help them clarify their beliefs and how they came to be the person they are. You may wish to start that process now.

Corey, Corey, and Callanan (1993) suggest that people contemplating careers in any helping profession ask themselves the following additional questions.

ISSUES

EXTRA

Continued

Another point of confusion was the use of athletes to endorse products. Students believed that the athletes did commercials for a variety of reasons, none of which involved making money by selling products. The teens listed these reasons why athletes appeared in commercials.

- It motivates them to play better.
- It's a reward for doing excellent work.
- It helps their team.
- It elevates their status and reputation. (p. 77)

In fact, many students thought that the athletes actually paid the sponsors for the privilege of appearing in commercials.

Students reported that they often chatted about commercials, even calling to alert each other when a good commercial was on. Most troubling was the students' response to Fox's final question:

"Is there anything else about commercials that we haven't talked about?"
"Yes!" they enthused, "We need new commercials!" I was startled by this answer until I realized how logical it was in the context of operant conditioning. Many young people who watch so many commercials, every day for nine months, with some repeated endlessly, develop a craving for new commercials. (p. 78)

Channel One, it appears, may be having deleterious effects on young people.

Other arguments against Channel One concern the proper role of commerce within the public sector. Is it right to give businesses a captive audience? Is it right for a public agency to implicitly endorse a product?

How might one apply the principles of autonomy, beneficence, nonmaleficence, and justice to this dilemma? Does Channel One foster self-determination, increased capacity for independence and self-regulation? Does it promote good for students, or at least do them no harm? Are there issues of fairness, equal access, or equal opportunity for students that need consideration?

If you were a teacher, and Channel One was being considered for your school, would you argue for or against it? Why?

- Are my values open to modification?
- Have I challenged my views, and am I open to challenge by others?
- Do I insist the world remain the same as it was earlier in my life?
- Do I feel so deeply committed to my values that I'm likely to push my clients to accept them?
- What is the role of religion in my life?
- How do my own values and beliefs affect my approach to working with clients? (pp. 61, 75)

A final recommendation is to increase your skills in perspective taking. Purposely seek out unfamiliar experiences and people, and try to understand the world from these other points of view. What are the values of others? How did they come to believe in them? What are their rationales? This does not mean you have to agree with them; you just need to increase your ability to see things as they see them. Recall how critical the skill of perspective taking is for both ethical action and successful relationships. An added bonus to this endeavor is that it will enhance your multicultural awareness. Getting better at perspective taking will take you giant steps forward in the quest to become an effective and wise teacher.

An Eastern European proverb says, if you want to know somebody's character, put them in a position of authority. As a teacher, you will be in a position of authority; you will create the environment in which students will live and breathe for months at a time. In this very public position, your character will be revealed. Take ample time between now and then to reflect on and clarify your own values and to provide yourself with multiple opportunities to gain the knowledge, dispositions, and skills needed to help your students, and yourself, develop morally.

SUMMARY

- Although interest in character education has been on the upswing in recent decades, Americans have always looked to schools to help shape students' moral capacities.
- Piaget pioneered research in children's moral development, and found two types of moral reasoning in children: heteronymous and autonomous.
- Kohlberg grounded his stage theory of moral development on Piaget and extended the framework to six stages: (1) punishment-obedience; (2) instrumental relativist; (3) good boy/good girl; (4) law and order; (5) social contract; and (6) universal principles. Some empirical research confirms this framework.
- Opponents of Kohlberg criticize the theory for its lack of gender and culture sensitivity and its failure to capture the potential for sophisticated moral reasoning on the part of younger children.
- Although the issue is controversial, teaching values in the classroom is unavoidable, because teaching involves rules and relationships. Every rule enforced and every nuance of relationship communicates values to students.
- Teachers should strive to communicate values necessary to functioning in our democratic society. Specifically, teachers should help students understand that their active participation as citizens is essential. Also important is the ability to understand divergent points of view and to enter into dialogue with those who differ.
- Perspective taking, emotional insight, and the ability to defer gratification, are key skills underlying moral reasoning and conduct.
- Research has revealed that mere exhortation will not make students ethical people. Opportunities to discuss moral issues, to share and understand differences of opinion, and to take moral action, all within a supportive classroom and school environment, are more likely to effect growth in ethical thinking and behavior.
- An important way that students learn is by modeling adults. Therefore teachers should be exemplary role models to afford students the chance to learn ethical behavior by imitation.
- Research on parenting has shown that an authoritative leadership style and an inductive approach to discipline are most conducive to promoting ethical conduct.

Teachers should develop authoritative, rather than authoritarian or laissez faire, leadership capabilities and learn how to discipline inductively.

- Moral discussion and service learning are two important ways to advance students' moral development.

- Teachers need to adhere to professional standards of conduct and to consider the principles of autonomy, beneficence, nonmaleficence, and justice in resolving moral dilemmas.

- Prospective teachers need to carefully reflect on their own values and the ways their values might interact in the classroom with those of students.

Readings for the Professional

DeVries, R. & B. Zan. *Moral Classrooms, Moral Children: Creating a Constructivist Atmosphere in Early Education*. New York: Teachers College Press, 1994.

This book shows how to advance young children's moral development through instructional practices.

Jackson, P. W., R. E. Boostrom, & D. T. Hansen. *The Moral Life of Schools*. San Francisco: Jossey-Bass, 1993.

This book offers detailed case studies of how morality is taught, explicitly and implicitly, in 18 elementary and high schools, both public and private.

Teachers and Their Work

Application and Portfolio Activities

Self-Assessments

Measuring Up to the Standards 436

Assessing Your Level of Moral Development 437

Observations

Professional Boards in Action 438

The Moral Tone of the Classroom 439

Interviews

The Unions and Professionalism 441

Students' Views about Ethics 442

Measuring Up to the Standards

Purpose
What are the standards for teacher preparation in your state? What does your community expect you to learn in an accredited teacher education program? The purpose of this exercise is to help you find out.

Directions
Obtain current standards for teacher preparation from your state's department of education or your university's curriculum library. Read the standards carefully. Write a summary of the standards.

Reflection
How do you feel about these standards you are expected to attain by the time you graduate with a degree in teaching? Are they higher or lower than you thought they would be? Do you feel comfortable with the prospect of teaching to these standards? Are there particular standards that you strongly agree or disagree with? If you have any strong negative feelings, how will you manage these as you pursue teacher education? Are there standards you find confusing or whose purposes are unclear? How might you go about clarifying these?

Assessing Your Level of Moral Development

Purpose   As we discussed in Chapter 13, teachers' level of moral development is related to their ability to create and maintain a democratic learning environment. It is important to be aware of one's own level of development and to seek to raise it if need be in order to achieve professional standards of conduct.

Directions   Read the dilemma below. Then tell whether you believe Steve should cheat on the test. Most important, justify your answer, explaining the reasoning behind your decision. Then compare your reasoning with the levels described in Chapter 13.

Steve, a high school junior, is working a night job to help support his mother, a single parent of three. Steve is a conscientious student who works hard in his classes, but he doesn't have enough time to study.

History isn't Steve's favorite course, and because of his night work, he has a marginal D average. If he fails his final exam, he will fail the course, won't receive credit, and will have to alter plans for work during his senior year. He arranged to be off work the night before the exam so he could study extra hard, but his boss called, desperate for Steve to come in and replace another employee who called in sick at the last minute. His boss pressured him heavily, so Steve went to work reluctantly at 8:00 P.M. and came home exhausted at 2:00 A.M. He tried to study, but he fell asleep on the couch with his book on his lap. His mother woke him for school at 6:30.

Steve went to his history class, looked at the test, and went blank. Everything seemed like a jumble. However, Lakeisha, one of the best students in the class, happened to have her answer sheet positioned so he could clearly see every answer by barely moving his eyes.

Based on what you've read here, is Steve justified in cheating on the test? Why or why not?

Reflection   At what stage of moral reasoning do you operate? Are you satisfied with this level? Is your moral reasoning adequate to the job of creating and maintaining a democratic classroom environment? What can you do to elevate your ability to reason about moral problems?

Professional Boards in Action

Purpose
The governance of teacher education is quite complex. This text has discussed, for example, the many constituencies that influence education, from federal to parental. It is a difficult job to coordinate the activities of so many entities. One important stakeholder in this process is the university. Colleges and universities are the major institutions that prepare new teachers. One way that they monitor teacher education and coordinate their activities is through universitywide committees. Understanding the issues, constraints, and trade-offs that go into the design and maintenance of teacher education programs will aid your own professional growth. The purpose of this exercise is to acquaint you with the governance of teacher education at the college and university level.

Directions
Sit in on a university advisory committee on teacher education or a similar committee in your department, college, community, state, or region. Keep a log of their discussion. Who is in attendance? What constituencies do they represent? Are students represented? What issues are discussed? What positions do participants take, and what are their arguments? What decisions are made? How will these decisions affect education majors? How will these decisions be communicated to education majors?

Reflection
What is your reaction to this experience? Evaluate the quality of the committee's work. What did they do well? What not so well? Justify your evaluation. What do you understand better now about the process of teacher education. What questions did this experience provoke?

The Moral Tone of the Classroom

Purpose   It is often difficult to make connections between abstractions like morality and the concrete world of classrooms. The purpose of this exercise is to aid you in making those connections.

Directions   Observe a classroom for about an hour. Look for evidence of how the teacher encourages autonomy, beneficence, nonmaleficence, and justice. Note teacher actions that embody these principles, as well as actions that run counter to them. At the end of the class, rate on a scale of 1 (low) to 5 (high) how well the teacher has established a positive moral tone.

Principle	Evidence For		Evidence Against
Autonomy			
	1	2	3	4	5
Beneficence			
	1	2	3	4	5
Nonmaleficence			
	1	2	3	4	5
Justice			
	1	2	3	4	5

Reflection   In what ways did this teacher foster autonomy, beneficence, nonmaleficence, and justice? Compare your findings with other students'. Together, compile a list of practices you have observed that foster these important ethical principles in classrooms. In what ways did this teacher impede these principles? Compile a further list of practices to avoid. Based on this experience, develop and discuss additional actions that you could take as a teacher to foster autonomy, beneficence, nonmaleficence, and justice in your own classroom.

The Unions and Professionalism

Purpose   The purpose of this exercise is to familiarize you with the perspectives and work of teachers' unions.

Directions   Interview a teacher who is active in union leadership, either in the NEA or the AFT. Use the questions below as a guide.

1.   What is your role in the union? Could you explain union membership rules here?

2.   Do you believe that teaching is a profession? Why or why not? There are four characteristics associated with professions: specialized body of knowledge, respect and status, autonomy, and accountability. How do you think teaching stacks up on those four attributes? What is the union doing to facilitate teaching as a profession?

3.   How does collective bargaining work? Are teachers in this district getting good raises lately? What factors influence teacher salaries here? What are the prospects for future salary raises?

4.   How does the grievance procedure work? Can you give me examples of some recent grievances in this district? What was the union's role? What was the outcome?

5.   What does your union see as its major priorities in the next few years? Why?

Reflection   How do you feel about the union after talking to a representative? Do you see it as a positive influence for education? Why or why not? How has this experience affected your interest in teaching as a career?

Students' Views about Ethics

Purpose

Essential to establishing a positive ethical climate in the classroom is a firm understanding of your students' moral capacities. The purpose of this exercise is to familiarize you with how students think about moral problems.

Directions

Interview two or three students in the age group that most interests you. Use the questions below as a guide.

1. Read aloud the cheating dilemma in the self-assessment section. Should Steve cheat or not? Why?

2. Read aloud the Heinz dilemma in Chapter 13. Should Heinz steal the drug or not? Why?

3. Here are some things that kids are usually not supposed to do in school. Which of these do you think are the worst, and which do you think aren't so bad?

    Copying someone else's homework.
    Copying on a test.
    Sidetalking.
    Taking cuts in line.
    Stealing somebody else's stuff.
    Lying to a teacher or other adult.
    Lying to a friend.
    Marking a desk or a wall.
    Passing notes to friends during class.
    Fighting.
    Making fun of another student.
    Teasing a younger student.
    Bullying.
    Grabbing, pushing, shoving.
    Breaking something that belongs to somebody else.

4. Have you known anybody who did any of those things? What happened? Are there other things students do that are wrong? Like what?

5. We've talked about the things you're not supposed to do. What about good things? What are some good things that you should do?

6. Are there ever times when you're not sure what the right thing to do is? Can you tell me about it? How did you decide?

Reflection

How would you assess these students' levels of moral development? If they were in your class, how would their level of ethical functioning affect your classroom organization, rules, and procedures? How might you maximize student involvement in rule making and decision making, while at the same time preserving a safe, orderly environment? What could you do as a teacher to help them grow in their capacity for moral reasoning and action?

Observing in Communities, Schools, and Classrooms

Importance of Observation

One of the most important parts of preparing to teach is to learn how to observe. This, of course, is something you do every day of your life. So, you may be wondering why we have included an entire appendix on observing. We believe there is a big difference between looking at an activity or situation and really *seeing* and understanding what is going on.

You have observed schools and classrooms for most of your life. However, as we explained in Chapter 4, you have participated as a *student* and have observed what goes on from in front of rather than behind the teacher's desk. This guide will help you develop the tools for observing what goes on in schools and classrooms, as well as in the communities in which they exist, from the viewpoint of a prospective teacher. Using this guide will help you learn to analyze and reflect on those activities and situations and to understand them in the context of the larger pedagogical, social, and political picture.

There are wide variations in teacher education programs in regard to how much field experience is planned for students and how early in their programs this component begins. In some cases, you may be given little or no planned or structured opportunity to observe school and classroom activities until you begin your student teaching. In other cases, your program may provide many and varied experiences. Today, many teacher educators and individuals preparing to teach believe that prospective teachers should be given plenty of opportunity to observe what professionals do in schools and classrooms. Whether or not your program provides early and systematic observation opportunities as part of your field experience, you can take the initiative for professional observation on your own. Many of the activities in the Application and Portfolio section at the end of each part in this text suggest how to arrange to observe in schools and classrooms. These activities include structured observation forms that help you to observe and understand what is going on. The forms will assist you in noticing and reflecting on what is taking place and

will help you develop your own professional ideas and expertise.

Observation Settings

As you learned in Chapter 7, the majority of your time as a teacher will be spent in your own classroom, teaching and working with students. It is important to keep in mind that much of what takes place in your classroom is affected by the school and community in which you teach. To be effective in your classroom, it is critical that you are aware of and understand community and districtwide factors that can influence your workplace. Likewise, there are various components of how the particular school in which you teach is run that will affect what you do in your classroom. Before reviewing guidelines for observing in these three settings, let us consider briefly some of the most important elements of each.

Communities

Community factors that influence your classroom include the prevailing socioeconomic status and the racial and ethnic makeup of the community and student body; the dynamics of the operation of the school board, including its interaction with the superintendent; the strength and impact of the teachers' association; and the relative influence of parent groups. You need to know what a community's values are and whether they are more likely to storm a school board meeting because of low standardized test scores or the elimination of an athletic team.

Schools

School factors that are important in teachers' daily lives include both the physical and the social environments. Components of the physical environment include the size, structure, and appearance of the building; the layout of classrooms and other work areas in the building; the amount and quality of educational equipment, especially technology; the placement of such crucial areas as the main office, guidance, and the media center; provisions made for teacher collaboration, such as lounges and offices;

and facilities provided for parent and community participation in school and related activities.

The social environment of the school includes the organizational structure of the school; the leadership style of the principal and his or her relationship with the teachers, other school personnel, students, and parents; teachers' relationships with each other and the extent of conflict or collaboration that exists; and teachers' attitudes toward and relationships with students and parents.

Classrooms

How well does a classroom promote self-regulated learning and democracy? This can be identified by such things as how the teacher arranges the classroom; work chosen for students to do; the amount of interaction permitted among students; the relationship between the teacher and the students; the amount of teacher talk versus student talk; the way in which the teacher uses the textbook; the kinds of questions teachers ask in their lessons; the kinds and amount of homework assigned; and the disciplinary measures the teacher uses.

Observation Processes

Whether you are observing at the community, school, or classroom level, there are several common components to the observation process. The following guidelines will be useful to you in carrying out an actual observation.

1. *Follow observation etiquette.*
   a. Arrange in advance with the person in charge to observe any activity that is not usually open to the public, such as a school meeting or a class.
   b. Arrive on time.
   c. Remember that you are a guest.
   d. Thank the responsible person for allowing you to observe.
2. *Focus your observations.* Determine in advance exactly what it is you want to observe. This is important because there are so many things taking place at such a rapid pace in observation contexts that you will be overwhelmed if you do not isolate a particular activity on which to concentrate. The observation and interview guides at the end of each part are designed to help you focus.
3. *Observe an activity from beginning to end.* Whether it is a school board, PTA, teachers' meeting, or a history class, it is important that you see the entire activity to understand the dynamics of the situation.

4. *Refrain from becoming involved in the activity.* Your primary purpose as an observer is to learn from what is taking place, not to influence events. That means it will be necessary for you to position yourself as unobtrusively as possible and to avoid both verbal and nonverbal involvement with the participants in the activity.
5. *Record your observations.* You may think you will remember what you observe, but this is not the case. Therefore, it is important that you keep careful records. Not only will these records be useful to you in the classes that may accompany your field experiences, they will also provide a wealth of information you can refer to during your first few years of teaching. The observation and interview guides in the text are structured to simplify the recording process. In addition, there are several other ways that you can record what you observe.

Methods of Recording Observations

Note Taking Taking notes on what you observe in order to later reflect on and analyze what took place is the simplest form of recording your observations. As you continue this activity over an extended period of time, you may find that what you record falls into regularly recurring categories, and thus your subsequent observations may become more focused. It is important that you identify when and where an observation takes place and that you record dialogue or other details as explicitly as possible. Note taking is the most frequent form of recording data in an interview with a single individual, but it can also be used during classroom or meeting observations.

Logs and Journals One specific way to take notes is in a log or journal. Many teacher education programs require students to keep logs or journals throughout their field experiences and designate the specific format in which they are to be kept. Typically, journals are kept on a daily basis and include the date, time, and place of the activity followed by a brief description of what took place. Journals usually provide space for analysis and reflection. It is expected that over time teacher candidates will review their logs or journals and reflect on personal growth.

Observation Guides Observation guides, such as those found in the Application and Portfolio Activities sections of this text, have been developed to help observers focus on specific components of an activity. These guides are most frequently used in classroom observations. They deal with activities ranging from classroom physical arrangements to teachers' questioning strategies, and they enable an observer to record what is observed in a systematic way.

Structured Observation Systems   Researchers have developed a number of observation instruments that have standardized responses to designated categories. Like observation guides, these are used primarily for observation in classrooms and may require training if they are to be used reliably. We examine two current forms of structured observation systems when we discuss observing in the classroom context.

Questionnaires   Often it is not possible to observe sufficient instances of a situation to know whether what you are seeing is a unique or a commonplace event. In these instances, you may want to gather additional information from a large number of individuals. Questionnaires are the most practical way to accomplish this goal. Questionnaires may have structured items in which respondents select one or more options from a defined set of specified responses. Alternatively items may be open-ended questions they complete with their own words.

Distinguishing between Recording, Interpreting, and Evaluating Data

During observations, it is important that you distinguish between recording *what you see* and *your interpretation of what you see*. Although ultimately the purpose of observation is to help you to make sense of classroom, school, and community life, during the observation itself, you must avoid the inclination to interpret or to evaluate what is taking place. It is important that you do your best to simply record the facts as you observed them. At a later time, you will have an opportunity to reflect on what you saw, interpret the events, and evaluate them for your own purposes. The following examples will help you distinguish between recording a factual description of what you observed and interpreting and evaluating the event.

Description: The substitute teacher sent the student to the principal's office.

Interpretation: The substitute teacher was unable to control the student's behavior.

Evaluation: The substitute is a poor teacher.

Description: The student was looking out the window while the teacher was talking.

Interpretation: The student was not paying attention.

Evaluation: The student was bored.

Description: The activities bulletin board outside the school displayed last month's dates.

Interpretation: Someone has failed to fulfill his or her responsibility to keep the bulletin board up to date.

Evaluation: The staff of the school does not care about the community's perception of the school.

Description: Twenty parents objected to the new high school discipline policy at the school board meeting.

Interpretation: Parents were angry about the way it was formulated.

Evaluation: Parents thought it was a bad process for developing policy.

Interviewing

Interviewing is also a useful tool for learning about teaching and schooling. Sometimes, you will want to interview a variety of individuals—such as students, teachers, administrators, or parents—about a specific school policy or event. For example, you are likely to get very different opinions about the school detention or suspension policies depending on whom you are interviewing. On other occasions, you may want to interview many members of the same group in order to get a broader picture regarding general attitudes and perceptions. An example of such a situation might be teachers' reaction to a new school requirement that progress reports must be written for all students in the middle of the semester, whether or not they are failing.

As with observation, there are some general guidelines for interviewing people in schools or in community settings. You will find that there are two types of interview opportunities: *impromptu* and *previously arranged*. The most common occasion for impromptu interviews will be immediately before or after an event or meeting. In the suggested observation activities discussed further on, we describe various circumstances in which you might carry on an impromptu interview. When you do, it is important that you be sensitive to just how much time the individual is willing to give you and try to arrange additional time if you have a lot of questions. For arranged interviews, like the ones described in the Application and Portfolio sections, it is important that you make an appointment beforehand, show up on time, and stay no longer than the amount of time agreed to. Additional guidelines for interviewing include the following.

1. Remember that you represent your teacher education program and college or university and want to make the best possible impression.

2. The information you collect should be considered confidential, to be shared only with your instructors and fellow students and usually without naming specific individuals interviewed.

3. Be polite when interacting with school personnel.

4. Dress professionally.

5. If possible, carry out the interview in a private place.

6. Thank the interviewee in writing.

There are generally two types of questions interviewers ask: *close-ended, factual questions* that solicit specific information and *open-ended questions* that ask for the interviewee's perceptions or opinions. If you are not already equipped with a ready-made guideline, it is important to have several questions prepared in advance rather than just asking people to tell you about something. It is true, however, that people will tell you interesting and worthwhile things which you could not have anticipated. If you are going to interview several individuals about the same event or issue, it is important to have a few standard questions in order to be able to compare their answers. In all cases, you should take notes about what respondents say, because it is easy to forget what you hear and from whom, especially if you are interviewing several people. The interview activities provided at the end of each part are structured with these guidelines in mind. Always feel free, however, to pursue in more depth particular responses that are interesting to you.

Observation Activities

This section describes additional observation activities you might conduct in three settings: communities, schools, and classrooms. Most teacher education programs provide many field experiences whose focus will be primarily classrooms and schools. But since it is extremely important that you have some understanding of the community in which schools and classrooms exist, we offer several that focus on the community level first.

Communities and Districts

Demography   There are countless ways in which you can become generally familiar with a community, starting with walking around the neighborhood in which the school is located. You should be able to get some idea of the socioeconomic status of the people living in the immediate area by observing such things as the type and condition of the housing, how much business and industry there is nearby, and the presence of such public buildings as libraries and community centers. Questions to ask yourself might include, Is there a downtown area with well-kept stores and a good deal of foot traffic, or do you find empty store fronts and the appearance of vagrancy and drug-dealing? Are the neighborhoods racially integrated, segregated, or predominantly one race? Does there seem to be a large number of senior citizens or younger families with children in the schools?

There are a variety of things that will affect what teachers do in the classroom that result from the geography of the community. For instance, if all the students in the district walk to school, there are fewer reasons for being late to school than if they are bused by the district or take public transportation. Likewise, their means of getting home after school will affect both teachers' discipline methods and whether or not they can provide after-school help. These general community observations are good for a start. In the following sections we list specific questions that will help you gain more detailed information about how communities affect school practices.

Municipal Government   Attend a meeting of the council in the city or town where your school is located. You can find out when these meetings are scheduled by calling the central office of the local government or by checking in the newspaper. You can get some idea of how welcome visitors to these meetings are by observing the following.

1. Are agendas and related materials available in advance of the meeting? Or are they on a table near the entrance of the room where the meeting is held?

2. Is the room arranged to facilitate communication between the council and citizens?

3. Does the council give citizens an opportunity to speak at both the beginning and the end of the meeting?

The relationship between the municipal government and the school board is extremely important, because they both depend on local and state taxes to carry out their functions. In addition, they frequently share services within a community, such as snow removal and grounds maintenance. As you listen to what takes place in the meeting, try to identify whether any of the business on the agenda is school related and, from that, whether there is a cooperative or hostile relationship between the two governing bodies. After the meeting is over, try to interview members of the municipal council to determine what the relationship with the school board is like. Does the council have a representative to the school board or the board to the council? Does the school district use the local police force for security at school events? Do the council and the school board plan together on budgets and tax rates?

School Board Meeting   At the end of Part I there is an observation activity relating to school boards. Some additional issues and questions are offered here to extend your learning about how school boards operate. You can determine when school board meetings take place by checking in the newspaper or by calling the school board office. Availability of the agenda, arrangement of the room, and opportunity for interaction between the board and the public are as important in these meetings as they were in city government meetings. As you observe, consider the following questions.

1. Does a single person seem to dominate the proceedings?
2. Does the board vote unanimously on most motions or is there a consistent split in the vote?
3. Do members of the board make efforts to see each other's point of view?
4. Does the board approve every recommendation of the superintendent with little or no debate or discussion?
5. Are there many members of the public present?
6. If they are given the opportunity to speak, do members of the public have generally positive or hostile interactions with the school board?
7. Who are the people who speak–senior citizens concerned about the impact of the school district budget on taxes or parents worried about school programs?

There are other dimensions of school board operations that will help you understand the impact that the community and the school board have on what takes place in schools and classrooms. As you observe the school board meeting, notice also the following.

1. What proportion of the meeting is spent discussing academic matters as compared to such matters as facilities, transportation, grounds, and athletic events?

2. Does the board operate with a committee structure or as a committee of the whole?
3. Are there any teacher representatives to the board? Student representatives?
4. What is the proportion of male and female representatives on the board?
5. Are there any minority board members?
6. Did any significant actions take place at the meeting?

As you did after the council meeting, when the meeting is over, try to talk to various members of the board. Find out whether there is a liaison to the council, what various board members see as school district problems, why they wanted to serve on the board, and what they hope to accomplish.

Organizational Chart   Prepare an organizational chart of the school district that shows the positions and the people in them and their relationships to each other. You may be able to acquire such a chart from the school board main office. Fill in some of the following information.

1. Districtwide policy or curriculum committees.
2. Regular or ad-hoc school board committees.
3. Committees common to all schools, such as site-based committees.

Use this chart to help answer the following questions:

1. What is the relationship of the board to the community?
2. What is the relationship of the superintendent to the board? To the community? To the teachers' association? To the parents?
3. How much input do the faculty and staff have in policy making and curriculum development?
4. How much autonomy do individual schools have?

Teachers' Association   In addition to the Part V interview with a teacher union leader, this observation will extend your learning about the roles unions play in the teaching profession. Find out whether the teachers in the district in which you are observing are represented by the AFT or the NEA. Arrange to attend a regular meeting. You can get some idea of the role of the teachers' association in the district through the following considerations.

1. What proportion of the members of the association attend the meetings?
2. Was a clear agenda prepared in advance?

3. Are there representatives present from all of the schools or primarily from a single school? Does one group seem to dominate the meeting?

4. Do actions planned by the teachers' association seem pro-active or reactive?

5. Does the association have a plan for ongoing professional improvement for its members?

Schools

Physical Facilities   Quality educational activities can go on in the humblest of surroundings. However, what physical facilities are like in a district will tell a great deal about what the community values. As you think about the schools you have attended or visited, probably the first things that come to mind is whether they were old or new, multistoried or spread out on a single level. There are a number of other aspects of school facilities that will help you to get an idea about a community's educational values and priorities.

1. Do the building and grounds appear well kept?

2. Is the main entrance to the school obvious and inviting?

3. Is it easy to find the main office once you enter the school, and are there signs to guide you to other areas?

4. Is the inside of the school clean?

5. How is the school decorated? Does it feature student work and accomplishments?

6. How many computer labs does the school have? How many gymnasiums?

7. What is the school library like? Is it centrally located?

8. Is there a teachers' lounge? Teachers' work areas?

9. Are there security personnel in the halls? Metal detectors?

10. Can teachers be seen standing outside their rooms as classes pass?

Organizational Chart   Just as you developed an organizational chart for the school district as a whole, it will be helpful to understand what takes place in the school itself by developing an organizational chart for it.

In addition to showing the relationships among the principal, assistant or vice principals, guidance, secretaries, teachers, maintenance and other support persons, and students, use the chart to consider the following.

1. Are there school committees that have any role in the policy making and/or governance of the school?

2. If so, are they composed of teachers, staff, parents, students, or a mix of individuals?

3. Are they "recommending" committees or do they actually make policy?

4. Who chairs the committees? Is this individual appointed by the principal or elected by the committee?

5. Does the principal or vice principal sit on any of these committees?

6. How are members selected for the committees?

7. Are there individuals in the school who have more influence on school affairs than their place in the organizational chart would indicate?

The answers to these questions will help you to understand the extent of traditional versus site-based governance and management taking place at the school where you observe. You can supplement what you learn from developing the organizational chart by interviewing some of the individuals on it—from the principal to the students—regarding their perceptions of school organization and governance.

Guidance   Although guidance may be a district-wide service, in most school districts it is concentrated at the high school level, where it generally serves the dual functions of counseling and career planning. Understanding how the guidance department works in a school can be crucial to providing students with help they need outside of the classroom. Notice the following aspects of how guidance works in the school in which you observe.

1. What is the makeup of the guidance department? Is there any attempt to have gender and racial balance comparable to the student body?

2. How are students divided among guidance counselors? For example, are they divided arbitrarily by the alphabet or grade, or are they divided by career interests, college-prep with one counselor, vocational track with another.

3. Does the guidance department appear to be primarily proactive or reactive? For example, is there an aggressive effort to help students identify the most appropriate colleges to attend, or do counselors wait for students to come to them for help? Is there a career-shadowing program in place?

4. Are there specific counselors who deal with substance abuse problems?

5. Are teachers familiar with the services the guidance department provides?

6. How much contact does guidance have with parents?

7. Does the district offer guidance services at the junior high or elementary level?

Cultural Sensitivity   The sensitivity of a school to cultural diversity can be identified by observing the facilities, programs, activities, and events and how they relate to students' backgrounds. Some questions to help you to focus on school culture follow.

1. How racially, ethnically, religiously, and economically diverse is the student body?

2. Is this diversity reflected in what is displayed on the walls in the halls of the school? How diverse are the faculty and staff?

3. Are there clubs that reflect student diversity?

4. Are specific sports teams, musical groups, and drama production crews predominantly one race or are they integrated?

5. Is there a clear effort by teachers to integrate culturally relevant activities into their curriculum?

6. Are newsletters, bulletin boards, and other communications in English only, or do they include other languages?

7. Are there other school events—assemblies, festivals, projects, or other—that recognize and celebrate cultural diversity?

Teachers' Lounge   The teachers' lounge or work area is another place you can learn about the school. Look at its location, size, and equipment.

1. Is it centrally located for teachers' routine use, or is it so far off in a corner somewhere that teachers seldom ever go there?

2. Is it large enough for a number of teachers to use simultaneously and be able to accomplish any work?

3. What equipment do teachers have?

4. Is there ready access to computers and copying machines?

5. Is the room comfortably furnished and inviting?

6. Do teachers use the room and appear to enjoy being there?

Another area that will yield information about a school is that of teacher talk in the teachers' lounge.

1. If teachers talk about students, curriculum, and classroom activities, do they share constructive ideas about students and new ideas about what works in their classrooms?

2. Do they seek help from each other with classroom problems?

3. How much information is shared about the activities of the teachers' association?

The teachers' lounge is probably the best place to learn about the power structure in a school.

1. Who is "in" and who is "out" with the principal?

2. Do the teachers generally see their relationship with the administration as collaborative or authority based?

3. How often does the principal come to the teachers' lounge?

4. Are there certain teachers who never use the teachers' lounge? Can you learn why? Do they congregate somewhere else?

5. Are there gender-based groups of teachers or groups based on other categorical differences? Do important decisions get made in any of these groups?

Teachers' Ethics   This is a most sensitive area to observe and one in which hasty interpretation or evaluation should be avoided.

1. Review the two components of the NEA Code of Ethics—Commitment to the Student and Commitment to the Profession in Chapter 13. Observe over a period of time whether there are any violations of the code. Record what you believe the violation is and what you think would have been appropriate for the teacher to do in that situation.

2. Identify any teacher behavior that you feel is unprofessional and explain why. Is this covered by the NEA Code of Ethics? Is there a category you would add to the code?

Classrooms

Classroom observations are the most complicated observations you will do. This is because there are so many individuals involved who are often engaged in a variety of fast-paced and complicated activities. Therefore, it is especially important that you do focused observations. There are a number of observation activities described here that focus on the main aspects of classroom activity: planning, managing, instructing, and assessing. Because of the complexity of the classroom, do not attempt to observe more than one activity during a class visit. For some of the activities, the best means of recording data is through notes. For others, use observation guides, such as those presented in this text, or structured observation systems. It is important to emphasize again, however, that while you are observing in classrooms, you should only record data, not attempt to interpret or evaluate it.

Planning   The old saying "if you fail to plan, then you plan to fail" is especially true in teaching. Unfortunately, planning is the most difficult aspect of teaching to observe, because so much of it is invisible mental work. However, most school districts provide teachers with some planning time every day. Ask a teacher to explain her planning process to you, and to show you any written plans she may use. Alternatively, while observing in a classroom, try designing the instructional plan that represents the lesson being taught. Share it with the teacher afterward, and see how closely it parallels her own.

Management   Observing the components of classroom management includes the physical arrangement of the room, the established rules and procedures, and the teachers' interactions with the students. The following questions will help you focus your observations about classroom management.

1. How is the room arranged? Are all the desks in rows facing the front of the room? Where is the teachers' desk? Are the desks movable? Does the teacher move them for different lessons? If so, is there an organized plan for moving them or is desk moving haphazard? Are there learning centers? Do students ever sit on the floor for classroom activities? Is equipment accessible and ready to use when it is needed?

2. Are classroom rules and procedures clearly posted? Do the students seem to know them? Do the procedures facilitate the smoothness of the classroom operation? Does the teacher enforce the rules?

3. Where does the teacher spend the most time? At the desk or moving around the room? During lessons does the teacher move toward student disturbances in an effort to stop them without interrupting the lesson? Does the teacher use the chalkboard during lessons? Does the teacher lose students' attention while her back is turned? Or does the teacher use an overhead projector to see the students while writing?

4. Does the teacher interact differently with different students? Try some of the following exercises to determine this?
   a. Count the number of times the teacher calls on boys or girls.
   b. Record whether there is any difference in the teachers' willingness to let boys or girls call out answers to questions without raising their hands.
   c. Who talks more in the class—boys or girls?

5. If the class is racially mixed, is there a difference in a , b, or c by race?

6. If the socioeconomic levels of students are known, does the teacher treat those who appear to be poor differently from those who appear more affluent?

Instruction   There are countless things to look at when observing the actual activity of classroom instruction. We suggest a few here.

1. Is the teachers' primary instructional method teacher-centered or does he or she use class discussion, group work, student reports?

2. What kinds of questions does the teacher ask? Open or closed ended? Seeking information, understanding, or evaluation?

3. How does the teacher answer student questions? With only the minimum amount of information necessary? Or does the teacher try to get students to find the answers to their own questions?

4. Does the teacher give the students the opportunity for guided practice of newly learned skills?

Assessment   As Chapter 6 described, assessment of learning takes various forms—from the teacher's moment-by-moment awareness of students' interest and responsiveness, to the lesson, to annual standardized tests. Although assessing student learning through regular end-of-unit tests or projects is an important form of evaluation, it is equally as crucial that teachers assess learning while it is in progress. Focusing on the following considerations will help you observe how much of this kind of assessing a teacher does.

1. Does the teacher seem to notice when the students are not paying attention? Does the teacher change what he or she is doing as a result?

2. Does the teacher make regular eye contact with all the students in an effort to determine whether or not they are following the lesson?

3. Does the teacher check student understanding in a variety of ways?

4. Are students expected to explain to each other or the entire class things they have just learned?

5. Do the students have any opportunity to assess one another's work and provide feedback?

6. Does the teacher walk around the room while students are doing seatwork to get an overall picture of how students are doing and to provide individual students with help?

7. How much homework does the teacher assign? Does he or she grade it and return it promptly? Is it reviewed in class? Do students have an opportunity to ask questions about graded homework, tests, or projects? Does the teacher provide informative feedback?

Parent Communication   An additional area of importance in classroom observation is the frequency, form, and quality of communication with parents and guardians. The most common form of parent communication is the report card, but there are a variety of ways schools can get information to parents. It is important as well to observe whether or not schools encourage parents to be involved in school activities and to provide information to teachers. The following questions will help you to identify the forms and quality of parent communication.

1. What are report cards like? Letter or numerical grades? Are there places for comments? Do students have to bring signed report cards back to school?

2. Are there parent conferences? If so, ask the teacher if you can sit in on one or more and observe the following:
   a. Are the students also present for the conferences? If so, do they just listen or are they encouraged to participate?
   b. Does the teacher have examples of student work to share with parents?
   c. Are the conferences scheduled for various times of the day in order for working parents to be able to participate?
   d. Are teachers responsive to parents who call and ask for conferences at other than regularly scheduled times?

3. Are teachers expected to call parents on a regular basis for things other than discipline?

4. Do parents volunteer in the classroom?

5. Does the teacher regularly send home a newsletter or some other form of communication about what is going on in class?

6. Do parents feel welcome in the teacher's class?

Getting Certified and Employed

The overwhelming majority of jobs in education are in the public schools, and employment in the public schools requires state certification. Although many states have reciprocity agreements, each state issues its own teaching certificates. Appendix B provides information about the steps involved in acquiring a certificate, and Appendix C gives the addresses of the offices of certification for each of the states. Also included are the steps you need to take to secure your first teaching position.

You may think that getting your certificate is not something you have to worry about for a few years—until you have completed student teaching and are ready to graduate, but that is not the case. You need to be aware of certification requirements from the beginning of your program to ensure that you meet the course and field experience requirements in the state in which you wish to be certified. These requirements generally fall into the following areas.

- General education.
- Subject area for certification.
- Professional education including student teaching and other field experiences.
- Competency tests.

At the same time you are acquiring your teaching certificate, you should begin thinking about your first teaching position in order to *collect materials for a professional portfolio* and to *identify through your field experiences the type of community and school in which you want to teach.*

Supply and Demand in the Teaching Profession

You may already have chosen the subject and level you want to teach, or you may be considering one or another subject and not be completely sure whether you want to teach at the elementary, middle, or high school level. To some degree your getting a job once you complete your program will be determined by how many openings there are and the number of qualified individuals available to fill them—what is referred to as supply and demand. In the teaching profession supply and demand are affected by a variety of factors, which are considered here.

Geography   Job availability varies by both section of the country and whether the district is located in an urban, suburban, or rural area. For example, sections of the country that experienced teacher shortages by the mid 1990s included the western and midwestern states. Generally speaking, areas of the country in which there is a high demand for teachers are those in which there is a substantial population growth or salaries are lower than average. Regardless of what section of the country you may be interested in, urban areas generally have more teaching jobs available than suburban areas, for the obvious reasons that there are more people in urban areas and teaching in inner-city schools is often highly challenging.

Subject Area   For those interested in teaching at the middle school or secondary level, job availability varies by subject area. The two fields in which there are often more qualified applicants than there are job openings are social studies and English. In contrast, the subject areas that continuously experience teacher shortages are science, mathematics, and foreign languages. Job availability in these subject areas varies by state, however. The more years of a subject that a state requires for high school graduation, the greater a demand there will be in that state for teachers of that subject.

Teaching Level   Overall, there is a greater demand for elementary teachers than for secondary teachers. This results from several factors. In the first place, the older students get, the more likely they are to drop out of school, which leads to decreasing enrollments in the upper grades. Second, it is often true that class size at the elementary level is smaller and greater numbers of fully certified instructional support people are employed. Finally, the turnover in elementary school positions is higher than in secondary positions.

Types of Teachers   Those areas of teaching in which there have been ongoing shortages are special education, bilingual education, and speech pathology. As the special needs population of students grows, especially in the inner city, these areas are likely to increase in demand.

Race and Gender   In all geographic areas, in subjects, and at all levels, there is a shortage of minority teachers, in particular, African Americans and Hispanics. As the population of minority students grows, the proportion of minority teachers in our schools declines. This is true at all levels from prekindergarten through twelfth grade. The picture is more complex in regard to gender. At the elementary level, teachers are overwhelmingly female, and school districts often seek additional male teachers on their staffs. At the secondary level, there are usually more males than females, especially in the areas of math and science. Additionally, there is a severe gender imbalance in administration, where both principals and central administrators are generally male.

As you begin your teacher preparation program, you need to take these factors into consideration as you decide where, whom, and what you want to teach. If you are sure you want to teach one of the subject areas for which the supply is greater than the demand—social studies or English—you may want to consider going to a geographic area in which the general demand for teachers is greater. Or, you may want to think about getting additional certification in an area such as reading or bilingual or special education. If you have more than one subject area that interests you, you may want to select the subject in which the demand is the greater. If you believe you would be equally happy teaching at either the elementary or the secondary level, it might be a good idea for you to take some extra coursework to qualify you for either.

Steps to Certification

Getting certified is not a difficult or complicated process as long as you know what it is you have to do and set out from the beginning of your teacher education program to do it. In this section, we outline the basic steps common to all programs and all states for acquiring initial certification and leading to permanent certification. Although some states give permanent certification immediately on graduation from college and completion of an approved teacher education program, a growing number require a period of successful teaching and/or additional course requirements before they will issue permanent certification.

Coursework   One of the most important resources available to you is your academic advisor. In addition, you should learn who the certification officer on your campus is and who is responsible for ensuring that you take the courses necessary to be certified in your state. Your academic advisor will help you plan your course schedule to complete the requirements for general education and your subject matter major. He or she should also be generally familiar with the certification process or be able to refer you to the individual in the school or department of education who handles certification. Carefully planning your coursework over the 4 or 5 years of your teacher preparation program will prevent your overlooking any requirements for certification.

All states require a college bachelor's degree and studies of subject matter and pedagogy for a regular teaching certificate. All but three states (California, Oregon, and Washington) have general education requirements. A growing number of states require coursework in special education (42 in 1996) and computer education (24 in 1996). Other general areas of study required by some states include health, drug, alcohol, and nutrition education (National, p. B–3). More specific requirements for initial elementary and secondary teaching certificates may include some of the following courses.

- Social foundations
- Philosophy of education
- Introduction to American education
- Educational psychology
- Human development
- Alternative ways of organizing schools
- Curriculum patterns and alternatives
- Nature of students' learning process/ developmental characteristics
- Structure of the school as an organization
- Development of basic repertoire of teaching strategies
- Methods of teaching elementary/secondary school subjects
- Methods of teaching reading
- Study of self (teacher) as learner
- Cultural diversity
- Technology in teaching (National, p. B–12)

Assessment Requirements

You will need to ask your advisor what teaching examinations your state and college require for entering into and/or completing the teacher education program. The majority of states require teachers to pass basic skills competency exams in reading, mathematics, writing, and subject matter. Nearly half have tests of general knowledge and knowledge of teaching. About a third include an assessment of teaching performance. In 1996, the following states and Washington, DC, required some form of assessment of teaching performance as part of initial certification: Alabama, California, Florida, Hawaii, Kentucky, Louisiana, New Jersey, Oklahoma, Oregon, South Dakota, Tennessee, and West Virginia (National, p. B–4).

Until recently, most states that required teachers to pass a competency exam before they were awarded initial certification used the National Teachers Exam (NTE) developed by the Educational Testing Services (ETS). However, that test has been replaced by a three-part series called Praxis. Praxis I is taken as a prerequisite for admission into a teacher education program and is a paper-and-pencil test of basic literacy skills in reading, writing, and mathematics. Praxis II is given at the end of the teacher preparation program and assesses professional knowledge and subject area knowledge in more than a hundred subjects. Praxis III is an assessment of classroom teaching performance and is more difficult to administer and evaluate than the other two. Thus, Praxis III is not widely used.

Field Experience

As of 1996, all but 12 states required field experience before student teaching. Those that do not are Arizona, Florida, Idaho, Maine, Maryland, Mississippi, Nevada, New Jersey, New York, Rhode Island, Utah, and West Virginia. Many states do not specify the amount of field experience required, indicating that it will be determined by individual institutions. In those that do, the amount ranges from a minimum of 40 hours to as many as 300 hours, or 2 full semesters (National, p. B–18).

Most states have some specific requirements regarding the final field experience of student teaching. Almost all states (except Alaska, Missouri, New York, West Virginia, and Wyoming) specify the amount of time for student teaching, ranging from 8 to 18 weeks or a specified number of clock hours, days, or semester hours of credit. Likewise, almost all states require that cooperating teachers meet minimum standards, and 14 states require that they be trained (National, p. B–19). Almost all states also require that a college-based supervisor visits student teachers. In all but 14 states (Arizona, Georgia, Idaho, Indiana, Kansas, Maine, Maryland, Missouri, Montana, Nebraska, New Mexico, New York, South Dakota, and Wisconsin) a student teacher is evaluated on the basis of a specific set of requirements. The individual responsible for evaluating the student teacher and recommending him or her for an initial certificate may be the college supervisor, the cooperating teacher, the school principal, or a combination of these (National, p. B–21).

Noneducational and Special Requirements for Teaching Certificates

Almost all states have some requirements for initial certification that are not part of the normal college preparation program (National, p. B–5). These include the following.

- U.S. citizenship
- Oath of allegiance
- Evidence of employment
- Recommendation of college/employer
- Minimum age
- A fee
- General health certificate
- TB test or chest X-ray
- Fingerprinting
- Screening for moral character

Reciprocity Agreements

There is always a possibility that you will find yourself teaching in a state other than the one in which you attend school. You need to be aware of the certification requirements in that state as well. In many cases, the state in which you receive your training will have a reciprocity agreement with the state in which you wish to teach.

The purpose of the Interstate Certification Agreement Contract is to assist teachers and other educators who move from state to state. It provides recognition of their educational training if they are state certified with appropriate experience or have completed state-approved teacher education programs. Currently 30 states, the District of Columbia, and Puerto Rico have signed contracts in one or more of the four educator categories: teachers, support professionals, administrators, and vocational educators.

Developing a Professional Portfolio

The way to increase the likelihood of your getting a job offer is to demonstrate to the principal and/or superintendent who interviews you that you are better prepared than other applicants. A *professional portfolio* is a collection of items you have selected throughout your teacher preparation program to demonstrate this. Some teacher preparation programs require such portfolios; many do not at the present time. However, the fact that it is not required in your program should not keep you from developing this important way in which to share your professional development with a prospective employer.

A professional portfolio is not to be confused with a course or program portfolio. Many course instructors or programs require that you keep a portfolio of your work for the primary purpose of showing your growth in knowledge and skills over a specified period of time. Thus, for a course, you may have both the first and the last papers you wrote so you and your instructor can assess your improvement in such skills as clearly stating your thesis, providing supporting points, and writing a comprehensive conclusion. Or your teacher education program may require you to complete a philosophical inventory in an introductory course and keep it in your program portfolio to consider in the final course as you write your own philosophy of education.

A professional portfolio, in contrast, provides your prospective employer with samples of your best work and documents that demonstrate the wide range of your preparation and qualifications. It is "a structured collection of evidence of a teacher's best work that is selective, reflective, and collaborative, and demonstrates a teacher's accomplishments over time and across a variety of contexts" (Wolf, 1991, p. 130). Following is a list of suggested items for a professional portfolio (Department, 1997; Shannon & Boll, 1997).

1. A current resumé.
2. Awards and/or certificates.
3. A summary of summer experiences or other extracurricular activities related to one's teaching success.
4. Evidence of membership in professional organizations.
5. A well thought out, succinct statement of one's philosophy of teaching that provides the basis for the selection of materials in the portfolio.
6. A complete unit, preferably one taught during student teaching.
7. A model lesson plan taught during student teaching, with an accompanying observation or evaluation form completed by the university supervisor.
8. A classroom management plan.
9. Photographs, drawings, diagrams, or descriptions of classroom activities carried out during student teaching.
10. Worksheets, activities, or games developed during student teaching.
11. A videotape of a lesson conducted during student teaching.
12. A reflective journal kept during student teaching.
13. A student evaluation tool developed during student teaching to monitor students' progress in some specified area, such as an observation checklist, criteria for evaluation of a student project, a student interview or questionnaire, or a formal written test.

Preparing a Resumé

The first contact a prospective employer will have with you is through your resumé, so you should prepare it carefully and thoroughly. Many colleges and universities have an office or individual responsible for helping students prepare their resumés. The appropriate time to contact that service is during the last year of your teacher preparation program.

Your resumé should include all the information your prospective employer will need in order to decide whether you are the best candidate for a position. It is important that you also focus on your own strengths. Your resumé should be typed, well-organized, and carefully proofread for content, grammar and spelling and punctuation errors. We recommend that it be no longer than two pages. The following items are included in most resumés.

1. A heading with name, address, phone number, and e-mail address.
2. Educational background, including dates, places, and majors for high school and college.
3. Date and location of student teaching.
4. Other work experience.
5. Awards, honors, certificates.
6. Membership in professional organizations and any offices held.
7. Extracurricular activities relevant to teaching.

8. Skills or competencies that will enable you to be a successful teacher.

9. Names of individuals as references (from whom you have acquired permission).

The Job Interview

There are several ways in which you may learn of an available teaching position. If you are interested in teaching in a particular school district, call or send a letter of inquiry to find out if there are any openings. Look through the local newspaper or professional publications that advertise for teachers. Also, the job placement office on your campus may bring recruiters from schools to interview applicants on campus. Regardless of how you acquire an interview, the interview itself will determine whether or not you receive a job offer. Therefore, it is extremely important that you prepare for it thoroughly.

Research the School District   It will help you in both your interview and your decision about whether to accept a job offer if you find out as much as possible about the community, the school district, and the school in which the position is available. You can get information about the community at the local library or through local newspapers. If school systems in your state are organized by counties, the office of the county superintendent of schools will be able to provide specific information about a district. Visit both the district office and the schools to get an idea of what they look like, and pick up any available literature. Talk with the secretaries in the central office and the individual schools. If you have friends in the district, interview them about their perceptions of the schools. Demonstrating to your interviewer that you have information about the district confirms that you are truly interested in working there.

Dress Appropriately   When you interview, present yourself in the most positive way possible. Although you may understand that teachers in the district where you are interviewing dress casually, your interviewer will expect men to wear suits and women to wear comparable professional attire. You should also be neatly groomed.

Preliminaries   Arrive for your interview early. This will give you an opportunity to speak with the receptionist or secretary and to observe what takes place in the waiting area, which will help you to get a feel for the school. When you are called in for the interview, it is appropriate to shake hands and wait to be asked to be seated.

Listen Carefully   Interviewing successfully entails carefully answering the questions your interviewer asks. In order to do this, you must be clear about what is being asked. If you do not understand a question, ask for clarification or elaboration, and be sure to give an answer. In addition to knowledge of subject area, school administrators often indicate that a critical quality for teaching is enthusiasm. Avoid getting off on tangents or giving too much information, however. Some frequently asked questions include the following.

- What is your philosophy of education?
- What are your strengths and weaknesses?
- What would you do in specific classroom situations?
- What extracurricular activities can you advise or coach?
- What are your future career plans?

You should also be aware of questions that interviewers cannot legally ask, such as your marital or parental status or your religion.

Ask Good Questions   Toward the end of an interview, most administrators will ask you if you have any questions. The purpose of the interview is not only for the district to determine if they want to hire you, but for you to determine if you would like to work there. You may want to know about such things as the size of the student body, the teaching staff, the average class size, what extracurricular activities are provided for students, what the grading and grade-reporting systems are like, the amount of teacher involvement in school decision making, the amount of parental involvement in the school, whether there are parent conferences, and what expectations there are for teachers beyond the classroom.

Provide Documentation   Take your professional portfolio to the interview with you. It will not be the first thing you show your interviewer, but as you are asked some of the questions we suggested you prepare for, you will be able to demonstrate your answers with documents or photographs from your portfolio. The videotape should be a copy so that you can leave it for the interviewer to watch at a later time.

Postinterview Etiquette   It is a good idea soon after the interview to send the interviewer a follow-up thank-you note and an expression of your interest in and qualifications for filling the available position. Not only is this courteous, but it leaves a positive impression on the interviewer who may be deciding among candidates.

Summary

Getting a teaching position that is satisfying, challenging, and enjoyable is something you should begin preparing for early on in your teacher education program. The first thing that you should do is become aware of the supply and demand in various teaching fields in order to be able to select the one that interests you most and in which you are likely to find employment. This may involve meeting one or more times with a college advisor, who should also be able to help you learn the certification requirements in your state and help you plan your coursework to meet them. In addition to getting certified, you will want to engage in those activities that will best prepare you for finding and securing a teaching position. These include developing a professional portfolio, preparing an informative and attractive resumé, and knowing how to participate effectively in a job interview.

State Licensing Agencies

Alaska Department of Education
Teacher Education & Certification
Juneau, AK 99801-1894
(907)465-2441

Teacher Certification Section
State Department of Education
P.O. Box 302101
Montgomery, AL 36130-3901
(334)242-9977

Teacher Education & Licensure
4 State Capitol Mall
Rms. 106B/107B
Little Rock, AR 72201
(501)682-4342

Teacher Certification Unit
1535 W. Jefferson St.
Phoenix, AZ 85007
(602)542-4367

Commission on Teacher
Credentialing
Box 944270
Sacramento, CA 94244-2700
(916)445-7254

Teacher Certification
201 E. Colfax Ave.
Rm. 105
Denver, CO 80203
(303)866-6628

Bureau of Certification &
Accreditation
P.O. Box 2219
Hartford, CT 06145-2219
(203)566-5201

Professional Development &
Certification Division
Townsend Bldg.
P.O. Box 1402
Dover, DE 19903
(302)736-4686/(800)433-5292

Teacher Education &
Certification Branch
Suite 101A
215 G St., N.E.
Washington, DC 20002
(202)724-4246

Bureau of Teacher Certification
Florida Education Center
Tallahasse, FL 32399
(904)488-2317

Division of Teacher Certification
1452 Twin Towers East
Atlanta, GA 30334
(404)657-9000

Office of Personnel Services
P.O. Box 2360
Honolulu, HI 96804
(808)548-3276

Office of Teacher Education &
Certification
State Dept. of Education
P.O. Box 83720
Boise, ID 83720-0027
(208)334-3475

Illinois State Board of Education
Teacher Education & Certification
100 N. 1st St.
Springfield, IL 62777
(217)782-2805

Indiana Professional Standards
Board
Teacher Certification Program
251 East Ohio, Suite 201
Indianapolis, IN 46204-2133
(317)232-9010

Practitioner Preparation &
Licensure
Grimes State Office Bldg.
Des Moines, IA 50319-0147
(515)281-3245

Teacher Education &
Accreditation
120 E. 10th St.
Topeka, KS 66612
(913)296-7933

Division of Certification
State Department of Education
Capital Plaza Tower
500 Mero St.
Frankfort, KY 40601
(502)564-4604

Higher Education & Teacher
Certification
P.O. Box 94064
Baton Rouge, LA 70804
(504)342-3490

Division of Certification &
Placement
Department of Education
23 State House Station
Augusta, ME 04333
(207)287-5944

Teacher Education & Certification Branch
Maryland State Dept. of Education
200 West Baltimore Street
Baltimore, MD 21201
(410)767-0100

Office of Certification
Department of Education
350 Main Street, P.O. Box 9140
Malden, MA 02148
(617)388-3380

Teacher/Administrator Preparation & Certification Services of Education
P.O. Box 30008
Lansing, MI 48909
(517)373-3310

Personnel Licensing
Capitol Square Building
550 Cedar Street
St. Paul, MN 55101
(612)296-2046

Division of Teacher Certification
State Department of Education
P.O. Box 771
Jackson, MS 39205
(601)359-3483

Teacher Education & Certification
Department of Elementary & Secondary Education
P.O. Box 480
Jefferson City, MO 65102
(314)751-3486

Teacher Education & Certification
Office of Public Instruction
P.O. Box 202501
Helena, MT 59620
(406)444-3150

Licensure Section
Department of Public Instruction
301 N. Wilmington Street
Raleigh, NC 27601
(919)733-4125

Education Standards & Practices Board
600 E. Boulevard Ave.
Bismarck, ND 58505-0440
(707)328-2264

Teacher Education & Certification
Department of Education
301 Centennial Mall South
P.O. Box 94987
Lincoln, NE 68509
1-800-371-4642

Bureau Of Credentialing
Division of Program Support
State Department of Education
State Office Park South
101 Pleasant Street
Concord, NH 03301
(603)271-2407

NJ Department of Education
Office of Licensing Cn 503
Trenton, NJ 08625-0503
(609)292-2070

Professional Licensure Unit
Department of Education Building
Santa Fe, NM 87503
(505)827-6587

Department of Education
1850 E. Sahara
Suite 207 State Mail Room
Las Vegas, NV 89158
(702)486-6455

Office of Teaching
State Education Department
Cultural Education Center
Room 5A-11
Nelson A. Rockerfeller Empire State Plaza
Albany, NY 12230
(518)474-3901

Division of Teacher Education & Certification
Ohio Department of Education
Ohio Department Building
Room 416
65 South Front Street
Columbus, OH 43215-4183
(614)466-3593

Professional Standards Section
Hodge Education Building Room 211
2500 North Lincoln Blvd
Oklahoma City, OK 73105
(405)521-3337

Teacher Standards & Practices Commission
255 Capitol St. N.E. Suite 105
Salem, OR 97310-1332
(503)378-3586

Bureau of Teacher Preparation & Certification
Pennsylvania Dept of Education
333 Market Street
Harrisburg, PA 17126-0333
(717)783-6736

Office of Teacher Education & Certification
Roger Williams Building
22 Hayes Street
Providence, RI 02908
(401)277-2675

Office of Education Professions
State Department of Education
Room 702
Rutledge Building
Columbia, SC 29201
(803)734-8317

Teacher Education & Certification
700 Governers Drive
Pierre, SD 57501-2291
(605)773-3553

Office of Teacher Licensing and Career Ladder Certification
State Department of Education
Gateway Plaza
710 James Roberts Pkwy 5th Floor
Nashville, TN 37243-0377
(615)532-4885

Division of Educator Preparation & Certification
Texas Education Agency
1701 N. Congress Ave.
Austin, TX 78701
(512)475-3568

Utah State Office of Education
250 East 500 South
Salt Lake City, UT 84111
(801)538-7740

Licensing Office
State Department of Education
Montepelier, VT 05620
(802)828-2445

Department of Education
Division for Compliance
Coordination
Office for Teacher Education and
Licensure
P.O. Box 2120
Richmond, VA 23216-2120
(804)225-2022

Professional Certification
Old Capitol Building
P.O. Box 47200
Olympia, WA 98504-7200
(360)753-6773

Office of Preparation
Building 6 Room 337
Capitol Complex
Charleston, WV 25305-0330
(304)558-7010

Licensing Team
Teacher Education Team
Department of Public Instruction
125 South Webster Street
P.O. Box 7841
Madison, WI 53707-7841
(608)264-9558

Wyoming Professional Teaching
Standards Board
Hathaway Building 2nd Floor
2300 Capitol Ave.
Cheyenne, WY 82002
(307)777-6261

Professional Associations

Arts

Music Educators National Conference
1902 Association Drive
Reston, VA 22091
(703) 860-4000

English & Reading

International Reading Association
800 Barksdale Road
Newark, DE 19714
(302) 731-1600

National Council of Teachers of English
1111 W. Kenyon Road
Urbana, IL 61801
(217) 328-3870

Foreign Language

American Council on the Teaching
of Foreign Languages
Six Executive Plaza
Yonkers, NY 10801
(914) 963-8830

Global Education

The American Forum
120 Wall Street
Suite 2600
New York, NY 10005
(212) 742-8232

Vocational Education

National Center for Research
in Vocational Education
University of California, Berkeley
2150 Shattuck Avenue
Berkeley, CA 94704
(510) 642-4004

History

National Center for History in Schools
UCLA, 231 Noore Hall
405 Hilgard Avenue
Los Angeles, CA 90024
(310) 825-8388

Mathematics

National Council of Teachers of Mathematics
1906 Association Drive
Reston, VA 22091
(703) 620-9840

Physical Education

National Association for Sport & Physical Education
1900 Association Drive
Reston, VA 22091
(703) 476-3410

Science

National Science Education Standards
2101 Constitution Avenue NW
HA 486
Washington, DC 20418
(202) 334-1399

Social Studies

National Council for the Social Studies
3501 Newark Street NW
Washington, DC 20016
(202) 966-7840

Abington School District v. *Schempp,* 374 U.S. 203 (1963).

Airasian, P. W. *Classroom Assessment.* New York: McGraw-Hill, 1991.

Airasian, P. W. *Classroom Assessment.* 2nd ed. New York: McGraw-Hill, 1994.

Airasian, P. W. *Assessment in the Classroom.* New York: McGraw-Hill, 1996.

Alexander, K., D. Entwisle, & S. Dauber. *On the Success of Failure: A Reassessment of the Effects of Retention in the Primary Grades.* New York: Cambridge University Press, 1994.

Allen, V. "Teaching Bilingual and ESL Children." In *Handbook of Research on Teaching the English Language Arts,* ed. J. Flood, J. M. Jensen, D. Lapp, & J. R. Squire. New York: Macmillan, 1991.

Alvin Independent School District v. *Cooper,* 404 S.W.2d 505 (9th Cir. 1984).

Ameral, M. & S. Feiman-Nemser. "Prospective Teachers' Views of Teaching and Learning to Teach." Paper presented at the annual meeting of the American Educational Research Association, New Orleans, 1988.

American Association of Colleges for Teacher Education. *Teaching Teachers: Facts and Figures (RATE I).* Washington, DC, 1987.

American Association of Colleges for Teacher Education. *Teaching Teachers: Facts and Figures (RATE II).* Washington, DC, 1988.

American Association of Colleges for Teacher Education. *Teaching Teachers: Facts and Figures (RATE III).* Washington, DC, 1989.

American Federation of Teachers. "Classnotes: High Standards Work for All." *American Teachers* 80 (1996), p. 2.

Ames, C. "Classrooms: Goals, Structures, and Student Motivation." *Journal of Educational Psychology* 84 (1992), pp. 261–271.

"An 'F' in World Competition." *Newsweek,* February 17, 1992, p. 57.

Anderson, C. "The Role of Education in the Academic Discipline of Teacher Education." In *Research Bases for the Graduate Preparation of Teachers,* ed. A. Woolfolk. Boston: Allyn & Bacon, 1989.

Anderson v. *Central Point School District No. 6,* 747 F. 2d 505 (9th Cir. 1984).

Anyon, J. "Social Class and the Hidden Curriculum of Work." *Journal of Education* 162 (1980), pp. 67–92.

Appeal of Mulbollen, 39 A. 2d 283 (Pa. Super. Ct. 1944).

Apple, M. W. *Teachers and Texts: A Political Economy of Class and Gender Relations in Education.* New York: Routledge, 1988.

Arends, R. I. "Challenging the Regularities of Teaching through Teacher Education." In *Current Perspectives on the Culture of Schools,* ed. N. B. Wyner. Boston: Brookline, 1991.

Arends, R. I. *Learning to Teach.* 3rd ed. New York: McGraw-Hill, 1994.

Artiles, A. J., M. P. Mostert, & M. Tankersley. "Assessing the Link between Teacher Cognitions, Teacher Behaviors, and Pupil Responses to Lessons." *Teaching and Teacher Education* 10 (1994), pp. 465–481.

Arundar v. *Dekalb County School District,* 620 F.2d 493 (5th Cir. 1980).

Azmitia, M. "Peer Interaction and Problem Solving: When are Two Heads Better Than One?" *Child Development* 59 (1988), pp. 87–96.

Baker, D., C. Semple, & T. Stead. *How Big Is the Moon?* Portsmouth, NH: Heinemann, 1990.

Baker v. *Owens,* 395 F. Supp 294 (M.D. N.C. 1975), aff'd, 423 U.S. 907 (1975).

Ball, D. L. (1988). "Knowledge and Reasoning in Mathematical Pedagogy: Examining What Prospective Teachers Bring to Teacher Education." Ph.D. diss., Michigan State University, East Lansing, 1988.

Banks, J. "Multicultural Education: For Freedom's Sake." *Educational Leadership* 4 (1992), pp. 32–36.

Banks, J. A. *Multiethnic Education: Theory and Practice.* 3rd ed. Boston: Allyn & Bacon, 1994.

Banks, J. "Multicultural Education: Its Effects on Students' Racial and Gender Role Attitudes." In *Handbook of Multicultural Education,* ed. J. Banks. New York: Macmillan, 1995.

Bannister v. *Paradis,* 316 F. Supp. 1985 (D. N.H. 1970).

Barker, R. & P. Gump. *Big School, Small School: High School Size and Student Behavior.* Stanford, CA: Stanford University Press, 1964.

Baumeister, R. F., T. F. Heatherton, & D. M. Tice. "When Ego Threats Lead to Self-Regulation Failure: Negative Consequences of High Self-Esteem." *Journal of Personality and Social Psychology* 64 (1993), pp. 141–156.

Baumeister, R. F. & L. Smart. "Relation of Threatened Egotism to Violence and Aggression: The Dark Side of High Self-Esteem." *Psychological Review* 103 (1996), pp. 5–33.

Baumrind, D. "A Developmental Perspective on Adolescent Risk Taking in Contemporary America." In *Adolescent Social Behavior and Health,* ed. C. Irwin, Jr. San Francisco: Jossey-Bass, 1987.

Beck, I. L. & McKeown, M. G. (1993). "Why Textbooks Can Baffle Students." *Learning* 1 (1993), pp. 2–4. Pittsburgh: University of Pittsburgh National Research Center on Student Learning.

Beck v. *James,* 739 S.W.2d 416 (Mo. Ct. App. 1990).

Benard, B. "Fostering Resiliency in Kids." *Educational Leadership* 51 (1993), pp. 44–48.

Benninga, J. S. (1988). "An Emerging Synthesis in Moral Education." *Phi Delta Kappan* 69 (1988), pp. 415–418.

Berk, L. E. *Child Development.* 2nd ed. Boston: Allyn & Bacon, 1994.

Berkowitz, M. "The Role of Discussion in Moral Education." Paper presented at the International Symposium on Moral Education, Fribourg, Switzerland, September 1982.

Berliner, D. C. "Implications of Studies of Expertise in Pedagogy for Teacher Education and Evaluation." Paper presented at the annual meeting of the Educational Testing Service, Princeton, NJ, 1988.

Berliner, D. C. & Biddle, B. J. *The Manufactured Crisis: Myths, Fraud, and the Attack on America's Public Schools.* Reading, MA: Addison-Wesley 1995.

Berman, P. & M. McLaughlin. *Federal Programs Supporting Education Change. Vol. 4: The Findings in Review.* Santa Monica, CA: Rand, 1975.

Bernstein, H. T. *A Conspiracy of Good Intentions: America's Textbook Fiasco.* Washington, DC: The Council for Basic Education, 1988.

Bestor, A. *Education Wasteland.* Urbana, IL: University of Illinois Press, 1953.

Bethel School District No. 403 v. *Fraser,* 478 U.S. 675 (1986).

Bettencourt, E. M. "Effects of Training Teachers in Enthusiasm on Student Achievement and Attitudes." Ph.D. diss. Eugene: University of Oregon, 1979.

Black, H. *Black's Law Dictionary.* 6th ed. St. Paul, MN: West, 1990.

B. M. v. *State,* 649 P.2d 425 (Mont. 1982), after remand, 698 P.2d 399 (Mont. 1985).

Board of Education of D.C. v. *Wilson,* 290 A.2d 400 (D.C. App. 1972).

Bolles, R. N. *What Color is Your Parachute.* Berkeley, CA: Ten Speed Press, 1996.

Bolman, L. G. & T. E. Deal. *Reframing Organizations.* San Francisco, CA: Jossey-Bass, 1991.

Book, C., J. Byers, & D. Freeman. "Student Expectations and Teacher Education Traditions with Which We Can and Cannot Live." *Journal of Teacher Education* 34 (1983), pp. 9–13.

Borko, H. & C. Livingston. (1989) "Cognition and Improvisation: Differences in Mathematics Instruction by Expert and Novice Teachers." *American Educational Research Journal* 26 (1989), pp. 473–498.

Boyd v. *Board of Directors of McGehee School Dist. No. 17,* 612 F. Supp. 86 (E.D. Ark. 1985).

Boyer, E. *The Basic School: A Community for Learning.* Princeton, NJ: The Carnegie Foundation for the Advancement of Teaching, 1995.

Bracey, G. W. "The Second Bracey Report on the Condition of Public Education." *Phi Delta Kappan* 74 (1992), pp. 104–117.

Bracey, G. W. "Curing Teen Violence." *Phi Delta Kappan* 77 (1995a), pp. 185–186.

Bracey, G. W. "The Fifth Bracey Report on the Condition of Public Education." *Phi Delta Kappan* 77 (1995c), pp. 149–160.

Bracey, G. W. "Research Oozes into Practice: The Case of Class Size." *Phi Delta Kappan* 77 (1995b), pp. 89–90.

Bracey, G. W. The Sixth Bracey Report on the Condition of Public Education. *Phi Delta Kappan* 78 (1995d) pp. 127–138.

Bracey, G. W. "International Comparisons and the Condition of American Education." *Educational Researcher* 25 (1996), pp. 5–11.

Bradley, A. "Signs Abound Teaching Reforms Take Hold." *Education Week.* April 5, 1995, pp. 23–24.

Bradshaw v. *Alabama State Tenure Commission,* 520 S.2d 541 (Ala. Civ. App. 1988).

Brendan v. *Independent School District 742,* 342 F. Supp. 1224 (D. Minn. 1972), aff'd 477 F.2d 1292 (8th Cir. 1973).

Breton, M. *What's Happened to Teacher?* New York: Random House, 1970.

Brice-Heath, S. *Ways with Words: Language, Life, and Work in Communities and Classrooms.* Cambridge, England: Cambridge University Press, 1983.

Brookover, W. et al. *School Social Systems and Student Achievement: Schools Can Make a Difference.* New York: Praeger, 1979.

Brophy, J. "Teacher Praise: A Functional Analysis." *Review of Educational Research,* (Spring 1981), pp. 5–32.

Brouilett v. *Cowles Publishing Company,* 791 P.2d 525 (Wash. 1990).

Brousard by Lord v. *School Board of City of Norfolk,* 801 F. Supp. 1526 (E.D. Va. 1992).

Brousseau, B. A. & D. Freeman. "How Do Teacher Education Faculty Members Define Desirable Teacher Beliefs?" *Teaching and Teacher Education* 4 (1989), pp. 267–273.

Brown, A. L. & A. Palinscar. "Guided Cooperative Learning and Individual Knowledge Acquisition." Technical report no. 372. Champaign, IL: Center for the Study of Reading, 1986.

Brown v. *Board of Education of Topeka, Kansas,* 347 U.S. 483, 495 (1954).

Bruner, J. *The Culture of Education.* Cambridge, MA: Harvard University Press, 1996.

Bruning, R. H., G. J. Schraw, & R. R. Ronning. *Cognitive Psychology and Learning.* 2nd ed. Englewood Cliffs, NJ: Merrill/Prentice-Hall, 1995.

Buckholdt, D. R. & J. S. Wodarski. (1978). "The Effects of Different Reinforcement Systems on Cooperative Behaviors Exhibited by Children in Classroom Contexts." *Journal of Research and Development in Education* 12 (1978), pp. 50–58.

Butts, R. F. & L. A. Cremin. *A History of Education in American Culture.* New York: Holt, Rinehart & Winston, 1953.

Callahan, R. *Education and the Cult of Efficiency.* Chicago: University of Chicago Press, 1962.

Carlson, R. *Reframing and Reform: Perspectives on Organization, Leadership, and School Change.* White Plains, NY: Longman, 1995.

Carnegie Corporation. *A Nation Prepared: Teachers for the Twenty-First Century.* New York, 1986.

Carter, K. "Teachers' Knowledge and Learning to Teach." In *Handbook of Research on Teacher Education,* ed. W. R. Houston. New York: Macmillan, 1990.

Cazden, C. B. *Child Language and Education.* New York: Holt, Rinehart & Winston, 1972.

Cazden, C. B. "Classroom Discourse." In *Handbook of Research on Teaching.* 3rd ed., ed. M. Whitrock. New York: Macmillan, 1986.

Chalk v. *United States District Court,* 840 F. 2d 701 (9th Cir. 1988).

Charters, W. W., Jr. "The Social Background of Teaching." In *Handbook of Research on Teaching,* ed. N. L. Gage. Chicago: Rand McNally, 1963.

Cherry, L. J. "Teacher-Student Interaction and Teacher's Expectations of Students' Communicative Competence. In *Language, Children, and Society,* ed. O. Garnica & M. King. New York: Pergamon Press, 1981.

Choy, S. P., S. A. Bobbitt, R. R. Henke, E. A. Medrich, L. J. Horn, & J. Lieberman. *America's Teachers: Profile of a Profession.* Washington, DC: U.S. Department of Education, 1993.

Civil Rights Division v. *Amphitheater Unified School District No. 10,* 680 P. 2d 517 (Ariz. App. 1983).

Clark, M. & P. Peterson. "Teachers' Thought Processes." In *Handbook of Research on Teaching* 3rd ed., ed. M. C. Wittrock. New York: Macmillan, 1986.

Cohen, E. *Designing Groupwork: Strategies for the Heterogeneous Classroom.* New York: Teachers College Press, 1986.

Coleman, J. *The Adolescent Society.* New York: Free Press, 1961.

Coleman, J. "The Children Have Outgrown the Schools." *Psychology Today.* February, 1972, pp. 72–82.

Coleman, J., E. Cambell, C. Hobson, J. McPartland, A. Mood, F. Weinfield, & R. York. *Equality of Educational Opportunity.* Washington, DC: U.S. Government Printing Office, 1966.

College Entrance Examination Board. *Equality and Excellence: The Educational Status of Black Americans.* New York, 1985.

Collins, M. L. "Effects of Enthusiasm Training on Preservice Elementary Teachers." *Journal of Teacher Education* 29 (1978), pp. 53–57.

Commission on Reading. *Becoming a Nation of Readers.* Washington DC: The National Institute of Education, U.S. Department of Education, 1985.

Conant, J. *The Education of American Teachers.* New York: McGraw-Hill, 1963.

Confrey, J. "What Constructivism Implies for Teaching." In *Constructivist Views on the Teaching and Learning of Mathematics,* ed. R. Davis, C. Maher, & N. Noddingo. Reston, VA: National Council of Teachers of Mathematics, 1990.

Cook, K. *State Laws and Regulations Governing Teacher Certification.* Bulletin no., 19. Washington, DC: Bureau of Education, 1927.

Coontz, S. (1995). "The American Family and the Nostalgia Trap." *Phi Delta Kappan* 76 (1995), pp. K1–K20.

Corey, G., M. S. Corey, & P. Callanan. *Issues and Ethics in the Helping Professions.* 4th ed. Pacific Grove, CA: Brooks/Cole, 1993.

Cottom, C. "A Bold Experiment in Teaching Values." *Educational Leadership* 53 (1996), pp. 54–58.

Counts, G. S. *Dare the World Build a New Social Order?* Carbondale: Southern Illinois University Press, 1932.

Council of Chief State School Officers. *The Council.* Washington, D.C.: author, 1995.

Cremin, L. A. *The Transformation of the School.* New York: Alfred A. Knopf, 1964.

Cremin, L. *Popular Education and Its Discontents.* New York: Harper & Row, 1990.

Crow, N. A. "Preservice Teachers' Biography: A Case Study." Paper presented at the annual meeting of the American Educational Research Association, Washington, DC, April 1987.

Cuban, L. *How Teachers Taught.* New York: Longman, 1984.

Cuban, L. "Reforming Again, and Again, and Again." *Educational Researcher* 19 (1990), pp. 3–13.

Cuban, L. *How Teachers Taught.* 2nd ed. New York: Teachers College Press, 1993.

Curti, M. *The Social Ideas of American Educators.* New York: Charles Scribner's Sons, 1935.

Curti, M. *The Growth of American Thought.* New York: Harper & Brothers, 1943.

Cypher, T. & D. J. Willower. "The Work Behavior of Secondary School Teachers." *Journal of Research and Development* 18 (1984), pp. 19–20.

Darling-Hammond, L. "Teaching Knowledge: How Do We Test It?" *American Educator* 10 (1986), pp. 18–21.

Darling-Hammond, L. "The Teacher Supply, Demand, and Standards." *Education Policy* 3 (1989), pp. 1–17.

Darling-Hammond, L. "Who Will Speak for the Children? How 'Teach for America' Hurts Urban Schools and Students." *Phi Delta Kappan* 76 (1994), pp. 21–34.

Darling-Hammond, L. ed. *What Matters Most: Teaching for America's Future.* New York: Columbia University, Commission on Teaching and America's Future, 1996.

Darling-Hammond, L. "What Matters Most: A Competent Teacher for Every Child." *Phi Delta Kappan* 78 (1996), pp. 193–200.

Darling-Hammond, L. & B. Barry. *The Evolution of Teacher Policy* (JRE–01) Santa Monica, CA: Rand Corporation, 1988.

Darling-Hammond, L. & V. Cobb. "The Changing Context of Teacher Education." In *The Teacher Educator's Handbook,* ed. F. Murray. San Francisco: Jossey-Bass, 1995.

Darling-Hammond, L. & A. Goodwin. "Progress toward Professionalism in Teaching." In *Challenges and Achievements of American Education,* ed. G. Cawelti. Alexandria, VA: Association for Supervision and Curriculum Development, 1993.

Darrell, L. R. "Estimating the Economic Worth of a 5th-year Licensure Program for Teachers." *Educational Evaluation and Policy Analysis* 12 (1990), pp. 25–39.

David, J. L. "The Who, What, and Why of Site-Based Management." *Educational Leadership* 53 (1995/96), p. 4.

Davis, O. L. ed. *Perspectives on Curriculum Development 1776–1976.* Washington, DC: Association for Supervision and Curriculum Development, 1976.

Deal, T. E. & A. Kennedy. *Corporate Culture.* Reading, MA: Addison-Wesley, 1982.

Deal, T. E. & R. Nolan. *Alternative Schools.* Chicago: Nelson-Hall, 1978.

DeAvila, E. & S. Duncan. *Finding Out/ Descubrimiento.* Corte Madera, CA: Linguametrics Group, 1980.

Debra P. v. *Turlington,* 564 F. Supp. 177 (M.D. Fla. 1983), aff'd, 730 F. 2d 1405 (11th Cir. 1984).

DeLisi, R. & J. Staudt. "Individual Differences in College Students' Performance on Formal Operations Tasks." *Journal of Applied Developmental Psychology* 1 (1980), pp. 201–208.

Delisle, J. *Gifted Children Speak Out.* New York: Walker, 1984.

Department of Education, State of Hawaii v. *Katherine D.,* 727 F.2d 809 (9th Cir. 1983).

Department of Teacher Education, Orlean Bullard Beeson School of Education, Samford University. "Preparing the Professional Portfolio." Paper presented at the meeting of the Eastern Education Research Association, Hilton Head, SC, 1997.

Destefano, J. "Social Variation in Language: Implications for Teaching Reading to Black Ghetto Children." In *Better Reading in Urban Schools,* ed. J. A. Figurel. Newark, NJ: International Reading Association, 1972.

DeVries, R. & B. Zan. *Moral Classrooms, Moral Children: Creating a Constructivist Atmosphere in Early Education.* New York: Teachers College Press, 1994.

Devries by DeBlaay v. *Fairfax County School Board,* 882 F. 2d 876 (4th Cir. 1989).

DeWijk, S. L. "Career and Technology Studies: Crossing the Curriculum." *Educational Leadership* 53 (1996), pp. 50–53.

Dewey, J. *Democracy and Education.* New York: Macmillan, 1916.

Diegmueller, K. "History Center Shares New Set of Standards." *Education Week* 15 (April 10, 1996), pp. 1, 14–15.

Dodd v. *Rambis,* 535 F. Supp 23 (S.D. Ind. 1981).

Doe v. *Renfrow,* 631 F. 2d 91 (7th Cir 1980), cert. denied, 451 U.S. 1022, at 1025 (1981).

Doe v. *Taylor Independent School District,* 975 F 2d 137 (5th Cir. 1991).

Doyle, R. "The Resistance of Conventional Wisdom to Research Evidence: The Case of Retention in Grade. *Phi Delta Kappan* 71 (1989), pp. 215–220.

Doyle, W. Classroom Tasks and Student Abilities. In *Research on Teaching: Concepts, Findings, and Implications,* ed. P. L. Peterson & H. J. Walberg. Berkeley, CA: McCutchan, 1979.

Doyle, W. "Classroom Organization and Management." In *Handbook of Research on Teaching,* ed. M. C. Wittrock. 3rd ed. New York: Macmillan, 1986.

Doyle, W. & K. Carter. "Academic Tasks in Classrooms." *Curriculum Inquiry* 14 (1984), pp. 129–149.

Eaton, W. H. *The American Federation of Teachers. 1916–1961: A History of the Movement.* Carbondale: Southern Illinois University Press, 1975.

Educational Testing Service. *America's Smallest School: The Family.* Princeton, NJ, 1992.

Edwards, C. P. "Social Experiences and Moral Judgment in Kenyan Young Adults." *Journal of Genetic Psychology* 133 (1978), pp. 19–30.

Edwards, N. & H. G. Richey. *The School in the American Social Order.* Boston, MA: Houghton Mifflin, 1963.

EEOC v. *Madison County Community School District No. 12,* 818 F. 2d 577 (7th Cir., 1987).

Eggen, P. & D. Kauchak. *Educational Psychology.* 2nd ed. New York: Merrill, 1994.

Elam, S. M. "The 22nd Annual Gallup Poll of the Public's Attitudes toward the Public Schools." *Phi Delta Kappan* 71 (1990), pp. 41–54.

Elam, S., L. Rose, & A. Gallup. "The 28th Annual Phi Delta Kappa/Gallup Poll of the Public's Attitudes toward the Public Schools." *Phi Delta Kappan* 78 (1996), pp. 41–59.

Elsbree, W. S. *The American Teacher: Evolution of a Profession in a Democracy.* New York: American Federation of Teachers, 1992.

Elson, R. *Guardians of Tradition.* Lincoln: University of Nebraska Press, 1964.

Emmer, E. T., C. M. Evertson, J. P. Sanford, B. S. Clements, & M. E. Worsham. *Classroom Management for Secondary Teachers.* 2nd ed. Englewood Cliffs, NJ: Prentice-Hall, 1989.

Emmer, E. T., C. M. Evertson, J. P. Sanford, B. S. Clements, & M. E. Worsham. *Classroom Management for Secondary Teachers* (3rd ed.), Englewood Cliffs, NJ: Prentice-Hall, 1995.

Evertson, C. M., E. T. Emmer, B. S. Clements, J. P. Sanford, & M. E. Worsham. *Classroom Management for Elementary Teachers.* 3rd ed. Englewood Cliffs, NJ: Prentice-Hall, 1995.

Evertson, C. M., W. D. Hawley, & M. Zlotnik. "Making a Difference in Education Quality Through Teachers Education." *Journal of Teacher Education* 36 (1985), pp. 2–12.

Fairbanks, C. & L. Hill. *Students Define Learning Disabilities for Themselves: A Collaborative Study of Labeling.* Paper presented at the Joint Conference on Learning Disabilities, Ann Arbor, Michigan, 1989.

Fee v. *Herndon,* 900 F. 2d 804 (5th Cir. 1990).

Feiman-Nemser, S. & J. Remillard. "Perspectives on Learning to Teach." In *The Teacher Educator's Handbook,* ed. F. Murray. San Francisco: Jossey-Bass, 1996.

Fernald v. *City of Ellsworth Superintending School Comm.,* 342 A.2d 704 (Me. 1975).

Fialkowski v. *Shapp,* 405 F. Supp. 946 (E.D. Pa. 1975).

Finn, J. D. & C. M. Archilles. "Answers and Questions about Class Size: A Statewide Experiment." *American Educational Research Journal* 27 (1990), pp. 557–577.

Finot v. *Pasadena City Board of Education,* 58 Cal. Rptr. 520 (1967).

Fischer, I., D. Schimmel, & C. Kelly. *Teachers and the Law.* 4th ed. White Plains, NY: Longman, 1995.

Fisher v. *Fairbanks North Star Borough School Dist.,* 704 P. 2d 213 (Alaska 1985).

Fitzgerald v. *Green Valley Area Education Agency,* 589 F. Supp. 1130 (S.D. Iowa 1984).

Florida Department of Education. *Florida Performance Measurement System for Teachers.* Tallahassee, FL: 1991.

Foldman, J. "Social Participation of Preschool Children in Same Versus Mixed-Age Groups." *Child Development* 52 (1981), pp. 644–650.

Force v. *Pierce City R-VI School District,* 570 F. Supp. 10920 (W.D. Mo. 1983).

Fordham, S. & J. Ogbu. "Black Students' School Success: Coping with the Burden of Acting White." *Urban Review* 18 (1986), pp. 176–206.

Fox, R. F. "Manipulated Kids: Teens Tell How Ads Influence Them." *Educational Leadership* 53 (1995), pp. 77–79.

Freedman, P. *A Comparison of Multi-Age and Homogeneous Grouping in Early Childhood Centers.* Urbana, IL: ERIC Clearinghouse on Elementary and Early Childhood Education. ERIC Document Reproduction Service No. ED 207 673, 1981.

Freeman, D. & H. A. Kalaian. *Profiles of Students Completing Teacher Education Programs at*

Michigan State University: Fall, 1986 through Spring, 1988. Program Evaluation Series No. 25. East Lansing: Michigan State University, College of Education, Office of Program Evaluation, 1989.

French, D. C., G. A. Waas, A. L. Stright, & J. A. Baker. "Leadership Asymmetries in Mixed-Age Children's Groups." *Child Development* 57 (1986), pp. 1277–1283.

Friedrich, E. ed. *Learning and Instruction: European Research in an International Context.* vol. 22. Oxford, England: Pergamon Press, 1987.

Fullan, M. *Change Forces.* New York: Teachers College Press, 1993.

Fullan, M. *The Meaning of Educational Change.* New York: Teachers College Press, 1982.

Fullan, M. *The New Meaning of Educational Change.* New York: Teachers College Press, 1991.

Galuszka, P. "Kentucky's Class Act." *Business Week,* 68 (April 7, 1997), pp. 90–94.

Gall, M. D. *Handbook for Evaluating and Selecting Curriculum Materials.* Boston: Allyn & Bacon, 1981.

"GAO Criticizes OCR Efforts to Limit Biased School Tracking." *School Law News,* May 9, 1991.

Garcia, E. E. 1993. "Language, Culture, and Education." In *Review of Research Education* 19 (1993). Washington, DC: American Educational Research Association.

Garcia, J. "The Changing Image of Ethnic Groups in Textbooks." *Phi Delta Kappan* 75 (1993), pp. 29–35.

Gardner, H. *Frames of Mind: The Theory of Multiple Intelligences.* New York: Basic Books, 1983.

Gardner, H. & T. Hatch. "Multiple Intelligences go to School: Educational Implications of the Theory of Multiple Intelligences." *Educational Researcher,* 18 (1989), pp. 4–10.

Gay, G. *Differential Dyadic Interactions of Black and White Teachers with Black and White Pupils in Recently Desegregated Social Studies Classrooms: A Function of Teacher and Pupil Ethnicity.* Washington, DC: U.S. Office of Education, 1974.

Geary, S. "Class Size: Issues and Implications for Policy Making in Utah." Policy paper sponsored by FOCUS Project, Department of Educational Administration, Graduate School of Education, University of Utah, Salt Lake City, UT, 1988.

Gelman, R. & R. Baillargeon. "A Review of Some Piagetian Concepts." In *Handbook of Child Psychology: Vol. 3 Cognitive Development,* ed. P. H. Mussen. 4th ed. New York: John Wiley, 1983.

General Accounting Office. *School Facilities: Conditions of America's Schools.* Washington, D.C.: Author, Report no. GAO-HEHS-95-61, 1995.

Getzels, J. W. "Images of the Classroom and Visions of the Learner." In *The Social Context of Learning and Development,* ed. J. C. Glidwell. New York: Gardner Press, 1977.

Getzels, J. W. & P. W. Jackson. "The Teacher's Personality and Characteristics." In *Handbook of Research on Teaching,* ed. N. L. Gage. Chicago: Rand McNally, 1963.

Gilligan, C. *In a Different Voice: Psychological Theory and Women's Development.* Cambridge, MA: Harvard University Press, 1982.

Glass, G. "Effectiveness of Special Education." Paper presented at Wingspread conference, Racine, WI, 1981.

Glass, G., L. S. Cahen, M. L. Smith, & N. N. Filby. *School Class Size: Research and Policy.* Beverly Hills, CA: Sage, 1982.

Glass, G. & M. L. Smith. "Meta-Analysis of Research on Class Size and Achievement." *Educational Evaluation and Policy Analysis* 1 (1979), pp. 2–16.

Glasser, W. *Control Theory in the Classroom.* New York: Harper & Row, 1986.

Glasser, W. *The Quality School Teacher.* New York: HarperCollins, 1993.

Glynn, S. M., R. H. Yeany, & B. K. Britton. eds. *The Psychology of Learning Science.* Hillsdale, NJ: Erlbaum, 1991.

Goldenberg, C. "Making Success a More Common Occurrence for Children at Risk for Failure: Lessons from Hispanic First-Graders Learning to Read." In *Risk Makers, Risk Takers, Risk Breakers: Reducing the Risk for Young Learners,* ed. J. Allen and J. Mason. Portsmouth, NH: Heinemann, 1989.

Gomez, M. "Prospective Teachers' Beliefs about Good Writing." Paper presented at annual meeting of the American Educational Research Association, New Orleans, 1988.

Goncz, B. & D. Kodzepeljic. "Cognition and Bilingualism Revisited." *Journal of Multilingual and Multicultural Development* 12 (1991), pp. 137–163.

Good, T. L. "Research on Classroom Teaching." In *Handbook of Teaching and Policy,* ed. L. Shulman, & G. Sykes. New York: Longman, 1983.

Good, T. L. & D. A. Grouws. "The Missouri Mathematics Effectiveness Project." *Journal of Educational Psychology* 71 (1979), p. 357.

Goodlad, J. I. *A Place Called School: Prospects for the Future.* New York: McGraw-Hill, 1984.

Goodlad, J. *Teachers for Our Nation's Schools.* San Francisco: Jossey-Bass, 1990.

Gottfredson, D., C. Fink, & N. Graham. "Grade Retention and Problem Behavior." *American Educational Research Journal* 31 (1994), pp. 761–784.

Grant, L. "Black Females' 'Place' in Desegregated Classrooms." *Sociology of Education* 57 (1984), pp. 98–111.

Graziano, W., D. French, C. A. Brownell, & W. W. Hartup. "Peer Interaction in Same and Mixed-Age Triads in Relation to Chronological Age and Incentive Condition." *Child Development* 47 (1976), pp. 707–714.

Green v. *County School Board of New Kent County,* VA, 391 U.S. 430 (1968).

Greenstein, F. I. *Children and Politics.* New Haven, CT: Yale University Press, 1965.

Griese, A. A. *Your Philosophy of Education: What Is It?* Santa Monica, CA: Goodyear, 1981.

Grossman, P. L. *The Making of a Teacher: Teacher Knowledge and Teacher Education.* New York: Teachers College Press, 1990.

Grove City College v. *Bell,* 465 U.S. 555 (1984).

Guthrie, J. W., W. I. Garms, & L. Pierce. *School Finance and Education Policy: Enhancing Educational Efficiency, Equality, and Choice.* 2nd ed. Englewood Cliffs, NJ: Prentice-Hall, 1988.

Guzick v. *Drebus,* 431 F. 2d 594, 600 (6th Cir. 1970), cert. denied, 401 U.S. 948 (1971).

Haberman, M. "The Pedagogy of Poverty versus Good Teaching." *Phi Delta Kappan* 72 (1991), pp. 290–294.

Hall v. *Tawney,* 621 F.2d 607, 613 (4th Cir. 1980).

Halperin, R. "Exemplary Curriculums Cross National Borders." *Educational Leadership* 53 (1996), p. 59.

Hamack, B. G. "Self-Concept: Evaluation of Preschool Children in Single and Multiage Classroom Settings." *Dissertation Abstracts International* 35 (1975), pp. 6572–6573.

Hamburg v. *North Penn School Dist.,* 484 A. 2d 867 (Pa. Commw. Ct. 1984).

Hanna, J. L. "Connections: Arts, Academics, and Productive Citizens." *Phi Delta Kappan* 73 (1992), pp. 601–607.

Hardman, M. L., C. J. Drew, M. W. Egan, & B. Wolf. *Human Exceptionality: Society, School, and Family.* 5th ed. Boston: Allyn & Bacon, 1996.

Harel, I. & S. Papert. *Constructionism.* Norwood, NJ: Ablex, 1993.

Hargreaves, A. *Changing Teachers, Changing Times: Teachers Work and Culture in the Postmodern Age.* New York: Teachers College Press, 1994.

Hartshorne, H. & A. May. *Studies in the Nature of Character. Vol. 1. Studies in Deceit, Vol 2. Studies in Self-Control; Vol 3. Studies in the Organization of Character.* New York: Macmillan, 1928–1930.

Hartup, W. W. "The Social Worlds of Childhood." *American Psychologist* 34 (1979), pp. 944–950.

Hawley, W. D. "The High Costs and Doubtful Efficacy of Extended Teacher-Preparation Programs." *American Journal of Education* 95 (1987), pp. 295–298.

Hazelwood School District v. *Kuhlmeier,* 484 U.S. 260 (1988).

Healey v. *James,* 408 U.S. 169, 181 (1972).

Heider, E. R., C. B. Cazden, & R. Brown. *Social Class Differences in the Effectiveness and Style of Children's Coding Ability.* Project Literacy Reports, no. 9. Ithaca, NY: Cornell University, 1968.

Henderson, J., N. Winitzky, & D. Kauchak. "Effective Teaching in Advanced Placement Classrooms." *Journal of Classroom Interaction* 31 (1996), pp. 29–35.

Hess, R. & T. McDevitt. "Some Cognitive Consequences of Maternal Intervention Techniques: A Longitudinal Study." *Child Development* 55 (1984), pp. 2017–2020.

Hess, R. D., & H. Azuma. "Cultural Support for Schooling: Contrasts between Japan and the United States." *Educational Researcher* 20 (1991), pp. 2–8.

Hess, R. D. & J. V. Torney. *The Development of Political Attitudes in Children.* Chicago: Aldine, 1967.

Heyns, B. *Summer Learning and the Effects of Schooling.* New York: Academic Press, 1978.

Hirsch, E. D., Jr. *Cultural Literacy: What Every American Needs to Know.* Boston, MA: Houghton Mifflin, 1987.

Hobson v. *Hansen,* 269 F. Supp. 401 (D.D.C. 1967), aff'd sub nom. *Schmuck* v. *Hobson,* 408 F.2d 175 (D.C. Cir., 1969).

Hodgkinson, H. L. *A Demographic Look at the Future.* Washington, DC: Institute for Educational Leadership, 1992.

Hofstader, R. *Anti-intellectualism in American Life.* New York: Knopf, 1962.

Holland, J. *Making Vocational Choices: A Theory of Vocational Personalities and Work Environments.* 2nd ed. Odessa, FL: Psychological Assessment Resources, 1992.

Holmes, C. & K. Matthews. "The Effects of Nonpromotion on Elementary and Junior High School Pupils: A Meta-Analysis." *Review of Educational Research* 54 (1984), pp. 225–236.

Holmes Group. *Tomorrow's Teachers: A Report of the Holmes Group.* East Lansing, MI, 1986.

Holmes Group. *Tomorrow's Schools: A Report of the Holmes Group.* East Lansing, MI, 1990.

Holmes Group. *Tomorrow's Schools of Education: A Report of the Holmes Group.* East Lansing, MI, 1995.

Hortonville Joint School District No. 1 v. *Hortonville Education Association,* 426 U.S. 482 (1976).

Horvitz, R. A. "Effects of the Open Classroom." In *Educational Environments and Effects: Evaluation, Policy, and Productivity,* ed. H. J. Walberg. Berkeley, CA: McCutchan, 1979.

Housner, L. D. & D. C. Griffey. "Teacher Cognition: Differences in Planning and Interactive Decision Making between Experienced and Inexperienced Teachers." *Research Quarterly for Exercise Studies* 1 (1985), pp. 2–16.

Howes, C. & S. A. Farver. "Social Pretend Play in Two Year Olds: Effects of Age of Partner." *Early Childhood Research Quarterly* 2 (1987), pp. 305–314.

Howsom, R. B., D. C. Corrigan, G. W. Denmark, & R. J. Nash. *Educating a Profession.* Washington, DC: American Association of Colleges of Teacher Education, 1976.

Illich, I. *Deschooling Society.* New York: Harper & Row, 1971.

Individuals with Disabilities Educational Act, 20 U.S.C. & 1401 (1991).

Ingraham v. *Wright,* 430 U.S. 651 (1977).

Jacklin, C. N. "Female and Male: Issues of Gender." *American Psychologist* 44 (1989), pp. 127–133.

Jackson, G. "The Research Evidence on the Effects of Grade Retention." *Review of Educational Research* 45 (1975), pp. 627–639.

Jackson, P. W. *Life in Classrooms.* New York: Holt, Rinehart & Winston, 1968.

Jackson, P. W., R. E. Boostrom, & D. T. Hansen. *The Moral Life of Schools.* San Francisco: Jossey-Bass, 1993.

Jefferson County School District 50-9-J, v. *Fair Dismissal Appeals Board,* 793 P.2d 888 (Ore. App 1990). 812 P.2d 1384 (Ore. 1991).

Jencks, C., et al. *Inequality: A Reassessment of the Effect of Family and Schooling in America.* New York: Basic Books, 1972.

Jenkins v. *Bishop,* 589 P. 2d 770 (Utah 1978) (per curiam).

Johnson, C. *Old-Time Schools and Schoolbooks.* New York: Macmillan, 1904.

Johnson, D. *An Investigation of Sex Differences in Reading for English-Speaking Nations.* Tech Rep. No. 109. Madison: University of Wisconsin, Research and Development Center for Cognitive Learning, 1976.

Johnson, D. & R. Johnson. *Learning Together and Alone.* 2nd ed. Englewood Cliffs, NJ: Prentice-Hall, 1987.

Johnson, J. A., V. L. Dupuis, D. Vusial, & G. E. Hall. *Introduction to the Foundations of American Education.* 9th ed. Needham Heights, MA: Allyn & Bacon, 1994.

Johnson, W. R. "Teachers and Teacher Training in the Twentieth Century." In *American Teachers: Histories of a Profession at Work,* ed. D. Warren. New York: Macmillan, 1989.

Jordan, C. "Creating Cultures of Schooling: Historical and Conceptual Background of the KEEP/Rough Rock Collaboration." Paper presented at the annual meeting of the American Educational Research Association, New Orleans, April 1994.

Jordan, J. "Nobody Mean More to Me Than You and the Future Life of Willie Jordan." *Harvard Educational Review* 58 (1988), pp. 363–374.

Joyce, B., R. Hersh, & M. McKibbin. *The Structure of School Improvement.* New York: Longman, 1983.

Joyce, B., R. Hersh, & M. McKibbin. *The Structure of School Improvement.* 2nd ed. New York: Longman, 1993.

Joyce, B. R. & R. T. Clift. "The Phoenix Agenda: Essential Reform in Teacher Education." *Educational Researcher* 13 (1984), pp. 5–18.

Juffras, J. & M. Rose. "Are You Ready for the New Title I?" *American Teacher* 79 (1995), pp. 6–7.

Katzmman v. *Cumberland Valley School District,* 479 A. 2d 671 (Pa. Commonwealth Court 1984).

Kagan, S. *Cooperative Learning Resources for Teachers.* San Juan Capistrano, CA, 1994.

Kahne, J. & J. Westheimer. "In the Service of What? The Politics of Service Learning." *Phi Delta Kappan* 77 (1996), pp. 593–599.

Kane, M. B. *Minorities in Textbooks.* Chicago: Quadrangle Books, 1970.

Karweit, N. "Retention Policy." In *Encyclopedia of Educational Research,* ed. M. Alkin. New York: Macmillan, 1992.

Katz, M. B., ed. *Education in American History: Reading on the Social Issues.* New York: Praeger, 1973.

Katz, P. A. & S. R. Zalk. "Modification of Children's Racial Attitudes." *Developmental Psychology* 14 (1978), pp. 447–461.

Keefe v. *Geanakos,* 418 F.2d. 359 (1st Cir. 1969).

Kellaghan, T. & G. F. Madaus. "National Curricula in European Countries." In *The Hidden Consequences of a National Curriculum.* Washington, DC: American Educational Research Association, 1995.

Kennedy, P. *Preparing for the Twenty-First Century.* New York: Random House, 1993.

Keyishian v. *Board of Regents,* 385 U.S. 589 (1967).

Kim, S. H. *The Effect of Cross-Age Interaction on Socially at Risk Children.* Ph.D. diss. University of Illinois, Urbana, 1990.

Kirkpatrick, W. "The Project Method." *Teachers College Record* 19 (1918), pp. 319–333.

Kitchener, K. S. "Intuition, Critical Evaluation and Ethical Principles: The Foundation for Ethical Decisions in Counseling Psychology." *The Counseling Psychologist* 12 (1984), pp. 43–55.

Klein Independent School District v. *Mattrox,* 830 F. 2d 576 (5th Cir. 1987).

Kliebard, H. M. "The National Interest and a National Curriculum: Two Historical Precedents and their Implications." In *The Hidden Consequences of a National Curriculum.* Washington DC: American Educational Research Association, 1995.

Knight, G. R. *Issues and Alternatives in Educational Philosophy.* Berrien Springs, MI: Andrews University Press, 1982.

Knowles, G. "The Context of Home Schooling in the United States." *Education and Urban Society* 21 (1989), pp. 5–15.

Koerner, J. *The Mis-Education of Teachers.* Boston: Houghton-Mifflin, 1963.

Kohlberg, L. "Moral Education in the School." *School Review* 74 (1966), pp. 1–30.

Kohn, A. *The Brighter Side of Human Nature.* New York: Basic Books, 1990.

Kohn, A. "Caring Kids: The Role of the Schools." *Phi Delta Kappan* 72 (1991), pp. 496–506.

Kounin, J. S. *Discipline and Group Management in Classrooms.* New York: Holt, Rinehart & Winston, 1970.

Kozol, L. *Savage Inequalities: Children in America's Schools.* New York: Crown, 1991.

Krug, E. A. *Salient Dates in American Education 1635–1964.* New York: Harper & Row, 1966.

Krupnick, C. G. *High School: Film Study Guide.* Cambridge, MA: High School II, 1995.

Labaree, L. W. & J. B. Whitfield. *The Papers of Benjamin Franklin.* New Haven, CT: Yale University Press, 1961.

Labov, W. "The Logic of Nonstandard English." In *Language in the Inner City: Studies of Black English Vernacular,* ed. W. Labov. Philadelphia: University of Pennsylvania Press, 1972.

Lanier, J. & J. Little. "Research on Teacher Education." In *Handbook of Research on Teaching,* ed. M. C. Wittrock. 3rd ed. New York: Macmillan, 1986.

Lantz v. *Ambach,* 620 F. Supp. 663 (S.D.N.Y. 1985).

Lawson, A. & D. Snitgren. "Teaching Formal Reasoning in a College Biology Course for Preservice Teachers." *Journal of Research in Science Teaching* 19 (1982), pp. 233–248.

Lee, V. E. & J. B. Smith. "Collective Responsibility for Learning and Its Effects on Gains in Achievement of Early Secondary School Students." *American Journal of Education* 104 (1996), pp. 1103–1146.

Leinhardt, G. *Towards Understanding Instructional Explanations.* ED 334150. 1990.

Leinhardt, G. & J. Greeno. "The Cognitive Skill of Teaching." *Journal of Educational Psychology* 78 (1986), pp. 75–95.

Leming, J. S. "In Search of Effective Character Education." *Educational Leadership* 51 (1993), pp. 63–71.

Lemon v. *Kurtzman,* 403 U.S. 602 (1971).

Leo, J. "Feel-good Reinforcement's no Substitute for Learning." *Seattle Times,* January 14, 1997, p. B–5.

Levine, M. *Viewing Violence: How Media Violence Affects Your Child in Adolescence Development.* New York: Doubleday, 1996.

Lewis, A. "Washington Commentary." *Phi Delta Kappan* 77 (1996), p. 4.

Lickona, T. "Four Strategies for Fostering Character Development in Children." *Phi Delta Kappan* 69 (1993), pp. 419–423.

Lieberman, A. *Building a Professional Culture in Schools.* New York: Teachers College Press, 1989.

Lieberman, A., ed. *The Changing Contexts of Teaching.* Chicago: The National Society for the Study of Education, 1992.

Lines, P. M. "An Overview of Home Instruction." *Phi Delta Kappan* 68 (1987), pp. 510–517.

Linn, M. C. & J. S. Hyde. "Gender, Mathematics, and Science." *Educational Researcher* 18 (1989), pp. 17–27.

Lipp v. *Morris,* 579 F. 2d 834 (3rd Cir. 1978).

Little, J. W. & M. W. McLaughlin, eds. *Teachers' Work: Individuals, Colleagues, and Contexts.* New York: Teachers College Press, 1993.

Lo, L. N. K. & C. H. Lee. "Which Road to Relevant Education?" *Educational Leadership* 53 (1996), pp. 60–63.

Loewen, J. *Lies My Teacher Told Me.* New York: The New Press, 1996.

Lortie, D. *School-Teacher: A Sociological Study.* Chicago: University of Chicago Press, 1975.

Lougee, M. D., R. Grueneich, & W. W. Hartup. "Social Interaction in Same and Mixed-Age Dyads of Preschool Children." *Child Development* 48 (1977), pp. 1353–1361.

Loving v. *Virginia,* 388 U.S. 1, 12 (1967).

Lucas, T. *Black English Discourse in Urban Contexts.* Ph.D. diss. Georgetown University, Washington, DC, 1987.

Macias, J. "Scholastic Antecedents of Immigrant Students: Schooling in a Mexican Immigrant-Sending Community." *Anthropology and Education Quarterly* 21 (1990), pp. 291–318.

Mancha v. *Field Museum of Natural History,* 283 N.E. 2d 899 (Ill. App. 1972).

Manners, P. A. & D. J. Smart. "Moral Development and Identity Formation in High School Juniors: The Effects of Participation in Extracurricular Activities." Paper presented at the annual meeting of the American Educational Research Association, San Francisco, April 1995.

Marcus, L. *The Treatment of Minorities in Secondary School Textbooks.* New York: Anti-Defamation League of B'nai B'rith, 1961.

Marcus v. *Rowley,* 695 F. 2d 1171, 1174 (9th Cir. 1983).

Mathematical Sciences Education Board. *Measuring Up: Prototypes for Mathematics Assessment.* Washington, DC: National Academy Press, 1993.

Mayer, R. E., V. Sims, & H. Tajika. "A Comparison of How Textbooks Teach Mathematical Problem Solving in Japan and the United States." *American Educational Research Journal* 32 (1995), pp. 443–460.

McAdams, R. P. *Lessons from Abroad.* Lancaster, PA: Technomic, 1993.

McCarthy, M. M. & N. H. Cambron-McCabe. *Public School Law: Teachers' and Students' Rights.* Boston: Allyn and Bacon, 1992.

McConaghy, T. "Newfoundland Schools: A Classic Struggle of Church versus State." *Phi Delta Kappan,* (1996) pp. 173–174.

McCormick, C. B. & M. Pressley. *Educational Psychology. Learning, Instruction, Assessment.* New York: Longman, 1997.

McCullar Human Rights Commission, 158 Ill. App. 3d 1011, 511 N.E. 2d 1375 (1987).

McGlaughlin v. *Board of Educ.,* 659 S.W. 2d 249 (Mo. Ct. App 1983).

McIntyre, D. J. & M. J. O'Hair. *The Reflective Roles of the Classroom Teacher.* Belmont, CA: Wadsworth, 1996.

McNeil, L. M. "Local Reform Initiatives and a National Curriculum: Where Are the Children?" In *The Hidden Consequences of a National Curriculum.* Washington, DC: American Educational Research Association, 1995.

Means, B., C. Chelemer, & M. Knapp. *Teaching Advanced Skills to At-Risk Students.* San Francisco: Jossey-Bass, 1991.

Melmed, P. *Black English Phonology: The Question of Reading Interference.* Philadelphia: Language-Behavior Research Laboratory, 1971.

The Metropolitan Life Survey of the American Teacher: 1984–1995. New York: Louis Harris & Associates, 1995.

Mills v. *Board of Education of District of Columbia,* 348 F. Supp. 866 (D.D.C. 1972).

Mitchell, D. E. & S. A. Beach. *How Changing Class Size Affects Classrooms and Students.* Policy brief no. 12. San Francisco: Far West Laboratory, 1990.

Mobley, C. *A Comparison of the Effects of Multi-Age Grouping vs. Homogeneous Age Grouping in Primary School Classes of Reading and Mathematics Achievement.* Ph.D. diss. Nova University, Ft. Lauderdale, FL, 1976.

Mongitore v. *Regan,* 520 N.Y.S.2d 194 (N.Y. App. Div. 1987).

Morine-Dershimer, G. "Patterns of Interactive Thinking Associated with Alternative Perspectives on Teacher Planning." Paper presented at the American Educational Research Association, San Francisco, April 1992.

Mounts, N. S., & J. L. Roopnarien. "Social-Cognitive Play Patterns in Same-Age and Mixed-Age Preschool Classrooms." *American Educational Research Journal* 24 (1987), pp. 463–476.

Murray, F. B. ed. *The Teacher Educator's Handbook: Building a Knowledge Base for the Preparation of Teachers* San Francisco, CA: Jossey-Bass, 1996.

Myers v. *Orleans Parish School Board,* 423 So. 2d 53 (La. Ct. App. 1983). review denied, 430 So. 2d 657 (La. 1983).

Naisbitt, J. & P. Aburdene. *Megatrends 2000.* New York: William Morrow, 1990.

Nanus, B. *Visionary Leadership.* San Francisco: Jossey-Bass, 1992.

National Association of State Boards of Education. *State Education Governance at a Glance.* Alexandria, VA: Author, 1995.

National Association of State Directors of Teacher Education and Certification. *Manual on Certification and Preparation of Educational Personnel in the United States and Canada.* Dubuque, IA: Kendall Hunt, 1996.

National Center for Education and Statistics. *America's Teachers: Profile of a Profession.* Washington, DC: U.S. Government Printing Office, 1993.

National Center for Education and Statistics. *The Condition of Education.* Washington, DC: U.S. Government Printing Office, 1994.

National Center for Education and Statistics. *The Conditions of Education.* Washington, DC: U.S. Government Printing Office, 1996.

National Center for History in the Schools. *National Standards for History.* University of California, Los Angeles, 1996.

National Commission on Excellence in Education. *A Nation at Risk: The Imperative for Educational Reform.* Washington, DC: U.S. Government Printing Office, 1983.

National Committee for Standards in the Arts. *Dance, Music, Theatre, Visual Arts: National Standards for Arts Education.* Reston, VA, 1994.

National Council for the Social Studies. *Expectations of Excellence: Curriculum Standards for Social Studies.* Washington, DC, 1994.

National Council of Teachers of English and International Reading Association. *Standards for the English Language Arts.* Urbana, IL, 1996.

National Council of Teachers of Mathematics. *Curriculum and Evaluation Standards for School Mathematics.* Reston, VA, 1989.

National Education Association. *Status of the American Public School Teacher.* Washington, DC, 1993.

National Education Association. *Rankings of the States.* Washington, DC, 1995.

National Educational Goals Panel. *Data for the National Educational Goals Report.* Volume 1: National data. Washington, DC: U.S. Government Printing Office, 1995.

National Governors' Association. *Educating America: State Strategies for Achieving the National Education Goals.* Washington, DC: 1990.

National School Boards Association. *Education Vital Signs.* Alexandria, VA, 1994.

Neil, A. S. *Summerhill: A Radical Approach to Childrearing.* New York: Hart Publishing Company, 1961.

New Braunfels Independent School District v. *Armke,* 658 S.W. 2d 330 (Texas Appl. 1983).

New Jersey v. *T.L.O.,* 469 U.S. 325 (1985).

Nieto, S. *Affirming Diversity.* New York: Longman, 1992.

Nikola-Lisa, W. & G. Burnaford. "A Mosaic: Contemporary School Children's Images of Teachers." In *Images of Schoolteachers in Twentieth-Century America: Paragons, Polarities, Complexities,* ed. P. Joseph & G. Burnaford. New York: St. Martin's Press, 1994.

North Haven Board of Education v. *Bell,* 456 U.S. 512 (1982).

Nucci, L. "Synthesis of Research on Moral Development." *Educational Leadership* 44 (1987), pp. 86–91.

Oakes, J. *Keeping Track: How Schools Structure Inequality.* New Haven, CT: Yale University Press, 1985.

Odden, A., et. al. "The Story of the Education Dollar." *Phi Delta Kappan* 77 (1995), p. 2.

Ogbu, J. U. "Understanding Cultural Diversity and Learning." *Educational Researcher* 21 (1992), pp. 5–14, 24.

Olesen v. *Board of Education of School District No. 228,* 676 F. Supp. 820 (N.D. Ill. 1987).

O'Neill, J. M. "Why Charter Schools Failed in Pennsylvania and Floated in New Jersey." *Philadelphia Inquirer.* January 19, 1997, p. 1.

Ordway v. *Hargraves,* 323 F. Supp. 1155 (D. Mass. 1971).

Osborn, M. "The Impact of Current Changes in English Primary Schools on Teacher Professionalism." Paper presented at the annual meeting of the American Educational Research Association, Chicago, April 1991.

Osborn, M. & P. Broadfoot. "A Lesson in Progress: Primary Classrooms Observed in England and France." *Oxford Review of Education* 18 (1992), pp. 3–15.

Osborn v. *Bullitt County Board of Education,* 415 S.W. 2d 607 (KY Ct. App. 1967).

Pallas, A., G. Natriello, & E. McDill. "The Changing Nature of the Disadvantaged Population: Current Dimensions and Future Trends." *Educational Researcher* 18 (1989), pp. 16–22.

Palmer v. *Board of Education of City of Chicago,* 603 F.2d 1271 (7th Cir. 1979). cert. denied, 44 W.S. 1026 (1980).

Parduci v. *Rutland,* 316 F. Supp. 352 (N.D. Ala. 1970).

Parkay, F. W. & B. H. Stanford. *Becoming a Teacher.* 2nd ed. Boston: Allyn & Bacon, 1992.

Pell v. *Board of Education of Union Free School District No. 1,* 313 N.E. 2d 321 (N.Y. 1974).

Pennsylvania Association for Retarded Children v. *Commonwealth,* 343 F. Supp. 279 (E.D. Pa. 1972).

People for the American Way. *Attacks on the Freedom to Learn.* Washington, DC: Author, 1991.

Perelman, L. *School's Out: Hyperlearning, The New Technology and the End of Education.* New York: William Morrow, 1992.

Perkins, D. K. *Smart Schools. From Training Memories to Educating Minds.* New York: Free Press, 1992.

Perkinson, H. J. (1991). *The Imperfect Panacea.* New York: McGraw-Hill, 1991.

Peter W. v. *San Francisco Unified School District,* 131 Cal. Rptr. 854 (Cal. Ct. App. 1976).

Peterson, I. "The Stuff of Protons." *Science News,* August 27, 1994, p. 140.

Peterson, P. L. "Direct Instruction Reconsidered." In *Research on Teaching: Concepts, Findings, and Implications,* ed. P. L. Peterson & H. J. Walberg. Berkeley: McCutchan, 1979.

Piaget, J. *Understanding Causality,* trans. D. Miles & M. Miles. New York: Norton, 1974.

Pickering v. *Board of Education,* 391 U.S. 563 (1968).

Pierce v. *Society of Sisters,* 268 U.S. 510 (1925).

Pintrich, P. R. & D. H. Schunk. *Motivation in Education.* Englewood Cliffs, NJ: Merrill, 1996.

Pipho, C. "Stateline: The Standards Parade." *Phi Delta Kappan* 77 (1996), pp. 655, 701.

Posner, G. J. *Analyzing the Curriculum.* New York: McGraw-Hill, 1992.

Postman, N. *The End of Education: Redefining the Value of School.* New York: Alfred A. Knopf, 1995.

Pratt, D. "Age Segregation in Schools." Paper presented at the annual meeting of the American Educational Research Association, Montreal, 1983.

Preston, J. A. "Feminization of an Occupation: Teaching Becomes Women's Work in Nineteenth Century New England." Ph.D. diss. Brandeis University, 1982.

Project 2061. *Benchmarks for Science Literacy.* New York: Oxford University Press, 1993.

Prosser, W., J. Wade, & V. Schwartz. *Cases and Materials on Torts.* 7th ed. St. Paul, MN: West, 1982.

Proviso Council of West Suburban Teachers Union, Local 571 v. *Board of Education of Proviso Township High Schools,* District 209 Cook County, 513 N.E.2d 996 (Ill. App. 1987).

Purkey, W. W. & J. M. Novak. *Inviting School Success: A Self-Concept Approach to Teaching, Learning, and Democratic Practice.* Belmont, CA: Wadsworth, 1996.

Putnam, J. & J. B. Burke. *Organizing and Managing Classroom Learning Communities.* New York: McGraw-Hill, 1992.

Pyle v. *South Hadley School Committee,* 824 F. Supp. 7 (D. Mass. 1993).

Rado v. *Board of Education of Borough of Naugatuck,* 583 A. 2d 102 (Conn. 1990).

Ramirez, D., S. Yuen, & D. Ramey. *Longitudinal Study of a Structured English Immersion Strategy, Early-Exit, and Late-Exit Transitional Bilingual Education Programs for Language Minority Children: Executive Summary.* Washington, DC: George Washington University, National Clearinghouse for Bilingual Education, 1991.

Raspberry, W. "Second and Third Thoughts about Black-Male Programs," *Seattle Times,* February 6, 1996, p. A–7.

Raths, L. E., M. Harmin, & S. B. Simon. *Values and Teaching.* Columbus, OH. Charles E. Merrill, 1966.

Ratteray, J. K. D. "Don't Overlook Black Independent Schools," *USA Today,* October 4, 1996, p. 13–A.

Ravitch, D. & C. Finn. *What Do Our 17-Year-Olds Know?* New York: Harper & Row, 1987.

Ray, B. D. "An Overview of Home Schooling in the U.S.: Its Growth and Development and Future Challenges." Paper presented at the annual meeting of the American Educational Research Association, San Francisco, March, 1989.

Reed, S. & R. C. Sautter. "Children of Poverty: The Status of 12 Million Young Americans." *Phi Delta Kappan* 71 (1990), pp. K1–K12.

Regents of the University of California v. *Bakke,* 438 U.S. 265 (1978).

Render, G. F., J. M. Padilla, & H. M. Krank. "Assertive Discipline: A Critical Review and Analysis." *Teachers College Record* 90 (1989), pp. 607–630.

Resnick, L. B. "Learning in School and Out." *Educational Researcher* 16 (1987), pp. 13–20.

Reuter, J. & G. Yunik. "Social Interaction in Nursery Schools." *Development Psychology* 9 (1973), pp. 319–325.

Reynolds, M. C., M. C. Wang, & H. J. Walberg. "The Necessary Restructuring of Special and Regular Education." *Exceptional Children* 53 (1987), pp. 391–398.

Rippa, S. A. *Education in a Free Society.* New York: Longman, 1984.

Rist, R. C. "Student Social Class and Teacher Expectations: The Self-Fulfilling Prophecy in Ghetto Education." *Harvard Education Review* 40 (1970), pp. 411–451.

Roberts v. *City of Boston,* 59 Mass. (5 Cush.) 198 (1849).

Roberts v. *Robertson County Board of Education,* 692 S.W.2d 863 (Tenn Ct. App. 1985).

Roderick, M. "Grade Retention and School Dropout: Investigating the Association." *American Educational Research Journal* 31 (1994), pp. 729–759.

Roopnarien, J. "The Social Individual Model: Mixed-Age Socialization." In *Approaches to Early Childhood Education,* ed. J. L. Roopnarien & J. E. Johnson. Columbus, OH: Charles E. Merrill, 1987.

Rosemond, J. "Helping with Homework Isn't Always Necessary." *Hartford Courant* (August 6, 1995), p. H.5.

Rosenholz, S. *Teachers' Workplace: The Social Organization of Schools.* New York: Longman, 1989.

Rosenshine, B. & N. Furst. "The Use of Direct Observation to Study Teaching." In *Second Handbook of Research on Teaching,* ed. R. M. W. Travers. Chicago: Rand McNally, 1973.

Rosenshine, B. & R. Stevens. "Teaching Functions." In *Handbook of Research on Teaching,* ed. M. C. Wittrock, 3rd ed. New York: Macmillan, 1986.

Ross, J. G. & R. R. Pate. "Factors Associated with Health-Related Fitness." *Journal of Physical Education, Recreation, and Dance* 58 (1987), pp. 54–78.

Rowan, B. "Comparing Teachers' Work with Work in Other Occupations: Notes on the Professional Status of Teaching." *Educational Researcher* 23 (1994), pp. 4–17, 21.

Rowe, M. B. "Wait-Time and Rewards as Instructional Variables: Their Influence on Language, Logic, and Fate Control. Part One: Wait-Time." *Journal of Research in Science Teaching* 11 (1974), pp. 81–94.

Rury, J. L. "Who Became Teachers? The Social Characteristics of Teachers in American History." In *American Teachers: Histories of a Profession at Work,* ed. D. Warren. New York: Macmillan, 1989.

Rutherford, F. J. & A. Ahigren. *Science for All Americans.* New York: Oxford University Press, 1990.

Rutter, M., B. Maughan, P. Mortimore, J. Ouston, & A. Smith. *Fifteen Thousand Hours: Secondary Schools and Their Effects on Children.* Cambridge, MA: Harvard University Press, 1979.

Ryan, D. *Characteristics of Effective Teachers.* Washington, DC: American Council on Education, 1960.

Ryan, K. & J. Cooper. *Those Who Can, Teach.* 7th ed. Boston: Houghton Mifflin, 1995.

Sadker, M. P. & D. M. Sadker. *Teachers, Schools, and Society.* 3rd ed. New York: McGraw-Hill, 1994.

Sadker, M. P., D. M. Sadker, & S. Klein. "The Issue of Gender in Elementary and Secondary Education." In *Review of Research in Education,* 17, ed. G. Grant. Washington, DC: American Educational Research Association, 1991.

Sarason, S. B. *The Culture of the School and the Problem of Change.* Boston: Allyn & Bacon, 1971.

Sarason, S. B. *The Case for Change: Rethinking the Preparation of Educators.* San Francisco: Jossey-Bass, 1993a.

Sarason, S. B. *You Are Thinking of Teaching? Opportunities, Problems, Realities.* San Francisco: Jossey-Bass, 1993b.

Sarason, S. B. *School Change.* New York: Teachers College Press, 1995.

"S.A.T. Score Differences between Men and Women." *Education Week,* September 7, 1994, p. 11.

Sato, N. & M. W. McLaughlin. "Context Matters: Teaching in Japan and in the United States." *Phi Delta Kappan,* 73 (1992), pp. 359–366.

Scheelhaase v. *Woodbury Cent. Community School Dist.,* 488 F.2d 237 (8th Cir. 1973), cert. denied, 417 U.S. 969 (1974).

Scherer, M. "School Snapshot: Focus on African-American Culture." *Educational Leadership* 49 (1992), pp. 17–19.

Schlesinger, A. *The Disuniting of America.* New York: Norton, 1992.

Schlosser, L. K. "Teacher Distance and Student Disengagement: School Lives on the Margin." *Journal of Teacher Education* 43 (1992), pp. 128–140.

Schmuck, P. & R. Schmuck. "Democratic Participation in Small-Town Schools." *Educational Researcher* (1990), pp. 14–19.

Schmuck, R. A. & P. J. Runkel. *Handbook of Organization Development in Schools and Colleges.* 4th ed. Prospect Heights, IL: Waveland Press, 1994.

Schmuck, R. A., P. J. Runkel, J. H. Arends, & R. I. Arends. *The Second Handbook of Organization Development in Schools.* Palo Alto, CA: Mayfield, 1977.

Schmuck, R. & P. Schmuck. *Group Processes in the Classroom.* 7th ed. Dubuque, IA: Brown & Benchmark, 1997.

Schon, D. *The Reflective Practitioner.* San Francisco: Jossey-Bass, 1983.

Schon, D. *Educating the Reflective Practitioner.* San Francisco: Jossey-Bass, 1986.

School Dist. No. 11, Joint Counties of Archuleta and La Plata v. *Umberfield,* 512 P.2d 1166 (Colo. Ct. App. 1973).

Scott v. *Board of Education,* Hicksville, 305 N.Y.S. 2d 601 (1969).

Sedlak, M. W. " 'Let Us Go and Buy a School Master:' Historical Perspectives on the Hiring of Teachers in the United States: 1750–1980." In *American Teachers: Histories of a Profession at Work,* ed. D. Warren. New York: Macmillan, 1989.

Sergiovanni, T. *Moral Leadership: Getting to the Heart of the Problem.* San Francisco: Jossey-Bass, 1992.

Sergiovanni, T. *Leadership for the Schoolhouse: How Is It Different? How Is It Important?* San Francisco: Jossey-Bass, 1996.

Shanker, A. "Where We Stand: Truths about Teaching." *The New York Times,* January 28, 1996, p. E–7.

Shanker, A. Where We Stand: What Standards? *The New York Times,* April 7, 1996, p. E–7.

Shannon, D. M. & M. Boll. "Designing and Implementing a Preservice Teacher Portfolio System." Paper presented at the meeting of the Eastern Education Research Association, Hilton Head, SC, February 1997.

Sharan, S. & Y. Sharan. "Cooperative Learning: Changing Teachers' Instructional Methods." In *Current Perspectives on the Culture of Schools,* ed. N. B. Wyner. Boston: Brookline, 1991.

Shatz, M. & R. Gelman. "The Development of Communication Skills: Modification in the

Speech of Young Children as a Function of Listener." *Monographs of the Society for Research in Child Development,* 38 (5, Serial No. 152), 1973.

Shepard, L. A. & C. L. Bliem. "Parents' Thinking about Standardized Tests and Performance Assessments." *Educational Researcher* 24 (1995), pp. 25–32.

Shulman, L. "Knowledge and Teaching: Foundations of the New Reform." *Harvard Education Review* 57 (1987), pp. 1–22.

Schuman v. *Cumberland Valley School District Board of Directors,* 536 A.2d 490 (Pa. Commonwealth Court 1988).

Sieber, R. T. "Classmates as Workmates: Informal Peer Activity in the Elementary School." *Anthropology and Education Quarterly* 10 (1979), pp. 207–235.

Silcock, P. "Primary School Teacher-Time and the National Curriculum: Managing the Impossible." *British Journal of Educational Studies* 40 (1992), pp. 163–173.

Simmons v. *Beauregard Parish School Board,* 315 So. 2d 883 (La. App. 1975).

Sinatra, G. M., I. L. Beck, & M. G. McKeown. "A Longitudinal Characterization of Young Students' Knowledge of Their Country's Government." *American Educational Research Journal* 29 (1992), pp. 633–661.

Singleton v. *Iberville Parish School Board,* 136 So.2d 809 (La. App. 1961).

Sizer, T. *Horace's School: Redesigning the American High School.* New York: Houghton Mifflin, 1992.

Skinner v. *Railway Labor Executives Association,* 489 U.S. 602 (1989).

Slavin, R. E. "Achievement Effects of Substantial Reductions in Class Size. In *School and Classroom Organization,* ed. R. E. Slavin. Hillsdale, NJ: Erlbaum, 1989.

Smelter, R. W., B. W. Rasch, & G. J. Yudewitz. "Thinking of Inclusion for All Special Needs Students? Better Think Again." *Phi Delta Kappan* 76 (1994), pp. 35–38.

Smith, M. L. & G. Glass. "Meta-Analysis of Research on Class Size and Its Relationship to Attitudes and Instruction." *American Educational Research Journal* 17 (1980), pp. 419–433.

Snarey, J. R. "Cross-Cultural Universality of Social-Moral Development: A Critical Review of Kohlbergian Research." *Psychological Bulletin* 97 (1985), pp. 202–232.

Snyder, T. D. *Digest of Education Statistics, 1988.* Washington, DC: National Center for Education and Statistics, 1988.

Sockett, H. "The Moral Aspects of the Curriculum." In *Handbook of Curriculum Research,* ed. P. Jackson. New York: Macmillan, 1995.

Sommerfield, M. "Corporate Gifts to K-12 Education up 13%." *Education Week* (September 29, 1992), p. 17.

Spring, J. *The Sorting Machine.* New York: David McKay, 1976.

Spring, J. *Conflict of Interest,* 2nd edition. New York: Longman, 1993.

Spring, J. *American Education.* 6th ed. New York: McGraw-Hill, 1994a.

Spring, J. *Wheels in the Head: Educational Philosophies of Authority, Freedom, and Culture from Socrates to Paulo Freire.* New York: McGraw-Hill, 1994b.

Spring, J. *American Education.* 7th ed. New York: McGraw-Hill, 1996.

Stanford, G. *Developing Effective Classroom Groups: A Practical Guide for Teachers.* New York: A & W Visual Library, 1977.

State ex rel. Gretick v. *Jeffrey,* 465 N.E.2d 412 (Ohio 1984).

State v. *Parker,* 592 A.2d 228 (N.J. 1991).

Statistics in Brief. *Student Victimization at School.* Washington, DC: U.S. Department of Education, 1995.

Stedman, L. "The Achievement Crisis Is Real: A Review of *The Manufactured Crisis.*" Education Policy Analysis Archives 4, World Wide Web: http://seamonkey.ed.edu/epaa, 1996.

Sterzing v. *Fort Bend Independent School Dist.,* 376 F. Supp. 657 (S.D. Tex. 1972), 496 F.2d 92 (5th Cir. 1974).

Stevenson, D. L. & Baker, D. P. "State Control of the Curriculum and Classroom Instruction." *Sociology of Education* 64 (1991), pp. 1–10.

Stone v. *Belgrade School District No. 44,* 703 P.2d 136 (Mont. 1984).

Stright, A. L. & D. C. French. "Leadership in Mixed-Age Children's Groups." *International Journal of Behavioral Development* 11 (1988), pp. 507–515.

Stringfield, S. "Attempting to Enhance Students' Learning Through Innovative Programs: The Case for Schools Evolving into High Reliability Organizations." *School Effectiveness and School Improvement Journal* 6 (1995), pp. 1–29.

Swann v. *Charlotte-Mecklenburg Board of Education,* 402 U.S. 1 (1971).

Sykes, G. & L. Shulman, eds. *Handbook of Teaching and Policy.* New York: Longman, 1983.

Takaki, R. *A Different Mirror: A History of Multicultural America.* Boston: Little, Brown 1993.

Tannen, D. *You Just Don't Understand: Women and Men in Conversation.* New York: Morrow, 1990.

Tannenbaum, M. *Concepts and Issues in School Choice:* Lewiston, NY: Edwin Ellen Press, 1995.

"Teachers as Examples." *Hartford Courant,* Monday, May 16, 1994, p. E–6.

Theobold, P. & E. Mills. "Accountability and the Struggle over What Counts." *Phi Delta Kappan* 76 (1995), pp. 462–466.

The Third International Mathematics and Science Study: Pursuing Excellence. World Wide Web: httpp://www.ed.gov/NCES/timss, 1996.

Tinker v. *Des Moines Independent School District,* 393 U.S. (1969).

Toffler, A. *The Third Wave.* New York: Bantam Books, 1980.

Tomasky, M. "Kids Say the Darndest Things." *New Yorker,* 29 (1996), pp. 58–62.

Tozer, S. E., P. C. Violas, & B. B. Senese. *School and Society.* 2nd ed. New York: McGraw-Hill, 1995.

Tyack, D. ed. *Turning Points in American History.* Waltham, MA: Blaisdell, 1967.

Tyack, D. B. *The One Best System.* Cambridge, MA: Harvard University Press, 1974.

Tyack, D., T. James, & A. Benavot. *Law and the Shaping of Public Education 1785–1954.* Madison, WI: University of Wisconsin Press, 1987.

Tye v. *Houston County Board of Education,* 681 F. Supp. 740 (M.D. Ala. 1987).

Urban, W. A. & J. Wagoner. *American Education: A History.* New York: McGraw-Hill, 1996.

U.S. Civil Service Commission v. *National Association of Letter Carriers,* AFL-CIO, 413 U.S. 548 (1973).

U.S. Commission on Civil Rights, *Statement of Affirmative Action for Equal Employment Opportunities.* Washington, DC, 1973.

U.S. Commission on Civil Rights, *Twenty Years after Brown: Equality of Educational Opportunity.* Washington, DC, 1975.

U.S. Department of Commerce, Bureau of the Census. *Statistical Abstract of the United States.* 112th ed. Washington, DC: 1992.

U.S. Department of Education. *National Household Education Survey.* Washington, DC: 1993.

U.S. Department of Education. *Sixteenth Annual Report to Congress on the Implementation of the Individuals with Disabilities Education Act.* Washington, DC, 1994.

Van Galen, J. A. "Ideology, Curriculum, and Pedagogy in Home Education." *Education and Urban Society* 21 (1988), pp. 52–68.

Vann, K. & J. Kunjufu. "The Importance of an Afrocentric, Multicultural Curriculum." *Phi Delta Kappan* 74, (1993), pp. 490–491.

Vasudev, J. & R. C. Hummel. "Moral Stage Sequence and Principled Reasoning in an Indian Sample." *Human Development* 30 (1987), pp. 105–118.

Veenman, S. "Perceived Problems of Beginning Teachers." *Review of Educational Research* 54 (1984), pp. 143–178.

Villasenor, A. *Teaching the First Grade Mathematics Curriculum from a Problem-Solving Perspective.* Ph.D. diss. University of Wisconsin, Milwaukee, 1990.

Villegas, A. M. *Culturally Responsive Teaching.* New Jersey: Educational Testing Service, 1991.

Vosniadou, S. "Conceptual Development in Astronomy." In *The Psychology of Learning Science,* ed. S. M. Glynn, R. H. Yeany, & B. K. Britton. Hillsdale, NJ: Erlbaum, 1991.

Vosniadou, S. & W. F. Brewer. "A Cross-Cultural Investigation of Children's Conceptions about the Earth, Sun, and the Moon: Greek and American Data." In *Learning and Instruction: European Research in an International Context,"* ed. H. Mandl, E. DeCorte, N. Bennette, & H. F. Friedrich. vol. 22. Oxford: Pergamon Press, 1990.

Wakefield, A. P. "Multi-Age Grouping in Day Care." *Children Today* 8 (1979), pp. 26–28.

Walker, A. *The Color Purple.* New York: Washington Square, 1982.

Walsh, M. "Parent-Rights Cases against Schools Fail to Make Inroads." *Education Week,* April 10, 1996, p. 11.

Ware v. *Morgan County School Dist. No. RE-3,* 748 P. 2d 1295 (Colo. 1988).

Warren, D. W. ed. *American Teachers: A History of a Profession at Work.* New York: Macmillan, 1989.

Way, J. W. "Achievement and Self-Concept in Multiage Classrooms." *Educational Research Quarterly* 6 (1981), pp. 69–75.

Webb v. *McCullough,* 828 F.2d 1151 (6th Cir. 1987).

Weick, K. E. "Educational Organizations as Loosely Coupled Systems." *Administrative Quarterly* 21 (1976), pp. 1–19.

Weinstein, C. S. "Teacher Education Students' Preconceptions of Teaching." *Journal of Teacher Education* 40 (1989), pp. 53–60.

Weinstein, C. S. *Elementary Classroom Management.* New York: McGraw-Hill, 1993.

West Virginia v. *Barnette,* 319 U.S. 624; 642 (1943).

Westbury, I. "Comparing American and Japanese Achievement: Is the United States Really a Low Achiever?" *Educational Researcher* 21 (1989), pp. 18–24.

Whaley v. *Anoka-Hennepin Independent School District No. 11,* 325 N.W.2d 128 (Minn. 1982).

Wheatley, M. J. *Leadership and the New Science.* San Francisco, CA: Berrett-Koehler, 1992.

Wheeler, N., G. Marcus, B. Cullen, & L. Konugres. "Baseline Chronic Disease Risk in a Racially Heterogeneous Elementary School Population: The 'Know Your Body' Program." *Preventive Medicine* 12 (1983), pp. 569–587.

Whiting, B. B. & C. Edwards. *Children of Different Worlds: The Formation of Social Behavior.* Cambridge, MA: Harvard University Press, 1988.

Whiting, G. G. The Genesis of Prosocial Behavior. In *The Nature of Prosocial Development,* ed. D. Bridgeman. New York: Academic Press, 1983.

Whittington, D. "What Have 17-Year-Olds Known in the Past?" *American Educational Research Journal* 28 (1991), pp. 759–780.

Willis, D. B. & P. Horvath. "The Teaching Profession: A View from Japan." *Educational Leadership* 46 (1993), pp. 64–68.

Willis, S. "Teaching Language-Minority Students." *Update.* Association for Supervision and Curriculum Development Newsletter 36 (1994), pp. 1, 4–5.

Wilson, S., L. Shulman, & A. Richert. "150 Different Ways of Knowing: Representations of Knowledge in Teaching." In *Exploring Teacher Thinking,* ed. J. Calderhood. London, England: Cassell 1987.

Wisconsin v. *Yoder* 406 U.S. 205 (1972).

Wise, A. "NCATE's Emphasis on Performance." *NCATE Quality Teaching* 5 (Spring, 1995), pp. 1–12.

Wise, A. "Building a System of Quality Assurance for the Teaching Profession." *Phi Delta Kappan,* 78 (1996), pp. 191–192.

Wise v. *Pea Ridge,* 855 F.2d 560 564 (8th Cir. 1988).

Witte, J. F., A. B. Bailey, & C. A. Thorn. *Third-Year Report: Milwaukee Parental Choice Program.* Madison, WI: University of Wisconsin, 1993.

Wittrock, M. C. ed. *Handbook of Research on Teaching.* 3rd ed. New York: Macmillan, 1986.

Wolf, K. "The Schoolteacher's Portfolio: Issues in Design, Implementation, and Evaluation." *Phi Delta Kappan* 73 (1991), pp. 129–136.

Woolfolk, A. *Educational Psychology.* 6th ed. Boston: Allyn & Bacon, 1995.

Wylie, C. "Finessing Site-Based Management with Balancing Acts." *Educational Leadership* 53 (1995), pp. 54–59.

Yinger, R. "A Study of Teacher Planning." *Elementary School Journal* 80 (1980), pp. 107–127.

Zahorik, J. & H. Dichanz. "Teaching for Understanding in German Schools." *Educational Leadership* 51 (1994), pp. 75–77.

Zirkel, P. A. & S. N. Richardson. (1988). *A Digest of Supreme Court Decisions Affecting Education.* Bloomington, IN: Phi Delta Kappan, 1988.

Zukerman, M. "Socialization in Colonial New England." In *Education in American History: Readings on the Social Issues,* ed. M. B. Katz. New York: Praeger, 1970.

ability grouping: organizing students by similarity of achievement levels for instruction purposes.

academic freedom: the right of teachers to select topics, materials, and teaching methodologies.

academic learning time: the amount of time students are actually learning the material during a lesson.

accountability: schools' and teachers' responsibility for student learning.

accreditation: a process used by an external agency to confirm that professional preparation programs meet agreed-upon standards.

achievement motivation: the basic human emotional need to accomplish mastery.

action zone: the area of the classroom from which teachers most often call on students, usually the front rows and center columns.

ADD: *see* attention deficit disorder.

adoption process: the process by which textbooks are selected, usually by committee at the state, district, or school level.

adult literacy: the proportion of people over 18 who have sufficient literacy skills to function in society.

advance organizer: an analogy or metaphor that serves to bridge students' prior knowledge with the content of a lecture.

advanced placement (AP): courses and examinations taken by high school students in order to receive college credit.

affiliation need: the basic human emotional need for attachment, friendship, and affection.

affirmative action: a plan that requires schools to take positive steps to bring about integration in schools, not simply eliminate policies and practices that resulted in segregated schools.

Afrocentric curriculum: a curriculum organized around the history, literature, and perspectives of Africa rather than Europe.

allocated time: the amount of time actually devoted to a given topic after time lost for unanticipated interruptions is deducted.

alternative certification: the practice of providing individuals who have liberal arts degrees a certificate to teach without completing a formal teacher education program.

American Association of Colleges for Teacher Education (AACTE): a professional organization concerned with improving programs of teacher education.

American Federation of Teachers (AFT): a national teachers' union with affiliates at the state and local levels concerned with protecting teachers' rights and improving working conditions and the quality of education.

angst: dread in the face of death.

anti-intellectualism: a perspective that devalues scholarly pursuits and things of the mind.

assertive discipline: a popular but flawed classroom discipline package that focuses on reward and punishment as the sole strategies for establishing classroom order.

assessment: strategies and techniques that teachers use to evaluate what students know and can do.

at-risk student: a student who can be predicted to have problems with school learning because of social background and/or handicapping condition.

attention deficit disorder (ADD): a learning disability diagnosed by a professional characterized by impulsive activities, inattentiveness, and an inability to take turns.

audiolingual method: a foreign language teaching technique in which students listen and respond to audiotaped conversations in the foreign language.

authentic assessment: a means of assessing student skill by having them actually perform the skill rather than take a test.

authoritarian: a form of discipline in which parents or teachers exert strict control over children despite children's emerging maturity.

authoritative: a form of discipline in which parents or teachers exert democratic leadership with children, setting boundaries but allowing for student input, and adjusting the boundaries appropriately as children mature.

autonomous morality: a Piagetian term referring to individuals at a relatively high stage of moral development in which they can interpret the behavior of others in terms of the others' intentions.

autonomy norm: the expectation in many schools that teachers can do as they want within the confines of their own classroom.

axiology: the branch of philosophy that attempts to answer the question, What is the nature of values and valuing?

back to basics: a movement that emphasizes teaching the basic subjects of reading, writing, and mathematics and de-emphasizes critical thinking.

basic school: the term used by Ernest Boyer to describe a restructured school that teaches a common core of learning within a community characterized by caring and interdependence.

behavioral disorder: a disability in emotional and social functioning.

bilingual education: a variety of instructional arrangements in which students are taught in both English and their native language.

board of education: the local governing body for school districts, elected or appointed by elected officials and responsible for making policy for the district and hiring and dismissing all school personnel.

bureaucracy: an organizational form characterized by fixed rules, specialization of functions, and hierarchical control systems.

captive clientele: those, such as students, who are required by law to be members of an organization, in this case, school.

career ladder: a situation in which work roles and positions are differentiated and/or hierarchically arranged and individuals advance from one position to the next as they gain experience and expertise.

Carnegie unit: a measure used to standardize high school study. One Carnegie unit denotes a class that meets for 1 semester 5 days a week for approximately 1 hour a day.

case law: the body of court cases out of which rulings are made that determine policy and practice.

cellular structure: the organizational arrangement in schools by which students are divided into age-graded classrooms and one teacher is assigned full responsibility for each classroom.

certificate: a license granted to teachers signifying they are prepared to teach particular subjects or at particular grade levels.

chain of command: the organizational hierarchy in a school system through which policies are implemented and problems handled.

character: moral excellence.

character education: a reform movement aimed at using schools to improve students' character and morals.

charter school: a public school designed by a group of individuals from the ground up in order to meet a specific purpose with clearly delineated outcome objectives for students, whose charter is renewed only if those objectives are achieved.

clarity: a characteristic of lectures in which the structure of the lecture is obvious, little extraneous information is introduced, there are few dangling or run on sentences, and transitions are smooth.

classroom climate: the emotional atmosphere of a classroom.

classroom management: the ability to establish and maintain order in the classroom using an array of strategies.

classroom meeting: a classroom management strategy that promotes student influence on classroom decisions.

cognitive process: human mental functioning.

collaboration: the act of working jointly with others.

collective bargaining: the process whereby the union that represents teachers in a school district negotiates a contract for everyone in the district.

competency exams: tests given to students or teachers that measure prespecified understandings or skills.

comprehension strategies: a series of techniques that help learners understand what they read.

concrete operations: the third stage of cognitive development in which preadolescent children demonstrate the principle of conservation and the ability to reason about objects.

constructivist perspective: a view that knowledge is not fixed but instead personal and social in nature and that individuals construct knowledge and meaning through experience.

cooperative learning: classroom activities in which students work in small groups and are responsible for completing collaborative projects.

core curriculum: basic curriculum requirements, usually developed at the state level.

cultural deficit theory: a hypothesis that accounts for minority children's school difficulties by attributing them to disadvantages in their culture, race, class, or language.

cultural difference theory: a hypothesis that accounts for minority children's school difficulties by attributing them to differences between their culture, race, class, or language and that of the dominant group.

cultural literacy: a term coined by E. D. Hirsch referring to the important names, dates, events, concepts, and products of Western society.

cultural socialization: a process of providing students with the ways and symbol systems of their culture.

culturally responsive teaching: adapting teaching to meet the needs of culturally diverse students.

culture carriers: individuals who carry and help preserve a group's or organization's culture from one generation to the next.

culture shock: the emotional reaction that first-time travelers to foreign countries experience as they encounter behavior patterns that violate their own cultural norms.

curriculum: the content of instruction.

curriculum alignment: the match between what is taught and what is tested.

curriculum fragmentation: a situation caused by a poorly planned, incoherent, or incomplete curriculum.

curriculum frameworks: guidelines for what should be taught, usually developed at the state level.

curriculum integration: interdisciplinary instruction.

dangle: a teacher behavior that disrupts a smoothly flowing lesson due to an unfinished sentence or thought.

Darwinism: the idea that life is continuously evolving, not static.

de facto segregation: segregation that results from residential patterns.

de jure segregation: segregation that results from laws and/or governmental actions intended to keep the races apart.

decoding: in reading, the process of identifying and pronouncing words correctly.

deductive logic: begins with general statements and moves to particular or specific instances of application.

deferred gratification: the ability to postpone satisfying an immediate desire.

demography: the study of population patterns; in education, generally concerned with racial and ethnic distribution of students.

desegregation: eliminating policies and practices that have caused neighborhoods and schools to be segregated by race.

difficulty level: the percent of questions answered correctly.

direct instruction: an approach to teaching skills in which lessons are highly goal directed and the learning environments tightly structured by teachers.

discipline: the aspect of classroom management concerned with responding to student off-task behavior and regaining cooperation.

discourse patterns: regularities in interpersonal communication.

discovery learning: an approach to teaching that encourages students to learn concepts and principles through their own inquiry and explorations.

discrimination: treating individuals on the basis of characteristics that are irrelevant to the activity in which they are engaged.

discussion: an instructional strategy involving more student than teacher talk aimed at encouraging critical thinking.

dominated communities: the outcome when majority power is exercised by a few people or one person and school boards generally represent the power elite.

due process rights: guaranteed by the Fourteenth Amendment in any effort by the state to deprive individuals of life, liberty, or property.

early-exit programs: a form of bilingual education in which students quickly move into regular English-language classes as soon as possible, usually by second grade.

effective teachers: teachers who have developed a broad repertoire of teaching approaches and consistently produce high achievement among their students.

emergency certificate: certificate given individuals that allows them to teach even though they do not have the required formal training.

emotional insight: the ability to read another's emotional state.

emotional intelligence: the ability to establish and maintain mutually satisfactory relationships.

engaged time: the amount of time students are actively involved during a lesson.

English as a Second Language (ESL): a form of instruction for language minority students in which they participate in special pull-out programs to learn English.

epistemology: the branch of philosophy that attempts to answer the question, What is the nature of knowledge and knowing?

equity pedagogy: teaching strategies aimed at helping all students learn.

Essentialism: the educational philosophy which holds that the purpose of schools is to preserve the knowledge and values of the past while simultaneously providing students with the skills necessary to live successful and meaningful lives in present society.

establishing rules and routines: the second stage of group development in which group members come to accept the standard operating procedures of the classroom.

establishing shared influence: the third stage of group development in which group members develop a sense of reciprocal influence.

ethics: the study of right and wrong.

ethos: the fundamental character or spirit of a culture; *see* school culture.

existentialism: the philosophy which holds that reality, knowledge, and values are totally individual.

extracurriculum: the content of schooling contained in planned, nonclassroom settings like athletics, clubs, and student government.

extrinsic rewards: rewards that stem from the external environment, such as salary, grades, or job security.

facilitating psychological membership: the first stage of group development in which group members strive for a sense of belonging to the group.

factional communities: communities in which two factions holding different values compete for power, and school boards are made up of members who have won hotly contested elections and rarely agree on any agenda items.

fair use doctrine: the privilege for others than the owner of a copyright to use the copyrighted material in a reasonable manner without his consent, despite the monopoly granted to the owner.

federal revenues: include direct grants-in-aid to schools or agencies, funds distributed through a state or intermediate agency, and revenues in lieu of taxes to compensate a school district for nontaxable federal institutions within a district's boundary.

feedback: information provided to students on the correctness and quality of their work.

flip-flop: a teacher behavior that disrupts smoothness of lesson delivery by starting one sentence, dropping it, and starting another, then dropping it and returning to the first one.

formal operations: the final stage of cognitive development in which adolescents acquire the ability to reason logically about abstractions.

formative evaluation: ongoing assessment of the success of instruction used by teachers to inform future lessons.

foundation plan: funding formula in which a state determines the cost of providing a basic level of education to all children, assesses how much the local district can raise toward this amount, and provides the difference.

fragmentation: a teacher behavior that disrupts momentum by using incomplete sentences or other unclear speech.

free appropriate public education (FAPE): required by the *Education for All Handicapped Children Act*, education designed to meet the needs of each individual child including special education and related services.

full bilingual programs: a form of schooling for language-minority students in which they receive part of their instruction in their home language and part of it in English on a continuing basis.

gemeinschaft: German term to describe community in which individual relationships are characterized by intimacy and informality.

gesellschaft: German term to describe community in which individual relationships are characterized by formality and contractual agreements.

good boy/good girl stage: Kohlberg's third stage of moral reasoning in which decisions are made based on living up to the expectations of others.

guided practice: a form of assisted performance in which students practice a new skill with the teacher nearby to provide immediate corrective feedback.

hands-off norm: the expectation in many schools that teachers will not interfere or criticize other teachers' work and practices.

hegemony: the domination of one class or group by another.

heroes and heroines: prominent individuals in a group or organization who embody the group's or organization's core values and beliefs.

heterogeneous grouping: instructional arrangements in which students of unlike ability are grouped together.

heteronomous morality: a Piagetian term referring to children at a low stage of moral development in which they rigidly adhere to rules without attending to intention.

hidden curriculum: the unspoken norms, values, and attitudes embedded in the official, operational, extra-, and null curricula.

higher-order questions: questions that call for deeper mental processing than is required in simple recall.

higher track: instruction provided specifically for students of higher academic ability.

history property: in education, the particular norms and sense of community that develop when classroom groups stay together for an extended period of time, coined by Doyle.

homogeneous grouping: grouping students of like ability together for instruction; *see* ability grouping.

idealism: the philosophy which holds that reality is based in ideas, knowledge is mental or spiritual, and values are determined through authority.

imbalance bias: a form of curriculum bias in which only one aspect of a complex situation is addressed.

immediacy property: Doyle's term to describe the fact that decisions must be made and actions taken very quickly in classrooms.

immersion program: a form of ESL instruction in which language-minority students are placed with their age mates in a regular classroom and given no special instruction in English.

improvement scoring: a cooperative learning assessment strategy that promotes individual accountability and positive interdependence.

in loco parentis: school officials acting in the place of the parents while students are involved in school activities.

inclusion: the practice of keeping special education students in regular education classrooms and bringing support services to the child, rather than taking the child to the support services.

independent practice: classroom activity in which students practice a new skill on their own.

individual accountability: an aspect of cooperative learning in which teachers structure learning activities so that all students learn the material.

individual educational program or plan (IEP): a plan that is jointly prepared by education officials and parents which must identify the child's needs, annual instructional goals and objectives, specific educational services to be provided, and evaluation procedures; reviewed annually.

inductive discipline: a discipline technique in which parents or teachers point out to children how their actions affect others.

inductive logic: examines the particulars or specifics in an attempt to develop generalizations.

inert communities: communities in which there is no visible power structure, little competition for positions on the school board, and little display of public interest in the schools, tending to produce sanctioning school boards that are relatively inactive, do not represent any factions within the community, and usually approve the recommendations of the school administrative staff.

influence need: the basic human emotional need to exert control over one's life.

in-service: the designation for teachers who have been certified and are currently employed as teachers; also, continuing education for practicing teachers.

instruction: the means by which curriculum is conveyed to students.

instructional assessment: techniques teachers use during lessons to ascertain student understanding.

instrumental relativist stage: Kohlberg's second stage of moral reasoning in which decisions are made based on whether the outcomes meet one's own needs.

interactive tasks of teaching: those aspects of teachers' work in which they provide face-to-face instruction to students.

interdependence: a situation in which individuals are mutually dependent on one another.

international baccalaureate: a special degree conferred on high school graduates who have completed an internationally organized curriculum.

intrinsic rewards: incentives that stem from within an individual, such as satisfaction, sense of accomplishment, or pure enjoyment.

invisibility bias: a form of curriculum bias in which the perspectives of nondominant groups are not included.

involuntary minority: groups that have been subordinated to the dominant group against their will.

IRE: the recitation discourse pattern of teacher initiation, student response, and teacher evaluation.

isolates: those students who have a hard time getting along with others and are rejected by their peers.

ITBS: Iowa Test of Basic Skills, a popular achievement test.

laissez faire: a form of discipline in which parents or teachers exert no control or guidance over children.

latchkey kids: school-age children who are not supervised by adults after school.

late-exit programs: a form of bilingual education in which students move into regular English classroom settings slowly, usually around sixth grade.

law-and-order stage: Kohlberg's fourth stage of moral reasoning in which decisions are made based on exactly following the existing moral code.

leadership tasks of teaching: those leadership aspects of teachers' work such as providing motivation, assessment and planning, and coordinating classroom activities.

least restrictive environment: mainstreaming children with handicaps into regular classrooms for as much of the school day as possible.

lecture: teacher-centered instructional strategy designed to convey large amounts of factual information.

legislature: the primary source of state educational policy, with broad powers to enact legislation

LEP: limited English proficiency.

lesson plan: organization of instruction for a particular lesson or period.

linguistic bias: a form of curriculum bias in which language is used in stereotypical ways.

literacy: the ability to read, write, speak, and listen in a particular language and to communicate visually.

literate environment: a classroom in which reading and writing take place routinely and often and for a variety of purposes and audiences.

local revenues: revenues from such sources as local property, income, and sales taxes, investments, income from student activities, textbook sales, transportation and tuition fees, and food service revenues.

logic: the study of the principles of reasoning.

logical consequences: a classroom discipline technique in which students experience a logical outcome of their inappropriate behavior rather than an imposed punishment.

logical construct: a concept based on a nonobservable inference from observable behavior used to examine reality. For example, intelligence.

logical positivism: a philosophical perspective that prizes objective ideas that can be proved over emotionally driven values that can not.

loosely coupled: a situation in which one part of an organization is not tightly tied or connected to other parts of the organization, and in which the parts operate somewhat independently of each other.

lower track: instruction provided specifically for students of lower academic ability.

lower-order questions: simple recall questions.

magnet schools: schools that have specific themes around which their programs are organized.

mainstreamed: children with handicaps are placed into regular classrooms for as much of the school day as possible.

mastery learning: an instructional strategy in which students are required to achieve a preset level of achievement, usually 80 percent correct on an objective test, before they may advance to the next unit.

mastery orientation: an individual's attitude toward achievement that involves linking success with effort.

metaphysics: the branch of philosophy that attempts to answer the question, What is the nature of reality?

microteaching: a situation in which individuals practice a particular teaching method in a scaled-down setting (with just a few students) and for a short period of time (usually 10 or 15 minutes).

momentum: teachers' ability to maintain appropriate lesson pace.

moral: commonly accepted standards of right and wrong.

moral discussion: an instructional strategy designed to promote moral reasoning.

moral education: using schools to improve students' ethics.

motivation: internal states that arouse action, cause behavior, or direct attention.

multicultural education: programs that strive to equalize educational and life chances of racial, class, cultural, and linguistic minority children, to promote understanding between members of diverse groups, to develop students' skills in cross cultural communication, and to encourage political action to redress social and economic injustice.

multidimensionality property: Doyle's term denoting the large number of types of events and tasks that go on in classrooms.

multiple intelligence: a theory proposed by Howard Gardner postulating that intelligence is not a unitary characteristic but rather a collection of different abilities.

NAEP: National Assessment of Educational Progress.

National Congress of Parents and Teachers (PTA): composed of mostly parents and organized into over 27,000 local units in all 50 states and the District of Columbia; works to advance the welfare of children and youth.

national curriculum: a proposed educational reform to determine curriculum nationally rather than locally.

National School Boards' Association (NSBA): the national association of school boards with affiliates at the state and county levels that provides information and services for their constituent members, solicits input from them, and lobbies legislators at the state and national level.

national standards: curriculum standards created at the national level by a board of political, business, and education leaders.

natural consequences: a classroom discipline technique in which students experience the natural result of their inappropriate behavior rather than an imposed punishment.

NCSS: National Council for the Social Studies.

NCTM: National Council for Teachers of Mathematics.

NEA: National Education Association, the larger of the two major teacher organizations, and mainly concerned with improving education and working conditions for teachers.

negligence: the basis on which the courts provide relief from a civil wrong in the form of damages.

normal school: schools created in the nineteenth century to prepare teachers.

null curriculum: everything that is excluded from the operational, official, and extra curriculum.

official assessment: data collection used for report card grades and instructional placement decisions.

official curriculum: the content of instruction dictated by formal documents like curriculum guides and frameworks.

open classroom: an approach to teaching involving more individual and small-group work, student choice, curriculum integration, and flexible use of space.

open education: an approach to education that emphasizes informal classrooms and methods so students can have more control over their learning and exercise their imagination and creativity.

operational curriculum: the content of instruction actually taught by teachers.

oppositional identity: the tendency of involuntary minorities to avoid adopting the behaviors and attitudes of the majority.

organization perspective: a view of schools as social organizations and as workplaces for teachers.

organizational tasks of teaching: those aspects of teachers' work involving interactions with other adults in the school setting for the purposes of schoolwide planning and coordination.

overdwelling: a teacher behavior that disrupts the momentum of a lesson by spending too much time on a particular issue.

pacing: the speed at which a lesson moves.

pedagogical content knowledge: knowledge about how to represent, explain, and demonstrate particular ideas in a content field.

pedagogy: the study of the art and science of teaching; also, the methods and approaches to instruction.

Perennialism: the educational philosophy derived from Realism

and Idealism which holds that schools should offer all children an academic curriculum based on the classics in order to prepare them to accept their appropriate places in society.

performance-for-grade-exchange: the contractual aspect of the relationship between teacher and students by which students do work and in return the teacher gives a grade.

performance orientation: an individual's attitude toward achievement that involves affirming one's self-worth by competing with and besting others.

performance tests: tests in which individuals are asked to demonstrate that they can perform particular skills, normally in life-like situations.

perspective taking: the ability to see things from another's point of view.

philosophy: the process of systematically reflecting on the world around one in an attempt to build a coherent set of beliefs and values with which to guide one's actions.

phonics: the aspect of reading involving letter-sound correspondences.

planned time: amount of time a teacher sets aside to cover a given topic.

pluralistic communities: communities in which competition exists among a variety of community interest groups; no single group dominates school policies and status-congruent school boards represent a wide variety of community groups that encourage open debate in hopes of reaching a consensus.

political socialization: the process of preparing students to accept and participate in their society's political system.

political vulnerability: a situation in which it is easy for citizens to

influence what goes on in organizations.

portfolio assessment: a means of assessment in which students collect samples of their work over time for evaluation.

positive interdependence: structuring group relationships such that for one person to succeed, all must succeed.

Pragmatism: the philosophy which holds that reality is physical and ever changing, knowledge is established consensually through the scientific method, and values are relative.

preoperations: Piaget's second stage of cognitive development characterized by inability to think logically about concrete objects.

preservice: designation for teachers while they are in professional training and before they are certified.

principal: the person in charge of a school responsible for its operation and performance.

privatization: turning the management of school services and/or entire schools over to private contractors.

probationary period: period of time, usually the first 2 or 3 years, during which teachers are evaluated annually for recontracting and must show competence, prior to receiving tenure.

problem-based instruction: a student-centered and interdisciplinary strategy in which instruction is organized around a particular problem.

procedural due process: requires fairness in procedures if the government threatens any actions that would deprive an individual of life, liberty, or property. Minimally, this requires notification of charges, opportunity to refute charges, and a fair hearing.

procedures: routines for carrying out everyday tasks in the classroom, like lunch counts or homework correcting.

process-product research: research characterized by studying the relationships between teacher behavior (process) and student achievement (product).

professional accountability: the amount of control that professional societies have over their members to assure they behave in ethical ways and use accepted practices.

professional autonomy: the amount of freedom provided to professionals to conduct their work in a manner they deem most appropriate.

proficiency testing: tests developed by states to evaluate students for the award of a high school diploma.

progressive taxes: those that require individuals to pay proportionate to their income.

Progressivism: the educational philosophy that holds that the purpose of the schools is to prepare students to live in a society that is in a constant state of change through a curriculum that is highly social and student-centered.

prosocial behavior: caring, helpful actions stemming from an understanding that another's needs are as important as one's own.

provisional certificate: certificate given to individuals allowing them to teach for a specified period of time.

proximity control: a classroom discipline technique in which teachers use their physical nearness to students to indirectly regain students' attention.

publicness property: Doyle's term for the fact that events in classrooms are in plain view and that every event has an audience.

pull-out programs: a way schools provide additional services to students with special needs by taking them out of their regular

classroom and placing them in a special class for short periods.

punishment obedience stage: Kohlberg's first stage of moral reasoning in which decisions are made based on whether or not one will be caught.

purposeful grouping: an aspect of cooperative learning in which teachers match their grouping of students to their instructional goal.

pursuing academic goals: the fourth stage of group development in which group members make the greatest gains in learning.

question level: refers to the type of thinking required to respond to a question.

racism: inequitable treatment of people based on race.

real estate taxes: primary source of funds for public schools.

Realism: the philosophy which holds that reality is physical and constant, knowledge is that which can be proven empirically, and values are determined by the natural order of the universe.

reciprocity agreements: an arrangement among various states to recognize each other's teaching certificates.

recitation: a discourse pattern in which a teacher asks a question, calls on a student to respond, and then evaluates the student's response.

Reconstructionism: an educational philosophy which holds that the purpose of the schools is to address the needs of society as a whole and make students social problem solvers and agents of change.

reflection: careful and analytical thought by teachers about what they are doing and the effects of their behavior on students and on society.

regressive taxes: those which place an inequitable burden on

low-income families and communities.

related services: transportation and such developmental, corrective, and other support services as may be required to assist the handicapped child to benefit from special education; includes the early identification and assessment of handicapping conditions in children.

repertoire: the mastery of a variety of teaching strategies.

resegregation: segregation of urban areas following "white flight."

reserved powers: those legal powers left to the individual states rather than held by the federal government as a result of the Tenth Amendment to the Constitution.

resilience: the psychological capacity to successfully endure adversity.

responsive teaching: an approach to teaching in which students are encouraged to identify problems and projects and to take responsibility for their own learning.

restrictive control values: a pattern of ethical thinking common in mathematics teachers in which premium is placed on cleanliness, obedience, politeness, responsibility, and self-control.

reverse discrimination: discrimination against nonminorities that results from attempting to correct for past discrimination against members of minority groups.

rituals and ceremonies: events conducted by groups and organizations that express and confirm the group's or organization's core values and beliefs.

role contradiction: a situation in which conflicting expectations exist for individuals performing the same role.

rules: principles to guide student and teacher actions in the classroom.

SAT: Scholastic Achievement Test, a popular assessment of basic skills and knowledge; also Stanford Achievement Test, a college entrance exam.

school culture: the ways members of a school think about social actions; the embedded beliefs, values, and attitudes of members of a school.

school effectiveness research: a type of process-product research characterized by studying the relationships between schoolwide processes and student outcomes, such as attendance and achievement.

schools as community: the perspective that views schools as places in which individuals are bonded together for natural reasons and members share common sentiments and traditions; contrasted to the view of schools as bureaucratic organizations kept together by fixed rules.

schools of choice: an arrangement in which students and their parents are able to select schools of their choice within a district, county, or state rather than their being assigned to specific schools based on their geographic location.

scope of bargaining: the areas about which collective bargaining takes place.

secular humanism: a philosophy maintaining it is possible to live an ethical life without recourse to a deity.

sensorimotor: Piaget's earliest stage of cognitive development in which infants and very young children develop their sensory and large-motor abilities.

separate but equal: the doctrine established by the *Plessy* v. *Ferguson* case of 1896 which maintained that separate facilities for blacks and whites did not violate the Constitution as long as those facilities were equal.

service learning: an instructional strategy designed to promote moral action.

SES: socioeconomic status; a group's income level relative to other groups in the society.

sexism: the inequitable treatment of people based on gender.

shared values and beliefs: attitudes and beliefs held by individuals who are interdependent with one another.

simultaneity property: Doyle's term for the fact that many things go on at once in classrooms.

site-based management: responsibility for governance and control of schools is decentralized to the individual school level based on the rationale that those most directly affected by decisions ought to participate in making them.

sizing-up assessment: data on students collected early in the school year.

skill: knowing how to do something.

smoothness: a teacher's ability to avoid problems that will interrupt the flow of a lesson.

social contract stage: Kohlberg's fifth stage of moral reasoning in which decisions are made based on the realization that rules are socially agreed upon and that moral actions should promote social good.

social-emotional development: the process of gradually acquiring skill in the affective domain as one matures.

social learning theory: a model for learning based on learning by imitation.

social organization of schools: that aspect of school that considers how the various part and subsystems are organized and interrelated.

social segregation: students self-segregate for nonacademic activities.

special education: additional educational services provided students who are handicapped in some way.

specialized knowledge base: special information mastered by professionals that allows them to perform their work effectively.

specific learning disability: a difficulty in learning in a particular domain in students of normal intelligence.

stage disparity: occurs when students in a single classroom operate at a variety of stages of moral reasoning.

state board of education: the state agency responsible for developing policies to implement educational legislation passed by the state legislature.

state department of education: the state agency responsible for implementing and monitoring policies made by the state board of education.

state revenues: include both direct funds from state governments and revenues in lieu of taxation; revenues in lieu of taxes are paid to compensate a school district for nontaxable state institutions or facilities within the district's boundary.

state-adoption states: those states that organize textbook adoptions at the state level.

stereotyping bias: a form of curriculum bias in which groups are portrayed in traditional, limited ways.

student subculture: the attitudes, beliefs, and ways of acting shared by students within particular schools and throughout the wider youth community.

student-centered instruction: instructional strategies in which students can influence content, pace, and learning activities.

subject-specific knowledge development: the pattern of learning over time in a particular content domain.

substantive due process: requires that state action depriving an individual of life, liberty, or property interests be based on a valid objective with means reasonably related to attaining the objective, intended to shield the individual against arbitrary governmental action.

Success-for-All: school-wide elementary program designed by Robert Slavin and colleagues in which every student is assisted to succeed academically.

summative evaluation: assessments of student understanding derived from tests and other formal means that are used to assign grades.

superintendent: chief executive officer of a school district, with the responsibility for carrying out the policies of the school board and seeing to the day-to-day operations of the district.

synergy: positive results achieved from working together or combined action.

teacher characteristics: distinguishing traits possessed by teachers believed to affect their effectiveness, such as warmth, fairness, empathy.

teacher disposition: a teacher's inclination or tendency to act in certain ways.

teacher enthusiasm: A set of behaviors used by teachers, such as using uplifting language and dramatic body movement, to make students interested in learning materials.

teacher expectations: attitudes and beliefs teachers hold about the capabilities of their students.

teacher-centered learning: includes instructional strategies in which the teacher determines content, pace, and learning activities.

teaching subculture: the attitudes, beliefs, and ways of acting shared by teachers within particular schools and throughout the teaching profession.

team teaching: a form of curriculum integration in which teachers share responsibility for each others' students and teach the curriculum together.

tenure: the legal right that provides teachers with a continuing contract in a school district.

thematic instruction: a form of curriculum integration in which instruction is organized around particular themes.

time on task: the amount of time students are engaged in particular learning activities.

Title IX: one of the education amendments, passed in 1972, mandating equal treatment for males and females.

tone: *see* school culture.

tracking: the practice of providing separate instructional environments for students of different academic abilities.

transition and closure: the fifth stage of group development in which the group works through issues attendant to the end of the group and the moving on to the next class.

transitional bilingual programs: a form of instruction for language minority students in which they participate in regular classes with their age mates but receive extra instruction in both English and their own language until they achieve English proficiency.

TTAS: Texas Teacher Assessment System.

unit plan: organization of instruction for an extended period of time.

universal principle stage: Kohlberg's sixth stage of moral reasoning in which decisions are based on one's own moral code which may or may not coincide with society's rules.

unpredictability property: Doyle's term for the fact that because there are so many different people and tasks in a classroom events can often take unexpected turns.

unreality bias: a form of curriculum bias in which a group is portrayed unrealistically.

user fees: fees for a variety of what are considered nonessential school services.

values clarification: instructional strategy by which teachers help students identify their values without imposing judgment.

voluntary minority: groups that have willingly and freely immigrated to a new country.

voucher: a promissory note provided by the government that can be redeemed by parents for a stipulated amount of money at the school of their choice.

wait time: the amount of time teachers pause after asking a question.

weighted formula: state funding of local districts that weights those characteristics of children known to increase the cost of schooling, such as being handicapped, disadvantaged, or in a special program, and provides additional funds for them.

white flight: the mass exodus of whites from inner-city areas following governmental mandates for integration.

withitness: a teacher's ability to spot problem behavior early.

zero reject: a situation in which no child with disabilities is to be excluded from an appropriate public education.

Aburdene, P., 302
Adams, J., 289
Addams, J., 221
Adler, M. J., 71
Ahlgren, A., 248
Airasian, P. W., 174, 175
Alexander, K., 177
Allen, R., 131
Allende, I., 147, 241, 248
Amarel, M., 50
Ames, C., 145
Anderson, C., 50
Angelou, M., 241
Anthony, S. B., 6
Anyon, J., 112
Apple, M., 392
Arends, R., 26, 98, 160
Artiles, A. J., 158
Ayres, L., 176
Azmitia, M., 61
Azuma, H., 145

Baillargeon, R., 61
Baines, H., 148
Baker, D., 118–119, 166, 167, 180
Baker, D. P., 259
Baker, J. A., 60
Ball, D. L., 50, 103
Bandura, A., 300
Banks, J., 146, 147, 149, 248, 263
Barker, R., 230
Barnard, H., 94, 382
Barth, R., 97
Baumeister, R. F., 102, 421
Baumrind, D., 423
Beach, S. A., 114
Beck, I. L., 141, 238
Beecher, C., 6
Bell, T., 237
Belsky, H., 296
Benavot, A., 368
Berk, L. E., 419, 423
Berkowitz, M., 424
Berliner, D., 158, 217–219, 220, 221, 225, 226, 227, 230, 232, 237
Berman, P., 230
Bernard, B., 139
Bernstein, H. T., 241
Best, R., 210
Bestor, A., 385
Bettencourt, E. M., 43
Biddle, B. J., 217–219, 220, 221, 225, 226, 227, 237

Black, H., 339
Bliem, C. L., 178, 179
Blume, J., 241
Bolles, R., 20
Book, C., 103
Boostrom, R. E., 433
Borko, H., 50
Boyer, E., 225, 226, 227, 230, 232, 233
Bracey, G. W., 116, 120, 175, 221
Bradley, A., 389
Brewer, W. F., 142
Brice-Heath, S., 127
Britton, B. K., 142
Broadfoot, P., 259
Brookover, W., 224
Brophy, J., 46
Brousseau, B. A., 102
Brown, A. L., 61
Brown, R., 291
Brownell, C. A., 60
Bruner, J., 97, 233, 287, 304
Buckholdt, D. R., 60
Burke, J. B., 105, 108, 153, 180
Burnaford, G., 38–39
Bush, G., 64, 205, 236, 252, 354
Byers, J., 103

Cahen, L. S., 115
Callanan, R., 428, 431
Cambron-McCabe, N. H., 337, 340, 345, 358, 359, 368
Campbell, E., 39
Carlson, R., 216
Carnegie, A., 221, 302, 399
Carter, J., 50, 110, 111, 386
Carter, J., 109, 277
Carver, G. W., 245
Cazden, C. B., 168, 291
Charters, W. W., Jr., 391
Chase, R., 408
Chelemer, C., 149
Cherry, L. J., 130
Choy, S. P., 138
Clark, M., 175
Clift, R., 398
Clinton, W., 64, 101, 205, 236, 258, 298, 386
Cobb, V., 409
Cohen, E., 131
Colburn, W., 200
Coleman, J., 39, 210
Collins, M. L., 43
Comer, J., 225

Conant, J., 204–205, 385
Cook, K., 383
Coontz, S., 291, 296
Cooper, J., 256
Corey, G., 428, 431
Corey, M. S., 428, 431
Cortines, E., 230
Cotton, J., 285
Counts, G. S., 73, 301
Cremin, L., 215–216
Crow, N. A., 102, 103
Cuban, L., 72, 94, 95, 97, 98, 213
Cullen, B., 255
Cypher, T., 23

Darling-Hammond, L., 139, 390, 381, 408
Darrell, L. R., 399
Darwin, C., 68, 71
Dauber, S., 177
Deal, T. E., 208, 209, 210
DeAvila, E., 131
DeLisi, R., 140
Destefano, J., 130
DeVries, R., 433
Dewey, J., 31, 68, 72, 74, 95, 117, 384
deWijk, S. L., 245
Dichanz, H., 52
Diegmuller, K., 252, 254
Dorner, A. M., 264
Douglass, F., 263
Doyle, R., 178
Doyle, W., 103, 108, 109, 110, 111
Dreikurs, R., 172, 173
Drew, C. J., 135, 138
Duncan, S., 131

Eaton, W. H., 384, 411
Edison, T., 263
Edwards, N., 7, 92, 198, 200, 201, 202
Edwards, C. P., 422
Egan, M. W., 135, 138
Einstein, A., 38, 68
Eisner, E., 392
Elam, S., 302
Elders, J., 298
Eliot, C., 203
Elsbree, W. S., 6
Elson, R., 262
Entwisle, D., 177
Erikson, E., 144
Escalante, J., 38
Evertson, C., 399

Fairbanks, C., 137
Feiman-Nemser, S., 50
Filby, N. N., 115
Fink, C., 177
Finkelstein, B., 95
Finn, J. D., 115–116
Fischer, I., 343, 344, 350, 359, 363, 368
Fordham, S., 210
Fox, R., 430
Frank, A., 241
Franklin, B., 198, 285
Freeman, D., 103
French, D. C., 60
Fullan, M., 230
Furman, S., 60
Furst, N., 43

Garcia, E. E., 130, 131, 263
Garcia, J., 124, 130, 131, 263
Gardner, H., 144, 225
Gates, W., 302
Gay, G., 126
Geary, S., 114
Gelman, R., 61
Getzels, J. W., 40, 91, 94, 97
Gilligan, C., 419
Gilmore, G., 69
Glass, G., 115, 208
Glasser, W., 35, 173
Glynn, S. M., 142
Godwyn, T., 198
Goldenberg, C., 101
Gomez, M., 50
Gompers, S., 221
Goncz, B., 131
Good, T. L., 39, 51
Goodlad, J., 39, 103, 104, 113–114, 122,
    125, 225, 226, 227, 230, 232, 233, 381,
    386, 398, 411
Goodrich, S. G., 92
Goodwin, A., 390
Gottfredson, D., 177
Graham, N., 177
Grant, L., 133
Graziano, W., 60
Greeno, J., 50, 158
Greenstein, F. I., 141
Griese, A. A., 80
Griffey, D. C., 50
Grossman, P. L., 35, 115
Grouws, D. A., 51
Grove, A., 384
Grueneich, R., 60
Gump, P., 230

Haberman, M., 49, 112, 296
Hansen, D. T., 433
Hardman, M. L., 135, 138
Harel, I., 55
Hargreaves, A., 80
Harmin, M., 414
Hartshorn, H., 414, 422
Hartup, W. W., 60
Harvard, J., 198
Hatch, T., 144

Havighurst, K., 296
Hawley, W. H., 399
Heatherton, T. F., 102
Heider, E. R., 291
Hesiod, 198
Hess, R. D., 141, 145, 292
Heyns, B., 291
Hill, L., 137
Hirsch, E. D., 73, 237, 284, 287
Hoffman, 296
Holland, J., 20
Hollins, E. R., 264
Holmes, C., 177, 381, 398, 399
Horwitz, R. A., 117
Housner, L. D., 50
Howsom, R. B., 398
Huberman, M., 392
Hummel, R. C., 419
Hutchins, R., 71
Hyde, J. S., 133, 134

Illich, I., 292, 293

Jacklin, C. N., 133
Jackson, P., 40, 103, 109, 433
Jackson, A., 5, 177
James, T., 368
Jefferson, T., 5, 199, 277, 278, 286
Jencks, C., 39
Johnson, D., 133
Johnson, L., 354
Johnson, W. R., 383, 385
Jordan, C., 131, 132
Joseph, P., 38
Joyce, B., 208, 215, 224, 398
Juffras, J., 146

Kagan, S., 131
Kahne, J., 424
Kalaian, H. A., 103
Karweit, N., 177
Katz, P. A., 263
Katz, M. B., 92
Kellaghan, T., 258
Kelly, C., 343, 350, 359, 363, 368
Kennedy, J. F., 208, 354
Kennedy, P., 302, 304
Kim, S. H., 60
King, M. L., 37, 208, 284, 418
Kirkpatrick, W., 95
Kitchener, K. S., 428
Klein, S., 133
Kliebard, H. M., 236
Knapp, M., 149
Knight, G. R., 80
Knowles, G., 106
Kodzepelic, D., 31
Koerner, J., 385
Kohlberg, L., 414, 415–420, 424,
    425, 432
Kohn, A., 420
Konugres, L., 255
Kounin, J. S., 172
Kozol, J., 237
Krank, H. M., 173

Krupnick, C. G., 171
Kunjufu, J., 244

Labaree, L. W., 199
Labov, W., 130
Lancaster, J., 94
Lanier, J., 391
Lawson, A., 140
Lee, C. H., 246, 409
Leinhardt, G., 50, 158
Leming, J. S., 414, 422
Leo, J., 229
Levin, H., 225
Levine, S., 296
Levine, M., 300
Lickona, T., 413, 421, 425
Lieberman, A., 233, 384
Lines, P. M., 106, 107
Linn, M. C., 133, 134
Lipman, C., 409
Little, J. W., 35, 391
Livingston, C., 50
Lo, L. N. K., 246
Locke, J., 68, 279
Loewen, J., 243
Lortie, J., 7, 14, 208, 209, 212, 390, 391
Lougee, M. D., 60, 61
Lucas, T., 130
Lyon, M., 6

Madaus, G. F., 258
Mailer, N., 69
Mann, H., 5, 6, 38, 94, 199, 277, 278, 286,
    381, 382
Manners, P. A., 423
Marcus, G., 255, 262
Matthews, K., 177
Maurer, R. E., 264
May, A., 414, 422
McAdams, R., 394
McAuliffe, C., 208
McCarthy, M. M., 337, 340, 345, 358,
    359, 368
McCaslin, J., 423
McConaghy, T., 288
McCormick, C. B., 418
McDevitt, T., 292
McDill, E., 291
McGuffey, W. H., 200, 201, 413
McKenzie, L., 255
McKeown, M. G., 141, 238
McLaughlin, M. W., 26, 35, 230
McNeil, L. M., 235, 242, 243
Means, B., 149
Melmed, P., 130
Mezzacappa, J., 408
Mignano, Jr., A. J., 180
Mills, E., 64
Mitchell, D. E., 114
Morine-Dershimer, G., 158
Mostert, M. P., 158
Murray, F. B., 93, 411

Naisbitt, J., 302
Nash, R. J., 254

Natriello, G., 291
Neill, A. S., 97
Nieto, S., 126
Nikola-Lisa, W., 38–39
Nolan, R., 210
Novak, J. M., 411
Nucci, L., 419, 420, 424

Oakes, J., 125
Ogbu, J., 127, 149, 210
Osborn, M., 259

Padilla, J. M., 173
Palincsar, A. M., 61
Pallas, A., 291
Papert, S., 55
Parkay, F. W., 38
Pate, R. R., 255
Peck, R., 75
Perelman, L., 293
Perkins, D., 233
Perkinson, H. J., 202, 277
Perot, R., 242
Pestalozzi, J., 72
Peterson, P., 117, 175
Piaget, J., 139–140, 144, 145, 414, 415, 420, 432
Pickering, M., 343
Pintrich, P. R., 430
Pitt, W., 289
Plato, 37, 38, 58, 66, 67
Posner, G. J., 243, 264
Postman, N., 301, 304
Pressley, M., 418
Preston, J. A., 4
Prodis, H., 365
Prosser, W., 367
Purkey, W. W., 411
Putnam, J., 105, 108, 153, 180

Rasberry, W., 229
Raths, L. E., 414
Ratteray, J., 229
Ravitch, D., 221, 252, 254
Ray, B. D., 106
Reagan, R., 237, 252, 354
Reed, S., 291
Remillard, J., 50
Render, G. F., 173
Reuter, J., 60
Reynolds, M. C., 137
Richardson, S. N., 368
Richert, A., 49
Richey, H. G., 7, 92, 198, 200, 201, 202
Rist, R. C., 41
Roderick, M., 178
Roopnarine, J., 60
Roosevelt, E., 208
Rose, M., 146
Rosemond, J., 223
Rosenholz, S., 212, 213
Rosenshine, B., 42, 47, 51
Ross, J. G., 255

Rousseau, J. J., 68, 72
Rowan, B., 390–391, 392–393
Rowe, M. B., 167
Rury, J. L., 4, 6
Rutherford, F. J., 248
Rutter, M., 208, 224, 296
Ryan, K., 256

Sadker, M. P., 133, 242, 261
Sadker, D. M., 133, 242, 261
Salinger, J. D., 241
Sarason, S. B., 35, 210, 230, 411
Sato, M., 26
Sautter, R. C., 291
Scherer, M., 245
Schimmel, D., 343, 350, 359, 363, 368
Schlesinger, A., 147, 248
Schlosser, L. K., 169
Schmuck, R., 105, 145
Schmuck, P., 105, 145
Schon, D., 50, 55, 58
Schunk, D. H., 430
Schwartz, V., 367
Sedlak, M. W., 5, 6, 7, 383
Semple, C., 118–119, 166, 167, 180
Senese, B. B., 276
Sergiovanni, T., 213–215, 224
Shanker, A., 38, 211, 247–258, 408
Sharan, Y., 98
Sharan, S., 98
Shatz, M., 61
Shepard, L. A., 178, 179
Shulman, L., 47, 49
Shunk, D. H., 430
Sieber, R. T., 109
Silcock, P., 259
Simon, S. B., 414
Sinatra, G. M., 141
Sizer, T., 122, 179, 225, 226, 227, 232, 289
Slavin, R., 61, 115, 154–155, 225
Smart, D. J., 423
Smart, L., 421
Smith, J. B., 409
Smith, M. L., 115, 398
Snarey, J. R., 419
Snitgren, D., 140
Snyder, T. D., 17
Spring, J., 98
Stanford, G., 105
Staudt, J., 140
Stead, T., 118–119, 66, 167, 180
Stedman, L., 219
Steinbeck, J., 241
Stevens, R., 47, 51
Stevenson, D. L., 259
Stright, A. L., 60
Stringfield, S., 222–223

Takaki, R., 149
Tan, A., 147
Tankersley, M., 158
Tannen, D., 133

Tannenbaum, M., 26, 407
Theobold, P., 64
Tice, D. M., 102
Toeffler, A., 302, 303
Tomasky, M., 301
Torney, J. V., 141
Tozer, S. E., 5, 276, 278
Tyack, D., 8, 9, 199, 201, 203, 204, 277, 279, 368

Urban, W. A., 198, 200, 301

Van Galen, J. A., 106
Vann, K., 243
Vasudev, J., 419
Veenman, S., 172
Villegas, 126, 127, 130
Violas, P. C., 276
Vonnegut, K., 344
Vosniadou, S., 142

Waas, G. A., 60
Wade, J., 367
Wagoner, J., 198, 200, 301
Wakefield, A. P., 60
Walberg, H. J., 137
Walsh, M., 241
Wang, M. C., 137
Washington, G., 252, 253, 263
Way, J. W., 61
Webster, N., 93, 200
Wehlage, J., 409
Weinfeld, F., 39
Weinstein, C. S., 102, 108, 156, 180
Westbury, I., 219
Westheimer, J., 424
Wheeler, N., 255
Whitfield, J. B., 199
Whittle, C., 430
Willard, E., 6
Willis, D. B., 250
Willower, D. J., 23
Wilson, S., 49
Winitzky, N., 26
Wise, A., 397, 398
Wittrock, M. C., 55
Wodarski, J. S., 60
Wolf, B., 135, 138
Wollstonecraft, M., 6
Woodridge, W., 198
Wright, R., 147

Yeany, R. H., 142
Yinger, R., 158
York, R., 39
Yunik, G., 60

Zahorik, J., 52
Zalk, S. R., 263
Zan, B., 433
Zirkel, P. A., 368
Zlotnik, M., 399
Zuckerman, M., 92

Academic focus, 212–213
Academic learning time, 159–160
Accreditation, 396–398
Achievement, 144–145
Action zone, 167
Adler, Mortimer, 71
Adoption process, 238
Advance organizer, 163
Affiliation, 144–145
Affirmative action, 281, 352
Afrocentric curriculum, 244–245
Allocated time, 159–160
Alternative certification, 16, 400
Anyon, Jean, 112–113
Assessing, 174–179
  alternatives, 178
  purposes, 174–178
    instructional assessment, 174–175
    official assessment, 175–178
    sizing-up assessment, 174
At-risk students, 48–49, 136–138
  the labeling controversy, 136–137
Attendance, mandatory, 5, 94
Attention deficit disorder (ADD), 136
Authentic assessment, 179
Authoritarian parents, 423
Authoritative parents, 423
Autonomously moral, 414
Autonomy norm, 98, 209
Axiology, 66–70

Back-to-basics movement, 73, 97
Barnard, Henry, 94
Behavioral disorders, 138
Branches of philosophy, 66
Brown v. Board of Education, 74, 281, 352–353
Bureaucracy, 29

Captive clientele, 212–213
Career ladder, 27
Career of teaching, 18–20
Cellular structure, 212
Central Park East Secondary School, 170–171
Channel One, 430–431
Charter schools, 228, 317–318
Chief state school officer, 307
Civil Rights Act, 74
Clarity, 163
Class size, 114–116

Classroom, present, 100–121
  ambiguity in teacher preparation, 111–112
  expectations, 101–103
    and how they shape perception, 101
    research on expectations of beginning teachers, 102–103
    and student learning, 101
    of the teacher, 101–102
  risk in teacher preparation, 111–112
Classroom differences, 112–121
  alternative classrooms, 117
  classrooms, other cultures, 120–121
  classrooms and other workplaces, 118–120
    mental versus technology, 119–120
    organization, 120
    solitary versus group, 118–119
  grade level and subject matter, 113–117
    teacher's conceptions of subject matter, 115–117
  social class, 112–113
Classroom discourse, 165–166
  questioning, 166
Classroom organization, 151–157
  long-range planning, 152
  and management, 157
  physical arrangement, 152, 156
  rules and procedures, 156–157
Classroom management, 157
Classroom properties, 108–110
  history, 110
  immediacy, 109
  multidimesionality, 109
  publicness, 110
  simulaneity, 109
  unpredictability, 109
Classroom similarities, 103–112
  classroom properties, 108
  life in classrooms, 103–104
  a place called school, 104
  social psychology of classrooms, 105, 108
    academic goals, 108
    psychological membership, 105
    rules and routines, 105, 108
    shared influence, 108
    transition and closure, 108

Classrooms, history, 91–99
  colonial era, 92
  impediments to classroom reform, 97–99
    the culture of teaching, 98
    organizational structures, 98
    schooling as social reform, 98
    teacher characteristics, 98–99
  inquiry-oriented teaching, 96–97
  late nineteenth-century to present, 94–97
    student-centered instruction, 95–96
    teacher-centered instruction, 94–95
  nineteenth century, 92–94
  open education, 96–97
Colonial roots, 92, 197–199, 277, 382
  academics, 198–199
  dame schools, 197
  Latin grammar schools, 198
  reading and writing schools, 197–198
Cohorts, 399
Common schools, 5–6, 199–202, 277–278, 382
  elementary school education, 200–201
    age-graded classrooms, 201
    textbook development, 200–201
  movement, the, 5–6, 277–278
  secondary schools, 201–202
  public support of, 202
Competency exams, 25
Comprehension strategies, 247
Concrete operations stage of development, 140
Conservation, 140
Constructivism, 31, 46–47, 51, 118
Contemporary era, 386–387
  autonomy and accountability, 386–387
  preparation and accreditation, 386
  specialized knowledge, 386
  teacher licensing and certification, 386
Cooperative learning, 163–169
Core curriculum, 239
Cultural compatibility, 128
Cultural deficit theory, 126
Cultural difference theory, 126–127
Cultural stereotypes, 74–75
Culture, 207

Curriculum, American, 246–259
　the arts, 255
　curriculum trends, 257–259
　　integrating across disciplines, 257
　　national curriculum, 248–259
　　thematic instruction, 257–258
　foreign language, 254–255
　language arts, 248
　mathematics, 248
　physical and arts education, 255–256
　science, 248–249
　social studies, 250–254
　vocational education, 256–257
Curriculum, control of, 235–246
　hegemony, 243–244
　local influences, 239–243
　　censorship, 241–242
　　parents and students, 240–241
　　principals, 240
　　school districts, 239
　　teachers, 242–243
　national influences, 236–239
　　national testing, 239
　　political forces, 236–237
　　professional associations, 237
　　publishing companies, 237–239
　　social forces, 237
　other countries, 244–246
　state influences, 239
Curriculum, definition, 235
Curriculum, legal basis for, 362–368
　access to student records, 365–366
　copyright laws, 363–365
　curriculum, 362–363
　liability, 366–368
　　abuse, 367–368
　　malpractice, 368
　　negligence, 367
　student testing, 363
Curriculum alignment, 175–178
Curriculum choices, 259–261
　selecting materials, 260
　subject matter, 259–260
　supplementing curriculum, 260–261
　　circumventing bias, 260–261
　　nontraditional materials, 261
Curriculum fragmentation, 399
Curriculum frameworks, 239

Dame schools, 4, 197–198
Dangles, 172
Darwin, Charles, 68, 71
Darwinism, 413
Decoding, 135
Deductive logic, 66
De facto segregation, 281, 354
Defer gratification, 422
De jure segregation, 281, 354
Democratic classrooms, 31
Demographic profile of teachers, 16–18
　gender, 16–17
　quality, 18
　race and ethnicity, 17–18
Dewey, John, 31, 68, 72, 95
Difficulty level, 166
Direct instruction, 51, 165

Discipline, 172
Discourse patterns, 104
Discovery learning, 97, 99
Discussion, 168–169
Dispositions of teachers, 40–44
　toward children, 41–42
　　caring, 41
　　expectations, 41–42
　toward colleagues and other adults,
　　43–44
　toward knowledge, 42–43
　　enthusiasm, 43
　　intellectual orientation, 42–43
Dominated communities, 308
Doyle, Walter, 108–111
Dreikurs model, 172–173

Early-exit programs, 249
Early Republic, 4, 382
Education, American, features of,
　275–276
　local control of education, 276
　public education, 276
　school system, 276
　secular orientation, 276
　universal education, 276
Education, American, periods in, 276–282
　colonial roots, 277
　common school era, 277–278
　the contemporary era, 282
　the Early Republic, 277
　the post–World War II era, 279–282
　　affirmative action, 282
　　extending higher education, 280
　　opportunities for children with
　　　handicaps, 281–282
　　opportunities for women and
　　　minorities, 280–281
　the progressive era, 278–279
Education, constitutional bases for,
　336–337
　first amendment, 337
　fourteenth amendment, 337
　fourth amendment, 337
　eighth amendment, 337
　tenth amendment, 337
Education, funding of public, 324–332
　accountability, 331
　collection of revenues, 324–329
　　collection inequities, 325–326
　　federal revenues, 324–325
　distribution of funds, 326–327
　funding practices, new, 311–332
　funding reform, 327–329
　inadequate infrastructure, 331
　increasing enrollments, 331
　resistance by public, 329–331
Educational voucher, 228, 313
Effective teachers, 36–53
　behaviors of, 44–46
　in Germany, 52–53
　perceptions of teachers, 37–39
　　by children, 38–39
　　by the media, 38
　　praise, 46
　　process-product research, 45

Effective teachers—*Cont.*
　research on, 39–50
　　making a difference, 39
　　personal qualities, 40–44 (*See also*
　　　Disposition)
　teachers' knowledge, 46–50
　　pedagogical content, 47
　teachers' thought processes, 46–50
　　expert teachers, 50
　　novice teachers, 50
　　reflective teachers, 50
　in the twenty-first century, 50–53
Emotional insight, 421–422
Emotional intelligence, 422
Engaged time, 159–160
English as a second language (ESL), 130
Erikson, Erik, 144
Epistemology, 66–70
Equity pedagogy, 147
ESL (English as a second language)
　programs, 249
Ethical, 68, 412–432
Ethics, professional, 425–432
　codes of ethics, 425–428
　ethical teacher, becoming an,
　　429–432
　moral problem solving, 428–429
Ethics in the classroom, 420–425
　legitimacy, 420–422
　teaching values, 422–425
　　additional tools, 425
　　classroom research, 423–424
　　moral development of teachers, 425
　　moral discussion, 424
　　parenting applied to teaching, 423
　　research-based principles, 422
　　service learning, 424–425
　　social learning principles, 422–423
Expectations, 41–42
Explaining, 161–162
Extracurriculum, 235
Extrinsic rewards, 25–27

Factional communities, 308
Feedback, 167
Flip-flops, 172
Formal operations stage of
　development, 140
Formative evaluation, 175
For-profit schools, 228
Fragmentation, 172
Free appropriate public education
　(FAPE), 357
Full bilingual program, 249

Gaining the floor, 167
Gay/Straight Alliance, 240
Gemeinschaft, 214–215
Gesellschaft, 214–215
Goodlad, John, 103–104, 113–114,
　121, 225
Government, federal, role of,
　318–320, 322
　executive influence, 320
　legislative influence, 318–320
　judicial influence, 320

Government, local, role of, 308–318
  policy development, 310–311
  principals, 310
  school boards, 308–309
    curriculum, 308
    finances, 309
    infrastructure, 309
    personnel, 309
    students, 309
  school district organization, 311–318
    charter schools, 317–318
    privatization, 318
    schools of choice, 313–317
    site-based management, 312–313
    traditional, 311–312
  superintendents and administration, 309–310
Government, state, role of, 306–307
  governors, 307
  legislature, 306–307
    chief state school officer, 307
    state boards of education, 307
    state courts, 307
    state departments of education, 307
Guided practice, 161–162

Hands-off norm, 98, 209
Heteronomously moral, 414
Hidden curriculum, 235
Historical nature of classrooms, 110–111
Home schooling, 106–107

Immediate nature of classrooms, 109, 111
Immersion programs, 249
Improvement scoring, 164
In-service, 239
Inclusion, 62–63, 146
Independent practice, 161–162
Individual accountability, 164
Individual educational program or plan (IEP), 358
Individualized educational plan (IEP), 146
Inductive discipline, 423
Inductive logic, 66
Industrial Age, 4
Inert communities, 308
Influence, 144–145
Information Age, 4
Instructing, 160–169
  classroom discourse, 165–169
  cooperative learning, 163–165
  discussion, 168–169
  informal interaction, 169
  lecture, 162–163
  questioning, 166–167
  recitation, 168
  repertoire, 161
    direct instruction, 161
Instructional Assessment, 174–175
Interactive tasks, 21
Interdependence, 43
Intrinsic rewards, 25–28
Involuntary minority, 127, 130
IRE (initiation, response, evaluation), 168
Isolates, 421–422

Jefferson, Thomas, 5, 199

Laissez-faire parents, 423
Late-exit programs, 249
Laws, effect on teachers, 337–342
  certification requirements, 338
  collective bargaining, 341–342
  grounds for dismissal, 339–341
    conduct unbecoming a teacher (unprofessional conduct), 341
    good and just cause, 341
    immoral conduct, 340–341
    incompetence, 339
    insubordination, 339–340
    reduction in force (riffing), 341
  interview process, 338
  tenure, 338–339
Leadership tasks, 21
Learning communities, 32
Least restrictive environment, 146
Lecture, 162–165
  advance organizer, 163
  clear presentation, 163
  review and questioning, 163
Legislation, early, 336
Limited English proficiency (LEP), 130
Literacy, 246–247
Literate environment, 246
Locke, John, 67–68
Logic, 66
Logical consequences, 173
Logical construct, 66
Logical positivism, 413
Loosely coupled, 30, 212

Magnet schools, 228, 313
Mainstream, 62, 146
Mann, Horace, 5, 38, 94, 199–200, 277–278, 381
Mastery orientation, 145
Meta-analysis, 114
Metaphysics, 66–70
Metropolitan desegregation, 281
Modeling, 161–162
Momentum, 172
Montessori school, 415–417
Moral, 412–432
Moral development, research on, 414–420
  Kohlberg's critics, 419–420
  Kohlberg's stage theory, 415–419
  Piagetan perspective, 414
Moral education, history of, 413–414
Motivation, 145
Motives for teaching, 12–15
  extrinsic, 13, 25–27
  intrinsic, 12–13, 25–28
Muliage grouping, 59–61
Multicultural education, 33, 146–147
Multidimensional nature of classrooms, 109, 111

National curriculum, 64–65
National standards, 63–65
Natural consequences, 173

Nongovernmental influences on school governance, 322–324
  business organizations, 323–324
  parent organizations, 323
  professional educational organizations, 323
  school boards' associations, 322–323
  teachers' organizations, 322
Normal schools, 6
Null curriculum, 235

Official curriculum, 235
Open-classroom approach, 117–118
  in Australia, 118
Open education, 97
Operational curriculum, 235
Oppositional identity, 130
Organizational perspective, 211
Organizational tasks, 21
Overdwelling, 172

Pacing, 166
Participation, 167
Planned time, 159–160
Planning, 157–160
  cycles of, 158–159
  and teachers' thought processes, 158
  and use of time, 159–160
Pedagogical content knowledge, 47–48
Pedagogy, 25, 98
  child-centered pedagogy, 96, 99
  teacher-centered pedagogy, 96, 99
Perennialism, 70–76
Performance assessment, 179
Performance-for-grade exchange, 110–111
Performance orientation, 145
Performance test, 25
Personal life histories, 431
Perspective taking, 421
Pestalozzi, Johann, 72
Philosophy of education, 56–79
  branches of, 66
  contemporary issues, 58–70
    content of teaching, 59–60
    education and testing of teachers, 65–66
    inclusion, 61–63
    method of teaching, 59–60
    national standards, 63
    pupose of education, 58
    relationship with students, 60–61
    role of teachers, 60–61
  defining a personal philosophy, 77–79
    choose and follow, 78
    mix and match, 78
    positioning, 78–79
  essentialism, 70, 72
  meaning of, 57
  perennialism, 70–72, 75–76, 78–79
  progressivism, 70–73, 75–76, 78
  reconstructionism, 70, 73–79
  relevance of, 57–58
  systems of, 66–69
    existentialism, 69–70
    idealism, 67–70
    pragmatism, 68–70
    realism, 67–70

Pluralistic communities, 308
Piaget, Jean, 139, 144–145, 414, 420
Politically vulnerable, 212–213
Portfolio assessment, 179
Positive interdependence, 165
Post-World War II era, 385–386
    criticism, 385
    teacher activism, 385–386
Preoperations stage of development, 140
Problem-based instruction, 165
Procedures, 156–157
Professionalism of teaching, 381–382
Progressive era, 383–384
    professional association, 384
    teacher preparation and licensure, 383
Progressivism, 70–72, 95–96, 99
Prosocial concern, 430–431
Proximity control, 172
Public nature of classrooms, 110–111
Puritans, 4, 67–68
Purpose, teacher's ultimate, 150
Purposeful grouping, 164

Question level, 166

Reciprocity agreements, 400
Recitation, 168
Redundancy, 163
Reflection, 150
Repertoire, 32, 150, 161–163
Resegregation, 354
Resilience, 138–139
Restrictive control values, 430
Reverse discrimination, 354
Rights of teachers and students,
        342–347, 350–362
    due process rights, 359
        of students', 359–362
        of teachers', 362
    freedom of association, 347, 350
        students, 347, 350
        teachers, 347
    freedom from discrimination, 351–359
        age discrimination, 356–357
        disability, discrimination based on,
            357–359
        gender discrimination, 355–356
        racial discrimination, 351–355
    freedom of expression, 342–345
        students' free speech rights,
            344–345
        teacher's free speech rights,
            343–344
    personal freedom, 350–351
    religious freedom, 345–347
Role contradictions, 209
Rousseau, Jean-Jacques, 68, 72
Rules, 156–157

School, purpose of, 285–287, 289–291
    potential, development of, 298
    reconstructing society, 290–291
    transmitting the culture, 286–287, 289
        cultural socialization, 287, 289
        political socialization, 286–287
School of choice, 313–317

School organization, 206–215
    culture of, 207–211
        components of, 208–209
        effects of, 210–211
        subcultures, 209–210
    as social organization, 211–213
        common organizational features, 211
        unique organizational features,
            211–213
School of philosophy, 66
School and social problems, 291–301
    child abuse, 296–297
    crime and violence, 298–300
    drug and alcohol abuse, 297
    family configurations and distress, 296
    kids and television, 300
    perspectives, 300–301
    social class and poverty, 291–296
    teen pregnancy, 297–298
School-based management, 312–313
School-effectiveness research, 223–224
Schools, modern, 202–205
    contemporary debates, 204–205
    creation of, 202–204
        the comprehensive high school,
            202–203
        standardization and reform, 203
            broadening curricula, 203–204
Schools, quality of, 215–221
    criticism and reform, 215–216
        Sputnik reforms, 215–216
    more positive view of schools,
            216–221
        citizen satisfaction, 219
        evaluating importance, 219–221
        student achievement, 217–219
Schools in the future, 222–232
    improving traditional schools,
            223–224
    innovative schools, 224–227
    twenty-first century, 227–232
        curriculum, 227
        grouping patterns and size,
            228–231
        leadership, 231–232
        roles and relationships, 227–228
Self-regulated learning, 31
Sensorimotor stage of development, 140
Service learning, 424
Shared values and beliefs, 208
Simultaneous nature of classrooms,
        109, 111
Site-based management, 312–313, 321
Situation ethics, 69
Sizing-up assessment, 174
Skill, 161
Small-group work, 168
Smoothness, 172
Social context of teaching, 31–32
Social learning theory, 422–423
Social organization, 207
Social reform, 301–303
Specific learning disabilities, 135
Stage disparity, 424
State adoption state, 238
State boards of education, 307

State departments of education, 307
Student development, 139–145
    affective domain, 144–145
        emotional needs, 144
        social-emotional development, 144
    cognitive domain, 139–140, 144
        development and culture, 145
        intellectual development, 139–140
        multiple intelligences, 140, 144
Student discipline and management,
        169, 172–174
    alternatives, 178
        authentic assessment, 179
        portfolios, 179
    classroom meeting, 173–174
    communication, 172–173
    discipline, 172–173
        assertive discipline, 173
        Dreikurs model, 172–173
        Jones model, 172
    cooperation and management, 169, 172
Student diversity, 124–139
    at-risk children, 138–139
    demographic trends, 138
    ethnicity and culture, 124–130
        cultural deficit theory, 126
        cultural difference theory, 126–127
        school patterns, 124–126
    gender, 132–134
        biological explanations, 133
        school patterns, 133
        sociological explanations, 133
        testing differences, 133–134
    language, 130–131
        dialect, 130–131
        English as a second language, 131
    resilient kids, 138–139
    schools' response to, 145–147
        inclusion, 146
        mainstreaming, 146
        multicultural education, 146–147
        pull-out programs, 145–146
    social class, 132
    special needs, 134–138
        emotional, 138
        intellectual, 134–137
        physical, 137–138
        teachers' responsibilities, 138
Student subculture, 209–210
Student success, 154–156
Subculture of teaching, 209–210
Subject specific knowledge
        development, 140–143
Summative evaluation, 175
Superintendent, 309–310
Synergy, 43

Tabula rasa, 68
Talk story, 128
Teacher, professional, 388–391,
        394–395
    features, 389–390
        accountability, 390
        autonomy, 390
        respect, status and income, 390
        specialized knowledge, 389–390

Teacher, professional—*Cont.*
  in the future, 408–409
    research and performance-based
      teacher education, 408–409
    restructured schools for student
      and teacher success, 409
    testing to assure teacher quality,
      409
  questioning the profession, 390–391,
    394–395
    accountability, 394–395
    autonomy, 391, 394
    respect and income, 390–391
    specialized knowledge, 390
Teacher-centered strategy, 161–162
Teacher enthusiasm, 43
Teacher organizations, 405–408
  American Federation of Teachers, 407
  collective bargaining, 407–408
  National Education Association,
    406–407
Teacher preparation, 395–405
  certification, 399–400
    alternative certification, 400
    initial certification, 399–400
  continuing education, advanced and
    national certification, 400–405
    advanced certification, 400–403
    national certification, 403
    tenure, 403–405
  phases of preparation, 395–396
  preservice preparation and
    accreditation, 396–399
    candidate selection, 396
    changing context, 398–399
    education program accreditation,
      396–398

Teacher supply, 15–16
  alternative certification, 16
Teachers' work, current, 20–28
  advancement opportunities, 25–28
  goals, 20–21
  in Japan, 26
  preparation requirements, 25
  rewards, 25–28
  role expectations, 34
  schedules, 22–25
  tasks, 21–22
  tools and technologies, 22
Teachers' work, history, 3–5
  colonial era, 3–5
    Anglican Church, 4
    northern colonies, 4–5
    Puritans, 4
    role expectations, 4–5
    southern colonies, 4–5
  nineteenth century, 5–7
    demographic changes, 5–6
    leaders, 5
    role expectations, 6, 9
    teacher training, 6–7
    women's access to education, 6
  twentieth century, 7–9
    demographic changes, 7
    psychology, influence of, 9
    role expectations, 9
    standardization, 7–9
    supervision of teachers, 8–9
  information age, 10
    current trends, 10

Teachers' workplace, 28–30
  organizational features, 29–30
    ambiguous goals, 29–30
    conflicting goals, 29–30
    loosely coupled, 30
    political visibility, 30
    political vulnerablility, 30
    underfunding, 30
  physical characteristics, 29
Team teaching, 257
Tenure, 27
Thematic orientation, 399
Think-pair-share, 167
Title IX, 134
Tracking, 125
Transactive discourse, 424
Transitional bilingual, 249

Unclear goals, 212
Unpredictable nature of classrooms,
  109, 111
User fees, 331–332

Values clarification, 414
Voluntary minority, 127, 130

Wait time, 166–167
Withitness, 172